A.T. Mann
The Round Art
The Astrology of Time and Space

Edited by Donald Lehmkuhl and Mary Flanagan

GALLEY PRESS
A Division of W. H. Smith Publishers Inc.
112 Madison Avenue
New York City 10016

Written, designed, illustrated and produced by A. T. Mann.

ISBN: 0 8317 7309 2
Manufactured in Hong Kong
FIRST AMERICAN EDITION

The author wishes to acknowledge the following: Harriet Wynter Ltd., for the photographs on pages 51 and 52; Lee Knowle for the illustrations on pages 48, 53, 54, 55, 56, 57, 58, 59, 60, 61, 62 and 78-79; Mary Evans Picture Library for the photographs on pages 228, 230, 231, 232, 234, 235, 236, 237, 238, 239, 240, 241, 242, 243, 244, 246, 247, 248, 250 and 251; The Radio Times Hulton Picture Library for the photographs on pages 233, 234, 235, 239, 246, 249 and 251; Camera Press Ltd. for the photographs on pages 229, 236 and 241; Patrick Wiseman for the photographs on pages 7 and 61; Painton Cowen for the photographs on pages 27 and 274; Arione DeWinter for the photographs on pages 233 and 245; Mary Flanagan for the print on page 136; and to the authors and publishers of the many books from which I have taken quotations.

Correction :
The illustration on page 72 (fig 111.32) should be coloured
as the illustration on page 74 (fig 111.34).

Table of Contents

To Mary and Ptolemy

Acknowledgements

My greatest acknowledgements are for the untold millennia of individuals who participated in forming the tradition of Astrology. From primeval wanderers worshipping the lights in the heavens to modern adherents and sceptics, virtually all of mankind have participated in the growth and transformation of this oldest pursuit of mind and spirit.

I thank Carl Gustav Jung for his life and work, which opened my eyes to the mechanics and mysteries of the psyche. The work of Rodney Collin provided the catalyst for the necessary re-evaluation of the place of man within our universe of space and time. The persistence, skill and dedication of Reinhold Ebertin vaulted astrology into the modern world, and laid a stable ground for all of my investigations.

I thank Roger Dean for his trust and assistance in allowing this book to be possible. Donald Lehmkuhl provided an inestimable service by bringing me into contact with Roger, and spent untold time and energy editing the text. Hubert Schaafsma assisted in the production and business management of the book. Martyn Dean provided valuable advice and support in production and printing. Nathan Dunbar helped me thoughout the layout and production as an assistant and friend.

The most valuable help and support came from Mary Flanagan. She edited the text throughout all of its stages, compiled the tables of correspondences, provided essential criticism on all matters covered by this book, and without her devotion, time and energy, this project would never have become a reality. For continuous moral and friendly support I thank Painton, Arione, Ann, Giugi and Sarah. I also express gratitude to the many hundreds of clients who have convinced me of the validity of astrological processes.

THE ROUND ART

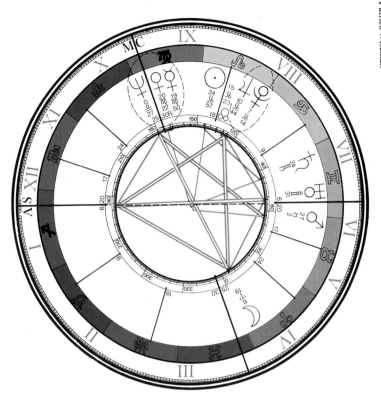

Patrick Wiseman

Element Distribution

Fire	5	8 pos
Air	3	
Earth	3	3 neg
Water	0	

Mode Distribution

Cardinal	2
Fixed	4
Mutable	5

House Distribution

Angular	4
Succedent	2
Cadent	4

A.T. Mann
18 August 1943
Auburn, New York, USA

Bowl Shape: Neptune leads
Ruling Planet: Jupiter Leo VIII

Fiery Grand Trine: ASC △ ☽ △ ♃ ♇

Biographical Outline

1943	A. T. Mann was born in Auburn, New York, USA on the 18th August at 3.05 pm. His father had been killed in action as a pilot in the World War four months earlier. He was raised by his mother and she remarried two years later. He has two half-brothers and two half-sisters.
1961-1966	He graduated from Cornell University in Ithaca, New York, receiving the degree of Bachelor of Architecture.
1966-1970	During this time he worked as an architectural designer for many offices in New York City and for The Architect's Collaborative in Rome throughout the winter of 1968-1969.
1970-1972	He travelled extensively through Europe, North Africa and overland to India. During this period he began drawing and painting mandalas and developed an interest in astrology.
1972	After returning to the USA, he taught himself the mechanics and practice of astrology. Finding the existing information and graphic material unsatisfactory for the proper understanding of the subject, he designed and implemented a unique system for interpreting and reading the horoscope. He also designed a Tarot deck and the KALA astrological calendar. His daughter Ptolemy was born on the 14th of December.
1973	A move to London, England, in September was followed by the formation of Phenomenon Publications, and the first Phenomenon Calendar for 1973-1974.
1974	The Phenomenon Book of Calendars 1974-1975.
1975	The Kala Calendar 1975-1976.
1977	The Phenomenon Book of Calendars 1978-1979 was published by Doubleday & Co. in the USA, and by Dragon's World in England. He exhibited a series of paintings, "Twelve Mandalas" at the 1977 Festival of Mind and Body which were eventually published as cards by Dragon's World.

Illustrations

Symbol Key

The Signs

Glyph	Sign	Symbol	Date	Logarithmic Time Scale Ages	Gender	House	Element	Mode	Colour
♈	**ARIES**	Ram	21 March to 21 April	Birth to 7 mths	Male	I	Fire	Cardinal	Red
♉	**TAURUS**	Bull	21 April to 22 May	7 mths to 1 yr 8 mths	Female	II	Earth	Fixed	Red-Orange
♊	**GEMINI**	Twins	22 May to 22 June	1 yr 8 mths to 3 yrs 6 mths	Male	III	Air	Mutable	Orange
♋	**CANCER**	Crab	22 June to 23 July	3 yrs 6 mths to 6 yrs 10 mths	Female	IV	Water	Cardinal	Orange-Yellow
♌	**LEO**	Lion	23 July to 24 August	6 yrs 10 mths to 12 yrs 10 mths	Male	V	Fire	Fixed	Yellow
♍	**VIRGO**	Virgin	24 August to 23 September	12 yrs 10 mths to 23 yrs 5 mths	Female	VI	Earth	Mutable	Yellow-Green
♎	**LIBRA**	Scales	23 September to 23 October	23 yrs 5 mths to 41 yrs 6 mths	Male	VII	Air	Cardinal	Green
♏	**SCORPIO**	Scorpion	23 October to 23 November	41 yrs 6 mths to Death	Female	VIII	Water	Fixed	Blue-Green, Turquoise
♐	**SAGITTARIUS**	Centaur, Archer	23 November to 22 December	Conception to 7 weeks after	Male	IX	Fire	Mutable	Blue
♑	**CAPRICORN**	Goat	22 December to 21 January	7 wks to 12 wks after conception	Female	X	Earth	Cardinal	Indigo
♒	**AQUARIUS**	Waterbearer, Man	21 January to 19 February	12 wks to 22 wks after conception	Male	XI	Air	Fixed	Violet
♓	**PISCES**	Fishes	19 February to 20 March	22 wks after conception to Birth	Female	XII	Water	Mutable	Red-Violet

The Planets

	Planet	Principle	Gender	Cycle	Rulership	Exaltation	Biological Correspondence	Colour
☉	**SUN**	Spirit	Male	1 year	Leo	Aries	Vitality, heart, circulation — Thymus	Orange, Gold
☽	**MOON**	Soul	Female	29½ days	Cancer	Taurus	Fertility, blood, bodily fluids — Pancreas	Indigo, Silver
☿	**MERCURY**	Mind	Neuter	88 days	Gemini, Virgo	Virgo	Motor-nerves, speech and hearing — Thyroid	Yellow
♀	**VENUS**	Harmony	Female	225 days	Taurus, Libra	Pisces	Gland products, hormones, veins — Parathyroid	Green
♂	**MARS**	Conflict	Male	687 days	Aries, Scorpio	Capricorn	Muscles, body, heat, sexuality — Adrenals	Red
♃	**JUPITER**	Expansion	Female	12 years	Sagittarius, Pisces	Cancer	Organs, nutrition, corpulence — Posterior Pituitary	Blue
♄	**SATURN**	Contraction	Male	29½ years	Capricorn, Aquarius	Libra	Bones, skin, aging, organ loss — Anterior Pituitary	Violet
♅	**URANUS**	Eccentricity	Neuter	84 years	Aquarius	Scorpio	Rhythm, nerves, brain meninges — Gonads	Light Yellow
♆	**NEPTUNE**	Sensitivity	Female	165 years	Pisces	Leo	Pineal Gland, aura, drugs	Light Green
♇	**PLUTO**	Regeneration	Male	270 years	Scorpio	Aquarius	Collective Unconscious	Light Red
☊	**MOON'S NODE**	Association	—	19 years	—	Gemini	Astral Body	—

THE ROUND ART

Ruler	Exaltation	Alchemical Process	Body Part	Acupuncture Meridian	Stone	Principle	Correspondences
Mars	Sun	Calcination	Head, Cerebrum	Kidney Meridian	Ruby	self-assertion	initiatory action, adventure, daring, impatience, aggression, the personality
Venus	Moon	Congelation	Throat, ears, Cerebellum	Triple Generator	Topaz	physical world	fertility, beauty, passivity, security, finances, stewardship, form, endurance
Mercury	North Node	Fixation	Arms, lungs, hands	Liver Meridian	Tourmaline	instinctive mind	communication, duality, imitation, facility, versatility, superficiality, mobility
Moon	Jupiter	Dissolution	Stomach, Breasts	Stomach Meridian	Moonstone, Amber	emotions and feeling	maternal urges, emotion security, dreams, the unconscious, home and family life
Sun	Neptune	Digestion	Heart, Spine	Heart Meridian	Cat's Eye	self-expression	exteriorization of the self, personal love, self-consciousness, pleasure, conceit, vanity
Mercury	Mercury	Distillation	Back, Intestines	Large Intestine	Peridot	discrimination	work, perfectionism, health and hygiene, diet, secondary education, analysis, prudence
Venus	Saturn	Sublimation	Liver, Kidneys	Circulation	Emerald	partnership	marriage, co-operation, public relations, enemies, persuasion, yielding, understanding
Mars, Pluto	Uranus	Separation	Genitals Bladder	Bladder Meridian	Turquoise, Snakestone	death and rebirth	metaphysical reality, passion, lust, violence inheritances, others' possessions, loss
Jupiter	South Node	Incineration	Thighs, Hips	Spleen Meridian	Jacinth	realization	higher mind, meditation, philosophy, religion extravagance, psychology, freedom, literature
Saturn	Mars	Fermentation	Knees, skin, bones	Gall Bladder	Black Diamond	perfected matter	organization, physical limitations, devotion power and success, society and government
Saturn, Uranus	Pluto	Multiplication	Ankles	Lung Meridian	Glass, Chalcedony	social consciousness	humanitarianism, collectivity, altruism, progressive ideas, utopianism, romanticism
Jupiter, Neptune	Venus	Projection	Feet	Small Intestine	Pearl	sensitivity	emotional receptivity, self-sacrifice, karma psychic abilities, drugs, seclusion, hospital

Stone	Metal	Plant	Personifications	Correspondences
Crysolith	Gold	Sunflower, Laurel	Father, men in general, paternal figures, leaders, masculine individuals, active people	Consciousness, individuality, creativity, activity, vitality, direction, leadership, objectivity
Pearl, Moonstone	Silver	Moonwort, Almond	Mother, women in general, maternal figures, the family, feminine individuals, inactive people	Unconscious, habitual or instinctive behaviour, domesticity, impressionability, moodiness, adaptability
Opal, Agate	Mercury	Vervain, Herb Mercury	Intellects, mediators, communicators, agents, hermaphrodites, travellers, tradesmen	Analytical and discriminative mind, criticism, diplomacy, writing and speaking, dexterity, multifaceted, diverse
Emerald	Copper	Myrtle, Rose	Young women, maidens, beauties, lovers, artists, musicians, poets, entertainers, decorators	Affections, physical attraction, harmonious sense, pleasure, creativity, sociability, sentimentality, good taste
Ruby	Iron	Absinthe	Young men, fighters, aggressive individuals, craftsmen, athletes, mechanics, surgeons	Force, aggression, creative and destructive powers, will-power, active urges, high energy, impulsiveness
Lapis Lazuli	Tin	Oak, Fig, Hyssop	Aunts and Uncles, officials, philanthropists, churchmen, the moral, gluttons, the wealthy	Benevolence, calm, mania, justice, constructive impulses, morality, optimism, philanthropy, higher aspirations
Onyx	Lead	Nightshade, Yew, Ash	Depressives, elders, inhibited individuals, authority figures, pessimists, the greedy	Concentration, maturity, senility, seriousness, economical, melancholic, isolated, reserved, guilty, constructive
Topaz	—	Aspen	Eccentrics, inventors, reformers, rebels, peculiar people, erratic people	Peculiarity, independence, rhythmic, innovative, individual, unusual, erratic, reformative, inventive
Beryl, Aquamarine	—	Lotus, Water Plants	Psychics, dreamers, visionaries, mediums, the sensitive, crooks, addicts, alcoholics	Expanded consciousness, psychic phenomena, drug states, reverie, fantasy, illusion, sensitivity, mysticism, fraud
Salt	Nuclear elements	Ivy, Oak	Magicians, revolutionaries, regenerators, propagandists, public figures, mass-murderers	Revolutionary processes, regeneration, wanton destruction, magical forces, propaganda, catastrophes, reactionary
—	—	—	Allies, socialities, groupies, kindred, jet-setters, relatives, schoolmates	Adaptability, convivial attitudes, socialism, fellowship, associative, familiar, communal

Preface

The Round Art: Space, Time and Astrology is an ambitious attempt to integrate relevant modern ideas in astronomy, psychology and physics with the traditional body of astrological knowledge. It is intended to reach the whole range of individuals interested in discovering astrology as a unifying mechanism for the personal, internal world of the psyche and the collective, external world of events and physical phenomena.

The structure of this book should allow equal access to those who have no previous knowledge of astrology as well as those who do know and practice the art. Each of the mechanisms and ideas of astrology is carefully paralleled by concepts from other areas of human thought, permitting helpful analogies to aid understanding. Astrology is not intended to be an isolated "occult" phenomenon or the exclusive province of those with psychic or mediumistic leanings, but rather a universal system of correspondences which is the common property of all men. The breadth of the presentation of astrology in The Round Art furthers this aim.

In Part II, *"The History of Astrology",* the emphasis is not placed upon the evolution of astrology alone, but rather upon the evolution of the myths, men and ideas from which astrology arose and blossomed throughout history. Astrology is an accumulation of many strands of experience and learning which interweave through the tapestry of civilization. It is impossible to separate astrology from the mainstream of human thought, as its practicioners and detractors alike have attempted to do over thousands of years.

To aid comprehension for those who are new to the subject or who have no interest in the calculation and construction of horoscopes, all of the technical procedures and accompanying information are removed from the text and accumulated in a series of *Appendices.* These Appendices explain how to calculate and construct Birth Horoscopes; how to determine Solar Arc Directions and Solar Returns for making accurate predictions; and how to correct inaccurate or unknown times of birth through the process of Rectification.

The ideas behind the procedure of *Interpretation* and *Prediction* are fully explained and documented, with numerous examples. These example analyses include: a complete Birth Horoscope interpretation of the psychologist *Carl Gustav Jung;* an analysis of the Personality of the contemporary psychiatrist *R. D. Laing;* complete Solar Arc Directions for the life of *Adolf Hitler;* a Solar Return yearly analysis for *Vladimir Illyich Lenin* during 1917-1918; and a Transit analysis of the day that *Richard Nixon* resigned the Presidency of the United States of America. These interpretations are all taken from the complete *"Tables of Correspondences"* in *Part VII,* and are also documented from biographies and autobiographies.

To illustrate the many facets of astrological analysis, the Horoscopes and pictures of 48 well-known individuals are included in *Part X.* These examples serve to present tangible evidence of astrological doctrines and provide useful comparisons to all interpretive statements made in the Round Art.

For individuals who wish to know the technique of giving an astrological reading or for those who practice astrology professionally, *Part IX, "The Reading",* explores the process in depth and makes relevant comparisons to psychoanalysis. The "transference" between the astrologer and his client, as well as the therapeutic results possible are compared to many of the major schools of psychology and psychiatry. As astrology is ultimately a self-analytical process, the implications of the entire astrological process are evaluated in their relevance to the individual.

An original conception of astrology is presented in The Round Art — the correlation of biological time to the horoscope. Using the transparent *Logarithmic Time Scale Disk* included in this book, it is possible to synchronize the life of the individual to the relativity of the space-time continuum by dating every planetary event from conception until death. This adds a new dimension to astrological interpretation and allows even the novice to make accurate analyses and predictions. The Time Scale also explains the derivation of the Signs of the Zodiac and the Houses of the Horoscope in a logical way for the first time. The Logarithmic Time Scale catapaults astrology from a primitive superstition to a science of life.

The texture of The Round Art is that of a dynamic learning process rather than a sterile recitation of doctrinal pronouncements, and should elevate astrology to its true position as the science and art of wholeness.

A. T. Mann   *London, 1978*

Part I   Introduction

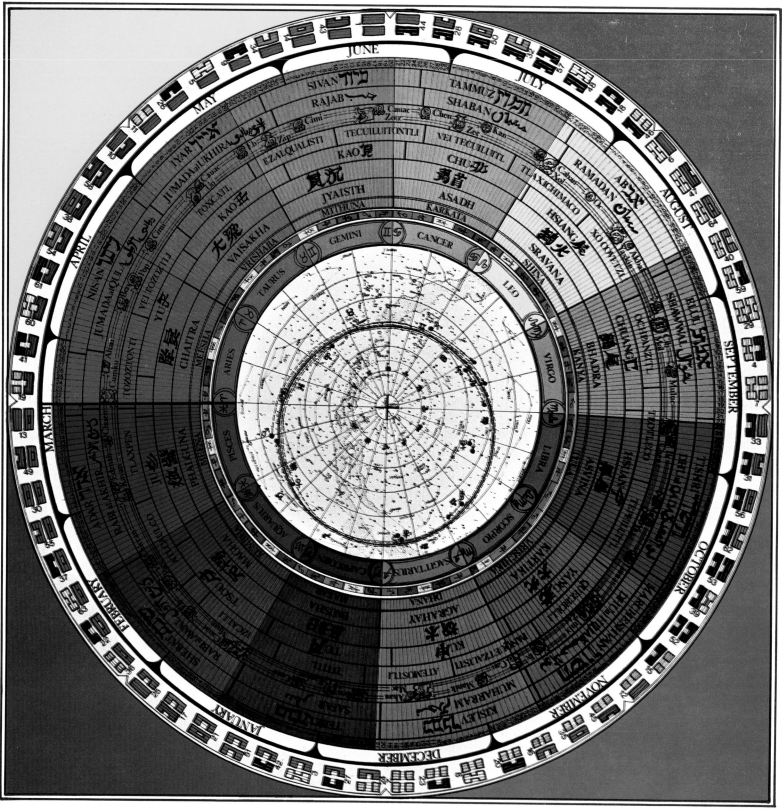

Figure I.1 Central poster from the Phenomenon Book of Calendars, 1979-1980.

 THE ROUND ART

Astrology is a mirror of the life of Man in the Universe. Since the first men became conscious it has existed as a symbol system which has proven startlingly central. It has attended the creation of civilizations and their destruction, interpenetrating them like a thread of Ariadne through the labyrinth of Time. Every world age has "rediscovered" astrology, adapted to its purposes and then abandoned it. Astrology, like Man himself, is capable of an infinite number of metamorphoses.

History is a representation of the stratified past of all men which functions within every individual, and astrology is a language which evokes history and its mechanisms. Man has passed through many transformations — from the instinctive reality of lower life forms up through the successive development of emotion, mind and spirit — and his wholeness is dependent upon each function occurring in its proper place. What in former civilizations were totem animals, gods and goddesses, or mythological heroes are now so abstracted and intellectualized that man is in a very real danger of cutting off all connection from his roots and hence eliminating all possibility of achieving or regaining his original totality. The universal memory of the paradisiacal Garden of Eden and the desire to recreate it is a recognition that man's Fall was from a unitary and undifferentiated state, where he lived in total communion with all other creatures, to one where the disastrous expulsion and complete separation are becoming an irreversible reality. The Garden of Eden is available to every individual, but it is to be found *within* before it is to be found *without*.

The desire to inhabit Eden once again has given rise to many of man's mythologies, religions, philosophical systems, civilizations and ways of "knowing". The historical preoccupation with religion signifies the desire to *link back* (Latin = *religio*) to our essence and, by extension, to the primal life force.

Astrology is ideally suited for the task of understanding and realizing our lost totality. Astrology has at various times functioned as a time-keeping device and predecessor of the calendar; a language of the gods; a basis for the cosmology of many major world religions; a repository for projected images of the gods; a synonymous term encompassing astronomy, geometry, mathematics and psychology; a prime diagnostic and therapeutic tool in medicine; and the mother of the mantic arts. As these represent central aspects of what we call civilization — the collective reality of man — they are ultimately reflections of our internal mechanism's attempt to define itself.

Modern theoretical physicists are belatedly discovering that "all the theories of natural phenomena, including the "laws" they describe, are creations of the human mind; properties of our conceptual map of reality, rather than of reality itself."[1] The profound interconnection and inseparability which links the mental, psychic and physical worlds, which has always been the central concept of astrology, is finally being accepted and verified experimentally.[2] The suppositions which physicists make, in order to permit their "models" to approximate an indescribable reality, are virtually identical to the ancient doctrines of astrology. The only difference is that as yet there has been very little effort on the part of physicists to extend the relevance of their models into the life of the psyche. Astrology is an attempt to orient man in the universe rather than a "pure science" which holds the formulation and proof of laws as paramount. Man has looked everywhere, including outer space, for the ultimate knowledge and typically has failed to realize that it has been under his nose all the time. To search for the meaning of life in subatomic particles or in the wastes of space is to avoid the search where it is most critical. The real issue is the *integration of our external and internal universes.*

The common factor linking astrology, physics and psychology is *Time.* Time has always been central to astrology, and since the beginning of this century it has become so for physics and psychology as well. Einstein's correlation of energy, matter and time in physics occurred at about the same period as the correlation of psyche and physiology by Freud and Jung. Once an hypothetical relationship was found in both cases, there immediately arose the necessity to integrate the Time Factor.

In physics the crucial test of the Relativity Theory was its bearing upon the origin of the universe and, by implication, the origin of life. Although Einstein found that there was no way to determine whether space and time were infinite or finite, he eventually decided that it was "more satisfying to have the mechanical properties of space completely determined by matter, and this is the case only in a closed universe."[3] This conclusion implies that the universe, being finite, has a beginning and an end, that spatially it has a constant curvature

[1] Capra, *The Tao of Physics,* p. 303.

[2] See the works of Michel Gauquelin, Landscheidt, and West and Toonder in the bibliography.

Figure I.1 Central poster from the Phenomenon Book of Calendars, 1979-1980. This diagram compares the calendar systems of the Western Civilian Calendar, the Hebrew Calendar, the Islamic Calendar, the ancient Mayan Calendar, the Aztec Calendar, the Chinese Calendar, the Chinese Astrological Calendar, the Hindu Calendar and the Hindu Astrological Calendar with the Zodiacal Calendar from Spring Equinox to Spring Equinox.

[3] Einstein, *The Meaning of Relativity,* 1922.

and, in respect to its time extension, is cylindrical. This indicates that time is also *circular*. The universe must have begun with an "event" and will proceed until it terminates in an "event" — just like the life of a man. Since space and time are a continuum, every moment succeeding the creation is linked in meaning to the whole "being" of the universe.

An identical process is in operation in psychology. Originally it was assumed that the psychology of the individual was totally determined by actions experienced during his life, whereas Carl Gustav Jung realized that there was a reservoir of information which preceded individual existence — a *Collective Unconscious* — a history of all men transmitted directly through archetypal behaviour, dreams, visions, fantasies and other unconscious mechanisms. The Collective Unconscious is the universe in relation to the individual psyche. Jung conceived both as circular mandalas moving through time, paralleling the shape of time in relativity. Existence anywhere in the universe gives relative access to the whole and the Collective Unconscious gives access to the universal psyche. Memories of the entire universe of space and time lie within everyone waiting for discovery and translation into virtually any frame of reference, into any language.

Astrology is a language which uses a series of symbols to create an identification between man and the universe. Where many of the earliest languages were operative as symbol systems, at the present time most have become crystallized as signs which, although being widely accepted, have become extremely confused. *Symbols* relate a meaning which is indeterminate, undefined, still alive and vital, but as symbols become clearly identified and universally accepted they gradually transform into *signs*, which have determinate meanings and are therefore static and lifeless. The Zodiac symbols, the alphabet of astrology, are perpetually in the midst of this transition and function both as symbols and signs. Their meanings are clear relative to each other in sequence, but their transposition into the individual psyche is continually changing. They have always functioned as symbols because every synchronistic or successive culture has adapted the identical sequence of stellar constellations to images which reflect the cultural and anthropomorphic roots of its people. When a culture begins to accept symbols as absolutes, they change into signs and lose their energy.

In early cultures correspondences between the times of the year and the equivalent animals which worked, were hunted, provided food, protection or were central to survival were common knowledge. Since they affected everyone vitally, they were also essential to the language the culture used. Gradually totem animals were identified with individuals who were most intimately connected with them, to the extent that there developed a natural identification of anthropomorphic archetypes with personality types. These "types" were transformed into social hierarchies which, at their purest level, were identifications with archetypal qualities allowing the culture to characterize any individual according to his dominant physical or hereditary qualities. Eventually the hereditary aspect became dominant, but originally it was a totally "objective" method of organization.

In the Twentieth Century our previous affinity with the land and animals from which our sustenance is derived has been eliminated almost totally from our cultural mainstream. Every individual is ostensibly "equal", and the trend is towards assimilation rather than differentiation. Personality types associated with the totem animals of our past are no longer accepted. The loss of identification with the physical world has produced a concomitent loss of psychological security, and the only contacts which do connect the individual back to the primal vitality have become more and more abstract and intellectualized. The attraction that astrology has upon millions of newspaper readers all over the world is a direct result of the dormant unconscious interest in the magic of the anthropomorphic images of astrology.

Astrology is the archetypal system for integrating the individual with the universe. It is a geometrically oriented system of Ideal values (the signs of the Zodiac) which defines the individual in terms of the Ideal. Through the selective emphasis of time and place it determines which combination of archetypal values are present and operative at any given time. This process is a *transference between the Ideal and the Real.* The realities of life are so complex and fragmented at the present time that they have only a symbolic relationship to the ideal. The interpenetration and mutual reaction of these archetypal values produces a whole which is far from being easily understood and totally predictable, but it does provide a matrix and a language which can assist the individual to discover the world within himself and the "missing links" back to his instincts. Astrology provides a mechanism for describing parallels

between men and between man and the universe. This is also true in psychology, where the terminology and identification of certain processes are not intended to limit and totally define the individual, but rather to provide a set of mutually accepted symbols and terms which allow a dialogue between the self and others.

This situation is similar to the way in which individuals are components of history and help define certain movements, while at another level they are only the thinnest veneer of its reality. We see history in symbolic form, and the individuals that make it are symbols, just as in our lives we seek to discover our own personal and universal symbolism, the meaning of ourselves. In both history and astrology the quest for meaning proceeds from the symbolic or ideal to the actual or real.

Astrology in our modern age is obviously undergoing a revival which is rapidly gaining strength and adherents all over the world. Many individuals and groups are rediscovering and beginning to practice anew myriad ancient religions (Druidism, Hinduism, Taoism, Buddhism, ecstatic Shamanism, Zen, Mystic Christianity and Christianity); ancient philosophies (Platonism, Pythagorean mathematics, Hermeticism, Alchemy and Magic); mantic arts (Tarot, I Ching, Geomancy, Palmistry, Graphology and Dowsing); and martial arts (Tai Chi Chuan, Judo, Karate, Kung Fu). This barrage of ways of confronting the Self and the world all try to communicate the same thing, through different languages. As a response to the chaos and conflict which increasingly dominate the world, these methods of liberation counterbalance the negation of life, but simultaneously are in danger of duplicating the legendary Tower of Babel's profusion and confusion of tongues. It is urgent to discover the undercurrents which link these pursuits to each other and individuals to the pursuits. By virtue of its historical evolution, astrology is a mother to many of these siblings and is in a unique position to catalyze their metamorphosis and synthesis.

This book is an attempt to combine historical and modern techniques of astrology with many specialized and artificial fragments which man has devised to discover the "truth" about himself. Astrological ideas will be correlated with depth psychology, physics, astronomy, genetics, mathematics, medicine and the arts to produce this link back to our roots. Astrology is the classical tour-de-force of correspondentia and analogy, and this book will explore and unite the many relationships these open to view.

Since astrology was originally an observational and graphic medium, the visual mechanism will be integrated into the texture of the book in such a way that it will evoke the participation of the senses and the emotions as well as the intellect. The images, symbols, diagrams and other supportive graphic material are as essential to an understanding of the process as the ideas transmitted through the words.

"We do not fear being called meticulous, inclining as we do to the view that only the exhaustive can be truly interesting."[4]

[4] Thomas Mann, *The Magic Mountain*.

Part II   The History of Astrology

Figure II.1 Stonehenge.

The History of Astrology

Astrology has a long and vital history which stretches back to the emergence of modern man from the savage and brutal Neanderthaler. Life in those ancient times was solely dictated by natural, instinctive drives. Man was different from the other animals, but simultaneously was deadlocked with them in the struggle for survival. The lack of physical strength, protective colouring, great speed or naturally lethal weaponry forced him to concentrate all of his mind and energy to *understand* the situation he found himself in. He was forced to heighten his awareness of himself and his environment in order to exist.

The main tool he had available to ensure his continuing survival was *communication.* Groups of early men held their own by being able to organize themselves with hand signals or speech, and in spite of overt shortcomings, they realized that extending and developing this tool greatly improved their survival chances. Not only did this advance allow men to communicate during the hunt, but it soon led to descriptions of the hunt around the fire afterwards, and eventually to verbal tradition. Each successive generation was able to benefit from the mistakes and innovations of previous generations, unless the mistakes were drastic ones. The experiences of the group began to be greater than the experiences of any individual in the group. This extension of consciousness signalled the most critical transition for early man because it made obsolete his former relationship to Time as pure present, and introduced the concept of the "passing" or "flow" of time. As formerly, like the animals, he lived from meal to meal and never conceived more than one meal ahead, *he began to think about tomorrow.*

> "Tomorrow and tomorrow and tomorrow
> Creeps in this petty pace from day to day
> To the last instant of recorded time.
> And all our yesterdays have lighted us
> The way to dusty death." [1]

[1] William Shakespeare, *Macbeth*.

The concept of 'tomorrow' meant that these men were forced to begin to consider *(sider = star)* when to hunt, when to gather berries and fruits, and when to migrate, instead of having totally instinctive impulses which held total governance. Instead of seeing the Sun as a wanton natural force which might not come again, they gradually realized that the Sun did return each day, and that through longer periods of time heat and light varied. This led to a comprehension of the *year,* when the spacing and sequences of survival tasks became even more complex and necessary.

The nomadic migrations throughout the year in search of game and other food gave way to more stable agrarian communities in the middle east, about 9000 BC. Changes in season determined the times for ploughing, sowing, reaping and storing grains and vegetables. By this time the tribes had diversified and fragmented, and were structured so that certain families performed specific duties within the whole tribe. This specialization mirrored the increasing breadth of interest and necessity of the early civilizations. One of the dominant activities within the tribe was observing and recording the heavenly movements. The Greek historian **Solon** recorded that astronomical observations and calculations were made nine thousand years before his time, which means that actual observations have been recorded continuously for over eleven thousand years.

Agrarian tribes utilized the cycles of the Moon as well as the Sun. Solar cycles were useful for measuring time during the day, seasons during the year and ages throughout the lifetime, while the Moon was necessary for cycles of planting and mating, predicting the rise and fall of rivers, and for scheduling festivals. The Sun was a cruel god of vitality and strength, and the Moon was a goddess of procreativity and destruction. Although there is speculation that they were both originally feminine or both masculine, they eventually were universally seen as a male and female pair of deities. The history of early civilizations shows a periodical fluctuation between the dominance of patriarchal solar deities and that of the feminine lunar 'earth mothers.' [2] As comprehension of the other visible planets ensued, the pantheons of the gods enlarged and diversified. The characteristics of the gods and goddesses were derived from planetary colours, patterns while moving across the sky, lengths of cycles, and from their mutual relationships.

The myths of these first civilizations were combinations of qualities they observed and

Figure II.1 Stonehenge (built approximately 2400 BC) shows a sophisticated knowledge of astronomy and geometry. The positioning of the stones prove that observations and calculations were accurately made by "primitive man".

[2] See Erich Neumann, *The Great Mother,* J. G. Frazer, *The Golden Bough,* and Robert Graves, *The White Goddess.*

projected onto the planetary bodies as well as encapsulated histories of their predecessors. The myths were complex and ambiguous tales which generated patterns of behaviour, rules of conduct, cultural values, and were symbolic of the natural cosmic forces which determined their health and welfare. Men believed the gods were forces to be appeased and sacrificed to, but due to their unconsciousness, they believed that the gods were within them at the same time. The identification was total and un-differentiated. The earliest kings of **Babylonia, Chaldea** and **Egypt** not only represented the Sun God, but *were* the Sun God in the flesh. There was no distinction between being and meaning. Events which occurred during the reign of a king were applicable to his entire nation, and making obeisance to the king was making obeisance to the god. Since the king and his consort, together with his main advisers, were equated with the gods and the planetary bodies in the sky, they were representatives and actualizations of the entire cosmos on earth.

The festivals which marked propitious times during the year coincided with rituals of appeasement, correct astronomical configurations and re-enactments of mythological events. The successful functioning of the kingdom depended upon the pattern of rituals the population were subjected to, and failures were seen as the affects of inaccurate timing. If the activities were not properly synchronized the god was not appeased, and so he vented his anger upon both the king and his people. Since the timing of the rituals was the responsibility of the priestly caste, this caste attained great power and control over the populations and even the kings. But, since the welfare of the people and the king all benefited from correct management, the delegation of power to the priests was accepted.

The establishment of the calendar and the origin of astrology were probably simultaneous. They coincided with the identification of the belt of fixed stars against which the Sun, Moon and planets moved; the Zodiac. The zodiac was a "celestial way" within which the creation of the world was eternally being re-enacted. The first Babylonian calendars were also zodiacs whose images were the totem animals which represented the twelve important divisions of the year. (Figure II.2) The Babylonians also defined the day and night as 24 hours and the circle as containing 360° degrees. In Babylonian calendars the months were simultaneously totem animals, planetary beings and the gods themselves. Because each yearly cycle was virtually identical, life was understood as an eternal repetition of mythological patterns which were originally determined by the gods, then re-enacted by their ancestors. There was no concept of individuality or separation from the divine cosmos because they believed that the patterns and ritual acts were universal, pre-existent and always attended by viligant monstrous deities who would punish them for any deviation.

Men saw themselves not as separate beings, but as integral components of the whole. As **Thomas Mann** states in his novel *Joseph and His Brothers:*

> "the task of the individual person (was) the filling out in present time and again making flesh certain given forms, a mythical frame that was established by the fathers . . . the life of the individual was more superficially separated from that of the tribe, birth and death represented a less radical shock to exisence; in short, . . . he displayed the phenomenon of open identity." [3]

Open identity allowed the entire cultural reality to permeate each person and made those who had open identities represent universal qualities. In the novel, Joseph's teacher Eliezer continually confused his own life with the lives of the other teachers with the same name who preceded him:

> "Joseph listened with a pleasure in no way marred by Eliezer's syntactical idiosyncrasies, and certainly not by the fact that the old man's ego was not clearly demarcated, that it opened at the back, as it were, and overflowed into spheres external to his own individuality both in space and time; embodying in his own experience events which, remembered and related in the clear light of day, ought actually to have been put in the third person. Is man's ego a thing imprisoned in itself and sternly shut up in its boundaries of flesh and time? *Do not many of the elements which make it up belong to a world before it and outside it?* The notion that each person is himself and can be no other, is that anything more than a convention, which arbitrarily leaves out of account all the transitions which bind the individual consciousness to the general? The conception of individuality belongs after all to the same category of concep-

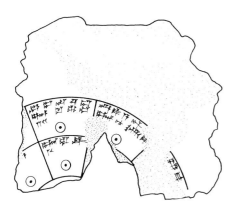

Figure II.2 Babylonian clay tablet. A fragment of a circular Zodiac divided into twelve segments attributed to the chief clerk of King Sargon II (722-705 BC). The fragment after L. W. King, *Cunieform Texts in the British Museum XXXIII, plate II.*

[3] Thomas Mann, *Joseph and His Brothers,* p. 81.

tions as that of unity and entirety, the whole and the all; and in the days of which I am writing the distinction between spirit in general and individual spirit possessed not nearly so much power over the mind as in our world of to-day which we have left behind us to tell of the other.'' [4]

[4] Thomas Mann, *Joseph and His Brothers,* p. 78.

Thus the ancients were totally integrated with the stars and the gods, and astrology was integral to their identity and the identity of their culture.

Egypt

From the beginning of the Egyptian dynasties, about 3200 BC, the connections between astrology-astronomy and the life of man were crystallized. The monuments of the Egyptians, particularly the Great Pyramid[5] and the magnificent Temple at Denderah, were temples of sacrifice and worship, symbols of the majesty and omnipotence of the pharaoh-god, and observation towers for the astronomer-priests. The siting and form of the Great Pyramid were correlated to astronomical values and its form embodied keys to the mysteries of the universe.[6] The hierarchy of geometrical forms was a reflection of a strictly hierarchial society where every person had his own position in what really was a vast, incredibly organized earthly representation of the universe. Religion, astrology, astronomy, and the calendar were all unitary in conception and practice.[7]

[5-6] See Figure II.3.

[7] See Schwaller de Lubicz, *The Temple in Man.*

The Egyptian myths were profoundly illustrative of the harmony between heaven and the Earth. The central myth of Egypt was the death and resurrection of **Osiris.** Osiris was the son of heaven and earth — the God of Death. He was slain by his dark brother Set, God of Evil, and cut into fourteen pieces which were then scattered throughout Egypt. His sister-wife Isis (Babylonian = *Ishtar)* was equivalent to Venus, the Goddess of Love and the planet which accompanies the Sun at its rising and setting. Isis found all of the parts of Osiris except the phallus, and preserved them with the appropriate rituals, while Horus (son of Ra, the rising Sun) killed Set in revenge. Through the labours of Isis, the gods bestowed immortality upon Osiris, and he became Judge of the Dead and governor of the initiatory mysteries which were later the basis for The Egyptian Book of the Dead.

This myth can be interpreted simply and traditionally as the death and rebirth of the Sun each day, but another variant is possible and even probable. The Egyptian civilization was agrarian and depended upon the annual flooding of the Nile for its survival. The precise timing of the flooding was the determining factor in the yearly calendar and ritual schedule. The indicator of this time was the heliacal (with the Sun) rising of the star Sirius. Sirius rose after the Sun for the months preceding the flooding of the Nile, and hence was not visible in the rays of the risen sun. Just as the flooding occurred, Sirius rose slightly before the Sun and could be seen leading the Sun into the day sky. The characters of the myth represented the planetary participants in this sacred day. Osiris was the star Sirius (O-sirius); Isis the planet Venus, which always rises with the Sun as the Morning Star; Horus was the rising Sun; and Set, the darkness and infertility of the night and of the season before flooding which the holy triad were trying to banish. The myth is a way of transmitting essential astronomical information from generation to generation.

The Egyptians believed that the universe was bound up with number, and that number was embodied in all tangible and intangible representations of the universe. The temples, the sacred art and the hieroglyphics were all correlated with numerical and astronomical-astrological realities, and communicated in such a way that the entire population could interface with the pharaoh in harmony. They were expressions of the unity which was the pervading factor in the universe. The laws of the planetary movements and the solar system were the same laws which governed men, and they believed that the closer the cosmic laws could be understood and followed, the more unified the entire civilization would be. The geometry determining planetary positions was identical to the geometry which determined human proportion or the shape and proportions of buildings. **Schwaller de Lubicz,** an orientalist and scholar, drew these conclusions to the great consternation of Egyptologists all over the world. He thought the prevailing technique of trying to superimpose interpretations from our cultural framework onto hieroglyphics was erroneous, and proposed a solution in which the hieroglyphs are coded astronomical information and a vocabulary of cosmic principles — the headdresses, postures and dress being keys to the knowledge the images contain. The

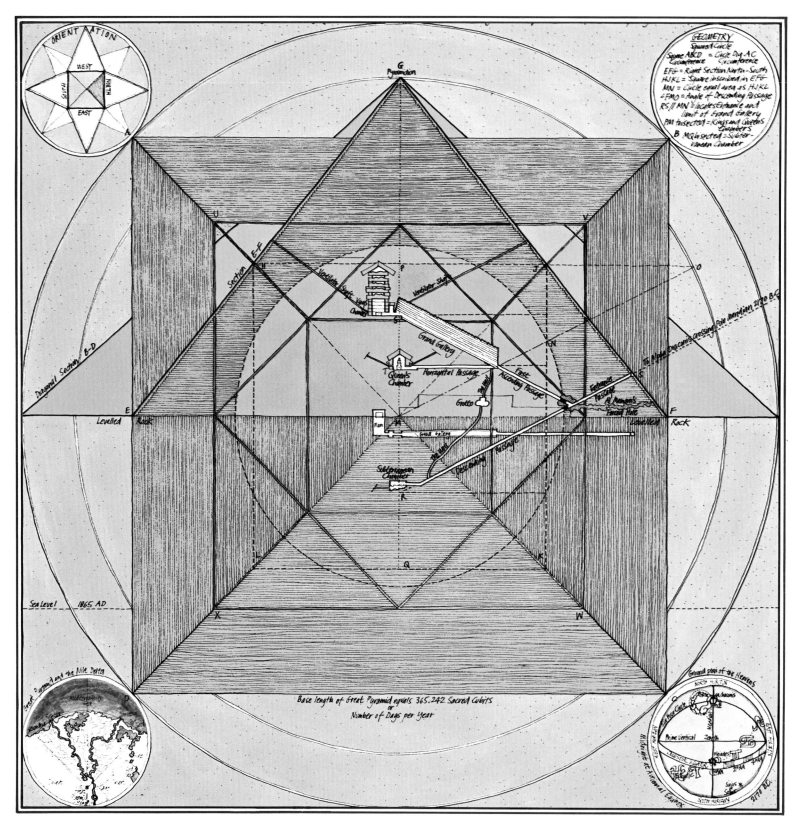

Figure II.3 The Great Pyramid.

temples are likewise reservoirs of astronomical-astrological heritage. (Figure II.3) The pyramids and pharaohs are not merely glorifications of earthly divinities, but also analogues of the nature of man in the universe.[8]

Classical Synthesis

The **Greek** civilization became the most powerful force in the known world. The Greeks synthesized the multitude of mythologies and religions which permeated the near east and the eastern Mediterranean, and were dominant partially because they knew how to subjugate conquered peoples by assimilating their mythologies.[9] The complex mythological Olympus echoed the wide-ranging cultural and military influence of the Greeks. Through the extreme multiplicity of overlapping and interpenetrating gods and goddesses there remained a firm identification of the major gods with the seven visible planetary bodies and with many of the other constellations in the skies. The seasonal transformations of Dionysius and the twelve labours of Hercules were both astrological-astronomical schemata like the Gilgamesh Epic, and mythologies were directly related to seasonal or planetary phenomena.[10]

The gods were a manifestation of the inherent need for protection the people felt during unsettled and barbarous times, and they likewise gained strength and prestige through the growth and prosperity of the people who worshipped them. Mythology was a retrospective and cumulative process. Wishes for expansion were associated with the equivalent characteristics of the gods of the region, and past successes were correlated with the potency of the gods. When tribes or cities were conquered, it was customary to destroy or to remove images of the existent gods, replacing them with the god-images of the conquerors. The myths of conquered people were altered to a subserviant position within the hierarchy of gods, and reduced to peripheral importance in the shadow of the conquering gods. Metaphors which expressed absorption were paternities, rapes, seductions and transformations. **Zeus,** for example, was supposedly the father to many hundreds of gods and goddesses, while chronologically a majority of his ''children'' existed demonstrably earlier than he did. His potency was indicative of the warlike bent of the Greeks. He was a syncretic image — he swallowed the previous mythological leaders, the Titans, who were definitely related to the seven planetary day names in the week, and replaced them with a twelvefold motif.[11]

The magical significance of names passed from the gods to a more personal level of operation. Often individuals were named after the gods, as were plants, trees, islands, and many other objects or ideas. The structure of language reveals direct connection to the very earliest religions and to astrology, as do alphabets throughout the world.[12] (Figure 11.4) The original formula, which implied the god's power over his subjects, encircling them with the magic of his name (via political power), has been reversed in astrology, which uses the name or symbol of the god to re-establish contact with the gods within the psyche.

The abstraction, clarification and distillation of the pantheon were paralleled by the similar action of Greek philosophers and scientists. They gathered ancient ideas from Babylonia, Chaldea, India, and Egypt together with various mythologies which transmitted concepts of their predecessors, trying to discover the *logic* (logos = word) behind them.

Pythagoras (531 – ? BC) used *number* to organize this assault upon the ancient beliefs. He explored the connection between natural numbers and the structure of mind and universe. Among his best-known aphorisms are, ''All things are number'', and ''God is a geometer''. The Pythagorean School utilized the mechanics of number as their major teaching and logical device. Natural numbers in their sequence have meanings which extend far beyond their mere qualities; they have an archetypal reality of their own. Man did not invent numbers, but rather they were *discovered* as an integral component of the mechanics of his own brain.[13] Numbers have their own internal logic like the series of numbers which form the Fibonacci Series, which has recently been found to govern the structure of plant life. There is a connection between natural numbers and the essence of life itself. Pythagoras has been verified as modern science uses number to describe everything in the universe. He believed that the mechanics of number arose from the cosmic *"music of the spheres",* the planetary harmony, and that the

[8] West and Toonder, *The Case for Astrology,* p. 40-53.

Figure II.3 The Great Pyramid was built at approximately 2170 BC. Although it served as the burial chamber of the Pharaoh Cheops, it also functioned as an astronomical observatory, a standard for Egyptian weights and measures, and an initiation temple. The entire geometry of the pyramid was based upon astronomical positions and movements.

[9] See Graves, The Greek Myths.

Figure II.4 The Evolution of the Alphabet. The evolution of early alphabets paralleled the form of the astrological glyphs we now use.

[10] See the Rape of Persephone and the legend of Adonis in Graves, *The Greek Myths,* and Frazer, *The Golden Bough.*

[11] Graves, *The Greek Myths,* p. 29.

[12] See Alfred Kallir, *Sign and Design.*

[13] Jung, *Letters II, 1951-1961,* p. 287.

musician who understood the numerological basis of music could evoke in his audience any emotion, sensation or idea. (Figure II.5)

Implicit in the series of signs of the zodiac, the quest of Gilgamesh, the labours of Hercules and the series of numbers from one to twelve are certain 'archetypal' (organic or integral) qualities. *Each number is a symbol* possessing its own particular correspondences and mechanisms, and it relates to every other number in certain specific ways. It participates in a *continuum,* a structure which unfolds in time, and contains meaning because it mediates between the physical world and the intellectual world. The properties of numbers allow their multiple meanings to be used interchangeably to create the whole fabric of the universe. The astronomer Sir James Jeans said in his connection, "he (God) is addicted to arithmetic".[14] The natural number sequence produces rhythms in meaning which approximate the action of life through time.

The psychologist **Carl Jung** was preoccupied with the qualities of the natural numbers and felt that they were a key to understanding the workings of the psyche. He saw in numbers a linking-up of all forms of judgement:

> "it appears that *whole numbers are individuals,* and that they possess properties which cannot be explained on the assumption that they are multiple units. The idea that numbers were invented for counting is obviously untenable, since they are not only pre-existent to judgement but possess properties which were discovered only in the course of the centuries, and presumably possess a number of others which will be brought to light by the future development of mathematics." [15]

These notions were transmitted by Pythagoras and his world view was based upon them, but he derived his divine ideas from the tradition of astrology which embodied them long before his time.

The cosmologies the Greeks inherited from the Chaldeans and Babylonians were simplified, although very accurate sightings and records had been made for millennia, as we have mentioned.[16] The Sun and Moon seemed to move across the vault of the sky, and the Greeks assumed that the Earth was the centre of the universe, and stellar bodies all revolved around it in concentric circles. Even though the Atomist **Democritus** (460-370 BC) proposed a model of the atom as a spherical nucleus surrounded by rapidly moving spheres, and **Aristarchus of Samos** (310-230 BC) extended the analogy to the Sun as centre of the solar system, the commonly accepted model was the Earth as the centre of the solar system (geocentric = Earth-centred) and not the Sun (helio-centric = Sun-centred). At this time Astrology included astronomy, geometry, mathematics and geography, and they all treated the Earth as a privileged vantage point, an attitude which still holds today, in spite of the Copernican revolution.

Plato (429-347 BC) develops in his dialogue *Timaeus* the ideas of Pythagoras in detailed but very abstract form. He believed that God used the four elements (fire, air, earth and water) to make a perfect world harmonized by its proportions. The gods were predominantly fire, and this fire permeated the other three orders of animals, birds and fishes and land animals as fire permeated the other three elements. The four elements were composed of triangular components and the atoms of these elements had the shape of the regular solids. (Figure II.6) The triangular parts were right-angled, one being half a square and the other being half an equilateral (equal-angled) triangle. Atoms of earth are cubes; of fire, tetrahedra; of air, octahedra; and of water, icosahedra. The other regular solid, the dodecahedron, was composed of pentagons and was designated as the Universe, although Plato also stated that the universe was a sphere. These elements could be inscribed within spheres within each other, making an image of the world. Eventually Kepler, almost two milennia later, tried to actualize this scheme and found that it approximated the planetary orbits in the solar system.[17] According to Plato every soul had its equivalent star in the sky and every body was composed of varying proportions of the elements, the soul and body being combined at birth and separated at death.

A universal structure governing all life forms in the universe has been sought through the ages, but this initial attempt is profound. The physicist **Werner Heisenberg** states, "According to Plato, it appears that the foundation of this apparently complicated world of elementary particles and force fields is a simple and lucid mathematical structure. All those

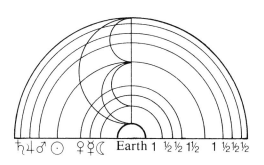

♄ ♃ ♂ ☉ ♀ ☿ ☾ Earth 1 ½ ½ 1½ 1 ½½½

Figure II.5 Pythagorean Musical Theory. Pythagoras related the intervals and harmonies of his diapasonal scale of music to the proportions of the planetary positions from the earth to the sphere of the fixed stars.

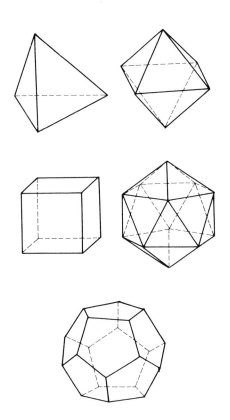

Figure II.6 The Five Platonic Solids.

[14] Russell, *The History of Western Philosophy,* p. 37.

[15] Jung, *Letters II, 1951-1961,* p. 328.

[16] Russell, *The History of Western Philosophy,* p. 208 & 212.

[17] See Moore, *The Atlas of the Universe,* p. 15., and Wolfgang Pauli, *The Influence of Archetypal Ideas on Kepler's Theories,* in *The Interpretation of Nature and the Psyche.*

heidt, *Cosmic Cybernetics*, p. 23.

man was integral to astrology before the time of Plato.

Plato also investigated the forces which make up the universe, principles of action or relative states of things, scaled from the most dense to the elements were Earth for the physical, Water for the emotional, Air for the intellect, Fire for the spiritual. At first it seems absurd to make these attributions when modern physicists and chemists have isolated and identified over 92 natural elements, but it does not when they are considered as *classes of phenomena*. The definition of Fire as energy, libido, spiritual impulse, vitality and the motivating factor of the elements in fact does hold up under the scrutiny of scientists. **Nigel Calder** in *"The Key of the Universe"* (1977), describing the very latest breakthroughs in particle physics, says: "With hindsight, the 'fire' of Heraclitus was not too different from the 'energy' from which everything was made according to twentieth-century physicists." [19] Water, traditionally defined as emotion, feelings, passivity and sensitivity, is a very close hit to the *wave nature* of energy and matter in the universe. There is also a close connection between emotions and waves via the rhythms of libido which affect sexuality.[20] Air, which is traditionally correlated with mind, intellect, communication and duality, is similar to the concept of *complementarity* between particle and wave nature. Earth, which governs the physical, matter, density and immovability, would naturally correlate with the *particle nature* of light and matter.

The pure geometric world-view culminated in the *Propositions of Euclid*. **Euclid** (c.?-300 BC) defined space, which he saw as a void, as a geometrically pure grid extending eternally in all directions with right-angle co-ordinates determining all positions. (Figure II.7) This attitude is totally static, and though not representative of the dynamics of space, prevailed as the standard view of the universe until Einstein two thousand years later.

The most important astronomer-astrologer in antiquity was Claudius Ptolemaius (called **Ptolemy,** c.100-178 AD), who was educated in Alexandria. His classic work on astrology, *Tetrabiblos* (Four Astrology Books) syncretized the information and ideas of the Egyptians, Chaldeans, Babylonians, and the Greeks, Pythagoras and Plato. This book remains the only source of ancient astrological thought, and is essentially a collection of "rules of thumb" used to make predictions at the time. He defined the astronomical reality of antiquity in the *Almagest,* which described the motions of the Sun, Moon and the planets around the Earth using the concept of "epicycles", interconnecting circular orbits which allowed accurate calculations for verifying the astronomical positions. The Earth was immovable in the middle of the solar system, the Moon rotated around it, then Mercury, Venus, the Sun, Mars, Jupiter, Saturn and the 'Empyrean', the sphere of the fixed stars. This complex structure in fact described the movements of all the planets quite accurately, and it stood as a model of the geocentric view of the solar system until 100 years after Copernicus. (Figure II.8) The privileged position of the Earth was a "given" to Ptolemy, and this assumption has been considered one of the most damaging structural ideas of astrology since the Renaissance. As we shall see later, in relating astrology to modern physics, it was a correct and verifiable hypothesis, and in fact represents the relativistic reality of the earth within the solar system.

Ptolemy believed that the function of man is to compare the order and regularity of astronomy to the

> "weakness and unpredictability of material qualities found in individual things. The movements of the heavenly bodies are a constant, observable and logical phenomenon which can be compared to the conditions and ambiance at certain times on earth. Just as the sun and the moon have definite relations to the seasons, the weather, and the ambient on a general level, so the movements of the other planets against the stars relate to more specific natures of things. As the interrelationships between the luminaries and the planets are very complex, so the relationships of these actions are to the quality of life on earth." [21]

His views about the general state of the knowledge of astrology during his time are that the greater forces and simpler natural orders related to stellar bodies are comprehensible even to ignorant men and some animals, while the lesser forces and orders are accessible only to those

[19] Calder, *The Key of the Universe,* p. 180.

[20] Jung, *Psychological Types, CW 6,* p. 175.

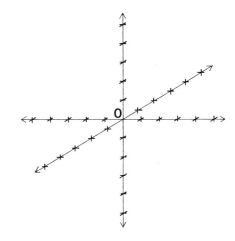

Figure II.7 The Euclidean Grid of Space. Any position in the universe can be determined by three reference numbers, according to Euclid.

[21] Ptolemy, *Tetrabiblos,* p. 134.

Figure II.8 The Ptolemaic System. The Earth was in the centre of the solar system, and the other planets, the Sun and the Moon revolved around it. *(London, 1708.)*

who necessarily make special observations, such as sailors, farmers and priests. Since at that time observations were still quite inaccurate, the correspondences possible were also commensurably inaccurate. But Ptolemy realized this:

> "If then, a man knows accurately the movements of all the stars, the Sun, and the Moon, so that neither the place nor the time of any of the configurations escapes his notice, and if he has distinguished in general their natures as the result of previous continued study, even though he may discern not their essential, but only their potentially effective qualities; and if he is capable of determining in view of all these data, both scientifically and by successful conjecture, the distinctive mark of quality resulting from the combination of all of the factors, what is to prevent him from being able to tell on each given occasion the characteristics of the air or the temperament of a man?" [22]

Ptolemy approached the predictive side of astrology in a very effusive manner, probably because at that time in history events *were* quite extreme in terms of individuals' fates. To relate Mars' positions to death by burning at the stake or the destruction by fire of a city is quite extreme to us, but in 150 AD, when the Roman Empire was on the verge of collapse, it may have been a common fate. Ptolemy's rules for the evaluation of horoscopes, the meaning of the signs and houses of the horoscopes and his method for determining weather were all used until the Renaissance. [23]

Tetrabiblos also presents the first system of astrological *houses*. In distinction to the signs of the zodiac — which are anthropomorphic representations of zones of the ecliptic — the houses are divisions relating to the stages in the life of the individual. (See Part V, The Houses of the Horoscope.) The names of the houses in Ptolemy are indicative of the approach in his time:

I.	Horoscope	VII.	Occident
II.	Gate of Hades	VIII.	Beginning of Death
III.	Goddess	IX.	God
IV.	Lower Midheaven	X.	Midheaven
V.	Good Fortune	XI.	Good Daemon
VI.	Bad Fortune	XII.	Bad Daemon

[22] Ptolemy, *Tetrabiblos*, p. 136.

[23] See the *Phenomenon Book of Calendars, 1978-1979*, p. 48.

The house names reflect the pagan attitude towards destiny and fate and the still potent relationship of the gods to man.

Christianity and Astrology

The advent of Christianity did not have any bearing upon the works of Ptolemy — he used exclusively pre-Christian sources. Christianity was only one of many religions vying for recognition within the Roman Empire. The effect of Christianity upon astrology was obviously parallel to its effect upon the attitudes of all men, being the final concentration of the god-image towards monothesism and the creation of a link between god and man which was "tangible". As Jung so perceptively observed, **Christ** was a symbol of the "Self", the total man. [24] The archetype of the Self unites the opposites and is a synthesizing device denoting psychic wholeness. Just as the Christ of the Gospels was representative of the god in man, he also pointed towards the potential of God residing in all men.

The **Old Testament** related the first stages in man's development from primordial unity through the paradisiacal Garden of Eden to the Fall, man's schism with the Creator. The metaphor is clearly about the diffusion of the religious impulse into the myriad gods of the near east in early times. The Old Testament follows the diversification of this unity in the histories of the Twelve Tribes of Israel, once again correlated with the twelve signs of the zodiac. This fragmentation of the family of Jacob symbolized the breakdown of the unified god-image into irreconcilable variations. [25]

The function of the **New Testament** was to utilize Christ as a reuniter of the fragments, his twelve disciples being another obvious extension of the twelve tribes — Christ is the thirteenth and their synthesis. Christ's prophesies of the Kingdom of Heaven on Earth work onwards in time, back toward the primordial unity, but most importantly towards the discovery of the timeless godhead within the Self. The image in the Book of Revelations is clear about

[24] See Jung, *Aion, CW 9, Part II.*

[25] *Genesis, XXVI-L.*

"In the midst of the street of it, and on either side of the river, was there the tree of life, which bare twelve manner of fruits, and yielded her fruit every month: and the leaves of the tree were for the healing of the nations."[26]

The twelve-fold path of astrology is a tool for the unification of man and god, and for man and man: the image of the Holy Jerusalem of completion.

Variations and developments of the god-image in history mark parallel developments in man's attitudes towards the Self. The pagan gods revelled in Olympian glee and sported with man for amusement, occasionally committing themselves briefly to altering his status, but usually becoming bored and consigning the poor mortal to eternal life as a swan, a laurel tree, or a stony mountain peak. This reflected man's feeling that he was a plaything of the infinite. The patristic Yahweh of the Jews, although less frivolous than most, was mortally demanding and outrageously vindictive towards his "chosen people". His baiting and torture of those closest to Him seemingly indicated a desire, difficult to sate, to experience His Grand Creation from the mortal coil, but in practice He did not deign to bridge the gap until His incarnation in Christ.[27] The Christian Trinity — Father, Son and the Holy Ghost — reflected a still masculine bias towards dogmatic paternalism and onesidedness which was corrected only when the Virgin Mary was assumed in 1950. The prototype of the Virgin, Sophia (= *wisdom),* was discredited by the Church as being gnostic.

The mathematics of the religion is also interesting. The Son is a mediating influence between two poles: the Father of Light and the Holy Ghost of the primal Darkness, the expansion of two into three. Within the trinity, the third is related back to the initial unity of the first and becomes extended to a fourth. This is an alchemical axiom called the "Axiom of Maria" which states, "Out of the One comes Two, out of Two comes Three, and from the Third comes the One as the Fourth."[28] Whereas the god-image is characterized as a trinity within the circle, the quaternity within the circle is a symbol of the Self.[29] The implication is that god-images are often whole but are not always so because they seek contact with man without achieving satisfaction, while images of the Self include both God and Man within their whole.

The relationship between three and four is as central to astrology as it is to religion. In astrology there are four elements and three modes which transmit influences (4 x 3 = 12). Early Christianity used both the trinitarian images of Father, Son and Holy Ghost, and the quaternarian imagery of the Four Horsemen of the Apocalypse, the four Evangelists, and the four Sacred Beasts. (Figure II.9) Interlocking number with meaning became the preoccupation of the next revitalizers of astrology, the alchemists.

The Alchemists

Following the flowering of Christianity and the Fall of the Roman Empire all of the ideas we have presented so far entered a state of isolation. The monastic Christian orders and the Arabic philosophers maintained and transmitted classical mathematics, astrology and astronomy separately. When these two mainstreams met after the Eleventh Century, the world picture had changed from the static classical view. The Hermetic revivalists, the Neoplatonists and survivors of many pre-Christian millenialist sects also joined to produce this change. As **Marie Louise von Franz** observes, the two major world views at the time were the time-bound rotating circles of astrology as envisioned by the Egyptians, Gnostics and Arabic alchemists, and the timeless geometric images which were static representations of the universal order derived from Pythagoras and Euclid.[30] The common link was *time,* which bridged the two world models. The prototype of the two models is derived from Plato. Plato assumed that there was a world of ideas (archetypes) which was purely god-created and composed of totally static geometric forms. When god desired to create the "real" world, he translated the pure model into a moving image which corresponded to the sequence of natural numbers. The thinkers and religious men from the 11th century until the 15th century described their cosmologies in terms of one of these two types of models, and usually represented them graphically.

The usual format for cosmological models was the circle, the *mandala* (Sanskrit for *circle).*

Figure II.9 The Four Sacred Beasts. The Bull, Lion, Man and Eagle adorn the rose window at St. Gabriel's Church in Tarascon, near Avignon, built approximately 1150 AD. (Photograph courtesy of Painton Cowen.)

[26] *Revelation XXII, 2.*

[27] See Jung, *Answer to Job.*

[28] Von Franz, *Number and Time,* p. 65., and Jung, *Psychology and Alchemy, CW 12,* p. 160.

[29] Jung, *Mysterium Coniunctionis, CW 14,* p. 207.

[30] Von Franz, *Number and Time,* p. 179.

Figure 11.10 Lausanne Rose Window. This window, built from 1225 to 1235 AD shows the use of circles and squares in the rose window. (Photograph courtesy of Painton Cowen.)

The mandala could represent any cosmological model in use at the time: Ptolemaic geocentric solar systems, Arabic astrolabes and navigational devices, the earliest clocks, personal horoscopes, rose windows and religious structures. Since people at the time assumed the connection between the ideal and the real, they also believed that the circular model indicated perfection and could therefore show both God and Self images. Astrology was renewed during this medieval age as a time-bound system, and its temporal orientation was especially prominent as the year 1000 AD had been associated with biblical prophesies about the end of the world. Astrology was a prime carrier of those projections.

Circular representations had a wide range of applications. Most accessible to the common people were the great rose windows of the cathedrals. (Figure II.10) The cathedrals were mirror images of the scholastic *summa* — a system of knowledge — and the Gothic cathedral was a device to enable the common people to understand the unity of imagery which the Church perpetrated.[31] The roses were images of the Self, and usually had representations of the Prophets, Disciples, Virgin and Child, Kings of Israel and images from the Old and New Testaments. (Figure II.11) The people could understand the hierarchies of the Bible as well as the order of their virtues by knowing the structure of the rose. **Dante's** *Divine Comedy* was also a mandala image of Heaven and Hell. The structure of these places was clearly described, as were the various virtues and vices which were associated with them. The images of the ideal world were available to the people through the mandalas.

The alchemists took the use of mandalas a step further. They attempted to create a miniature internal universe which reflected the external universe; the correlation of the microcosm and macrocosm. Initially this was a purely religious and intellectual pursuit, then represented the position of thinkers who found that Christian orthodoxy excluded their ideas, and eventually became heretical in the eyes of the Church. The mandala models of the alchemists were images of the universal mind which came closer and closer to the real world. While these images carried projected contents of the abandoned instinctual reality, "at the same time, the projection of this mandala image (the horoscope) onto the heavens began to be withdrawn, only to be projected anew onto another region: the mystery of nature."[32] The earliest chemistry models were images of the *unus mundus* (the unity of existence). The alchemists began to investigate not only the static realities underlying life, but also the temporal manifestations.

The mandala represented the *opus*, the process of the "work". Marie Louise von Franz discusses a mandala of the opus, the so-called *"Chrysopoiea of Cleopatra"*, in *Number and Time*. (Figure II.12) The three circles contains clues to the great work; the innermost carrying symbols for Sun, Moon and Mercury; the second an inscription saying, "The serpent is the One which possesses the poison according to the two symbols"; and the outermost, "One is the Whole and by its means the Whole (exists) and toward it the Whole (tends) and if the Whole should not comprise the Whole (everything) it would be nothing." The outer circle is the zodiac and the ourobouros of time encompassing the unity of the universe.[33] Life is the circular process of discovering unity behind appearances in the outer world. Jung studied alchemy, and concluded that the alchemists were not only the predecessors of modern chemists, but also of modern psychologists. Their process was simultaneously external and internal, and its intent was to create wholeness which encompassed both pairs of opposites.

The underlying idea of magic was that the circle can co-ordinate a multitude of diverse or opposing values around its periphery. By placing any desired idea, power, information or product in its proper location round the circle, the effect produced would "constellate" within the soul of the magician. The magician identified with the entire range of contents around himself and was able to assimilate any alien or missing content which came to him. Facsimiles of worldly things — metals, colours, stones and other materials — would sympathetically evoke their clarifying effects. The circle could extend the consciousness of the magician or locate and restrengthen weakened parts of the whole. The *Talisman* was an individual aspect of the unus mundus which drew the meditator to concentrate his being upon the part of his nature which was most in need of contact with the higher consciousness. (Figure II.14) The object was communication and coincidence with the centre of the mandala in its aspect as the Self. The talisman corresponded to the personal horoscope of the magician as it indicated which planet or sign quality was deficient, and allowed easy determination of what influence was needed (and when) as correct compensation. It was used together with the

[31] Yates, *The Art of Memory,* p. 90.

[32] Von Franz, *Number and Time,* p. 178-9.

[33] *Ibid,* p. 179.

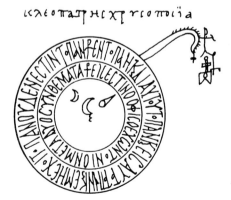

Figure II.12 Chrysopeia of Cleopatra. (After the drawing by M. Berthelot, *Collection des anciens alchimistes grecs,* Paris 1887-1888, as reproduced in von Franz, *Number and Time,* p. 180.)

procedure for the diagnosis and treatment of illness. Each bodily part and major organic or glandular system is attributable to specific signs (body parts) or planets (organ or gland system). The rulerships of all vegetable remedies, minerals, precious stones, colours, fabrics, herbs and animal substances were also catalogued by Paracelsus. The individual horoscope indicates correlations between illness and cure, or fragmentation and wholeness. The remedy might be a talisman with a diagram complete with its colours, geometric forms, metals and stones. For instance, wearing a green robe with an emerald set in copper on a Friday (Vendredi) would evoke Venusian qualities, and promote love and affection. The objects an individual surrounds himself with continually evoke qualities of which he may or may not be conscious. The magician tried to retain total awareness.

Subtle imbalances can be equilibrated easily when they first appear in an individual, but if they are not recognized they begin manifesting in physical form, finally becoming disease. Paracelsus believed that disease started on the finest spiritual-mental level with a feeling of loss of harmony and gradually proceeded into the less fine emotional level, until finally the physical body was effected. Once physical symptoms appeared, the disease had already reached an advanced stage and the physician had to produce a remedy which operated on all levels simultaneously. He was forced to treat the soul as well as the body.

Figure II.13 Paracelsus.

The Memory Art

The Greeks and Egyptians had few written manuscripts, which made the ability to memorize information a necessity. The Greeks included in the necessary areas of knowledge the "art of memory".[34] To memorize according to their method, one pictures a familiar building or room and — using a preset sequence of columns, objects or niches — places "ideas" of the information on the key objects. Greek actors used the classical theatre seats as memory places or images. When a certain speech was required, the appropriate place in the theatre was pictured and the speech reconstructed as the information was retrieved. Using this system actors could memorize long dramas and always have them available. The staging of the drama was a reciprocal memory technique for the audience, who also were unable to have manuscripts. The positions of the actors, their costumes and gestures all related to their speeches and their role as memory images. All of these devices enhanced understanding of the drama and allowed it to be imprinted on the memory of the audience. Morality plays were ways of influencing the unconscious of the population during the Middle Ages.

A variant memory system, originated by **Metrodorus of Scepsis** (106-43 BC), was based upon astrology. In her definitive book, *The Art of Memory,* **Frances Yates** discusses Metrodorus:

> "I suspect that Metrodorus was versed in astrology, for astrologers divided the Zodiac not only into twelve signs, but also 36 decans, each covering ten degrees; for each decan there was an associated decan-figure. Metrodorus probably grouped ten artificial backgrounds (loci) under each decan figure. He would thus have a series of *loci* numbered 1 to 360, which he could use in his operations. With a little calculation he could find any background *(locus)* by its number, and he was insured against missing a background, since all were arranged in numerical order. His system was therefore well designed for the performance of striking feats of memory." [35]

The memory art was perfected by Metrodorus, and he was reputed to be able to repeat everything he heard verbatim. Many of the foremost medieval scholars, religious men and magicians used memory systems and freely applied them to whatever series of images they desired. Among these were **St. Thomas Aquinas, Albertus Magnus, Ramon Lull, Simonides** and many others.

The magus **Giordano Bruno** (1548-1600) felt that every man carried an image of the universe within his soul, and the establishment of access to it conferred memory, healing, power and enlightenment. Bruno was a follower of the Corpus Hermeticum (Body of Hermes), and wrote many works on the art of the magical memory, the major being *De umbris idearum . . . .* (Shadows), and *Sigillus Sigillorum . . .* (Seals). Bruno used rotating cir-

[34] See Frances Yates, *The Art of Memory.*

[35] Yates, *The Art of Memory,* p. 54, and L. A. Post, *Classical Weekly,* p. 109.

Figure II.11 Chartres Cathedral North Rose Window. Built in 1145 AD, this window shows the Virgin held by her Mother surrounded by the Doves of the Spirit, the Kings of Israel and the Twelve Prophets.

Figure II.14 Lunar Talisman. This talisman is dedicated to Mother Luna, and displays her colours, astrological symbols, animals, orientations and other glyphs.

Figure II.11 Chartres Cathedral North Rose Window.

Figure II.14 Lunar Talisman.

Figure II.16 Planetary Sigils.

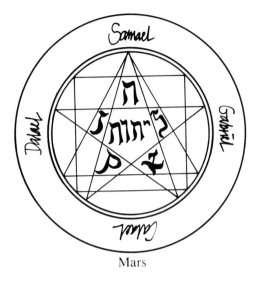

Mars

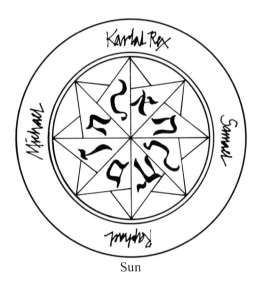

Sun

cular diagrams which combined series of letters and were called "memory wheels". (Figure II.15) His major memory system was a huge mandala composed of circles divided into the following sections:

1. 360 divisions, one for each degree, all with images.
   Each group of ten degrees is one decan with its image.
   Every three decans constitute an astrological sign with its image.
2. Forty-nine images for the planets, seven for each planet.
3. Images for the twenty-eight mansions of the moon, or "stations".
4. Images for the thirty-six astrological houses, which are connected with the traditional calendar.

These images form a complete moving representation of the entire universe and can reflect any event or quality in its proper place. Bruno used astral systems together with mnemonic techniques to improve the memory, but on a higher level he was searching for methods of organizing the psyche. He made many sigils, which combined astrological information with memory devices, making a bridge between the two magical worlds. (Fig. II.16) The progress of Bruno's magical ideas tends towards more complex representations, until he attempted to duplicate a universal memory system which was encyclopaedic.[36]

The two major memory arts are the *Square Art* which uses rectilinear buildings as loci for their places, and the *Round Art* which uses the scheme of the celestial sphere to represent not only static images, but also images which have a temporal order. The round art uses magicized images and talismans, stellar effigies, images of the virtues and vices, while the square art is involved with corporeal things and inanimate objects. The square art is 'artificial' while the round art is 'natural', and **Robert Fludd** (1547-1637) believed the round art to be the more efficacious, as it is more complex and intellectually satisfying, and comes closer to the lyrical nature of men. Fludd believed that the obvious connection between the two would produce a more stable whole. The combination of the ars rotunda and the ars quadrata — rectilinear buildings within spherical universes and solar systems — is the *Theatre of the World*.[37] The theatre which was the supreme culmination of memory technique was the Globe in London, covered by canvas embroidered with the images of the zodiac. All the world was a stage.

The Renaissance

The renaissance was a time for unification of the psyche. This "Age of Humanism" saw man as a reflection of the divine proportion which pervaded architecture, painting, sculpture and drama. **Nicolas Copernicus** (1473-1543) proposed a return to a heliocentric model of the solar system. Although an astrologer, Copernicus advanced the theory that the Sun was stationary at the centre of the solar system, and movements of the Sun and the stars were caused by the rotation of the Earth on its axis and its revolution around the Sun. (Figure II.17) He still believed in "uniform circular motion" and simplicity: unfortunately, neither were true. It took one hundred years for the mathematics of the Copernican theory to be proven. It took the Church as long as the mathematical proof to accept the theory because they felt it removed man from the centre of the universe and undermined the divinity of the Church.[38] Although the astrologers and the Church agreed upon geocentricity, the Church classified astrology as highly suspect and probably heretical. The impact this had upon astrology was so critical that it had to go 'underground' to escape the censure of the Church.

Johannes Kepler (1571-1630) finally proved the Copernican theory by using elliptical orbits for the planetary bodies. This was the final deviation of the real from the ideal. Even though after this time the planetary orbits were still graphically indicated as being circular, the circle became an abstraction which indicated a merger of the real and the ideal. The true distinction was mathematical. Kepler was simultaneously a good Protestant and a sun-worshipping Pythagorean, as Wolfgang Pauli's paper, *"The Influence of Archetypal Ideas on the Scientific Theories of Kepler"*, shows clearly. Kepler also practiced astrology, as proven by his writings and an extant horoscope drawn for Wallenstein. Kepler thought that astrology was valuable but required a re-evaluation. He cautioned those who would reject it totally. A commentary after the title in his *Tertius interviens,* states: "A warning to sundry Theologos,

[36] Yates, *The Art of Memory*, p. 289.

[37] Yates, *The Art of Memory*, p. 314-319 and Yates, *The Theatre of the World*.

[38] Russell, *The History of Western Philosophy*, p. 528.

just repudiation of star-gazing superstition, throw out the child with the bath and thus unknowingly act in contradiction to their profession." [39] Kepler believed that the soul, *vis formatrix* or *matrix formativa,* had a specific reaction to certain harmonious proportions which stellar rays cast in the horoscope, corresponding to specific rational divisions of the circle. The light rays were effective, but the influences of the planets and stars emitted no special influences due to their distance from Earth. The soul knew the harmonious proportions instinctively without conscious reflection, because the soul, being circular, was an image of God in Whom these proportions and the geometric truths existed from all eternity. [40] The soul was impressed by the external forms of the rays, and retained a memory of them from birth. In *Harmonices mundi* Kepler states:

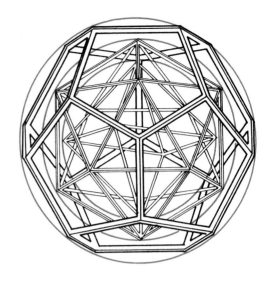

> "Inasmuch as the soul bears within itself the idea of the zodiac, or rather its centre, it also feels which planet stands at which time under which degree of the zodiac, and measures the angles of the rays that meet on earth; but inasmuch as it receives from the irradiation of the Divine essence the geometrical figures of the circle (by comparing the circle with certain parts of it) the archetypal harmonies (not, to be sure, in purely geometrical form but as it were overlaid or rather completely saturated with a filtrate of glittering radiations), it also recognizes the measurements of the angles and judges some as congruent or harmonious, others as incongruent." [41]

The human soul at birth flows into a pre-existent form, and evaluates all planetary influences for the rest of life in accord with the original state of the soul.

Besides formulating his three laws of planetary motion by 1619 explaining why elliptical orbits were necessary to prove the heliocentric theory of Copernicus, Kepler was also interested in proving the cosmic and scientific significance of the Pythagorean solids. He constructed diagrams which showed regular solid figures inscribed within spheres and inscribed within each other, and derived from them an approximation of the distances of the planets from the Sun, although it was not quite accurate. (Figure II.18) His book *Harmonices mundi* (Harmonies of the World) stated his Third Law, but also was concerned with the Pythagorean "harmony of the spheres", and this admixture of the scientist and the mystic was potent. Although philosophically classical, he ushered in the era of scientific method by combining the patient collection of many facts and bold guessing. [42]

Kepler signalled the final split between the humanist-magical-astrological viewpoint and the scientific-mechanical-objective viewpoint. The split paralleled the schism of **Luther** from the Church, where the traditional-liturgical and abstract-individual orientations were separated from each other. This severed the roots of the medieval attempt to unify the real and the ideal.

The use of the telescope by **Galileo** (1564-1642) and the basic theories of gravitation and mechanics of **Isaac Newton** (1642-1727), both of whom were astrologers, further accentuated the split. The vast improvement in observation could have elevated astrology, but served to discredit it, and its intelligent practitioners were forced either to withdraw from their studies or to mask these studies behind other arts or "sciences".

Francis Bacon and **Shakespeare** both integrated stellar doctrines and magical ideas into their works, but the advent of Cartesian logic and its acceptance in the Seventeenth Century forced the separation of mind from matter, and led towards the devaluation of art in favour of science. The importance of matter overshadowed the centrality of the spirit, completed the obliteration of astrology and vaulted the mechanistic world-view into dominance. The "Royal Art" of astrology was not able to accept these materialist strictures, and it degenerated into fortune-telling by madmen or gypsies.

William Lilly (1602-1681) was the best-known English astrologer of his time, and published *"An Introduction to Astrology"* (1647), which was the only text on astrology which had virtue until the end of the Nineteenth Century. He was integral to the trend — started in the Seventeenth Century — for transferring the source of astronomical information from observation to the tables of almanacs. (Figure II.19) This signalled the end of the direct contact of the astronomer-astrologer with the heavens themselves. After this date observation was virtually nonexistent for practicing astrologers. Lilly's almanacs created quite a stir, particularly when he predicted the Great Fire of London in 1666 so accurately that he was brought to court and charged with complicity. He also correctly prognosticated the beheading of King Charles I.

[39] Pauli, *The Interpretation of Nature and the Psyche,* p. 179-80.

[40] Ibid, p. 180-81.

[41] Kepler, *Harmonices Mundi,* Book IV (Frisch, V, p. 256); and Pauli, *Ibid,* p. 182-83.

[42] Russell, *The History of Western Philosophy,* p. 528.

Figure II.15 Figura Intellectus.

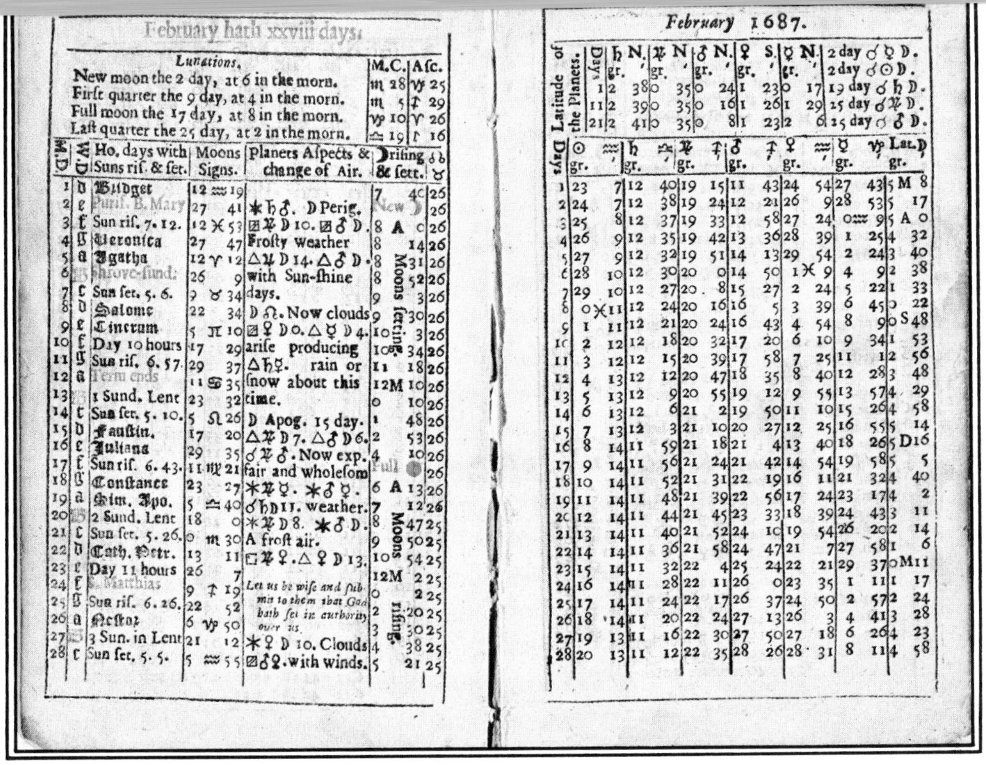

Figure II.19 John Wing's 1629 Almanac. (In the collection of the Author.)

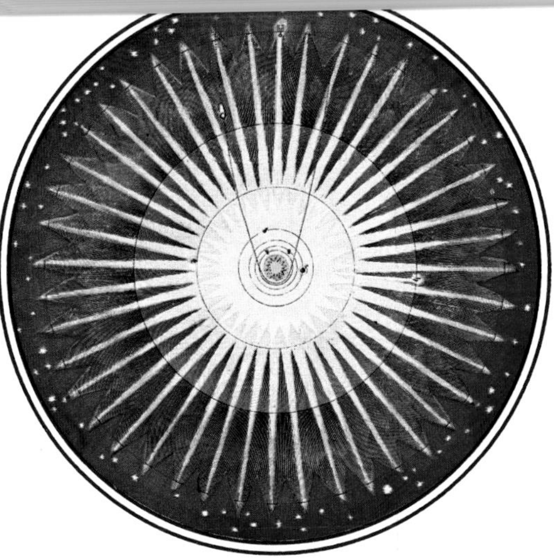

Figure II.17 The Copernican Heliocentric System.

He advised the King to quit London, but obviously the advice was not taken. His book was neglected until it was reprinted by a Nineteenth Century astrologer, **Zadkiel**, in 1852. Although many astrologers flourished during these times, the majority were quacks, and those who were not often ended their lives at the stake or in seclusion from authority.

The Theosophical Revival

Astrology lay dormant until the foundation of the Theosophical Society by **Helena Petrovna Blavatsky** (1831-1891). Madame Blavatsky was Russian and travelled extensively in the far east — Tibet, India, China and Ceylon. Her mission, she believed, had been determined by a secret "White Brotherhood" of enlightened lamas in the mountains of Tibet who communicated with her psychically. Her function was to reintegrate eastern religious ideas with western consciousness. Her handbook was the *Secret Doctrine* (1893), which described a world view encompassing millions of years and thousands of civilisations, and she gave credit to astrology as an essential language in the renewal, although she did not practice it herself. The damage this movement did to astrology was incalculable — due to the shady spiritualistic overtones she encouraged — but it did serve to awaken public interest in the life of the psyche as a compensation for the deadly Darwinian materialism of the Victorian Age.

Astrologers who received their initial impetus from the Theosophical Society were affected by the extraordinarily moralistic attitudes fostered by Madame Blavatsky. As a result, their texts on astrology were laden to overfilling with flowery back-pedalling which inevitably induced associations of old ladies sitting around a shadowy table conjuring up the spirits of their deceased husbands. The foremost astrologer of the Society was **Alan Leo** (William Frederick Allan, 1860-1917), whom Margaret Hone describes as the "Father of Modern Astrology".[43] Alan Leo wrote extensively on "Esoteric Astrology", and the following is a sample of his attitude:

Figure II.15 Figura Intellectus. This meditative mandala is based upon a diagram made by Giodano Bruno in 1588. Every possible permutation of the Sun and Moon in the twelve signs of the zodiac is shown in the rotating windows.

[43] Hone, *A Modern Textbook of Astrology*, p. 295.

"The time has come when the Chaldean and Assyrian religions shall once more be revealed, and the truth with regard to our destiny, as told by the stars, unfolded. The Wisdom Religion has now in the west taken firm root among those who have thrown off the heavy chains of conventionality, and its leaders by their force of reason and purity of life have now the power to turn the tide of evolution into the channels of progress and liberty. But their theories of fate and freewill, and the law of action and reaction, need the practical demonstration of this law through the aid of Astrology." [44]

Although well-meaning, the Theosophical astrologers and their organization, the Astrological Lodge of London, reflected the inability of "modern" man to see the individual as a whole, incorporating both positive and negative sides of his character. This dilemma was rectified by the psychology of the unconscious at the turn of the Twentieth Century.

Psychology and Astrology

Sigmund Freud (1856-1939) studied with individuals in Europe who attempted to find connection between the life of the psyche and physiological processes. The experimenters of the Nineteenth Century, **Charcot, Mesmer** and **Wundt,** had tried chemical means, hypnosis, restraint, and many other techniques to establish this connection, but none were able to see the two together as a unity. The missing connection discovered by Freud was dreams, the mediating language between waking consciousness and the subconscious.

Freud discovered that the conscious attitude was derived from both environmental-parental factors and an inherent "racial memory" of the developments during mankind's primordial epochs which were acted out through childhood. The child in his development acted out the gradual civilization of mankind against the background and tempering influence of the family. The essential dominant, he believed, was sexuality, and his *"psychanalysis"* [45] was a *reductive* process of stripping away all influences which masked or qualified the sex drive. Connections between the child and his parents were conditioned by basic mythological themes, the central ones being the incestuous *Oedipus* and *Electra Complexes*. The impossibility of the maturing child to gratify his or her sexual drives upon the parents gave rise to unconscious inhibitions, transmitted through actions which masked the instinctive motives, misdefined words (Freudian slips) which betrayed the true feelings and, most importantly, dreams.

In Freud's psychanalysis, the analyst had a distinctly paternal relationship with his patient, and the medium of communication was *"free association"*. Dream or fantasy material was related by the patient, and then stripped of its overlaid meanings and guises by the analyst. The gradual reduction of extraneous material yielded the nature of the central sexual drives and consequent frustrations which had forced the patient to misinterpret the external world and his place in it. The *neurotic* substituted imaginary situations and meanings for reality. The intent of the therapy was eventually to free the patient from his afflictions by talking them out. Freud was the founder of modern psychology, but his attitude towards sexuality as the central motif eventually hardened into rigid doctrine. Many of his students were forced to reject his oversimplification and dogmatic paternalism.

Alfred Adler (1870-1937) adopted the idea of the *"will to power"*. Sexuality was an instinctive drive and modern man had a striving for dominance which overshadowed the instincts. This dominance characterized man just before the World Wars, but still failed to recognize the necessity to *balance* instinct, sexuality and consciousness.

Carl Gustav Jung (1875-1961) broke off from Freud in 1913 due to his concept of libido *(psychic force* or *energy)*. Jung maintained that the life force was capable of functioning through sexuality, but that sexuality was not the only or ultimate channel through which it could operate. He conceived of a *Collective Unconscious,* which was an inherited mythological substratum of associations which are the common property of all men. It complemented the *Personal Unconscious,* which is the sum total of acquisitions of personal life — everything forgotten, repressed, subliminally received, thought or felt. By structuring two types of unconsciousness as parts of a unitary whole, Jung had combined two of Freud's main interests in a reasonable way. Jung stated the following in his *"Psychological Types"* (1923),

[44] Alan Leo, *Practical Astrology,* p. v.

[45] Freud's original spelling. The term later became *psychoanalysis.* Jung, *Letters I, 1906-1950,* p.10.

"What lies behind sexuality or the power instinct is the *attitude* towards sexuality or power. In so far as an attitude is not merely an intuitive (i.e., unconscious and spontaneous) phenomenon but also a conscious function, it is, in the main, a view of life. Our conception of all problematical things is enormously influenced, sometimes consciously but more often unconsciously, by certain collective ideas that condition our mentality. These collective ideas are intimately bound up with the view of life and the world of the past centuries or epochs. Whether or not we are conscious of this dependence has nothing to do with it, since we are influenced by these ideas through the very air we breathe. Collective ideas always have a religious character, and a philosophical idea becomes collective when it expresses a primordial image. Their religious character derives from the fact that they express the realities of the collective unconscious and are thus able to release its latent energies. The great problems of life including, of course, sex are always related to the primordial images of the collective unconscious. These images are balancing or compensating factors that correspond to the problems which life confronts us with in reality." [46]

The *archetypes* are the common primordial images which carry our conceptions of the world. The archetype is a "mnemic deposit, an imprint or engram, which has arisen through the condensation of countless processes of a similar kind." [47] These archetypes can be in the form of mythological motifs, psychic expressions of the physiological or anatomical disposition, or *ideas,* in the classical Greek sense.

Jung used astrology throughout his life, reasoning that because much psychological knowledge had been projected onto the heavens, it must have a profound bearing upon the core of psychological truth, and can be successfully withdrawn from the heavens.[48] He recognized in the signs of the zodiac libido symbols which depicted the typical qualities of the libido at any given moment. The psychic and hereditary predisposition of the individual is expressed through the horoscope. Since he treated astrology in a totally scientific manner, he cautioned that it must not be taken too literally. It is an apt tool *only when used intelligently.* In a letter to Andre Barbault in 1954, he explained the connection between astrology and psychology quite succinctly:

> "There are many instances of striking analogies between astrological constellations and psychological events or between the horoscope and the characterological disposition. It is even possible to predict to a certain extent the psychic effect of a transit. One may expect with a fair degree of probability that a given well-defined psychological situation will be accompanied by an analogous astrological configuration. Astrology, like the collective unconscious with which psychology is concerned, consists of symbolic configurations: the 'planets' are the gods, symbols of the power of the unconscious." [49]

Astrology is an apt tool for forging the link back to man's basic reality and, used with psychology, can assist in the achievement of psychic wholeness.

Jung was also very concerned with *mandala symbolism*[50] as a representation of a Self in pictorial form within a mathematical structure. The horoscope is a mandala in which the circle is the Self and its mechanisms — including divisions into dark and light halves, a system of correspondences, a time sequence around the periphery, atemporal connections through the centre of the circle, specific identifications with the personality, the Ego, the parents and the environment, and a mathematical structure capable of supplying analysis, hypothesis and verification. It is an image of the individual and his relationship to the *unus mundus.*

The advantages of the interconnection between astrology and psychology are manifold. Astrology can utilize terminology and mechanisms which have been identified by psychology, and transmit them along a framework that operates through time. The sequence within which psychological states unfold through time is helpful in pinpointing connections to the whole, and the relativity of the parts to the whole. Astrology can utilize the methods of analysis, and the implications of the *transference* between the doctor and the analysand which psychology has explored in depth.[51] Jung considered both psychology and astrology as natural sciences, and this makes them of the same family — astrology being the mother returned to the fold after many millenia as a black sheep.

[46] Jung, *Psychological Types, CW 6,* p. 220.

[47] Jung, *Psychological Types, CW 6,* p. 443-44.

[48] Jung, *Letters I, 1906-1950,* p. 24.

[49] Jung, *Letters II, 1951-1961,* p. 260.

[50] See Jung, *Archetypes and the Collective Unconscious, CW 9, Part I,* VI, 3.

[51] See Jung, *The Practice of Psychotherapy,* and Freud, *Introductory Lectures, III.*

Figure II.20 The Einsteinian Curved Universe. (After Nigel Calder's diagram in *The Key to the Universe.*)

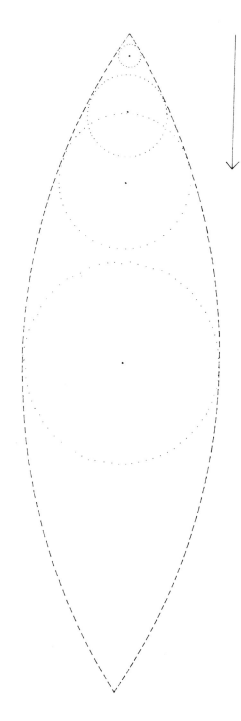

Astrology and Physics

As psychology broke through the "haze of unknowing" about man and psyche, the concept of the physical world was totally altered by the *Theory of Relativity* (1904) of **Albert Einstein** (1879-1950). Before the publication of this work, the concept of space — the only view for the previous two thousand years — was Euclidean. Space was seen as from an ideal vantage point and the geometry of space was uniform everywhere. This concept was an 'absolute space principle' which had been accepted since the Greeks and did not recognize Time, except as an additional dimension. Einstein integrated time with space through his "field theories".

Instead of the universe as a void containing solid particles, the particles are understood as concentrations of energy, and have *fields* which influence the space around them. Fields are produced by the motion of the particles — which themselves are charges rather than substance — and their motion produces an electric current. Einstein related the particles to their fields, their currents, and their surrounding space as a unified whole. The energy of which the entire universe is composed can transmute itself into any of myriad energy forms, all mutually interdependent.

The field concept not only deals with electric and magnetic fields (of charged bodies and currents), but also with gravitational fields. Whereas electromagnetic fields attract and repel, gravitational fields not only attract massive bodies to other massive bodies, but affect the space around as well. By attracting equally in all directions, gravitational fields of bodies *curve* the space around themselves. This situation is mutual however, as it is a condition of space that it is curved and cylindrical along its time axis. (Figure II.20) Therefore, "the geometrical properties of space are not independent, but depend upon the distribution of masses within it." [52] This implies that *matter, its fields, and space are all interdependent parts of the whole.* The relativity of parts to the whole means that any vantage point in the universe can be affected by the whole as well as affecting the whole. The universe is an energetic fabric which is dynamic, and all its parts relate to one another.

This concept is very interesting vis-a-vis astrology. Since the matter of our body is in reality a web of energy which is moving through time and space, it has electrical, electro-magnetic, magnetic and gravitational fields in operation simultaneously. The centre of the fields is the physical body of the individual, and the curved field surrounding the body is the Self, represented in astrology by the horoscope circle. The fields centred in the body are affected by the space and other objects around them, and equally they affect the space around themselves. The energy of the organism is equivalent to the libido (psychic energy) which Jung postulated. Libido can transform itself into any number of forms or types of activity, just like the energy motivating the fields.

> We would be better advised, . . . , when speaking of libido, to understand it as an energy value which is available to communicate itself to any field of activity whatsoever, be it power, hunger, hatred, sexuality or religion, without ever being itself a specific instinct." [53]

Matter is the concentration of a field and a disturbance of the perfect state of the field. In astrology the planets can be seen in this way. The planets concentrate and geometrically distort the hypothetically perfect field. The essence in both cases is the *order* and *symmetry* of the field.[54] The total state must be described rather than local states. *In the horoscope the total picture must take precedence over the individual planets and signs.* The planets distort the total field as events distort the flow of our lives but, as in physics, the relationship is mutual and reversible.

The concept of *time* is altered by Relativity. Time in classical mechanics is an absolute reference system like pure space. This means that events happen in an "objective sequence" which would be identical for all observers. Einstein proved that events will be ordered differently by each individual observer. This forces time as well as space into the realm of the subjective description of events by an observer.

Each individual horoscope in astrology has its own spatial and temporal frame of reference. The events happening to an individual are always *relative to him*. This idea and Jung's definition of a symbol are striking: "The symbol has a large number of analogous

[52] Einstein, *The Meaning of Relativity,* (1922).

[53] Jung, *Symbols of Transformation, CW 5,* p. 137.

[54] Capra, *The Tao of Physics,* p. 225.

variants, and the more of these variants it has at its disposal, the more complete and clear-cut will be the image it projects of its objects."[55] Space and time in modern physics are inseparable and codependent — the space-time continuum. Time is a fourth dimension which is defined relative to the other three spatial dimensions. In astrology, the horoscope relativizes the space and time of the individual throughout his life.

One of the most persistent criticisms of astrology has been its use of the geocentric framework, in apparent violation of the Copernican theory of the heliocentricity of the solar system. In the heliocentric theory the Earth is in no way a privileged vantage point, and movements of the Earth are relative to the Sun. Due to relativity theory, however, the Earth has returned gloriously to the centre, as the entire universe must be observed relative to the (Earth-bound) observer. In recent astrophysics, study of phenomena like the expansion of the universe, red shift, and the various theories of the origin and demise of the universe (Big Bang theory) have further verified this relativity. According to the astrophysicist **Brandon Carter,** *"our situation in the universe **must** be privileged, to some extent."*[56] Calder says: "Radio energy fills space, produced by the cooling effect of the Big Bang. The fact that it is more or less uniform in all directions does not mean that the earth is at the very centre of the universe — although *by definition it is at the centre of the observable universe."*[57] The diagram opposite from Calder's book is clearly an analogy to the astrological horoscope, fully verified and vindicated by the physicists. (Figure II.21)

Two essential principles in modern particle physics are *uncertainty* and *complementarity.* Both are concerned with the duality of all things. The nature of light, matter and electromagnetic radiation is such that they appear as both particles and waves. Electrons are assumed to be particles orbiting around a nucleus, also a particle, but they perform in a manner that could only be considered wavelike when seen through time. The wave pattern is determined by the period of movement of a particle, but the exact location of the particle can only be determined by locating the crest of its equivalent wave. (Figure II.22) In physics a particle and a wave are complementary. To determine mathematically where a particle is located is *uncertain;* it can only be found to exist "probably" at any predicted position. This probability factor qualifies all computation in physics. Either the position of a particle or its momentum can be known, but *never both of them together.* Physics is a statistical reality.

The following quote from **Capra** indicates how this bears upon astrological prediction:

> "The uncertainty in the location of an event in time thus becomes related to an uncertainty in energy in the same way as the uncertainty of a particle's location in space is related to an uncertainty in momentum. This means that we can never know both the time at which an event occurs and the energy involved in it with great accuracy. Events occurring inside a short time span involve a large uncertainty in energy; events involving a precise amount of energy can be localized only within a long period of time.[58]

In predictive astrology the times of events and their qualities are also probabilities. Astrological prediction can indicate with certainty either the time when an event is likely to manifest itself or how important the event is to the individual, but rarely both at the same time. In using *transits* (the actual positions in the sky of planets compared to the birth horoscope) the exact time of an event can be determined, but it is difficult to know the amount of energy involved. The same transit can on one occasion produce a near-fatal accident, and at another time not even be noticed. *Directions* (planets moved through the horoscope according to particular keys, such as one degree per year of life) can indicate the specific quality and charge of an event, but usually are only accurate to within a number of months. The solution to this dilemma is identical in both physics and astrology — the two viewpoints are seen as being complementary. Each specific viewpoint is only partially correct and has a limited range, while a complete picture is an integration of both. The physicist **Pauli** stated that it is "most satisfactory for physics and psyche to be complementary."[59]

The complementarity of opposites is a universal theme, an archetype. The unconscious and consciousness have this relationship just as particles (quanta) and waves do. Jung developed models of the psyche which are very similar to those of physics. Complementarity is central to Chinese Taoism, which uses a pair of contrasting qualities *yin* and *yang* to describe the dynamic universe. (Figure II.23) It also permeates alchemy, particularly the *coniunctio,* the

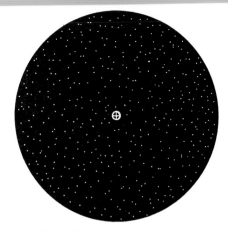

Figure II.21 The Radio Astronomy Universe. The Earth has retained its position at the centre of the Universe.

Figure II.22 Waves and Particles. The particle, when seen through time, appears as a wave.

Figure II.23 The Chinese Yin-Yang Emblem.

[55] Jung, *Symbols of Transformation, CW 5,* p. 124.

[56] Calder, *Key of the Universe,* p. 176.

[57] *Ibid,* 170.

[58] Capra, *Tao,* p. 164.

[59] Pauli, *Kepler,* p. 210.

◁THE ROUND ART▷

[60] See Jung, *Mysterium Coniunctionis, CW 14.*

resolution of the opposition between the King and Queen.[60]

The *conservation of energy* is another key concept which functions both in physics and astrology. Energy adopts many forms (light, heat, electricity, electro-magnetism, etc.) and is eternally changing. The one constant of energy processes is the conservation of the total energy within a closed system. No matter how complex exchanges or transformations are, no energy is ever lost or gained. Mass is composed of dynamic patterns of energy, and therefore participates in this conservation also. Our bodies, objects we possess, the Earth we live on, and stellar bodies are all produced by the dance of energy in the universe — many levels of energetic processes interacting. In astrology every description of events or states is subject to the conservation of the energy involved, and to the levels of interpretation necessary to describe the total energetic situation. The circle of the horoscope can be a closed system within which energy circulates or is activated by external forces, and events are exchanges of energy from one part of the psyche to another. The symbols of astrology are indications of energetic processes which interact with each other, paralleling events in the life. External situations are reflections of inner energetic processes which are seeking acknowledgement (consciousness). The energy which appears to belong to external objects is actually projected onto them by the individual, and is eventually withdrawn through realization, maintaining the conservation. Difficulties in allowing energy to flow in and out freely results in blockages, the source of virtually all psychological and physical ailments.[61]

[61] See Wilhelm Reich's writings.

Recently, particle physicists have entered a bizarre universe which has invalidated their previous conception of things. The search for "unified field theories" which explain all processes, or "elementary" particles (building blocks) has led towards the ideologies of ancient mystics and religious seekers whom scientists particularly condemn. Scientists are beginning to realize that their theories of natural phenomena, their "laws", and their mathematics are all *creations of the mind itself* rather than "objective" reality. This change in attitude is a recognition of the central importance of understanding the relative position of the observer and the observed. The complete picture of reality utilizes many hypothetical models of reality. Only when they are interchangeable with all others can they be valid for our understanding. The tangible is yielding to the intangible, and the musings of millenia of mystics are beginning to sound quite real. Physical energy and psychic energy are obviously reflections of each other, aspects of a unity underlying reality. It seems very late in the game for our modern physicist to admit:

> "Carried to its logical extreme, the bootstrap conjecture (a total view of the universe) implies that the existence of consciousness, along with all other aspects of nature, is necessary for self-consistency of the whole." [62]

[62] Quote of Geoffrey Chew from Capra, *Tao,* p. 317.

Astrology has always recognized these "facts of life".

Reinhold Ebertin and Cosmobiology

Reinhold Ebertin (1901-   ) states that Cosmobiology:

> "is a scientific discipline concerned with the possible correlations between cosmos and organic life and the effects of cosmic rhythms and stellar motions upon man, with all his potentials and dispositions, his character, and the possible turns of fate; it also researches these correlations and effects as mirrored by the earth's plant and animal life as a whole. In this endeavour, cosmobiology utilizes modern-day methods of scientific research, such as statistics, analysis and computer programming." [63]

[63] Ebertin, *Combination of Stellar Influences,* p. 11.

Cosmobiology emerged from Germany in the 1940's as the first truly scientific school in the history of astrology. Ebertin realized that it would never be possible to describe human conditions and psychology in a qualitative fashion, as chemistry describes the properties of certain substances, but that interpretations necessarily must be optimised by continual verification and re-evaluation. His textbook for the interpretation of aspects (the angular relationships between planets) is called *The Combination of Stellar Influences* (1940), abbreviated *CSI*. It standardised the interpretation of all planetary configurations in a form which allows extremely accurate prediction as well as analytical information. He describes each pair of stellar bodies relative to their Cosmic Constellation, Principle, Psychological Correspondence,

Biological Correspondence, Sociological Correspondence and Probable Manifestations. Each category has positive and negative definitions graded from least to most effective shades of value. The scope of the information permits very precise identification of any configuration and its constituent factors.

The essence of Ebertin's interpretive method is the use of *mid-points;* the axes between each pair of planetary positions in the cosmogram (horoscope), which are treated as *sensitive points* in interpretation. (Figure II.24) The sensitive mid-point is activated when a third stellar body passes over it or in geometrical relationship to it. The combination of a third factor to the initial pair creates a parallel to a *complex* or *constellation* in psychology. Complexes are the basic structural elements in the psyche. They are combinations of archetypes (planetary bodies) which have certain definite relations with each other, and determine individual behaviour. They are networks of associations which are often produced by difficulties throughout the life, and can be activated by words, events, personalities, etc. Complexes carry the driving power of the psychic life, and are only problematic when the individual is not conscious of them. The major function of both psychology and astrology is to identify these patterns of behaviour and allow them to enter consciousness. The constellation of planets in astrology is equivalent to the complex of contents in psychology.

In order to evaluate the "cosmic state" of a planetary body, all its combinations with other bodies must be analyzed and interpreted. Each planetary body is evaluated according to the astrological sign it is in, its relative position in the horoscope, the other planets which pair up with it, and the total constellation of which it is a part. The increase in precision achieved by Ebertin comes from the use of three or more planetary bodies simultaneously, rather than the traditional method, which only compares pairs of bodies. In the process, he undervalues the sign positions and houses (positions in the horoscope relative to the rising sign) to the extent that they are virtually eliminated from interpretation. Ebertin would also like to eliminate the traditional term "interpretation" as the following quote illustrates:

> "It is not possible in cosmobiological usage to do without the word 'interpretation' entirely, simply for the reason that it is a long-established term. We do, however, want to take it to mean the compilation of the statements contained in the elements and their combination." [64]

The shift from the traditional method of interpretation, which only stresses the meaning of the planetary body in its sign and house in the horoscope, to the predominant use of aspect connections mirrors a similar shift in modern physics. The *S-matrix theory* is a resolution of the difficulties (uncertainty) of relativity theory and quantum mechanics, and *shifts the emphasis from objects to processes.* The types of connection, the "tissue of events" which define the universe, are given more importance than the objects (which are difficult to define anyway):

> "Each reaction (aspect) involves particles (planetary bodies) which link it to other reactions (other aspects) and thus build up a whole network of processes (horoscope constellations)." [65]

In both astrology and physics the connections within the network cannot be determined with certainty, but are associated with *probabilities.*[66] This shift in viewpoint has had a revitalizing affect upon astrology as it brings astrological ideas more in line with the dynamic nature of the universe as seen by "science".

Ebertin suggests that cosmobiology be used as an analytical tool for psychologists, counsellors, doctors and businessmen, and he links it intimately with one's family, medical and psychological history. He also sees a personal use for the extended scope of cosmobiological analysis. The procedure he recommends implies the formation of an overall meaningful picture of oneself, and "represents the attempt to form a link between mythic and symbolic thought and the natural sciences and, therefore, to synthesize ancient astrological tradition and modern psychological conceptions." [67] This is precisely what is needed.

Ebertin's system has created a large network of cosmobiologists, and has involved many scientists and medical researchers in corroborating and continually correcting his data through thousands of test cases. In this respect astrology has been put back on its feet as a verifiable natural science which also utilizes intuitive mechanisms. He has followed *The Combination of Stellar Influences* with a series of highly technical texts dealing with the other major areas

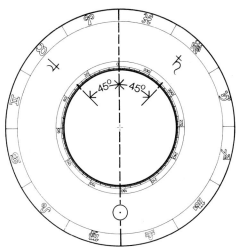

Figure II.24 Planetary Midpoints. The axis between the positions of Jupiter and Saturn intersects the circle at two opposite points. In this case the Sun is at one end of the axis. The Sun then qualifies the midpoint Jupiter/Saturn.

[64] Ebertin, *Man in the Universe,* p. 66.

[65] Capra, *Tao,* p. 277. My parentheses.

[66] *Ibid,* p. 278.

[67] Ebertin, *CSI,* p. 11.

of cosmobiological interest. These valuable works are listed below:

Applied Cosmobiology (1972)
Transits (1928 German, 1952 English translation)
Directions (1931 German, 1976 English translation)
Man in the Universe (1973)
The Annual Diagram (1973)
Rapid and Reliable Analysis (1970)
Fixed Stars and their Interpretation (1971)

These books are essential information for every modern astrological or cosmobiological practitioner or querent.

While the methodology of Ebertin is extraordinarily accurate, there are still certain problems which remain. The method is very complex, as individuals are, but the complexity tends towards such detail in analysis that it becomes overwhelming. There are many factors available which, while being accurate, are exceedingly difficult to order in time through the life. What the method gains in completeness, it loses in succinctness. Somewhat like modern medical analysis-diagnosis, it is so concerned with the microcosm of fragments that the classic overall pattern becomes easily obscured. The horoscope must evoke in the individual awareness of his total being, not merely the composite parts. Life is a dynamic process, and the nature of this process must be discovered and presented as fluidly as possible. "The Round Art" presents an interpretive approach to astrology which uses the technical facilities of Ebertin and attempts to restore the *wholeness* implicit in the process.

Research and Astrology

In the last thirty years there has been an upsurge of interest in astrology within the scientific community. Many of the time-honoured mechanisms of astrology seem to offer explanations or avenues of approach to problems which the strictly scientific approach does not. In most cases, scientists doing research in their specialties discovered that they were moving towards astrological viewpoints without any previous knowledge of astrology, except as an ancient heresy. The extension of the scientific world-view into the depths of space and the recesses of the subatomic world produced a necessity to discover how the many levels of physical and psychological realities interact. Many formerly isolated scientific "branches" have converged upon each other. Physics was successively applied to astronomy, biology, medicine, botany and genetics, and much research is now concerned with, and concentrated on, the areas where the fields of study overlap. The intelligent scientist has discovered that he must consider many frames of reference beyond the specific problems with which he is directly concerned and eventually must include ever wider spectra of influences in his hypotheses, experiments and calculations.

Astrology has traditionally been concerned with the relation between the microcosm and the macrocosm, and scientists are realizing that this is the essence of their work as well. Many astrological assumptions which previously served to discredit its approach in the scientific community are now being statistically proven *by scientists themselves.* Probably the most convincing example of this is the French statistician **Michel Gauquelin,** who set out twenty-five years ago to disprove — once and for all — basic astrological ideas. He correlated astrological data for tens of thousands of doctors, politicians, athletes and soldiers, and against his overtly negative attitude towards astrology, convinced himself that it rested upon *statistically verifiable premises.*

One of his experiments was based upon the traditional astrological correlation of the military and the planets Mars and Saturn. In the horoscopes of 3,142 military leaders he found Mars and Saturn coinciding with the major vertical and horizontal axes of the horoscope in enough cases to prove statistically that the principle was valid. He also found the athletic prowess associated with Mars in the axes of 1,485 athletes.[68]

Astrology maintains that heredity can be determined from the horoscope. This was verified by Gauquelin in an experiment which compared planetary factors in the horoscopes of 15,000 married couples and their children. He found a statistically significant correlation between parental and filial planetary positions.[69] Gauquelin has written three books which accurately

[68] Gauquelin, *L'Influence des Astres* (1955).

[69] West and Toonder, *The Case for Astrology,* p. 163.

document his researches, and believes that he rediscovered a science which astrology never realized was there. His attitude towards this smacks of very peculiar superstitions. His statistics proving certain hereditary correlations with planetary positions only make him suspect that the scientific community has not approached the problem correctly, but not that this validates the hypotheses of astrology as a whole. He insists:

> " . . . modern science has still much to teach us about the rapport between man and the cosmos; let us continue along the new road opposed to astrology, upon which we have begun, but this time accompanied by qualified experts." [70]

[70] Gauquelin, *Die planetaire Hereditat,* p. 168-69.

He also vents his spleen on the practitioners of astrology:

> "If astrology's clientele is gathered from people who are credulous or in distress, the practitioners of the doctrine who spread it among us are generally not so much credulous as alienated. Beside the ordinary charlatans who use it as a 'hustle' to make a lot of money, *there are any number of deranged people who waste their time in vainly trying to revive this ancient conception of the world.* The latter are serious cases, and there is no point in arguing with them over principles. Fanatics, the deranged, and the mentally sick, they make a sad and discordant group."
> For in the question of belief in the stars, the psychiatric angle should not be overlooked. Ravings about astrology are regularly symptommatic of certain mental illnesses, particularly those which include mystical ravings as well. For these people, the sky and the heavenly bodies are even more alive than they were in the ancient days of Babylon." [71]

[71] Gauquelin, *Astrology and Science,* p. 152, My italics.

This conclusion is consistent with the attitude of virtually all scientists.

Their initial impulse upon rediscovering planetary correlations is to try to assimilate astrology into science *without giving it any verification in its own right.* Gauquelin believes that he is the guiding light of a "new" science which of course has virtually nothing to do with astrology. Eight pages after the preceeding diatribe about the raving of astrologers, he seems to loosen up and rave a little himself:

> "Finally, we shall see that their (other scientists') patient observations have led to overwhelming consequences for modern science, since they transform the very concept of what constitutes determining factors in science. Naturally in the course of this march back from astrology the way may sometimes seem overgrown, and it is easy to get lost in the labyrinths of the new science. But only by following this difficult path will we be able to introduce scientific truth again into this province of charlatan astrology." [72]

[72] *Ibid,* p. 160.

The heart of this problem of acceptance as a natural science is directly related to the generally poor account most astrologers give of themselves, and to the obvious generalization of newspaper "horoscopes" which vast numbers of individuals all over the world consult every day. Ebertin mentions in CSI that in 1972 two-thirds of the population of the Federal German Republic (40,000,000 people!) read their daily horoscopes in magazines and newspapers, and know at least their sun-sign. The conclusions drawn from this are very misleading, because there are many practising astrologers who are aware of the scientific approach and utilize the scientific method in their work.

The correlation of statistical factors is necessary in astrological interpretation, but is only part of the whole process. The intuition of the astrologer plays a considerable part in the correct analysis, just as intuition is essential in scientific thinking. **Albert Einstein** described the discovery of physical laws: "There is no logical way to the discovery of these elemental laws. There is only the way of intuition, which is helped by a feeling for the order lying behind appearances." **Schiller** remarked, "Again and again the imaginary plan on which one attempts to build up order breaks down and then we must try another. Imaginative vision and faith in ultimate success are indispensable. The pure rationalist has no place here." The above quotations are from the *Art of Scientific Investigation* by W. L. W. Beveridge,[73] and the book mentions many more examples of highly influential scientists who acknowledge the necessity of intuition in even the most mundane scientific work. *In astrology this attitude is assumed.*

[73] Collin, *The Theory of Celestial Influence,* p. 350-51.

Carl Jung performed an astrological experiment as part of his paper *Synchronicity: An Acausal Connecting Principle.*[74] The astrological experiment took 180 married couples and

[74] Jung, *The Structure and Dynamics of the Psyche, CW 8.*

compared the relative positions of the Sun, Moon, Venus and Mars of each partner, attempting to find significant correlations accepted by traditional astrology. The traditional correspondence signifying marriage is either a coincidence or opposition of the Sun and Moon. The results proved statistically that the correlations in the samples corresponded with astrological expectations. In checking his statistical technique, Jung felt that even though the results corresponded with his expectations, it could almost be said that he *unconsciously arranged* and manipulated the material. As a result he repeated the experiment using a slightly different statistical method and found that the marriage correlations were very close to chance but *not* significant. While this was not encouraging to astrology, which Jung used personally, in the process he hit upon an interesting idea. Since his research was connected to his concept of *synchronicity*[75] which postulates acausal connections between mind and matter, he realized that the results were in fact affected by the expectations of his co-worker and himself. He concluded that this synchronistic effect is "simply there" and that it can bever be excluded from any experiment. The expectations of the observer in all experiments produce an incalculable transformation of the data.[76] In astrology the involvement of the observer (the astrologer) is taken into consideration, as will be shown in the section of this book dealing with The Reading, Part IX.

Jung discovered that the parapsychological experiments of **J. B. Rhine,** of Duke University, were also conditioned by this "synchronistic" factor. In Rhine's tests for parapsychological aptitude (guessing hidden cards), he found that as the subject performed more tests his interest flagged, and the decreasing accuracy of response reflected this. The more the experiment was repeated on any subject, the poorer his responses were against chance. The implication is that there is an inseparable connection between the experimenter and his experiment, and that this must be understood. This relationship is acknowledged in astrology and can be used to the advantage of both the astrologer and his client. This is the *mantic* (divinatory) nature of astrology — the connection between the mathematical and psychic processes which are components of every whole. Jung mentioned that the mantic arts create favourable conditions for the occurrence of meaningful coincidences. Astrology is a blend of the rational and irrational, united by an underlying mathematical structure.

Gauquelin is representative of a scientist who does not know astrology, but backs into its territory. On one level he does a great service to astrology, but from the viewpoint of the astrologers, it is unfortunate that the experiments he chooses to use involve the isolation of many factors of the horoscope. The scientific is interested in isolating certain microcosmic situations and in pretending that they are momentarily disconnected from the outside, while the astrologer knows that no situation can ever be isolated. The essence of astrology is that the horoscope *must* be seen as a whole web of interconnecting factors, and concentration upon only one aspect can be misleading. This constitutes a criticism of science since it is never possible to isolate any phenomenon in the universe.

Jung represents another situation — that of the scientist who does not exclude astrology although he is aware of the problems that have been inherited by its practitioners. He used astrology throughout his life, but was extremely wary of announcing his interest because of astrology's "unscientific" connotations within the psychiatric community. He is unique because he represents one of the very few individuals who try to combine astrology and science science.

Research is also being done by astrologers themselves using statistical methods. Foremost in this regard are the German schools. The Hamburg School of **Witte** started by compiling vast numbers of test horoscopes and cataloguing them. Witte's attitude towards the statistics was sound, but became obsessive. He found that his statistics indicated influences affecting individuals which could not be explained by the ten known planets, and he mathematically located four "transneptunian" planets, Hades, Cupido, Zeus and Cronos. He also calculated ephemerides (position tables) for these hypothetical planets. He investigated horoscopes which used mirro-images of the planetary positions together with the standard positions. Due to his extremely "scientific" approach, he was led totally off the path.

The school which has done the most in a scientific regard is the Cosmobiological Institute of Ebertin. Ebertin catalogued thousands of cosmograms and carried out exhaustive analyses of them. In CSI he mentions that there is no interpretive factor which has not been verified by his researchers. The language and vague approach of the Theosophists is rejected, and the

[75] The connection between an inner event — a dream or fantasy — and an outer event that is simultaneous and conveys the same *meaning*.

[76] See Capra, *The Tao of Physics,* p. 86.

work is therefore without the objectionable, unverified information which permeates virtually all previous textbooks on interpretation. Following are listed some of the many scientists who have worked with Ebertin:

1. **Dr. Theodor Landscheidt** — His book *Cosmic Cybernetics* studies the correlations between Cosmobiology and mathematics, theoretical physics, cybernetics, astronomy, information theory and music. He experimented with mathematical statistics as a Cosmobiological tool for predicting solar eruptions. He also correlated the periodic table of the elements to the planets.
2. **Dr. H. G. Muller-Freywardt** — He correlated Cosmobiological information with the human body and its relationship to diagnosis and medical treatment.[77]
3. **Dr. Med. Baron von Klockler** — He compared the stellar relationships to biological, organic, psychological and sociological information.[78]
4. **Dr. Walter Koch** — *The Doctrine of Aspects.*[79]
5. **Hermann Jaeger** — He is an engineer concerned with astrological planting time experiments.[80]

There are many other scientists and doctors who are involved with astrologically related research. While they will only be listed with a brief precis of their researches, there are five books which contain impressive detail about these researchers and their relationship to astrological thought and practice.

    A. *The Case for Astrology,* by John West and Jan Toonder.   *(CA)*
    B. *Astrology and Science,* by Michel Gauquelin.   *(AS)*
    C. *Cosmic Cybernetics,* by Dr. Theodor Landscheidt.   *(CC)*
    D. *The Jupiter Effect,* by John Gribbin and Stephen Plagemann.   *(JE)*
    E. *Natural Birth Control,* edited by Art Rosenblum.   *(NBC)*

The following is a list of the major contributors to the establishment of a definitive link between science and astrology, and those who have researched the rhythms of life with which astrology is vitally concerned.

6. **Dr. Eugen Jonas,** Head of the Czechoslovakian government-sponsored Birth Control Research Centre — He did research with 30,000 women, discovered that a method of astrological birth control worked, and proved its effectiveness to be 97.7%. He also developed a means to predict the sex of an unborn child based upon the moon position in the zodiac at conception which was proven 87% effective. *(NBC)*
7. **John M. Addey** — He researched 970 octogenarians and established that they had a statistically proven dominance of separating aspects. He also wrote a book on wave analysis and harmonics in astrology. "Addey's work demonstrates that almost all the principal factors of traditional astrology — the aspects, the houses, the significance of degree areas, the positions of the planets within the houses — are based upon realities, and that these realities are, to a certain extent, amenable to the statistical approach." *(CA, p. 169.)*
8. **Dr. Rudolf Tomaschek,** physicist and astrologer — He developed statistical proof that earthquakes and planetary harmonics can be predicted accurately. He found that 134 earthquakes have occurred throughout history when Jupiter, Uranus and Pluto are in 90° relationships to each other, thus verifying the traditional interpretation of the square aspect. *(CA, p. 180.)*
9. **Donald O. Bradley** — He found that clergymen have a majority of planets in the seventh harmonic (every seven degrees) in their horoscopes. *(CA, 168.)*
10. **John H. Nelson,** RCA electrical engineer — He discovered that magnetic storms which effect health happen when planets align in 0°, 90° and 180° angles, and their harmonics, in 93% of cases. His experiments were made by measuring radio disturbance, and showed that disturbance-free fields are produced when planets are either 60° or 120° apart. The first three angles mentioned are considered inharmonious and the last two are harmonious in traditional astrology. *(CC, 179-80.)*
11. **Prof. Giorgio Piccardi,** Florence University — He found that the rate of precipitation in colloids followed a definite and predictable cyclical pattern throughout the yearly time period. A connection was also proven between precipitation and the latitude in which the experiment was performed. Since the human body is over 80% water, this implied a connection to man as well. *(CA, p. 182.)*
12. **Dr. Maki Takata,** Toho University, Tokyo — He proved that the composition of human blood changes in relation to an 11-year sunspot cycle. The same changes occurred in the daily rotation of the Earth, concentrating upon the time of sunrise (the ascendent in astrology). "Man is a living sundial." *(SA, 224.)*
13. **Frank A. Brown,** Northwestern University biologist — He experimented with the biological clocks of oysters and attributed this clock to celestial rhythms which operated independently of light and location. When oysters were moved a thousand miles from their coastal location, they opened on their natural tidal schedule. Similar patterns were found to exist in rats and potatoes. *(CA, p. 171-72.)*

[77] Ebertin, *The Combination of Stellar Influences,* pages 16-20.

[78] *CSI,* p. 14.

[79] *CSI,* p. 13.

[80] *CSI,* p. 7.

14. **Dr. Abraham** and **Dr. Walther Menaker** — They found a connection between lunar periodicity and human reproduction. *(CSI,* p. 9.)

15. **Dr. Leonard J. Ravitz,** Duke University — Electrical potential emitted in normal and insane people coincided with the phases of the moon and the seasons. "These energy reserves may be mobilized by periodic universal factors (such as the forces behind the moon) which tend to aggravate maladjustments and conflicts already present." *(CA,* p. 173.)

16. **Prof. K. D. Wood,** University of Colorado — Alignments of the Earth, Venus, and Jupiter have a tidal effect which produces solar flares. *(JE,* p. 110.)

17. **Prof. Jakob Eugster** — He found cosmic radiations effect seed germination. *(CSI,* p. 8.)

18. **Avinadav Levit,** Russian scientist — The universe can be regarded as a gigantic cybernetic system (information theory) containing organizational links. *(CC,* p. 57.)

19. **Robert B. Evans** — A definite connection was found to exist between information and energy in the universe. (Information is energy.) *(CC,* p. 77.)

20. **Hoyle, de Beauregard, V. Ambartsumian, Levit, Ducroq, Narlikar,** and **Reiser** — They all believe that our galaxy is organized like a cybernetic system, and information can be transmitted by planetary or galactic bodies. *(CC,* p. 61.)

21. **Firsof,** Russian astronomer — He discovered theoretical particles, "mindons", which link matter with spirit. *(CC,* p. 77.)

22. **Rudolf Hauschka,** anthroposophist chemist — He found that the nature of substance can be related to the astrological concept of the four elements, and to planetary harmonics. *(CA,* p. 216-17.)

23. **H. C. Willet** (USA) and **Y. Arai** (Japan) — They independently discovered a connection between solar activity and short-range weather prediction. *(SA,* p. 185.)

24. **H. Casper,** biologist — He found a connection between Moon phases and mosquito breeding. *(SA,* p. 190-91.)

25. **Dr. de Rudder,** University of Frankfurt-am-Main — Epidemic diseases and meteorological activity correlate. *(SA,* p. 200.)

26. **Dr. Poumaillax, Dr. M. Viart,** Russian **Prof. N. V. Romenski** — They found a connection between myocardial infarctus and solar flares. *(SA,* p. 200-01.)

27. **Prof. Helmut Berg,** University of Cologne — He discovered that magnetic disturbances and solar flares indicate times when lung disease and pulmonary hemorrhages become critical. *(SA,* p. 201.)

28. **Prof. H. Bartels,** Berlin — He found that microbiotic reactions, weather changes, and chemical reactions depend upon solar flares. *(SA,* p. 236.)

29. **Prof. A. L. Tchijewsky,** University of Moscow, and later **Dr. Robert O. Becker,** Syracuse Veterans Hospital — They both discovered that historical epidemics of typhus, cholera, smallpox and the great plagues were determined by the times of sunspot maxima. *(SA,* p. 204.)

30. **Volynski** and **Vladmirsky,** Russian researchers — They found that human cardiovascular and nervous functional disorders occur at the same time as geomagnetic disturbances. *(CC,* p. 72.)

31. **C. P. Weizsacker** — His theory of Primary Entities shows a continuity in action from subatomic dimensions to the universal expanses (the microcosm is the macrocosm). *(CC,* p. 24.)

32. **Dr. R. A Challinor,** University of Toronto — There are harmonic variations in the length of days over each year. Six months are a half harmonic, and four months are third harmonics. The day length is greater in spring and the fall at the equinoxes. *(JE,* p. 63.)

33. **Vernon Clark,** American psychologist — He carefully prepared a monitored experiment with twenty astrologers and showed that although the odds against correct prognostication of occupation and predictions of illnesses were 100-to-1, they performed much better than chance. *(CA,* p. 193.)

34. **Hans Jenny** — Originated Cymatics — the study of wave forms. That vibrations effect the shape of magnetic particles upon plates implies the existence of the actual harmony of the spheres.

35. **Prof. Edward R. Dewey** — He discovered that conjunctions of Jupiter, Saturn, Uranus, and Pluto coincide with times of maximum sunspot activity. *(CA,* p. 186-87.)

36. **Prof. Ellsworth Huntington,** Harvard University — He found that atmospheric phenomena are cyclical, and are closely associated with psychic rhythms. *(AS,* p. 185.)

37. **Dr. Edson Andrews** — Discovered in 1000 tonsillectomies that 82% of the bleeding crises occurred between the first and last quarters of the lunar cycle. *(CA,* p. 174., and CSI, p. 8.)

38. **Dr. Abram Hoffer,** University Hospital, Saskatchewan — He found that neurotics have peak experiences in January and July, and depressives in March. *(CA,* p. 174.)

This imposing list of researchers is only a sampling of individuals all over the world who are in some way involved with experiments which are related to astrological mechanisms, and many of those listed can be considered refutations of many criticisms of astrology.

Part III   The Structure of the Zodiac

Figure III.1 The Celestial Sphere.

The Celestial Sphere

"The mystery is in the sphere. But the sphere consists in correspondence and reintegration; it is a doubled half that becomes one, that is made by joining an upper and a lower half, a heavenly and an earthly hemisphere, which complement each other in a whole, in such a manner that what is above is also below; and what happens in the earthly represents itself in the heavenly sphere and contrariwise. This complementary interchange of two halves which together form a whole and a closed sphere is equivalent to change — that is, revolution. The sphere rolls — that is in the nature of spheres. Bottom is soon top and top bottom, in so far as one can speak of top and bottom in such a connection. Not only do the heavenly and the earthly recognize themselves in each other, but, thanks to the revolution of the sphere, the heavenly can turn into the earthly, the earthly into the heavenly, from which it is clear that gods can become men and on the other hand *men can become gods.*"[1]

The Chaldeans believed that there was a tree growing at the centre of the world; its branches of crystal formed the sky and drooped to the sea around the periphery of the world. The Phoenicians believed that the world was like a revolving tree over which was spread a vast blue tapestry embroidered with stars. To the Turko-tatars the sky was a tent; the milky way was the 'seam', the stars were holes and windows through which the gods descended to man.

In the middle of the sky is the *Divine Tent Pole*, the pole star Polaris. The sky appears to rotate around Polaris; this moved many ancient cultures to describe the pole star as the *"Nail Star"*, the *"Sky Nail"*, the *"Golden Pillar"*, the *"Sky Pillar"*, the *"Iron Pillar"*, the *"Solar Pillar"*, the *"Yggdrasil World Ash Tree"*, *"Mount Meru"*, the *"Ziggurat"*, the *"Pyramid"*, the *"World Axis"* or the *"World Tree"*.[2] Ultimately these concepts designate the *Centre of the World*.

The night sky appears to be composed of many spots of light, varying in size and brightness, which are all equidistant from the observer. They appear to travel around the pole star in circles, as if along the inside surface of a large rotating sphere surrounding the earth. (Figure III.2) The movements of the Sun, Moon, planets and fixed stars are all registered upon this *Celestial Sphere*.

The celestial sphere is a convenient framework for recording astronomical-astrological information. It should be imagined as a huge hollowed-out crystal, the centre of which is coincident with the centre of the Earth. (Figure III.1) The celestial sphere moves with the Earth on its journey through space, and they both rotate around a common axis, the *Polar Axis,* which skewers both spheres through their north and south poles. The celestial sphere can be imagined as being any size. Since the distances of the heavenly bodies are so great in reference to the Earth, their position upon the surface of the celestial sphere is identical either from the centre of the Earth or any position on the surface of the Earth. The position of any observer on Earth is identical with an imaginary observer in the exact centre of the Earth. The movements of planetary bodies across the surface of the celestial sphere are called *directions*.

Originally it was thought that the celestial sphere itself rotated while the Earth remained static, but the use of the celestial sphere was not invalidated by the realization that the Earth moves around the Sun. The celestial sphere is a datum plane for the Earth and any cosmic influences beyond the celestial sphere produce alterations in the field of the Earth, to which the celestial sphere is analogous. It is also analogous to the magnetic halo which surrounds the Earth.

Influences are registered upon the individual as they are registered upon the celestial sphere: at a distance. The question of whether astrology is correct in assuming that actions at a distance can have effects on Earth has been an age-old criticism. Recent research by Giorgio Piccardi of the University of Florence has been concerned with this question. He correlated information showing how external radiations affect the earth's field and influence climate. His conclusion of the effect of far-distant bodies upon life on Earth is that:

"... certain phenomena which take place in geophysical space and all of the phenomena which take place in solar space and astrophysical space *act at a distance.* No matter what the nature of far-off spatial phenomena their action is exercised by means of radiations of an electromagnetic or corpuscular nature, or by means of variations in the general field, electrical, magnetic, electro-magnetic or gravitation. All of this may be listed as distant actions."[3]

The celestial sphere which transmits the influences of the stellar bodies to Earth is similar on a

Figure III.2 Circumpolar Motion. A time exposure photograph taken at night shows the rotation of the circumpolar stars around the Pole Star.

[1]Thomas Mann, *Joseph and His Brothers*, p. 124.

[2]Mircea Eliade, *Shamanism*, p. 259-65.

[3]Piccardi, *The Chemical Basis of Medical Climatology*, p. 120.

personal level to the idea of the *aura,* the field which surrounds each individual and registers influences from the external world.

It is necessary to understand the mechanics of the celestial sphere to compute the astrological horoscope. In this book we will describe the characteristics of the celestial sphere and the horoscope through images and words, and the actual mathematics of the construction of the horoscope will be fully explained in Appendix A.

The astrological *horoscope* (Greek *= hour-pointer)* is a two-dimensional representation of the positions of the Sun, Moon, planets and signs of the zodiac at the exact moment of birth. Its calculations are based upon the time, date and place of birth. The horoscope is representative of the orientation of an individual in space and time. Because the entire solar system is moving through space with the Earth making a complete rotation each day, the task of orienting the horoscope is similar to the *astronomer orienting his telescope* towards the heavenly bodies. The *Individual* (traditionally called the Native) is the subject of the horoscope; the *Observer* in astronomy refers to the time and location of a particular observation.

In order to understand the true orientation of the individual we must consider two complementary viewpoints. These are the subjective viewpoint of the individual on Earth perceiving the universe around him, and the objective viewpoint of an imaginary observer exterior to the galaxy which contains the solar system. The first is from the inside looking out; the second is from the outside looking in.

These two relative viewpoints were represented by Renaissance astronomer-astrologers by mechanical devices called *"armillary spheres"*, *"celestial spheres"* and *"globes"*. (Figures III.3A, 3B and 3C)

The celestial sphere was a solid sphere which had the positions of the fixed stars, including the band of stars which defined the plane of the solar system — the *zodiac,* (from the Greek *zoidiakos kyklos* = wheel of the animals) — inscribed upon its surface. The celestial sphere rotated upon an axis synchronous with the Earth's axis, and so the movements of stars could be determined by rotating it at the same rate as the Earth itself rotates.

The armillary sphere was a skeleton of the celestial sphere showing the reference circles by which stellar positions were translated into geocentric co-ordinates. The Earth was usually indicated by a miniature sphere in the centre of the armillary sphere, and this device was used to 'sight' the positions of stellar bodies during observation. The armillary sphere represented the subjective viewpoint.

The globe was a solid sphere representing the Earth, bounded by a set of reference circles corresponding to those on the armillary sphere. The globe was the Earth as seen from space; it represented the objective viewpoint.

All of these devices were used to make observations and construct horoscopes prior to the publication of printed almanacs or ephemerides — computed tables of daily planetary positions. Once the printed tables became available, astrologers ceased making their own observations and also ceased using the mechanical observational aids we have discussed. While this increased the accuracy of horoscopes, it simultaneously split astrologers from the actual heavens — until in this century most astrologers would not have the faintest idea what existed in the sky. Aleister Crowley discussed astrology with the well-known astrologer Evangeline Evans in the United States, and said of her that she "did not know that the solar system was essentially a disk. She thought the planets were stuck at random in the sky like so many plums in a suet pudding."[4]

[4]Crowley, *The Complete Astrological Writings*, p. 8.

Figure III.3A Armillary Sphere (Photograph courtesy of Harriet Wynter Arts and Sciences.)

Figure III.3B Celestial Sphere. (Photograph courtesy of Harriet Wynter Arts and Sciences.)

Figure III.3C Terrestial Globe. (Photograph courtesy of Harriet Wynter Arts and Sciences.)

Divisions of the Celestial Sphere

The celestial sphere is divided and used according to a branch of mathematics called *spherical astronomy*. Most divisions of the celestial sphere are created by plane surfaces passing through it, producing circles. The two kinds of circles are *Great Circles,* which are formed by a plane intersecting the centre of the celestial sphere, and *Small Circles,* formed by planes intersecting the celestial sphere but not passing through the centre. (Figure III.4)

Figure III.4 Great Circles and Small Circles. A great circle is a plane passing through the celestial sphere which intersects the centre. A small circle is a plane passing through the celestial sphere which does not intersect the centre. The yellow plane defines a great circle and the orange plane defines a small circle.

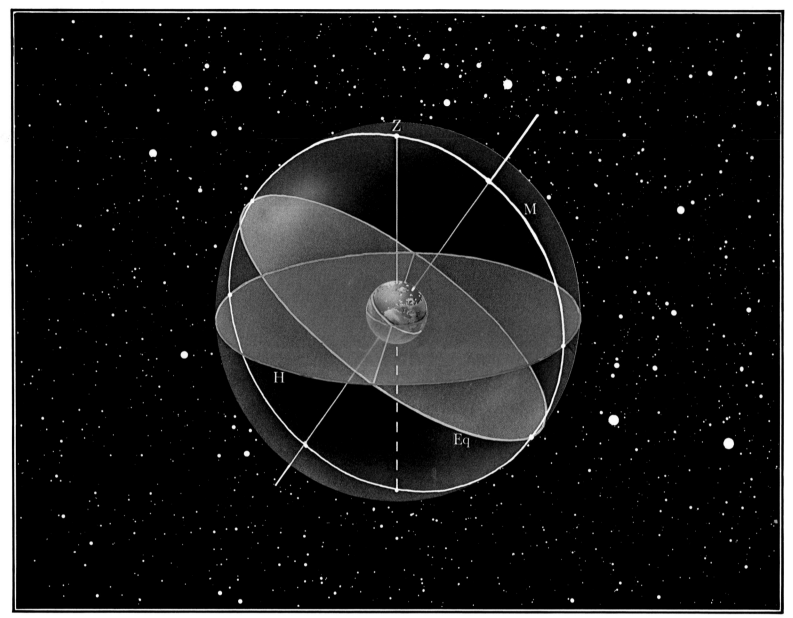

Figure III.5 Major Divisions of the Celestial Sphere. The Zenith is determined by a plumb-line at the individual's location on Earth. The plane of the Horizon is red. The plane of the Equator is yellow.

The two most basic frames of reference for an individual on Earth are the direction of the Earth's rotational axis and the direction of gravity. (Figure III.5) The direction of the Earth's rotation is common to all observers on Earth and is determined by observation of the stars near the poles, the circumpolar stars — usually the *Big Dipper* or *Ursa Major,* also known as the Great Bear. The terrestrial poles projected onto the celestial sphere are the north and south **Celestial Poles.** The circumpolar stars appear to rotate around the celestial poles. The direction of gravity is relative to an individual's position on Earth and can be found with a plumb line. The direction of gravity determines the plane of the **Horizon** relative to the individual.

The **Equator** is a great circle perpendicular to the axis of the Earth and equidistant from the terrestrial poles. The terrestrial equator on the Earth is equivalent to the **Celestial Equator** on the celestial sphere.

THE ROUND ART

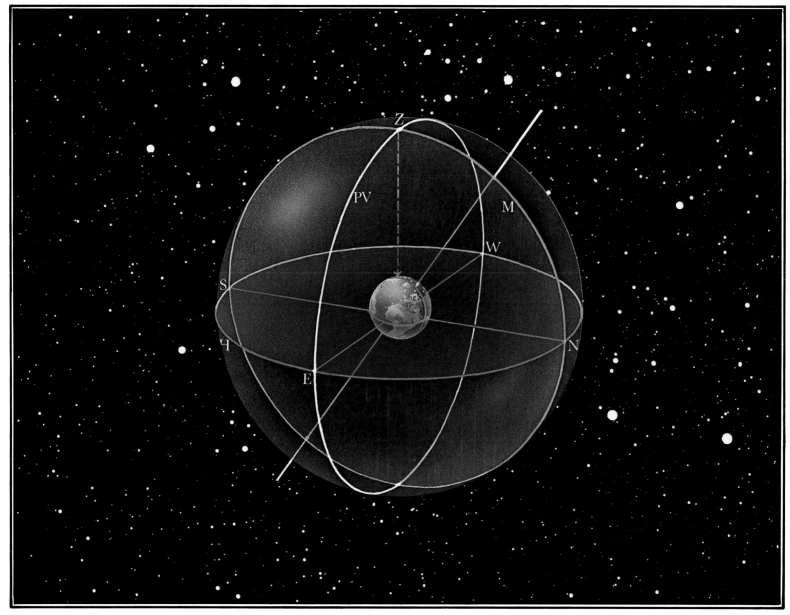

The **Horizon** is a great circle formed by a plane perpendicular to the direction of gravity that intersects the centre of the celestial sphere. Where the equator and the horizon intersect, a line is produced.

The position on the celestial sphere directly over the observer (determined by plumb line) is the **Zenith.** Its opposite point is the **Nadir.**

The **Meridian** is a circle passing through both the zenith and the north and south celestial poles. The meridian depends upon the longitude of the individual, and not upon his latitude.

The **Cardinal Points** are four primary points of intersection on the horizon plane. (Figure III.6) The north and south points are intersections of the horizon by the meridian, and the east and west points are intersections of the horizon and the equator. When planetary bodies coincide with the meridian on the surface of the celestial sphere they are *Culminating.*

Figure III.6 The Cardinal Points. The Cardinal Points (North, East, South and West) are defined by the intersections of the Horizon plane by the Meridian and the Prime Vertical. The Horizon plane is red. The plane of the Meridian is orange. The intersections of these planes are brilliant red lines radiating from the Earth.

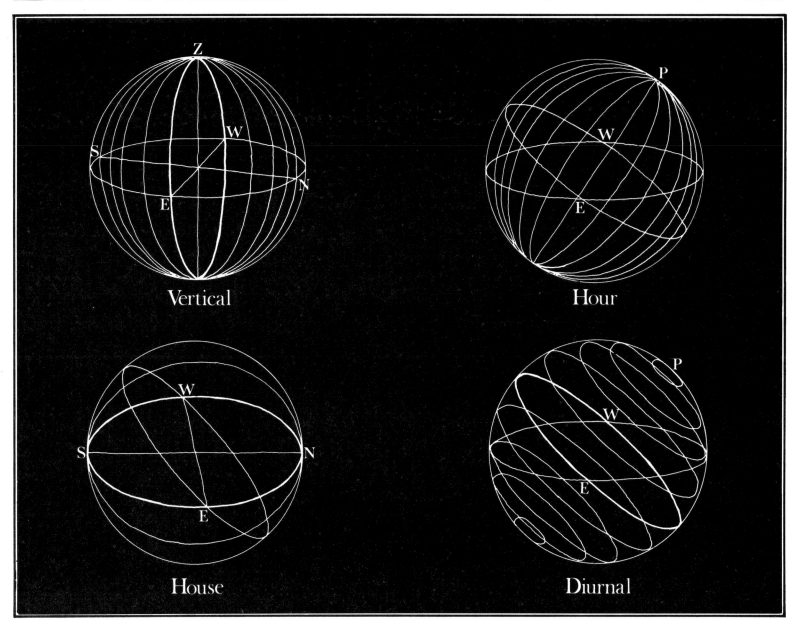

Vertical

Hour

House

Diurnal

Figure III.7 House, Hour, Diurnal and Vertical Circles.

In addition to the meridian, there are other great circles called **Vertical Circles,** which are perpendicular to the horizon plane and intersect the zenith and the nadir. (Figure III.7) The great circle intersecting the zenith, nadir and the east and west points on the horizon plane is the **Prime Vertical.**

Hour Circles are great circles which pass vertically through the celestial poles. The hour circle which passes through the zenith and nadir is the meridian. **House Circles** are great circles which intersect the north and south points of the horizon. The house circle intersecting the east and west points is the horizon, while the house circle passing through the zenith, nadir and the poles is the meridian. **Diurnal Circles** are small circles parallel to the equator.

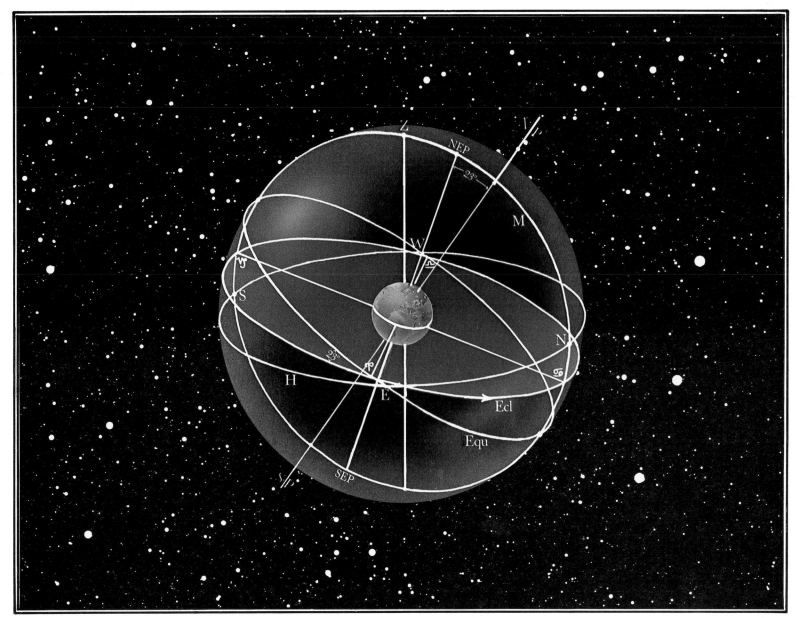

The **Ecliptic** is a secondary great circle which indicates the plane of the solar system, the plane which the Sun apparently follows on its journey around the Earth. (Figure III.8) The plane of the ecliptic is inclined at an angle of 23½° to the plane of the equator. Due to this inclination, the path of the Sun around the Earth does not follow the equator but the ecliptic, producing the seasons through the year. The intersections of the ecliptic and the equator determine the *Equinoxes*. When the sun passes these points of intersection, day is equal in length to night.

Figure III.8 The Ecliptic is tilted from the plane of the Equator at an angle of 23°. The plane of the Ecliptic is yellow, and the equinoctial and solstitial points are brilliant lines radiating from the Earth.

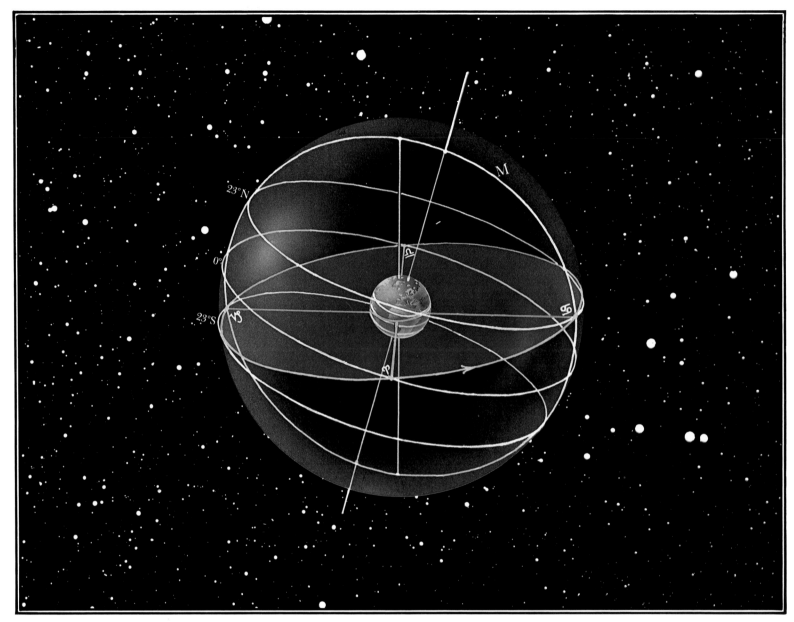

Figure III.9 The Tropics. The Tropics are defined by the intersections of the Ecliptic and the Equator, and by the points farthest north and south of the Equator. The Ecliptic is a yellow plane.

The *Vernal (Spring) Equinox* is the point where the Sun passes the equator moving from south to north — at about the 21st of March each year — and is equivalent to 0° Aries astronomically and astrologically. (Figure III.9) The *Autumnal (Fall) Equinox* is the point where the Sun passes the equator moving from north to south — at about the 21st of September each year — and is designated 0° Libra astronomically and astrologically. While on the equinoxes the Sun moves along the equator, throughout the remainder of the year it moves along small circles either north or south of the equator. The farthest point south on the ecliptic is 23½° below the equator, and is designated the *Tropic of Capricorn*. When the Sun reaches the Tropic of Capricorn on about the 21st of December each year, the point of intersection is the *Winter Solstice* and it is designated 0° Capricorn. The farthest point north of the ecliptic is 23½° above the equator and is called the *Tropic of Cancer*. When the Sun intersects the Tropic of Cancer, about the 21st of June each year, the point of intersection is the *Summer Solstice* and 0° Cancer. At both the solstitial points the Sun moves along diurnal circles which coincide with the tropics. Through the rest of the year, the Sun appears to move eastwards along the ecliptic at slightly over 1° per day, completing the entire circuit in

THE ROUND ART

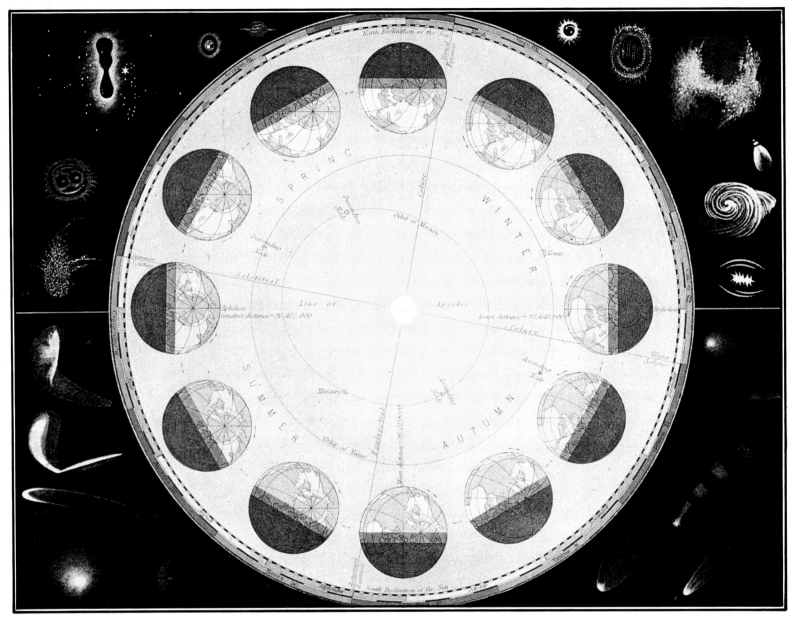

Figure III.10 The Four Seasons. The tilt of the Earth's axis relative to the plane of the Solar System creates the seasons. In the Summer, the northern pole faces the Sun, while in the Winter the northern pole faces away from the Sun.

365¼ days, which is one *solar year.*

The seasons are produced by the deviation of the equator and the ecliptic. The axis of the Earth tilts at a 23½° to the plane of the Earth's orbital plane. (Figure III.10) During the winter the northern pole of the Earth is pointing away from the Sun, producing cold weather in the northern hemisphere, while during the summer the northern pole points *towards* the Sun, producing warm weather in the northern hemisphere. In the southern hemisphere the seasons are reversed as it is affected by the opposite polar orientation. During the equinoctial times the weather is either changing from winter to summer or vice versa, and is generally temperate. The length of day is also affected by the tilting of the Earth's axis. When the Sun is at either equinox, day and night are equal; 12 hours of day and 12 hours of night. When the Sun coincides with the summer solstice it produces the longest day of the year, when there are 16 hours of day and 8 hours of night. The winter solstice is the shortest day of the year, when the day is only 8 hours and the night is 16 hours. Throughout the year the length of daylight time is growing shorter from summer solstice until winter solstice and longer from winter solstice until summer solstice.

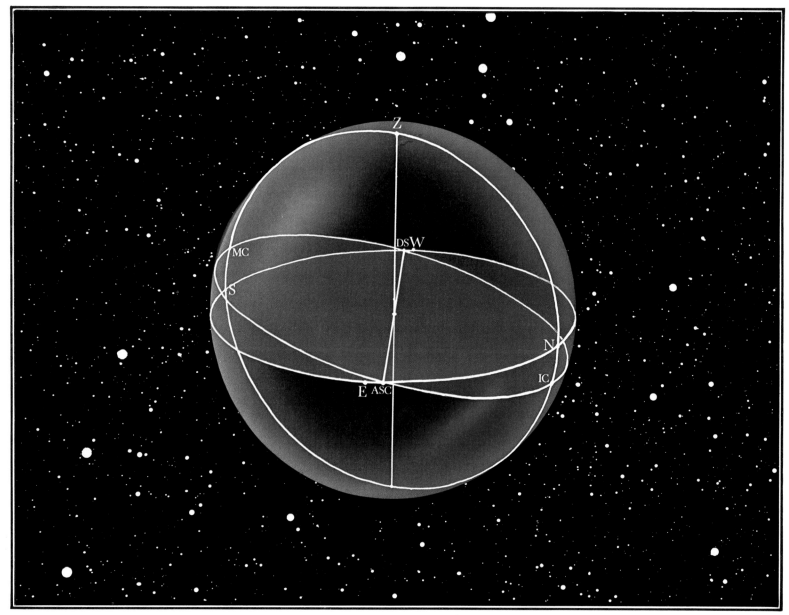

Figure III.11 The Primary Points. The horizontal line in the horoscope is equivalent to the line of intersection between the Ecliptic plane and the Horizon plane. The Ecliptic is orange and the Horizon is yellow. The brilliant orange line is the intersection. The horoscope itself is an abstraction of the plane of the Ecliptic.

The intersection of the meridian with the ecliptic produces two primary positions in the horoscope: the upper arc of intersection is the **Midheaven** *(Medium Coeli or MC)* which is the highest point in the sky, and the lower arc of intersection is the **Lower Midheaven** *(Immum Coeli or IC)* which is its opposite point. (Figure III.11) While the MC is the point of highest elevation in the sky for any given day, the Sun can only be directly overhead when the observer is between the two tropics on the Earth. As the observer moves north or south from the tropics the position of the Sun at noon on the summer solstice becomes progressively lower until, as one approaches the poles, the Sun appears to be following the horizon even at its highest points during the year.

The point where the horizon intersects the eastern arc of the ecliptic is called the **Ascendant** *(ASC),* which is equivalent to sunrise. Its opposite point, where the horizon intersects the western arc of the ecliptic, is the **Descendant** (DSC), equivalent to sunset. At the equinoxes the ascendant and the descendant are coincident with the east and west points on the equator. The ascendant is dependent upon both the terrestrial longitude and latitude of the individual.

The horoscope is a two-dimensional representation of the ecliptic, and the cardinal points

THE ROUND ART

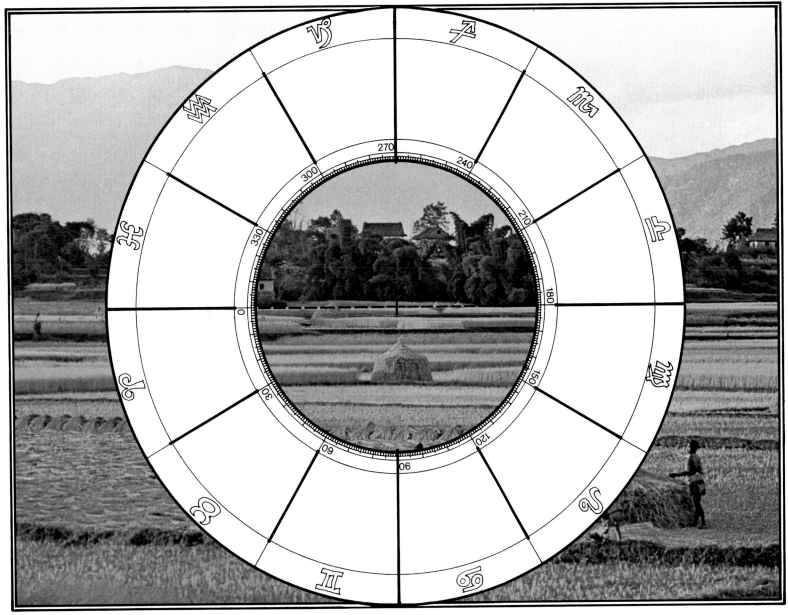

Figure III.12 The Orientation of the Horoscope.

are called *angles*. The angles are the Ascendant, Midheaven, Descendant and Lower Midheaven. The horizon is a line between the ascendant and the descendant — the intersection between the planes of the horizon and the ecliptic. The horoscope is always oriented with the ascendant (east) to the left and the descendant (west) to the right. (Figure III.12) South is at the top of the page, while north is at the bottom. This is an astrological convention, except in Ebertin's method. The meridian is a line which connects the MC and the IC. Although the archetypal position of the meridian is perpendicular to the horizon, this seldom happens because of longitude and latitude. The celestial sphere is an ideal set of circular co-ordinates always seen from elliptical viewpoints since the Earth itself is actually elliptical.

The four cardinal points in the plane of the ecliptic are north, south, east and west points equivalent to 0° of the astrological signs Cancer, Aries, Capricorn and Libra. There are correspondences between these two systems. The four cardinal points correspond to the four seasons and important hours of the daily cycle. The ascendant is equal to the vernal equinox and sunrise; the MC to the winter solstice and noon; the descendant to the autumnal equinox and sunset; and the IC to the winter solstice and midnight. Planets in the horoscope are conditioned by their proximity to these points. The two most critical points of intersection in the horoscope are the Ascendant and Midheaven, called *"Personal Points"*.

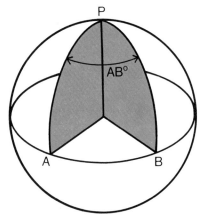

Figure III.13 Measurement on the Celestial Sphere.

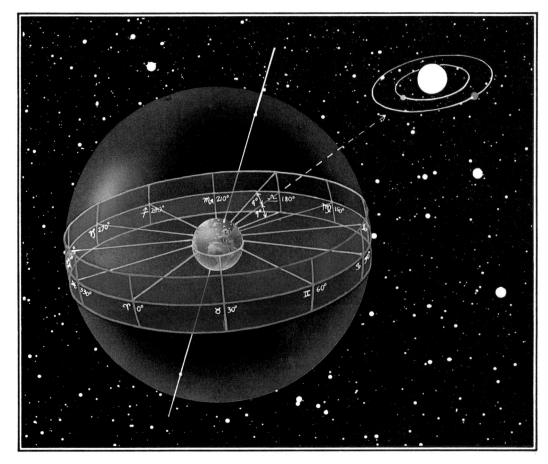

Figure III.14 The Zodiac Band. The Zodiac Band is red, and extends 9° above and below the plane of the Ecliptic. The plane of the Ecliptic is yellow. When the Sun is in a particular astrological sign, it resides in the appropriate 30° segment of this band.

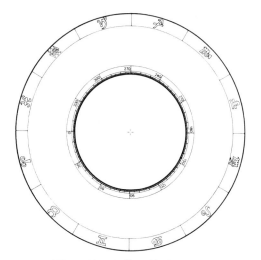

Figure III.15 The Zodiac Circle.

Measurement on the Celestial Sphere

Great circles are used for measurement because on the surface of a sphere the shortest distance between two points is along a great circle connecting them. (Figure III.13) Spherical measurements are made either in degree arcs or angles, which are equivalent designations. A spherical angle is an intersection between a pair of great circles which have common poles. The angle their planes subtend is equivalent to "degrees of arc" on the surface of the sphere connecting the planes by diurnal circles.

The most common division of great or diurnal circles is by degrees, minutes and seconds. The great circle is divided into 360 degrees (°), each degree is divided into 60 minutes (′), and each minute is divided into 60 seconds (′′). Both the ecliptic and the equator are divided into 360 degrees.

The **Zodiac** is a band extending approximately 9° on either side of the ecliptic, and the **Signs** of the zodiac are divisions of the ecliptic by twelve equal arcs. (Figure III.14) Each sign is composed of 30° of arc. The degree which begins each of the signs is called the *Cusp* of the sign. Thus the equinoctial point 0° Aries is the cusp of Aries.

The yearly solar cycle of 365¼ days is equated with the circle of the zodiac of 360 degrees. (Figure III.15) Since the path of the Sun around the Earth is elliptical, the Sun appears to move at different rates throughout the year. As a result, the co-ordination between the zodiac and the calendar is not a static affair, but a flexible one. Following are the twelve **Signs of the Zodiac** and their approximate times in the solar year.

Symbol	Sign	Degree Position	Date of Entry
♈	Aries, Vernal Equinox	0°	21 March
♉	Taurus	30°	20 April
♊	Gemini	60°	21 May
♋	Cancer, Summer Solstice	90°	22 June
♌	Leo	120°	23 July
♍	Virgo	150°	24 August
♎	Libra, Autumnal Equinox	180°	23 September
♏	Scorpio	210°	24 October
♐	Sagittarius	240°	23 November
♑	Capricorn, Winter Solstice	270°	22 December
♒	Aquarius	300°	20 January
♓	Pisces	330°	19 February

Figure III.16 Longitude and Latitude.

It must be carefully noted that the signs of the zodiac refer to the 30° divisions of the ecliptic in both astronomy and astrology, and *not* to the series of constellations which carry the same names. This point will be fully clarified later in this chapter.

A translation must be made between the measurement of distance around the terrestrial sphere and degrees of arc around the celestial equator. The rotation of the Earth about its axis is our prime measure of time, and it is correlated with the distance around the equator. The Earth makes a complete rotation every 24 hours, and since the equator is composed of 360° of arc, *one hour of time equals 15° of arc.* As each zodiacal sign is 30°, each sign division is equal to two hours of time. The exchange of unit designation in astronomical and astrological calculations between degrees of arc and time, both of which use minutes and seconds as secondary units, will be covered in the Appendix.

Measurement around the equator uses hour circles which converge on the polar axes. These hour circles correspond with the meridians of Longitude on the terrestrial sphere. (Figure III.16) Longitude on Earth is measured by the degrees east or west of the Greenwich (England) Meridian which has been designated as the world reference point. New York is 73°58'30'' of longitude west of Greenwich Meridian, while Peking is 116°28'15'' east of Greenwich. Likewise New York is 4 hours 55'54'' west, and Peking is 7 hours 45'53'' east of Greenwich in time. *One degree of arc equals 4 minutes of time.*

The complementary grading from the north pole to the south pole is Latitude. Latitude is measurement in degrees north or south of the equator by diurnal circles parallel to the equatorial circle. The maximum is obviously 90° north or south, which coincides with the poles.

All measurements of longitude and latitude are indicated by the letter N (North), S (South), E (East) or W (West) after the number of degrees and before the number of minutes and seconds. Thus 45 degrees, 15 minutes, 28 seconds West of Greenwich is indicated 45°W 15'28''. Time measurements in hours, minutes and seconds are indicated 5:54.27 or if they happen to be a longitude or latitude equivalent, 05 W 16'37''.

The Precession of the Equinoxes

The rotation of the earth around its polar axis produces day and night. The inclination of the polar axis results in the seasons. The Earth can be likened to a huge gyroscope which orients itself at a particular angle even though it is hurtling through space in its orbit around the Sun. At the present time, the North Pole points at the star Polaris, but this has not always been so, mainly because the axis of the earth *wanders* and *wobbles.* (Figure III.17)

The wandering of the Earth's axis was known by the Egyptians and later "discovered" by the Greek astronomer Hipparchus (born approximately 190 BC.). The wandering produces a slow western motion of the equinoctial points through the ecliptic. Since the equinox is defined by the moment when day is exactly equal to night and the Sun passes the equator along the ecliptic, this equinoctial point of 0° Aries was originally assumed to be always coincident to the beginning of the constellation Aries. The Egyptians found that the orientation of the Earth and the Sun was not quite identical at the Vernal Equinox each year and discovered after many years of observation that this equinoctial point moved *backwards* through the zodiac relative

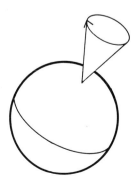

Figure III.17 The Axial Wobble of the Earth.

Figure III.18 The Platonic Months.

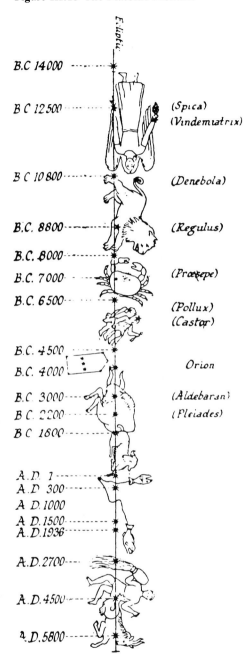

B.C 14000

B C 12500 — (Spica)
(Vindemiatrix)

B C 10800 — (Denebola)

B.C. 8800 — (Regulus)

B.C. 8000 —

B.C. 7000 — (Praesepe)

B.C. 6500 — (Pollux)
(Castor)

B.C. 4500 —
B.C. 4000 — Orion

B.C. 3000 — (Aldebaran)
B C 2200 — (Pleiades)

B C 1800 —

A.D. 1 —
A.D. 300 —
A.D. 1000
A.D. 1500 —
A.D. 1936 —

A.D. 2700 —

A.D. 4500 —

A.D. 5800 —

to the constellations. The complete revolution through the zodiac takes about 25,500 years — a *Platonic Year.* As the vernal equinox moves clockwise through the twelve signs, the length of time required to traverse each sign is about 2,120 years — a *Platonic Month.* (Figure III.18) The Vernal Equinox *pointer,* the cusp of Aries, only coincides with the constellation Aries once every 25,500 years. Hipparchus fixed the position of the vernal equinox as 0° Aries independent of the actual constellation the vernal equinox occurred in.

The Vernal Equinox at the present time is on the border between the constellation Pisces and the constellation Aquarius. When the pointer enters the sign Aquarius, the "Age of Aquarius" which has been so anxiously heralded will begin. Each precessional sign bestows certain characteristics upon the two thousand year period it governs. The "Age of the Ram" preceded the Piscean Age of the last two thousand years,[5] and that age was dominated by the early civilizations which used the ram for their totem and sacrificial animal. The age before used the Taurean Bull as its prime symbol, and so on. The book *Hamlet's Mill* by Giorgio Santillana and M. von Dechand is about the mythology of the precessional process and its implications for modern man.

This question of the precession of the equinoxes has produced great criticism of astrology since astrology uses the standards set up by Hipparchus, but *astronomers still use exactly the same frame of reference.* Within astrology there has also been controversy about this which has culminated in many astrologers using the *Sidereal Zodiac* (corrected to the constellation the equinox actually falls in). This means that all astrological and astronomical information must be altered back one sign. An individual born on the 23rd of March and designated an Aries is to the sidereal astrologer actually born in Pisces, etc. The method which Hipparchus instituted and which astrologers and astronomers prefer is the use of the *Tropical Zodiac* based upon the time of the vernal equinox.

The resolution of this problem lies in the fact that astrology does not attribute effects to the constellations themselves, but rather defines the signs as 30° segments of longitude along the ecliptic. The positions of the signs are not related to the constellations but rather to symbolic representations based upon the sequence of the seasons. The correlation of the signs with the seasons is of great and central importance in the horoscope. Births in the spring and the quality of "springtime" contain the active forces of the sign Aries independent of the real astronomical zodion in which the sun stands in at the vernal equinox.

The vernal equinox point is now passing slowly into the sign Aquarius from the sign Pisces, but this does not mean that the spring has lost its potency. As Jung observed,

> "The fact that astrology nevertheless yields valid results proves that it is not the apparent positions of the stars which work, but rather the times which are measured or determined by arbitrarily named stellar positions. Time thus proves to be a stream of energy filled with qualities and not, as our philosophy would have it, an abstract concept or precondition of knowledge."[6]

> "Careful investigation of the unconscious shows that there is a peculiar coincidence with time, which is also the reason why the ancients were able to project the succession of unconsciously perceived inner contents into the outer astronomical determinants of time. This is the basis for the connection of psychic events with temporal determinants, so it is not a matter of an indirect connection, but of a direct one. Conjunctions, oppositions, etc., are not in the least affected by the fact that we arbitrarily designate Pisces 1 as Aries 1."[7]

The effects of proton radiation from the Sun also correlate with seasonal influences and prove that there is a seasonal identification which is still valid.[8] The precession of the equinoxes is representative of the influences of larger cycles of time.

Circles and Cycles

> "Formation, transformation, Eternal Mind's eternal recreation."[9]

> ". . . when intersected by a plane, the sphere displays in this section the circle, the genuine image of the created mind, placed in command of the body which it is appointed to rule; and this circle is to the sphere as the human mind is to the Mind Divine, that is to say, as the line is to the surface; but both, to be sure, are circular."[10]

The Round Art of astrology is bound up with the mechanics of the sphere and the circle. The sphere and the circle have been accepted by virtually all civilizations at all times as the

[5]See Jung, *Aion, CW 9,* Part II, on the symbolism of the Piscean Age

[6]Jung, *Letters I, 1906-1950,* p. 138.

[7]*Ibid,* p. 138.

[8]Jung, *Letters II, 1951-1961,* p. 429.

[9]Goethe, *Faust Part II,* p. 79, translated by Philip Wayne.

[10]Kepler, *Harmonices mundi, Book V,* Frisch, Vol. V, p. 223.

ultimate image of the Ideal. The ancients ascribed the universe to the sphere and Fire to the point, its focus. The sphere is the most perfect manifestation of the all-wise Creator and the circle is its two-dimensional representation. The circle represented the cosmos (as in astrology), the *world-egg, gold,* the *Self,* eternal motion as the snake *Ouroboros* biting its tail, the *shining* or *illuminating body that dwells in the heart of man*[11] and the *universal balsam.* (Figure III.19)

The Sun is represented by the circle with a point in the centre indicating the heart of the physical universe. (Figure III.20) St. Bonaventura maintains in his Itinerarium that "God is an intelligible sphere whose centre is everywhere and whose circumference is nowhere". The sphere and the circle have no end, and symbolize the purest manifestation of the absolute in its aspect of transfiguration and rebirth.

Kepler was obsessed by the circle and the sphere, although he was the individual who recognized that there were no perfectly circular or spherical shapes or movements in the universe. He described the relationship of the circle to its centre:

> ". . . the centre point is, as it were, the origin of the spherical body; the outer surface the image of the innermost point, as well as the way to arrive at it; and the outer surface can be understood as coming about by an infinite expansion of the point beyond itself until a certain equality of all the individual acts of expansion are reached. The point spreads itself out over this extension so that point and surface are identical, except for the fact that the ratio of density and extension is reversed. Hence there exists everywhere between point and surface the most beautiful harmony, connection, relation, proportion and commensurability. And, although centre, surface and distance are manifestly three, yet they are One, so that no one of them could be even imagined to be absent without destroying the whole."[12]

The circle signifies unity and is the image of the Self as a whole — the mandala. (Figure III.21) "There is no linear evolution to the psychic goal of wholeness; there is only circumambulation of the Self."[13] The process of astrology is also circular. The nature of this image is profound.

In the history of man from the Babylonians to the modern age, the circle has been of paramount importance, having been used to represent cosmologies, symbols, languages, religions, buildings, mandalas and physical processes. Modern physicists have hypothesized that the Big Bang which created the universe from a central point produces a spherical universe.[14] (Figure III.22)

The relationship between the centre point and the circumference indicates the nature of the centre as focus and of the periphery as dispersion, bridging the gap between the Ideal and the Real. The centre is the *scintilla,* the *breath of life* of the whole. It corresponds to the yolk of the egg; the seed in the fruit; the Sun in the solar system; the heart in man; the nucleus in the atom; and all these are the germ and focus of the whole being. Jung says that the "centre is the goal, and everything is directed towards that centre, etc."[15] The circle is the extension of the point as Kepler observed, a prerequisite of its existence and the location of its essence. St. Bonaventura's idea is a recognition that any point in the universe can be the centre, concurring with Einstein, and conversely, that any collection of energies, masses or transformational elements have an implicit centre somewhere. *Any reference point is the centre and all centres are interchangeable.*

The Argentinian author Jose Luis Borges describes this interchangeability in his short story *The Aleph.* A man discovers that the centre of the universe, the Aleph point, is located in his cellar. The Aleph gives its beholder simultaneous access to everything that has or ever will happen in the universe. Since the Aleph point can encompass everything within itself, any point in the universe of space and time can also be an Aleph point. The identification of man's centre with God is also the basis of all meditative and religious systems, ever since the primordial shamans believed that their tentpoles were the axes of the universe. The Aleph point is accessible to everyone.

Nothing in the psycho-physical universe remains the same. Time is the perception of this dynamic reality, totally relative to its perceiver. To be one with the universe, one must be coincident to it and therefore lack this relative position.[16] Lacking this relative position, time ceases to exist. Jung calls this the limit of possible experience, the confrontation of the ego with the "emptiness" of the centre. "The ego dissolves as the reference-point of cognition. It

Figure III.19 The Ouroboros and the World Egg.

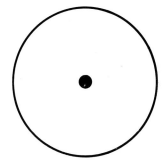

Figure III.20 The Symbol of the Sun.

[11]Jung, *Mysterium Coniunctionis, CW 14,* p. 47.

[12]Kepler, *Ad Vitellionem paralipomena,* p. 6-7., from Pauli.

[13]Jung, *Memories, Dreams and Reflections,* p. 222.

[14]Calder, *The Key to the Universe,* p. 169, quoting the physicist George Gamow in 1946.

[15]Jung, *MDR,* p. 224.

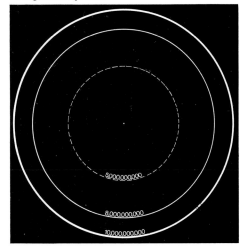

Figure III.22 The Circular Universe.

[16]**Samadhi** in the Hindu terminology is such a state.

Figure III.21 Tibetan Buddhist Mandala.

cannot coincide with the centre, otherwise we would be insensible; that is to say, the extinction of the ego is at best an endless approximation. But if the ego usurps the centre it loses its object (inflation!)."[17] Astrology, religion, psychoanalysis and physics are all concerned with this confrontation with the centre.

We are forced to maintain the flow of time, making us continually change position and create movement. Even if we are perfectly still, as in meditation, we are actually flying through space on a rotating sphere. According to the nature of time, this movement, having a beginning, must also have an end. This process of moving from beginning to end is a *Cycle*. The cycle is the circle moving through time. Electrons revolving around the atomic nucleus when viewed from the side form waves, the expression of the cyclic nature of the atom in time. (Figure III.23) When the movements of the nucleus and the electrons are assumed to be suspended they have a particulate nature, but since they never can be stopped in their tracks they also have a dual wave nature. Light, electro-magnetic radiation, sound and mass all behave in this way because there is always movement through time. One could say that the entire universe is subject to cycles and behaves according to the flow of time.

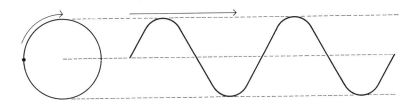

Figure III.23 Wave Motion and the Circle.

Every cycle can be broken down into its component smaller cycles. Nuclei and electrons have been broken down into even smaller particles and their intrinsic cyclic waves. The atom and its cycles combine to produce molecules which have their cycles. Every cycle in the universe is a component of larger cycles. Their continual interplay from the original primordial unity creates the diversity of the universe.

Man's reality is bound by two such cycles. The fastest cycle he can perceive is the velocity of light and the slowest is the lifetime of the universe. These extremes determine the extent of his perceptions and he is in the exact centre of them. Everything within the universe is bounded by perceptions of the cycles which are faster or slower. The extremes defining *our* reality are equivalent to the Heaven and the Hell of our universe. From any vantage point these limits apply, and if one reaches the extent of one's perceptions, the extent of one's universe, the very act of attainment merely creates a new set of boundaries. Unity is the only boundless reality.

By calibrating and subdividing component cycles and comparing them with each other we create various systems by which we evaluate life. The Periodic Table of the Elements, the Electro-magnetic spectrum, horological time, music and mathematics are all examples. (Figure III.24) In music the range of notes which the ear can register defines the limits. The limits of vision are determined by the cycles which the eye can register. All of these cyclic systems can be seen as analogous to each other and simultaneously extensions of each other. Upon this the physicist, the mathematician, the musician and the astrologer should agree, as it represents the essence of their world. Each individual tries to relate his dominant cycles with all other other perceptible cycles around him, with the aim of bridging the universes within universes and creating one contiguous whole. The process of life is return to the original unity through the circle.[18]

In the East, the circle of qualities is called the *Wheel of Life*, the *Samsara Round*. The force of creation which impels every living being to participate in the sequence of qualities is *Karma*. Freedom from the bondage of karma, and hence liberation from the samsara round, is equivalent to identification with the unity of all things — the centre of the wheel. The liberated individual identifies with the peripheral qualities equally and understands that they represent the illusion of earthly life. He identifies with the whole through the centre, rather than with any of the separate parts. In astrology the same process is true.

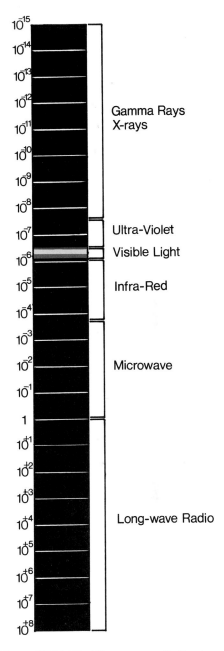

10^{15}
10^{14}
10^{13}
10^{12}
10^{11} Gamma Rays
            X-rays
10^{10}
10^{9}
10^{8}
10^{7} Ultra-Violet
10^{6} Visible Light
10^{5} Infra-Red
10^{4}
10^{3}
10^{2} Microwave
10^{1}
1
10^{+1}
10^{+2}
10^{+3}
10^{+4} Long-wave Radio
10^{+5}
10^{+6}
10^{+7}
10^{+8}

Figure III.24 The Electro-magnetic Spectrum.

Figure III.21 Tibetan Buddhist Mandala. This Seventeenth Century mandala shows Mahakala, the Great God of Time, dancing with his female consort within the Sacred Precinct of the four elements.

As the signs of the zodiac were identified with totem animals and the archetypal activities of the various societies in the dawn of historical time, they were infinitely more integral to the common man than today. In the modern world most basic survival instincts have been suppressed, complicated and abstracted, while some have been totally annihilated. The need to identify with the *processes of life* in such a way that they become real and comprehensible to the individual is glaring. Overcomplexity binds the individual even more strongly to the round of life because he is unconscious of its existence, and humdrum routines trap most individuals. It is necessary to associate astrology with the psychological or physiological mechanisms which have replaced forgotten survival instincts.

Every individual has certain astrological qualities working within him and affecting his life. The extent to which he is *aware* of these qualities indicates the scope of his reality. The enlightened man sees all the diverse qualities around him as necessary fragments of the whole. Astrology espouses identification with the whole range of qualities and through this, a total view, a liberation from fragmentation. Every man is unique, but is made of the same psychic and physical components as all other men, varying in proportion. Identification with all men is paradoxically the way to individuality.

Duality

Jung discovered that events occur *simultaneously* in the dream state, implying that in the unconscious there is no time. Upon waking the dreamer reorders the sequence of images in time as he would have logically seen them in the context of his life. This is a key to their interpretation as it indicates how the conscious mind communicates with the unconscious. The unconscious is coexistent with the Einsteinian "block" universe, the Unity. Mystical experiences are also timeless. *The waking state of consciousness is the creator of duality.* When we are unconscious we are integral to the entire space-time continuum, but as soon as we wake there is a duality between the time-bound conscious reality and the timelessness of the unconscious. The task of the individual is to integrate these two states. The desire for the reconciliation of opposites, the mysterium coniunctionis, the alchemical marriage, samadhi, or the unified field theory, are all ways to the centre and unity.

The duality of man is reflected in the physical world. The simplest atom, hydrogen, is composed of one proton and one electron. Fertilization is the meeting of one female ovum with one male sperm, followed by the process of cell division where the cells split into twos, always doubling. The wave has a peak and a trough, a maxima and a minima. Psychic contents double and redouble as they reach the threshold of consciousness.[19] Particle and wave. Night and Day. Black and white. The list is virtually endless. Everywhere in the universe duality reigns.

The expression of duality in the physical world produces the concept of symmetry. Marie Louise von Franz in *Number and Time* devotes a chapter to "The Number Two as the One-Continuum's Rhythm by Which Symmetries and Observables are Engendered."[20] Plato and the mathematician Brouwer believe that the concept of two-ness is the root of mathematical thought.[21] In geometry, two creates bilateral symmetry and plane projection.[22] She mentions that symmetry is integral to polarity in dynamic situations, and that mathematically the poles engender each other.[23] Light resolves into an electron pair with electron and positron.[24] In physics symmetry is a valuable tool for classifying particles, groups of particles, the interactions of particles and is connected to the previously mentioned conservation laws.[25] Double guardians adorned most ancient temples. Janus, the two-headed Roman god, both ended the old year and initiated the new. Two also forms the basis of many thought systems such as the Yin-Yang duality of the I Ching and Taoism; the God-Devil dualism (privatio boni) in Christianity; the essence of Gnosticism; and the binary logic which governs electronic computers and genetics in the chromosomes. All of these paired situations imply Time, which brings us back to the nature of the circle and the cycle. Through the reciprocity of parts in duality, the poles always contain the possibility of the hidden unity which was lost in their creation. Every part contains the essence of the whole. This is expressed in the alchemical relationship, "As above, so below."

The most important pairs of opposites in the structure of the horoscope are the

[19]von Franz, *Number and Time,* p. 92.

[20]von Franz, *Number and Time,* p. 87.

[21]*Ibid,* p. 87.

[22]*Ibid,* p. 88.

[23]*Ibid,* p. 89.

[24]*Ibid,* p. 91.

[25]Capra, *The Tao of Physics,* p. 263-4.

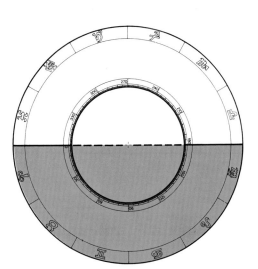

Figure III.25 The Horizon.

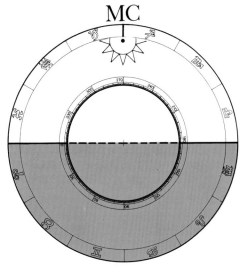

Figure III.26 The Midheaven-Noon Point.

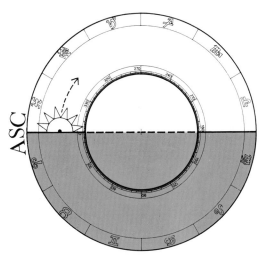

Figure III.27 The Ascendant-Sunrise Point.

hemispheres. The horizon is the ascendant-descendant axis in the horoscope and divides it into an upper and a lower half. (Figure III.25) The upper half indicates influences which affect the individual directly through the thin film of the earth's atmosphere and governs *consciousness, objectivity* and *direct influences* upon the individual. It corresponds with daytime and the waking state. The strongest point in the upper hemisphere is the MC point, equivalent to noon, when the influences at the MC are shining vertically down upon the individual through the thinnest part of the atmosphere. (Figure III.26) The MC is equivalent to the *Ego* and *Ego-consciousness*. The ego is will, the driving force of individuality and the governor of consciousness, being located in the approximate centre of the field of consciousness (the upper hemisphere). When any planet is in the MC, its influences are strongest.

The lower hemisphere is the opposite of the upper. Planets move clockwise through the horoscope each day, and so the upper hemisphere indicates the movements from sunrise (the ascendant), past noon (the MC) to sunset (the descendant). As soon as the Sun sets under the western horizon (the descendant), *it* must pass its influences through the entire mass of the earth to reach the individual These influences from the lower hemisphere are *unconscious, subjective* and *indirect*. The IC is opposite the MC, is analogous to midnight, and is the centre of the field of the unconscious. Planets at the IC are least strong, darkest and most subliminal.

The ascendant is mediator between the two hemispheres, and the synthesizing agent uniting the upper conscious and objective hemisphere with the lower unconscious and subjective hemisphere. (Figure III.27) It is equivalent to the *Personality* in the sense of the Greek *persona, a mask* — the way the individual sees himself and a reflection of the way he feels he is seen by the external world. The ascendant is the device by which contents from the unconscious make themselves known to consciousness. The personality is essentially a blending function and since it also governs the *physical body* and *appearance* through which all psychic material is transmitted, it is a vital and important position.

The other hemispherical division is around the vertical axis between the MC and the IC. This axis distinguishes the eastern (occidental) half from the western (oriental) half of the horoscope. (Figure III.28) Once again it is easy to use the path of the Sun as a metaphor for movements. When the Sun (or any other planetary body) is at the IC point, its influence is weakest and most unconscious. As the Sun traverses the left half of the horoscope, it becomes gradually stronger until it reaches the ascendant, when it "rises" above the horizon, and reaches its peak of strength at the MC. The left hemisphere indicates influences which are *ascending* or getting stronger, and are gaining in consciousness. This is the hemisphere of the *Individual Psyche* which contains all contents of a personal nature. The ascendant (personality) is the centre of the field of the individual psyche. The whole individual psyche is constituted of conscious and unconscious contents of a personal nature and archetypically is connected with the signs from Capricorn to Cancer.

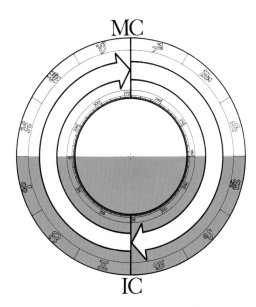

Figure III.28 The Occidental and Oriental Halves of the Horoscope.

As the Sun reaches the MC point of maximum strength, it begins to wane through the right hemisphere losing most of its force passing under the horizon at the descendant until it again returns to the IC. This hemisphere indicates all influences which are descending, losing consciousness and energy. This is the hemisphere of the *Collective Psyche,* which contains all contents of a collective nature and indicates the attitude towards collective values. The collective psyche is constituted of conscious and unconscious contents of an impersonal nature, the image of the outside world, and is associated with the signs from Gemini to Sagittarius.

The twelve Signs of the Zodiac produce six pairs of opposites around the circle of the horoscope. (Figure III.29) They represent opposite times of the year, and astrologically their meanings are opposite and complementary. The pairs of signs and their respective seasons in CSI follow:

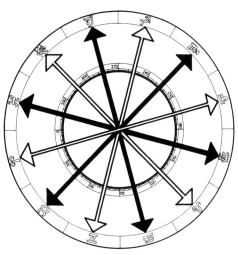

Aries (March-April = germination and unfolding
Taurus (April-May) = strengthening and creation of form
Gemini (May-June) = diversity and flourishing
Cancer (June-July) = fertilization pollination
Leo (July-Aug) = ripeness and completion
Virgo (Aug-Sept) = harvest

Libra = (Sept-Oct) = fallow fields and adjustment time
Scorpio (Oct-Nov) = life terminating processes, seed retention
Sagittarius (Nov-Dec) = hibernation and advent
Capricorn (Dec-Jan) = torpidity and crystallization
Aquarius (Jan-Feb) = fasting time and lent
Pisces (Feb-Mar) = rains swelling the planted seeds

Figure III.29 Paired Signs.

There is also an alternating pattern of gender throughout the signs. (Figure III.30) If the signs are numbered from one to twelve starting with the equinoctial sign Aries, the odd signs are *masculine, positive, extravert* and *active* while the even signs are *feminine, negative, introvert* and *passive*. The accompanying diagram indicates this alternation. Through every cycle around the signs of the zodiac, the gender and mode of operation is continually alternating. This parallels the fact that every individual is governed by chromosomal proportions and there is only a slight variance between man and woman. Each of us has almost equal qualities of masculinity — femininity and the differences are a function of how dominant those qualities are in response to external influences. The sexual balance often reflects itself in the degree of extraversion or introversion of the individual. Sexuality is also qualified by the concept of libido (psychic or sexual energy). Libido, as we have discovered, is never static and tends to apply itself to whatever channels of activity present themselves. The sexuality of any individual also follows this pattern. Sexuality is always changing from activity to passivity and back again, whether the individual is conscious of it or not.

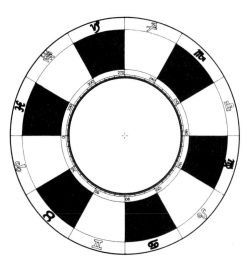

Figure III.30 Alternating Gender Through the Signs. The positive signs are white and the negative signs are black.

No individual is totally represented by any one sign of the zodiac, as the "Sun-Sign" newspaper astrologers would have us believe. There are nine planetary bodies in addition to the Sun. Besides this, the cross-correspondence of the opposing signs is always brought into play in each individual. Every sign has such an intimate relationship with its opposite that it is often difficult to separate basic sign qualities from the reflective qualities which it absorbs from its opposite. If an individual manifested the purest qualities of any sign, it would imply that he was totally on the periphery of the horoscope circle. In reality, it is not possible to exist exclusively around the periphery as this would imply that the individual is totally mechanical and one-sided. At the same time it is not possible to exist in the centre of the circle, for the reasons we covered before, and also because it would imply manifesting *none* of the archetypal sign qualities. During life the opposite of every sign quality is activated either from the centre of the individual or through the "carrier" of another individual or individuals in his environment. Since it is not possible to be exclusively on the periphery or in the centre, *every individual is somewhere between the periphery and the centre of his being*. Life is as much concerned with experience in dancing in the charged zone between the opposites as it is with specific qualities indicated astrologically. Individuals who are highly focussed are closer to the centre, while those who are dispersed are closer to the periphery.

When the opposites become irresolute within the individual, one side of the opposition tends to try to annihilate the other, which, if successful, produces dementia praecox, or its popularized name, schizophrenia. Schizophrenia is a state of extreme unconscious fluctuation between the psychic poles. The extreme acted out at any given time seems the only reality and the other pole of the personality is forgotten even though the "new" personality is predominantly a compensation for unconscious qualities of the first one. Every individual experiences compensatory qualities in his own actions and thoughts — the expression of his inner striving for unity. The beautiful actress feels physically inferior; the billionaire lives like an animal; the honest politician is essentially nasty and disreputable; the company treasurer runs off with the funds; etc. Astrology seeks to initiate a process of *conscious* compensation instead of one-sidedness or a dependence upon external compensation.

Quaternities

The combined division of the zodiac by the ASC-DES and MC-IC axes produces a division by four, a *quaternity*. The quaternity is extremely important in psychology, religion, astrology and mathematics.

> "The quaternity is an archetype of almost universal occurrence. It forms the logical basis for any whole judgement. If one wishes to pass such a judgement, it must have this fourfold aspect."[26]

[26]Jung, *Psychology and Religion, CW 11*, p. 167.

Jung considered that (the quaternity) constituted an essential psychic mechanism in the search for wholeness. One is unity, Two is duality and the play of opposites, Three is mediator between the initial two, but Four is both an echo of One and Four in its own right as a culmination — a model of wholeness.

Most spatial orientation systems and models of the universe use four points in their structure. The cardinal points of the compass; the number of dimensions in the Einsteinian universe; the four forces in nature, (nuclear, gravitational, electro-magnetic and weak); the number of elements, according to Plato; faces of the Great Pyramid; all Cross shapes (religious images, cathedrals); the four psychological types of psychic orientation (thinking, feeling, sensation and intuition); the four triplets of 'quarks' in physics; the four base acids which compose DNA and RNA and its cross-section; the faces of the square representing Earth; the four ancient castes; the four Evangelists and sacred animals; and the religious systems of many pre-Christian cultures are all examples of the orienting faculty of the quaternity.

The cross of the two axes in the circle are the symbol of earth ($\oplus$) in astrology. Each quadrant is defined by an overlap of a horizontal and a vertical hemisphere and its opposite quarter. If we generalize, the upper hemisphere is *conscious,* the lower is *unconscious,* the left is *individual,* and the right is *collective.* Therefore, the spring signs Aries, Taurus and Gemini represent the quadrant of *unconscious individuality;* the summer signs Cancer, Leo and Virgo represent the *unconscious collective* values; the autumn signs Libra, Scorpio and Sagittarius represent the *conscious collective;* and the winter signs Capricorn, Aquarius and Pisces represent the *conscious individual* qualities. (Figure III.31) The disposition of planets through the horoscope activates from one to all four sets of qualities, and indicates the general orientation of the individual. Analysis according to these quadrant values constitutes the first step in the Interpretation of the horoscope, and will be defined in detail in the chapter on *Interpretation, Part VIII.*

Jung uses the term *Individuation* to denote the process by which a person becomes an *Individual.* Since I have chosen to use this designation for the person who is the subject of the horoscope, instead of the traditional term *native,* it should be clearly defined as I believe that this state of being is the major objective of astrology as well as psychology. The term individual implies that the person is a *separate, indivisible unity* and that he or she has successfully resolved the paired opposites of the quaternity which are the integral psychic structure of the Self. Jung defines the structure of the individual in his book, *The Structure of the Unconscious, CW 9, Part I:*

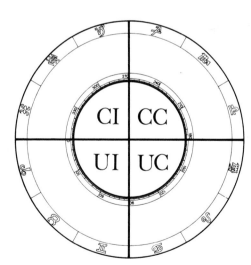

Figure III.31 The Four Quadrants and their Psychological Designations.

1. Individuality manifests itself partly as the principle which selects, and sets limits to, the components adopted as personal. (Components tending towards differentiation from the collective)
2. Individuality is the principle which makes possible, and if need be compels, a progressive differentiation of the collective psyche. (Components tending towards general collective values)
3. Individuality manifests itself partly as an obstacle to collective productivity and partly as resistance to collective thinking and feeling. (Personal elements in different individuals can resemble each other and even amount to an identity, largely cancelling out the individual nature of those personal components, and begin to become collective)
4. Individuality is that which is peculiar and unique in combinations of general (collective) psychological components.

Since conscious and unconscious contents of the psyche are divided into both individual and collective components, psychic unification is never only a resolution of any one pair of opposing hemispheres but rather a creative combination of all the quadrants. The integration of the individual through the horoscope necessitates comprehension of the whole while still recognizing the nature of the parts. The individual must be able to differentiate himself from the collective without cutting himself off from it entirely. It amounts to transfering the quaternity from the outside world to the inside world of the psyche. *"Individuation does not shut one out from the world, but gathers the world to one's self".*[27]

[27]Jung, *The Structure and Dynamics of the Psyche, CW 8*, p. 226.

Triplicities and Quadruplicities

The quaternity of interlocking hemispheres is a structural disposition within which the signs operate, but the signs are subject to other orders of organization as well. The signs have an order which operates within their sequence, and also an order which is a function of the geometry of the circle divided into twelve. The dualities constitute both the pairs of opposites, and the alternating gender every other sign. We will now concern ourselves with divisions of three and four. These orders of organization are called *Triplicities* and *Quadruplicities*. (Figure III.32)

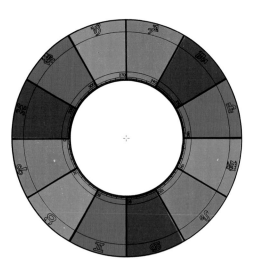

Figure III.32 The Triplicities of Fire (Red), Earth (Yellow), Air (Blue) and Water (Green).

The triplicities are formed by the four elements — Fire, Earth, Air and Water — each of which governs three signs. The quadruplicities are formed by the three modes of operation: Cardinal, Fixed and Mutable; and each mode governs four signs. Three and Four interact in both of these orders and this is the cause of some misunderstanding in the terminology of traditional astrology. The names Triplicity and Quadruplicity refer to the number of signs which each order contains rather than the operation they perform. This must be made quite clear, as our attitude is dynamic and not the traditional static one. The four triplicities are composed of triangles within the circle, while the quadruplicities are composed of squares within the circle. (Figure III.33) Plato recognized that the elements were composed of triangles. Robert Fludd, the alchemist, realized that "The quadratic number is likened to God the Father in whom the mystery of the whole sacred trinity is embraced."[28]

[28]Pauli, *The Interpretation of Nature and the Psyche*, p. 227.

Figure III.33

The philosphical implications of the relationship between three and four have been already mentioned in the History chapter, referring to the "Axiom of Maria". They are archetypal ordering factors and their relationship is clearly demarcated: "As Jung observed, all quaternary numbers are essentially bound up in a qualitative way with the symbols of the process of 'becoming conscious of wholeness', and triadic numbers are similarly connected with the principles of intellectual and physical movement."[29] The triplicity of elements defines qualitative symbols of the process, while the quadruplicity of modes defines the principle of movement. Following is a table of the twelve signs and their element and mode designations, as well as their general characteristics.

[29]von Franz, *Number and Time*, p. 101.

I.	Aries	Cardinal	Fire	Self-Assertion
II.	Taurus	Fixed	Earth	Undifferentiated Matter
III.	Gemini	Mutable	Air	Instinctive Communication
IV.	Cancer	Cardinal	Water	Familial Feeling
V.	Leo	Fixed	Fire	Self-Exteriorization
VI.	Virgo	Mutable	Earth	Differentiated Matter
VII.	Libra	Cardinal	Air	Sublimated Communication
VIII.	Scorpio	Fixed	Water	Intensified Feeling
IX.	Sagittarius	Mutable	Fire	Self-Realization
X.	Capricorn	Cardinal	Earth	Perfected Matter
XI.	Aquarius	Fixed	Air	Idealistic Communication
XII.	Pisces	Mutable	Water	Isolated Feeling

[30]Landscheidt, *Cosmic Cybernetics,* p. 26-27.

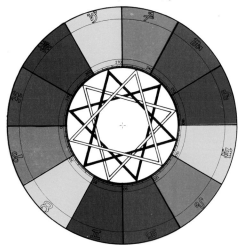

Figure III.34 The Grand Trines.

The three triplicities of four elements divide the zodiac into three *Octaves.* In each octave the elements progress in the same sequence: Fire, Earth, Air and Water. To Plato, they were a mathematical system of successively greater densities underlying Nature. To Robert Fludd, the elements were proportional to each other as they ascended from Earth. The physicist Werner Heisenberg states that: ''in all elementary processes, from which all natural phenomena evolve, four different groups are to be distinguished.''[30] As each element has the same relative position in each octave around the circle, the three signs of each triplicity are at equal thirds of the circle (120°) from each other, producing equilateral triangles, called *Grand Trines.* Each grand trine is composed of the cardinal, fixed and mutable sign of each element. (Figure III.34)

The sequence is initiated by the *Fiery Grand Trine:* Aries, Leo and Sagittarius. (Figure III.35) Fire signs indicate the spiritual and creative energy which motivates each octave. They determine the vitality as pure force, and are related to the Intuitive function in psychology as well as libido (life-force). The fire signs are positive, active and masculine.

They project their energy into the *Earthy Grand Trine:* Taurus, Virgo and Capricorn. (Figure III.36) The earth signs are material, the physical world as beauty and illusion, matter in all its forms as well as perceptions and attitudes towards the physical world. Psychologically earth is related to the function of Sensation, the operation and interrelationship between the senses and physical stimulus. The earth signs are negative, passive and feminine.

The combination of fire and earth produces the *Airy Grand Trine:* Gemini, Libra and Aquarius. (Figure III.37) Energy applied to matter produces movement, which in turn breeds communication, intellect, relationship, rhythmic activity and duality. Psychologically air is related to the Thinking function which is abstract, conceptually connective, ideological and separate from the object of thought. The air signs are positive, active and masculine.

The dissolving and synthesizing of the previous three elements occur within the *Watery Grand Trine:* Cancer, Scorpio and Pisces. (Figure III.38) The water signs are emotional responses which imply a valuation and are characteristically unconscious, subjective, sensitive, irrational and reactive. Psychologically they are related to the function of Feeling which accepts or rejects. The water signs are negative, passive and feminine.

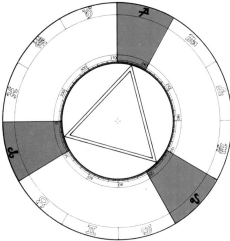

Figure III.35 The Fire Grand Trine (Aries, Leo and Sagittarius).

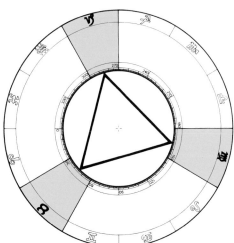

Figure III.36 The Earth Grand Trine (Taurus, Virgo and Capricorn).

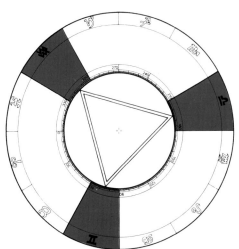

Figure III.37 The Air Grand Trine (Gemini, Libra and Aquarius).

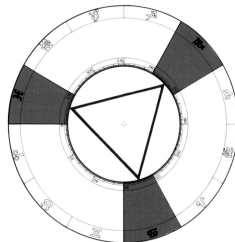

Figure III.38 The Water Grand Trine (Cancer, Scorpio and Pisces).

Each quadrant of the horoscope and the signs is sub-divided into three signs which represent three modes of operation. These modes are principles of movement and repeat in the same sequence within each quadrant. The interaction of these forces constitutes the "dynamics" of the zodiac. Historically, trinities have been used to define the dynamics of religion, physics, logic and alchemy. The Christian Church recognizes the Trinity of Father, Son and Holy Ghost. Hinduism has a triune godhead of Brahma, Vishnu and Shiva and the energetic processes of rajas, tamas and sattvas. In alchemy the Royal Marriage involves the King (salt), the Queen (sulphur) and the mediating agent Mercurius (mercury). In colour printing all colours are made from red, yellow and blue. All particles in particle physics are composed of triplets of red, blue and white quarks. The double helix in genetics is made of two spiralling chains and a central axis. The Hebrew Kabbalistic Tree of Life structures the universe in three pillars of Justice, Mercy and Mildness. In all of these cases the trinity is dynamic. The signs in each quadruplicity occupy the same relative position in each quadrant and are disposed at 90° angles from each other, forming squares and crosses, called in astrology the *Grand Crosses.* (Figure III.39) Each of the three modes — Cardinal (initiating), Fixed (static) and Mutable (changing) — and their Grand Crosses contain one of each element.

The *Cardinal Grand Cross* is coincident with the quadrant divisions, the cardinal points, the equinoxes and the solstices, and the angles of the horoscope. (Figure III.40) The cardinal grand cross is active, kinetic and initiates the movement in each quadrant. Aries is the cardinal fire sign, Cancer the cardinal water sign, Libra the cardinal air sign, and Capricorn the cardinal earth sign.

The *Fixed Grand Cross* is the most stable mode and occupies the centre of each quadrant, governing sustaining, centrifugal and dominating influences. (Figure III.41) Taurus is the fixed earth sign, Leo the fixed fire sign, Scorpio the fixed water sign and Aquarius the fixed air sign.

The *Mutable Grand Cross* is unstable, flexible, mediative, as it is bounded by the cardinal and fixed crosses. (Figure III.42) Mutable signs are imitative, externally influenced and constantly changing. Gemini is the mutable air sign, Virgo the mutable earth sign, Sagittarius the mutable fire sign and Pisces the mutable water sign. According to the precession of the equinoxes, the mutable cross has been in the equinoctial and solstitial positions for the last two thousand years during the 'Piscean Age', certainly known for its changes in attitude.

Each zodiacal sign is a component of both of the two systems of organization, as well as being defined by the oppositions and gender. These interpenetrating organizational systems allow the signs to be *simultaneous* and *dynamic,* making them better able to represent the dynamic character of the individual.

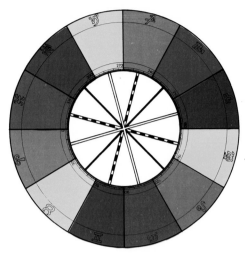

Figure III.39 The Grand Crosses.

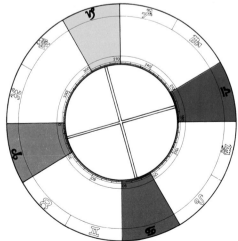

Figure III.40 The Cardinal Grand Cross (Aries, Cancer, Libra and Capricorn).

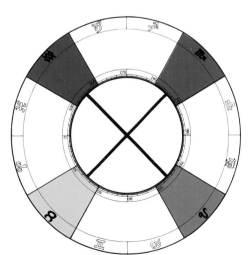

Figure III.41 The Fixed Grand Cross (Taurus, Leo, Scorpio and Aquarius).

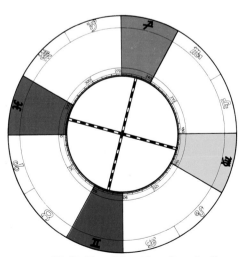

Figure III.42 The Mutable Grand Cross (Gemini, Virgo, Sagittarius and Pisces).

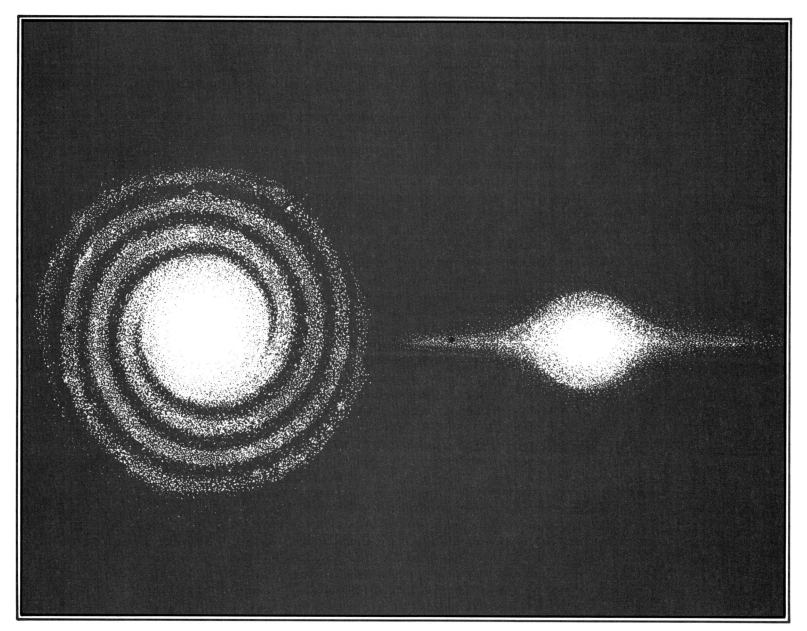

Figure III.43 The Milky Way Galaxy. Our galaxy is shown as it would be seen from the end on and from above. The position of the Sun is indicated by the red dot.

[31]Landscheidt, *Cosmic Cybernetics,* p. 16.

The Celestial Sphere and the Universe

The celestial sphere is the datum sphere of the Earth and is subject to many external forces. The Earth is the centre and reference point for man, but in the entire universe there are many greater centres to which the Earth and even the Sun are subservient. As the Earth rotates upon its axis and revolves around the Sun, so the Sun rotates around its axis, and revolves around its Sun within the Milky Way Galaxy. Our Sun, which is spiralling disk nebula is only one of billions in the Milky Way. The Sun is approximately two-thirds of the way from the centre of the Milky Way towards the edge and has a vast orbit around the galactic centre. (Figure III.43) The Sun actually travels around the galactic centre at 19.5 kilometres per second, taking the earth and the other planets with it.[31] An external observer would see the solar system through time as a brilliant spiralling filament (the Sun) surrounded by other coloured filaments (the planets) spiralling around it, and with still other almost invisible filaments around them (the planetary moons). (Figure III.44) Rodney Collin likens the vision to "a gossamer-fine web woven from the eccentric paths of innumerable asteroids and comets, glowing with some sense of living warmth and ringing with an incredibly subtle and harmonious music."[32] To illustrate this requires the path to be roughly a cylindrical spiral, but actually it would be a great funnel through time as all bodies in the universe fall away from each other at close to the speed of light. This gigantic vortex is the *vas* (vessel) into which we plummet at death, but also the womb from which we emerge at birth.

The aforementioned vision is as it would be seen by an "objective" external observer. If seen from our central interior 'subjective' viewpoint, it appears that the celestial sphere, on the surface of which the entire universe is inscribed, is receding from us at almost the speed of light. . . the universe through time is an exploding sphere towards the future and a dark vortex towards the past.

As the solar system spins through time and space in its spiral, so does the entire Milky Way galaxy and all the other galaxies in the universe. The plane of the solar system is tilted in respect to the Earth at an angle of 23½°. The plane of the solar system in respect to the Milky Way is tilted at an angle of 55°.[33] The Sun's axis is tilted in respect to the plane of the solar system at an angle of 7°. This complex system of tilts produces a whole range of compensating motions which ultimately resembles a huge gyroscope orienting itself in time. Since the solar system and the Milky Way are continually moving, the only reference system to which we can refer is the stars *which lie outside the Milky Way.*

The reference plane of our solar system is a pattern of stars lying around the periphery of the Milky Way: the Zodiac. The constellations of the zodiac are so far away even from the Sun that they only appear to be close to each other. The stars which compose the constellation Ursa Major (Great Bear) are tightly grouped from our viewpoint, but in reality the star Alkaid in that constellation is as close to the other stars as we are.

Like all the other stars within the Milky Way galaxy, our Sun revolves around the Galactic Centre, a journey which takes an estimated 225,000,000 years! As the journey is so long, the galactic centre is a very stable orientation point for us in the universe. Studies which have been made recently verify that radiation is emanating from the galactic centre, and that it is affecting the Sun and Earth. Dr. Theodor Landscheidt considers the galactic centre as the centre of the system superior in order to the Sun, and has correlated data relating its location to the effects it has on man. Its position correlates with solar eruptions and earthquakes, and it is prominent in the horoscopes of eminent politicians.[34]

The galactic centre is presently located at 26°30′ Sagittarius according to radio astronomers.[35] The Milky Way is a spiral nebula with flattened edges and a greater thickness towards the centre, so when we look towards Sagittarius we see a greater density of stars than when we look in the opposite direction towards Gemini. Sagittarius is thus the centre of vitality and source of energy from which the Sun derives its force as well. When we face Gemini we are facing away from the source of those radiations, away from the focus of the galaxy. This constitutes an objective value system for determining the sign qualities. "They are in fact a measure of our inclination towards the focus of our galaxy, as definite as the hours of the day are of our inclination towards the Sun."[36]

[32]Collin, *The Theory of Celestial Influence*, p. 38.

[33]*Ibid*, p. 10.

Figure III.44 The Spiral Path of the Solar System through Time. The central white line is the path of the Sun through space. Mercury is light yellow, Venus is light green, Earth is green-blue, Mars is red, Jupiter is blue, Saturn is violet, Uranus is deep yellow, Neptune is deep green and Pluto is deep red. The Asteroid Belt, between Mars and Jupiter, is a haze of tiny fragments which produces a glowing zone within which the Sun and the inner planets move.

[34]Landscheidt, *Cosmic Cybernetics*, p. 17-18.

[35]*Ibid*, p. 17.

[36]Collin, *The Theory of Celestial Influence*, p. 13.

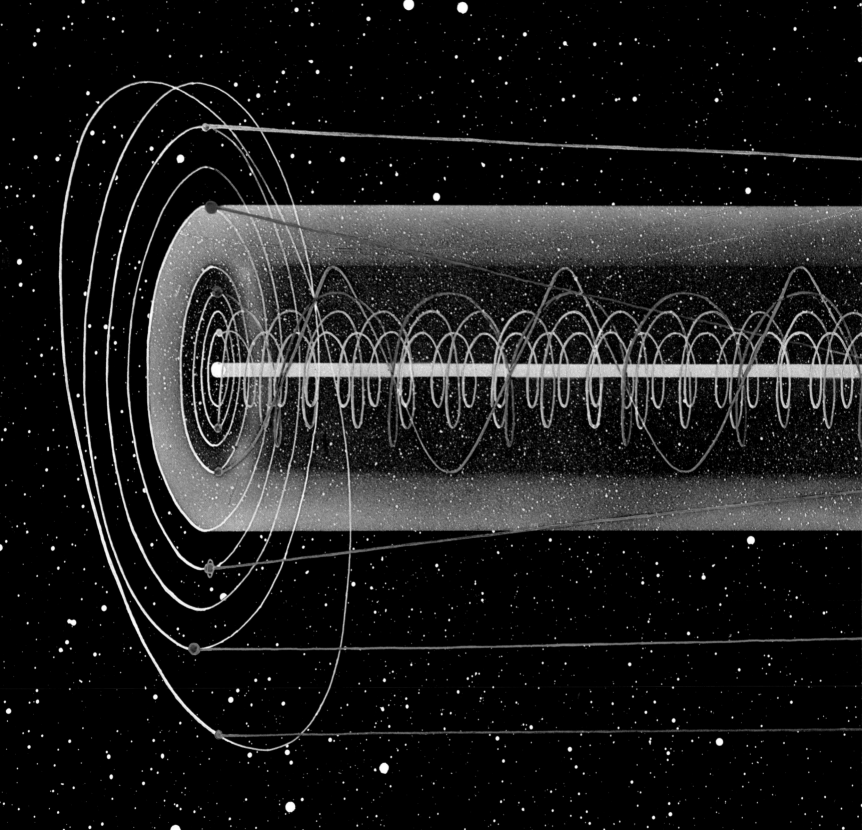

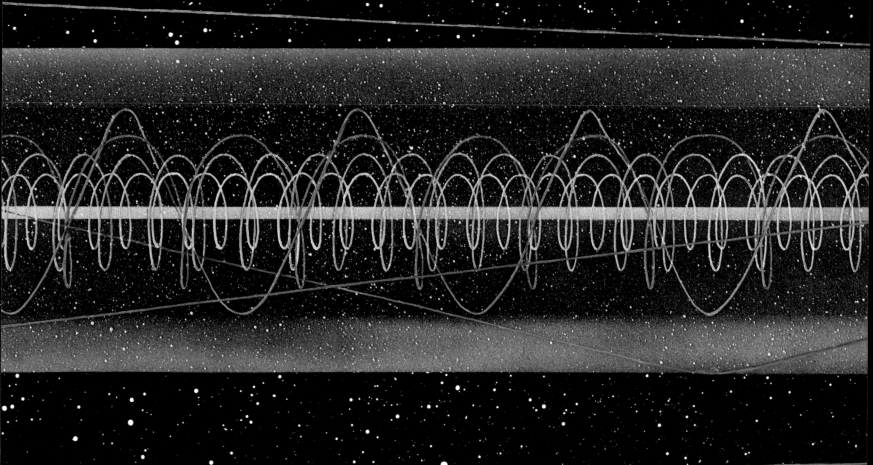

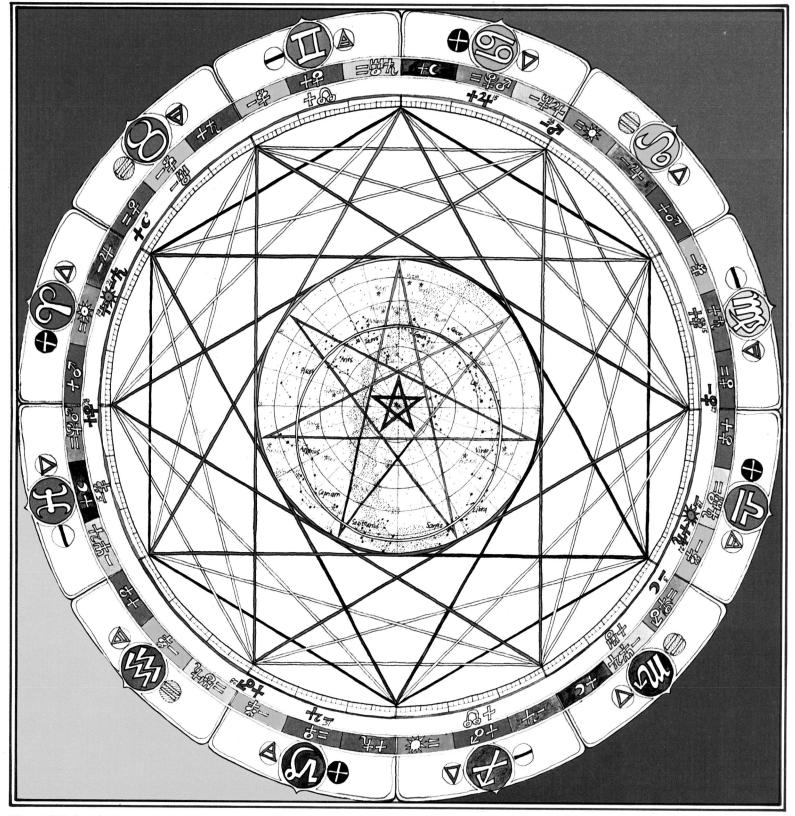

Part IV

Figure IV.1 Cosmic Geometry.

The Planets

"The day-star, sonorous of old,
Goes his predestined way along,
And round his path is thunder rolled,
While sister-spheres join rival song."[1]

[1] Goethe, *Prologue in Heaven,* translated by Wayne, p. 39.

The first attribution of planets to gods was recorded by the Babylonians in the Third Millenium BC. They likened the movements of the planets through the field of the fixed stars to 'stray goats' wandering at the beck and call of the shepherd god, Marduk. Their mythology coded the movements of the planets to their history. When certain configurations occurred it was assumed that the equivalent gods were mating or battling with each other, just as the Babylonians did in ordinary life. The planetary movements formed the basis of their calendar, feast schedule, religion and history, combined in a vocabulary to which everyone could have access.

The movements of the planets were correlated to the colours and qualities of the gods associated with them. **Shamash** the Sun was the charioteer who held the reins of the world and carried his light across the sky each day through the gates of morning and evening. **Sin,** the goddess of the Moon, governed wisdom through her ability to change shape, and though she was married to Shamash, she soon left him to wander on her own. She was associated with agriculture because she formed a sickle at certain times of the month. She was associated with sailors because her reflection was seen in the waters of the sea at night. Mercury was very difficult to see, being never more than 25° away from the Sun and thus usually obscured by the light of the Sun. He was called *gud-ud* or *Mushtaddallu,* the messenger, and the *shining bull* because he had phases like the Moon. Venus was the *Morning Star* or *Evening Star* as she also followed the Sun on his journey, and was called *dil-bad,* which means 'herald' or 'proclaimer'. She was the first star in the sky at night and often rose before sunrise, the times the Babylonians considered most propitious for love-making — hence her governance of procreation. Because of his red colour, Mars was related to the high summer heat, pestilence and death and was identified with the god **Nergal.** Jupiter was called the **White Star** or **Chief Oracle-giver** *(molobabar* or *sag-me-gar).* He was considered the *'most high god',* and due to his cycle was absent from the sky for one month each year. He had a complement of his own planets (the moons of Jupiter) and was a small replica of the solar system. Saturn was associated with 'time' as he took over twenty-nine years to pass around the zodiac, and was the *Star of the Sun (kakkab shamshi),* the nocturnal equivalent of Shamash. When Jupiter and Saturn were close to each other they were called the *'two great stars'.* As their light varied when they ascended or descended through their cycles they were called by different names which indicated a range of powers and equivalent cosmic situations.

When planets were not seen at night in their accustomed positions, the Babylonians found fixed stars which represented them. Each of the planets had their 'deputy' stars. There were also names indicating which planets stood near each other, particularly Venus and Mars. Venus had 'crowns' of different colours to represent her various positions. She had a yellow crown when near Mercury, a red one near Mars, a white one near Jupiter and a black 'sun-crown' near Saturn. The planets were more sympathetic when they were near fixed stars of the same colour. (This practice is astonishingly similar to modern use of spectrographic analysis.)

According to the Greeks, the planets moved within a series of crystal spheres surrounding the Earth. (Figure IV.2) These spheres were ordered outwards from the Earth to the realm of the fixed stars, the *'Empyrean'.* While the planetary spheres moved, the Empyrean remained static and was used to compare the movements of the other spheres. The sphere of the Moon was closest to the Earth, followed by the spheres of Mercury, Venus and the Sun. Beyond the Sun were the spheres of the *'superior planets'* — Mars, Jupiter and Saturn. Thus the Sun was in the central sphere 'escorted' by Mercury and Venus in his cosmic dance. To this day the planets Mercury and Venus are considered *'inferior planets',* while the outer planets Mars, Jupiter and Saturn are *'superior planets'.* The concept of the spheres continued until the late Renaissance.

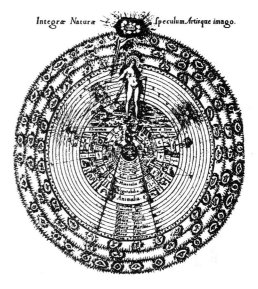

Figure IV.2 The Spheres of the Empyrean. (From Fludd's *Collectio Operum.)*

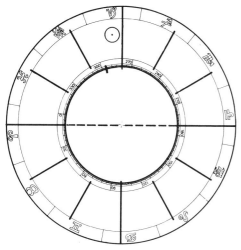

Figure IV.3 Rotating Circles of the Signs and the Houses. The Sun is in the Xth House and the Sign Capricorn.

The following table shows the correlations of the seven planets with their equivalent gods.

Planet	Babylonian	Hindu	Egyptian	Greek	Roman
Sun	Shamash	Surya	Ra	Helios	Apollo (Sol)
Moon	Sin	Chandra	Chomse	Artemis	Diana (Luna)
Mercury	Nabu	Hanuman	Thoth	Hermes	Mercurius
Venus	Ishtar	Lalita	Hathoor	Aphrodite	Venus
Mars	Nergal	Mangala	Horus	Ares	Mars
Jupiter	Marduk	Indra	Amoun	Zeus	Jupiter
Saturn	Ninurta	Brahma	Sebek	Kronos	Saturnus

The Nature of the Planets

Within the structure of the Signs and corresponding Houses of the Horoscope, the *Planets are Archetypes and Catalytic Agents.* The wheels of the Signs and the Houses rotate against each other, while the position of each planet links a certain sign with a certain house. (Figure IV.3) Chiefly, the link is between the spatial aspect of the signs and the temporal aspect of the houses, with the planet indicating how an influence or event operates. The way in which these influences are carried by the planets is parallel to the way the archetypes function as symbols of the powers of the unconscious.

The *archetypes* are defined by Jung as "symbolic expressions of the inner unconscious drama of the psyche which become accessible to man's consciousness by way of projection — that is, mirrored in the events of nature."[2] They are dynamic units of psychic energy which channel material originating in the outside world into perceptible inner images and symbols. As symbols they carry many layers of meaning which can refer to action patterns, events, states of being, personifications and ideas, but the essential quality of archetypes is that they are *regulatory mechanisms* of the growth and evolution of man. They are equivalent to 'patterns of behaviour' in Biology and symbolize the sum of the experiences of mankind. They are autonomous (self-governing) in that they exist in everyone and are theoretically the same in everyone, but in practice are moulded by the conscious mind of each individual. They attract from the unconscious the contents which are best suited to them at any given time, place or situation. Archetypes act as transformers of psychic energy (libido), converting activities in the outside world into higher forms within the psyche, and operate as the gods did for primitive man — as symbols of the powers of the unconscious.

> "This is no matter for astonishment, since these images are deposits of thousands of years of experience of the struggle for existence and for adaptation. Every great experience in life, every profound conflict, evokes the accumulated treasure of these images and brings about their inner constellations. But they become accessible to consciousness only when the individual possesses so much self-awareness and power of understanding that he also reflects on what he experiences instead of just living it blindly. In the latter event, he actually lives the myth and the symbol without knowing it."[3]

Just as the ancients believed that the gods were forces of nature which governed them in total domination, so the archetypes are governors of man's behaviour. The more unaware the individual is of these underlying forces, the more he is ruled by them and acts in an instinctive manner. In his journey through the houses he raises the quality of libido to ever higher levels, but the more instinctual and unconscious he is, the further back towards childhood is his centre. 'Possession' by archetypes — where the level of awareness precedes even the birth moment — is equivalent to the total unconsciousness of the womb. (Hysteria is derived from the Greek *hystera = womb.*)

The planets have ascending levels of meaning just as the signs and houses do. These levels range from the instinctive activities of the animals up through the awakening of consciousness in man to his identification with the gods.

> "The ascent through the planetary spheres . . . means something like a shedding of the characterological qualities indicated by the horoscope, a retrogressive liberation from the character imprinted by the archons.[4]

[2] Jung, *Archetypes and the Collective Unconscious, CW 9,* Part I, p. 6.

[3] Jung, *Psychological Types, CW 6,* p. 220.

[4] Jung, *Mysterium Coniunctionis, CW 14,* p. 230.

This journey signifies the overcoming of psychic obstacles, represented by planetary gods or daemons, and to pass through the process was to be free from compulsion — to be like a god. The god-like reality is absolute synchronism of psychic reality and physical events throughout the life.

The Planets and Their Symbols

The planetary symbols are derived from the circle and its divisions as is the structure of the horoscope.

The circle is an image of wholeness — the psyche and the universe. It represents *Pure Spirit, the Quintaessentia.* As the entire universe is crystallized from the circular space-time continuum, the **Sun** is an image of *concentrated Spirit.* The symbol of the Sun is a circle with a point in the centre — the focus and creator of the solar system simultaneously. (Figure IV.4)

Division of the circle vertically produces the half-circle or crescent of the *Soul.* (Figure IV.5) The Soul is reflective like the two halves, and is a metaphor for the **Moon.**

The spirit and the soul are related to each other as the Sun is to the Moon — as source and reflection. They are complementary aspects of the same primordial unity. The Greek word *anemos* 'wind' refers to the 'breath of life' and from this root are derived the two Latin words *Animus, 'spirit'* and *Anima, 'soul'.* The spirit and the Sun are masculine and active, while the soul and the Moon are feminine and passive. As Jung observed in *"The Structure and Dynamics of the Psyche"* the two words 'spirit' and 'soul' are central to all cultures, religions and languages but are virtually impossible to define exactly as they are *symbols of the essence.* Both have an almost infinite number of analogous variants, and in many cultures (Indian and German) they are even reversed in gender. In German the Sun is feminine and the Moon is masculine, while in India the Sun is considered negative and the Moon positive. The astrological relationship between the Sun and the Moon is analogous to the masculine-feminine polarity which exists within every individual.

The introduction of a horizontal line produces a cross within the circle. (Figure IV.6) The cross represents matter and the body, while the cross within the circle is the symbol of **Earth** — *Matter within Spirit.*

The resultant symbols are the *circle of spirit,* the half-circle or *crescent of soul* and the *cross of matter.* (Figure IV.7) All planetary glyphs are derived from the interplay between these symbols. Their essential meanings can be found by analyzing their individual components. All life derives from spirit, soul and matter in varying proportions.

Venus is feminine and is composed of the circle of spirit above the cross of matter — *spirit over matter equals love and harmony.* (Figure IV.8)

Mars is the complement of Venus. Mars is masculine and his glyph is the cross of matter over the circle of spirit — *matter over spirit indicates desire and conflict.* (Figure IV.9) Venus and Mars are the feminine-masculine duality translated into the physical world.

Mercury mediates between the essential Sun-Moon pair and the physical Mars-Venus pair, and is therefore hermaphroditic and neutral. The symbol for Mercury is the circle of spirit with the crescent of soul above and the cross of matter below. (Figure IV.10) The *spirit mediates between the soul and the body.* Since Mercury uses all three basic symbols, it is a synthesis of all of the other planets and the relationships among them.

The next pair of planets, Jupiter and Saturn, concern the relation between soul and body. **Jupiter** is the soul elevated over the cross of matter indicating *expansion through wisdom.* (Figure IV.11) **Saturn** is the cross of matter above the crescent of soul, and indicates *contraction through material reality.* (Figure IV.12) Jupiter frees the soul from the dominance of matter, while Saturn indicates the restriction of the soul — its bondage to matter. Jupiter and Saturn are duality as amplification. Jupiter is the expansion of mania and Saturn is the contraction of depression. Together they *modulate* contents of the unconscious.

The three known major planets beyond Saturn are *higher octaves* of the first seven planets. Like the musical scale and the spectrum of light the basic personal octave of planets is seven in number. The first seven planets can be seen with the naked eye and were the *'Seven Sacred Planets'* of the ancients, while the three others must be seen through telescopes and have been discovered in the last two hundred years. The slowest of the first octave of seven, Saturn,

Figure IV.4 The Glyph of the Sun.

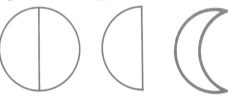

Figure IV.5 The Glyphs of the Moon.

Figure IV.6 The Glyph of the Earth.

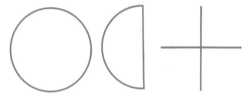

Figure IV.7 The Three Primal Symbols.

Figure IV.8 The Glyph of Venus.

Figure IV.9 The Glyph of Mars.

Figure IV.10 The Glyph of Mercury.

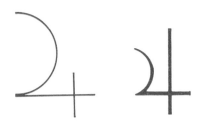

Figure IV.11 The Glyph of Jupiter.

Figure IV.12 The Glyph of Saturn.

Figure IV.13 The Glyph of Uranus.

Figure IV.14 The Glyph of Neptune.

Figure IV.15 The Glyph of Pluto.

takes 29½ years to make a complete revolution around the zodiac and therefore can be totally experienced within the lifetime.

The fastest of the outer three planets is Uranus, which takes 84 years to make one revolution. Since Uranus, Neptune and Pluto take so long to revolve, they indicate the connection of the individual to his generation. Uranus takes about 7 years to pass through one sign of the zodiac, Neptune takes about 14 years and the irregular Pluto takes from 12 to 30 years. Since they affect entire generations, their influences are mainly collective and their purpose is to enlighten the individual to the long-term forces acting upon him.

Uranus is the higher octave of Mercury. Mercury governs the mind and communication, and since Uranus has an eccentric orbit and was first discovered through calculation and logic, it governs the ability to integrate eccentric or unusual contents into the psychic whole. The symbol of Uranus is the cross of matter bracketed by two crescents of soul, surmounting the circle of spirit. (Figure IV.13) Although matter is dominant over the spirit, it has outlet through the wholeness of the soul. *The Spirit is transformed through conditioned matter.*

Neptune is the crescent of soul speared upon the cross of matter. (Figure IV.14) Its lower octave Venus governs harmony and love, and Neptune indicates harmony and love transmitted through the medium of the soul. Matter is surmounted by soul, but simultaneously penetrates it. Neptune therefore is the *psychic reality and the super-natural.*

Pluto is the higher octave of Mars, and as Mars is desire and conflict, Pluto represents desire operating on an extreme level. It governs revolution and transformation through the destruction and rebuilding of existing patterns. The symbol of Pluto is, like Mercury, a composite of all three symbols — the crescent of the soul with the circle of spirit above and the cross of matter below. (Figure IV.15) The soul mediates between the two and the hierarchy of Pluto is equivalent to the original hierarchy of the three symbols. *Spirit dominates matter through the medium of the soul.*

As the symbolic representations of the planets involve a triple interaction of spirit, soul and matter, they can be understood as a series of dynamic processes which exist in the psyche. The quality and reaction each planet transmits are analogous to processes within the universe which physics also describes, but they are translated into the medium of human expression. Matter can be related to the particulate or quantum nature of light and matter in the universe, soul to the wave nature, and spirit to the energy which motivates the entire process. *The planetary symbols are formulae which express the dynamics of life and the psyche.* Particle physicists understand that all processes in nature are events which are only partially explained by any one of these principles, and usually require all three. Astrology has integrated into its mechanism this mode of descriptive symbolism. The nature of the 'field' of each planet is indicated by the manner in which energy is transmitted. The horoscope indicates the location of all ten planets and their interrelationships — the total field of the individual psyche with the individual planets indicating *modulations* of the basic field.

The use of the octave of seven is highly important. Crystal lattices in nature are based, according to their symmetry, upon a *sevenfold axial system.* This ordering factor in crystalline structure is similar to the order of the planetary archetypes, as was recognized by the earliest mystics in their planetary glyphs or talismans. The crystal lattice is an ideal structure which actual crystals never conform to exactly although it orders their growth, just as the planetary archetypes provide an *ideal* structure for the individual of which everyone is a permutation. Jung compares the sum of the archetypes of the Collective Unconscious to the crystal lattice which is preformed in crystalline solutions. The solution is liquid, but nonetheless the crystal forms and matures in accordance with the inherent geometric nature of the solution.[5] The space-time continuum has a preformed order which we are subject to as are all other life forms. The structure of our solar system is a crystallized version of the cosmic archetype.

The three 'trans-Saturnian' planets fit within the next higher octave which begins to mirror the structure of the first octave. There is a necessity to these three planets which is integral to dynamic astrology and which cannot be ignored. This has to do with the reciprocity of man's mind with the Universal Mind — they reflect and affect each other. The heavenly bodies affect our lives and behaviour, as we have seen in Part II. At the same time, we have an effect upon the nature of the universe around us through our *consciousness of it.* This is true in both particle physics[6] and psychology.

[5] Jung, *The Structure and Dynamics of the Psyche, CW 8,* p. 311.

[6] Capra, *The Tao of Physics,* p. 303.

As our comprehension of the universe and ourselves becomes more all-encompassing, we include more and more initially alien and unknown images, symbols, concepts and identities based upon ideas we have gradually discovered. Jung calls this process the *constellation of latent archetypal images.*

> "In psychological terms the constellations in the sky are where the archetypes of the collective unconscious appear in projection, in such a way that, in contrast to myths, fairytales, and other elaborations of the archetype, its time-quality is also taken into consideration. An archetype is constellated, i.e., becomes a realizable power having real effects, only when a specific attitude of consciousness prevails."[7]

When the three outer planets were discovered (Uranus in 1781, Neptune in 1846 and Pluto in 1930), one could say that their discovery was simultaneously the result of an extension of the collective state of consciousness on Earth and the psychic need for a symbol to account for the transformational nature of life at that time. There is always synchronicity — an equivalence of meaning — in the process of discovery.

Uranus' discovery coincided with the beginning of the Industrial Revolution and the upsurge of scientific invention, which it governs. It also accompanied a time of dramatic change in society, the time of the American and French Revolutions. Neptune coincided with the realization that deviations in the orbit of Uranus posited the existence of another outer planet. At this time the dogmas of ideal social systems (Utopianism, Marxism and Communism) were forming, and the link between psyche and physiology was explored through Mesmerism, hypnotism and spiritualism, all of which Neptune governs. Pluto coincided with the total destruction and transformation of the Great World Wars. The discovery of these three planets clarified influences which could not be explained by an exclusively personal mechanism, but rather by a collective process affecting all mankind. Since our atomic and genetic structure contains formations identical to the cosmic structure, we could even say that *we discovered the trans-Saturnian planets within ourselves and then searched without for their actual 'physical' forms.* In fact, all three were initially predicted and then subsequently discovered. A sarcastic comment on the pragmatism of science voiced by Charles Fort casts light upon 'discoveries': "One of the greatest of all secrets was for ages blabbed by all the pots and kettles in the world, but to no purpose, because it was not yet 'steam-engine time'."[8]

[7] Jung, *Archetypes and The Collective Unconscious, CW 9,* p. 300.

[8] *The Books of Charles Fort,* p. 207.

[9] Collin, *The Theory of Celestial Influence,* p. 40.

[10] Collin, *The Theory of Celestial Influence,* p. 145.

Planets and Glands

Besides the archetypal nature of the planets, they also have direct influences upon the physiology of the individual. The procession through the houses creates a temporal or philogenetic structure in the lifetime, and the planets refer to the growth of the cells, glands and functional elements within that structure.

The solar system can be considered a huge step-down transformer of solar energy which produces an effective range of magnetic fields governing all life processes on Earth. The tracks of the planetary bodies around the Sun create magnetic fields charged with induced current and the Earth receives these as an *archetypal magnet.*[9] As Collin noticed, this parallels the working of the endocrine gland system in the human body. (Figure IV.16)

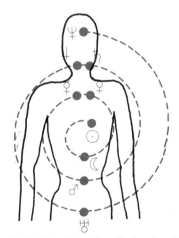

> "The seven major glands in order of their distance from the heart obey the same laws as the planets in the order of their distance from the Sun, and each gland is revealed to be a sensitive instrument, which not only transforms human energy to the tension required for its function, but is tuned to a similar instrument on a cosmic scale and obeys its guidance."[10]

Each gland controls many nerve plexi in a threefold octaval arrangement corresponding to three systems in the body — cerebrospinal for consciousness, sympathetic for unconscious operation and parasympathetic-vagus for instinctive control. There are activations of the glandular systems occurring through all three octaves in the horoscope, governed and adjusted by planetary locations and movements.

The most basic example of this is heredity, which accords with the planetary situation at conception.

Figure IV.16 The Spiralling Endocrine Gland System in the Body. (After Rodney Collin, *The Theory of Celestial Influence,* p. 138.)

> "(The first aspect) is set working through the arrangement of chromosomes in

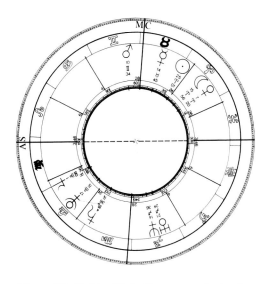

Figure IV.17 The Birth Horoscope shows the positions of the planets at birth.

[11] Collin, *The Theory of Celestial Influence,* p. 145.

[12] Collin, *The Theory of Celestial Influence,* p. 146.

[13] Jung, *Mysterium Coniunctionis, CW 14,* p. 230.

the egg at the critical moment of conception, and is determined by the disposition of the planets at that time. This arrangement decides exactly what — out of the infinite resources of the race — the man-to-be shall inherit from his parents and ancestors."[11]

The planetary positions and relative strengths at the equally critical moment of birth are responsible for the individual 'type'. At birth the glands each receive a different but exact impetus and are set in operation and fixed in that setting for life. (Figure IV.17)

Collin mentions a wonderful analogy for understanding the unfolding of the planets during the life, comparing it to a safe with a combination lock of many rollers, each in continuous movement but at different speeds. At the moment of birth the lock becomes 'set' at a particular combination, and even though the rollers continue to move throughout the life, the combination registered at birth remains the only permanent key to the safe that will enable it to be opened and the contents examined.[10] The 'combination' at birth is an indicator of the shape, size, colour and other qualities which determine the *character of the individual.*

This essence of the individual registered at birth is his *type.* Historically there have always been correlations of planetary qualities with types.

> "to the alchemists the connection between individual temperament and the positions of the planets was self-evident, for these elementary astrological considerations were the common property of any educated person in the Middle Ages as well as in Antiquity."[13]

These types are even now integral terms in our language. *Lunatics* are affected by the Moon, *martial* people by Mars, the *jovial* by Jupiter, the *saturnine* by Saturn, the *venereal* by Venus, and *solitaries* by the Sun. The planetary type is determined by the relative strengths of the planets in the horoscope, usually with one type dominant, although everyone has all of the types latent within. In many individuals there will be no distinct or dominant type due to a parity of conditions.

The endocrine glands unfold at specific times throughout the life. In the Theory of Celestial Influence, Rodney Collin defines this process based upon the spiralling diagram of the glands and their progressive excitation around the logarithmic circle. (See Part V, The Houses of the Horoscope.) After conception each stellar body continues its movement and, as it completes its cycle, manifests to the resonance of the fundamental tone registered at conception. The locations of these resonant times signal transitions in life which Collin terms *shock points.* (Figure IV.18)

Figure IV.18 Glandular Release Cycles.

Planet	Gland	Age of Registration
Moon	Pancreas	58 days after conception
Mercury	Thyroid	130 days after conception
Sun	Thymus	80 days after birth
Venus	Parathyroid	10½ months
Mars	Adrenals	2 years 1 month
Jupiter	Posterior Pituitary	12 years 6 months
Saturn	Anterior Pituitary	29 years 6 months
Uranus	Gonads	84 years
Neptune	Pineal	165 years
Pluto	?	270 years

The first two shock points occur during Gestation. From the first cell divisions until one lunar month after conception the embryo develops germ-layers until the logarithmic spiral begins with the formation of the entoderm, and the ovum has travelled into the uterus, beginning its differentiation of parts.

The first is the *Moon cycle,* indicating the operation of the Pancreas at 58 days after conception. The Pancreas is associated with the lymphatic system and digestion, and corresponds to water balance affecting the emotions.

The *Mercury cycle* at 130 days governs the operation of the Thyroid Gland, which regulates combustion and heat in the body. This corresponds to the first involuntary movement and to individual blood circulation.

The *Sun cycle* is 85 days after birth (365 days minus the 280-day gestation equals 85 days) and indicates the Thymus Gland which sets in motion the growth of the child, and his focusing and reception of light.

The *Venus cycle* is 10/12 months after birth, and signals the working of the Parathyroid Gland. The Parathyroid governs mediating and stabilizing mechanisms, and promotes muscle tone and nerve formation.

The *Mars cycle* occurs at 25 months after birth and governs the Adrenal Glands. They activate the medulla and cortex, manifesting heightened sensitivity and producing the 'fight and flight' mechanism.

The *Jupiter cycle* at 12½ years old governs the Posterior Pituitary Gland. This controls involuntary muscles and the nutritive rhythm of the body, ending the stage of 'mothering'.

The *Saturn cycle* at 29½ years old governs the Anterior Pituitary Gland. This gland affects the end of growth, crystallization of the skeletal system and the function of abstract thought. The individual must realize the limitations of his physical and mental vehicle, and learn to control himself during middle age.

The first seven planets are generally the only planets to make entire revolutions during the lifetime. The three outer planets have such vastly longer cycles that man can only experience portions of their periods and generations are required to gauge their effects.

The *Uranus cycle* at 84 years old governs the Gonads. They regulate sexuality by modulating the Venusian Parathyroids and the Martial Adrenals, and indicate generational fluctuations of sexuality.

The *Neptune cycle* of 165 years relates to the Pineal Gland, the 'Third Eye' of eastern religions. The Pineal Gland governs extra-sensory perception (ESP) and psychic equilibrium.

The *Pluto cycle* of 270 years governs collective evolution and, on the individual level, magical power and control over the masses.

The glands operate as a web of relationships, continually balancing each other. Although there is an order of operation inherent in the glandular system, there are also reciprocal influences which are continually communicated from outside of the individual. Physical health and well-being is the synchronization between the inner glandular mechanism and external influences.

Planetary Correspondences

The nature of the individual's relation to the archetypes is the basis of planetary definitions and their implications. The planets affect the individual by *Projection*. Projection is an automatic process whereby an unconscious content transfers itself to an object and then seems to belong to the object.[14] An individual often sees his actions as having been determined by others — father, mother, brothers, sisters, lovers, mates, children, business associates, the world at large, or by the 'gods'. In reality, the individual projects himself unconsciously onto these others — identifying aspects of himself with those of others because he cannot understand and accept them as being his own.

[14] Jung, *Archetypes and the Collective Unconscious, CW 9, Part I,* p. 60.

The Sun indicates not only the Father himself, but also the relation to the archetype of father. The father is seen as all-powerful and omniscient — the essence of the wise man — when in reality the young child only *projects those characteristics onto him.* This is the *'father-imago'* rather than the physical father. Since the Sun indicates the energy of the individual, the way he relates to his father is indicative of how he relates to his own vitality. If the relationship is fluid and healthy, his vitality is free-flowing. If there is a blockage in communication, it implies that the individual is in some way cut off from his centre. The quality of the relationship to 'father' is much more important than the specific qualities of the genetic father.

In the early part of life, Sun qualities are usually the exclusive province of the father, although there are other individuals who can function as paternal figures. The individual can associate the paternal imago with the mother, older brothers, uncles, doctors or others when the father is either weak or absent during childhood. If no individual fulfils the projection, it is transferred onto the world at large. Upon reaching school age the individual projects the father-imago onto teachers, athletic coaches, heroes, or even media creations. In higher education it is then transferred onto professors, intellectual heroes or political figures. When the individual begins working, he passes the projection onto superiors, the wealthy and the powerful within his world. In partnerships the partner often receives fatherly projections, particularly in the case of women, when the husband is older or more experienced. The original father-imago sets a precedent which all later cases usually adhere to.

Later in life projections are gradually withdrawn as the individual realizes his or her essential nature. The imagos are discovered to be *within* rather than without, and the behaviour which formerly was attributed to others becomes identified as an emanation from the individual himself. Those who remain unconscious of the archetypes continue to project their essential mechanisms into the outside world. Inability to become conscious of projections results in *neurosis* or *possession,* where the projection maintains its reality independent of the individual and becomes cut off from the psychic centre. Parts of the psyche are then inaccessible and the archetype becomes autonomous — an insuperable barrier to wholeness. Feelings of dissatisfaction, incompleteness and total dependency upon others are all warnings of this situation.

If an individual cannot find within himself a necessary archetypal quality, he will seek a personification of that archetype outside himself — in a person, idea, event or object which evokes the missing qualities. This continually applies for all of the planets and their archetypes.

The Sun

The Sun is one of billions of stars in the Milky Way galaxy which produce heat and light by interior chemical and nuclear reactions. It is the centre of our solar system, around which the nine major and a multitude of minor planets revolve. Although the Sun is composed of all the constituent elements from which the other planets are made, it is so hot that the elements exist in a high condition of ionization, called 'plasma'. The central process within the Sun is a continual atomic chain reaction produced by hydrogen, the simplest element, colliding with the atoms of heavier elements. Heat and light are created by the disintegration of the heavier elements into their constituent parts. All life is maintained by the conversion of the energy thus liberated.

The Sun also produces electro-magnetic fields of enormous strength, as its composition and temperature make it an ideal current carrier. It has recently been discovered by the Pioneer expeditions that the magnetic field of the Sun spirals out to the orbit of Pluto, 3.7 billion miles away, as a 'solar wind'. (Figure IV.19) The planets acts as transformers of the solar energy, their size and the elements which compose them being a guide to their conductivity. This polyphase transforming action is sympathetic to the organization of the glands of our bodies, as we have seen. The Sun is the source of light, life and energy in the solar system.

Mythologically the Sun was a wanderer making endless treks across the sky. His life-giving qualities were often represented as rays or arms reaching down to give the breath of life directly to man, a motif similar to the solar wind.

In astrology he governs *spirit, will, energy, vitality, wholeness, self-integration, rulership, organization* and *power.*

Physiologically he corresponds to the *heart, circulatory system, the spine, health and vitality in general and the heart meridian in acupuncture.* Solar eruptions have been correlated with the incidence of heart attacks. He also rules the Thymus gland.

In a horoscope the Sun represents vitality and the will to live. His personifications are the *Father, older friends, teachers, creative individuals, gurus, kings, rulers, people who lead, officials* and *male partners.* The imago is the creative, masculine, objective, conscious and rational essence within everyone. In psychology he is *libido,* the energy which metamorphoses continually into ever higher forms. Images of breath, fire, flame, wind and lightning all indicate the presence of libido and the archetype of the Sun. The trials and tribulations of the hero, god-man or superman are all symbolic of libido and the Sun's eternal quest. The Sun is also phallic as an indication of its procreative power and masculine force. The Sun is, above

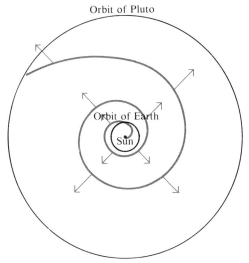

Figure IV.19 The Solar Wind. (Not to scale)

all, *Consciousness* separated from and yearning to recapture its opposite *Unconsciousness,* symbolized by the Moon.

> "It seems to us that he is first and foremost a self-representation of the longing of the unconscious, of its unquenched and unquenchable desire for the light of consciousness. But consciousness, continually in danger of being led astray by its own light and of becoming a rootless will 'o the wisp, longs for the healing power of nature, for the deep wells of being and for unconscious communion with life in all its countless forms."[15]

[15] Jung, *Symbols of Transformation, CW 5,* p. 205.

The Sun rules the sign Leo and the Vth house as the source of libido and self-consciousness. He is exalted in Aries and the Ist house where the Self is most forcibly asserted.

The Moon

The Moon is the only satellite of the Earth and reflects light and energy from the Sun. Its cycle is the *month* which divides the year into approximately twelve parts as do the signs. There are three types of month of varying lengths. The *sidereal month* is the period of the Moon's complete revolution relative to the stars, (Figure IV.20) and its length is 27 days 7 hours 43 minutes (27.3 days). The sidereal month has been statistically confirmed to coincide with the period of human ovulation by the Swedish scientist Svante Arrhenius. The sidereal month indicates the Moon-Earth relationship. The *synodic month* is the period from New Moon (when the Sun and the Moon have the same longitude) to New Moon and is also called the *lunation cycle.* (Figure IV.21) The synodic month is 29½ days and is the most important lunar month for astrology. During the transit of the Sun through each sign of the zodiac, a New Moon occurs combining the influences of the Sun and Moon with the Earth. The synodic month is divided into four *phases* from New Moon (Sun and Moon at the same longitude), to First Quarter (Sun and Moon 90° apart), to Full Moon (Sun and Moon 180° apart), to the Last Quarter (Sun and Moon 270° apart), and back to New Moon. Since each of these phases are approximately seven days in length, this quarter-cycle was probably the basis of the seven-day week originated by the Babylonians.

The Moon affects water on Earth through the tides. When New Moon occurs, both Sun and Moon are exerting gravitational forces upon the Earth from the same direction, while at Full Moon the Sun and the Moon are pulling from opposite directions producing a 'tug of war'. (Figure IV.22) At these times high tides occur. The lower neap tides happen at the quarter phases. It has been proven that during Full Moons the likelihood of hemorrhages, births and the bleeding of ulcers is greatly increased. Electrical potential is also greatest during New and Full Moons. The cycle of the moon phases has a direct influence upon life through the amount of light reflected at night. During the day preceding, the day of, and the day after New Moon, the Moon is totally invisible as it travels with the Sun. During this time each synodic month, nocturnal activity is reduced to a minimum. The ancients believed that the goddess of the Moon, Selene, was taken down into the underworld during New Moon and it was revered and dreaded. Before the time of Christ, Middle-Eastern religions were primarily lunar, and there may be a connection between the three-day interval between the death and resurrection of Jesus Christ and the 'death and resurrection' of the Moon. In Islam the month still begins when the first sliver crescent is sighted after the New Moon.

Due to the westward movement of the Earth through the zodiac, the Moon rises about 58 minutes later each day. At the First Quarter sunset the Moon is directly overhead in the sky and the Moon sets at midnight, illuminating half of the night. At Full Moon the Sun sets in the West as the Moon is rising in the East, illuminating the sky for the entire night. This allowed early man maximum nocturnal mobility, and many festivals were held at the Full Moon. Animals which hunted at night obviously preferred New Moon, when they were hidden. The lives of sailors, farmers, fishermen and hunters are directly affected by these cycles, and although in the present age the daylight quotient is irrelevant because of electricity, lunar cycles continue to affect us unconsciously.

The *calendar month* does not have any direct relationship to the activity or periods of the Moon but was derived by Julius Caesar's transposition of lunar months of 29½ days to the solar cycle. The months in the Julian calendar are composed of either 28, 29, 30 or 31 days and

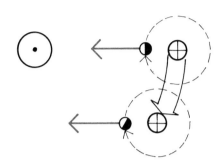

Figure IV.20 The Sidereal Month.

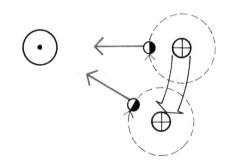

Figure IV.21 The Synodic Month Lunation Cycle.

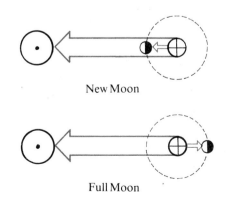

New Moon

Full Moon

Figure IV.22 New Moon and Full Moon.

bear no relation to actual lunar periods.

Mythologically the Moon governed fertility as the Great Goddess, the Triple Goddess and Luna.[16] Growth, fertility, conception, decay and death were her domain and she had both light and dark qualities related to her monthly changes. Her light aspect was benevolent and maternal, while her dark aspect was the savage, bloodthirsty avenger Kali of Hindu myth. The Greek goddess Artemis was the patroness of fishermen and sailors, and her representative priestesses took a yearly consort representing the Sun God, who was sacrificed to her each Winter Solstice. Eventually the "tanist's" reign was extended to eight years, as after one hundred lunar cycles the solar and lunar calendars coincide. The worship of the Moon has variously been dominant over solar cults, just as the Sun and Moon alternate in potency in the sky. Her ambiguity is related to her simultaneous roles as mother and consort of the Sun.

The Moon governs the *feminine essence, the Unconscious, feelings, emotions, rhythm, instinctual responses, reflection, passivity, the Soul, motherliness, the family* and *heredity.*

Physiologically the Moon is related to the *stomach, fertility, the lymph glands, the cerebellum, blood serum, the breasts and bodily fluids.* She also governs the ovaries and the Pancreas gland.

In the horoscope, the Moon governs *changeability, fluctuation of moods, sensitivity, the feelings, form sense, memory and maternal instincts.* Her primary personification is the Mother-imago.[17] This archetype is collective and sheltering, ignoring individuality, and in her negative aspect is possessive and domineering. The Moon indicates *women in general, maternal feelings, nurses, nannies, the wife, the family, home, women relatives, daughters, cooks, seamen, travellers* and *domestics.* She has a key role in astrology as she is a transmitting agent for all events. Each month, the Moon circles the entire horoscope and activates the life cycle on an emotional level, particularly affecting latent tensions and forcing them to externalize through the feelings. The Moon establishes the *tone* of the life.

The Moon rules the sign Cancer and the IVth house, her feminine archetype being at 'home' there. She is exalted in Taurus and the IInd house as the giver of form and beauty.

Mercury

Mercury is the planet closest to the Sun, being never more than 28° away from a geocentric viewpoint, and is the smallest and hottest planet in the solar system. Mercury has a very short period of revolution, moving around the Sun every 88 days. Viewing Mercury is very difficult, as it is usually either in front of or behind the Sun and totally obscured. When Mercury is within 3° of the position of the Sun in the horoscope, its influence is so drastically diminished that it is called *combust* and the mentality suffers. Mercury is seen either as an evening star or as a morning star. The orbit of Mercury is very eccentric, paralleling the essential randomness of Mind. The Mariner 10 expedition which photographed Mercury in 1974 found that the planet was like the Earth on the inside and like the Moon on the outside. This is reflected in its symbol — the solar disk topped by the crescent moon surmounting the cross of matter, representing the Earth.

Mercury has a very cold side facing away from the Sun and a hot side facing it. The Mariner spacecraft found that it rotates every 59 days, so that it rotates three times during two revolutions. Mercury has a dipole magnetic field very similar to the Earth's and reflects sunlight, infrared radiation and radio waves like the Moon. As its rotation period is 59.65 days, it is equal to two synodic months, and the revolution period around the Sun of 88 days is equal to three synodic months. Mercury is thus related to the Moon by its periods and the Sun by its proximity — justifiably the mediator between the two.

Mythologically, Mercury is shown with winged feet and helmet, carrying the caduceus of entwined snakes (libido). As the "Messenger of the Gods" he represents Mind, rapidity of thought, intellect, intelligence and discriminative powers. In Roman mythology Mercury is also the god of merchandizing and the marketplace. The alchemical Mercurius is the hermaphroditic intermediary in the coniunctio between the King (Sol) and the Queen (Luna). He is a consolidating element, but at the same time ambivalent and unreliable. As the Egyptian Hermes Trismegistus he invented writing and language, and is the patron of medicine. (As the symbol of the American Medical Association. Figure IV.23)

[16] See Robert Graves, *The White Goddess,* and Sir James Frazer, *The Golden Bough.*

[17] See Jung, *"Symbols of the Mother and Rebirth",* in *Symbols of Transformation, CW 5.*

Figure IV.23 The Caduceus.

Mercury governs the *intellect, communication, mental and nervous processes, dexterity, ambiguity, writing* and *diplomacy*. Negatively, Mercury indicates *untruthfulness, unreliability, diffusion of energies* and *weakness of mental processes*.

Physically, Mercury governs the *nervous system,* particularly the *motor nerves, organs of speech and hearing and the Thyroid gland controlling respiration and metabolism.* As metabolism affects time sense, Mercury has control over perceptions of time. The dual nature of Mercury is reflected in the brain mechanism. The solar cerebrum and the lunar cerebellum are joined by the mercurial *pons,* a neural bridge which both links them and governs their alternation. Secretions of the thyroid gland regulate Mercurial interconnections by transmitting impulses to the nerve stem and then the body. Mercury is the primal linkage in man.

In the horoscope Mercury exemplifies hermaphroditic qualities. When Mercury is in masculine signs or houses, it adopts masculine qualities, while when in a feminine sign or house it adopts feminine qualities. Planets aspected to Mercury also give their gender to it. The fluctuation in gender is analogous to its rhythmic spin in orbit.

Personifications of Mercury are *agents, mediators, intellectuals, middlemen, advisors, ambassadors, interpreters, authors, teachers, pupils, attorneys, brothers and sisters, and people who deal with nervous disorders* like *analysts, psychologists, therapists* and *sympathetic listeners.* The psychological archetype of Mercury is the 'Trickster' who, while having positive qualities of communication, is mainly a vehicle for the negative Shadow, which complements the light aspect of everyone.

Mercury is the ability to mediate between essential masculine and feminine qualities within the individual, as the Mercurial function of children is to mediate between parental viewpoints. Mercurial figures in life continually change, never form absolute alliances and are always ready to alter existing viewpoints.

Although Mercury revolves around the Sun in 88 days, it is so close to the Sun that it travels with the Sun from our viewpoint. It therefore takes about one year to pass with the Sun through the zodiacal signs. Since it can never be more than one sign away from the Sun, the mental faculties which it governs are always similar to the solar region of the zodiac. There is always proximity between spirit and mind.

Mercury rules Gemini and the IInd house positively as the agent of instinctive communication and duality, and the sign Virgo and the VIth house negatively as discrimination and criticism. He is also exalted in Virgo and the VIth house as the ultimate application of mental discrimination.

Venus

Venus is approximately the same size as the Earth, but is never more than 47 degrees from the Sun. It is bright due to its carbon dioxide atmosphere and reflects the Sun effectively, making it the brightest planet after the Sun and Moon. Venus is unique among planets as it is the only one to rotate in a retrograde direction. The Sun as seen from Venus would rise in the West and set in the East. It rotates much more slowly, in 243 Earth days, than its atmosphere does in 4 days. This blindingly rapid gaseous atmosphere is what we see rather than the planet itself and it has even been compared to a 'cloudy crystal ball'. Venus is visible when it is an evening star or morning star.

Mythologically, Venus was the goddess of Love as the consort of the Sun god. As Ishtar, Ashtraoth or Astarte she governed sexual love, and as Aphrodite, she governed conjugal bliss. Venus was masculine to the Hebrews, Phoenicians and the Egyptians and under the name Lucifer, the 'light-bringer', introduced the day as the morning star. He is often shown as a bearded Aphrodite in early Greek and Roman sculpture.

Venus governs *love, harmony, artistry, feminine sexuality, attraction, affection,* and *the ability to integrate existing influences into a unified whole.* She also rules *physical beauty* and *art,* metaphors of the illusory clouds which hover over her surface.

Physiologically Venus governs *physical beauty* and the *hormones* which regulate and equilibrate our bodies. She also rules the *Parathyroid Gland* which *stabilizes growth processes* and *promotes nervous balance*. Venus creates well-being, and tends towards relaxation and passivity.

In the horoscope Venus indicates the female aspect of the male-female polarity in the physical world. As the Sun and the Moon are the essential opposition, Venus and Mars are its tangible carriers. Venus is feminine sexuality — the ability to take a given physical situation and make it harmonious. In women's horoscope it shows other women they are physically attracted to and reveals the feminine aspect of men they are attracted to. For men it determines women they are physically attracted to and reveals the feminine component of men they are attracted to. Psychologically, Venus is related to the principle of *Eros* (Cupid), which is a propensity for connectedness and relationship to the psyche. This is in distinction to the *Logos* of her opposite Mars, which is objective interest.

Personifications of Venus are *physically attractive individuals* or *one's own physical appearance*. Early in life these tend to be friends or characteristics of friends of the mother — *nurses, nannies, companions, artistic individuals, attractive people* and *individuals who think the child is beautiful*. Later this is transferred to everything which exerts attraction and to *lovers, socialities, maidens* and *'beautiful people'*. She also governs *artists, musicians, godmothers, feminine relations, entertainers, dancers, diplomats, pacifists* and *romantics*. The core of all Venus qualities is the physical appearance.

Libra and the VIIth house are ruled by positive Venus, where relationship and flattery function at their strongest. The negative Venus rules Taurus and the IInd house, where the harmony is applied to the physical world. Venus is exalted in Pisces and the XIIth house as her sense of harmony and relationship is dependent upon external appearances.

Mars

Mars is the next planet beyond Earth and has two moons, Deimos and Phobos. The surface composition of Mars is mainly iron and aluminium giving it a reddish-orange colour. The advancing and receding polar caps together with linear markings criss-crossing the surface give it a mysterious appearance. These 'canals' have now been proven to be the result of wind-blown dust which has striated. It takes Mars 687 days to revolve around the Sun and 780 days to move through the signs of the zodiac.

Mythologically Mars has always been connected with war, due to its reddish colour. The Babylonians called him *Nergal,* and he governed summer heat, pestilence, fire and blood. The Romans called him *Ares* as the warrior-god.

Physiologically Mars corresponds to the *muscular system, red blood corpuscles, body heat* and the *sexual organs*. In a sexual context Mars is the *genito-urinary tract* and specifically the *testes,* while Venus is the ovaries. Mars is also the *Adrenal Gland* governing the fight and flight mechanisms of aggression and retreat. The errant but brilliant psychologist Wilhelm Reich believed that the ability to experience the involuntary release of orgasm was the prime factor in maintaining healthy tone in the body and psychology of the individual and this implies utilization of the Martial function. Mars produces *inflammatory illnesses, high fevers, burning and scalding,* and through its connection to Iron and Steel (the Mars metals) indicates *surgical operations*. The sign position of Mars in the horoscope indicates the most likely part of the body for broken bones and operations together with the opposite sign by reflex action.

Mars is the opposite of Venus. As Venus indicates the ability to take a given situation and make it harmonious, Mars indicates the inability to accept and work with prevailing circumstances. The Mars *desire for change* produces conflict. This manifests as the masculine, aggressive sexual drive. Mars indicates men linked to the individual and the masculine sexual drive in women. His personifications are *men in general, strong women, fighters, doctors and surgeons, people who work with metals, athletes, craftsmen, mechanics, blacksmiths, technicians, engineers* and *labourers*. It also represents *male relatives,* especially *brothers, adventurers* and all those who actively affect the world. Mars corresponds to the *Logos* principle as well as to the Hero archetype which is unconcerned with personal expression but concentrates upon battling all comers. This is a manifestation of the unadulterated ego forcing itself upon the world.

Mars rules the positive sign Aries and the Ist house, indicating the aggression, self-assertion and egocentricity resident there, as well as the negative Scorpio and the VIIIth house where the desire for change becomes self-destructive. Mars is exalted in Capricorn and the Xth house

where desire for material possession and worldly power are paramount — force allied with desire.

Jupiter

Jupiter is beyond the asteroid belt and although more than 1000 times larger in volume than the Earth, it is much less dense — virtually a huge balloon in space. Jupiter is composed mainly of hydrogen and helium, like the Sun, and contains most of the matter in the solar system which did not go into the formation of the Sun. Jupiter is essentially liquid molecular and metallic hydrogen with a small molten iron-silicate core and is surrounded by a very thin dense atmosphere. The fluids which compose it are highly conductive, so Jupiter has a very strong magnetic field, a complex system of radiation belts and transmits many radio waves. This radiation is akin to the Sun's, justifying the identification of Jupiter with the *King of the Gods.* The sidereal period is 11 years 315 days, also equating it with the twelve months of the solar year. The yearly transit of the Sun obscures Jupiter for one month when it passes behind the Sun and the ancients believed that at this time he had disappeared to heaven. Every 399 days when the Earth moves into a critical conjunction with Jupiter, its magnetosphere ejects cosmic-ray electrons which reach the Earth through the spiralling solar wind. These conjunctions indicate the times when transmission is strongest. Therefore Jupiter energizes the Earth with its cycle. Jupiter's thirteen moons make it a miniature solar system, also suggesting its parity with the Sun.

Mythologically Jupiter was the King of the Gods, the Greek *Zeus.* He impregnated virtually everything that moved as well as many immovable objects, giving life everywhere. He conquered the Titans by utilizing weather and storms, but later became sunny and beneficent. He was associated with justice and expansion, and his nature was warm and moist. An interesting myth (which recent investigations of Jupiter support) is that Zeus impregnated with the 'winds', and was responsible for fertilizing winds in nature. The stream of magnetism is carried upon the equivalent of the solar wind. The expansive nature of the god is also sympathetic to the giant gaseous nature of the planet.

Physically Jupiter governs the *lungs, liver, spleen, kidneys* and the *blood* through the *nutrition* and *weight gain.* The action of the Jupiterian *Posterior Pituitary Gland* regulates the *circulation of fluids* in the body and the *growth principle.* A predominance of Jupiter in the horoscope indicates *corpulence* and *extreme indulgence.* In early cultures the liver was the 'seat of the animal soul' as regulator of sensation. The purity of the liver indicated control over desire.

Astrologically Jupiter represents the ability of the organism and the spirit to *expand,* in distinction to the contractive nature of his opposite, Saturn. He is associated with people who *benefit* the individual, and are *optimistic* or *generous.* Early in life he refers mainly to *godfathers, the father's relations, uncles, guardians* and the *expansive qualities* of the child. Later he is linked with *religious teachers, churchmen, ascetics, indulgers, the wealthy, philosophers, fortune hunters, connoisseurs, aristocrats, officials, judges, attorneys* and *teachers.* Jupiter represents the individual nature which extends beyond the physical world, although it also indicates enjoyment of the sensations. Psychologically he is equivalent to the archetype of the *Wise Old Man,* concerned more with principles and ideas than with their external manifestations. He does not fight, but reasons and meditates. He is the *Teacher* in dreams, the all-knowing guide of the psyche.

Jupiter governs the signs Sagittarius and Pisces. In Sagittarius and the IXth house, his positive places, he is the realizer of the higher self, while in his negative sign Pisces and the XIIth house he is the philosophical detachment of the old man in seclusion from the external world. He is exalted in Cancer and the IVth house, the religious nature of the soul permeating the feelings.

Saturn

Saturn is the sixth planet from the Sun, and because of its brightness, was the furthest planet known until the discovery of Uranus in the Eighteenth Century. Saturn is near Jupiter in size and is distinguished by its rings, extremely thin layers of ice particles that look like a halo. This is compatible with the ancient idea of Saturn as the 'cold and dry' planet. Saturn radiates more heat that it receives from the Sun, although considerably less than Jupiter. As Saturn rotates, the rings change angle until at some stages they become invisible. (Figure IV.24) The composition of the planet is probably ammonia and methane gas. Saturn has ten satellites, one of which, Titan, is as large as Mars. Saturn takes 29 years 167 days to revolve around the Sun, and its synodic period is 378 days.

Mythologically Saturn is identified with the Greek god *Chronos,* the god of Time. He is pictured as *Old Man Time* with his sickle. It was believed by the Babylonians that he was the closest god to the Empyrean. He was also connected with agriculture and dense metals, but lost these rulerships because he was extremely bad-tempered and evil, and was replaced by Zeus. This myth was transmitted through the story of Chronos devouring all of his children except Zeus, who was cleverly saved and eventually conquered him.

Physically Saturn rules the *bone structure* and the *aging process.* He is responsible for the *loss of organs,* the *constriction of activity which aging produces, rheumatism, calcination of bones, hardening of arteries* and the *loss of teeth.* He operates through the *Anterior Pituitary Gland* which limits growth and the scope of the entire endocrine gland system in the body. His cycle of 29½ years signals the beginning of old age and the *crystallization* of the organism.

In the horoscope Saturn is the complement of Jupiter. He is the *restricting* or *contracting* influence which balances Jupiterian expansion. Saturn is depressive as Jupiter is manic, and governs *melancholy, reserve, limitation, seriousness, economy, authority* and the ability to accept and work with *the limitations of life.* At best be can channel and produce the concentration necessary to transcend the physical vehicle through discipline and awareness of the mechanism of time. Personifications of Saturn are initially *older people* around the child — *grandparents* especially. People who are *older, more serious, limiting or limited, authoritarian, dogmatic, more experienced,* or *more highly concentrated* are ruled by Saturn and indicate *projections of the individual's own limitations.* Saturn's influence occurs when the individual cannot limit and concentrate his own energies, necessitating an outside agency which will restrict him without his knowledge or control. Saturn can be beneficial only when clearly perceived. Psychologically he is nonpersonal, objective, independent and wary of the unconscious. There is a difficulty with emotions and a tendency to withdraw from all contact.

Figure IV.24 The Angles of Saturn's Rings.

Saturn rules the positive sign Aquarius and the XIth house in his self-abnegation and abstraction, and the negative Capricorn and the Xth house in his concentration upon the material world and the tendency to hoard. Saturn is exalted in Libra and the VIIth house as Time is the great equilibrator and equalizer which forces sublimation.

Uranus

Uranus is the first of the three 'outer' planets in the solar system. It was discovered in 1781 by William Herschel during a telescopic survey of the heavens, and originally was called *Herschel.* Uranus is half the size of Saturn and twice as far from the Sun — more than 19 times further than the Earth. Like the other outer planets, it is composed of shells of minerals and an atmosphere of hydrogen and helium. The planet is yellowish through the telescope and has five moons which orbit in retrograde motion, contrary to the direction of all other planetary and satellite motions. Its highly eccentric orbit led to the discovery of Neptune and Pluto, as their motions are the cause of Uranus' perturbations. Uranus is also distinguished because its axis is tilted at an 82° angle to the plane of the ecliptic.

Mythologically the planet relates to *Ouranos,* the primeval god of the Universe. He was the son of Mother Earth and the father of the Titans, who eventually castrated him. He was the original sky god and first patriarch. He also created the first polarity by throwing his sons, the Cyclopes, down as far into the underworld as he was high in the sky.

Physiologically Uranus governs the *rhythms* of the body which are transmitted through his lower octave Mercury. He rules the *membranes of the brain* and *nervous system,* affecting the transmission of electrical impulses from the brain to the body. This rulership includes the *'etheric body'* of man — his electro-magnetic field. Uranus also rules the *rhythm of libido* on the molecular level — the *motive force of sexuality* — combining the feminine Venusian

Parathyroid with the masculine Martial Adrenals. The resultant rhythm affects all other glands and their overall balance.

Uranus governs *eccentricity, invention, rhythms, independence, intuition, mobility, peculiarity* and *impulsiveness.* He indicates the ability to integrate all influences which do not fit into the 'personal' picture of the individual. The necessity to recognize and utilize one's own peculiarities and intuitions is vital to creativity. As the planets up to Saturn are purely personal, Uranus is the first of the generational planets which indicate the effects of collective communication and pressures. Failure to accept the eccentric impulses of Uranus produces randomness and a lack of originality. Uranus personifications are *inventors, eccentrics, rebels, those working with electricity and electronics, atomic energy (Uranium), technicians, inspired individuals* and *independent people.* As the discovery of Uranus coincided with the use of electricity and the Industrial Revolution, his characteristics reflect those profound alterations of the previous static state of the world. The effect these developments had upon the collective character through communication and transportation necessitated a total re-evaluation of the position of the individual in society.

Uranus rules the positive Aquarius and the XIth house through its passion for innovation, change and abstraction, and is exalted in Scorpio and the VIIIth house through its perceptions of the universal rhythms, which are the basis of metaphysics.

Neptune

Neptune is three times farther away from the Sun than Saturn and is difficult to see even with telescopes. Neptune was predicated as a reason for the peturbations in the orbit of Uranus and was found to exist within one degree from its predicted location in 1846. Neptune is about the same size and composition as Uranus, but has only two moons. The period of Neptune is 164.8 years, and it moves through each sign in about 14 years, only advancing two degrees per year. The Sun is in conjunction to Neptune every 367 days, just over one solar year.

Mythologically Neptune was the Roman version of the sea god *Poseidon,* the brother of Zeus. They both wielded thunderbolts, but Poseidon's was translated into a three-pronged trident when he became the governor of seafarers and the sea.

Physically Neptune governs *drugs, the pineal gland, the solar plexus* and the *aura.* The *Pineal Gland* is connected with psychic reality and higher levels of perception. Neptune communicates through the aura, its colour and shape indicating the strength and weakness of the psychic field. The effects of Neptune are mainly subliminal with their prime manifestations occurring through the *psychic faculty (ESP), dreams* and *fantasies.*

Neptune governs *psychic activity, mediumship, dreams, fantasies, illusion, extreme sensitivity, drugged states, alcoholism, refinement* and the *immaterial world.* Personifications of Neptune are *mediums, psychics, anaesthetists, mystics, sensitive people, chemists, filmmakers, drug-addicts* and *alcoholics.* Neptunian influences are transmitted through liquid media, for which the psychic continuum can be seen as a metaphor. In dreams, images of water and immersion indicate the activity of the unconscious, while drowning indicates submersion in the unconscious.

In the horoscope Neptune indicates impulses from the unconscious or obscure sources which affect the individual. *Anaesthetics* administered at birth produce the *sensitivity* associated with Neptune and indicate much psychic activity throughout the life. Drugged states are attempts to achieve unconscious communication through external agencies, as is alcoholism. Neptune influences can even be produced by internal chemical action, foods prepared by others, clothing belonging to others or even dwellings inhabited by others. The positive manifestations are delicate and indicate understanding of inner processes, while negative ones denote delusion, illusion and hypersensitivity.

Neptune rules Pisces and the XIIth house since solitude and subjection to external influences evoke sensitivity to the inner psychic world.

Pluto

Pluto is the outermost planet in the solar system, so far away that even though its existence was predicted in 1919, it was not discovered until 1930 by Percival Lowell. Its original symbol was taken from the initials of his name, ℙ. It cannot be seen through telescopes at all and can only be photographed. The orbital plane of Pluto is inclined from the ecliptic by 17° and its orbit is so elliptical that it occasionally moves inside the orbit of Neptune, one billion (1,000,000,000) kilometers within its mean orbit! The period of Pluto is 247.7 years, but due to its elliptical orbit it takes only about 12 years to pass through some signs and as many as 33 years to pass through others. This extreme fluctuation makes it very unpredictable. Pluto is known to have a triggering effect upon solar activity which produces natural catastrophes.

Mythologically Pluto was *Hades,* the god of the Underworld. He had the mask of invisibility and never knew what was happening in the world of men, save only through their curses and cries. Hades consorted with the witch Hecate and her magical companions, and their effects over men were absolute and inevitable.

Physically Pluto rules the *Collective Unconscious* and the *processes of regeneration.* He governs the *antibodies* and *defensive systems* in the body which allow cells and organs to heal themselves after they have been damaged. He also has rulership over *generational illnesses* (tuberculosis, syphilis, cancer, sycosis) which are race-poisons inherent in the genetic disposition of entire generations of individuals.[18] Pluto cycles indicate drastic changes in life style and values which stem from the collective unconscious and percolate through to individuals.

As Pluto has no traditional meaning, his correspondences must derive from the prevailing circumstances at the time of its discovery. The era of *authoritarian governments* stamping out individuality, the *World Wars, sophisticated mechanical and atomic weaponry, gangsters* and *wildly fluctuating economic situations* in the world are all associated with Pluto. He indicates the ability to destroy an existing behaviour pattern and to create a new one from its ruins. He indicates *force majeure, revolution, regeneration,* and *the hidden forces which affect whole societies.* He also governs magical control of the masses and contact with the deepest collective unconscious values. If the radical changes indicated by Pluto are not harmoniously effected, the results are often *violent* and *overtly destructive.*

In the horoscope Pluto indicates times in the life when a new beginning follows a drastic change in conditions or a fanatical adherence to certain ideas produces tensions which alter everything. In the first part of life he usually indicates *changes in residence, financial condition of the parents, or breakdowns of the parents' marriage.* His personifications are *people who affect the masses, activists, magicians, propagandists* and *all individuals who deal with large groups of people.* He also governs *revolutionaries* — those who prod one to change — people who are able to transform themselves, and *fanatics.* While Pluto affects primarily the masses and the forces they exert upon the individual, he can also indicate *individual recognition* and *communication with collective values* through unconscious contact. Pluto individuals are *reformists* who have wide-ranging influence upon others, but this always implies that they are unable to change themselves and are projecting their desire onto the outside world. Pluto is the fanatical attitude of the great reformers in history who have tried to alter or conquer the world to conform to their own madness (Caligula, Hitler, Stalin, Luther and Napoleon). In psychology Pluto is the psychotic or obsessional drive to destroy evil, the shadow aspect of the individual himself, and as a result is usually self-destructive and viciously violent.

Pluto rules the sign Scorpio and the VIIIth house defining the ultimate destruction and regeneration. Pluto is exalted in Aquarius and the XIth house where social change is usually accompanied by the death and transformation of the preceding social system.

[18] See the works of Samuel Hahnemann, the originator of Homoeopathy.

The Moon's Nodes

The Moon's apparent path around Earth intersects the ecliptic at two points, called the Nodes. When this path intersects the ecliptic where the Moon is moving from south to north, the point of intersection is called the North Node or the Ascending Node. When the Moon passes from north to south its intersection is called the South Node or the Descending Node. Every time the Moon crosses one of its nodes — approximately every 13 days — the position of the node has moved backwards through the zodiac. The complete cycle of the nodes takes about 18 years. Its position changes about 3' per day.

The Moon's Nodes are critical influences in Indian astrology. The North Node is called the Dragon's Head or Rahu, and is considered to govern positive occurrences or good luck. The South Node is called the Dragon's Tail or Ketu, and governs negative occurrences or bad luck. The Indians liken the nodes to a great dragon which entwines the ecliptic.

Since the nodes indicate the collective movement of the Moon through long periods of time, it is most reasonable to relate them to *associations, adaptability to groups including the family* and to *societies of individuals with common aims.* Personifications of the nodes are *socialites, groupies, compulsive joiners, those who encourage group or family coherence,* and *organizers.*

In the horoscope the North Node is usually the position indicated as the South Node is always exactly opposite. The North Node is exalted in Sagittarius and the IXth house where the ultimate community spirit is manifested in religion. The South Node is exalted in Gemini and the IIIrd house where the ambivalence of Gemini is contradictory to group realities.

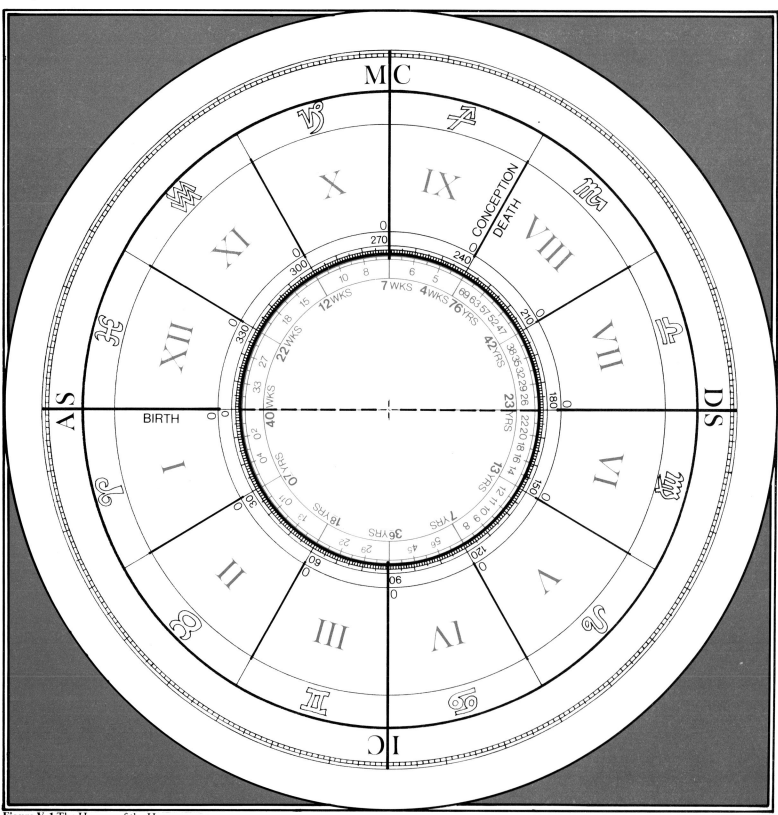

Figure V.1 The Houses of the Horoscope

Time Standards

> . . . he resolved to have a living image of eternity, and when he set in order the heavens, he made this image eternal but moving according to number, while eternity itself rests in unity: and this image we call Time.[1]

[1] Pythagorean Creation Myth.

The signs and the structure of the celestial sphere are primarily concerned with the physical structure of astrology. The houses are complementary considerations which involve the nature of *Time.* To explore the effect of time upon the mechanics of astrology, it is necessary to investigate how time is measured.

The most basic method of measurement is derived from the movement of the Earth around its axis. The *day* is determined by one complete rotation of Earth — its *diurnal rotation.* Since the Earth moves around the Sun as well as around its own axis, there are two types of 'day'. The *Sidereal Day:* (sideris = star) the interval between the position of a certain star directly overhead until it returns to the same position; and the *Solar Day:* the interval between sunrise on two successive days. The sidereal day is 23 hours 56 minutes and 3.455 seconds long; the solar day is exactly 24 hours long. The difference in length between these two 'days' is four minutes. This is caused by the fact that in the period of time that it takes the Earth to make one rotation, the Sun has moved approximately one degree along the ecliptic. For the Earth to regain the same orientation relative to the Sun, it must travel an additional four minutes. Thus the sun returns to the meridian four minutes later each successive day. *Solar Time* is convenient for day-to-day timekeeping on Earth because it extends from noon to noon each day, while *Sidereal Time* (Star Time) is convenient for stellar timing because it moves with the stars. Either time system alone would not allow the range of information necessary to astronomy or astrology.

There are other complications. A *clock* is defined as any mechanical device which can be synchronized to the periods of time designated as sidereal day or solar day. Ostensibly clocks keep accurate time, but in reality this is impossible as there is a large variance in the length of the day throughout the year, and the time of the Sun's movement through the individual signs of the zodiac varies throughout the year. Even the length of the year varies over large periods of time. The irregularity of the Earth's rotation makes time some seconds faster or slower over centuries, possibly due to the motion of the liquid interior of the Earth. The Earth's orbit around the Sun is also irregular, and so the Sun appears to increase its speed from early January until early July, and slows down from July until January.[2] There is a factor of *wobble* of the earth's axis which produces an increase in day length slowly but steadily each year. Scientists take all of these factors into account, but there are many varieties of standard time.

The time used by astronomers and navigators is *Basic Universal Time (UTO),* which includes wobble and the effects of precession. They also use *Universal Time One (UT1),* which excludes effects of wobble. Since 1955, an independent standard has been found which excludes almost all inertial effects called *Atomic Time (AT),* but even atomic clocks, due to Relativity theory, continue to depend upon their gravitational system, latitude, distance from the Sun and other factors. According to Relativity theory it is impossible for there to be any absolute time. Time is a *democracy of regular motion* where a majority of clocks are chosen to be accurate.[3] This lack of standardization is due to the standards of all astronomical times being based upon "circular motions with respect to an absolutely non-rotating framework."[4] This reference system (which science finds essential for all astronomical time standards) is the same reference system continually criticized in astrology as "Ptolemaic" and primitive!

In 1956 a new definition of time was internationally agreed upon and adopted. The new measure was named *Ephemeris Time (ET),* and altered the definition of the second from its previous 1/86400th of the day to 1/31556925.9747 of the tropical year of 365.242199 . . . days. This differs primarily because it is computed and not measured by observation. The name *ephemeris* means 'tabulation', 'calendar', 'diary' or 'daily', and the ephemeris is an almanac which displays in daily tables the relation among sidereal time, solar time and the positions of the planetary bodies and stars. Ephemeris time is satsifactory to the scientific

Figure V.1 The Houses of the Horoscope. This is the archetypal position and order of the Houses in relation to the Signs of the Zodiac. The Roman numerals indicate the house numbers.

[2] Gribbin and Plagemann, *The Jupiter Effect,* p. 62-63.

[3] Fraser, *Voices of Time,* p. 415.

[4] Ibid, p. 415.

community, and ephemerides are published about one year in advance by joint British-American Naval Observatories. Since sidereal time advances about 4 minutes each day on solar time, the ephemerides indicate the sidereal time for every solar noon. Planetary and stellar positions are also indicated for solar noon.

Since the length of the solar day varies within the year, a *Mean Solar Time* was devised at the beginning of this century. Mean solar time is the average length of the solar day throughout the year, and although it virtually never coincides with rotational days, it does coincide with the total yearly circuit of the Sun around the ecliptic on the celestial sphere. This is the time standard to which watches and clocks are set. It is at best a rough approximation to those of you who possess the "incredibly accurate" cesium quartz crystal watches!

Standard Time Zones

If a traveller went around the world in the nineteenth century, he would have had to change his clock at virtually every city he entered, for each country and city in the world set its clocks at 12 o'clock when the Sun was exactly overhead. As we know, when it is noon on one side of the Earth, it is midnight on the opposite side. Time changes with longitude. The convention agreed upon when world-wide travel became easier was called *Zone Time*. It assumed a one-hour change in standard time at twenty-four intervals around the Earth. These intervals were 15° increments of longitude.

Because the standard was often disrupted by local regulations and ordinances, it was decided in 1880 that there should be a world-wide time standard. The zone time of the meridian passing through Greenwich, England became the meridian from which all zone times were measured. This standard was called *Greenwich Mean Time (GMT),* and Greenwich was designated 0° Longitude. Every 15° increment from Greenwich Meridian is a *Standard Time Zone,* defined by an even number of hours east or west of Greenwich. Every clock within each zone is set to the standard time for the zone, eliminating most confusing local times. The most complete work for the use of astrologers in determining standard time zones is a series of manuals by Doris Chase Doane which list the countries of the world and give information about which times are used and when they were instituted.[5]

[5] See *Time Changes in the USA; Time Changes in Canada and Mexico; Time Changes in the World.*

The Standard Time Zones around the world are indicated on the adjacent world map. (Figure V.2) The zones east and west from Greenwich meet in the mid-Pacific Ocean at a meridian 180° opposite Greenwich called the *International Date Line.* A traveller crossing the International Date Line changes his calendar a day ahead when travelling from east to west, and a day behind from west to east. If this were not done, a journey by supersonic aircraft around the world would allow an individual to travel forward and backward in time!

Since it is necessary to translate all local birth times into GMT to calculate the horoscope, the standard zone times are essential information. For places east of Greenwich, the number of hours away from GMT must be subtracted from the local time to get GMT, while places west of Greenwich must add the hours of the zone standard to local time to get GMT. The exact calculations are slightly more complicated and are explained in Appendix A.[6]

[6] See page 275.

Another variant which affects Standard Time is *Daylight Savings Time* in the USA, *Summer Time* in the United Kingdom and their equivalents in many other countries throughout the world. Standard zone time is turned ahead one hour during the summer months to preserve daylight. The working day starts an hour earlier to take advantage of the earlier rising of the sun. The usual practice is to move the clocks in spring and autumn according to the rhyme, "Spring Ahead; Fall Back". When summer time is in effect, an additional hour must be subtracted from the local standard time to find GMT.

During the Second World War, both the USA and the United Kingdom also used *War Time* throughout the year to save electricity and get everyone in bed earlier than usual. War Time was also one hour ahead of standard time. During War Time (from 1941 until 1945 in the UK) the United Kingdom also used Summer Time, making a two hour difference from GMT, the standard time in the UK. It was called *Double Summer Time* instead of War Time. From 1967 until 1972 the UK experimented with using Summer Time all year long, as the latitude of the islands is such that day is quite short in the winter. It is particularly amusing that the country which was responsible for the idea of standard time is the one which has found myriad ways to

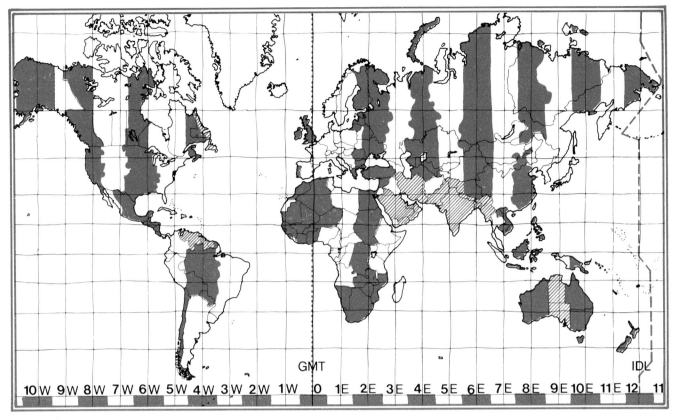

Figure V.2 The Time Zones of the World.

deviate from it.

These standardizations of time are critical to astrology as ephemerides are calculated for GMT, and may be used throughout the world. All local birth times are translated easily into GMT and planetary positions determined by a similar technique.

The Horoscope

The *horoscope* is a two-dimensional representation of the three-dimensional celestial sphere. (Figure V.3) The circle represented by the horoscope is the ecliptic and the page upon which it is drawn is the plane of the solar system relative to the Earth. The horizon is an horizontal line through the horoscope. Conventionally the eastern point of the horizon, the ascendant, is to the left and its opposite western point, the descendant, is to the right. The meridian is also a straight line which is archetypally vertical and perpendicular to the horizon. Since the intersection of the meridian and the ecliptic is rarely exactly 90°, the meridian is usually not perpendicular to the horizon but leans either east or west. The upper intersection of the horoscope circle (ecliptic) and the meridian is the Midheaven (MC) and is south, while the Lower Midheaven (IC) opposite is north.

The original derivation of the word 'horoscope' is the Greek *horoskopos,* meaning 'hour-pointer'. The function of the horoscope is to indicate the orientation of an individual to the zodiac and to the planetary bodies at the time and place required. The two criteria which determine this orientation are the zero point of the ecliptic, 0° Aries, and the sidereal time of the event. Sidereal time is calculated to determine the position of the Ascendant and the MC in degrees of longitude relative to the 360° zodiac.

The *Houses* of the horoscope are twelve *approximately* 30° divisions related to the position of the Ascendant on the ecliptic, just as the signs are exactly 30° divisions of the ecliptic relative to the Vernal Equinox point. (Figure V.4)

The simplest way of finding house positions is to add successive 30° arcs to the degree of the Ascendant, producing twelve *Equal Houses*. The houses are numbered with Roman numerals

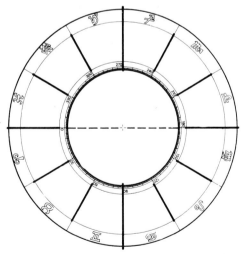

Figure V.3 The Horoscope.

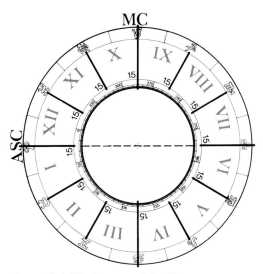

Figure V.4 The Houses of the Horoscope.

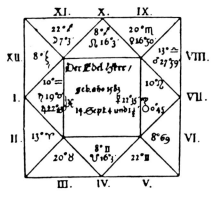

Figure V.5 The Square Horoscope.

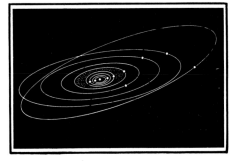

Figure V.6 The Off-Centre Geocentric Viewpoint.

[7] See Ebertin, Witte and the system of this book.

from I to XII in a counterclockwise direction from the Ascendant to differentiate them from sign designations. The Ascendant is the cusp of the Ist house, the IC is the cusp of the IVth house, the Descendant is the cusp of the VIIth house, and the MC is the cusp of the Xth house. Cusps are the same degree and minute as their opposites. The position of the Ascendant determines the Descendant by the addition of 180°, the cusp of the IInd house plus 180° indicates the position of the VIIIth house, etc. If the Ascendant is 15° Aries the Descendant is 15° Libra, and if the IIIrd cusp is 15° Gemini, then the IXth cusp is 15° Sagittarius. *Tables of Houses* give the Ascendant position for every sidereal time at any latitude and the cusps of the Xth, XIth, XIIth, IInd and IIIrd houses. The opposite house cusps are determined by adding 180° to them.

In the northern hemisphere the signs from Cancer to Sagittarius take longer to pass the Ascendant and are called signs of *long ascension,* while the signs from Capricorn to Gemini take less time and are called signs of *short ascension.* This is produced by the tilt of the Earth's axis. In the southern hemisphere they are reversed, i.e., the signs Cancer to Sagittarius are signs of short ascension,and the signs Capricorn to Gemini are signs of long ascension. On the equator these differentiations do not exist.

The graphics of the horoscope have gone through many transformations in history. Originally the horoscope was only calculated and drawn for the pharoah or king, and the prognostication was relevant for the entire population. During Chaldean and Babylonian times the horoscope was constructed by direct observation and transferred to stone or clay. There are circular representations of the zodiac dating from the time of King Assurbanipal in the Seventh Century BC, but most ancient astrological and astronomical information was codified in rectilinear tables (Egypt) or horoscopes in a square format (Romans). The square format was used until the early Twentieth Century. (Figure V.5) It was a table for displaying the necessary information and was not intended to be a picture of the actual heavens. The increase in the accuracy of calculations during this century has shifted the trend towards circular horoscopes with greater specificity and truer representation of the information conveyed. In some astrological systems developed during the past forty years, the horoscope diagram is an analytical tool in its own right.[7] Astrologers usually assume that it does not really matter which representational system is used (Margaret Hone, Jeff Mayo, Alan Leo and Donna Marie Lorenz), but we will see that this is far from being the case.

Systems of House Division

Renaissance celestial spheres were exactly spherical, as it was assumed that the movements were Ideal. Even the discovery by Kepler that all planetary bodies travel in elliptical paths with two foci, and never perfect circles, did not change the convention of representing them as circular. The irregularity of elliptical movements is nonetheless transferred to the perfect celestial sphere during observation. The resolution of this discrepancy between the *Ideal* celestial sphere and the *Real* elliptical planetary movements lies in the system used to determine the location of the house cusps. As the concept of elliptical movement was refined, the early simplified 'equal house' system gave way to house systems which recognized this irregularity. This trend was also supported by the geocentric viewpoint of astrology because the earth was off centre in the solar system and revolving in an elliptical orbit. (Figure V.6) The solar system is seen from an ellipse revolving within other elliptical paths. Even if the solar system were perfectly circular, due to our position,it would not appear to be so, as it would be like observing a perfect circle from some point between the centre and the periphery.

The relative roles of the signs and the houses clarify this situation. The signs of the zodiac are *divisions in space* of the celestial sphere and even though their arcs can be translated into time,they remain predominantly spatial. The houses of the horoscope should be understood as *divisions in time.*

All astrological influences are produced by cyclical periods marked by the interval between successive returns of stellar bodies to their original position in the zodiac and harmonics of intermediate points in the cycle. The zodiac is a circular grid and the houses are pointers which move around the grid continually and represent our base of observation. (Figure V.7)

In the horoscope planetary positions are indicated by their longitude on the ecliptic, and all

THE ROUND ART

cyclic movements are referred to these positions. After the moment of registration of the horoscope, the planetary bodies continue to move counterclockwise through the signs of the zodiac. Except for the Moon, which moves about 13° each day, the other planets and the Sun never move more than 2° per day. Planetary positions do not alter drastically in a day with respect to their sign position in the zodiac. They do, however, make a total revolution relative to the Earth once every twenty-four hours. The Sun, Moon and planets continuously move around us in a clockwise direction.

Every day each degree of the zodiac passes the horizon and every planetary body passes the Ascendant. The Sun moves through the signs at the rate of about 1° per day and is on the eastern horizon at sunrise. From sunrise to sunrise on successive days the Ascendant pointer moves the full 360° *less* the distance the Sun has moved in the intervening time. It takes the Ascendant approximately 4 minutes to move one degree, the same as the difference between the solar and sidereal days. The position of the Ascendant at sunrise advances one degree through the zodiac per day during the year, exactly as the Sun does. The advance of four minutes per degree is a way of indicating the exact time during the day that the individual is born. The Ascendant is used as the reference point because it is specific for the local time, the geographical longitude and the latitude. The primary house systems are all based upon the position of the Ascendant. The MC can be used as a pointer, but has the disadvantage of not reflecting the latitude.

To visualize how the signs and the houses interrelate we must see them as two circles moving upon each other in time. (Figure V.8) The house circle remains horizontal with the Ascendant pointer to the left, while the circle of the zodiac revolves in a clockwise direction. The planets all move their few degrees each day counterclockwise through the zodiac, but appear to be moving rapidly in a clockwise direction. The small counterclockwise movement through the signs can be considered an *Essential* movement reflecting the actual movements of the planetary bodies, while the clockwise movement is *Personal,* reflecting the rotation of the Earth on its axis. The *essence* of the individual progresses very slowly and is hidden by the apparently greater movement of the *personality.*

In addition to the Ascendant pointer, the position of the Sun within the two rotating circles is an indicator of the time of day. The Sun passes through the twelve houses in twenty-four hours or through one house in approximately two hours. If we assume an "equal house" division of the horoscope, each house cusp indicates a two-hour interval around the horoscope. At the equinoxes when day is equal to night, sunrise (Ist house cusp) is 6 AM, midnight (IC) is 12 at night, sunset (VIIth house cusp) is 6 PM, and the MC (Xth cusp) is noon. (Figure V.9) The intermediate cusps are then; XIth cusp = 10 AM, XIIth cusp = 8 AM, the IInd cusp = 4 AM, etc. It is helpful to use this as a visual guide to horoscope interpretation.

There are many ways of projecting the angular position of the Earth onto the circle of the ecliptic. While the cusps and lengths of the zodiacal signs are fixed as equal 30° arcs, the cusps of the houses are not fixed except in the very earliest systems before 200 AD, where they were also considered equal. The house cusps are determined by dividing *either* the prime vertical, the ecliptic, the equator, or a diurnal circle into equal arcs and then transferring them onto the ecliptic. While the ascendant is the same with most methods, the intermediate house cusps vary considerably. In traditional astrology the difference is a matter of individual preference, but this is an unsatisfactory situation.

The ascendant correlates time with geographical latitude, while the meridian (MC) indicates sidereal time independent of the latitude. Sidereal time is reflected in a fixed movement of the MC around the equator at the rate of 1 hour for each 15° of longitude. When the vernal equinox point of 0° Aries passes the meridian at noon it is 0 hours sidereal time on the equator. The ecliptic is inclined at 23½° angle to the equator, so the Tables of Houses are used to translate sidereal time on the equator to degrees of longitude on the ecliptic.

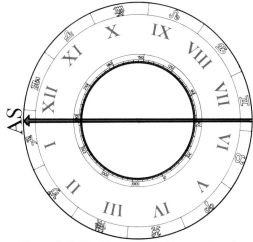

Figure V.7 The Houses as Pointers. The orientation of the Houses is determined by the degree of the zodiac on the Ascendant.

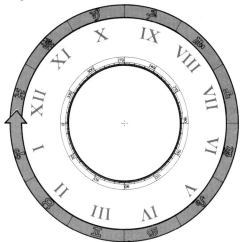

Figure V.8 The Movement of the House Circle.

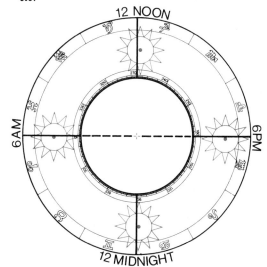

Figure V.9 The House Positions of the Sun in a Daily Cycle.

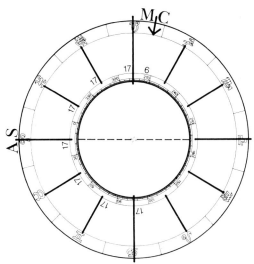

Figure V.10 The Equal House System.

A Brief History of House Systems

The clearest way to present the major methods of house division is chronologically, as they are the result of a continuous evolution.

The **Equal House System** *(modus equalis)* was codified by Ptolemy in the Second Century AD. This system is the simplest to use. It divides the space of the ecliptic into twelve equal arcs beginning with the ascendant. Each cusp is found by adding 30° increments of longitude to the longitude of the ascendant. If the ascendant is 17° Aries, the IInd cusp is 17° Taurus, the IIIrd cusp is 17° Gemini, etc. (Figure V.10) The problem with the equal house system is that the position of the MC rarely coincides with the cusp of the Xth house and wanders anywhere from the VIIth house in the west to the XIIth house in the east, depending on whether signs of short or long ascension are rising. The advantage of Equal House System is that it is simple to calculate (See Charles E. O. Carter, Margaret Hone and Jeff Mayo), while the disadvantage is the assumption that house qualities are equal for every individual.

The house system of **Porphyry** (233-303) was the first to use the *quadrant method* of determining house cusps. Since the ascendant and meridian are rarely perpendicular to each other, the quadrant method assumes that the division by these two axes produces two pairs of unequal quadrants which must then be subdivided into three houses each. (Figure V.11) The quadrants are called *semi-arcs* and are designated as *diurnal semi-arcs* or *nocturnal semi-arcs,* and these also into eastern or western diurnal or nocturnal semi-arcs. Porphyry finds the intermediate house cusps by trisecting each semi-arc on the ecliptic (dividing the semi-arc by three). To find the XIth house cusp one adds to the longitude of the MC one-third of the eastern diurnal semi-arc, and for the XIIth cusp two-thirds of the diurnal semi-arc. To find the IInd house cusp, one-third of the eastern nocturnal semi-arc is added to the longitude of the Ascendant, etc. This system divides the *space* of the semi-arcs to discover the house cusps.

The house system of **Campanus** (died 1297) divides the prime vertical into twelve equal 30° arcs and these are projected onto the ecliptic by house circles through the polar points. (Figure V.12) This system is also a division of the space of the prime vertical.

The house system of **Regiomontanus** (1436-1476) divides the equator into equal arcs of 30° and projects these arcs onto the ecliptic using great circles through the polar axis. (Figure V.13) This system is tied to the equator and is also space-oriented.

The house system of **Morinus** (1583-1656) is a projection method but does not use quadrant division. In this system the Ascendant is not the pointer but is found by adding 90° to the longitude of the MC. The equator is divided into equal arcs which are projected onto the ecliptic by great circles through the ecliptic poles. This system is also spatial.

The house sytem of the monk **Placidus** (died 1688) is a departure from all the earlier systems. The **Placidean** system has been the most popular for the last two centuries because most ephemerides use it (Raphael's Ephemeris has used this system since 1820). This system is not projective. The cusps are located on the ecliptic by means of diurnal circles which intersect the arc from the horizon to the meridian. (Figure V.14) As the arcs divided are diurnal circles, the calculation is based upon *the time taken to cover a given space* on the ecliptic and the time taken for each degree of longitude to rise on its own parallel of declination (diurnal circle). As a result, *this system is the only one defined by temporal parameters.*

The house system of Walter **Koch** (1895-1970) is called the **Birth-Place Method.** It is an intersection technique like the Placidean, based upon arcs of "quasi-ecliptics" between the equator and the horizon equivalent to equally spaced vernal equinox positions. Koch tried to "clarify" Placidean calculations, but in the process had to use "quasi-sidereal times". This house system is being researched by Ebertin's organization and is the first new house-division technique to be developed in three hundred years.

In the book *Tools of Astrology: Houses,* by Donna Marie Lorenz, from which much of the above information was gleaned, she astutely mentions that:

> "All of this stresses the importance of the *empirical* approach in the matter of houses. An empirical approach requires taking individual charts and dividing the houses according to each of the different methods so that the differences become visible. Claims based solely upon the geometry or on algorithms used to construct tables of houses can carry little weight with those concerned with validity of results."[8]

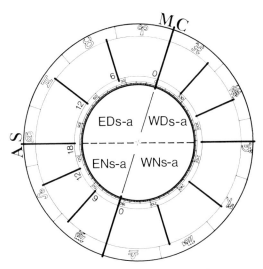

Figure V.11 The Quadrant Method of House Division.

[8] Lorenz, *Tools of Astrology: Houses*, p. 28. An algorithm is a set of arithmetic rules.

THE ROUND ART

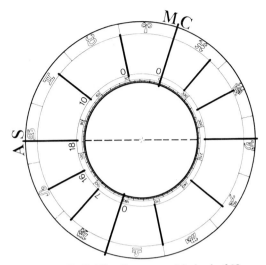

Figure V.12 The Campanus Method of House Division.

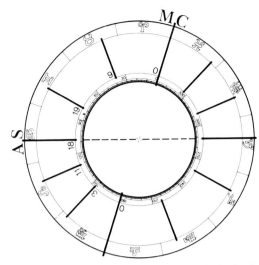

Figure V.13 The Regiomontanus Method of House Division.

This is the critical point. Within the context of traditional astrology, the various methods of house division are a random selection to almost all astrologers or students of astrology because their *interpretations of house systems are extremely unspecific.* The following portion of this chapter shows the way to utilize the characteristics of the time-oriented Placidean house system in a *space-time synthesis.* The signs represent the spatial aspect of the continuum, while the Placidean houses represent the temporal aspect. The two together form a whole which synchronizes with the nature of the universe.

The Interpretation of Houses

The function of the houses in traditional astrology is very unclear, although it is critical. The uniform lack of clarity is borne out by the following 'definitions' of the houses by well-known practitioners and authors:

> "Traditionally the houses are called *mundane* houses because they refer to everyday life-on-Earth activities."[9]

> "They differ altogether from the signs, for only under very rare conditions can they completely coincide with them (although they do so more or less approximately *once during each day*)."[10]

> "Hence, the first house, as counted from that degree, will correspond in meaning to that of the first sign, but, whereas the *sign-meaning* will give an understanding of a MODE of action or behaviour, the *house-meaning* will give an understanding of the SPHERE OF LIFE to which this may be expected to relate."[11]

> "In our journey from the cradle to the grave we carry the twelve houses with us in the auric atmosphere surrounding us, as the air envelopes the flying earth. Each house mirrors part of the life; each holds some of our life lessons; each represents how we have worked or shirked before in a given department of life's tasks."[12]

> "The *houses* relate particularly to the material interests and conditions, while the signs tell us more of the spiritual qualities which manifest as character, temperament and tendencies."[13]

> "There was nothing appertaining to the life of man in this world which, in one way or other, hath no relation to one of the twelve houses of heaven; and as the twelve signs are appropriate to the particular members of man's body, so also do the twelve houses represent, not only the several parts of the man, but his actions, quality of life, and living. And the curiosity and judgement of our forefathers in astrology was such that they have allotted to every house a particular signification; and so distinguished human accidents (events) throughout the twelve houses."[14]

It can be readily seen that there is little idea to what the houses do pertain.

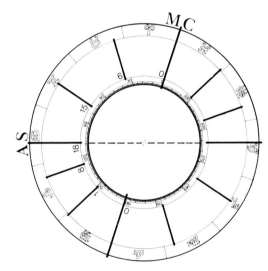

Figure V.14 The Placidean Method of House Division.

[9] Jeff Mayo, *Astrology,* p. 98.

[10] Alan Leo, *Practical Astrology,* p. 57.

[11] Margaret Hone, *The Modern Textbook of Astrology,* p. 89.

[12] Max Heindel, founder of the Rosicrucian Fellowship in America, *Message of the Stars,* p. 76.

[13] Llewellyn George, *A to Z Horoscope Maker and Delineator,* p. 32.

[14] William Lilly (1674), *An Introduction to Astrology,* p. 27.

[15] Rele, *Directional Astrology of the Hindus,* p. 57.

[16] Ptolemy, *Tetrabiblos,* p. 217.

[17] Eisler, *The Royal Art of Astrology,* p. 39.

[18] Lilly, *An Introduction to Astrology,* p. 27-34.

[19] Mayo, *Astrology,* p. 99.

[20] Ebertin, *The Combination of Stellar Influences,* p. 41-42.

The traditional definitions of the twelve houses are related to the qualities of the signs in their archetypal order. This archetypal order occurs when the vernal equinox point 0° Aries on the ecliptic coincides with the Ascendant, and an equal house system is used. This can also occur on any day on the equator when the sideral time is 18:00 hours. In this archetypal position the Ist house cusp is 0° Aries, the IInd cusp is 0° Taurus, the IIIrd cusp is 0° Gemini, . . . the XIIth cusp being 0° Pisces. The opposite illustration shows this arrangement. (Figure V.15)

There is no recognition in traditional astrology that any sequence is involved in the house designations. They seem to be randomly determined activities which roughly correspond with the 'influences' of the signs. The definitions of the signs are also subject to vague speculation. The following table of house definitions will bear this out.

HOUSE SYSTEM DEFINITIONS

House	Sign	Indian[15] BC	Ptolemaic[16] 150 AD	Firmicus Maternus[17] 400 AD	Lilly[18] 1647 AD	Jeff Mayo[19] 1964	Ebertin[20] 1940
I	Aries	Physical appearance	Horoscope	life (vita)	life of man stature, colour	self-centred interests	Personality Childhood
II	Taurus	Inheritance, wealth	Gate of Hades	business (lucrum)	estate-fortune wealth, in-laws	possessions and personal security	Material foundations of life
III	Gemini	Bad Luck	The Goddess	brothers (fratres)	brethren, letters neighbours	relation of self to environment	Relationships in the environment
IV	Cancer	Mother	Lower Midheaven	father (genitor)	father, lands, the end of life	self, possessions, relatives	Partental home, Heredity of traits
V	Leo	Intellect, mind Memory	Good Fortune	sons (nati)	children, plays, ambassadors	recreation and exposition of self	Assurance of progeny through sex-urge
VI	Virgo	Enemies	Bad Fortune	health (valetudo)	sickness, servants, uncles, cattle	service to community health	Work, teamwork, co-operation
VII	Libra	Death of Wife	Occident	wife (uxor)	marriage, enemies, duels, lawsuits	personal identity with others	Union, partnership, marriage
VIII	Scorpio	Death, losses	Beginning of Death	death (mors)	death, estates, wills	sacrifice, shared resources	Birth and death
IX	Sagittarius	Good luck	God	religion (pietas)	voyages, learning, visions, dreams	new horizons for the self	Spiritual life, religion
X	Capricorn	Father, journeys	Midheaven	reign (regnum)	royalty, mother, honour, authorities	status, material responsibility	Aims, vocation, old age existence struggle
XI	Aquarius	Personal gains	Good Daemon	good deeds (benefactum)	friends, courtiers, hope, confidence	identification with group objectives	Wishes, hopes, ties through friendship
XII	Pisces	Expenditure, and bondage	Bad Daemon	jail (carcer)	private enemies, secrets, prison	self-abnegation, escapism, confinement	Seclusion, solitude, the close of life

While throughout history these house interpretations agree with each other, their sources are unclear. The signs and their qualities are derived from seasonal identifications, but there is no equivalent derivation for the houses. We will soon see that *there is a way of relating signs and houses together in a natural sequence.*

The key to the interpretation of the houses is *Time.* The houses are the temporal aspect of the space-time continuum with which astrology is identified, and when the houses are correlated to times in the life of the individual, their derivation becomes clear.

Time and the Individual

The Ancient philosophers believed that Time was absolute. It was a linear dimension beyond space, exactly the same for everyone. A day, month or year were all absolute standards which never changed. As men became able to measure time more accurately this notion was reinforced. They believed that if clocks were distributed throughout space that they would eternally coincide. This was implicit in the Euclidian geometry of space. This view persisted until the Theory of Relativity identified the interconnection between space and time, and buried the idea of the absoluteness of time.

Our concept of time is so definite and clearly 'objective' that it seems to exist independent of our lives. What we perceive as the Time machines can measure for us is in reality a *measurement of space.* The amount of sand passing through an hourglass, the mechanical movements of clockwork, or the decomposition of certain crystals or radioactive elements are totally determined by the time scale of the parts. Even in cesium or quartz crystal clocks an extraordinarily elaborate system of calculation is necessary to determine the correct time. Among the variables are: the latitude; the height above sea level; the distance of the Earth from the Sun; the distance of the Earth from the Moon; and many others. The best possible timepieces, which exist in controlled conditions in subterranean vaults, only give a *standard frequency* from which the variations can be predicted and allowed for. *Time as an absolute does not exist.*

One of the analogies Einstein used to define the relativity of space and time was a pair of synchronized clocks which moved relative to each other and to an observer. He discovered that the faster they moved relative to the observer, the longer the time intervals became. Clocks in motion slow down. Scientific experiments with subatomic particles have proven that the velocity of a particle totally determines not only the 'time' of the particle, but the length of its lifetime as well.[21] As the curvature of the space-time continuum varies throughout, it affects time intervals as well as lengths. Time flows at different rates everywhere. The interesting point for astrology is that this differential in time is always relative to the observer.

In the extreme case of collapsing stars, the gravitational concentration increases until not even light can escape, producing an *event horizon* around it through which neither light nor time can escape: *A Black Hole.* A reasonable assumption about the mystery of the Black Holes is that time slows down until it stops, which seems to be equivalent in our terms to *Death.*

Besides the problem of relativity, a further dilemma exists. Theoretical physicists Dirac and Jordan discovered that there is an infinitesimal difference between time as calculated by atomic clocks and time as computed in ephemeris time. This is caused by the diminution of the gravitational constant through time. Comparing standard time with a corrected time subject to constant gravitation involves a logarithmic difference where "the age of the universe, if it is ten thousand million years in one time scale, may be infinite in the other one".[22] Time is a function of the perpetually changing continuum within which we exist.

The relativity of time has been recognized by scientists as the phenomenon of *Biological Time.* Biological time relates time perceptions to the frame of reference of any living creature or entity, and indicates an awareness of duration and location within the general spatial and temporal continuum: the *time sense* of life. Biological time is the transformation of perceived sequences into duration.

It has been statistically proven that although there is an astonishing variation in the length of lifetimes of organisms from the microseconds of atomic particles to the aeons of galaxies, the rate at which these organisms live their lives is constant. The same proportional enfold-

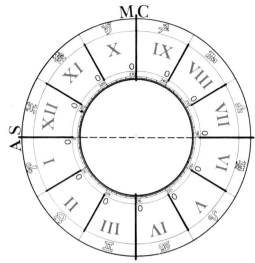

Figure V.15 The Archetypal Order of Houses.

[21] Capra, *The Tao of Physics,* p. 178.

[22] Frazer, *Voices of Time,* p. 412.

[23] *Ibid,* The works of Sacher, Rubner, Fischer, Griffin and Liss support this idea.

[24] Collin, *The Theory of Celestial Influence,* p. 32 and 353.

[25] *Voices of Time,* p. 185.

[26] von Franz, *Number and Time,* p. 250.

[27] Fischer, *Voices of Time,* p. 362.

[28] Fischer, *Voices of Time,* p. 363.

ment affects all organisms equally.[23] The factor which links these extremes of being is *metabolism.* Metabolism is proportional to the brainweight, body weight, respiration rate and lifespan of any organism. Rodney Collin in *The Theory of Celestial Influence* identified the proportion between lifespan and breath for many levels of organisms from cells through Man, Nature, the Earth, the Sun and the Galaxy, and discovered that they follow a precisely integrated scale.[24]

Collin uses an analogy of a flying gnat, which lives for half a day but sees the *flow* of its life at exactly the same rate that we do. We see the gnat moving almost as fast as we can perceive, and the gnat sees us as immovable objects. When a gnat is in a rainstorm the water particles falling around it move at the same rate as a glacier would to us! The gnat's world and time perception is such that the air is virtually solid, and therefore it is "walking on air". The rate of life and perceptions of time are consistent from organism to organism *throughout* the universe.

As our perception of time relates to our metabolism, the fact that our metabolism gradually slows down from the moment of our conception until the moment of our death means that *our time sense is continually changing* as well. The gradual decrease in metabolism is parallel to a gradual change in time sense through life against which changes of mood, excitation, drug states, psychological states, external stimuli and thought processes make local and temporary alterations or variations.[25] This is similar to the mechanics of music where a uniform order and duration is altered by changes in the harmonics, intensities, pitch, timbre, rests and timing devices. Many differentiations in our realities are attributable to fluctuations in our metabolism which we produce or are subjected to.

This is supported by recent ideas that our concepts of time are based upon one fundamental rhythm which reverberates through the universe and permeates the very energy of which everything is composed. This *temporal periodicity* of the physicist Eddington is inherent in the "lattice" structure of time and is perceived by us as *rhythm.* The view of time as rhythmic is echoed in biological time as well. All organisms have their own internal clocks functioning like electro-magnetic oscillators which are independent of their surroundings.[26] These clocks could be situated in glands, in cells or even inherent in the substances from which life is made. The controversy of whether time is an a priori category of our mental functioning or is an intellectual construction is related to this.

An experiment by Rolland Fischer related the alteration of metabolism to changes in time sense, spatial sense and their juxtaposition.[27] He admistered drugs to his test cases which either accelerated or retarded their metabolism. When a person is given a stimulant (amphetamines, cocaine, LSD), his metabolic rate increases, the respiration rate increases, and the rate at which his eyes receive images increases. Receiving proportionally more images in an equivalent amount of time than usual produces an overestimation of duration and a sense that time is passing slowly. (If normally the person received six images per second and in the excited state received nine images per second, he would then think that every second actually contained a second and a half of perceptions.) If a tranquillizer is administered the metabolic rate decreases, the respiration rate decreases, the rate at which the eyes receive images decreases and consequently fewer images are perceived in the same time. This produces an underestimation of the passage of time, and time seems to "fly" by.

This alteration also affects spatial sense. As the subject is stimulated the rates of bodily functions increase, time becomes extended and this produces a simultaneous *expansion of space, particularly nearby space.* Experiments with handwriting in both control and excited states show a reversal of the size and space occupied. The more stimulation, the larger the letters and the more total space on the page is occupied. The more sedation, the smaller the letters and the less space is occupied. This indicates an intimate link between our metabolic rate and our relationship to space-time. Fischer summarizes with a startling conclusion:

> "Alterations in interpretations of space-time are not only concomitant with the states of excitation and tranquilization induced by drugs which raise or lower the metabolic rate. Other contrasting pairs of modi such as *youth* and *old age* also produce high and low metabolic rate respectively and thus concomitant changes in interpretation of space-time. The seeming contradiction that time passes more slowly for the young and faster for the old is resolved in the light of the above explication."[28]

THE ROUND ART

Rodney Collin's similar ideas were derived from the studies of the biologist Pierre Lecompte de Noüy during the First World War. De Noüy experimented with the rate at which wounds healed according to the age of the wounded. As metabolic processes tend to slow down with age, the older the wounded person was, the longer the healing of a wound took. The body loses its ability to consume and process oxygen, and the period in which tissue can regenerate itself lengthens. "De Noüy calculated the impression of the 'passage' in time for a twenty- and fifty-year-old man to be four and six times faster respectively than for a five-year-old child."[29] An hour of childhood is *not* the same as an hour in old age.

Collin reasoned that because the time-scale of a large cell, the ovum, is one thousand times faster than the time-scale of a grown man, only when a man approaches death do his perceptions reach full breadth and comprehension. Approaching the end of life time seems to pass a *thousand times faster than at conception.* He compared this to the acceleration of a falling body gaining momentum and stated that measuring life by years is very misleading because less and less is put into them the nearer one is to death. *He corrected this false perspective by grading the lifetime from the lifetime of the ovum, one lunar month, to the time of death, one thousand lunar months, with a logarithmic progression.*

In a logarithmic scale the divisions 1, 10, 100, 1000 are equal to 1, 2, 3, 4 in an arithmetic scale. (Figure V.16).

Figure V.16 Logarithmic Proportions.

1	2	3	4
1 lunar month	10 lunar months	100 lunar months	1000 lunar months
Conception	Birth	7 years Childhood	77 years Death

"These limits of one and one thousand months, indeed, remind us of the two other intermediate points. Man is born ten lunar months after his conception; and his childhood is generally accepted as coming to an end after one hundred (7 years). These are clearly the key-points in his life. So that we now have our scale marked 1, 10, 100, 1000; thus dividing man's whole career into three logarithmically equal parts — Gestation, Childhood and Maturity."[30]

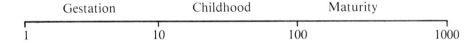

These three periods of development in the life are *Octaves.*

"During the prenatal peiod of *gestation* the physical body gradually is formed, and at last launched into independent existence in a different medium, the air. During *childhood,* personality is formed upon the basis of the physical body, and the combination launched into independent existence in the world of men. During *maturity,* the psycho-physical organism so created works out its various possibilities, and when these are complete, it is launched into eternity."[31]

The life is a continual unfolding of successively finer vehicles (bodies) with which the individual comprehends the universe. Simultaneously, the intensity of each successive octave diminishes through life.

The reason why the intensity diminishes is related to the mathematics of biological time. As we live, each successive day's experiences must be compared against a larger and larger number of previous days. The experiences of each day are appended onto this reservoir of memories and gradually become assimilated into them as a "block of memories" called the *Past.* As we age, the number of days we have experienced increases so profusely that most if not all individual day experiences during the life disappear into the whole.

The life process begins at Conception and is advanced by the time birth occurs, although we

[29] Collin, *Thê Theory of Celestial Influence,* p. 156-57; Fischer, *Voices of Time,* p.360; and de Noüy, *Biological Time,* p.121.

[30] Collin, *The Theory of Celestial Influence,* p. 157.

[31] Collin, *The Theory of Celestial Influence,* p. 157.

usually use the Birth moment as a datum point in time. In days after conception each successive day is a smaller and smaller proportion of the total life experience — the second day is ½ of the life, the third day is ⅓, the fourth day ¼, the end of the first month of life is 1/30th, the day of birth is 1/280th of the life, etc., until at the age of 29 years old each successive day is on the order of 1/10,000th of the lifetime!

As we age, time appears to be passing more quickly and contracting. These perceptions are not the exclusive property of the senile, but are a gradual acquisition of all of us as we age. The meaning of this proportional enfoldment during the life is that *the earlier in life events or influences are, the more important they are.* The earliest influences are most vivid and influential because at the time they represent major and critical experiences. After years of childhood and maturity they are overlaid by thousands of other days of experiences and begin to disappear into the unconscious, blurring all the while.

As we age, we continually re-evaluate our entire past. Subsequent events often pressure us to alter our memories of critical past events to make our lives seem more consistent. In describing our personal experiences and exploits, they are embellished or altered "for the sake of a good story". The actual event which is essential to our memory of ourselves is eventually lost behind our own distortions.

The principle aim of astrology is to identify the archetypal structure of the life and to create an honest attitude to one's individuality. In this sense astrology is similar to psychoanalysis, which seeks to uncover the essential nature of the psyche which motivates the individual. We must understand the process of our life and rediscover the bridge of memories back to the very time of conception to allow us to make of it a unified whole.

Collin set up the logarithmic scale of man's life in circular form. (Figure V.17) The circle, graded logarithmically, represents man's life according to biological time instead of calendar years. In this circle of life the moment of conception *coincides* with the moment of death, implying that there is a vital connection between them. Collin explains this with a clever analogy which gives life a new dimension:

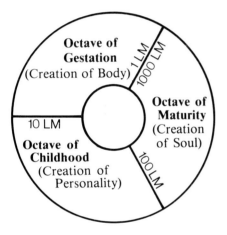

Figure V.17 The Circular Logarithmic Scale of Rodney Collin.

> "Earlier we compared birth and the end of childhood to the two critical points at which steam changed to water and water to ice. The moment of death and conception could be then likened to a point at which, in a single flash, the ice passed back through all the other stages, split into oxygen and hydrogen, and in the same instant condensed as steam again. The energy of death appears to have some similar effect on the whole being of man, splitting it into its component parts of body, essence, personality and life, and in the same instant rejoining that which survives in a different way. The instant at which all the unfulfilled causes set up in the past life are torn from the corpse by death is the same terrible instant of impregnation when the genes, or signature of the body, will rush together into their new pattern. *This is That.*"[32]

Collin sees the recurrence of life in time as the direct extension of phenomena which occur in faster cycles in the body. Since the lifetime of the molecules of which we are made is a fraction of one second, as every molecule in our body dies it is replaced by another which is virtually identical and possesses the memory of the original. This process of replacement is continually going on. The entire *molecular body* of man dies and is recreated *with every breath*. Each molecular body possesses habits, likes, dislikes, and the identity of the former body. In the same way the *cellular body* is reconstituted each night and retains the same form, constitution and health. The deviation in each successive body is so minimal that it takes years of breaths or decades of nights to make an appreciable change. Man is continually dying and being reborn, and the factors which constitute his life are being continuously passed on as *traces in time* both to offspring and to the "next life" in time.[33] Life is a pattern in the space-time continuum. It never disappears, but rather finds new forms. The energy and information dissipated in death is always reformed somewhere else in the continuum. One could call this the *Conservation of Life in Time.*

---

[32] Collin, *The Theory of Celestial Influence,* p. 336.

Astrology and Logarithmic Time

The triple octave time-scale which Collin developed is remarkably similar to the structure of the horoscope and can in fact be superimposed upon it with extraordinary results. The diagram in The Theory of Celestial Influence called *"The Clock of Human Life"*[34] can be made to coincide with the astrological signs and houses. In the horoscope the ascendant is equivalent to the time of birth, so the Birth Moment in the time-scale is coincident with it. When the two diagrams are superimposed, the octaves in the time-scale exactly coincide with the octaves of the four elements in the horoscope. (Figure V.18)

The **Octave of Childhood** (Creation of Personality) includes the first four signs Aries, Taurus, Gemini and Cancer. The **Octave of Maturity** (Creation of Soul) includes the signs Leo, Virgo, Libra and Scorpio. The **Octave of Gestation** (Creation of Body) covers the signs Sagittarius, Capricorn, Aquarius and Pisces. These groups of signs relate very closely with the qualities of their groups. Collin did not correlate this diagram with astrology so we must proceed alone from this point.

Each of the three octaves is divided logarithmically into four sections equivalent to the twelve zodiacal divisions. Every house has a specific time period to which it corresponds. The basis for calculation is the *lunar month* of 28 days, producing octaves of 280 days (10 lunar months) (Gestation), 2800 days (100 lunar months) or 7 years (Childhood), and 28000 days (1000 lunar months) or 78 years (Death). In our time-scale, the time during Gestation is indicated in weeks after conception. All times after birth are indicated in years and months. These divisions relate to the average timings during life. Once an understanding of the average sequence of the signs and houses is found from the time-scale, the variations which determine individual qualities will be discussed and correlated to the Placidean Method of house division in the horoscope.

Once the time-scale of logarithmic ages synchronizes with the horoscope we can compare the qualities of the signs and houses to their designated age period. The parallels are immediately very clear and answer a question about astrology and the signs which has never been resolved: *where did the sign and house qualities come from?* They come from the archetypal logarithmic ages to which they refer!

The sign Aries means self-assertion, personality, physical appearance and early environment: this corresponds to the time period in the logarithmic scale from Birth until 7 months old. Taurus, from 7 months old until 1 year 8 months is the time when a child begins crawling and investigating the physical world. Gemini, from 1 year 8 months until 3 years 6 months governs communication, and the child begins talking during this time. Cancer, from 3 years 6 months until 7 years old, governs the parents, the family and emotions. Leo is traditionally correlated with self-exteriorization, gameplaying and education and occurs during the time of primary education approaching puberty, from 7 until 13 years old. Virgo, governing discrimination and distillation coincides with secondary education and choosing a life path between the ages of 13 and 23.

At the age of 23 the subjective and unconscious half of the horoscope below the horizon has been experienced and the individual becomes *objective* for the first time. (Figure V.19) Libra governs partnership and marriage, and is correlated to the time from 23 until 42 years old. Scorpio is associated with death and the deacclimation from the life (metaphysics), from 42 until Death. It is particularly appropriate as Scorpio is the indicator of death, but is very confusing because it is not at the end of the twelve signs. Our structure clarifies this logic. The cusp of Sagittarius is related to the death moment and conception.

The last four signs in our logarithmic scale operate upon two levels. They traditionally govern the octave of "higher mind", which indicates the activities of an individual who transcends the "average". Sagittarius governs philosophy, psychology and religion; Capricorn governs fame, honour and position in the world; Aquarius governs societies, friends and humanitarian pursuits; and Pisces governs institutions and the psychic faculties. In our logarithmic time-scale, these four signs govern the *Octave of Gestation,* the time we spend in our mother's womb. *The experiences, feelings and attitudes of the mother during Gestation are the precursers of the existence of a higher reality in the life.* This is borne out in the increasing interest in recent years in the importance of natural childbirth and the prenatal state.[35] The work of Freud and Jung in psychoanalysis, and the multitude of therapies extant

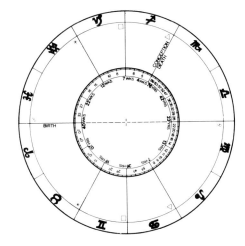

Figure V.18 The Logarithmic Scale and the Horoscope.

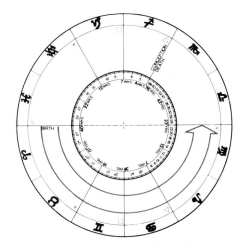

Figure V.19 Twenty-Three Years Old.

[33] See Nietzsche, *On Eternal Recurrence,* Plato, *Timaeus* and, Collin, *TCI,* 334-342.

[34] Collin, *The Theory of Celestial Influence,* p. 138.

[35] See R. D. Laing, *The Facts of Life;* The *"Birthing"* psycho-therapeutic process of Elizabeth Fehr; the birth technique of Dr. Frederick Leboyer, *Birth Without Violence;* and many others.

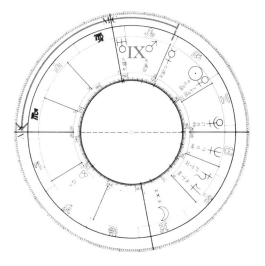

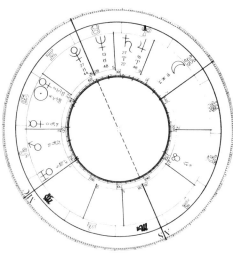

Figure V.21 The Navamamsha Chart of Conception Moment.

in the USA all imply the great importance of gestation time. (See Part IX, The Reading.)

Logarithmically, the time from Birth until Death is only two-thirds of the lifetime. The third of the horoscope which governs Gestation, from Conception until Birth, has a double set of meanings. Since the Logarithmic Time Scale is related to principles of movement in space and time which are essential in the nature of the universe, its form can be represented graphically.

The circle of the horoscope is a two-dimensional diagram, but in reality it is dynamic like the solar system. In addition to the movement around the circle through the lifetime, *the entire circle also moves through space and time* as the solar system moves through the galaxy. To indicate this movement, we extend the circle of the horoscope through time, forming a cylinder like the physicists' illustration of the shape of the space-time continuum.[36] This cylinder shows the passage of the individual field (the horoscope) through time.

If we logarithmically grade the length of the resultant cylinder as we have graded the periphery of the circle, we have a space-time diagram of the lifetime. The horoscope at birth is a section through the cylinder, as it is also a section through the spiralling path of the solar system. In both cases the central axis corresponds to the position of the individual. The axis around which the luminaries and planets seem to revolve is actually not a straight line, but in fact a very gradual spiral. This mirrors the spiral path of the Sun through space. This path extends through space and time all the way back to its origin, and will continue to travel along the axis until its demise. This spiral path is the *Long Body of the Solar System* which we have already discussed in Part III. The positions of the planetary bodies at any time are represented as a section through this spiralling circus. The ascendant is shown as a section in Figure V.20.

In the West the birth time is the conventional time of reference for all individuals, but in the East the conception moment is often used. Both events are indicated on the graded cylinder, but the difficulty of determining the time of conception moment forces us to use the birth time.

In the East, conception was considered the sacred moment, and techniques which combined religious dicta and astrology determined the exact time. The technique they used is related to our system, and is called the *Navamamsha Chart*. In the Navamamsha Chart the horoscope at birth is used as a base, but the degree and sign of the cusp of the IXth house is put on the ascendant. (Figure V.21) *This corresponds to the Conception point in the logarithmic time scale!*[37] The horoscope for the Conception moment indicates the person's *essence,* while the horoscope datum point in use in the West indicates the *personality*. The West is more involved with personality than essence, which is why we will use the ascendant as the prime reference plane. Within the graded cylinder any plane taken at any time of the life will relate to the whole through time. The cylinder extends backwards in time from the ascendant-birth time to the conception point and forwards towards the death moment.

If the archetypal life of man is superimposed upon the logarithmic cylinder, the Conception point is one octave behind (clockwise) the Ascendant point around the circumference of the circle, and one octave below the plane of the birth horoscope. Life is a spiral path around the circumference of the cylinder. (Figure V.22) The path begins with the Conception moment, continues through the Ascendant, intersects the cusp of Leo (7 years old), one octave above and one third around the cylinder and intersects the Death moment *exactly three octaves above the Conception Point.* As each new octave is entered during the life, the *previous octaves below become Memory.* The "mechanical man" who does not extend his reality beyond the life of his physical body remains within the three lower octaves. He is conceived, born, matures and dies without creating a Soul, and his life terminates at the Death point in the cylinder. There is a fourth octave available to the man who creates a Soul during the lifetime.[38] This octave is *Universal Consciousness* and indicates the ability to create a transcendent reality. This transcendent reality is the *higher octave of the Octave of Gestation* — outside of time, three octaves above the Gestation time. (Figure V.23) This universal consciousness is equivalent to Jung's "Collective Unconscious" — a repository of universal psychic contents of all men as a layer below the Personal Unconscious. When this octave is entered in the time scale, all three previous octaves become available to consciousness and the individual becomes "realized". Access to Universal Consciousness lies through the extension described in the Axiom of Maria.[39] The fourth is simultaneously beyond the third, and coincident to the first. The soul is the motivating force behind the movement through the cylinder

[36] Nigel Calder, *The Key of the Universe,* p. 173.

[37] Dr. V. G. Rele, *Directional Astrology of the Hindus as propounded in the Vimshottari Dasa,* p. 56-57.

[38] P. D. Ouspensky, *The Fourth Way,* and *In Search of the Miraculous;* Collin, *The Theory of Celestial Influence* and *The Theory of Eternal Life.*

[39] See "Alchemists" in Part II.

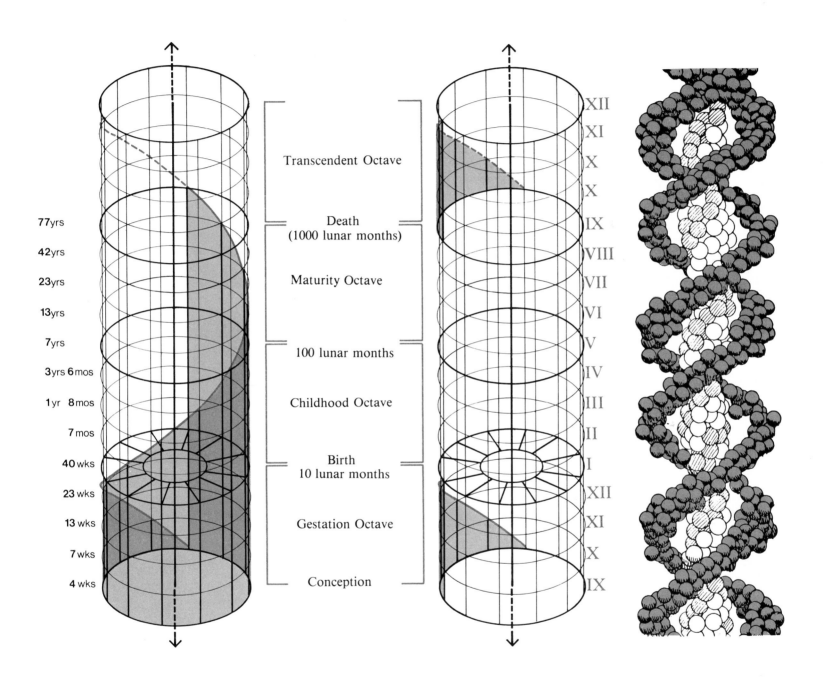

Figure V.20 The Logarithmic
Cylinder of Life.
Figure V.22 The Golden
Path of Life.

Figure V.23 Transcendent
Reality as the Higher Octave
of Gestation.

Figure V.24 The DNA
Double Helix.

40 The anima is the personification of the feminine component of man's personality and is identified with the Soul.

and the key to the Transcendent Octave, as the following analysis of an alchemical vision by Jung shows:

> "Thus by the Red Sea, he met the animal soul in the form of a monstrous quaternity symbolizing, so to speak, the prima materia of the self, and as the phoenix, rebirth. The mystery alluded to here is not only the encounter with the animal soul but, at the same time and in the same place, the meeting with the anima,[40] a feminine psychopomp who showed him the way to Mercurius and also how to find the phoenix."[41]

The prenatal time is the source of the Archetypes of the Collective Unconscious, and the "Home of the Soul". In the logarithmic spiral the Soul is found by comprehending the quaternity of octaves. Events that occur via the mother during Gestation are prototypes of the transcendent life of the individual. As events during Gestation have already happened, attaining universal consciousness is their *reflection outside time — in Eternity.*[42] The longing for rebirth is identical to return to the womb, the descent into the underworld and the realm of the collective unconscious. Libido is freed from incest fantasies and rechannels itself into a spiritual realm. "Thus man, as a spiritual being, becomes a child again, and is born into a circle of brothers and sisters."[43]

All events during Gestation are interpreted on two levels. First, as the sequence of intuitions, feelings, thoughts and sensations which the mother experienced and transmitted directly to the developing child, and secondly as the transcendental journey of the soul through the "Realm of the Mothers".[44] The four signs governing Gestation (Sagittarius, Capricorn, Aquarius and Pisces) are defined on both levels, with the implicit understanding that they are images of each other. They are connected not by identical events, but by an *equivalence of meaning.* The Fourth does relate back to the First, as the alchemists, magicians and churchmen believed.

The logarithmic spiral and the paths of the planets resemble the double helix of the DNA-RNA molecule which programs all life. The double helix can be represented as series of spheres moving along its length, as ribbons, or as a tinker-toy-like model connected with chemical bonds. (Figure V.24) In any representation it is analogous to the movement of the solar system through time and the logarithmic spiral of life. The length of the DNA chain is measured in Angstroms (Å) (wavelengths), and in the logarithmic cylinder the measurement is similarly scaled in lunar cycles. The DNA chain is additive (or even possibly logarithmic), and records the entire building process of life back to the beginning of the universe. Each successive life and the multitude of experiences which it encapsulates is added as impulses onto an existing chain which created the life form.

If the length of a single cell's DNA strand were extended, it would be miles long. The strand exists in every cell nucleus and transmits its memory to other cells through the messenger-RNA strand (a duplicate version of DNA) to the cytoplasm, where it activates and controls chemical and physical building processes. Theodor Landscheidt recognized this genetic coding as a cybernetic system, a control model of information, and this diagram we have constructed potentially allows the information of the genetic memory to be compared to the information in the life of an individual, transmitted by his horoscope. *Our model is a link between the macrocosm of the solar system and the microcosm of the DNA heliacal structure of man's genetics.*

The information transmitted through the galaxy is processed through our solar system to man through *Resonance.* The genetic code is a resonant circuit paralleling the movements of the planets, the Sun and ultimately the whole galaxy. As Landscheidt states:

> "I have hit upon the working hypothesis that the Sun always functions as an attuned gravitational resonance aggregate when the planets are clustered around the Sun in configurations corresponding to the oscillations or harmonic vibrations of the gravitational waves. Then the whole system vibrates like an antenna sensitive enough to receive gravitational transmissions from the galactic centre."[45]

41 Jung, *Mysterium Coniunctionis, CW 14*, p. 213.

42 See Plato, *Timaeus.*

43 Jung, *Symbols of Transformation, CW 5*, p. 226.

44 Goethe, *Faust Part II*, p. 78.

45 Landscheidt, *Cosmic Cybernetics*, p. 62.

The gravitational waves vibrate like quadrupoles, and the form of their vibrations is described by angles of 90, 180 and 360 degrees, the positions of the grand cross in the horoscope! Landscheidt further divides the basic angles until he has twelve elements, similar to the genetic elements in DNA, composed again of three groups of four elements each. Our model is a

unified model of the universe.

In the following detailed exposition of a lifetime according to the astrological logarithmic time-scale these relationships will be explored and amplified. *Astrology has been unconsciously correlated to biological time,* and this will be demonstrated. For the sake of clarity, we will start the process of the life with the first sign Aries, and when we come to the last four signs Sagittarius, Capricorn, Aquarius and Pisces, we will describe them on both levels.

The logarithmic times of the first five signs are virtually identical to the periods of development which the child psychologist Piaget discovered in his clinical studies on childhood. Therefore, many references will be made to a survey of Piaget's work by Ruth M. Beard, *An Outline of Piaget's Developmental Psychology* (abbreviated *OPDP).*

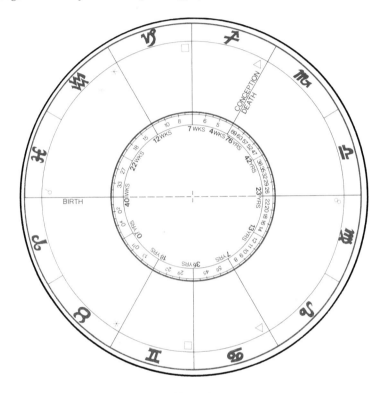

The Logarithmic Time Scale

The time scale is primarily associated with the houses of the horoscope, and is also the root of the definitions of the signs of the zodiac. The two systems are reflections of each other; the signs as *qualities in life* and the houses as the *time sequence of life.* The wheel of logarithmic time remains oriented to the ascendant and the traditional houses, while the wheel of the signs rotates upon it. The archetypal activities occupying developmental periods in the life — the signs — are oriented differently in time for every individual. The ascendant in the individual horoscope is a pointer indicating the sign stage of development of the personality. For example, individuals with Aries ascending live an archetypal process of development. The personality of Libra ascending is determined by partnerships. Sagittarius ascending associates the personality with philosophy, psychology or religion, etc. Planets and personal points which occupy a sign or house reflect the developmental qualities of the archetypal time period as follows:

(It must be noted that the structure of the horoscope involves many factors which qualify the house designations. The distribution of the ten planets, which are catalytic influences or archetypes, qualify the influences during each house period to produce the range of effects mentioned as possibilities. The pattern we are describing is a process, and does not refer to any specific individual.)

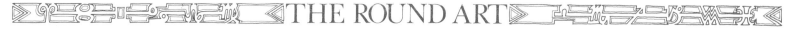

Ist House — ARIES
The Ram
Cardinal Fire Sign
Birth until 0 years 7 months

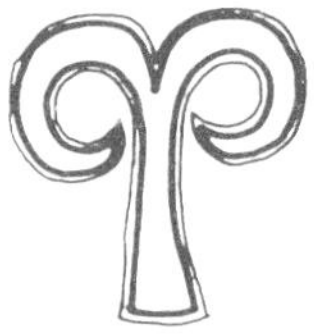

Figure V.25 The Glyph of Aries.

Aries corresponds in traditional astrology to *self-assertion, the personality, the physical body shape and appearance* and *the early family environment.* The first house indicates a child's ability to assert himself (ASC ♂ ☉ ♈) and the influences which affect this process.

If the qualities of the birth moment are supportive (♃ ♈) the individual will always believe, independent of circumstances in later life, that the environment around him will be supportive. The personality is determined by the quality of the birth moment and the nature of the environment immediately afterwards: the *physical conditions of the birth* — easy natural childbirth (♀ ♈); difficult delivery (♇ ♂ ♅ ♈); surgery (♂ ♅ ♈); medication of the mother (♆ ♈); home delivery (☾ ♈); hospital delivery and handling (♆ ♈); the individuals participating in the delivery and the treatment of the child, etc; *the physical appearance,* (ASC) *sex of the child* and the *reactions to this of people present at birth or soon after* — including immediate recognition and contact with the mother in natural childbirth (☾ ☿ ♈); many adoring relatives complimenting the mother and child immediately (♃ ♀ ♈); delivery of a sedated mother with doctors and nurses handling the process (♆ ♈); parental approval or disapproval of sex (☉ ☾ ♈), size or physical appearance; separation of the baby from the mother (♄♅♈) and immediate relocation in a children's ward away from contact (♀ ♈), etc. ; and the most important facts, the *attitudes and projections* of those performing and witnessing the birth, including the parents, towards the newborn baby (joy (♃ ♈); concern (♄ ♈); hate (♇ ♈); anxiety (☿♄♈); bliss (♀ ♃ ♈); jealousy (♂ ♇ ♄ ♈); indifference (♆ ♈); boredom (♄ ♈); no response (♄ ♈); etc.). All participants at the birth are critical as *they represent components of the personality* of the baby and have a direct bearing upon the individual throughout his later life.

Other factors include the treatment directly after the birth including the cutting of the umbilical cord, the pain of circumcision (♂☉♈), the period of time spent and the conditions in hospital and the name the infant is given. The personality of the child is directly affected by all of these factors and he will grow to *see himself as he was seen by others during this time.*

The newborn child has highly developed sensitivities, although he is immobile during the first seven months (♄ ♀ ♆ ♈). Until about 90 days after birth he cannot focus light properly (☉♈), so he must in some way indicate his needs, his feelings of pleasure and discomfort and adopt a life pattern which is satisfactory within his environment. Piaget believes that these first acquired adaptations and the "primary circular reactions" are formed at about 0 years, 2 months, and that secondary circular reactions like eye and hand co-ordination begin at 0 years 4 months.[46]

[46] *OPDP,* p. 20-21.

If the child is given attention and support during his first seven months, he will assume throughout his life that others will support his personality. If he is immediately placed in an infant's ward in the hospital, isolated from his mother and generally ignored he will feel for the rest of his life that it is difficult to assert himself and that others will ignore his efforts.

IInd House — TAURUS
The Bull
Fixed Earth Sign
0 years 7 months until 1 year 8 months

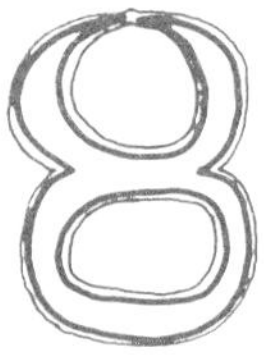

Figure V.26 The Glyph of Taurus.

Taurus governs the *physical world, undifferentiated matter, pure substance, the senses and perception, endurance, security, finances* and *property.* During the Taurus time the child has asserted his personality and begins to apply his energies towards the physical world. He gradually discovers his senses and uses them to investigate the physical world within and around himself through smell, touch, sight, taste and hearing. He becomes aware of the *object* (☉ ♉), and applies his senses in sequence to all familiar and unfamiliar objects around him.[47] (☿ ♉)He investigates spatial relationships by hiding and finding objects (♂ ♉).

The child begins to equilibrate and position his body at 1 year 3 months old.[48] He becomes familiar (♀ ♉) with objects within his reach and then extends these familiarities outwards, inventing rituals of exploration (♂ ♉). The permanence of objects, including the object-like quality of his own body is discovered by the end of this time. "His world has become a solid universe of co-ordinated objects including the body itself in the capacity of an element."[49]

The nature of the child's involvement with the physical world during this time determines his attitudes towards the *physical world* and his *body* throughout life. If the child is limited in the range of sensations available (♄ ♉), he will continue to feel limited access to and control over the physical world around him. The greater the variety of food (☾ ♀ ♉), objects, individuals and environments (♃ ☉ ♉)he is allowed to investigate,the broader his physical viewpoint. This obviously has a direct bearing upon later attitudes towards ownership (☉ ♂ ♉), stewardship (♀ ♉) and financial matters (♃♄ ♉).

The quality of objects, sounds, sights, smells and foods experienced during Taurus forms the basis for the "aesthetic sense" (♆♀♉). Contact with music heightens rhythmic awareness, with beautiful objects or exotic textures and colours the form sense improves, and with varieties of foods the palate will be broader and more adventurous (♃ ♉).

Individuals who have strong contact with the child during this time will be considered as *sensual objects of the perceptions* (☾ ♉); and so the degree of physical contact with others will determine sensuality and interest in touching others later in life (☾♀♉). The child who has these sensations withheld or minimalized will always experience difficulty relating to the physical and will feel distanced or frigid sexually (♄♂♉). Modern "grope" therapies are attempts to correct damage incurred during this time of the life by encouraging a childlike level of physical communication.

[47] *OPDP*, p. 18.

[48] *OPDP*, p. 25.

[49] Piaget, 1955, *OPDP*, p. 25.

IIIrd House — GEMINI
The Twins
Mutable Air Sign
1 year 8 months until 3 years 6 months

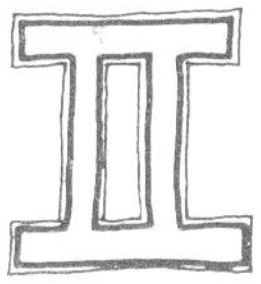

Figure V.27 The Glyph of Gemini.

Gemini means *instinctive mind, communication, movement, adaptability, brothers and sisters, short journeys, mimicry, multiplication and diversity.* The Gemini stage is a synthesis of the two previous stages. The assertion derived from Aries is applied to the physical world of Taurus producing *movement,* and by extension, *communication.*

The child discovers that in addition to confronting an object on a sensual level, he can make it do things for him (♄ ♊). Instead of picking the object up, looking at it, tasting it, feeling it, rotating it and then putting it down and moving towards something else as in Taurus, he begins to involve more than one object at a time in his perceptions (☿ ♊). He begins to represent one thing by another (☉♊) — *tying thinking to action.* Piaget calls this stage the *Preconceptual stage of concrete actions.*[50]

The most representative process of this time is *speech* (☿ ♊). The child during Taurus discovers the range of sounds he can make playing with the air, but in Gemini he begins to realize that he can represent himself through sounds and words. The impetus is *imitation of others* (☾♆♊), leading to the naming and describing of objects and actions (☿ ♊) as people around him do. This advance is the *co-ordination of movements to objects* (☿ ♊). Initial communication is vague, but through trial and error it becomes a comprehensible process with an emphasis upon mimicry.

When he cannot assimilate the name of an object or action, he *accommodates it into his fantasies* (♆ ♊). Play takes on a symbolic meaning and the ability of the child to adapt his reality to external situations determines the extent of these fantasies. When understanding is difficult (♆ ♄ ♊), the fantasy world is entered and the content assimilated into it. Reasoning

[50] *OPDP*, p. 17.

proceeds from one step to the next without any comprehension of overall groupings of steps. Every step in understanding is *dualistic* between assimilation and accommodation, which clarifies the traditional connection of Gemini to the "Twins". Whether or not he actually has a twin, the child finds one in himself in a fantasy world.[51]

The ability of the child to establish a method of communication (☽ ♃ ☿ ♊) indicates his later proficiency, and the *mode* of communication he prefers during this time he will always prefer. Jung describes the operations of children at this stage as the attempt of the basic energy value, *libido* (♂ ☉ ♊), to transfer its direction from the rhythmic sucking (♀ ♊) of the earlier nutritional stages into more highly developed activities, via the hand.[52] Libido eventually transfers itself into sexual functions at puberty, but it must make intermediate developments first. The rhythmic activity which takes over from the nutritive is *speech* (☿ ♊). Inability to make this transfer forces libido to regress into earlier stages — thumbsucking (♀☽ ♊), the banging of objects or an overstimulation of the fantasies. Valid outlets for the libido are music (♀ ♊), singing (☿ ♀ ♊), dancing and play (☽♃♊). The connection of rhythmic processes with speech allows natural energies to channel themselves into higher forms and allows earlier attitudes to combine and permute naturally. *Freudian slips* (♅ ♊) probably have their bases in this time and indicate faulty transformation (♇ ♊). It is consistent to archetypal Gemini qualities that there is usually a confusion between the activities and ideas of the child, and the activities and ideas of others (☉ ☿ ♊). This is the unconsciousness of the imitative process.

This time traditionally indicates relationship to brothers (♂ ♊) and sisters (♀ ♊). This is borne out because the family (☽ ♊), particularly those closest in age to the child, provide *models* (♀ ♊) which the child imitates. He gradually extends his field of awareness through each sign during his life: in Aries establishing contact with himself, in Taurus with objects and in Gemini with other individuals close to his own age. The child prefers the companionship of other children because *adults live at a vastly different rate* which the child finds difficult to understand. He sees adults moving so slowly that they barely enter his consciousness. A two-year-old child cannot imagine why an adult will sit reading for hours, when to him that constitutes aeons. If there are no brothers, sisters or close friends, the models must inevitably be adults. The child is still extremely egocentric and believes that all other individuals are parts of himself. Piaget remarks that eldest children and only children acquire larger vocabularies and are capable of higher attainments because they receive more adult attention, which becomes integrated into their view of themselves.[53] Other children or adults in close contact with the child during this time affect the type of communication which the child will eventually manifest. If the external models (☉ ☽ ♊) are not conducive to the child's inherent attitudes or are absent altogether (♄ ♊), the child has no model, and the subsequent level of communication is instinctive and random (♆ ♊).

[51] See Lewis Carroll, *Alice in Wonderland*.

[52] Jung, *Symbols of Transformation*, *CW* 5, p. 143.

[53] *OPDP*, p. 52.

IVth House — CANCER
The Crab
Cardinal Water Sign
3 years 6 months until 7 years

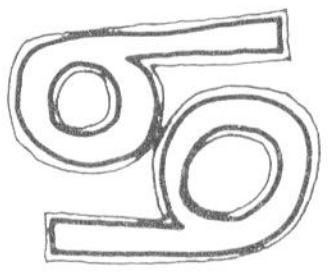

Figure V.28 The Glyph of Cancer.

Cancer governs the *family, feelings, the parents and particularly the mother, fertilization, receptivity, heredity, conditions in old age, intuition and the psychic world*. The communication in Gemini is almost totally unconscious because the child is not concerned about whether or not there is any response to his communications. At around 4 years old the child begins to realize that his communications produce either positive (♃ ☽ ♀ ♋) or negative (♂ ♄ ♅ ♇ ♋) emotions in others and, by reflection (☽ ♋), in himself. He begins to look beyond imitation and communicates to produce effects in others (♀ ♋). Constructive responses (☽ ♀ ♃ ♋) produce a positive emotional "set" in the child, while destructive responses (♂ ♄ ♅ ♇ ♋) produce a negative "set". The child is *feeling* (valuing) the quality of his position in the family (☉ ☽ ♋) by his ability to communicate to others.

Cancer is the summation and termination of the first octave. The individual influences of the first three signs are valued against each other, and a feeling towards the personality is connected with a response to the ability to communicate. Feelings and their mode of expression determine the *tone of the personality*. The child, realizing that communication produces emotional responses in others — supportive (☾♃♋), interested(♅♇♋), angry (♂♀♋), blasé (♆♋), bored (♄♋), violent (♂♇♅♋), etc.— also begins to realize that the *structure of the home and family is predominantly emotional* (☾♋). The family (☾♋) is a structure within which the child should be able to make any communication and receive supportive emotional response. The quality and intensity of the feelings are intimately tied to the freedom to communicate them and the security (♃♋) — or lack of it (♄♋) — which results from the family structure.

Piaget calls this the *Intuitive Stage,* when the thinking of the child becomes dominated by immediate perceptions in his environment (♀♋). He begins to seek reasons behind the beliefs and actions of himself and his family — his emotional relativity.[54] Since he still cannot make more than simple relationships (one to one), he concentrates on one aspect of the emotions of the family at a time and finds it difficult to extend his thinking or feeling beyond that. He begins to imitate the family reality he observes with dolls (♀♋), acting out family scenes and applying sequences to play. He can understand one person's viewpoint at a time, but cannot understand reciprocal relationships. He sees the consequences of his actions first and then invents the causes.[55] The judgements of parents are "absolute rules" and his reality becomes continuous to the world of his parents (☉☾♋). He can conceive only of processes or relationships as "paired". (Figure V.29) He sees his parents as a pair, but can relate only to one of them at a time. He internalizes many actions, and relationships of surrounding and enclosure assume great importance — his own room or space, etc.

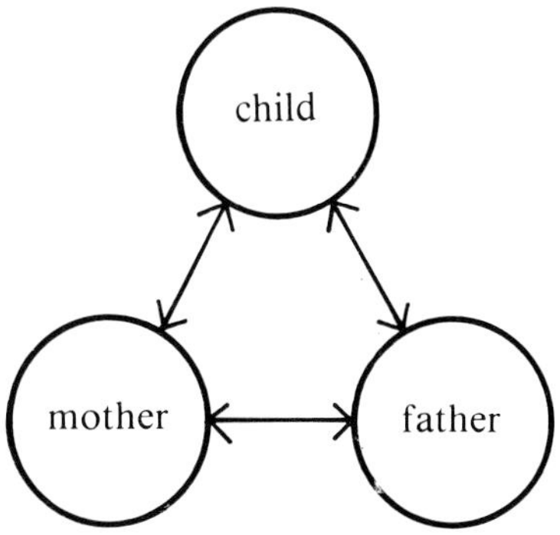

Figure V.29 Paired Relationships in Cancer.

The way the child perceives his family situation (☾♋) and the quality and nature of his home life (☾♋) determines the quality of his domestic reality for the rest of his life. The individual is inclined unconsciously to re-create the situation of his childhood home and family structure, much as he may or may not have actually liked them. In this sense, the hereditary pattern (IVth house) of the family is reflected in its structure.

At this time the child's attitudes and feelings towards his parents orient him within the family. As every individual is composed of both masculine (☉♂♄♋) and feminine (☾♀♋) characteristics, the tendency to relate to one parent or the other reflects an inherent duality. The most desirable situation is for the child to relate equally to both parents (☉♂☾♋), but in reality this virtually never happens.

The connection between the individual and his parents is at the core of psychology. Freud posed an Oedipus Complex which proposes the repression of incest between son and mother, and an Electra Complex between daughter and father as the principal source of parental identification. Jung understood these relationships as archetypal functions of being, and called them *anima* (soul) and *animus* (mind, spirit). They personify the unconscious, instinctive patterns of the opposite sex in every individual.

During the Cancer time the child begins to form a stronger identification with one or the other of his parents, due mainly to the tendency for thinking in terms of paired relationships. The choice is identification with the mother (☾♋) as representative of the eternal feminine, the soul, or the maternal *Eros* in the case of males, and identification by the female with the masculine, rational, discriminative, paternal *Logos* of the father (☉♋). Each child tends to *project*[56] onto the parents certain qualities which contain the key to his own ability later in life to manifest both masculine and feminine parts of the Self. The way a child understands the relationship between his mother and father (☉☾ aspects) is a function of the way he relates to the two images in himself. Cancer is at the centre of the field of unconsciousness, so many individuals remain unconscious of their identification with one or both parents for life.

The assumption made in astrology is that during this time the "archetypal" male child imitates the characteristics he sees in his father and finds his mother very mysterious and compelling. He relates to his family and home as he sees his father, and to the outside world as he relates to his mother. Later in life he unconsciously seeks personification of the characteristics of his mother in other women. The personification is compensation for the qualities which he associates with "mother", but does not possess. The female child relates to her mother as to her home and family, and tries to find the imago of her father in the outside world in the form of teachers, boyfriends, lovers and husband.

Every individual lives permutations of this archetypal situation. Where the child relates

[54] *OPDP*, p. 57.

[55] *OPDP*, p. 59.

[56] An unconscious, automatic process whereby an unconscious content of the subject transfers itself to an object, which then seems to possess those qualities.

most strongly with the parent of the opposite sex, for the male the result is effeminacy (♀♋) and possibly homosexuality (♅♋). For the female the phenomenon of animus possession results from relating primarily to the father, which produces intellectuality (☿♋) and excessive judgement and discrimination (♄♋). Possession by either anima or animus is a mythological theme which everyone experiences to some degree in their lives. The whole range of possible relationships to the parental imago extends from total absorption to a complete lack of relationship. Some individuals see their parents as identical (☉♂♋), producing an hermaphroditic attitude (☿♆♋).

In the horoscope the usual rule is that the parent of the same sex is indicated by the IVth house, while the parent of the opposite sex is indicated by the Xth house. Sun and Moon in the horoscope correspond to the father and the mother. Their placement qualifies parental attitudes indicated by the IVth and Xth houses — a quaternity of values.

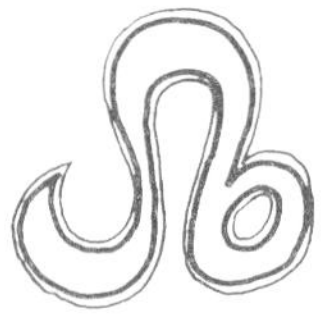

Figure V.30 The Glyph of Leo.

Vth House — LEO
The Lion
Fixed Fire Sign
7 years until 13 years

Leo governs *Self-consciousness, pride, the affections, love of the self and others, creation, acting, confidence, education, publications, speculation* and *game-playing*. After the completion of childhood at about seven years old, Leo brings the *exteriorization of the Self* (☉♌) into the world beyond the security of the family. The child begins to apply his personality to those outside the family circle, and this begins through *games* (☉☿♃♅♆♌).

Until the age of seven the child usually plays alone, or, even when in the company of other children is isolated 'in company'. During Leo the idea of co-operation replaces the isolation of the individual fantasy world. Previously, the ball-playing child would throw the ball across the yard, run and get it, and then throw it again. This is the residue of the "circular reactions" which Piaget associates with younger children. During this time the child begins to establish a rapport (☿♌) with other children. The circular reaction includes others, and manifests in enticing a neighbourhood child to "play ball". They decide upon rules — "You stand there and I'll stand here . . . Throw the ball to me and I'll throw it back to you" — and play. Playing with others becomes the prime mode of communication (☿♌), and the rhythmic nature of the games becomes a channel through which libido (♂♌) moves into a higher sphere. The rules (♄♌) define the function of each participant, and the more complex the game the more specialized is the participation of each child. Children make rules and act out parts (♆♌), often acting out every part in turn. Gradually the child discovers that he *likes* (♀♌) certain games because they allow him to exteriorize himself, while he *doesn't like* (♄♌) other games because they do not allow him an opportunity to express himself.

Piaget considers this time the stage of *Concrete Operations,* when physical actions are internalized as mental actions or operations and these become models of action ingrained in the child's behaviour. "Children do not obey rules until seven years old."[57]

[57] *OPDP,* p. 45.

The interest in classifying, serializing and acting out quite complex relationships is a *trial and error* process (♅♌) and not a testing of hypotheses. The hierarchy of games parallels the hierarchy of personal relationships. Some children like to play only by their own rules (☉♂♌), while others prefer to relinquish the responsibility for making rules (☾♌). Eventually the child finds that he prefers playing with certain children rather than others because they agree upon gameplaying attitudes. Individuality (☉♌) is determined by the roles the child plays in games and the other children he chooses to play with. This is the basis for *affectionate relationships* (♀♂♌), where the child likes to play certain games with certain *friends* (♀♌). Involvement in gameplaying forms the pattern for interpersonal relationships in later life.

The child goes to school (☿♌) for the first time at about seven years old to learn the games and rules by which his school, religion, race and nation operate. He accepts some of the rules (♃♌) but has a lack of respect for others (♄♇♌). There are inevitably some conflicts (♂♅♌), as there were in learning parental rules. The acceptance or rejection of rules is an indicator of the attitude towards education. Primary school forces the child to play and learn according to standards of behaviour. His ability to learn is connected to the ability to accept programming. As the child exteriorizes himself more fully, he is immediately subjected to more and more specific controls (♄♌) that channel and concentrate his energies in directions which the society is committed to uphold. The child becomes aware that the essence of all societies is a hierarchy of classes, elites and orders of succession (♀♃♌), and that school activity will always be compared to a norm.

The ability of the child to accept and work within the game-playing structure of school and the world determines his game-playing attitudes for the rest of his life. The rôles (ASC☉ ♌) he tends to choose or to be forced into — even though they become infinitely more complex — are prototypes of the rôles he plays throughout his adult life. Since game-playing extends past the time of puberty, these attitudes include the procreative instincts (☉☾♂♀♌). The desire to reproduce is often connected to a desire to have children who must play according to one's own rules.

Teaching (☿♌) is the desire to implement the rules one accepts in the outside world in the conditioning of others. Speculation (♃♆ ♇♌) is game-playing where one risks financial security, and gambling (☉ ♃♌) is also an extension of this motif.

VIth House — VIRGO
The Virgin
Mutable Earth Sign
13 years until 23 years old

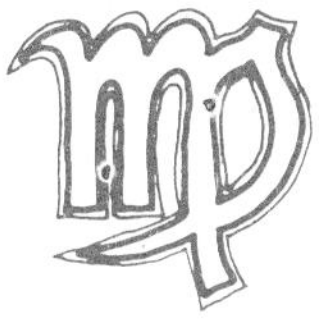

Figure V.31 The Glyph of Virgo.

Virgo governs *distillation, discrimination, work, health, service, criticism, differentiated matter, servants* and *diet.* Virgo begins at the advent of puberty, when the body re-enters the life equation. As the first earth sign Taurus signifies pure substance and undifferentiated matter, Virgo indicates the differentiation of the physical world. It is the time for making distinctions (☿☉♍), establishing a relationship between the mind and the body (ASC♇☉♍), refining attitudes and establishing work habits (♂♄♍).

During puberty (☿♍) the individual gradually begins to cut off from the parental home and its laws. He has to make his own choices (☉☾♍). It is the quest of the hero, where the first obstacle is leaving home and the parents.[58] The establishment of communication between the already developed mind (☿♍) and the rapidly maturing body (♃♍) is reflected in work attitudes (♂♄♍). If the individual sees his body as something which *works for him,* then in work situations he expects others to be subservient to him (☉♃♇♍). If, however, he sees his body as something which *he works for* and which determines his actions, he expects to work for others (☿♍). The interdependencies between these two extremes define the ability of the individual to make his own choices and his own way in the world.

When an individual during this time is able to determine a workable relationship between his body and his mind, his *health* (☉☿♍) will be good. The inability to understand what the body requires — resulting in confusion (♆♍) or conflict (♂♇♍) — indicates a tendency towards bad health through the life. Choices of food (☿☾♍), clothing (☿♀♍), exercise (♂♃♍) and companionship (♀♂♍) also affect the state of the health. All choices must operate in concert. The individual must see his being and his body as a whole rather than as a set of unrelated parts. The cohesiveness or fragmentation of the adult is often dependent upon which approach is chosen.

During Virgo the individual goes through his secondary and university education (☿♍), if the previous work stage has not precluded it. Piaget calls the time from 12 years until 15 years the period of *Formal Operations* (♄♍). Increased collaboration (♃♍) and reasoning (☿♍) among oneself and others leads to "those simultaneous relationships of differentiation and reciprocity which characterize the co-ordination of viewpoints."[59] The use of hypotheses and tests brings recognition that the laws of elders (♄♍) are not absolute (♇♍) and are subject to change (☿♍). There is much argument (☿♂♍) for the sake of argument, with the incidental effect of changing views, in higher secondary schools and universities. This signals a reintegra-

[58] See the legend of Parsifal.

[59] *OPDP,* p. 98.

tion of the fantasy world of childhood with systems (♃ ♄ ♍) which lie behind the procedures and rules accepted by society. Concrete experiences (♄ ♍) are translated into verbal (☿ ♍) and symbolic modes (♅ ♍) of expression, allowing transformations from one system to another. Finally, the rhythmic libido functions of the Leo game-playing time are translated into work activities (♅ ♂ ♍).

Virgo signals the end of dependence upon the family and the preparation for emergence into the realm of consciousness. The individual's ability to apportion interests (☉ ☾ ☿ ♄ ♍) in life's activities during this time has a profound affect upon his later development. The tendency is to concentrate (♄ ♍) upon local and specific dilemmas and not to understand that all eventually are to be combined. The pressure in most "modern" societies is for the individual to isolate himself (☾ ♍) and channel his activities into specialized directions (♄ ♍). Choices made before 23 years old often are binding for the remainder of life.

VIIth House — LIBRA
The Scales
Cardinal Air Sign
23 years until 42 years

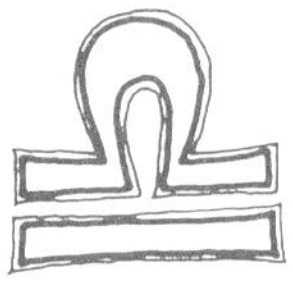

Figure V.32 The Glyph of Libra.

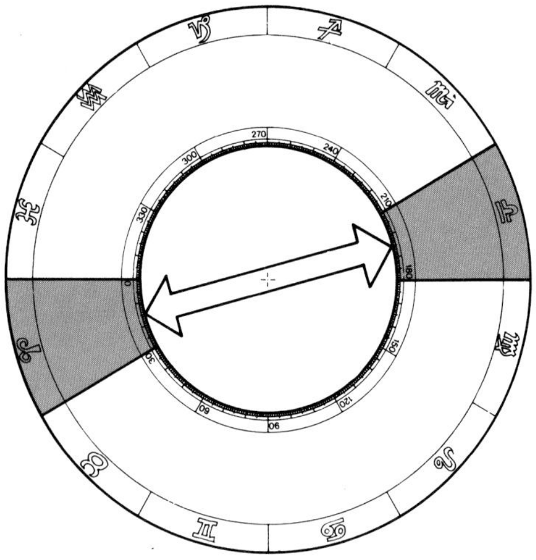

Figure V.33 Libra Opposite Aries.

Libra governs *partnership, communal relations, the public, obligations, sublimation, justice, business relationships, enemies* and *sociability.* At 23 years old, a very interesting phenomenon happens to the individual. From the moment of birth until the beginning of Libra, he has passed through the entire lower half of the horoscope, which is *unconscious* and *subjective.* During this time he is unconscious of himself and unable to see himself as others see him. The primordial survival instincts have been masked and assimilated throughout the first 23 years. Thomas Mann in his novel *Lotte in Wiemar* reconstructs an imaginary monologue of Goethe in which this point is made: ". . . for in me the most dangerous native tendencies have been subdued, civilized, purified, applied and compelled to good and great ends, by dint of a character sprung from somewhere altogether."[60]

From when the nucleus of the personality is formed at birth until 23 years old, it develops according to external conditions and parental criticism. But, there is little consciousness of exactly where this will lead. The beginning of Libra is exactly opposite the Ascendant logarithmically (Figure V.33), so by the time the individual has finally accepted his personality at 23 years old, *the way he sees himself is exactly opposite to the way he really is.* The youth qualifies his instinctual direction in life by adhering to the many guidelines his parents and society impose upon him, and the personality is affected by this response. This, coupled with the difficulty of adopting other viewpoints, produces the beginning of objectivity and true consciousness, as he must recognize the balance between the way he appears and the way he really is. Recognition of this polarity constitutes an essential realization upon which the depth and quality of life depends. The remaining half of the horoscope is a series of compensating factors which potentially reconcile this inherent opposition. All experiences, ideologies and conditioning received during the first 23 years must become conscious and their influences met directly and resolved.

The ability of the individual to realize this confrontation (☿ ♎) leads to potential wholeness, while to deny its existence produces an internal clash (♂ ♅ ♇ ♎) which remains for the rest of the life. The libido — which has been transformed through the life process — must at this time enter the sphere of consciousness, otherwise it regresses backwards into childhood. Individuals and collective values (♃ ♄ ♎) that have determined one's development must be seen from this time on as *images* (♀ ♎) of qualities already possessed. In this sense, all external images, behaviour patterns, events and persons in the first half of life are evocations of the individual's inherent structure. From 23 years old on, these contents must be reintegrated (☿ ♎).

Earlier events in life are necessary developments and trials (parental relationships, physical appearance, degree of education, communicative ability, drives, conflicts, etc.). They must be seen, accepted and integrated without being changed. This is essential, otherwise the energies

[60] Mann, *Lotte in Wiemar,* p. 217.

are blocked and forced to repeat earlier situations. Many individuals try to deny their earliest life (♄♎) and become caught in tape-loops which endlessly replay the same scenes in slightly different guises. Earlier situations which are too painful to analyze and become conscious of are repressed, forgotten, submerged in the unconscious and eventually split off from the conscious personality. Libra is the period during which early influences are confronted (♂☾♎) and assimilated (☉☿♎) as a necessary pre-requisite of individuality. From this time on, experiences and situations from early life are evoked again and their effects posed again.

Libra governs *partnership* (☉♎) and *sublimation* (☾♎). It is a compensation (☿♎) to its opposite house and sign Aries, which indicates self-assertion. To the degree that the individual established and asserted himself during the first seven months of his life, he must *give away as much of himself in partnerships as he received when his personality first registered.* The function of partners, whether business (♄♎) or marital (♀♂♎), is to provide an image of the qualities opposite to the individual's which must be balanced. The circumstances of the first months are a direct precursor of the partnerships that are to be formed during Libra. If the individual was sheltered during Aries in a nuclear family, then he will tend to duplicate that relationship during Libra by being content (♀♎) with one partner (♄♎). The conservation of actors in the drama must be maintained. If the child received an exorbitant amount of attention and was confused by the multiplicity of parental imagos, then he will pass from relationship to relationship (☊♎) during Libra (♅♎). If attention was withheld during Aries, the individual will either withhold his attention from his partner (♄♎), or seek a partner who withholds attention from him. It is important to stress that these mechanisms are almost always totally unconscious.

If the individual does not himself compensate for Ist House experiences, he is attracted to a partner who forces compensation (♇♂♎). Psychic parity (♆☾♎) is always maintained — subject to the same conservation laws as physics. If the individual does not meet his karma head on (♆☾♎), some carrier of the influences appears as if by magic. If his birth and subsequent attention were public knowledge (☉♃☊♎), the individual in Libra would never be satisfied with any one partner (♄♎) unless that partner were sufficiently collective (☊♎). The individual would form a partnership with the *public* (☊♂♎). This is true for most individuals in the "public eye": politicians (☉♂♅♇♎), actors (♂☿♎), actresses (♀♎), athletes (♃♎), beauties (♀♎), the wealthy (♃♄♎) and the notorious (♅♇♎). This explains the difficulty those individuals have maintaining one-to-one relationships. No other person can ever produce enough force or variety to make the individual sublimate. In forming a partnership with the public-at-large (♃☊☉♎), the assertion of the Individuality becomes inextricably connected with the collective.

Working partnerships (☉♂♄☊♎) are usually the first stage of sublimation. As the complexities of the modern world (♅♎) multiply it becomes more and more difficult for any one individual to perform virtually any task. He is forced to seek other individuals (♂☉♎) who possess the qualities which he lacks (☾♀♎). In a well-run business (♃♎), every individual is a component of the whole, although theoretically there are certain tasks which he can perform and no one else can. This situation is reciprocal. It is necessary for each individual to sublimate himself (☾☿♎) to the whole operation, while not losing track of his individual position. The person who can understand the whole (☿♀♃♎) while performing his task has an advantage over those who only comprehend their personal requirements (☉ASC♎). This is analogous to life in general. As most businesses are structured on a "pyramid" system, the further up the pyramid the individual advances the more necessary a total picture is — but the more difficult it is to achieve. As we have seen earlier, the ultimate task of Libra time is to maintain individuality in collective situations, always differentiating between and combining the two. This is appropriate to the Libran symbol, the *Scales* or *Balance.* A common misinterpretation of Librans is that they desire to be or have a partner. In reality, *Libra is the relationship itself. Partnerships are tools for balancing the psyche and not ends in themselves.*

Marriage (♀☉☾♎) is a partnership subject to strict legal (♄♎) and moral (♄♎) controls. This institution regulates the formation (♀♎), maintainance (☉♃♎) and dissolution (♅♇♎) of nuclear partnerships and forces all married couples to abide by the same rules (♄♎). While this may be necessary in the larger frame of reference of a whole civilization, it unfortunately does not always recognize the re-evaluation of rôles and the necessary individuality of the participants. The higher partnership must lay stress upon the transformative effect (♇♎) and potential freedom (♅♎) of the individual within the relationship, rather than just imposing (♂☉♎) other collective rules of behaviour.

Modern movements (♅☊♇♎) such as Women's Liberation, Gay Liberation and communal marriages (♀♅♎) still sacrifice the individual (☉♎) to the collective (♇♎), whatever their 'higher' motives. The inability (♅♎) or lack of desire (♆♎) to sublimate the self (♀♎) to *any* of these structures results in confrontation with the public image (☿♎) or the law (♃♄♎); the implication that one is an Enemy of the Collective. Obviously Socialism, Communism, Facism and Democracy are paragons of this last attitude.

> "It is perfectly natural, for example, that Marxism and Fascism must lead to the establishment of two types of historical existence: that of the leader (the only 'free' man) and that of the followers, who find, in the historical existence of the leader, not an archetype of their own existence but the lawgiver of the gestures that are provisionally permitted them." [61]

[61] See Mircea Eliade, *The Myth of the Eternal Return,* p. 157.

This situation is a direct embodiment of the oppostion between Aries and Libra.

VIIIth House - SCORPIO
The Scorpion
Fixed Water Sign
42 years until Death

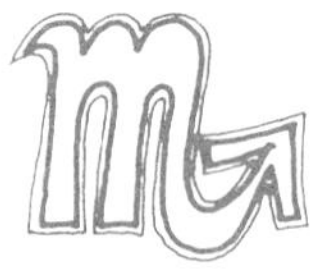

Figure V.34 The Glyph of Scorpio.

Scorpio governs *life processes, death, karma, regeneration, occultism, astrology, survival, legacies, shared resources, passionate sexuality* and *perversity.* Scorpio is opposite the Taurus time and, as Taurus determined contact with the physical world, Scorpio indicates the necessity of eventually *withdrawing from the physical world altogether* (ASC☉♏) in preparation for death (♇♏). To the extent that the individual established an identification with body and possessions in Taurus, this time governs his ability to accept the ultimate ineradicable loss. If the physical reality is overvalued (♃♏), the quality of death reflects and exaggerates the inability (♄♏) and unwillingness (♆♏) to relinquish the body. If the physical reality is properly understood (☿♏) the transition (♇♏) will be commensurably less difficult. (It actually is for some individuals!)

As the first water sign Cancer is an emotional response to the creation of a personality within the family, its higher octave Scorpio is the *emotional response to the ability to create a Soul* (☾♏). The Soul is an image of eternity which enters life at conception and returns to the infinite at death. It is a symbol of the *unus mundus* and the vehicle which allows the individual to become universal. In Egyptian burial rituals the *ka* (soul) of the deceased was guided to the infinite so it would not remain lost in the earthly world.[62] The following fragment describes the soul during resurrection, and is attributed to Petrus Bonus:

> "Because our soul was generated on the horizon of eternity, before it united with the body . . . in the resurrection *coniunctio* the body will become wholly spiritual, as will the soul itself; and they will become one, just as when water blends with water and will thenceforth never more separate in eternity."[63]

[62] The origin of "wandering souls" and "ghosts".

[63] von Franz, *Number and Time,* p. 290.

There are Egyptian and Chinese legends of the soul returning to the stars after completing the journey through the signs of the zodiac.

If the individual in Scorpio has not extended his reality beyond the limitations of matter (♄♏), suffering (☾♆♏) and punishment (♂♄♇♏) ensue at death. The weighing of souls (☿♏) by Osiris, the judge of the dead (♃♏), symbolized such a process, and if the soul of the deceased was impure (♇♏), it was passed to adjacent monsters to be eaten (☊♏). The *Divine Comedy* of Dante is also a symbolic description of the descent and ascent of the soul of the pilgrim. Scorpio governs the many methods of liberation (♄♇♏) and the equivalent dangers (♂♇♏) inherent in the failure to liberate (♄♏) before the end of the life.

During Scorpio the accumulation of actions which have not been "paid for" during life come back to the individual at last. Issues which have been suppressed (♄♏) or avoided (♆♏) for the entire lifetime are evoked in old age and take their toll. The occult and astrology are Scorpionic as they present the individual with aspects of himself which formerly were hidden (☉☾♆♏), and provide techniques for confronting them. Unless steps are taken throughout life to resolve *karmic debts* (♄ ♏) — the resultant effects of the actions of a lifetime — the end of life will be quite difficult (♂ ♄ ♅ ♇ ♏). For then the individual must balance himself at the time when he has the least energy and desire to do so. The *individual must be conscious of the need to give his essence and body back to the universe* just as he received them at the beginning of life.

As Taurus governs one's own possessions, energies and emotions, Scorpio governs the twilight of life when one is totally dependent upon the energy (☉♏), possessions (♂ ♄ ♏) and emotions (☾♏) of others. The Biblical "as ye give so shall ye receive" is appropriate. Scorpio qualities indicate this principle of dependency: either acceptance (☿♏) or the frustration of non-acceptance (♄ ♏). The perversions (♀ ♂ ♆ ♏) occasionally associated with Scorpio grow from recognition of the inability to possess personality (ASC ♏), power (☉♂ ♇ ♏) or objects (♀ ♄ ♏). The metaphysics (♄♏) of all early religions, primitive Christianity and even the Alchemists were geared to this impasse which affects everyone, but this has been neglected in the modern world in favour of its opposite pole, materialism. *The Infinite cannot be possessed.*

*The following four signs and houses operate on two simultaneous levels, as in our analysis of the logarithmic cylinder of the lifetime. Therefore they are identified both in relation to their relevance during the Gestation Octave — when all influences are received through the medium of the mother — and also in the Transcendent Octave — a higher reflection or reverberation of Gestation. In all horoscopes the process of gestation is a prototype of later developments, and usually only the context must be altered to yield accurate images of the higher mind derived from mother. The events of the Gestation Octave are connected to the Transcendent Octave not by cause and effect, but by an **equivalence of meaning.***

IXth House — SAGITTARIUS
The Centaur-Archer
Mutable Fire Sign
Conception until 7 weeks after Conception

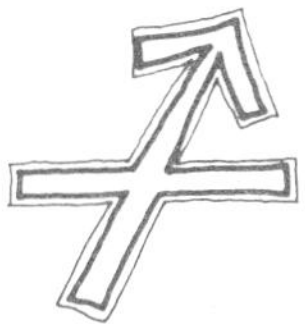

Figure V.35 The Glyph of Sagittarius.

Sagittarius governs *higher mind, meditation, philosophy, psychology, religion, foreign affairs, initiation, self-realization* and *long journeys.* As the first fire sign Aries is the assertion of Self, and the second fire sign Leo is the exteriorization of Self, Sagittarius is the *Realization of Self.* As the opposite Gemini is instinctive communication, Sagittarius is meditative access to the centre of the self.

The time scale begins with one lunar month — the lifetime of the ovum — after Conception. The scale of time during this month is so rapid that it is in fact a microcosm of the entire life. The cell divisions of the fertilized ovum create a pattern within a *molecular* scale of time which expands throughout the *cellular* scale of the lifetime. The first month sees the ovum pass through fish, reptile and other prehuman stages of evolution while attached to the uterine wall of the mother. At the end of the first lunar month, the *human development begins and the logarithmic time scale starts.*[64]

While the bodily functions of the embryo are being formed, impulses are received by the mother which reflect the process, but they are almost totally unconscious. The ovum forms itself into three spiral germ-layers which are prototypes of the three main body systems. The coincidence of these systems with the enfolding of the mother's consciousness is quite vivid.

> "The three germ-layers which develop from the first multiplication of cells fold around upon each other. From the germ-layer forming the inner coil (entoderm) develop the functions connected with the first three glands, namely, growth, digestion and respiration; from the germ-layer forming the middle coil (mesoderm) develop the functions connected with the next three, namely, blood circulation, involuntary and voluntary movement; from the

[64] Collin, *The Theory of Celestial Influence,* p. 162.

germ-layer forming the outer coil (ectoderm) develop the functions connected with the last three, namely, mind, emotion and reproduction."[65]

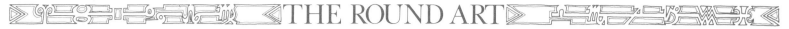

[65] Collin, *The Theory of Celestial Influence,* p. 140.

By one lunar month the nervous, muscular, vascular, digestive and skeletal systems are operative, the mouth opens, the liver begins functioning, and the embryo becomes a foetus.[66] By seven weeks after Conception, the end of Sagittarius, the foetus lives in the amniotic fluid and possesses all the human systems. Its sex has been determined and the face is fully human.

[66] Rugh and Shettles, *From Conception to Birth,* p. 41.

During this first seven weeks of pregnancy, the mother is usually not aware (♆ ♐) that she is pregnant. (38 days is the very earliest this can be felt.) She is undergoing hormonal changes (☽ ♀ ♐) and a transformation in viewpoint (☿ ♐) which are only gradually recognized. This unconsciousness during the most sensitive time of gestation allows the developing foetus to grow with a minimum of conscious influence from the mother. One could almost say that the purity of the initial development excludes the mother until the embryo has become strong enough to accept her consciousness. The mother receives extremely sensitive communications from the foetus (☽ ♀ ♆ ♐), but initially does not know to what to attribute them (♆ ♄ ♐). They emanate from inside her but have no definition. Her attitude (☉ ☿ ♐) becomes oriented towards discovering her position within her family (☽ ♐) and the world at large (♇ ☊ ♐). She feels unidentifiable impulses which change her consciousness (☉ ♐) and attitudes (☿ ♐), and she feels peculiar (♆ ♐). Sexual drives (♂ ♐) fluctuate between total chastity (♄ ♐) and wanton desire (♂ ♐), seemingly without motive. The mother's ability to read all of these clues of the coming of her child are relevant to the philosophical aspirations (♃ ♐) of the child. This sets the scene for a definite recognition of the child's existence at the end of Sagittarius.

In trying to 'place' herself within her universe, the mother is responding to the parallel attempt of the foetus to orient itself within the womb (☿ ♐). The quality and temper of the mother's awareness (☉ ♐) and sensitivity (☽ ♐) during this time is a gauge of the quality of the life of her child. As for the mother's psychology (☽ ♐), she experiences the higher octave of *her own gestation octave.* The conception moment is a metaphor for the 'death' of her previous state, and a rebirth (♃ ♐) into a new state, requiring a total re-evaluation. It is a foreign experience to her even if she has already had children and she feels that it is coming from "somewhere else" — anywhere, except from within her. She relives her own gestation and has the option of making a transcendent reality of the process. If she responds at the higher level, then her child will be oriented towards the awareness which characterizes Sagittarius (☿ ♃ ♐). If the process is totally instinctual (☽ ♐) and mechanical (♄ ♐), her offspring will reflect that instead. The mother's attitude towards herself before she realizes that she is pregnant, represents the child's abilities to understand himself philosophically (☉ ♐) later in his life.

The mother unconsciously experiences the evolution of these functions within her body and psyche, and the eventual development of the child mirrors her ability to abandon herself to those inner perceptions. The Sagittarian time ends when the mother recognizes that she is pregnant and becomes conscious of the fact. The MC represents the Ego of the child at the moment when this realization happens. In the East, it is believed that the Ego enters the body 49 days after conception, which corresponds to our timing.

On the Transcendent Level the sign and house of Sagittarius indicate the rebirth of the individual (♇ ♐) upon gaining a soul. The process the mother experiences during gestation is mirrored in the *Initiation Process.* The individual must undergo initiation in order to pass through the death moment (shock point) at the end of Scorpio.

Originally initiation was the transition from youth to adulthood in ancient societies, or the transition from the personal life of childhood to the collective life of the tribe. Initiation happened (and still does in certain areas of Africa, South America, Asia, Australia and the Southwestern United States) at puberty. It is the induction of the child into the mysteries of the tribe. As Mircea Eliade points out, there were mysteries for females and for males, corresponding to the two levels of the Sagittarian time.

The young child was stripped of childhood's clothing, name, identification marks (hair styles, painting on the body and markings of other sorts), possessions and toys. He was forcibly removed from his parents' home and experienced trials of survival in the wilds, in caves, or in the desert. During his trials he was required to prove his manhood by performing real or symbolic acts — killing violent totem animals (bears, wolves, lions, etc.); experiencing severe pain (exposure, ritual torture, whipping, suspension, drugged states or isolation); or performing acts of bravery to be expected of him when he matured. In some instances he was ritually mock-murdered, physically injured, drugged with poisons or buried alive in coffins or caves for days. The intent of these tests was to force the initiate to recognize the temporal nature of the body.

Upon successful completion of the trials, the initiate was then instructed by priests, magicians or shamans in the cosmology (♅ ♐) and rituals (☉ ♐) which were essential to the survival and well-being of the tribe. After assimilating the teachings, the initiate was ritually marked, given a new name, and reborn into the tribe. Examples of this are numerous — the Egyptians, the Mithraic cults, the Babylonians, Shamans, the Greek cults of Dionysius, Hercules and the oracular deities, Buddhists, Hindus, Aztecs, Mayans, and the Christian initiation.

The women had their own initiations (☾ ♀ ♐) which were connected with the procreative process. They underwent similar rituals involving pain, isolation and stigmatism. The equivalent to the initiatory circumcision for men was a ritual cutting of the feminine genitals at puberty. The women's mysteries were an outgrowth of the taboo associated with menstruation. Women were often sent away to be alone during their period, and the first occurrence of the menstrual blood was attended by an initiation. This concerned not only the menstrual myths, but the mysteries of conception and gestation.[67]

A surviving example of initiation is Christian Ritual, where the sacrifice and rebirth of Jesus are celebrated through the transformation symbolism of the Mass.[68] Initiation can have many alternatives, and all of them have one quality in common: *they force the individual to extend his reality beyond the physical body and experience death during life.* Although almost all ancient traditions have been lost or perverted beyond recall, in our times the initiation may be accomplished in many ways.

Through psychology (☉ ♃ ♐) or psychotherapy (☿ ♃ ♐) the primal experiences of birth and death are relived within controlled circumstances.[69] Accidents (♅ ♐) or near-death through operations can produce the shock necessary. Psychedelic drugs or plants (♆ ♐) can also key off the process.[70] It can happen through traumatic emotional, intellectual or physical events or crises. The actor who is able totally to abandon his own personality in creating a character is experiencing the process, unconsciously or consciously.[71] The historian who lives in the past pursuing his studies is also forced to recognize that his "real" life is being transcended. Anyone who, even momentarily, eradicates his identity and experiences the consequent feeling of death and its terrors has at least glimpsed the transcendent world. Awareness of death is necessary to circumambulate the periphery of the Self and its analogous horoscope circle.

Psychology, philosophy and religion are implicit in the idea of initiation. Psychology (☉ ♅ ♐) is knowledge of the nature of the psyche which allows the individual to comprehend the Self. Philosophy (☉ ♃ ☿ ♐) is the study of knowledge which leads to speculation concerning the death and rebirth of the Self through the analogy of ideas. Religion (♃ ♐) is "linking back" through life and history to the beginning via ritual. Comprehension by the mother through the Sagittarian stage of gestation from any of these viewpoints leads to a dominance of those attitudes throughout the life of the child.

[67] See Eliade, *Myths, Dreams and Mysteries,* Chapters VII and VIII, and Esther Harding, *Women's Mysteries.*

[68] Jung, *Psychology and Religion: West and East, CW 11, "The Transformation Symbolism of the Mass".*

[69] See R. D. Laing; Arthur Janov; Elizabeth Fehr; Esalen; etc.

[70] Huxley, *Heaven and Hell;* Leary and Alpert, translation of *The Tibetan Book of the Dead.*

[71] See *"A Double Life",* the film starring Ronald Coleman.

Xth House — CAPRICORN
The Goat-Fish
Cardinal Earth Sign
7 weeks until 12 weeks After Conception

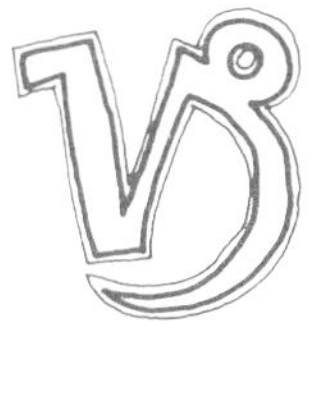

Figure V.36 The Glyph of Capricorn.

Capricorn governs *perfected matter, crystallization, concrete relationships, organization, the father, the public, fame and fortune, ambition, aspirations* and *pragmatism.* The *Midheaven (MC)* indicates the ego, ego-consciousness, the individual nature, desire and the life-force, and coincides with the cusp of the Xth house. As Taurus is undifferentiated matter and Virgo is differentiated matter, Capricorn is *perfected matter.* Its opposite Cancer governs

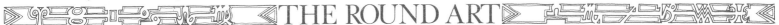

the mother, the home and the manipulation of the father, and so Capricorn governs the father, the outside world and the manipulation of the mother.

Capricorn is the natural position of the MC and is the strongest house position in the horoscope. The MC is the dividing line between the individual (left) and collective (right) hemispheres in the horoscope and is the integrator between them, as the Ascendant was the mediator between the Conscious and Unconscious hemispheres. The actual position of the MC is rarely vertical, so the side of the horoscope in which it falls is an indication of the orientation towards altruism of the Sagittarian side and ambition on the Capricornian side. The Ego and the MC register about seven weeks after Conception, at the moment when the mother becomes conscious of actually carrying a child (☿ ♑). The nature and qualities of the Ego of the child are directly determined by the nature of that moment, and the Xth house of Capricorn reflects the repercussions of this realization.

The mother can realize her pregnancy in a variety of ways, and they directly affect the child's Ego and objectives in life. The mother can *sense* the existence of the child, producing a materialistic reality in the child (earth sign MC). She can *think* she is pregnant and be confirmed (air sign MC); *intuit* a change in energy which leads to verification (fire sign MC); or *feel* that she is pregnant (water sign MC). The element on the MC of the child's horoscope indicates the psychological type which governs his Ego. The sign of the MC further qualifies the nature of the Ego and the response of the mother to the pregnancy. The exact sign on the MC evokes the archetypal characteristics of the stage of life indicated.

The Ego is determined by the initial *attitude* (☾ ☿ ♑) of the mother, the reaction when she informs others — particularly the father — and all repercussions of this process. The degree of acceptance and the blending of attitudes indicates the degree of acceptance of the Ego by the individual during his life. If there is a difficulty accepting the pregnancy (☾ ♄ ♆ ♑), the child unconsciously fights his destiny (♄ ♑). Those to whom the mother first confides are personified facets of the objectives of the child. The reactions of other individuals to the pregnancy indicate the responses the individual will receive to his desire to assert his Ego. In the horoscope, individuals affecting this time are indicated by planets either near the MC or in aspect to the MC.

The Ego includes all *projections* upon the child-to-be in respect of gender (♀ ♂ ♑), predominance of parental genetic characteristics (☉ ☾ ♑), character (ASC), position in the world (☉ ♑), intelligence (☿ ♑), appearance and destiny. Although these notions are usually quite inflated, the individual is eventually affected by them later in his life. (It is well-known that Napoleon's parents realized at his birth that he would become the Emperor of the World, which Napoleon himself later verified.) Napoleon had Sun in the Xth house. The individual reflects these projections even if his actual life does not seem to verify them. (Walter Mitty!) Strong reactions to the pregnancy produce a strong Ego; weak or nonexistent reactions have the opposite effect.

During this time many critical physiological changes are evident — the determination and primary formation of the sex glands in the foetus, the formation of the cerebrum and the neocortex,[72] the operation of the pancreas, the teeth and skeleton. As parts of the body correspond to astrological signs (See the Tables of Correspondences, Part VI, pages 136-161), they are influenced directly during their development by the psychology and physiology of the mother. The standard medical view is that there is absolutely no affect of the mother upon the child's development in the womb and vice versa, which is obviously ridiculous.[73]

As Capricorn governs the father (☉ ♑), he has a critical effect during the process by supporting the mother (☾ ♑), making financial arrangements (♄ ♑), selecting doctors and nurses (♂ ♄ ♑), finding space for the child in the home (♀ ♑), caring for the welfare of the mother and disseminating knowledge of coming birth to the world. The specific response of the father to the knowledge that he will be having a child, and his ability to solve practical matters (♄ ♑) during this time, determines the child's ability to make a place for himself in the physical world when he matures. If the parents keep the knowledge to themselves (♅ ♆ ♑), the individual will feel it difficult to make an impression in the world. If they broadcast the fact to everyone (♃ ☉ ☿ ♇ ♑), the likelihood is that the individual will be well-known. The way in which parental projections are received influences the way the individual's objectives will be eventually received. Complete protection (☉ ♑) or isolation (♄ ♑) of the mother produces equivalent qualities. If the parents are bound by religious (♃ ♑) or cultural (♀ ☊ ♑) rules to

[72] Sagan, *The Dragons of Eden.*

[73] Rugh and Shettles, *From Conception to Birth*, p. 54.

proceed in certain prescribed ways, the controls will be transmitted.

On the transcendent level, the registration of the MC is equivalent to the recognition that an initiation has actually happened (♅ ♃ ♑). The situation is central to Zen Buddhism, where the initiate has the requisite experiences, but must accept that he knows. In Zen this realization is often transmitted by paradoxes or through shocks like the well-known slaps administered by the masters. Since it is a purely internal process only confrontation with the "reality" of the process can ground its existence. The ego must be integrated into the whole and accepted as a determinant without being the only determinant. The parents must have the "right attitude" to the process — neither too dominant (☉ ♂ ♄ ♑) nor too passive (☽ ♀ ♆ ♑). The images (♀ ♑), beliefs (♃ ♑) and ideals (♃ ♑) of the parents are felt by the developing foetus, but the final test is whether the individual can later see that the parents acted consistently with their parental imagos. The tendency is to blame parents for situations which affect the psyche of the individual, but they must also be understood as primary carriers of archetypal information. This is the application of the transcendental reality to actual behaviour in the life of the individual.

XIth House — AQUARIUS
The Waterbearer or Watersnake
Fixed Air Sign
12 weeks until 23 weeks after Conception

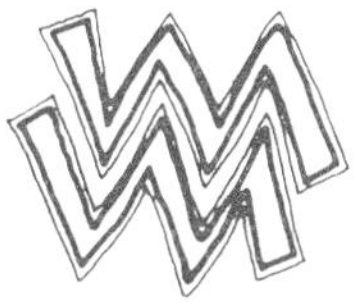

Figure V.37 The Glyph of Aquarius.

Aquarius governs *humanitarianism, altruism, selflessness, idealism, planning, wishes, plotting, ideal and group relationships, abstraction, coldness, social matters, friendships* and *friends.* The first air sign, Gemini, governs instinctive mind, the second air sign Libra governs partnerships, and the last air sign Aquarius governs *idealistic relationships.* Leo, the opposite of Aquarius, is related to the exteriorization of the Self, and is egocentric, while Aquarius is impersonal, altruistic and humanitarian.

At approximately 19 weeks after conception the respiration and involuntary movement systems are functional (☿ ♒). This signals the quickening of the foetus — the first movement. The reality of a child at this stage is investigated by Professor Liley in this extract from the *International Herald Tribune,* 5 November 1975:

> "The womb is neither the dark nor silent place which most of us imagine. The process of learning to suck, to drink, to use the lungs and limbs begins in the womb, in one environment, in preparation for emergence into another environment when born. The unborn child is responsive to pain and touch and cold and sound and light. He drinks the amniotic fluid more if it is artificially sweetened, less if it is given an unpleasant taste. He gets hiccups, and sucks his thumb. He wakes and sleeps. He gets bored with repetitive signals but can be taught to be alerted by a first signal for a different one."[74]

[74] Liley, *International Herald Tribune,* 5 November 1975, p.5.

After the parents have organized the physical environment (♄ ♒), the mother is allowed freedom of time (♃ ♒). She is liberated from most physical exertion and has a period of about ten weeks to herself while she is still mobile.

This time is usually altruistic (♃ ♒) and idealistic (♃ ♅ ♒). The mother is in a unique situation (♅ ♒) with respect to everyone else. It is a rare time in a woman's life because her drives to procreate or to have intimate relationships based upon sexual needs are already satisfied. Her activities are centred around the unborn child (☽ ☿ ♒). She is attracted to other women (♀ ♒) who have undergone similar experiences, who share her ideals (♃ ♒), or who are receptive listeners (☽ ☿ ♒). She continuously plans her own life and her child's (☿ ASC ♒), but only in general terms. Most of her energies are concentrated (♄ ♒) inside herself. She feels that she should continue to function normally in the family and world, but she is also distinctly different. She is concerned with the *idea of life* — this attitude is characteristically Aquarian.

The Ideals that the mother holds during this time (♃ ♆ ♒) determine the ideals of the individual. Her plans (☿ ♒) and projections (♆ ♒) become the plans of the child, as does the process of planning. The mother's interest in group situations (☊☉♒) reflects her interest in alternate points of view (♅♒), and this determines the *breadth of viewpoint* of the individual and his ability to confront multiple relationships (☉☊☽♒).

On the transcendent level, Aquarius indicates the process after the individual has applied and integrated his higher perceptions into the practical structure of his life during Capricorn. In Capricorn the higher realities are predominant, and in Aquarius *principles* (♃♒) are everything. The ability to renounce personal and selfish motives in favour of group realities, and to give totally to the group, are indicated by the behaviour of the mother during Aquarius time.

Aquarius relationships are more of community interest (☊♒) than self-oriented exchanges. The individual attempts to live his "ideal". The degree to which he looks towards collective values to formulate his ideal, or support to act it out, is determined in gestation. Innovations, utopian lifestyles, communities and inventive social systems are all (♅♒) produced when the individual tries to affect the collective without actually relinquishing his individual values.

The choice of methods of approach is critical in the present *"Aquarian Age".* The danger is that collective realities (♇♒) will totally annihilate the individual, as he is already well devalued. The Aquarian Age espouses humanitarian ideals (♃♒) of goodness and light, but that is only one side of Aquarius.

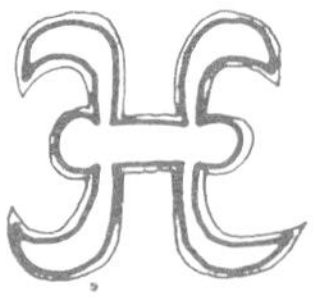

Figure V.38 The Glyph of Pisces.

XIIth House — PISCES
The Fishes
Mutable Water Sign
22 weeks After Conception until Birth

Pisces governs *self-sacrifice, seclusion, loneliness, extreme receptivity, subjection to external influences (drugs, alcohol, etc.), mediumship and the psychic world, extra-sensory perception, karma, debts of destiny, escapism, institutions* and *inertia.* The first water sign Cancer is the emotional response to the creation of a personality, the second water sign Scorpio is the emotional response to the creation of a Soul, and Pisces is the response to the ability to create a child on the lower octave and a transcendent reality on the higher octave. The opposite of Pisces is Virgo, which implies discrimination and choices, while Pisces is indiscriminative (☿♓) and totally subject to outside influences (♆♓). The contents of the gestation period are collected in Pisces, as well as the contents from the entire cycle of signs and houses. Jesus Christ — closely associated with the Piscean Age (approx. 1 AD until 2000 AD) — exemplified this doctrine by taking the sins of the world upon himself.

During this time the mother is at her most vulnerable and extremely receptive to external influences (☽♓). The child begins to gain bulk and the mother gains enough weight to hinder her mobility (☽♃♓). The increase in water content increases her sensitivity (☿♆♓) to lunar cycles, which produces an emotional orientation (♀☽♓) and makes her more aware (☿♓) of her restricted situation (♄♓). Her reality becomes introverted (♄♓) as she is restricted to less and less activity and travel. The contraction combines with the increased water content to produce a gradual *dissolution of the outside world* (♆♓). The child's increased activity (☿♓) is inversely proportional to the immobility of the mother (☽♄♓) and parallels an increase (♃♓) in psychic contact between child and mother (♆♓).

The mother during this time gradually relinquishes control over external situations: her outside contacts (☊♓), her active position within the family (☽♓) and sexual contact with her husband (♂♀♓). She becomes successively more reliant upon others (☽♃♓), until towards the very end of gestation she is almost as helpless (♄♆♓) as the child she will bear. Her entire system becomes attuned to the requirements of the child, reflected in introversion and the feelings it invokes.

As her reality becomes more concentrated (♄♓), she becomes highly influenced by dreams and psychic projections (☽♆♓) emanating from the inner world of the child. She has contact with doctors (♄♂♓), midwives (☽♓) or natural childbirth instructors (☿♓) who try to condition her to childbirth. She is subjected to examinations (☿♓); restrictions (♄♓); visits to hospital (♆ ⌗). According to the method of childbirth, she is treated either very impersonally or very sensitively. Her reactions to the type of treatment she receives indicates the ability of the child to respond to external pressures. If the mother accepts natural childbirth, she will retain awareness through the birth.

Individuals in her environment become protective of her during this time and she is carefully monitored. This time should be glorious and expansive (♃ ⌗), although there often is a reciprocal feeling of loneliness and isolation (☉ ☽ ☿ ♄ ♆ ⌗). The ability of the mother to maintain her composure and sense of humour as well as to accept her disconnection from others is critical. She must be willing to sacrifice herself (☽ ⌗) to her child and to make a close unconscious bond with him.

There is always a conservation of psychic energy: as the unborn child comes closer to consciousness in birth, the mother comes closer to her unconscious. The critical point for the mother is to find the finest possible level of reality and balance. She will realize at the moment of birth, even though there will be many others present, that she alone will undergo the process with the child. When it is totally up to her, as it should be, the timing is instinctive. More frequently in recent times the doctor controls the time and manner of the birth (♄ ♆ ⌗). The free will of the mother to allow the birth to happen naturally is substantially affected and possibly subverted. Natural childbirth occurs when the mother and the child are the only criteria. The ability of the mother to find support and security in her family, from her husband and friends — to feel secure for the critical time of birth — is paramount.

Astrologically the last ten degrees of the XIIth house above the Ascendant are included in the personality. (Figure V.39) This is the last six weeks of gestation and represents hidden components of the personality of the child (ASC ⌗). The behaviour of the mother during this time indicates the ability of the child to deal with crises by himself during his future life. Optimally the environment gells around the mother as birth approaches, providing her with the perfect context for the birth. Individuals in her environment should be subservient to her in order to allow her to remain in touch with her inner, instinctual nature.

As the day of the birth approaches, the most critical factor in determining the personality of the child is the *time* during the day when the mother is at her most relaxed. There is a known correlation between moments of relaxation and the expansion and dilation of the cervix. The most prevalent natural time of birth is just before sunrise, when the rhythms of nature are at their slowest and when sleep is deepest. Births at this time have the active participation of the Sun, as it is close to the horizon. Ideally, the child is the selector of the birth moment and transmits appropriate signals to the mother, and she should be as receptive as possible to these signals. Any external pressures (♂♀⌗), practical requirements (♄ ⌗) or psychological forces (♆ ⌗) affecting her during this time can directly alter (♀ ⌗) or even sever (♅ ⌗) the intimacy between her and her child.

When the choice of time does not rest with the child and mother at all, the personality of the child and the quality of the birth itself will be forced and uncomfortable. The standard procedure in most hospitals is for the mother to be separated (♄ ⌗) from all but her husband (if he is allowed to be with her), placed in a barren "preparation room", and given a glucose drip in her arm to hasten labour. If the mother is anaesthetized (♆ ⌗), she is not even aware that the birth is happening, and if only a local anaesthetic is used, she will be vaguely aware. In either case the child will not be able to make connection with her as the anaesthetic affects him as well.

Many doctors and psychologists are realizing that birth has a profound effect upon the individual. Since our society — virtually under total control of the medical profession anyway — has chosen to depersonalize the birth process for the sake of "safety" and convenience, they subsequently depersonalize the entire population.[75] Doctors believe they should have choice of time, place and method of delivery, totally ignoring the sublime natural process which has operated perfectly well since the creation of the human species. The minimal risk to the child or mother seems to have been exaggerated in favour of programming and mechanizing the population at large.

Psychological damage at birth is extremely difficult to remedy later in life, and the bewildering range of psychotherapies which either directly or indirectly attempt to resolve "birth traumas" (♂ ♅ ♀ ASC ⌗) are indicative of the situation.[76] The *Primal Scream* therapy of Ar-

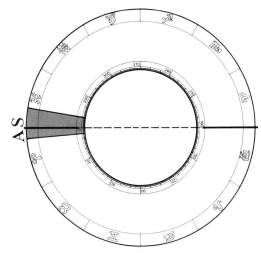

Figure V.39 The Zone of Influence of the Ascendant.

[75] See the works of Laing and Leboyer.

[76] See Part IX, The Reading, under "Psychoanalysis and the Time Scale".

thur Janov and the *Rebirthing* of Elizabeth Fehr concern themselves with the birth moment, but often can only approximate the conditions affecting the child and mother during birth. The 'cure' often happens within the same disoriented context as the birth itself, allowing a momentary release of tension but not a resolution of the larger issues, such as the individual's *consciousness of the experience.*

The preparation of the mother in the months leading up to the birth moment has a central significance. An understanding of the process and of breathing exercises can alleviate many fears (♂ ♄ ♇ ♓) and feelings of uncertainty (♆ ☾ ♓) in the mother and lessen the necessity of reliance upon drugs (♆ ♓) and the medical inducement of birth (♅ ♓). We seek the warmth and security of the womb throughout our lives, unconsciously or consciously, and it would be a disastrous state of affairs if even that last sacred place were not peaceful and secure. Mass paranoia is the inevitable result of depersonalized birth.

The transcendent octave of Pisces indicates Will immersed in the *Universal Solvent.* During Aquarius the individual relinquishes selfish inclinations, and in Pisces he prepares for his emergence into eternity, as the child in the womb awaits emergence into the air. Pisces governs withdrawl from life (☉ ☾ ♓), the "void" and the loneliness of old age (♄ ♓). In the far East it was traditional for people in old age to terminate their worldly attachments, to give up their families and friends, and to retire as penniless wanderer-beggars (saddhus) in the mountains. This was a symbolic giving of themselves back to nature and a recognition that they were on the verge of returning into the great womb of the universe, from which all life comes and returns.[77]

[77] See Eliade.

With the end of Pisces the circuit of the signs and houses is complete. We re-experience this entire cycle every day as the earth makes its rotation, each month when the Moon completes her cycle, and each year with the circuit of the Sun. Including the longer cycles of the further planets, this temporal matrix and all the individual permutations of it determines our lives: *it is our lives.*

The Mechanics of the Logarithmic House System

The progression through the houses gains a totally new logic when the ages of development are determined. The major advantage is that *developmental times* can be located very accurately. Due to the mathematical proportion of the logarithmic time scale, each house in sequence occupies slightly less time than the total lifetime up to the beginning of the house. Therefore, each successive logarithmic house occupies half of the lifetime by its end. This process is cumulative through life. The influences and experiences of each house period build upon the foundation of all previous houses, always in an approximate one-to-one ratio. Piaget recognized this gradual accretion in children since "the structure built at a younger stage evolves gradually into an integral part of the structure of the following stage."[78] In traditional astrology the houses are disconnected from each other and there is no such cohesiveness. Life can be seen as a linear succession of events, but in Piaget's view, as in the Author's, the events in the life only *qualify* the underlying structure; the development of *the structure is the focus.*

[78] *OPDP,* p. 16.

Jung supports this structural view through his libido concepts which define the nature of the energies which activate the process. If at any stage the energies cannot transform into the next higher level (house) through being checked or inhibited, they block the libido which then regresses.

> "Or, to be more precise, if there is an inhibition of sexuality, a regression will eventually occur in which the sexual energy flowing back from this sphere activates a function in some other (previous) sphere. In this way energy changes form."[79]

[79] Jung, *Symbols of Transformation, CW 5,* p. 158.

The inability of the individual to transform libido can force him to regress from adulthood into childlike states where the libido did have valid outlets. The more complete the blockage, the further back the focus of the energies moves until in severe psychotic states the individual regresses to before his birth, producing a catatonic or epileptic state resembling life in the womb. Likewise, as each stage yields to the next higher stage, it carries something of its previous character into the new form. The maintenance of the fluidity of the process is essential for psychic health.

A wonderful illustration of this is the way that primitive man made these transformations. His agricultural rituals during the time of the Earth Mother cults (approx. 25,000 BC until historical times) were re-enactments in the fields of the processes of procreation. Often the farmer and his wife made love among the tilled furrows before planting to ensure the fertility of the crops. In the work of tilling and sowing the seed, hunger and incest intermingled as if sperm were seed and furrows were the womb of the Great Mother. Firemaking with sticks, grinding grains with mortar and pestle, and rituals of craftsmen, were all analogous sexual acts transferred into higher realms.

The time scale as described is archetypal and general for the precise ages at which the sequence of houses registers. The choice of the Placidean system of house division resolves the transition of this *Ideal* sequence into the *Real,* because in dividing the ecliptic unequally according to divisions in time *every individual has different transition times from house to house.* The sizes of the houses in time can vary to a large extent — from half to twice the archtypal time. (Figure V.40) Some individuals develop faster than the norm during certain times of their life, while others lag behind and catch up later. The disposition of the houses in each horoscope indicates the rate of development for the individual while the sequence always remains the same. Piaget remarks:

> "the order of the periods of development is constant; one structure cannot appear before another . . . . But the age at which a stage can appear cannot be absolutely fixed, for it is always relative to the environment which may encourage, impede or even prevent its appearance."[80]

We have an advantage over Piaget because the ages of transition can be determined without first-hand knowledge of the environment.

The major complaint about the Placidean house system is resolved by the use of the Logarithmic Time Scale. The Placidean house system becomes distorted from equal houses as the location moves north or south of the equator. Certain houses become more than twice their normal 30° size, while others in the same horoscope contract to a third of theirs. The expanded houses often stretch over three signs and enclose one entire sign. (Figure V.41) When this occurs, the enclosed sign is said to be *Intercepted.* Since opposite houses are equal in size, a pair of signs are always intercepted. When a pair of houses expand, there are also two opposite houses elsewhere in the horoscope which contract. The further north or south of the equator, the more likelihood there is of a pair of intercepted signs within expanded houses, especially above 45° latitude. Since the sizes of the houses are not evaluated in traditional astrology, the distortion of the Placidean house system is an irrelevant factor. *In the Logarithmic Time Scale the distortion is an essential factor.*

The distortion of the houses affects the density of developmental phases in life. An expanded house in an individual's horoscope implies that the developmental phase indicated occupies more time than it would archetypally. Likewise the opposite house and time of life increases in duration. To balance this expansion, the houses in the same horoscope which compact indicate rapid developmental phases. This is seen clearly in the horoscope of Karl Marx. (Figure V.42 and Horoscope 32 in Part X.) The Ist house in his horoscope expands almost to the archetypal time of the end of the IInd house — 1 year 8 months. The young Marx spends more than twice the usual time asserting his personality in the Ist house. He therefore requires an equivalently large VIIth house (from 23 years old until his death) of sublimation and public affairs to balance this exaggerated assertive drive. As the Ist and VIIth houses expand, the IIIrd, IVth, IXth and Xth houses compact. Other examples of this phenomenon are the horoscopes of Marcel Proust (Horoscope 37 in Part X), Rasputin (Horoscope 39 in Part X), Rimiski-Korsakov (Horoscope 46 in Part X) and Queen Victoria (Horoscope 40 in Part X).

The exact locations of house cusps are determined by overlaying the transparent Logarithmic Time Scale included in this book on the horoscope to be analyzed. (Figure V.43) The Birth moment on the scale coincides with the Ascendant on the horoscope, and the ages when the cusps occur may be read off the inner circle.

For increased accuracy, a table is included in Appendix E, which shows the exact age for every five-degree increment from Conception until the cusp of the Vth house; and for every degree from the Vth house cusp to the age of 101. To use this table, each cusp is defined in degrees from the Ascendant. The degree found is then located in the table, and the equivalent age is read off. Cusps from Conception until the Ascendant are defined backwards (clockwise)

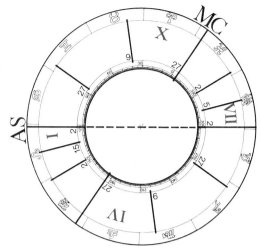

Figure V.40 House Size Variance.
Figure V.41 Interception.

[80] *OPDP,* p. 16.

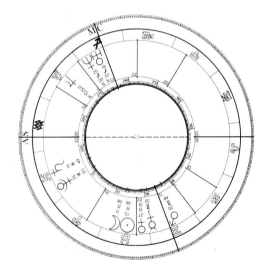

Figure V.42 The House Divisions of Karl Marx.

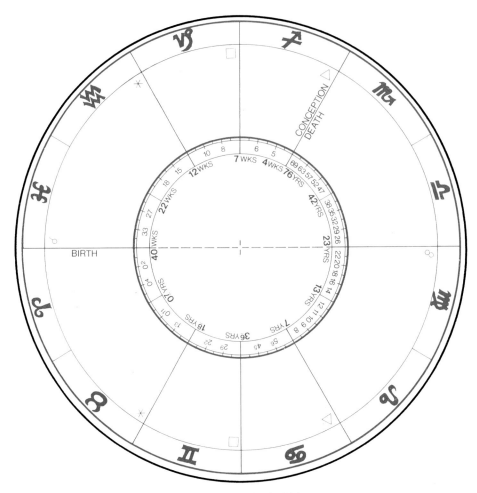

Figure V.43 The Logarithmic Time Scale Disk

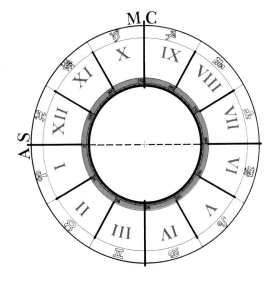

Figure V.44 Degrees of the House Cusps.

from the Ascendant. Thus the archetypal Conception point is 240° (−120°), the archetypal MC (Xth house cusp) is 270° (−90°), and the Ascendant is 360° (0°). The complete list of archetypal house cusps related to degrees from the Ascendant is as follows: (Figure V.44)

House Cusp	Sign	Degree	Archetypal Logarithmic Scale Ages
IX (Conception)	Sagittarius	240°	Conception (40 weeks before Birth)
X (MC)	Capricorn	270°	7 weeks after Conception (33 weeks before Birth)
XI	Aquarius	300°	12 weeks after Conception (28 weeks before Birth)
XII	Pisces	330°	22 weeks after Conception (18 weeks before Birth
I (ASC-Birth)	Aries	360° (0°)	Birth
II	Taurus	30°	0 years 7 months
III	Gemini	60°	1 year 8 months
IV	Cancer	90°	3 years 6 months
V	Leo	120°	6 years 10 months
VI	Virgo	150°	12 years 10 months
VII	Libra	180°	23 years 5 months
VIII	Scorpio	210°	42 years 3 months
IX (Death)	Sagittarius	240°	75 years 11 months (Death)

The locations of the house cusps in the horoscope of Carl Jung (Figure V.45 and Horoscope 25 in Part X) are as follows: (The AS on the Time Scale disk is aligned with Jung's Ascendant, 0° Aquarius)

House Cusp	Sign Position	Degrees from ASC	Age
IX (Concept)	3 Sco	273°	7 weeks (33 weeks before birth)
X (MC)	28 Sco	298°	12 weeks (28 weeks before birth)
XI	18 Sag	318°	18 weeks (22 weeks before birth)
XII	6 Cap	336°	24 weeks (16 weeks before birth)
(I (ASC)	00 Aqu	0°	Birth
II	23 Pis	53°	1 year, 5 months
III	3 Tau	93°	1 year, 11 months
IV	28 Tau	118°	6 years, 10 months
V	18 Gem	138°	10 years
VI	6 Can	156°	14 years, 6 months
VII	00 Leo	180°	23 years, 5 months (always the same age)
VIII	23 Vir	233°	66 years, 3 months
IX (Death)	3 Sco	273°	—

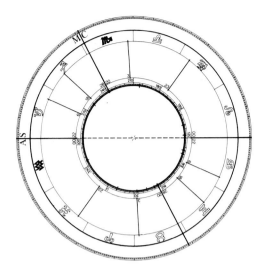

Figure V.45 Jung's House Cusps

The Ascendant is always the time of birth, and the cusp of the VIIth house is always the age of 23 years old. However the houses in the lower half of the horoscope distort, all individuals resynchronize at 23. The Ascendant-Descendant axis (the horizon) is the only reference which never changes.

To determine ages during gestation, the figure — determined by either the Time Scale disk or the table — refers to the age after conception in an archetypal individual. The ages of these house cusps must be calculated by subtracting them from the usual 40 week gestation period. The IXth house cusp in Jung's horoscope coincides with the archetypal MC, which is 7 weeks after conception (40 − 7 = 33 weeks before birth).

All of the house cusp times derived from the horoscope are accurate and verifiable except the IXth house cusp indicating the death moment. Because an individual may die at any time during the entire horoscope circle, the positions of all cusps are nevertheless indicated. *The time of the death moment is not to be taken literally.* Conception and death — the beginning and end of life — are the most complex events in life, and they are both very difficult to predetermine. Their causes involve the whole, and as such cannot be indicated by parts of the whole *unless all the parts agree.*

In the same way that the ages of the house cusps can be found using the Logarithmic Time Scale, the ages at which the planets register can also be found. The ages of the planets in Jung's horoscope (Figure V.46) are as follows:

Planet	Sign Position	Degrees from ASC	Age
Mars	21 Sag	321°	18 weeks after Conception (22 before birth)
Saturn	24 Aqu	24°	0 years, 6 months after birth
Node	11 Ari	71°	2 years, 2 months
Neptune	3 Tau	93°	4 years, 0 months
Moon	15 Tau	105°	5 years, 0 months
Pluto	23 Tau	113°	6 years
Mercury	13 Can	163°	16 years, 8 months
Venus	17 Can	167°	18 years, 1 month
Sun	3 Leo	183°	24 years, 10 months
Uranus	14 Leo	194°	30 years, 11 months
Jupiter	23 Libra	263°	————————————(past the end of the LTS)

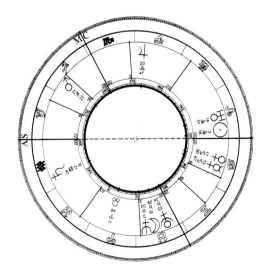

Figure V.46 Jung's Planetary positions

Occasionally planets occur in the horoscope past the known time of an individual's death. In Jung's horoscope, Jupiter in Libra is in the VIIIth house beyond the end of his lifetime. This implies that an influence exists which qualifies not only the later stages of his life, but also continues to function after his death.

Before interpreting any horoscope, the locations of the house cusps and the planets are determined by the preceding method. The enormous advantage of being able to date the elements in a horoscope is profound.

Figure VI.1

Correspondence Tables

The Correspondence Tables are the groundwork for all astrological interpretation. In the following pages of tables, a wide range of information is correlated to the planets in each of the twelve signs and houses.

In most astrological textbooks, separate tables are included for the planets in the signs and for the planets in the houses. Due to the mechanism of the Time Scale, this unnecessary duplication may be eliminated. Each pair of pages refers both to planets in the signs *and* the houses. The qualification required is the application of the metaphors given to the particular ages as found with the Time Scale. This produces a narrowing of characteristics for the individual interpretation, and also facilitates a correct view of each planetary event. If the metaphors listed for any planet in its sign are clearly off base for a required age in life, it may be assumed that the indication refers to another individual or an outside influence.

The correspondences for each sign of the zodiac include:
— Psychological Correspondences and Events.
— Historical or contemporary individuals with each planet or personal point in the sign.
— Historical or contemporary individuals with each planet or personal point in the equivalent house.
— Health Correspondences, including the Body Parts and Organs ruled by the sign and house, and the typical Diseases and Symptoms produced by each planet in the signs and houses.
— Physical Description for each ascending Face of 5°, as well as a general physical description of the sign itself when ascending.
— A set of correspondences drawn from medieval, Renaissance and modern attributions of signs to plants, animals, gods, etc.

ARIES

Aries/Ist House

The Ram

(Birth — 7 Months)

Cardinal Fire Sign	**Ruler** : Mars	**Exalted** : Sun	**Calcination**
Hieroglyph : 冈	Hebrew : ח	Greek : ε	Arabic : כ
Colour : Red	Animal : Ram, Owl	Plant : Tiger Lily	Gem : Ruby
Tarot : Emperor	Perfume : Dragon's Blood	Geomancy : Puer	Weapon : The Horns
Egyptian God : Chnoum	Roman God : Mars	Greek God : Ares	Genii : Papus

---

	Psychological Correspondences and Events	Aries Personalities
ASC ♈ Ascendant Aries/Ist House	restless environment, assertive power, ambition, ardour, quick temper, forceful speaker; rash, fanatical, independent, versatile, quarrelsome, aggressive, violent.	Rasputin, Savonarola, Douglas MacArthur, Bolivar, Janis Joplin, Steve McQueen
MC ♈ Midheaven Aries/Ist House	established individuality, awareness of objectives, ambition, confidence; precipitate, conceited, optimistic, domineering.	John I, Bismarck, John Dillinger, Goya, Rudolph Hess, John Wayne, Mae West
☉ ♈ I Sun Exalted Aries/Ist House	energy, leadership, urge to do, consciousness of objective, audacity, passion; enterprising, ruthless, bold, hasty, pompous, combative, insensitive.	Baudelaire, J.S. Bach, Charlemagne, Marlon Brando, Charles Chaplin, Max Ernst, Toscanini
☽ ♈ I Moon Aries/Ist House	will influences feeling, strong personality, lust for power, travel; impulsive, restless, primal, passionate, energetic, rebellious, independent, anarchistic.	Galileo, Henry VIII, Nietzsche, Al Capone, Marlon Brando, John Kennedy, Robespierre
☿ ♈ I Mercury Aries/Ist House	verbal aggression, repartee, quick-wit, over-work, enthusiasm, active intellect, nervousness, faux pas; observant, critical, precocious, sarcastic, eloquent, tactless.	Hitler, Khrushchev, Emile Zola, Charles Chaplin
♀ ♈ I Venus Detriment Aries/Ist House	creative power, love adventures, love at first sight, flirtations; demonstrative, ardent, generous, warm-hearted, passionate, idealistic.	Queen Victoria, Marilyn Monroe, Jean Harlow, Gloria Swanson, Isadora Duncan Shirley Temple, Christine Jorgensen
♂ ♈ I Mars Ruler Aries/Ist House	fighting spirit, ambition, destructive urge, quick temper, quarrelsome, impulsiveness; independent, domineering, adventurous, macho, brutal, irascible, courageous, insatiable, coarse.	Maximilian, Oliver Cromwell, Zola, Moshe Dayan, Douglas Fairbanks, Sam Houston, Joe Namath, Daniel Webster
♃ ♈ I Jupiter Aries/Ist House	frankness, honesty, leadership, travel; generous, optimistic, self-sufficient, speculative, aspiring, capable, ambitious, noble, adventurous.	Richard I, Amerigo Vespucci, Fidel Castro, Brahams, Jackie Gleason
♄ ♈ I Saturn Fall Aries/Ist House	ambition, diligence, endurance, selfishness, self-restraint, seriousness, defiance; reserved, unsympathetic, humourless, self-reliant, lonely, hard-hearted.	Peter the Great, Stalin, Dostoievsky, Douglas MacArthur, Lyndon Johnson, Helen Keller, Katherine Hepburn
♅ ♈ I Uranus Aries/Ist House	self-will, sudden energy, quick comprehension, fanaticism, hysteria, compulsive changes; restless, erratic, violent, utopian, reforming, original, inventive, abrupt, tactless.	Cromwell, Andrew Jackson, Verlaine, R.L. Stevenson, Sarah Bernhardt, Steve McQueen
♆ ♈ I Neptune Aries/Ist House	inspired realizations, insanity, highly sensitive, long journeys, addictions, aimlessness; unselfish, mystical, confused, intense, imaginative, uncontrolled.	Rasputin, Albert Schweitzer, Houdini, Toulouse-Lautrec
♇ ♈ I Pluto Aries/Ist House	power drive, extraordinary energy, self-assertion, rage, fury, destruction, sub-conscious urges; domineering, insatiable, compulsive, violent, maladjusted.	Nietzsche, U.S. Grant, Cromwell, Buffalo Bill Cody, Jesse James, R. L. Stevenson
☊ ♈ I Moon's Node Aries/Ist House	self-expression, wish to rule, love affairs, honours, wealth, associative urge, social success; extroverted, social, ardent, enthusiastic, organizing.	Churchill, Freud, Mao Tse-tung, Jung, James Dean, Nixon, Hess, Schweitzer, Neil Armstrong, Mae West, Jack London

ARIES

Physical Description

General Description
Lean, spare body, rather tall, strong limbs, large bones, thick shoulders, long face, sharp piercing sight, dark eye-brows, reddish and wiry hair, swarthy complexion, rather long neck.

First Face
1 – 5 degrees
Middle stature, thin, rather low, broad forehead, high cheeks, narrow chin, hooked nose, reddish or dark hair, swarthy red complexion, black eyes.

Second Face
5 – 10 degrees
Grave aspect, steady eye, not great stature, big boned, rather lean, brown or swarthy complexion, long visage, mole or mark on the face. 14th degree; good, pleasant face.

Third Face
10 – 15 degrees
Moderately lean, middle height, long visage, dark hair, grey hollow eyes, good face. Venus; oval visage.

Fourth Face
15 – 20 degrees
Middle stature, neat, well-proportioned, fresh round face, light brown hair, grey eyes. Mars; ruddy complexion. Sun; high forehead. Mercury; long face, freckled, curly hair. Uranus; dark hair.

Fifth Face
20 – 25 degrees
Middle stature, dark hair, dark skin, long face, distorted teeth, bent legs, whole body hooks forward. Mars; strongly made. Mars in Aries; hollow eyes. Saturn in Aries; hoarse voice, high forehead.

Sixth Face
25 – 30 degrees
Good stature, rather tall, austere countenance, thick eyebrows, curling black hair, wide mouth, large nose, well-set body, manly face with a scar. Uranus; long visage, large teeth, distortion.

1st House Personalities

Alexandra, Wagner, Cellini Maximilian, Maria Callas, Orson Welles

Alexandra, Machiavelli, Elizabeth Browning, Proust, Charles Chaplin, Phineas T. Barnum, Tennessee Williams

Francis Bacon, Debussy, Robert Burns, Paganini, Charles Darwin, J.J. Rousseau, Erasmus, Mark Twain, Bob Dylan

Dante, Wagner, James Joyce, Sophia Loren, Rita Hayworth, Dolly Madison, Melina Mercouri

Hemingway, Byron, John Barrymore, Daniel Boone, Custer, Sherman, Neil Armstrong, Amelia Earhart, Joe Namath, Princess Anne

Brahms, DeGaulle, Disraeli, J.P. Morgan, Michaelangelo, Elvi Presley, Errol Flynn, John Paul Jones, Burt Lancaster

MacArthur, Marx, Franco, Lenin, Lincoln, Hussein, Jung, Cezanne, Montgomery Clift, Yul Brynner

Cromwell, Isaac Newton, Balzac, Leonard Berstein

Jane Austen, Richard Burton, Fred Astaire, Isadora Duncan, Havelock Ellis, Handel, W.B. Yeats, Marilyn Monroe, E.A.Poe

Rasputin, Cesare Borgia, Goethe, Olivier, Brigitte Bardot, Judy Garland, Prince Charles

Adenauer, Al Capone, Henry Ford, M.L. King, Henry Miller, F. Scott Fitzgerald, Alexandra

Health Correspondences

Body Parts and Organs
head and brain, cerebral hemisphere, head organs, eyes, arteries of head and brain, cranium, bones of face, teeth, pineal gland, optic nerve.

Diseases and Symptoms
headaches, neuralgia, coma, trance, brain disease, cerebral haemorrhages, acne, epilepsy, migraines, toothache, smallpox, baldness, eruptions, measles, delirium, ringworm.

Sun Aries Diseases
brain fever, blood congestion, fainting, headaches, acne, insanity, hysteria.

Moon Aries Diseases
insomnia, headache, lethargy, weak eyes, convulsions, rapid pulse.

Mercury Aries Diseases
brain diseases, vertigo, spasms, nervous headaches, facial neuralgia.

Venus Aries Diseases
catarrh, mucus, kidney congestion, lethargy, head disordered by cold, swellings on face, head tumours, chin afflictions.

Mars Aries Diseases
fevers, violent headaches, sunstroke, congestion, brain inflammation, delirium, pains in the head, insomnia, eye rheums, head wounds and scars, inflammations.

Jupiter Aries Diseases
dizziness, cerebral congestion, sleepiness, thrombosis, fainting, gum ulcers, strange dreams, obesity, plethora, sanguinary fevers, boils on face.

Saturn Aries Diseases
emaciation, headache, colds, catarrh, deafness, chills, cerebral anaemia, toothache, tooth decay, tartar. fainting, skull fractures, falls.

Uranus Aries Diseases
demonical complaints, injury from lightning, electricity and explosives, acute and sporadic pains in the head, abnormal growth, eye diseases, abscesses in brain.

Neptune Aries Diseases
insanity, trances, sleep-walking, blindness, hysteria, coma, fainting, hallucinations, addictions, nightmares, obscure diseases, smallpox, sleeping sickness.

☉

☽

☿

♀

♂

♃

♄

♅

♆

♇

TAURUS

Taurus/IInd House

The Bull

(7 Months — 1 Year 8 Months)

Fixed Earth Sign	
Hieroglyph :	
Colour : Red-Orange	
Tarot : Hierophant	
Egyptian God : Osiris, Hathoor	

Ruler : Venus	
Hebrew :	
Animal : Bull	
Perfume : Storax	
Roman God : Castor & Pollux	

Exalted : Moon	
Greek :	
Plant : Mallow	
Geomancy : Amisso	
Greek God : Hera, Aphrodite	

Congelation	
Arabic :	
Gem : Topaz	
Weapon : The Labour	
Genii : Cisera	

Psychological Correspondences and Events

ASC ♉
Ascendant
Taurus/IInd House
love of beauty, harmonious environment, land, security, domesticity, obstinancy, avarice; practical, self-reliant, sensual, depressive, indulgent, dogmatic, prejudiced, egotistical, taciturn, magnetic.

MC ♉
Midheaven
Taurus/IInd House
persistent pursuit of aims, striving for security, slow development, difficult to please, strong will; tenacious, stubborn, artistic, conservative, plodding, patient.

☉ ♉ II
Sun
Taurus/IInd House
material outlook, endurance, fear of change, constancy, love of Nature and the beautiful; pleasure-loving, gentle, loyal, pragmatic, reliable, sensual, kindly, extravagant, indulgent, obstinate.

☾ ♉ II
Moon Exalted
Taurus/IInd House
constancy, deep emotions, acquisitiveness, strong maternal image, appreciation of beauty, firmness; cautious, affectionate, melancholic, easily injured, tranquil, stable, loving.

☿ ♉ II
Mercury
Taurus/IInd House
formal thinking, logic, endurance, patience, sense of form; dogmatic, acquisitive, sensible, deliberate, one-sided, thorough, ponderous, thick-headed.

♀ ♉ II
Venus Ruler
Taurus/IInd House
physical beauty, personal attraction, need to be loved, good taste, luxury; affectionate, faithful, conservative, artistic, precious, grasping, indolent, materialistic.

♂ ♉ II
Mars Detriment
Taurus/IInd House
capacity for work, practical abilities, foresight, executive ability, earning power, persistence; materialistic, acquisitive, irritable, intense, passionate, vindictive, surly, productive.

♃ ♉ II
Jupiter
Taurus/IInd House
good humour, wealth, hedonism, gluttony, comfort, trusteeship; generous, liberal, good-hearted, wasteful, over-indulgent, exploitative, jovial.

♄ ♉ II
Saturn
Taurus/IInd House
enduring energy, application of method, economy, property, security, stability, money worries; conservative, inhibited, miserly, reliable, restricted, grasping.

♅ ♉ II
Uranus Fall
Taurus/IInd House
unusual finances, gains and losses, ingenuity; resourceful, inventive, intuitive, determined, headstrong, fanatical, jealous, speculative.

♆ ♉ II
Neptune
Taurus/IInd House
form sense, good taste, speculation, ill luck, receptivity, luxury, indolence; soft-hearted, impractical, imaginative, addictable (drugs, nicotine, etc.), patient, aesthetic.

♇ ♉ II
Pluto Detriment
Taurus/IInd House
great gains and losses, dependency on money and property, acquisition, economics, finances determine destiny; exploitative, materialistic, lascivious, insatiable.

☊ ♉ II
Moon's Node
Taurus/IInd House
permanent unions, preserved alliances, affluent partners, material advantages through others; self-seeking, exploitative, devoted, loyal, reliable.

Taurus Personalities

Beethoven, George Washington, Hearst, R.F. Kennedy, Orson Welles, Jackie Gleason

Trotsky, Marcus Aurelius, Vermeer, Balzac, Albrecht Durer, Picasso

Balzac, Freud, Hearst, Hitler, Shakespeare, Brahms, Orson Welles, Rudolph Valentino

Milton, Ibsen, Proust, Marx, Edison, Garbo, Edgar Cayce, Jung, Hans Christian Anderson, Fred Astaire

Raphael, Bertrand Russell, J.P. Morgan, Robert Browning, Audubon, Lyndon Johnson, Barbra Streisand, Orson Welles

Durer, Wagner, Verlaine, W.B. Yeats, Liberace, Douglas Fairbanks, Dolly Madison, Duke of Windsor, Madeleine Grey

Marcus Aurelius, Catherine the Great, Hitler, Edison, Nureyev, Thoreau, Trotsky, Thomas Huxley

Vermeer, Christopher Wren, Howard Hughes, Frank Lloyd Wright, Phineas T. Barnum,

Benjamin Franklin, Pablo Picasso, Louis Pasteur

J.S. Bach, Beethoven, Napoleon, Van Gogh

Isadora Duncan, Herbert Hoover, Picasso, Pablo Casals, Thomas Mann

Cecil Rhodes, Stalin, Trotsky, Einstein, Herbert Hoover

Franco, Goering, Tito, Hoover, Caruso, Jean Harlow, Jackie Kennedy, Ronald Reagan, Oscar Wilde, Grace Kelly,

TAURUS

Physical Description

General Description	Short, full stout body, broad brows, large eyes, full face, thick lips, short neck, thick broad hands and shoulders, wide nose and mouth, dark curling hair, swarthy complexion.
First Face 1 – 5 degrees	Low middle stature, slightly curly black hair, swarthy complexion, dark eye-brows.
Second Face 5 – 10 degrees	Low middle stature, long face, broad forehead, full cheeks, distorted teeth, dark brown hair, swarthy complexion, stooping shoulders, melancholy appearance.
Third Face 10 – 15 degrees	Small stature, pale, swarthy complexion, small eyes, downward-looking countenance, frowning eye-brows, large forehead, thick lips, almost flat nose, thin beard, broad stooping shoulders.
Fourth Face 15 – 20 degrees	Middle stature, proportionate, pleasant oval face, chestnut hair, large forehead, grey eyes, women generally beautiful.
Fifth Face 20 – 25 degrees	Short, reddish complexion, facial eruptions, oval face, black hair, arms, hands, fingers, legs and feet rather short, fleshy body.
Sixth Face 25 – 30 degrees	Robust, square visage, brown complexion, mark or scar on face, low middle stature (5 feet 9 inches), black hair. 26th degree; eye defects, rude behaviour.

IInd House Personalities

Catherine the Great, Michaelangelo, Marx, Andrew Carnegie, Stalin, Valentino, Lyndon Johnson, Joe Kennedy, Mae West

Michaelangelo, Byron, Marx, Lenin, Aristotle Onassis, Joe Kennedy, Lyndon Johnson, Liz Taylor, Zsa Zsa Gabor

Leeuwenhoek, Leonardo da Vinci, Ralph Nader, George Lincoln Rockwell

Renoir, Vermeer, Brahms, Oscar Wilde, Trotsky, Hugh Hefner, John L. Lewis, Aristotle Onassis

Louis XIV, Machiavelli, Catherine the Great, Cesare Borgia, MacArthur, Vermeer, Edison, Ralph Nader

Raphael, Byron, Durer, Nietzsche, Toscanini, Thomas Husley, Wm. Jennings Bryan

J.S. Bach, Dickens, Caligula, Christopher Wren, Fidel Castro, Moshe Dayan, Jules Verne, Rembrandt, Huey Long, F.L. Wright

Vermeer, Byron, Liberace, Picasso, Rodin, Hearst, George Lincoln Rockwell

Isaac Newton, Amerigo Vespucci, Dostoievsky, Wren, Hans Christian Anderson

Durer, Renoir, Cellini, Nasser, Eisenhower, Adenauer, Rodin

Stalin, Coco Chanel, Walt Disney, Helen Keller, Gershwin, John L. Lewis, Bob Hope

Health Correspondences

Body Parts and Organs	neck, throat, larynx, tonsils, lower jaw, ears, lower teeth, occipital region, cerebellum, cartoid artery, jugular vein, thyroid, tongue, vocal cord, chin.
Diseases and Symptoms	goitre, diphtheria, croup, apoplexy, tonsilitis, constipation, difficult menses, cough, swollen neck glands, hoarseness, throat inflammation, laryngitis.
Sun Taurus Diseases	diphtheria, nose polyps, eye diseases (29), sore throats, croup, venereal disease, melancholia, scrofula, enlarged thyroid, swellings in neck, congestion of kidneys.
Moon Taurus Diseases	throat cancer, neck swellings, sore throat, disturbed menses, bronchitis, eye disorders (29°), genito-urinary disorders, gluttony, laryngitis, miscarriage.
Mercury Taurus Diseases	stuttering, hoarseness, deafness, nervous genito-urinary afflictions, swellings in the neck.
Venus Taurus Diseases	mumps, occipital headaches, goitre, tonsilitis, genital inflammation, swollen throat glands, throat ulcers, enlarged veins of neck.
Mars Taurus Diseases	mumps, tonsilitis, suffocation, adenoids, diphtheria, nose bleed, infected larynx, excessive menses, prostate diseases, scrofula, pains in neck, neck wounds and scars.
Jupiter Taurus Diseases	obesity, gourmandizing, apoplexy, ringworm, carbuncles, ulcerated gums, nasal catarrh, nose bleed, flatulence, spasms, illness as result of excess eating and drinking.
Saturn Taurus Diseases	phlegm, diphtheria, mumps, croup, lower tooth decay, choking, throat strictures, stiff neck, dislocated or broken neck.
Uranus Taurus Diseases	spasmodic throat disorders, disturbed thyroid, abnormal growth, wry neck, spasmodic contractions in neck, neck cramps, tetanus, hysteria.
Neptune Taurus Diseases	disorders or wasting of throat tissue, goitre, disturbed thyroid, obscure diseases of neck and throat, malformed sexual organs, septic throat, swollen tonsils.

 GEMINI

Gemini/IIIrd House The Twins

(1 Year 8 Months — 3 Years 6 Months)

Mutable Air Sign		Ruler	: Mercury	Exalted	: South Node	Fixation	
Hieroglyph	:	Hebrew	:	Greek	:	Arabic	:
Colour	: Orange	Animal	: Magpie, Hybrids	Plant	: Orchid, Hybrids	Gem	: Tourmaline
Tarot	: Lovers	Perfume	: Wormwood	Geomancy	: Albus	Weapon	: The Tripod
Egyptian God	: Twin Murti	Roman God	: Janus	Greek God	: Apollo Diviner	Genii	: Hanabi

Psychological Correspondences and Events

Gemini Personalities

ASC Ⅱ
Ascendant
Gemini/IIIrd House
quick responses, versatility, mimicry, vivaciousness; adaptable, mobile, talkative, inconstant, communicative, artistic, superficial, highly-strung, restless.

George Bernard Shaw, Voltaire, Garbo, Astaire, Audrey Hepburn, Bob Hope, Phyllis Diller, Olivier

MC Ⅱ
Midheaven
Gemini/IIIrd House
manifold aims, periodic creativity, changing goals, multiple professions; indecisive, talented, facile, unstable, dilatory, eclectic.

Oscar Wilde, Thomas Mann, Andy Warhol, Walt Disney, Marlene Dietrich, Roddy McDowell

☉ Ⅱ Ⅲ
Sun
Gemini/IIIrd House
eagerness to learn, versatility, dexterity, identity crises; articulate, educable, inquisitive, charming, unreliable, nervous, glib, pretentious, vacillating, dishonest, scintillating, dishonourable.

Durer, Stravinsky, Thomas Mann, Thomas Hardy, A. Conan Doyle, Isadora Duncan, Christine Jorgensen, Walt Whitman

☽ Ⅱ Ⅲ
Moon
Gemini/IIIrd House
manifold expressions of feeling, multiple relationships, mobile, multi-faceted, superficial loves; moody, inconstant, restless, nervous, manic-depressive, flirtatious, contradictory.

Rossini, Pablo Casals, Louis Pasteur, Jack Benny, Bette Davis, Joanne Woodward, Shirley Temple

☿ Ⅱ Ⅲ
Mercury Ruler
Gemini/IIIrd House
versatility, inquiring mind, wide reading, speaking and writing, business talent, lack of thoroughness; witty, naughty, facile, articulate, intellectual, flippant, inquisitive, clever.

Karl Marx, Emerson, W.B. Yeats, Hawthorne, Bob Dylan, Errol Flynn, Harry Truman, Rosalind Russell

♀ Ⅱ Ⅲ
Venus
Gemini/IIIrd House
charm, courtesy, sympathy, many loves, social sense; ingratiating, silly, flirtatious, superficial, attractive, flighty accommodating, adaptable, cooperative.

Henry VIII, Catherine the Great, Bob Dylan, J.F. Kennedy, Duchess of Windsor

♂ Ⅱ Ⅲ
Mars
Gemini/IIIrd House
mobility, mental energy, biting criticism, sarcasm, scattered energy, mockery; hasty, nervous, talkative, michievous, restless, quarrelsome, cynical, irreverent.

Toulouse Lautrec, Conan Doyle, Bob Hope, F.D. Roosevelt, John Barrymore, James Joyce, Amelia Earhard, Phyllis Diller

♃ Ⅱ Ⅲ
Jupiter Detriment
Gemini/IIIrd House
popularity, sociability, tact, charm, many contacts, travel; carefree, mannered, conceited, hypocritical, superficial, empty, obliging, sweet.

Jane Austen, Jackie Kennedy, Puccini, Moliere, Stravinsky, Dickens

♄ Ⅱ Ⅲ
Saturn
Gemini/IIIrd House
logic, thoroughness, serious study, conscientiousness, awkwardness, lack of adaptability, shyness; intellectual, abstract, cold, detached, studious, serious.

Dante, Francis Bacon, Sigmund Freud, Kahlil Gibran, J.Q. Adams

♅ Ⅱ Ⅲ
Uranus
Gemini/IIIrd House
quick comprehension, desultory manner, bizarre interest, short-lived pursuits, neophilia; agitated, nervous, original, sharp-witted, eccentric, scientific, restless.

Jane Austen, Paderewski, Puccini, Voltaire, A. Conan Doyle

♆ Ⅱ Ⅲ
Neptune
Gemini/IIIrd House
sensitivity, sense of humour, weak memory, whimsy; fantastical, sprightly, fey, confused, imaginative, mystical, vague, untruthful, scattered-brained, unrealistic.

Shakespeare, Haydn, Max Ernst, Bette Davis, Fred Astaire

♇ Ⅱ Ⅲ
Pluto
Gemini/IIIrd House
ingeniousness, specialized writing, plagiarism, socially ruthless, organization, oratory, mass suggestion; brilliant, witty, critical, subversive, magnetic, adventurous, hateful.

Louis XIV, Newton, William of Orange, Hemingway, Mar Ernst, Cary Grant, Alfred Hitchcock, Bob Hope

☊ Ⅱ Ⅲ
Moon's Node Exalted
Gemini/IIIrd House
multi-faceted relationships, ideas from others, cultivation of contacts, superficial associations; relatives and neighbours, shortlived contacts, education, preferment.

Proust, Cecil Rhodes, Calvin Coolidge, Bertrand Russell, Rose Kennedy, DeGaulle, Errol Flynn, Olivier

GEMINI

Physical Description

General Description Tall, upright, well-made, strong, active, sanguine complexion, hazel eyes, very dark hair, long arms and legs, short fleshy hands, quick-step, females have fine eyes.

First Face
1 – 5 degrees Stiff, long, lean, thin, red swarthy face, dark or reddish hair, round shoulders, nimble-tongued, bow legged. 5th degree; pockmarked.

Second Face
5 – 10 degrees Thin, trim, almost round visage, chestnut hair, voluble tongue, good appearance overall. 7th degree; dark complexion. Moon with Saturn or Mars; danger of facial injuries.

Third Face
10 – 15 degrees Short, red round face, strong, well-composed, short curling hair, dark hair, large mouth, goggle eyes, distorted teeth, thick shoulders, short thick legs. 12th degree; fat. Moon with Saturn or Mars; facial injuries.

Fourth Face
15 – 20 degrees Full stature, sandy hair, fresh countenance, rather corpulent, roundish visage, sparkling eyes, delicate composure, tooth decay.

Fifth Face
20 – 25 degrees Good proportion, lean, black hair, long visage, narrow chin, brown complexion, black eyes, black beard, long slender legs.

Sixth Face
25 – 30 degrees Neat person, clean oval visage, bright hair, whitish complexion. 27th degree; disgraceful. 29th degree; dark.

IIrd House Personalities

Dickens, Churchill, Isaac Newton, Truman Capote, Walt Disney, Hugh Hefner

Thomas More, Dolly Madison, J.P. Morgan, George Gershwin, Nureyev, Bing Crosby, F. Scott Fitzgerald

Dickens, G.B. Shaw, Vermeer, Haydn, W.B. Yeats, Karl Marx, Pasteur, Cary Grant, Walt Disney

Jefferson, Liszt, Picasso, Ravel, Casals, Valentino, Yehudi Menuhin, Gypsy Rose Lee Mae West

Andre Gide, Benjamin Franklin, Dillinger, Pasteur, Rachmaninoff, Isadora Duncan, Fred Astaire

J.S. Bach, Pablo Casals, Rimbaud, Walter Scott, Julie Andrews

Khrushchev, James Joyce, Nasser, Pope Paul VI, Bertrand Russell, Peter Sellers

Durer, Einstein, Nietzsche, Goethe, Pasteur, Edward Kennedy, Will Rogers

Dante, Toscanini, Vermeer, Cellini, Houdini, Louis Armstrong, Nureyev

Napoleon, Disraeli, Voltaire, R.F. Kennedy, Paganini, Orson Welles, Martin L. King, Jr., Hitchcock, Abraham Lincoln

Dali, Stravinsky, Houdini, F.D. Roosevelt, Olivier, Grace Kelly, Burt Lancaster, Rita Hayworth, Jack Benny

Health Correspondences

Body Parts and Organs arms, hands, fingers, shoulders, lungs, thymus, upper ribs, clavicle, scapula, humerus, bronchial tubes, nervous system, speech, trachea, dorsal region of spine, ulna.

Diseases and Symptoms pleurisy, bronchitis, asthma, tuberculosis, pericardium infection, accidents to arms, shoulders, hands, chest disorders, consumption, disordered mind, dropsy.

Sun Gemini Diseases pleurisy, tuberculosis, bronchitis, lung anaemia, pulmonitis, congestion, injured hands, structural defect of lung. ⊙

Moon Gemini Diseases lung catarrh, asthma, pneumonia, rheumatism of the arms, lung cancer, injury of arms, weak arms, ulcers on hands, nervous diseases, lame or swollen hands. ☽

Mercury Gemini Diseases gout in arms and shoulders, bronchitis, asthma, asphyxiation, pleurisy, arm diseases, paralysis of arms, neuralgia in hands. ☿

Venus Gemini Diseases warts, dropsy, pulmonary inefficiency, eruptions on hands. ♀

Mars Gemini Diseases lung haemorrhages, pneumonia, acute phthsis, cough, fractured hands or collar bone, itching, fever, rashes (nervous), pain in arms, accidents to hands and arms. ♂

Jupiter Gemini Diseases pleurisy, lung congestion, inflammation of lungs, pulmonary apoplexy, swollen hands. ♃

Saturn Gemini Diseases rheumatism, bronchitis, asthma, pleurisy, consumption, sciatica, asphyxiation, broken arms, atrophy of arms and arm muscles. ♄

Uranus Gemini Diseases spasmodic asthma, convulsive hoarse dry cough, colds, paralysis of arms and hands, nervousness, deformities of arms and hands, nervous breakdown. ♅

Neptune Gemini Diseases disorders or glands in arms, deformed hands, nervous diseases, weak-mindedness, afflictions in glands of hand, mental disorders. ♆

♇

CANCER

Cancer/IVth House

The Crab

(3 Years 6 Months — 6 Years 7 Months)

Cardinal Water Sign	**Ruler**	: Moon ∏	**Exalted** : Jupiter	**Dissolution**
Hieroglyph : ●	Hebrew :		Greek : 𝑛̂	Arabic :
Colour : Yellow-Orange	Animal : Crab, Turtle, Sphinx		Plant : Lotus	Gem : Amber, Moonstone
Tarot : Chariot	Perfume : Onycha		Geomancy : Populus & Via	Weapon : The Furnace
Egyptian God : Khephra	Roman God : Dionysius		Greek God : Artemis	Genii : Phalgus

Psychological Correspondences and Events

		Cancer Personalities
ASC ♋ Ascendant Cancer	sensitivity, rich home life, dependency, shyness; mediumistic, impressionable, moody, changeable, sympathetic, protective, humble, dedicated, affectionate, gentle, introverted.	Debussy, Walt Whitman, Madame Blavatsky, Dali, Judy Garland, Will Rogers, Shelley Winters
MC ♋ Midheaven Cancer	simplicity, tactfulness, modesty, thrift; responsible, concerned, conservative, dedicated, emotional, slow, clinging, avaricious.	John Wesley, Christopher Wren, Robert E. Lee, Elizabeth Taylor, James Dean, Jean Harlow, Woodrow Wilson, Ingrid Bergmann
☉ ♋ IV Sun Cancer/IVth House	receptivity, domesticity, family ties; sensitive, maternal, emotional, nostalgic, tender, conservative, contemplative, reserved, comfortable, paranoid, religious, grasping.	Garibaldi, Proust, Rembrandt, Rubens, M.B. Eddy, Susan Hayward, Louis Armstrong, Rose Kennedy
☽ ♋ IV Moon Ruler Cancer/IVth House	emotional strength, depth of feeling, attachment, devotion, affection, motherliness, the Unconscious; domestic, impressionable, hypersensitive, despondent, mediumistic, religious, artistic.	Emily Bronte, Gustav Mahler, Baudelaire, Goya, Paganini, Pushkin, Thomas Mann, Eleanor Roosevelt, John Paul Jones
☿ ♋ IV Mercury Cancer/IVth House	perception, memory, thinking influenced by feeling, slow but retentive intellect; psychological, irrational, sentimental, profound, diplomatic, discreet, poetic, agreeable.	Jung, Maximilian, Alfred Tennyson, Pearl Buck, John Paul Jones, Rose Kennedy
♀ ♋ IV Venus Cancer/IVth House	love, devotion, love affairs, dependent relationships, family, the arts; affectionate, demonstrative, indulgent, exploited, romantic, imaginative, unselfish, dreamy.	Josephine, Pushkin, Mata Hari, Balzac, Florence Nightingale, Puccini, Helen Keller, Louis Armstrong, Princess Anne
♂ ♋ IV Mars Fall Cancer/IVth House	intense emotions, temper tantrums, troubled home-life, lacks persistence, accidents; impulsive, instinctual, bold, ambitious, irritable, sensuous.	Byron, John Calvin, Toscanini, Balzac, Pope John XXIII, John Wesley
♃ ♋ IV Jupiter Exalted Cancer/IVth House	receptivity, abundance of feeling, attachment, contentment, quiet pleasures, good humour; religious, prolific, just, good-natured, charitable, kindly, sociable, relaxed, intuitive.	Galileo, Franz Liszt, Proust, Valentino, Aristotle Onassis, Alexandra
♄ ♋ IV Saturn Detriment Cancer/IVth House	repressed emotion, difficult family life, archaeology, domestic economy; dissatisfied, paranoid, guilty, jealous, independent, lonely, introverted, resentful, melancholic, suspicious.	Michaelangelo, Galileo, Ibsen, Nostradamus, Marcus Aureluis, Wilhelm Furtwangler
♅ ♋ IV Uranus Cancer/IVth House	domestic troubles, parental estrangement, wanderings, peculiar associations; rebellious, independent, eccentric, impatient, restless, changeable, erratic.	John Wesley, Lenin, Paganini, Alexandra, Byron
♆ ♋ IV Neptune Cancer/IVth House	inspiration, sensitivity, compassion, spiritualism, discontent, anxiety, changes of residence, soul-suffering; emotional, addictable, imaginative, refined, self-sacrificial, unstable, spiritual, psychic.	James Pike, Rubens, John Paul Jones, Goethe, Goya, Hugh Hefner, Orson Welles,
♇ ♋ IV Pluto Cancer/IVth House	heredity moulds destiny, unusual task, solitary research, emotions squandered; magnetic, contemplative, fated, destructive, insatiable, dominating, possessive, melodramatic.	Martin Luther King Jr, Nureyev, Liberace, James Dean, Susan Hayward, Sophia Loren, Edward Kennedy
☊ ♋ IV Moon's Node Cancer/IVth House	family ties, continued parental contact, soul unions, ancestry confused, discordant family life; attached, dependent, obliging.	Hitler, Elizabeth II, R.F. Kennedy, Picasso, Joe Kennedy, Charles Chaplin, Bette Davis, Lyndon Johnson

CANCER

Physical Description

General Description
Small stature, strong and well-set, fair, pale, round face, small features, delicate voice, brown hair, grey eyes, bad teeth, upper body larger than the lower, slender arms, weak constitution.

First Face
1 – 5 degrees
Middle stature, large, full, fleshy body, oval face, swarthy, brown hair, indifferently handsome. 4th degree; light, middle to small stature.

Second Face
5 – 10 degrees
Little stature, square visage, reddish swarthy complexion, dark brown hair, curly hair, strong voice, broad forehead, dimple in the chin.

Third Face
10 – 15 degrees
Middle stature, swarthy complexion, black hair. Mars; curly hair, long and thin face, slender, shrill voice, high cheek bones.

Fourth Face
15 – 20 degrees
Lean, thin, black swarthy visage, drawling, affected speech, crook-legged, splay footed, heavy eye-brows, downward-looking.

Fifth Face
20 – 25 degrees
Lean visage, boldness, great lips, high forehead, long hooked nose and chin, little beard, dark brown or sandy hair, slender legs, incomposed body.

Sixth Face
25 – 30 degrees
Long freckled face, full forehead, large nose, full eyes, narrow chin, wide mouth, thin stooping body, low middle stature, broad shoulders, dark curling hair. Sun or Mars; red or yellow hair.

IVth House Personalities

Jane Austen, Nehru, Proust, Tolstoi, Martin Luther, Howard Hughes, Kahlil Gibran

Mahler, Mozart, Napoleon, Nietzsche, Picasso, Tolstoi, Howard Hughes

Victor Hugo, Nehru, Eugene O'Neill, Proust, Ravel, Carl Sandburg, Cervantes, Wm. Penn

Eugene O'Neill, Puccini, Dickens, Leonardo, Schiller, Madame Blavatsky, Poe, Sara Bernhardt

General Patton, John Calvin, Zola, Valentino, Alain Delon

Thomas More, Nostradamus, Proust, Rembrandt, Valentino, Thomas Beckett, John Adams, Prince Philip

Francis Bacon, Chopin, Garibaldi, J.P. Morgan, Martin Luther, Mary Baker Eddy, James Dean, Prince Philip

Baudelaire, Lord Nelson, Schubert, Turner, Bulwer-Lytton, Maria Callas, Joseph Smith, Mae West

Freud, Garbaldi, Pope John XXIII, Verlaine, Martin Luther, Chopin, Charlotte Bronte, Neil Armstrong, Baudelaire, Bulwer-Lytton

Caligula, Peter the Great, DeGaulle, Poe, Dostoievsky, Nietzsche, Rommel, Custer, Houdini

George VI, Marie Curie, DeGaulle, Mahler, Greta Garbo, Ingrid Bergmann

Health Correspondences

Body Parts and Organs
aesophagus, stomach, diaphragm, pancreas, breasts, lacteals, upper liver lobes, thorasic duct, womb, ribs, sternum, albumen, axillae, digestive organs.

Diseases and Symptoms
lowered vitality, catarrh, dipsomania, gastric catarrh, indigestion, gas, cough, hiccup, dropsy, melancholia, hydrophobia, hysteria, gall stones, jaundice, cancer.

Sun Cancer Diseases
anaemia, dropsy, gastric fever, disordered stomach, dyspepsia, organic stomach defects, bloated stomach, obesity.

Moon Cancer Diseases
stomach cancer, dropsy, obesity, bloating, epilepsy, digestive troubles, convulsions, breast cancer, colic, overdeveloped breasts.

Mercury Cancer Diseases
nervous indigestion, nervous dyspepsia, phlegm, flatulence, drunkenness, cold stomach, gluttony.

Venus Cancer Diseases
distended stomach, gastric tumours, nausea, adenoma, disorders of stomach veins.

Mars Cancer Diseases
milk fever, stomach inflammations, dyspepsia, stomach haemorrhages, pains in breast and stomach, disorders of stomach muscles, irritable stomach, injuries to breast.

Jupiter Cancer Diseases
gourmandizing, dyspepsia, liver complaints, jaundice, dropsy, scurvy, corrupt blood, cancer of liver, gastric tumours, distended stomach, appetite disorders.

Saturn Cancer Diseases
pyorrhea, dyspepsia, gastric ulcer, breast cancer, nausea, belching, scurvy, jaundice, gall stones, anaemia, lack of pepsin, stricture of aesophagus, gastric catarrh.

Uranus Cancer Diseases
hiccups, dry stomach cough, wind spasms, gas, flatulence, colic, cramps in stomach, accidents to breast, disorders of stomach membranes, breast disorders.

Neptune Cancer Diseases
dipsomania, weak stomach, disorders of stomach glands, and secretions, malfunction of pylorus.

LEO

Leo/Vth House

The Lion

(6 Years 7 Months — 13 Years)

Fixed Fire Sign		**Ruler**	: Sun	**Exalted**	: Neptune	**Digestion**	
Hieroglyph	:	Hebrew	:	Greek	:	Arabic	:
Colour	: Yellow	Animal	: Lion	Plant	: Sunflower	Gem	: Cat's Eye
Tarot	: Fortitude	Perfume	: Olibanum	Geomancy	: Fortuna Major & Minor	Weapon	: The Discipline
Egyptian God	: Ra-Hoor-Khuit	Roman God	: Helios	Greek God	: Apollo	Genii	: Zeirna

Psychological Correspondences and Events

ASC ♌︎ Ascendant Leo
self-glorification, leadership, courage, extroversion, hedonism, generosity, nobility; impressive, fun-loving, confident, magnetic, dignified, open, fair, motivated, pretentious, arrogant, pushy.

MC ♌︎ Midheaven Leo
self-confidence, social climbing, optimism, egotism; organized, ambitious, generous, proud, domineering, rigid, selfish, aspiring.

☉ ♌︎ V Sun Ruler Leo/Vth House
formative energy, self-expression, creativity, self-confidence, wealth of ideas, organization, leadership; domineering, proud, honourable, haughty, candid, forceful, ardent, childless.

☽ ♌︎ V Moon Leo/Vth House
instinctive or intuitive creativity, love of grandeur, self-aggrandizement; confident, generous, passionate, sociable, luxurious, hedonistic, magnanimous, warm-hearted, lively, popular, responsible.

☿ ♌︎ V Mercury Leo/Vth House
good humour, enthusiasm, creative thinking, foresight, determination; aspiring, dignified, positive, expansive, voluble, speculative, bossy, anti-intellectual, extroverted.

♀ ♌︎ V Venus Leo/Vth House
love relations, games, pleasure, amusement, quick contacts; hedonistic, vain, indulgent, squandering, free, generous, merry, vivacious.

♂ ♌︎ V Mars Leo/Vth House
formative power, zeal, ardour, egotism, ambition, gambling, ruthlessness; self-assured, responsible, fearless, audacious, possessive, domineering, frank, brutal, determined, speculative, macho.

♃ ♌︎ V Jupiter Leo/Vth House
self-confidence, optimism, big ideas, speculation, benevolence, prestige, grandeur, prominence; lofty, noble, vain, pretentious, wasteful, spendthrift, inflated.

♄ ♌︎ V Saturn Detriment Leo/Vth House
inhibited expression, underdeveloped pleasure principle, ambition, selfishness, unhappy love, overwork, loss of children; shy, loyal, simple, ungratified, determined, awkward.

♅ ♌︎ V Uranus Detriment Leo/Vth House
spirit of enterprise, boldness, love of freedom, egomania, gambling, craves adventure, peculiar loves, loss of children; individualistic, obstreperous, unconventional, headstrong, self-willed, forceful.

♆ ♌︎ V Neptune Exalted Leo/Vth House
enthusiasm, love of beauty, peculiar or clandestine pleasures, acting, scandal, self-glorification, gambling, seduction, theatre and opera; wasteful, theatrical, pretentious, lavish.

♇ ♌︎ V Pluto Fall Leo/Vth House
dynamic emotions, authority, despotism, prominence, will to power, rule by force, extraordinary achievements; aggressive, tactless, brutal, powerful, boisterous.

☊ ♌︎ V Moon's Node Leo/Vth House
popularity, speculations with others, many children, festivities and entertainments, many love affairs, organization; wasteful, over-extended, social.

Leo Personalities

Cecil B. DeMille, Mae West, Douglas Fairbanks, Picasso, Phineas T. Barnum, Nureyev, Aleister Crowley

Rubens, Bertrand Russell, J.F. Kennedy, Elvis Presley, Frank Sinatra, Frank Lloyd Wright

Napoleon, Mussolini, G.B. Shaw, Jung, Shelley, Mick Jagger, Aldous Huxley, Debussy, Madame duBarry, Mae West

Catherine the Great, Frederick the Great, Nero, Louis XIV, Gypsy Rose Lee, Moshe Dayan, Barbra Streisand

Henry VIII, Castro, Hemingway, Mae West, George Wallace, Mussolini, Louis Armstrong

Andy Warhol, Truman Capote, Shelley, Louis XIV, Coco Chanel

Henry Ford, Himmler, Robespierre, Disraeli, U.S. Grant, Sophia Loren, George Wallace

Shakespeare, Christopher Marlowe, Rachmaninoff, Lyndon Johnson, J.P. Morgan, Nelson Rockefeller, Rex Harrison

Frederick the Great, Joe Kennedy, Billy Graham, J.F. Dulles

Shelley, Jung, Rossini, Isadora Duncan, Thomas Beckett

Josephine, Richard Burton, Maria Callas, Robert Burns, Liberace, Hugh Hefner

Muhammad Ali, Christopher Columbus, Leonardo de Vinci, Voltaire, Prince Charles, Mick Jagger

Eichmann, J.F. Dulles, Gandhi, Onassis, Paul Newman, Gide, Johnny Carson, Frank Lloyd Wright

LEO

Physical Description

General Description Large, noble body, full majestic stature, broad shoulders, austere, oval face, ruddy fierce countenance, yellow bushy hair, large staring eyes, quick sighted, strong voice, resolute.

First Face
1 – 5 degrees Short, thick, well-set body, square ruddy visage, brown hair, curly hair, good proportioned features, well-made nose, pleasant eyes, red lips, nimble tongue, strong, compact body.

Second Face
5 – 10 degrees Middle stature, good features, clear skin, roundish visage, flaxen hair, grey eyes, straight full body, breasts, expands with age. 8th degree; large. 9th degree; stiff.

Third Face
10 – 15 degrees Swarthy complexion, dark hair, large forehead, hanging eye-brows, black eyes, prominent cheek-bones, distorted teeth, mark near the chin, full stature, consumptive appearance.

Fourth Face
15 – 20 degrees Tall, slender, high forehead, chestnut hair, long face, pale complexion, slender legs, great eater. 16th degree; low and stiff. 17th degree; stiff. 19th degree; tall.

Fifth Face
20 – 25 degrees Comely, tall, lusty, full face, straight brown hair, majestic carriage and deportment. 21st degree; stiff and low. 22nd degree; middle stature, rather light complexion.

Sixth Face
25 – 30 degrees Tall, thin, pock-marked, swarthy face, dark eyes and hair, broad shoulders, short arms and legs, awry gait. 26th degree; tall and light. 27th degree; stout, dark, but good looking.

Vth House Personalities

Sarah Bernhardt, Casanova, F.D. Roosevelt, Clark Gable, Jean Harlow, Shirley Temple, Bette Davis, Duke of Windsor, Prince Charles

Liszt, Douglas, Fairbanks, Jackie Kennedy, Laurence Olivier, Marie Antionette, Albert Schweitzer, Bob Hope

Mozart, Mendelssohn, Pushkin, Verdi, Robert Browning, Will Rogers, Schweitzer

Dietrich, Edvard Greig, Haydn, Marie Antoinette, Carl Sandburg, Gloria Swanson

U.S. Grant, Nasser, Richard III, Verdi, Duke of Wellington

Catherine the Great, Cellini, Rose Kennedy, Pope Pius XII, Ocar Wilde

Duke of Wellington, Beethoven, Dietrich, Andy Warhol, Stalin, Goebbels, Calvin Coolidge

Proust, T.E. Lawrence, Rasputin, Richard I, Savonarola, Martin Luther, Castro, Coleridge, Verlaine, William of Orange

Phineas T. Barnum, Byron, Schubert, Beethoven, Tennessee Williams

John D. Rockefeller, Schiller, Leonard Bernstein, Al Capone, Cezanne

Eichmann, Bob Dylan, Janis Joplin, Wm. F. Buckley, Nureyev, Robert Mitchum, Paul Newman, Robert Redford

Health Correspondences

Body Parts and Organs	heart, dorsal spine and nerves, spinal cord, aorta, blood circulation, equilibrium in the body, spleen, superior and inferior vena cava, vital forces, wrists.
Diseases and Symptoms	anaemia, palpitation, fainting, aneurysm, spinal meningitis, arterio-sclerosis, curvature of the spine, back diseases, blood disorders, high fevers, dizziness, heart disease.
Sun **Leo** **Diseases**	backache, heart palpitation, madness, spotted fever, afflications of dorsal vertebrae, organic heart trouble, eye trouble (6°).
Moon **Leo** **Diseases**	backache, bad circulation, convulsions, eye trouble (6°), scrofula, swoonings, heartburn, heart dilation, palpitation due to haste and excitement.
Mercury **Leo** **Diseases**	back pains, fainting, palpitation, heart neuralgia.
Venus **Leo** **Diseases**	spinal diseases, backache, enlarged heart, heart dilation, palpitations due to excesses.
Mars **Leo** **Diseases**	muscular rheumatism of the back, enlarged heart, palpitations, heart pains, suffocation, fainting, inflammation of pericardium, damage to heart.
Jupiter **Leo** **Diseases**	apoplexy, fatty heart valves, weak back, arterio-sclerosis, spinal sclerosis, swollen ankles, heart ailments due to wrong diet, enlarged heart.
Saturn **Leo** **Diseases**	curvature of the spine, weak back, arterio-sclerosis, sclerosis of spinal cord, chronic heart disease, atrophy of heart, weak heart, endocarditis, heart afflicted by grief.
Uranus **Leo** **Diseases**	palpitation, spasmodic heart action, spinal meningitis, weak valves, infantile paralysis, obstruction of blood, fainting, nervous heart afflictions, irregular heart action.
Neptune **Leo** **Diseases**	afflicted depressor nerves of heart, enlarged heart, suppression of heart action through drugs and narcotics, heart trouble through tobacco.

☉

☾

☿

♀

♂

♃

♄

♅

♆

♇

 VIRGO

Virgo/VIth House　　The Virgin

(13 Years — 23 Years)

Mutable Earth Sign		Ruler	: Mercury	Exalted	: Mercury	Distillation	
Hieroglyph	: ****	Hebrew	:	Greek	: **'**	Arabic	: ﺱ
Colour	: Yellow-Green	Animal	: Anchorites, Solitaries	Plant	: Narcissus	Gem	: Peridot
Tarot	: Hermit	Perfume	: Narcissus	Geomancy	: Coniunction	Weapon	: Lamp & Wind
Egyptian God	: Virgin Isis	Roman God	: Ceres	Greek God	: Demeter, Persephone	Genii	: Tabris

Psychological Correspondences and Events

ASC ♍
Ascendant
Virgo
discretion, stability, caution, reserve; observant, critical, shy, articulate, precise, painstaking, hygenic, pedantic, prejudiced, tidy, anxious.

MC ♍
Midheaven
Virgo
striving for a secure livelihood, tidiness, organization, dissatisfaction, intellectual professions, susceptible to flattery; hypersensitive, petty, conservative, unspontaneous, moral.

☉ ♍ VI
Sun
Virgo/VIth House
method and analysis, diligence, correctness, orderliness, criticism; intellectual, nervous, precise, studious, fussy, verbal, scientific, remote, self-righteous, practical, technical, fastidious, dissatisfied.

☽ ♍ VI
Moon
Virgo/VIth House
head rules heart, simplicity, correct behaviour, coldness, prudery, hypochondria, reserve; articulate, practical, methodical, pedantic, anxious, hyper-sensitive, undemonstrative.

☿ ♍ VI
Mercury Exalted Ruler
Virgo/VIth House
thirst for knowledge, practical thinking, expert knowledge and specialized skill, biblophilia; scientific, precise, intellectual, patient, analytical, well-read, careful, detached, sceptical, intelligent.

♀ ♍ VI
Venus Fall
Virgo/VIth House
repressed feelings, moral sense, indecisive love; fastidious, pure, discriminative, quiet, restrained, dissatisfied, tasteful, decorous, polite.

♂ ♍ VI
Mars
Virgo/VIth House
business, detail work, compulsive organizing and arranging, exploitation, adaptation; scientific, orderly, irritable, nervous, astute, materialistic, tidy, critical, edgy.

♃ ♍ VI
Jupiter Detriment
Virgo/VIth House
urge to learn, organization, teaching, teamwork, medicine, ambition; ethical, moral, upstanding, prudent, philosophical, discriminating, materialistic, honest, professional, thorough.

♄ ♍ VI
Saturn
Virgo/VIth House
care and attention, accuracy, acting alone, misanthropy, seriousness, science; cold, humourless, overly cautious, meticulous, misunderstood, nagging, fault-finding, sedentary.

♅ ♍ VI
Uranus
Virgo/VIth House
individual working methods, reforming urge, unusual profession, mechanical genius, troubled employment; scientific, eccentric, intellectual, occult, subtle, original, brilliant.

♆ ♍ VI
Neptune Detriment
Virgo/VIth House
intuitive understanding, healing powers, hypochondria, chemistry, botany, planning, pathological sensitivity, seclusion, weak psyche; gentle, patient, discreet, deceitful, addictable.

♇ ♍ VI
Pluto
Virgo/VIth House
inquisitive mind, fanatical zeal, accumulated detail, scientific objectives; brilliant, incisive, ascerbic, hyper-critical, investigative, profound, impossible.

☊ ♍ VI
Moon's Node
Virgo/VIth House
associations in teaching, science and health, small animals, research, disagreements through criticism; health, employees, gain through service, working relationships.

Virgo Personalities

Mozart, Raphael, Charlotte Bronte, Dietrich, Calvin Coolidge, Helen Hayes, Mary Astor, Howard Hughes, Peter Sellers

Benjamin Farnklin, Dostoievsky, Stalin, John D. Rockefeller, Luther Burbank

Elizabeth I, Goethe, Tolstoi, Schoenberg, Prince Albert, Ivan the Terrible, Richelieu, Dante, Augustus Caesar, Walter Reed

Luther Burbank, Tolstoi, Dietrich, Swift, Gertrude Stein, Katherine Hepburn

Lyndon Johnson, Tolstoi, Joe Kennedy, Aristotle Onassis, Ules Verne, Gershwin

Goethe, Nietzsche, Proust, Emily Bronte, Helen Hayes, Deborah Kerr

Joan of Arc, Nietzsche, Walter Scott, Clara Barton, Aristotle Onassis, Patton, Frank Lloyd Wright

Thomas Jefferson, Dumas, Houdini, John Wilkes Booth, Chaing Kai-shek

Handel, thomas More, Cesare Borgia, Brahms, Nathaniel Hawthorne, Tito, DeGaulle

Leeuwenhoek, Vermeer, Stravinsky, Einstein, Kahlil Gibran, James Joyce

Jane Austen, John Milton, King Hussein, Neil Armstrong, Edward Kennedy, John Lennon, Dolly Madison

Durer, Erasmus, Machiavelli, J.J. Rousseau

Marie Curie, Christiaan Barnard, Toscanini, Brando, Muhammad Ali, J. Edgar Hoover, Dietrich, Patton, Zsa Zsa Gabor

VIRGO

Physical Description

General Description	Middle stature, slender, brown ruddy complexion, dark brown hair, round face, delicate features. small shrill voice, round head, well-composed body.
First Face **1 - 5 degrees**	Rather tall, brown complexion, thin beard, brown hair, broad forehead, Roman nose, narrow chin, long slender legs and feet. 1st and 2nd degrees; often tall. 4th degree; good stature.
Second Face **5 - 10 degrees**	Tall stature, oval face, brown complexion, sometimes pale, pleasant countenance, a good looking person.
Third Face **10 - 15 degrees**	Comely appearance, full middle stature, round face, clear complexion, flaxen hair.
Fourth Face **15 - 20 degrees**	Rather tall, oval visage, broad forehead, large nose, wide mouth, full lips, swarthy complexion, slender waist, long legs.
Fifth Face **20 - 25 degrees**	Tall, long thin visage, freckled face, narrow chin, high cheek bones, black eyes, large nose and nostrils, thin lips.
Sixth Face **25 - 30 degrees**	Short, full oval face, brown complexion, chestnut hair, high forehead, sometimes a Roman nose.

VIth House Personalities

Christiaan Barnard, C.G. Jung, Kipling, Voltaire, E.B. Browning, Chopin

Milton, Jules Verne, Alexander Graham Bell, Einstein, Franklin, Charlotte Bronte, Leeuwenhoek, Mark Twain

Marie Curie, Jung, John Keats, Lenin, Voltaire, Spinoza, Bertrand Russell, Franklin Roosevelt, Kipling

Keats, John Lennon, Mendelssohn, Mozart, Proust, Schumann

Marie Curie, Spinoza, Shaw, Proust, Thoreau, Kipling, James Joyce, Voltaire, Stalin, Howard Hughes

Florence Nightingale, James Pike, Pushkin, Jules Verne, Rossini, Joan Sutherland, Frank Lloyd Wright

Erasmus, Thomas Mann, Marie Curie, Anastasia, Bismarck, Charlotte Bronte, Onassis, Howard Hughes

Leonardo da Vinci, Mozart, Kant, Adenauer, Robert Fulton

Thomas Huxley, Keats, Paderewski, Ravel, Rossini, Berlioz, Helen Keller

Rembrandt, Jonathan Swift, Handel, Freud, Emerson, Edison, Nelson Rockefeller

Jane Addams, Ceil Rhodes, Schweitzer, Einstein, Freud, Hermann Goering, Barry Goldwater, George Wallace

Health Correspondences

Body Parts and Organs	abdominal organs, assimilations, duodenum, food and diet, bowels, pylorus, large and small intestines, lower dorsal nerves, nails, peristalsic action of bowels, spleen.	
Diseases and Symptoms	appendicitis, peritonitis, malnutrition, tapeworm, typhoid, cholera, bowel diseases, colic, diarrhoea, dysentery, enteric fever, hernia, indigestion, sterility.	
Sun Virgo Diseases	incorrect assimilation, bowel diseases, typhoid fever, dysentery.	☉
Moon Virgo Diseases	bowel disorders, abdominal tumours, dysentery, peritonitis, cancer of the bowels, irregular bowels.	☽
Mercury Virgo Diseases	flatulence, colic, short breath, nervous disorders, gas, nervous dyspepsia, neuralgic pains in the bowels, hyperaesthesia.	☿
Venus Virgo Diseases	impeded peristalsic action, worms, tapeworm, dysentery, intestinal tumours.	♀
Mars Virgo Diseases	typhoid fever, bowel inflammation, worms, peritonitis, diarrhorea, ventral hernia, appendicitis, fever of the bowels, gastroenteritis.	♂
Jupiter Virgo Diseases	enlarged or ulcerated liver, jaundice, weak back, consumption, abscess in bowels, diarrhoea, intestinal tumours.	♃
Saturn Virgo Diseases	intestinal peristalsis, abated absorption of chyle, leukaemia, obstruction of ileum caecum and transverse colon, gripe, appendicitis, melancholy, ileac passion.	♄
Uranus Virgo Diseases	flatulence, abdominal cramps, colic, cramps in bowels, intussusception, spasmodic intestinal pains, nervous dyspepsia.	♅
Neptune Virgo Diseases	hypochondria, dropsy, wasting of bowel glands, bowel disorders from use of drugs and opiates, consumption of bowels.	♆
		♇

 LIBRA

Libra/VIIth House

The Balance

(23 Years — 42 Years)

Cardinal Air Sign
Hieroglyph :
Colour : Green
Tarot : Justice
Egyptian God : Maat

Ruler : Venus
Hebrew :
Animal : Elephant
Perfume : Galbanum
Roman God : Themis

Exalted : Saturn
Greek :
Plant : Aloe
Geomancy : Puella
Greek God : Themis

Sublimation
Arabic :
Gem : Emerald
Weapon : The Cross
Genii : Sialul

	Psychological Correspondences and Events	Libra Personalities
ASC ♎ **Ascendant** **Libra**	harmonious environment, attractive appearance, charm, flattery, work aversion, vanity, craves approval; agreeable, sociable, indolent, meddlesome, pleasure-loving, saccharine, relaxed, gushing.	George VI, Stephen Foster, Jean Harlow, Liz Taylor, Hans Christian Andersen, Alain Delon, Lana Turner
MC ♎ **Midheaven** **Libra**	advancement through others, fortunate connections, cooperation, craves recognition, shared enterprises; harmonious, reliant, diplomatic, exploitative, artistic, fortunate, manipulating.	Shelley, Madame duBarry, Haydn, Robert Browning
☉ ♎ VII **Sun Fall** **Libra/VIIth House**	harmony, public spirit, partnerships, litigations, lacks self-reliance, fears solitude, popularity; charming, amenable, hyper-social, adaptable, diplomatic, mannered, vain, dependent, political.	R.D.Laing, Brigitte Bardot, Gandhi, Crowley, Cesare Borgia, Nietzsche, Liszt, Himmler, Pope Paul VI, Paracelsus, Trudeau
☾ ♎ VII **Moon** **Libra/VIIth House**	vivid expression of feelings, need for love, dependent on partner, seeks pleasure and amusement; affectionate, romantic, courteous, kind, refined, luxury-loving, vague, silly, unreliable.	Marie Antoinette, Madame duBarry, Valentino, Rose Kennedy, Duchess of Windsor, Disney, J. Austen, Oliver W. Holmes
☿ ♎ VII **Mercury** **Libra/VIIth House**	public relations, charm, creativity within existing patterns, learns through others, team-work, justice, tactful mediation, compassion; eclectic, diplomatic, well-spoken, unoriginal, vapid.	F. Scott Fitzgerald, Johann Strauss, Verdi, Maurice Chevalier, Jenny Lind
♀ ♎ VII **Venus Ruler** **Libra/VIIth House**	lively manner, love affairs, artistic skill, sociability, taste, scattered affections, infidelity, luxury, easy life; attractive, vain, foppish, amorous, cordial, high-living, frivolous.	Edward VII, Rimbaud, Rita Hayworth, Oscar Wilde, Grace Kelly, Bizet, Paderewski
♂ ♎ VII **Mars Detriment** **Libra/VIIth House**	urge to associate, team-work, male partner, the law, rivalry, enmity, entangled affections, passionate love, separations, controlled by opposite sex; ardent, idealistic, professional, impulsive, frank.	G.B. Shaw, Andy Warhol, John Lennon, R. D. Laing, Ingrid Bergmann, Dulles, Johnny Carson
♃ ♎ VII **Jupiter** **Libra/VIIth House**	enjoyment of social contact, justice, the Law, public work, conversation, happy marriage, reliance on others; temperate, mild, charitable, well-meaning, philanthropic, cultured, benign.	George Washington, Winston Churchill, Bach, Handel, Wilhelm Furtwangler
♄ ♎ VII **Saturn Exalted** **Libra/VIIth House**	sense of duty, older serious partners and colleagues, enmities, love difficulties, estrangements; loyal, industrious, conscientious, serious, intellectual, reliable, restrained, inhibited, honourable.	Franco, Khrushchev, Huey Long, Goering, Mao Tse-Tung
♅ ♎ VII **Uranus** **Libra/VIIth House**	free love, inspiration, public reforms, compulsive attachments, political, difficulties, short-lived partnerships, enmity, peculiar marriage-views, divorce; magnetic, quick-tempered, imaginative, restless, intuitive.	Machiavelli, Tiberius, James II, T.E. Lawrence, E.B. Browning, Furtwangler
♆ ♎ VII **Neptune** **Libra/VIIth House**	receptivity, refined feelings, easily attracted, platonic love, romanticism, love disappointments, odd relation of self to public; idealistic, dreamy, tender, poetic, seducible sympathetic, sweet.	Robert Burns, Byron, Shelley, Paganini
♇ ♎ VII **Pluto** **Libra/VIIth House**	fated partnerships, celebrities, fame, extraordinary power of assertion, personal magnetism, manifestation of genius; seductive, fascinating, disruptive, ruthless.	George Washington, John Adams, Casanova, Thomas More, Michaelangelo
☊ ♎ VII **Moon's Node** **Libra/VIIth House**	love affairs, team-work, public welfare, profit through others, gain through partner, inability to be alone, contention with partner; communal, social, dependent.	John Dillinger, John Glenn, Kipling, Eleanor Roosevelt, John Lennon, Cary Grant, Prince Philip

 # LIBRA

Physical Description

General Description
Tall and elegantly formed, round face, beauty, slender, lank, auburn hair, flaxen hair, generally blue eyes, fine clear complexion.

First Face
1 – 5 degrees
Rather tall, slender, oval visage, pale complexion, grey eyes, well formed nose and lips, chestnut hair.

Second Face
5 – 10 degrees
Same stature, more corpulent, clearer complexion.

Third Face
10 – 15 degrees
Middle stature, longish visage, brownish complexion, broad forehead, full grey eyes, brown hair, long arms and fingers, long nose, freckles, generally good features.

Fourth Face
15 – 20 degrees
Very comely, inclining to tallness, slender waist, round visage, clean white complexion, neat lips and nose, grey eyes, light or flaxen hair, long arms, hand and fingers, white soft skin, a lasting beauty.

Fifth Face
20 – 25 degrees
Much like the former, a redder blush, fresh countenance, a comely and perfect beauty.

Sixth Face
25 – 30 degrees
Much like the former two faces, somewhat taller, beautiful body.

VIIth House Personalities

R.D. Laing, Freud, Charles Manson, Adolf Hitler, Christopher Marlowe

Elizabeth II, Mao Tse-tung, Mussolini, Marilyn Monroe, Jean Harlow, Valentino, Pushkin

J.F. Kennedy, John Lennon, Marlowe, Tyrone Power, Rosalind Russell

Mary Astor, Liz Taylor, Jackie Kennedy, Verlaine, Mary Stuart, Charles Manson, E.B. Browning

Marlon Brando, Al Capone, Robespierre, Tito, Toscanini, John L. Lewis

Machiavelli, Trotsky, J.F. Kennedy, Cicero, Marilyn Monroe, Rex Harrison, Nureyev

Ivan the Terrible, Czar Nicholar II, John Calvin, Voltaire, Yeats, Prince Albert

Louis XVI, Wagner, Napoleon, Goya, Garbo, Madame Blavatsky, Josephine, James Dean, Liz Taylor

Madame Blavatsky, Casanova, Mussolini, Wagner, Wilde, Madame duBarry, Charles Chaplin

Gurdjieff, Chopin, Mozart, Mahler, Louis XIV, Gandhi, Billy Graham, Helen Keller, Moliere, Stalin

Winston Churchill, Hearst, Bogart, James Dean, Hugh Hefner, Fred Astaire, Andy Warhol

Health Correspondences

Body Parts and Organs
adrenals, kidneys, suprarenals, lumbar, vasomotor system, skin, distillation of urine, external generative organs, lumbar nerves, haunches to buttocks, reins.

Diseases and Symptoms
eczema, skin diseases, kidney and bladder disorders, aneuria, diabetes, abscesses, lumbago, nephritis, weak back, stone in bladder or kidneys, syphilis, vein diseases.

Sun Libra Diseases ☉
skin eruption, Bright's disease, weak kidneys, skin diseases.

Moon Libra Diseases ☾
Bright's disease, kidney abscesses, uraemia, insomnia, disturbed renal circulation.

Mercury Libra Diseases ☿
suppressed urine, renal paroxysms, lumbago, renal colic, nervous disorders of kidneys.

Venus Libra Diseases ♀
uraemia, polyuria, headaches, gonorrhoea, flatulence.

Mars Libra Diseases ♂
nephritis, excess urine, renal stones, kidney haemorrhages, hot urine, pyelitis, fevers from kidney diseases.

Jupiter Libra Diseases ♃
melancholy from weak adrenal secretion, renal abscesses, diabetes, skin eruptions, kidney tumours, amyloid kidneys, over-worked kidneys.

Saturn Libra Diseases ♄
ataxia, stones, gravel, Bright's disease, malnutrition, suppressed urine, disturbed renal circulation, cirrhosis of kidneys, skin eruptions, prolapsed kidneys.

Uranus Libra Diseases ♅
venereal skin eruptions, hallucinations, spasmodic kidney action, floating kidney.

♆

♇

SCORPIO
Scorpio/VIIIth House   The Scorpion

(42 Years — Death)

Fixed Water Sign		Ruler	: Mars & Pluto	Exalted	: Uranus	Separation	
Hieroglyph	: 〜〜〜〜	Hebrew	: ⅃	Greek	: ♈	Arabic	: ☾
Colour	: Blue-Green	Animal	: Eagle, Wolf, Scorpion	Plant	: Cactus	Gem	: Snakestone, Turquoise
Tarot	: Death	Perfume	: Siameze Benzoin	Geomancy	: Rabaeus	Weapon	: Obligatory Pain
Egyptian God	: Typhoon, Set, Ptah	Roman God	: Vulcan	Greek God	: Hephaestos	Genii	: Nantor

Psychological Correspondences and Events

ASC ♏
Ascendant
Scorpio

aggressive environment, passion, industry, reserve, caution, quick decision, violence; hot-blooded, secretive, magnetic, sexual, conservative, wilful, brutal, untiring, impulsive.

MC ♏
Midheaven
Scorpio

perseverance, industry, independence, ambition; self-willed, acquisitive, energetic, ruthless, compulsive, destructive, domineering, purposeful.

☉ ♏ VIII
Sun
Scorpio/VIIIth House

will power, tenacity, excess of energy, sensuality, cynicism, enmity; self-destructive, moody, vindictive, jealous, forceful, dynamic, quick-tempered, dangerous, magnetic, impenetrable.

☾ ♏ VIII
Moon Fall
Scorpio/VIIIth House

self-destruction, conflict with mother, death wish, extremes of self-control and liscentiousness, intense emotions, jealousy; passionate, one-sided, obstinate, vicious, possessive.

☿ ♏ VIII
Mercury
Scorpio/VIIIth House

sharp criticism, interest in difficult problems, intense concentration, scepticism, disputes, money troubles; sarcastic, insulting, cunning, argumentative, practical, penetrating, acidic.

♀ ♏ VIII
Venus Detriment
Scorpio/VIIIth House

strong attraction, fanatic lover, extremes of self-control and liscentiousness, legacies, intemperance, illness, squandered energy, withholds love, depravity; passionate, jealous.

♂ ♏ VIII
Mars Ruler
Scorpio/VIIIth House

survival instinct, power mania, ambition, ruthlessness, violence, destruction, sexual energy, dissipation; brutal, sadistic, danger-loving, forceful, irresistible, indestructible.

♃ ♏ VIII
Jupiter
Scorpio/VIIIth House

striving for possessions and pleasures, money from partner and from others, conceit, peaceful death, sex life; pleasure-loving, self-indulgent, materialistic, subtle, proud, emotional.

♄ ♏ VIII
Saturn
Scorpio/VIIIth House

metaphysics, melancholy, unhappy love, transformation, poverty, long life, intrigues, occult investigations, necrophilia; self-willed, resourceful, cautious, shrewd, pyschic, persistent, morose, twisted.

♅ ♏ VIII
Uranus Exalted
Scorpio/VIIIth House

fearlessness, great gains and losses, peculiar death, legacy troubles, strength of character, the occult, resistance; bold, stubborn, sharp-spoken, danger-loving, acute, rebellious.

♆ ♏ VIII
Neptune
Scorpio/VIIIth House

subconscious forces, keen senses, metaphysics, wrong-doing, soul-sickness, depression, drugs, debauch; secretive, emotional, seducible, mediumistic, escapist, perverted.

♇ ♏ VIII
Pluto Ruler
Scorpio/VIIIth House

fanaticism, tragic events, record achievements and endurance, rage, fury of destruction; transforming, maniacal, daemonic, homicidal, inspired, explosive, influential, subversive.

☊ ♏ VIII
Moon's Node
Scorpio/VIIIth House

associations, fighting for a common aim, subversive groups, sexual relationships, undermined cooperation, secret relations, groups advocating violence or practising deception.

Scorpio Personalities

Fidel Castro, Mata Hari, Freud, Richard III, Casanova, Maria Callas, Emily Bronte, Elvis Presley, Joan Crawford, Paganini

Rommel, Al Capone, George Lincoln Rockwell, Darwin, Rodin, Houdini

Trotsky, Goering, Goebbels, Rommel Tiberius, Picasso, Dostoievsky, Cellini, Marie Curie, Christiaan Barnard, M. Luther

John Wilkes Booth, Goering, Nostradamus, Rembrandt, Mae West, Henry Miller, Steinbeck, Liz Taylor

Charles Manson, Goebbels, Tiberius, Schiller, Eugene O'Neill, Mark Twain, R.L. Stevenson, Katherine Hepburn

George VI, Billy Graham, Charles Manson, Schiller, Keats

Goebbels, Marie Curie, Rembrandt, King John I, Schweitzer, Gurdjieff, T.E. Lawrence

Napoleon, Bogart, Disraeli, Mata Hari, Crowley, Adenauer, Elvis Presley, Rossini, Schweitzer

J. Edgar Hoover, Caligula, Pope Paul VI, Luther, R.F. Kennedy, Christine Jorgensen, Marilyn Monroe

Goering, Goebbels, J. Edgar, Hoover, Poe, Tito, Robert E. Lee, Casanova, Khrushchev, Francis Bacon, Mae West

Cesare Borgia, Machiavelli, Schubert, Keats, Hawthorne, Berlioz

Henry VIII, Paracelsus, Ignatius Loyola

Mussolini, Douglas Fairbanks, Lindbergh, Liberace, Kahlil Gibran, John Steinbeck Lenin, Nasser, Huey Long

 # SCORPIO

Physical Description

General Description
Strong, robust, corpulent, broad face, middle stature, dusky complexion, brown bush hair, dark eyes, thick neck, coarse hairy legs, often bow-legged, active.

First Face
1 – 5 degrees
Middle stature, rather short round full face, straight chestnut hair, pale complexion, grey eyes, compact, comely, excellent features, good countenance.

Second Face
5 – 10 degrees
Like the former, not beautiful, thick waist, plump visage, thick short legs.

Third Face
10 – 15 degrees
Slender, dark brown hair, brown complexion, greyish eyes, broad forehead.

Fourth Face
15 – 20 degrees
Slender, short, broad shoulders, dark hair, slightly curly hair, tawny or swarthy complexion, downward look.

Fifth Face
20 – 25 degrees
Little, gross, oval face, pale complexion, dark straight hair, good features, proportionate.

Sixth Face
25 – 30 degrees
Thick, well-made, square face, frowning, surly, broad forehead and chin, thick overhanging eye-brows, swarthy or ruddy complexion, sandy hair, inclining to red or yellow, middle stature.

VIIIth House Personalities

Edgar Cayce, Ibsen, James Pike, Jack London, J.F.Kennedy, Shelley,, Charlotte Bronte, Emily Bronte, Rachmaninoff, J.D.Rockefeller

Freud, Henry VIII, Nostradamus, Thoreau, Patton, Caruso, Pasteur, Robert Mitchum, Emily Bronte

J.D. Rockefeller, Ronald Reagan, Rachmaninoff, R.L. Stevenson

Baudelaire, Christine Jorgensen, Grace Kelly, Mata Hari, Shelley, Tiberius

Rommel, George Marshall, G.L. Rockwell, Marilyn Monroe, Baudelaire, John Glenn, Rodin

Carl Jung, Madame Blavatsky, Houdini, Alfred Hitchcock

Freud, Billy Graham, Rommel, Muhammad Ali, Rimbaud, R.D. Laing

Catherine the Great, Ivan the Terrible, Tiberius, Muhammad Ali, de Maupassant, Swedenborg, Toulouse-Lautrec

Rachmaninoff, Bach, Casals, Queen Victoria, Gloria Swanson

Julius Caesar, Hitler, Bismarck, Churchill, Galileo, Nostradamus, Newton

Yeats, Brigitte Bardot, Fidel Castro, Einstein, Chiang Kai-shek, Franco, J. Edgar Hoover

Health Correspondences

Body Parts and Organs
bladder, genitals, rectum, descending colon, prostate, nasal bones, cervix, excretion, genito-urinary system, sphincter, coccyx, uterus, scrotum, penis, vagina.

Diseases and Symptoms
bladder disorders, colitis, drunkenness, epidemics, venereal diseases, irregular or difficult menses, hernia, syphilis, nose disorders, piles, priapism, prostate diseases.

Sun Scorpio Diseases
genito-urinary diseases, menstrual disorders, uterine and ovarian afflictions. ☉

Moon Scorpio Diseases
disturbed menses, bladder troubles, hydrocele, throat troubles, poisoning, syphilis, miscarriages. ☾

Mercury Scorpio Diseases
pains in bladder and genitals, nervous menstrual trouble. ☿

Venus Scorpio Diseases
venereal diseases, female complaints, uterine prolapsis or tumours, painful menstruation. ♀

Mars Scorpio Diseases
excessive menses, renal stones, enlargement of prostate, inflammation and ulceration of ovaries, uterus, vagina and urethra, cystitis, accidents or injuries to genitals. ♂

Jupiter Scorpio Diseases
enlarged prostate, uterine tumours and abscesses, dropsy, hydranemia, strangury, abscess in urethra. ♃

Saturn Scorpio Diseases
sterility, suppressed menses, constipation, haemorrhoids, fistula, undeveloped genitals. ♄

Uranus Scorpio Diseases
miscarriages, abortions, venereal diseases, difficult births, malformed genitals, nervous afflictions of menses, epidemics. ♅

Neptune Scorpio Diseases
afflictions to nerves of the genito-urinary tract, ill health through drug abuse, epidemic diseases. ♆

♇

SAGITTARIUS

Sagittarius/IXth House   The Archer

(Conception — 7 Weeks)

Mutable Fire Sign		Ruler	: Jupiter	Exalted	: North Node	Incineration	
Hieroglyph	: ⊬	Hebrew	: ﬡ	Greek	: ع	Arabic	: س
Colour	: Blue	Animal	: Centaur, Horse, Dog	Plant	: Rush	Gem	: Jacinth
Tarot	: Temperance	Perfume	: Lign-aloes	Geomancy	: Acquisitio	Weapon	: The Arrow
Egyptian God	: Nepthys	Roman God	: Jupiter	Greek God	: Chiron the Centaur	Genii	: Rishuch

Psychological Correspondences and Events

ASC ♐
Ascendant
Sagittarius

enthusiasm, joie-de-vivre, broad aims, good humour, expansiveness, independence, travel, love of nature; sporting, garrulous, haphazard, social, gentlemanly, messy, lively, adventurous, articulate.

MC ♐
Midheaven
Sagittarius

aspiration, idealism, high standards, planning power, extended thought, spiritual growth; ambitious, noble, changeable, future-orientated, utopian, optimistic, impractical, undependable.

☉ ♐ IX
Sun
Sagittarius/IXth House

mobility, positivity, aspiration, love of freedom, imagination, intellect, taste, success abroad, travel; philosophical, generous, idealistic, undisciplined, scattered, witty, unreliable, open.

☾ ♐ IX
Moon
Sagittarius/IXth House

vivid inner life, striving for wisdom, voyages, manic-depression; changeable, inconstant, imaginative, jovial, frank, free, restless, quick, kind-hearted, sociable.

☿ ♐ IX
Mercury Detriment
Sagittarius/IXth House

philosophy, learning, broad outlook, legal troubles, scattered mentality, occupational difficulties; garrulous, hasty, unstable, sincere, freedom-loving, irreverent, inconstant, clever, fickle.

♀ ♐ IX
Venus
Sagittarius/IXth House

romantic imagination, quickly-responding emotions, outdoor entertainments, many loves, scattered emotions, easily attracted; light-hearted, impressionable, popular, generous, literary, harmonious.

♂ ♐ IX
Mars
Sagittarius/IXth House

love of contest and sport, need to convince others, extravagance; impetuous, adventurous, frank, mobile, argumentative, brave, unconventional, tactless, hasty, competitive.

♃ ♐ IX
Jupiter Ruler
Sagittarius/IXth House

nobility, tolerance, religious and moral aspirations, broad plans, foresight; humanitarian, just, expansive, positive, good-humoured, philosophical, speculative, wasteful, extravagant, kindly.

♄ ♐ IX
Saturn
Sagittarius/IXth House

dignity, devotion, asceticism, honour, seriousness, religion, the Law; easily hurt, high-minded, just, doubting, agnostic, sincere, earnest, reflective, moral.

♅ ♐ IX
Uranus
Sagittarius/IXth House

religious reform, strange and advanced ideas, imagination, risk-taking, inventiveness, love of liberty, unorthodox beliefs; unconventional, progressive, adventurous.

♆ ♐ IX
Neptune
Sagittarius/IXth House

presentiment, clairvoyance, travel, idealism, over-active mind, lack of discrimination, dreams, visions; mystical, prophetic, religious, literary, over-sensitive, vague, unrealistic.

♇ ♐ IX
Pluto
Sagittarius/IXth House

higher knowledge, spiritual pioneering, revolutionary ideas, striving for the unattainable, love of travel; fervid, iconoclastic, reforming, progressive, brilliant, uncontrollable.

☋ ♐ IX
Moon's Node Fall
Sagittarius/IXth House

joint utopian ideas, associations of kindred souls, legal teamwork, educational and humanitarian groups, dreams, voyages; political, egalitarian, academic, idealistic.

Sagittarius Personalities

Thomas More, Shelley, Haydn, Nietzsche, Rhodes, Elizabeth I, General Custer, M.B. Eddy, G. Washington, Carver, Gypsy Rose Lee

Karl Marx, Daniel Boone, DeGaulle, Swift, Duke of Wellington, R.L. Stevenson

Milton, Spinoza, Palladio, Blake, Brahe, Nobel, Pope John XXIII, Churchill, Beethoven, Jimi Hendrix, Keith Richard

Neil Armstrong, Mozart, Beethoven, Brahms, Liszt, Balzac, Einstein, Copernicus, Houdini, Gary Cooper, T.E. Lawrence

Spinoza, Rudyard Kipling, Voltaire, Mao Tse-tung, Jane Austin, Wm. Buckley

Jonathan Swift, R.L. Stevenson, Mark Twain, Mary Stuart, Melina Mercouri, Cary Grant

Louis XIV, Jules Verne, Eugene O'Neill, Robert Redford, Janis Joplin

Copernicus, Gurdjieff, Thoreau, Paganini, Toulouse-Lautrec, Yeats, Brando, Nelson, Spencer Tracy

Charles Darwin, M.L. King Jr, Spinoza, Zola, Gandhi, Frank Lloyd Wright

Martin Luther, Patrick Henry, Dali, Galileo, Charles Lindbergh, Oscar Wilde

Isaac Newton, Garibaldi, Walt Whitman, William Penn, Kit Carson

John Paul Jones, Lafayette, Goethe, Robert Burns, Mozart

Pope John XXIII, Billy Graham, Cecil deMille, Hemingway, Alfred Hitchcock, Truman Capote

SAGITTARIUS

Physical Description

General Description

Strong, active, well-formed body, rather tall, face long and handsome, fine clear eyes, ruddy or sunburnt complexion, chestnut hair, subject to baldness especially at the temples, Grecian nose, stoop.

First Face
1 – 5 degrees

Tall, broad shoulders, full breasted, thick waist, long face, broad forehead, large eyebrows, yellowish complexion, freckles, large nose and mouth, curling brown hair. Mars; mark or scar in the face.

Second Face
5 – 10 degrees

Middle stature, proportionate body, full reddish face, light brown hair, broad forehead, dark eyes, neat mouth and nose.

Third Face
10 – 15 degrees

Medium height, full fat face and body, well-set limbs, fair complexion, grey eyes, light eyebrows, light or flaxen hair, small mouth and lips, well-proportioned.

Fourth Face
15 – 20 degrees

Lusty, strong, good stature, longish face, freckled, brownish complexion, hollow eyes, broad forehead, thick lips, brown hair, long arms, flattish nose, modest countenance.

Fifth Face
20 – 25 degrees

Middle stature, well-proportioned, clear complexion, oval face, light chestnut hair, large grey eyes, thin lips, pleasant countenance.

Sixth Face
25 – 30 degrees

Rather tall, pleasant countenance, round face, clear skin, mixed red complexion, good features, hooked nose.

IXth House Personalities

J.S. Bach, Khrushchev, Mahler, Nostradamus, Raphael, Rembrandt, Rubens

Brahms, Cervantes, Galileo, Luther, Isaac Newton, A. Conan Doyle

Balzac, Nietzsche, Schubert, Henry Miller, F. Scott Fitzgerald, Hawthorne, Jack London

Josephine, Elizabeth I, Eleanor Roosevelt, Rossini, Rubens, F. Scott Fitzgerald

Dostoievsky, Rubens, Shelley, Coco Chanel, John Wesley

Beethoven, John Calvin, Einstein, Erasmus, Keats, Shelley, Richard I, Metternich, F.D. Roosevelt, Mark Twain

Trotsky, Dulles, John Audubon, Lyndon Johnson

Francis Bacon, Gandhi, Victor Hugo, Pushkin, Blake, Swinburne

Milton, Nelson, Pope Paul VI, Rubens, Edgar Cayce

Thomas Mann, Beethoven, Thomas More, Pope Paul VI, Schubert, Calvin Coolidge

Hitler, Dulles, James Pike, Khrushchev, Nelson Rockefeller, Oscar Wilde, Amelia Earhart, Rose Kennedy

Health Correspondences

Body Parts and Organs

hips, thighs, sciatic nerve, arterial system, especially Iliac arteries, coccygeal and sacral bones, gluteous and sartorius muscles, pelvis, femus, sacrum.

Diseases and Symptoms

injuries to hips and thighs, baldness, disorders of lower extremities, falls, coxalgia, dislocation of femur, danger from animals, gout, hip diseases, leg disorders.

Sun
Sagittarius
Diseases

sciatica, paralysis of limbs, eye troubles (8°), pulmonary diseases, swoonings, ulcers in legs, arthritis in hip and thigh, hyperaesthesia.

Moon
Sagittarius
Diseases

blood infections, hip diseases, broken femur, asthma, over-active stomach, lameness, gout in legs, deformed thighs.

Mercury
Sagittarius
Diseases

pains and swellings in hips and thighs, coughs, neuralgia in legs, weak legs.

Venus
Sagittarius
Diseases

hip tumours, hip gout, eruptions on legs.

Mars
Sagittarius
Diseases

fractured femur, accidents and injuries to hips and thighs, sciatica, thigh ulcers, cuts on hips and thighs, broken legs, lameness, pains in legs, dislocated hip.

Jupiter
Sagittarius
Diseases

rheumatism in hips and thighs, gout, pains and swellings in legs.

Saturn
Sagittarius
Diseases

hip and thigh contusions, drying up of hip joint, sciatica, dislocated hip, gout, bruises, aches, falls, lameness, broken legs, obstruction of circulation in legs, arthritis.

Uranus
Sagittarius
Diseases

paralysis of lower limbs, obstruction of circulation in legs, cramps in thighs, numbness in legs, contortions, accidents to thighs.

Neptune
Sagittarius
Diseases

disorders of glands of the leg, wasting of legs, rheumatism of hips or thighs.

CAPRICORN

Capricorn/Xth House The Goat

(7 Weeks — 12 Weeks)

Cardinal Earth Sign	**Ruler : Saturn**	**Exalted : Mars**	**Fermentation**
Hieroglyph : O	Hebrew : ע	Greek : O	Arabic : ع
Colour : Indigo	Animal : Goat, Ass	Plant : Indian Hemp	Gem : Black Diamond, Jet
Tarot : Devil	Perfume : Musk	Geomancy : Carcer	Weapon : The Secret Force
Egyptian God : Khem	Roman God : Bacchus	Greek God : Pan	Genii : Sezorbil

Psychological Correspondences and Events

ASC ♑
Ascendant
Capricorn
concentration, tenacity, expediency, seriousness, inhibition, work capacity, bad humour; goal-conscious, reserved, hard-working, ambitious, unhappy, pragmatic, unspontaneous, anxious.

MC ♑
Midheaven
Capricorn
self-confidence, loneliness, tenacity, overwork, ambition, selfishness; self-centered, sober, prosaic, unimaginative, conscientious, driven, ungratified, reliable.

☉ ♑ X
Sun
Capricorn/Xth House
toughness, endurance, ambition, goal-consciousness, egocentricity, sense of duty, vocational interests; hard-working, objective, selfish, serious, industrious, materialistic, loyal, inflexible, lonely, tenacious.

☽ ♑ X
Moon Detriment
Capricorn/Xth House
emotional repression, lack of gratification, patience, responsibilities, professional concerns, depression; reticent, undemonstrative, loyal, possessive, practical, cautious, reserved, steadfast, inhibited.

☿ ♑ X
Mercury
Capricorn/Xth House
logic, concentration, ambition, patience, thoroughness; shrewd, self-seeking, pragmatic, cunning, melancholic, suspicious, economical, painstaking, industrious, discriminating.

♀ ♑ X
Venus
Capricorn/Xth House
form sense, constancy, fidelity, self-control, older partner; social-climbing, materialistic, possessive, distrustful, cold, jealous, loyal, undemonstrative, inhibited, joyless.

♂ ♑ X
Mars Exalted
Capricorn/Xth House
ambition, success, zeal, self-reliance, authority, executive ability, prominence; sober, industrious, acquisitive, enterprising, heroic, bold, energetic, determined, directed, independent, defiant.

♃ ♑ X
Jupiter Fall
Capricorn/Xth House
leadership, responsibility, material stability, good birth, authority, government and industry, correctness; constructive, capable, organized, egocentric, esteemed.

♄ ♑ X
Saturn Ruler
Capricorn/Xth House
will-power, self-restraint, concentration, paternalism, ambition, slow advance, diplomacy, money failures; melancholic, serious, cautious, strict, suspicious, acquisitive, ambitious, dissatisfied, repressed, unfeeling.

♅ ♑ X
Uranus
Capricorn/Xth House
fanatical concentration, zealous aims, strange career, executive ability, independence, initiative; penetrating, profound, resolute, enterprising, headstrong, authoritative.

♆ ♑ X
Neptune
Capricorn/Xth House
deep research, meditation, strange objectives, religious problems, family troubles, psychic experiences, scandal, notoriety; mysterious, crooked, deceptive, depressive, underhanded.

♇ ♑ X
Pluto
Capricorn/Xth House
untiring struggle for recognition, power-mania, end justifies means, independence, dangerous positions; dictatorial, successful, inventive, single-minded, fanatical, isolated.

☊ ♑ X
Moon's Node
Capricorn/Xth House
business organizations, responsible to others, positions of authority, social climbing, exploitation, loss, deception, clear objectives.

Capricorn Personalities

Machiavelli, Charles Darwin, Rodin, Jonathan Swift, Chiang Kai-shek

Peter the Great, John Tyler, Orson Wells, Barbra Streisand, Charles Richter

Al Capone, Richard Nixon, Mao Tse-tung, Stalin, Nasser, Gurdjieff, Cezanne, Adenauer, Muhammad Ali

Julius Caesar, Augustus Caesar, Napoleon, Hitler, Rasputin, Eichmann, Patton, Darwin, John XXIII, Ivan the Terrible, G.L. Rockwell

Cicero, Daniel Webster, Thomas Beckett, Louis Pasteur, Wilhelm Furtwangler

Beethoven, Schubert, Elvis Presley, Henry Miller, Nero, Dostoievsky, Zsa Zsa Gabor, Toulouse-Lautrec

Einstein, Edison, Louis Pasteur, Bell, Tolstoi, Theodore Roosevelt, John Wayne, Admiral Byrd

Hitler, Richard Nixon, Beethoven, Patrick Henry, Thomas Beckett

Rasputin, Proust, Bertrand Russell, Verdi, Jonathan Swift, Spencer Tracy, Andy Warhol

Julius Caesar, Eichmann, Dostoievsky, Henry VIII, Thomas Huxley, Howard Hughes

John I, Tolstoi, Dostoievsky, Thomas Huxley, Madame Blavatsky

Napoleon, Duke of Wellington, Metternich, Bloody Mary

J.F. Kennedy, Humphrey Bogart, Al Capone, Douglas MacArthur, Nasser, Stalin, Trotsky, John L. Lewis

 # CAPRICORN

Physical Description

General Description
Tall, slender, long thin face, upturned jaw, sloping forehead, thin beard, dark hair, long neck, narrow chin and breast, weak knees, crooked legs.

First Face
1 – 5 degrees
Tall, thin face, pleasant countenance, dark hair, little mouth, freckles, dark complexion.

Second Face
5 – 10 degrees
Small stature, long face, pleasant look, brownish complexion, sad hair.

Third Face
10 – 15 degrees
Like the former, taller, fatter, awesome and majestic, a commanding aspect.

Fourth Face
15 – 20 degrees
Round face, fatness, clear skin, brown hair, freckled, neat mouth.

Fifth Face
20 – 25 degrees
Fatter, taller, fairer, more beautiful than the former faces, excellent features, good proportion. Saturn; dark and thin.

Sixth Face
25 – 30 degrees
Excellent middle stature, fair and clear complexion, flaxen hair, excellent proportions, admirable features, beautiful.

Xth House Personalities

Napoleon, George Washington, Charlemagne, Fidel Castro, Louis XIV, Balzac, Nietzsche, Princess Anne

Wagner, Schubert, Jane Addams, Mary Astor, Ethel Barrymore, Clara Barton, Dumas

Einstein, Thomas Mann, Durer, Emerson, Martin Luther King Jr, Rimski-Korsakov

Beethoven, Max Ernst, Mahler, Goethe, Goya, Dali, Durer, van Gogh, Ingrid Bergmann

Ivan the Terrible, Joan of Arc, Cezanne, A.G. Bell, Douglas Fairbanks, F.L. Wright

Augustus Caesar, Balzac, Khrushchev, Rubens, George VI, Schubert, Barnum, DeMille

Copernicus, Darwin, Winstein, Disraeli, Hitler, Nixon, J. Edgar Hoover, Napoleon

Marx, Ludwig II, Moshe Dayan, Gurdjieff, Michaelangelo, Dante, Gabriel Rosetti, Gladstone

Picasso, Aleister Crowley, Sarah Bernhardt, Nostradamus, Jean Harlow, Marlowe, Shelley, Rita Hayworth, Rimsky-Korsakov

Richard I, Khrushchev, Muhammad Ali, Ernest Hemingway, Errol Flynn, Warren Beatty, James Dean

Maria Callas, Calvin Coolidge, Gandhi, Moshe Dayan, John Glenn, Alfred Hitchcock, Mae West, Charles Manson

Health Correspondences

Body Parts and Organs
skin, knees, bones, cutaneous system, joints, knee-cap.

Diseases and Symptoms
sterility, rheumatism, chronic diseases, cutaneous complaints, dislocations of knee and leg, depression, eczema, gastric disorders, hypochondria, impetigo.

Sun Capricorn Diseases
rheumatism, bone diseases, skin diseases, digestive troubles, lame knees, sprains.

Moon Capricorn Diseases
articular rheumatism, skin eruptions, gout in knees, weak legs and knees.

Mercury Capricorn Diseases
rheumatism of knees, pain in back, skin disease, melancholy, neuralgia in knees or legs, pain in knees.

Venus Capricorn Diseases
gout in knees, skin diseases on legs.

Mars Capricorn Diseases
carbuncles, erysipelas, smallpox, synovitis, measles, chicken pox, pimples, inflammatory skin diseases, knee fractures, broken legs, knee accidents, ankylosis, gout.

Jupiter Capricorn Diseases
skin disease, melancholy, liver degeneration, swollen knees, weak legs, adenoid trouble.

Saturn Capricorn Diseases
diseases of capella, chronic trouble with knee joint, rheumatism, erysipelas, skin gout, bursitis, ague, sprains, broken legs, fractures, arthritis of leg joints, numbness.

Uranus Capricorn Diseases
accidents of legs or knees, cramps in knees, deformed knees, paralysis of lower legs, leprosy.

Neptune Capricorn Diseases
arthritis of leg joints, lack of control over knees.

AQUARIUS

Aquarius/XIth House The Waterbearer

(12 Weeks — 22 Weeks)

Fixed Air Sign		Ruler	: Saturn, Uranus	Exalted	: Pluto	Multiplication	
Hieroglyph	:	Hebrew	:	Greek	:	Arabic	:
Colour	: Violet	Animal	: Man, Peacock, Eagle	Plant	: Olive	Gem	: Glass, Chalcedony
Tarot	: Star	Perfume	: Galbanum	Geomancy	: Tristitia	Weapon	: The Censer
Egyptian God	: Ahephi	Roman God	: Juno	Greek God	: Ganymede	Genii	: Aiglun

---

	Psychological Correspondences and Events	**Aquarius Personalities**
ASC ♒ **Ascendant** **Aquarius**	reforms environment, communal sense, sociableness; group-orientated, friendly, reasonable, progressive, sympathetic, good-hearted, pleasant, intellectual, inventive, radical, eccentric.	T. Jefferson, Karl Marx, Jung, Wellington, Catherine the Great, Mary I, Robespierre, Alexander the Great, Mary Pickford
MC ♒ **Midheaven** **Aquarius**	mania for innovations, many plans, scattered energies, humanitarianism, vague ideas; modern, aspiring, unrealistic, undisciplined, hopeful, future-orientated, unrealized.	Spinoza, Rousseau, Jules Verne, W.B. Yeats, Lord Byron, Bob Dylan
☉ ♒ XI **Sun Detriment** **Aquarius/XIth House**	idealism, humanitarianism, readiness to help others, knowledge of human nature, intuitive understanding; sociable, sympathetic, detached, democratic, universal, scattered, political, impractical, cranky.	Dickens, Abraham Lincoln, Thomas More, F.D. Roosevelt, Mia Farrow, R. Reagan, John L.Lewis, Havelock Ellis, Furtwangler
☾ ♒ XI **Moon** **Aquarius/XIth House**	wealth of ideas, concern for others, abundant hopes and wishes, dislike of solitude, many friends, generous spirit, sympathetic to new methods; civilized, humane, political, superficial, indiscriminate, inane.	Mary Baker Eddy, Lenin, John Lennon, Yeats, Voltaire, A.C. Doyle, Carl Sandburg
☿ ♒ XI **Mercury** **Aquarius/XIth House**	progressive thinking, quick understanding, ramification, enthusiasm, originality, reformer, inventor, organizer; fresh, lively, involved, well-informed, sociable, utopian, comprehensive, intellectual, studious.	Handel, F.D. Roosevelt, Schubert, Steinbeck, Gertrude Stein, John L. Lewis
♀ ♒ XI **Venus** **Aquarius/XIth House**	progressive views on love, good friends, easy contacts, free love; cultured, refined, sociable, easy-going, amenable, superficial, scatty, naive, indiscriminate.	Gertrude Stein, Robert Burns, Byron, James Joyce, Wolfgang, Mozart
♂ ♒ XI **Mars** **Aquarius/XIth House**	male friends, new methods, reform, team-work, compulsive joining, disagreements among friends; high-spirited, contradictory, inconstant, superficial, enthusiastic.	Adlai Stevenson, Tito, Woodrow Wilson, Christiaan Barnard, Charles DeGaulle,
♃ ♒ XI **Jupiter** **Aquarius/XIth House**	prominent friends, patronage, help from others, good-fellowship, liberality; congenial, good-humoured, humanitarian, sympathetic, philanthropic, genteel, obliging, curious.	Queen Victoria, J.J. Rousseau, Walt Whitman, Madame Blavatsky, Charles DeGaulle
♄ ♒ XI **Saturn Ruler** **Aquarius/XIth House**	realization of plans, practical idealism, false friends, impressive speech, faithfulness, quiet determination; affable but detached, thoughtful, humane, reasonable, deliberate, organized.	Alexander Hamilton, Howard Hughes, Thomas Mann, Albert Schweitzer, Jung, Rilke, Crowley, Byron
♅ ♒ XI **Uranus Ruler** **Aquarius/XIth House**	progressive mind and spirit, originality, mental ability, inventiveness, neophilia, intuition, imagination; collective, rebellious, changeable, trouble-making, scientific, peculiar.	Joan of Arc, Mark Twain, Orson Welles, Leonard Berstein, Johannes Brahms, Ibsen
♆ ♒ XI **Neptune Fall** **Aquarius/XIth House**	strange attractions, search for soul unions, dependent on others, noble aims, idealism, unfounded hopes, wild enthusiasm; helpless, drifting, deluded, insincere, easily swayed, fraudulent.	John Calvin, Emile Zola, Rodin, Einstein, Edison, R.L. Stevenson
♇ ♒ XI **Pluto Exalted** **Aquarius/XIth House**	strongly communal, revolutionary activities, political involvements, advance through others, popularity, exaggerated plans; exploitative, dynamic, organized, rebellious.	Ivan the Terrible, Cervantes, Elizabeth I, Shelley, John Keats, Byron, Schubert
☊ ♒ XI **Moon's Node** **Aquarius/XIth House**	multi-faceted relationships, numerous friends, love of social contact, lack of independence, compulsive joining, helpful associations; sociable, communal, helpful.	Brigitte Bardot, Moshe Dayan, A.C. Doyle, Isadora Duncan, Einstein, F.S.Fitzgerald, Ralph Nader, Carl Sandburg

 # AQUARIUS

Physical Description

General Description
Well-set, stout, robust, strong, healthy, rather tall, never short, delicate fair complexion, long face, clear but not pale, sanguine, hazel eyes, sandy or dark flaxen hair.

First Face
1 – 5 degrees
Tall, long visage, brown complexion, long arms and legs, dark hair, wide mouth, Roman nose, dark eyes.

Second Face
5 – 10 degrees
Not so tall, slender, reddish face, rough skin, dark brown hair, long visage, wide mouth and nostrils. Mars; mole on the top of the nose. 8th degree; tall.

Third Face
10 – 15 degrees
Tall, slender, thin, thin visage, broad forehead, reddish face, narrow chin, curly hair.

Fourth Face
15 – 20 degrees
Thick middle stature, rather clear visage, full face, wide mouth and nostrils, chestnut hair, short arms and legs. Jupiter; tall. Mars; fiery appearance, mark on the face.

Fifth Face
20 – 25 degrees
Leanness, thin visage, long nose, narrow visage, narrow forehead, high cheeks, overhanging upper jaw. Saturn; melancholy appearance.

Sixth Face
25 – 30 degrees
Good looking, middle stature, good complexion, comely appearance, full face, round visage, light hair.

XIth House Personalities

Metternich, Tito, A. Warhol, Dali, Swift, Coco Chanel, Douglas Fairbanks, Jackie Gleason, Gary Cooper, Bob Hope

Churchill, Martin Luther King Jr, Spinoza, Ronald Reagan, Verdi, Orson Welles, Stravinsky

Edward VII, Mao Tse-tung, Walter Scott, Walt Whitman, Gary Cooper

Cecil B. DeMille, Stravinsky, Andy Warhol, Balzac, Tchaikovsky, Janis Joplin, Coco Chanel

Mao Tse-tung, Melin Mercouri, Napoleon, Harry Truman, Fidel Castro

Andy Warhol, Paul Cezanne, Alfred Tennyson, Moshe Dayan, Henry Ford, Paderewski

Charles Manson, Ronald Reagan, Richard III, Rodin, Balzac

Thomas Mann, Thomas More, Rimsky-Korsakov, Orson Welles, Disraeli, John Foster Dulles

Moliere, Elvis Presley, Brahms, Puccini, Stravinsky, Errol Flynn

Casanova, Dali, Goebbels, Patrick Henry, Tito, Wagner, Andy Warhol, Stravinsky

Caruso, Pope John XXIII, James Joyce, Lyndon Johnson, Nehru, Peter Sellers, Cary Grant

Health Correspondences

Body Parts and Organs
ankles, calves, the circulation, the breath, eyesight, Achilles tendon, tibia, fibula, shin bone.

Diseases and Symptoms
accidents to calves and ankles, circulatory disorders, blood diseases, extraordinary diseases, nervous diseases, varicose veins, dropsy.

Sun Aquarius Diseases ☉
sprained ankles, varicose veins, dropsy, heart palpitations, poor circulation, blood disorders, hyperaesthesia.

Moon Aquarius Diseases ☽
varicose veins, leg ulcers, dropsy, fractured ankles, poor blood, blood poisoning, lameness.

Mercury Aquarius Diseases ☿
shooting pains in legs, varicose veins, corrupt blood, lame ankles.

Venus Aquarius Diseases ♀
varicose veins, swollen ankles, poor blood.

Mars Aquarius Diseases ♂
blood poisoning, varicose veins, fractured leg or ankle, weak ankles, inflamed blood.

Jupiter Aquarius Diseases ♃
milk leg, swollen ankles, fevers from too much blood, high blood pressure, blood poisoning, poor circulation.

Saturn Aquarius Diseases ♄
weak ankles, sprains, cramps in ankles and joints, bad teeth, excema, fractured ankles, weak ankles, arthritis, in ankles, impeded circulation.

Uranus Aquarius Diseases ♅
unusual diseases, cramps in ankles, spasmodic circulation.

Neptune Aquarius Diseases ♆
blood diseases.

♇

PISCES
Pisces/XIIth House
The Fishes

(22 Weeks — Birth)

Mutable Water Sign	
Hieroglyph : ⊓	
Colour : Red-Violet	
Tarot : Moon	
Egyptian God : Anubis	

Ruler : Jupiter, Neptune
Hebrew : ק
Animal : Fishes, Dolphin
Perfume : Ambergris
Roman God : Neptune

Exalted : Venus
Greek : ς
Plant : Opium Poppy
Geomancy : Laetitia
Greek God : Poseidon

Projection
Arabic : ف
Gem : Pearl
Weapon : The Magic Mirror
Genii : Tarab

Psychological Correspondences and Events

ASC ♓ Ascendant Pisces
self-sacrifice, lack of self-confidence, determined by external influences, depression, vagueness, laziness, quiet comforts; receptive, peculiar, lonely, simple, passive, weak, sympathetic, gentle.

MC ♓ Midheaven Pisces
waiting and hoping, passive attitude, advance through luck, lack of clarity, lack of goal-consciousness; unambitious, impressionable, philosophical, procrastinating, tolerant, kindly.

☉ ♓ XII Sun Pisces/XIIth House
the inner life, seclusion, institutions, self-sacrifice, universal love, mysticism, poetry, music, passivity; reserved, secretive, compassionate, empathetic, tender, negative.

☾ ♓ XII Moon Pisces/XIIth House
yielding, surrender, feelings of inferiority, hyper-sensitivity, addiction, loneliness, danger of exploitation, attraction to the mysterious and occult; seducible, sentimental, self-doubting, dreamy, moody.

☿ ♓ XII Mercury Fall Detriment Pisces/XIIth House
fantasy, imagination, influenced by ideas of others; intuitive, retentive, discursive, mediumistic, philosophical, poetic, musical, humourous, versatile, refined.

♀ ♓ XII Venus Exalted Pisces/XIIth House
the longing for love, subjection to emotional and sexual influences, love of music and art; seducible, exploited, gentle, tender, indulgent, charitable, inspirational, compassionate, genial.

♂ ♓ XII Mars Pisces/XIIth House
lack of energy, procrastination, working silently or without recognition, dissipation, sexual fantasies, revelling, depravity, drugs and alcohol; romantic, easily tempted, poisonous, secretive, occult.

♃ ♓ XII Jupiter Ruler Pisces/XIIth House
altruism, contentment, solitude, tolerance, capacity for enjoyment; compassionate, generous, selfless, imaginative, beneficent, charitable, visionary, indolent, wasteful.

♄ ♓ XII Saturn Pisces/XIIth House
difficult work in seclusion, struggles, timidity, isolation, melancholia, fear of failure, inferiority complex; modest, self-underrating, depressed, ungratified, serious, retiring.

♅ ♓ XII Uranus Pisces/XIIth House
mysticism, revelling ecstasy, subconscious forces, intuition, estrangement, peculiar experiences, strange diseases; misunderstood, secretive, visionary, original, investigative.

♆ ♓ XII Neptune Ruler Pisces/XIIth House
art, reverie, reserve, mysticism, inner life, craving for alcohol, nicotine, etc., subject to externals; mediumistic, neurotic, contemplative, over-emotional, escapist, rhapsodic, broad-minded, vague.

♇ ♓ XII Pluto Pisces/XIIth House
desire for seclusion, universalism, volcanic emotions, self-destruction, revelations, longing for death, withstanding temptation, epidemic diseases; metaphysical, secretive, extravagant, profound, apocalyptic.

☊ ♓ XII Moon's Node Pisces/XIIth House
secret associations, occult groups, institutions, undone by relationships, harmful communities, subversive societies, enemies, restraint through others.

Pisces Personalities

Alfred Hitchcock, Tennessee Williams, Calvin, George Washington, Eichmann, Valentino, R.D. Laing

Pope Pius XII, Anastasia, Brigitte Bardot, Berlioz, Enrico Caruso, Marier Curie

Caruso, Ravel, Edgar Cayce, Einstein, Chopin, Renoir, Copernicus, Voltaire, Washington, Liz Taylor, Nureyev,

Wolfgang von Goethe, Helen Keller, Mahler, Michaelangelo, Ravel, Shelley, Rimsky-Korsakov

Harry Houdini, Victor Hugo, James Joyce, Ravel, Renoir, Tennessee Williams

Elizabeth Browning, van Gogh, E. Cayce, Mendelssohn, Mary Pickford, E.A. Poe, Hans Christian Andersen

Marilyn Monroe, Christine Jorgensen, Liz Taylor, Elizabeth Browning, Casanova, Ava Gardner, Milton, Steinbeck, Nietzsche

Leonardo, Goethe, Newton, Rembrandt, Laing, Welles, Lincoln, Cellini, Verlaine, Cervantes, Florence Nightingale

Jesse James, Queen Victoria, Karl Marx, Prince Albert, Barbara Stanwyck

Schubert, Peter Sellers, Tchaikovsky, Cezanne, Judy Garland, Nostradamus

Gustav Mahler, Puccini, Rimbaud, Wilde, A. Conan Doyle, Ivan the Terrible

Franz Liszt, Hugo, Robert E. Lee, Clara Barton, Baudelaire

Edgar Cayce, Pablo Casals, Mata Hari, Edward Kennedy, Valentino, H. Ellis, Tennessee Williams

PISCES

Physical Description

General Description
Short, thick-set, pale, delicate complexion, flabby face, rather large, thick shoulders, stooping gait, clumsy step, dark hair, ill-shaped head, not well made, sleepy eyes, large eyebrows, short arms and

First Face
1 – 5 degrees
Tall, middle proportions, broad shoulders, long face, dark brown hair, eyes sunken, high nose, large mouth, narrow chin. Mars; pock-marks.

Second Face
5 – 10 degrees
Great stature, full visage, clear skin, pleasant look, light hair, large eyebrows, long legs, arms, fingers and feet, wide mouth. Mars; pock-marks.

Third Face
10 – 15 degrees
Pleasant and neat, full oval face, clear skin, large and fair eyebrows, large forehead, brown hair, short stature, not thick.

Fourth Face
15 – 20 degrees
Strong middle stature, long visage, swarthy complexion, freckled, broad forehead, large eyebrows, black eyes, narrow chin, straight black hair, short arms, legs, fingers and feet.

Fifth Face
20 – 25 degrees
Incomparable and delectable, excellent proportions, round visage, grey eyes, well-formed nose, dimpled chin, smiling, chestnut hair.

Sixth Face
25 – 30 degrees
Small, thin, consumptive, freckled or pimpled face, tawny skin, black hair, sometimes excessively fat.

XIIth House Personalities

John Wilkes Booth, Bob Dylan, Havelock Ellis, Judy Garland, Gandhi, Queen Victoria, Tchaikovsky

Anastasia, Isadora Duncan, Havelock Ellis, Greta Garbo, B. Bardot, W.B. Yeats, Alfred Tennyson, Queen Victoria, Dylan

A. Conan Doyle, J.Edgar Hoover, Peter Sellers, Pearl Buck, Al Capone, Dumas

Jane Adams, Clara Barton, Tennyson, Duchess of Windsor, Bob Dylan

Adolph Eichmann, Bloody Mary, Elvis Presley, Queen Victoria

R.D. Laing, Edward VII, Jackie Gleason, Louis XIV, Spinoza, Tennessee Williams, Bob Dylan

Al Capone, Marcus Aurelius, Schubert, Toulouse-Lautrec, Mark Twain, Bob Dylan

Charles Manson, Nostradamus, Poe, Voltaire, Erasmus, Bernhardt, Casanova, T. Williams

Max Ernst, Dali, Doyle, James Pike, Rasputin, Muhammed Ali, Montgomery Clift, Alain Delon

A. Conan Doyle, T.E. Lawrence, Jack London, George Wallace, Christopher Columbus, Patton

Rochard Burton, Muhammad Ali, Dietrich, van Gogh, Himmler, Herbert Hoover, Howard Hughes, Marilyn Monroe

Health Correspondences

Body Parts and Organs
feet and toes, lymphatic system, glandular system, synovial fluids, mucus, gastro-abdominal system (reflex action with Virgo), tarsus and metatarsus bones.

Diseases and Symptoms
alcoholism, boils, bunions, chilblains, colds (from wet feet or living in cold places), deformed feet or toes, dissipation, dropsy, forgetfulness, insanity.

Sun
Pisces
Diseases
typhoid fever, intestinal troubles, colds, foot and mouth disease, lethargy, diseases of the lymphatic system, swimming and boating accidents.

Moon
Pisces
Diseases
drinking, drug addiction, weak feet, foot ulcers, colds as result of wet feet, oedema, lethargy, boils.

Mercury
Pisces
Diseases
gout, feet cramped and tender, colds as result of wet feet, neuralgic pains in feet, neuroses.

Venus
Pisces
Diseases
tender feet, chilblains, gout.

Mars
Pisces
Diseases
deformed feet, bunions, corns, blisters, accidents to feet, drowning, bromidrosis, bowel inflammation, diarrhoea, deformed feet, loss of foot, narcotic addiction.

Jupiter
Pisces
Diseases
swollen feet, alcoholism, addiction, enlarged feet, hyperidrosis.

Saturn
Pisces
Diseases
cold feet, rheumatism, bunions, tuberculosis, consumption, crying spells, accidents to feet, afflicted foot bones, club feet, flat feet, deformed feet.

Uranus
Pisces
Diseases
deformed feet, cramps in feet and toes, paralysis of feet, hyperidrosis, contortions.

Neptune
Pisces
Diseases
overstimulated pineal gland leading to drink, drugs, delirium, overdoses, enlarged feet, disorders of foot glands, psychosomatic diseases, wasting of foot tissues.

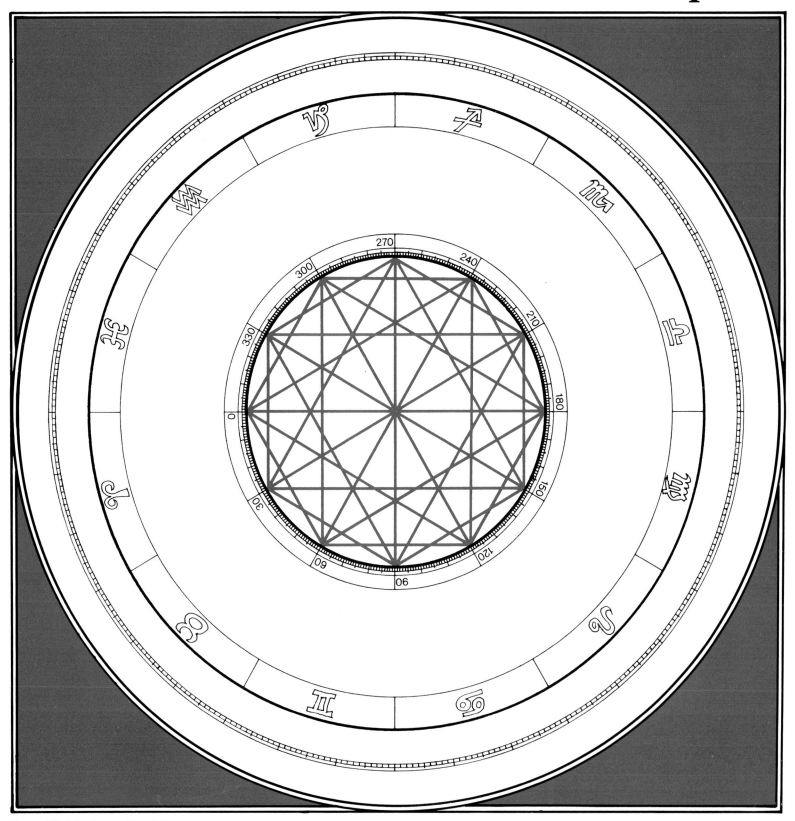

Part VII

Figure VII.1 An Aspect Mandala.

The Aspects

> "(In modern physics), one now has divided the world not into different groups of objects but into different groups of connections . . . . What can be distinguished is the kind of connection which is primarily important in a certain phenomenon. The world thus appears as a complicated tissue of events, in which connections of different kinds alternate or overlap or combine and thereby determine the texture of the whole."[1]

The positions of the ten planets are the datum points in astrology. The planets are linked to each other by *Aspects*. Aspects are angular relationships between planets as seen from the Earth. These aspect angles are technically measured from the centre of the Earth, but because the other stellar bodies are so immensely far away, they are of equal size everywhere on the Earth's surface. Aspects are derived from the ideal geometric patterns which determine the relationships between the signs — The Grand Trine and the Grand Cross — and are expressions of the proportional harmonies which exist in space and time. The various aspects used in astrology are derived by dividing the 360° circle by the whole numbers 1, 2, 3, 4 and 6, producing angles of 360° (0°), 180°, 120°, 90° and 60°. (Figure VII.1) The aspects represent vibrational patterns which reverberate throughout the universe.

The aspect angles are integrating factors between planets. The entire web of aspects defines the degree of integration within the individual psyche. Since every planet has a sign location in space and a house location in the Time Scale, the *aspects connect the qualities and times of events.* As an analogy to music, the signs of the zodiac are equivalent to the scale of twelve semitones (seven whole tones and five half tones), the houses to the key a piece is played in (based upon one of the twelve notes in the scale) and the planetary positions to the individual notes. (Figure VII.2) Harmonies and dissonances in a musical composition are equivalent to aspects. The aspects are latent relationships within the circle of the horoscope as harmonies and dissonances are latent within the notes on a piano keyboard.

In psychology, complexes are equivalent to these inherent structural patterns.

> "A complex is an unconscious or half-conscious cluster of representations, laden with emotion. A complex consists of a nucleus and a surrounding field of associations. A complex can be acquired by personal experience or its nucleus can be formed by an archetypal content."[2]

> "Complexes behave like secondary or partial personalities possessing a mental life of their own."[2]

The complex is thus a network of emotionally-charged associations, determining individual conditioning and personal history, which is continually reactivated throughout life. In astrology the complex is composed of a series of planets around the periphery of the horoscope which are related to each other by aspects, and the nuclear core of the complex is the archetypal meaning of the planets involved. Series of planets which aspect each other are called *Constellations*. Constellations show how the formal archetypal patterns in the horoscope manifest themselves in reality.

Aspects

The aspect from which others arise is the **Conjunction** (☌), indicating two or more planets in the same degree of the zodiac — the aspect of *Unity*. (Figure VII.3) It is the purest aspect as it joins the influences of planets involved so that they always operate simultaneously. The alchemical term 'coniunctio' referred to what is now called a 'chemical combination' and implies that the components involved will never separate. They are bound together by their mutual attraction and repulsion, like the King and Queen in alchemical symbolism, and the coniunctio is the "archetype of the union of opposites".[3] Whether the planets are sympathetic to each other or not, they are irrevocably joined.

In the conjunction, two or more planets are joined and altered in the process. They work in unison, mutually change each other and react at the same time. Conjunctions usually indicate situations where it is difficult if not impossible to separate the individual components. This is

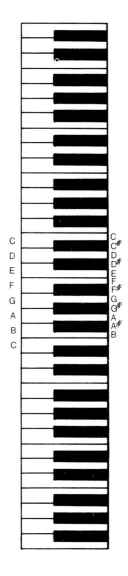

Figure VII.2 The Piano Keyboard and its Intervals.

[1] Werner Heisenberg, *Physics and Philosophy*, p. 96.

[2] Jung, *Psychology and Religion, CW 11,* par. 21.

[3] Jung, *The Practice of Psychotherapy, CW 16,* p. 169.

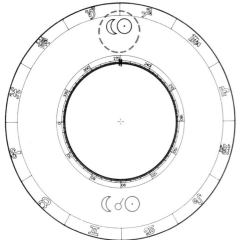

Figure VII.3 The Conjunction.

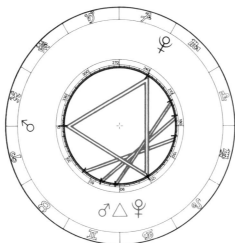

Figure VII.4 The Trine Aspect.

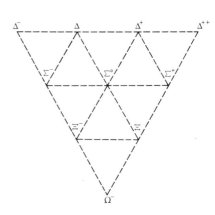

Figure VII.5 The Baryon Decuplet. (After Capra, *The Tao of Physics,* p. 268.)

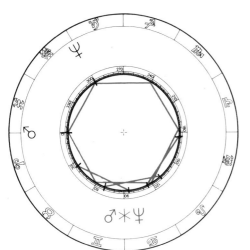

Figure VII.6 The Sextile Aspect. When many sextiles are linked within the horoscope they remain near to the periphery.

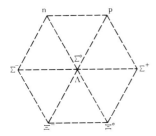

Figure VII.7 The Meson Octet. (After Capra, *The Tao of Physics,* p. 267.)

4 Capra, *The Tao of Physics,* p. 268.

true whether principles, personifications, inner mechanisms or other correspondences are being combined. For example, in a conjunction between Jupiter and Saturn, Jupiter is the principle of expansion or mania, while Saturn is the principle of contraction or depression. The two together produce manic-depression. In this state the individual is subject to extremes of elation and melancholy and is unable to equilibrate the two. Should an expansive situation occur, it would be compensated by an equivalent contraction at virtually the same time.

Two other sets of aspects derive from the *Grand Trine* and the *Grand Cross.* The Grand Trine and its harmonic, the Sextile, are geometrically stable shapes and indicate harmonious, static states of being. The Grand Cross and its harmonic, the Square, are unstable shapes indicating tension relationships which tend to be irrational and problematic.

The basic component of the Grand Trine is the **Trine** ($\triangle$), one leg of the equilateral triangle within the circle, and it indicates two planets 120° apart. (Figure VII.4) The trine implies a fluid exchange of energy and equal communication in both directions. Trines produce *balanced relationships, supportive situations,* but, being essentially static, usually lack motivation. The trine is indicated by a double (green) line connecting the planets involved. It indicates two planets which support each other at similar developmental stages of consecutive octaves in the life, usually in signs of the same triplicity of elements. Due to the geometry of the trine, its aspect lines never cross the centre point of the horoscope and are only adjacent to the core of the psyche. Trines are communications which allow the individual knowledge of his periphery, but only shed light upon the centre by implication.

The triangular shape is used in particle physics to describe the interaction of the basic force-carrying particles, the quarks. (Figure VII.5) The equilateral triangle obeys the laws of particle interactions of symmetry — each apex is in total equilibrium with the others. The quantity of charge remains constant in any location or time, maintaining an internal conservation of energy.[4] The grand trine and the trine are shapes where the planets involved will always remain the same before, during and after any interaction or event. Momentum is conserved, total energy is conserved and the orientation is conserved. These figures indicate symmetrical patterns which tend to conserve their meaning.

The bisector and harmonic of the trine is the **Sextile** ($\ast$), which is two planets 60° apart. (Figure VII.6) The sextile is half of the trine and adds *understanding* to trine relationships. It indicates a fairly harmonious situation which manifests as either an aesthetic or intellectual connection. This aspect links planets in a particular element with the signs of the same gender once-removed on either side. They connect positive signs to positive and negative to negative — like rapport between members of the same sex. They indicate the midpoint of the trine, and are even more peripheral, following the circumference of the circle very closely. The sextile is shown as a single (green) line.

A series of sextiles around the circle produces an inscribed hexagon — an important shape in particle physics and genetics. The subatomic particles, mesons and baryons, when arranged

5 Capra, *The Tao of Physics*, p. 268.

6 See Jung, *Mysterium Coniunctionis, CW 14.*

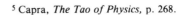

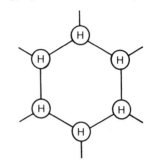

Figure VII.8 The DNA Molecule. This genetic molecule contains both an hexagonal bond and a pentagonal bond.

Figure VII.9 The Benzine Ring of Hydrocarbons.

according to quantum numbers expressing their charges produce hexagonal patterns. (Figure VII.7) These patterns are symmetrical, and within them particles are opposite their anti-particles in total balance. All particles in each pattern are positioned by their rotational forces, hypercharges and have the same quantum numbers.[5] The mesons and baryons are composed of triangular quarks just as the sextiles are made of the harmonic of the trine aspect. In the genetic double helix the base pairs of acids are diagrammed as hexagons in crystallographic studies, with the shape indicating the nature of their chemical bonding. (Figure VII.8) Hexagonal shapes also determine the structure of the benzine ring of hydrocarbons in organic chemistry. (Figure VII.9) This shape, from which the sextile emerges, is stable in the physical world and also in the horoscope.

The primary component of the Grand Cross is the **Opposition** (☍), which is a pair of planets 180° apart. (Figure VII.10) The opposition is the aspect of *maximum tension,* as the planets are in opposite signs and houses in the horoscope. They mutually antagonize, but simultaneously complement, each other. It implies two events and principles in life which are antithetical and occur at opposite times. The usual tendency is polarization, where one planet is activated and dominates at the expense of the other. Energy flows from one end of the opposition to the other like a see-saw, producing instability and frustration, eventually leading to unconsciousness of one of the two polar values. Each planet in an opposition contains some of the qualities of its opposite, but there is usually no awareness of this in the individual. The attraction of opposites is the counter-tendency to this division and its resolution involves the equilibration of the two poles through *consciousness* of the split. The opposition is indicated in the horoscope by a double (red) line through the centre of the circle, and the energy which the aspect produces emanates directly from the centre of the psyche.[6]

The opposition is related to the vast range of polar situations which exhibit attraction and repulsion. The continual movement of energy and particles in the universe is the direct result of this shifting. The opposition is the primary motive force in the universe and the horoscope.

The bisector and harmonic of the opposition is the **Square** (□), which is two planets at right angles to each other (90°). (Figure VII.11) Energy moves from one planet to the other via the centre, making a right-angle shift in direction along the way, indicating *tension* and *motivation.* In the square aspect *energy is liberated.* Squares operate through the same quadruplicity, but also through antithetical elements — from positive sign to negative sign and vice versa. For example, the signs square to the cardinal fire sign Aries are the cardinal water sign Cancer and the cardinal earth sign Capricorn. Positive fire is either drowned by negative water or smothered by negative earth. In square aspects the gender of each component will be different, producing tension and disruption. They release energy from the centre through contrast and incommensurability, and the result is usually an event. Within the overall structure of the horoscope, squares activate complexes and issue the energy which sustains life. They are often disruptive, but if they are properly utilized, they produce creative energy. The square is

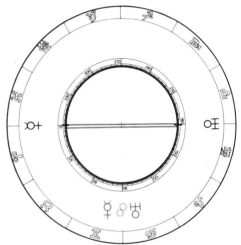

Figure VII.10 The Opposition Aspect. The opposition aspect passes through the centre.

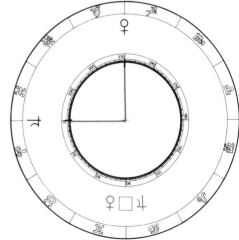

Figure VII.11 The Square Aspect. The signs square to Aries are Cancer and Capricorn, both of which are feminine and passive.

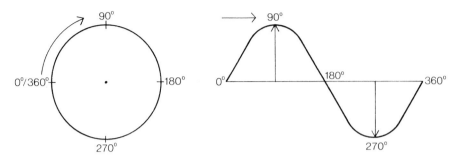

Figure VII.12 Gravitational Waves as a quadrupole vibration.

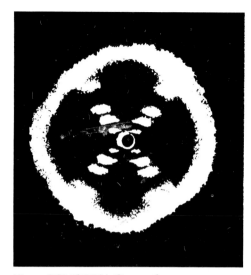

Figure VII.13 DNA Crossection.

[7] Landscheidt, *Cosmic Cybernetics*, p. 62.

[8] Watson, *The Double Helix*, p. 36.

[9] von Franz, *Number and Time*, p. 132.

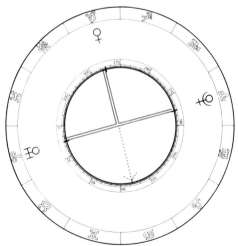

Figure VII.14 The T-Square.

[10] Ebertin, *Man in the Universe*, p. 38.

shown as a right-angled single (red) line connecting the planets involved.

Oppositions and squares are *dynamic* aspects and are parallel in nature to dynamic structures in the universe. The quaternity of the grand cross is reflected in many physical and psychological situations. Gravitational waves vibrate like quadrupoles, and their vibrations form at the points which mark the corners of a square within the circle. (Figure VII.12) These angles, 0°, 90°, 180° and 360°, correspond to the positions in the grand cross and determine the resonance of the whole solar system.[7] When planets are clustered on these points they agitate solar flare activity by corresponding to the harmonic vibrations of the gravitational waves. Resonance communicates information and is probably transmitted to the body through individual cells as well as in the gene elements in RNA and DNA. An X-ray photograph taken of DNA in the B form by Rosalind Franklin shows the cross pattern clearly.[8] (Figure VII.13) DNA is constructed of two base pairs of the acids adenine-thymine and guanine-cytosine, which bond together in the double helix, again reflecting the cylindrical spiral of the horoscope through time, the bonds acting as square or opposition aspects. There is also a quaternity in thermodynamics expressing the relationship between Work, Space, Heat and Matter.[9]

The **T-square** is a combination shape produced by one planet square to two others in opposition — the grand cross with one leg missing. (Figure VII.14) Often the imaginary position or sensitive point where the fourth planet would be is a highly important position in the horoscope, almost as though the t-square were yearning for completion, an evocation of its missing quality. Like grand crosses, the t-square is composed of planets in signs of the same mode and is designated by that mode — Cardinal T-square and Mutable T-square.

Although we have explained the major aspects used in this book, there are many other minor aspects. Many of the other aspects are smaller harmonics of the ones already discussed and are derived so that every pair of planets in the horoscope can be related in some way to each other. While this increases the total number of aspect relationships, it has the disadvantage of overcomplexity and does not recognize that individuals have qualities which *do not relate* to each other.

Ebertin places great importance upon the harmonics of the square and opposition aspects and excludes almost totally trines and sextiles. These aspects are the **Semi-square** (∠) of 45° and the **Sesqui-square** (⧠) of 135°. These points bisect the squares producing division of the circle by eight, and indicate minor tensions.

The harmonics of the trine and sextile are the **Semi-sextile** (⊻) of 30° and the **Quincunx** or **Inconjunct** (⊼) of 150°. These aspects indicate slightly harmonious contacts.

Division of the circle by five produces another family of aspects, the **Quintile** of 72°, the **Biquintile** of 144°, the **Sesquiquintile** or **Trecile** of 108° and the **Semiquintile** of 36°. These aspects are almost never used. Another virtually unknown aspect is the **Nonogon** of 40°, which is a division of the circle of the zodiac by nine. These aspects are reputedly beneficial, but their worth is highly tenuous.

An aspect of a totally different sort is the **Parallel,** which indicates two planets in the same degree of declination above or below the equator. It is similar to the conjunction. While this has been used often, its importance is difficult to prove.[10]

Orbs of Influence

The strongest and most critical manifestation of an aspect occurs when the angle between the aspected planets is exactly 0°, 60°, 90°, 120° or 180°, but since aspects function throughout the entire lifetime there is a margin allowed on either side of the exact aspect — the *Orb of Influence.* Providing the aspecting planets fall within a specified range, the aspect functions, although the closer to exactitude they are the more effective they will be. Orbs vary according to the planets involved and the type of aspect.

The Sun and Moon are large bodies and move rapidly through the zodiac and so are given an orb of 8° on either side.

The Personal Points, the Ascendant and the MC are the most important house positions, so they are also given an orb of 8°.

The inner planets, Mercury, Venus and Mars move rapidly but are quite small and have orbs of 5°.

The outer planets, Jupiter, Uranus, Neptune and Pluto move very slowly through the zodiac and are given orbs of 4°.

The Dragon's Head, the Moon's ascending node, has an orb of 3° as it moves extremely slowly.

The orb of each planet extends both before and after its longitudinal position. Therefore, a planet will be in trine to the Sun when it is between 112° and 128° away (120° − 8° = 112° and 120° + 8° = 128°). (Figure VII.15) When two planets with different orbs are aspected, the larger orb is used.

Orbs for aspects are: for the conjunction, trine and opposition a maximum of 8° while for the smaller sextile and square, a maximum 5°.

These orbs of influence are guidelines rather than hard-and-fast rules, so conditions may affect their use. When three or more planets are grouped together so that they each are conjunct to their neighbours, but the first and last planets are beyond each other's orbs (Figure VII.15), it is assumed that they are all mutually conjunct: a *Satellitium.* In interpretation, judgement is often dominant over rules.

Another factor which modifies the quality and operation of aspects is the differing rates of motion of the planets involved and whether they are moving towards or away from exactitude. (Figure VII.15) If a fast-moving planet (Sun, Moon, Mercury, Venus or Mars) is approaching the orb of a slower-moving planet, it is *Applying* to the exact aspect and is growing stronger towards its 'culmination'. When the two planets become exact the aspect is fully felt. As the faster moving planet moves past the exact aspect it is *Separating* until it passes the outside limit of the orb. Applying aspects in the birth horoscope indicate potential situations, while separating aspects indicate situations which have already happened. An awareness of the relative speed and direction of all planetary movements is required, as the dynamics of astrology are determined by continual flux rather than static situations. Applying aspects are indicative of the *Potential* of an aspect, the exact aspect is a *Discharge* and a separating aspect is an *After-effect.* The phase of operation has a profound effect upon interpretation and the slower the planets involved, the more important the phase of their operation.

Because of the Time Scale positions of each planet, the orbs of the aspects are doubly important. This is due to the compaction of time through the lifetime. *The period of time equal to a 5° orb in the horoscope increases with age.* While a 5° orb is equivalent to five days during the beginning of Gestation, in the VIIIth house it equals five years. An aspect in operation during Gestation will apply, become exact and separate within days while an aspect at the age of 45 will take up to ten years to apply, become exact and separate. This mechanism must be considered in the interpretation of all aspects.

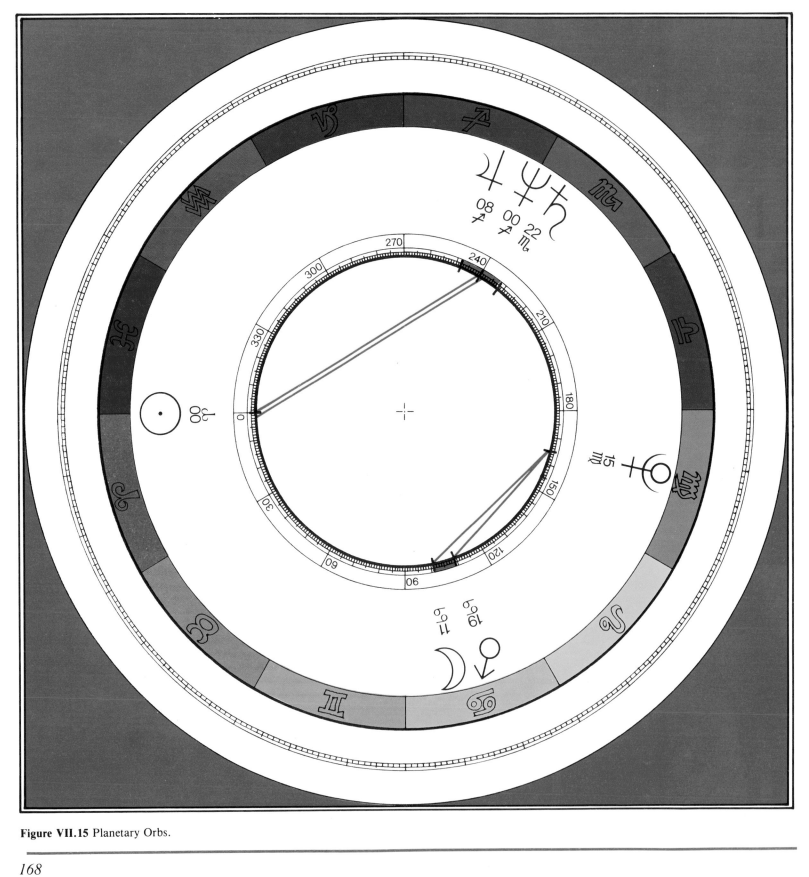

Figure VII.15 Planetary Orbs.

Determining Aspects in the Horoscope

When the positions of the planets have been determined and placed in their correct sign and house in the horoscope diagram, the aspects must then be indicated. (See The Construction of the Birth Horoscope, Appendix A.) When the planets are positioned, a mark is made on the 360° wheel and the aspects are then initially indicated as pencil lines between these marks. Conjunctions are easiest to find and are indicated by a dotted line around all the planets involved. The trines, oppositions and sextiles are all indicated by straight lines drawn between the aspecting planets, but squares are shown as a right-angled line intersecting the centre-point of the horoscope. The correct procedure for determining all the aspects is as follows:

1) Starting with the Ascendant, each planet is taken in turn and its aspects found.
2) Although finding aspects can eventually be done by eye alone, initially the Plastic Time Scale Disk is used. (Figure VII.16) On this disk all of the sensitive points of aspect are indicated. The disk is aligned with the Birth Moment (0° Aries) exactly on each planet in turn, and any other planet which falls within the correct orb of the seven sensitive points will form an aspect.
3) The aspect lines are drawn in pencil.
4) For clarity, the aspect lines should then be redrawn with double green lines for all trines, single green lines for all sextiles, double red lines for all oppositions and single red lines for all squares. This allows differentiation between the static aspects and the tension aspects during the interpretation.

See the sample horoscopes in Part X for many examples.

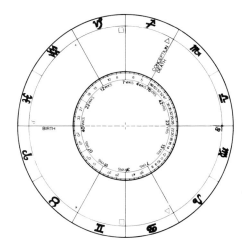

Figure VII.16 The Time Scale Disk.

The Dynamics of Constellations

In determining the influence of any planet, all of its combinations must be taken into consideration. Each planet in a constellation affects the others, and the type of aspects which join them determine the *dynamics of the constellation* — the flow of energy through them.

One of the greatest problems in traditional astrology is the definition of conjunctions as neutral, sextiles and trines as harmonious and squares and oppositions as disharmonious. These simplifications are not verified by experience because the qualities of the planets involved in the aspects are often much more important. A trine between Saturn (limitation) and Mars (desire or conflict) should traditionally be harmonious, but in practice indicates a 'static limitation of desire' or 'repressed desire'. The inherent difficulties of any aspect between Mars and Saturn will always function, and the trine, being essentially static, would indicate that the Mars-Saturn situation is long-term and will not be worked through easily. The same pair of planets in square produces the same potentially destructive energy, but because the square is dynamic it will force an event and liberate energy. Often the 'harmonious' aspects can be suffocating, while the 'tension' aspects are positive and invigorating.

Instead of applying terms like 'good', 'bad', 'harmonious' or 'inharmonious' to types of aspects, one should understand the aspects as *processes* which either encourage or inhibit the flow of energy. Events do not just happen, but are manifestations of the total psyche unfolding through time, always providing 'keys' to the whole. Each experience must be placed in its proper relationship to the centre. Separating any event from this context is misleading. Inferences derived from the birth horoscope are reasoned from the general to the particular rather than built up of many fragments.

This is similar to the recognition by physicists that the search for the 'elementary' particles is futile because the essence of the universe is dynamic and not static. The existence of the observer conditions the processes being observed — every individual is the entire universe and contains the processes which operate in it. In astrology, life must be seen as a web of events which, although experienced in linear succession through time, also have connections *outside time*. The aspects are connections that operate beyond the purely causal path around the periphery of the horoscope — they penetrate the centre from which the periphery is derived. Their connections transmit meaning, and meaning is the essence of life.

Since the planets are archetypal, the aspects which connect them must connect the whole range of manifestations each planet represents, whether it be a psychic mechanism, a pattern of behaviour, an action, an event, a personification, an idea or a physical condition.

Figure VII.15 Planetary Orbs. The Sun is at 0° Aries. Neptune is positioned at 0° Sagittarius, and is in exact trine to the Sun. Jupiter is 112° from the Sun, and Saturn is 128° from the Sun, and they define the maximum orb of the trine aspect. Jupiter is moving away from the exact aspect, and is Separating. Saturn is moving towards the exact aspect, and is Applying. Although Jupiter and Saturn are 16° apart, because Neptune is in their common centre, they can all be assumed to be mutually conjunct. The sensitive point for a sextile to Pluto is 15° Cancer. Therefore, the Moon is Applying to the exact aspect and Mars is Separating from the exact sextile to Pluto.

The overall *aspect pattern* indicates whether the flow of energy or libido is likely to proceed on to a higher form or be blocked by a planetary event and forced to regress. Certain planets encourage flow while others tend to produce blockages. The planets which encourage the flow of energy are the Sun, Moon, Mercury, Venus, Jupiter and to a lesser extent, Neptune. Those which create blockages are Mars, Saturn, Uranus and Pluto. The Personal Points, ASC and MC, are totally conditioned by their signs and by the planets which aspect them, and thus are neutral.

The conjunction aspect is neutral and determined by the qualities of the planets involved. The sextile and trine encourage flow. The square and opposition aspects tend to disrupt flow. The movement within the individual horoscope must be diagrammed and its flow determined. The mechanism which allows analysis is the use of *planetary pictures* of the constellations.

Planetary Pictures

The usual method for relating planets to each other in interpretation is to evaluate each pair of planets. Textbooks usually give pairs of planetary definitions, thus:

Sun/ASC =	Moon/ASC =	Mercury/ASC =	Venus/ASC =	Mars/ASC =
Sun/MC =	Moon/MC =	Mercury/MC =	Venus/MC =	Mars/MC =
Sun/Moon =	Moon/Mercury =	Mercury/Venus =	Venus/Mars =	Mars/Jupiter =
Sun/Mercury =	Moon/Venus =	Mercury/Mars =		
Sun/Venus =	Moon/Mars =	Mercury/Jupiter =	etc.	
Sun/Mars =	Moon/Jupiter =	Mercury/Saturn =		
Sun/Jupiter =	Moon/Saturn =	Mercury/Uranus =		
Sun/Saturn =	Moon/Uranus =	Mercury/Neptune =		
Sun/Uranus =	Moon/Neptune =	Mercury/Pluto =		
Sun/Neptune =	Moon/Pluto =	Mercury/Node =		
Sun/Pluto =	Moon/Node =			
Sun/Node =				

[11] Charles Carter, *Astrological Aspects.*

In the use of paired interpretations each constellation must be broken down into its component pairs and then gradually reconstructed.[11] This method has been used for thousands of years, but for the interpretation of constellations of more than two planets there is a superior technique. Reinhold Ebertin proposes this alternative in *The Combination of Stellar Influences.*

Ebertin made the interpretation of aspects more definitive by including, whenever possible, at least one other planetary position to each pair — a third quality which makes a trinity of values. To combine other planets with an initial pair, Ebertin uses the axis between the pair, the *Mid-point,* as discussed in Part II of this book. The use of mid-points is accompanied by the use of *planetary pictures,* which are diagrams illustrating how groups of planets are conjoined. There are three types of mid-points which demonstrate this.

1) *Direct Mid-points* or *Half-sums* occur when a planet is placed exactly in the centre of a pair (Figure VII.17):

Sun ————————————	Jupiter ————————————	Moon
15° Aries	15° Gemini	15° Leo
60°		60°

In this example the Sun and Moon are trine, and as Jupiter is sextile to both, it is also a direct mid-point of Sun/Moon. Ebertin also uses direct mid-points where the central planet is exactly on the axis of a pair of planets any distance apart, independent of whether they make aspects or not (Figure VII.17):

Mercury ————————————	Jupiter ————————————	Saturn
0° Aries	15° Gemini	0° Virgo
75°		75°

The direct mid-points are written: Jupiter = Sun/Moon or Jupiter = Mercury/Saturn.

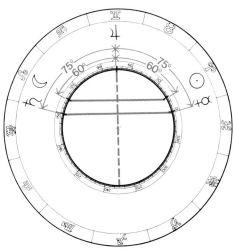

Figure VII.17 Direct Midpoints.

2) *Indirect Mid-points* occur when two pairs of planets have the same axis, whether or not there is a planet at that sensitive point (Figure VII.18):

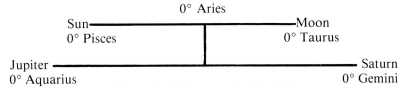

The indirect mid-points are written: Sun/Moon = Jupiter/Saturn.

3) There are also indirect mid-points when a third planet aspects the midpoint (Figure VII.19):

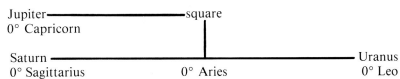

The indirect mid-point is written: Jupiter 90 = Saturn/Uranus or Jupiter = Saturn/Uranus.

Ebertin utilized Witte's method for making planetary pictures but recognized that the use of mid-points exclusively without traditional aspects is limited:

> "Whereas the Hamburg School of Astrology rests almost entirely upon the interpretation of the planetary pictures, neglecting the traditional aspects at the same time, such a procedure is just as partial according to our modern findings as if one ignored the mid-points or half-sums and judged the aspects only. Numerous investigations and experiments have proved that the simultaneous use of both half-sums and aspects leads to successful results. Moreover the inclusion of a third interpretive factor also restricts the number of possible interpretations, thus leading to a more exactly defined statement as to the correctness of the interpretation."[12]

Witte also defined each constellation by one possible event, often quite extreme in interpretation, a practice which Ebertin correctly questioned. As an antidote Ebertin developed the structural ideas of Witte to include a whole series of interpretive factors for each constellation. In CSI, each combination is defined according to the following six factors:

Cosmic Constellation = the pair of planets involved

Principle = the combined principles of the pair of planets

Psychological Correspondence = psychological states corresponding to positive, negative and neutral combinations

Biological Correspondence = the biological mechanism involved and the physical states produced

Sociological Correspondence = the personifications of the pair

Probable Manifestations = a range of events produced by the configuration

In addition, each cosmic constellation is compared to every other planet and personal point, producing a very specific picture of every possible combination (1117 factors). The information given in CSI was fully documented and proven over forty years by Ebertin and his associates, and they have been constantly reviewed and revised, fully satisfying the claims made in the introduction: "(CSI) has established itself as a standard reference work for the reliable and conscientious interpretation of cosmograms (horoscope) and planetary configurations."[13] In this light, although some guides to aspect interpretation are given in this book, it is suggested that CSI is a necessary tool for all astrological work, and should be used in conjunction with this book.

While the work of Ebertin has made astrology experimentally and practically viable, there are still mechanisms which (he recognizes) are in need of revision. He points out that the house systems are the weakest point in astrology and he virtually eliminates them in his interpretation considering them 'very dubious and biased'. We will remedy this problem by combining the structural ideas and information of Ebertin with the Logarithmic Time Scale house system, producing a possibility of total analysis. The planetary pictures will use only the traditional aspects which have implicit mid-point natures — the conjunction, the sextile-trines and the square-oppositions — and order them through the life by the Time Scale.

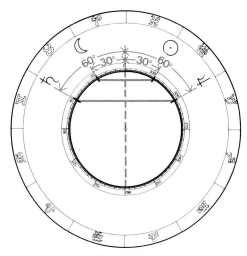

Figure VII.18 Indirect Midpoints.

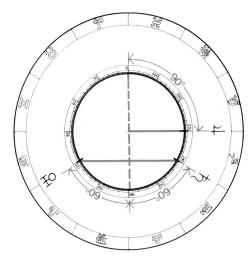

Figure VII.19 Indirect Mid-points with an asepcting planet.

[12] Ebertin, *CSI*, p. 27.

[13] Ebertin, *CSI*, p. 35.

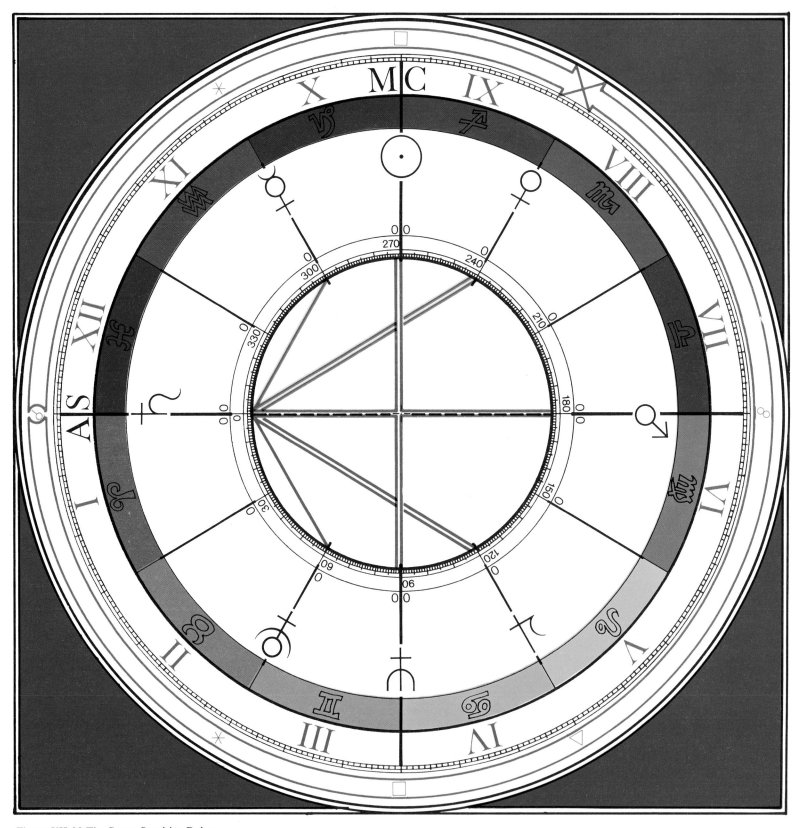

Figure VII.20 The Seven Sensitive Points.

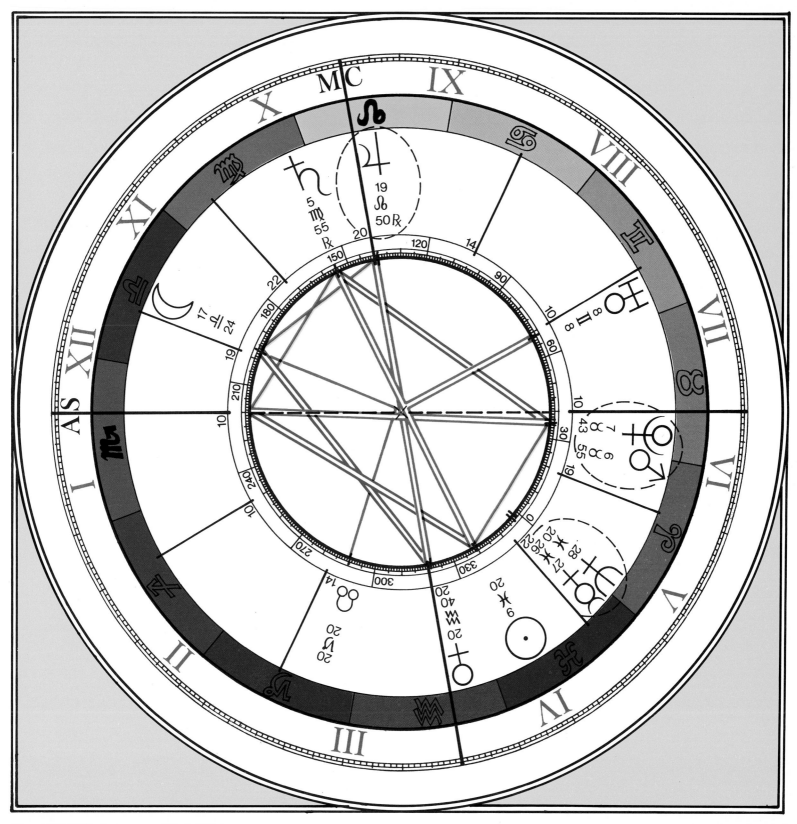

Figure VII.21 The horoscope of Rudolf Steiner

THE ROUND ART

Figure VII.20 The Seven Sensitive Points. The arrrow indicates the direction of time through life. Sinister aspects operate against the direction of the arrow, while dexter aspects operate in the same direction.

Planetary Pictures and the Time Scale

The application of the Time Scale to the aspects produces a system of 'sensitive points' in the horoscope, all of which can be related to specific times. The actual position of a planet in the birth horoscope indicates its prime manifestation, and the planets it aspects will coincide with the sensitive points it makes at other times. Each planet has seven sensitive points which may or may not be activated by other planets in aspect.(Figure VII.20) These sensitive points are two sextiles on either side, two squares on either side, two trines on each side and one opposition, all of which are indicated on the clear plastic Time Scale Disk. When any planet in the horoscope is aligned with the Ascendant-Birth Moment on this disk, all of the sensitive points and aspecting planets are indicated.

As an example, if — in an imaginary horoscope — Saturn is exactly conjunct the ASC at 0° Aries and seven other planets are placed upon the seven sensitive points around the horoscope, the following situation exists.

A. Saturn and the ASC function at the moment of birth, their qualities combining to determine the personality.

B. Venus, Sun and Mercury are *Sinister aspects* (left-hand) which occur during Gestation before the birth moment.

C. Pluto, Neptune, Jupiter and Mars are *Dexter aspects* (right-hand) which occur during Childhood and Maturity, with Mars happening at the time in the life opposite the Birth Moment, at 23 years old. All of these planets register after the Birth Moment.

D. Venus and Mercury will be supportive qualities leading up to the birth and the Sun will be a tensioning quality affecting birth.

E. Pluto and Jupiter will be supportive qualities which result from the birth but occur during Childhood.

F. Neptune will be a tension during Childhood resulting from the birth.

G. Mars will indicate a reversal and an extreme tension reciprocating the birth qualities.

The interpretation of the ASC would include all of the planetary aspects which occur before and after birth. As each of the planets is defined at its correct time, all the planets also partake of the ASC qualities. In every case there is a distinction between the *sinister aspects occurring before the event* and the *dexter aspects happening after the event* in question, until towards the end of the life, all of the aspects are sinister. (Figure VII.20). As each planetary position is reached the nature of the specific planet will either support the flow or impede it, according to its aspects: *Every aspect is qualified by planets occurring either before or after it in the lifetime.* The 'present moment' is a juncture between the individual's past and future.

When a sensitive aspect point occurs where there is no planet the original influence is transmitted, without any qualification, into a different age. As Saturn conjunct ASC in our example indicates 'restriction by an older person', at every sensitive point there will be an older person who restricts the individual in some way (Not necessarily the same person who did this at birth).

Here is an analogy to musical structure. The life is like a concerto where a theme is repeated many times. The essence of the theme remains the same, but each time it is repeated various instruments are dominant and it can sound entirely different. As the concerto develops, the theme becomes more complex and varied, but still evokes the original theme. The more complex the concerto (or the life) the less readily identifiable the theme, secondary and tertiary themes become, unless the individual experiencing them is able to perceive the *structure*. In both music and life the concerto is heard many times and in many different situations, played by different instrumentalists and led by varying conductors, but the essential structure is always there. The structure is qualified by the consciousness of the listener.

The analogy can be also extended to include singing and dance. Vocal accompaniment continuously plays off on the music — sometimes coinciding, sometimes contradicting, sometimes independent of the music, but always relevant to it.The dance is an accompanying movement and a physical manifestation of the musical structure. Jung remarked that dancing for primitives was a summation of their entire life and culture and a natural gradient for their libido. The ritual of life and survival was likened by them to a dance. Dancing recapitulated their whole existence all the way back to the movement within the mother's womb.[14] Events, patterns and participation are all reflected in the horoscope's aspect-pictures — a concerto of life.

14 Jung, *Symbols of Transformation, CW* 5, p. 154.

In many cases constellations exist by themselves within the overall horoscope, and often there are many independent constellations. This is the case in the horoscope of the occultist Rudolf Steiner. (Figure VII.21 Horoscope 43 in Part X.) The Sun in Pisces occurs at seven years old and is aspected to the ASC by trine (119°), to Saturn in Virgo by opposition (176°), to Mars and Pluto in Taurus by sextile (57°) and to Uranus in Gemini by square (89°). These six planetary positions are interconnected with each other but are separate from the remaining planets in his horoscope. This major constellation permeates his life but he has two other constellations which alternate with it. Jupiter is conjunct the MC, sextile Moon in Libra and in opposition to Venus in Aquarius. Mercury and Neptune are conjunct in Pisces but do not have any other aspects.

For structuring the major constellation, any pair of planets can be used as a 'reference pair', but since the opposition is the strongest aspect and Saturn a dominant planetary influence, the best starting point would be the Sun/Saturn pair. We would then compare the other four planets to this base pair and blend the resultant information.

    Sun/Saturn = ASC   (by trine and sextile)
             = Uranus   (square to both, producing a T-square)
             = Mars & Pluto (by sextile and trine)

Since in this example we are analysing the *structure of the constellation,* we continue to try to understand the mechanics of the aspects independent of their actual interpretations. If the Sun is the reference point at 7 years old, Saturn refers to the early part of Gestation and the ASC to the birth moment. These influences precede the Sun and indicate the context within which it operates. The aspects to Mars and Pluto at 21 years old and to Uranus at 41 years old are reactivations of the Sun and refer to situations which galvanize the constellation. Mars, Pluto and Uranus are all highly active and tend to precipitate explosive events. The Sun will combine influences from Steiner's past and future, transmitted through a childhood event, probably concerning his father. In analyzing Saturn all the other planets will be *potential,* while from the viewpoint of Uranus they have all happened and can be considered *actual.* Linking the potential to the actual is the essence of the present and leads to a perspective which sheds light upon the nature of the individual. *The aspects are relative temporal relationships.*

To determine more specifically the Sun's effect within Steiner's life, other pairs can be used for reference. The Sun can be paired with any of the planets in the constellation, that is, Sun/ASC to the birth moment, Sun/Mars or Sun/Pluto at 21 years old, or Sun/Uranus to 41 years old. These pairs will qualify very specifically the impact of the Sun (paternal imago) upon the earlier and later events. When all the sets of aspects are found and interpreted relative to their respective ages, the blend will lead to a very complete picture of Steiner. We will discover in the chapter on Interpretation that by structuring the entire horoscope in this way, the necessary choices can be made easily and accurately.

Sun Aspects

	Sun/Conjunction Aspects	Sun/Positive Aspects
☉/ASC Sun/Ascendant	strong personality, self-confidence, a good front, seeking the lime-light, cheerful disposition, recognition, public life, showing off, desire to be important; happy, extraverted, irrepressible,	popularity, ambition, charm, fortunate contacts, gaining recognition; affable, harmonious, positive.
☉/MC Sun/Midheaven	Authority, fame, consciousness of goal, self-awareness, strong father, late developer; strongly fated, self-conscious, directed, one-pointed, ambitious, individualistic, dogmatic.	happy in profession, easy advancement, earned success, striving for a goal, self-knowledge, positive attitude, success; well-adjusted, ambitious, aspiring, fortunate.
☉/☾ Sun/Moon	one-sidedness, special abilities, misunderstood person, close parental tie, lowered vitality; highly strung, sensitive, egotistical, ambitious, mono-maniacal, self-obsessed.	harmonious person, happy marriage, strong constitution, good parental relations, harmonious home; well adjusted, calm, optimistic, bouyant, adaptable.
☉/☿ Sun/Mercury	good learning capacity, knowledge, intelligence, curiosity, egocentric mind; quick-witted, reasonable, well-informed, literary, scientific, capable, ingenious, talkative.	No Aspects Possible
☉/♀ Sun/Venus	love affairs, artistic ability, romanticism, praise, recognition, help through the opposite sex; attractive, amorous, warm-hearted, refined, kindly, demonstrative, artistic.	No Aspects Possible
☉/♂ Sun/Mars	desire to be in the lime-light, moral and physical strength, competition, danger, feats of endurance, positions of prominence; self-assertive, decisive, hot-blooded, enthusiastic, impulsive.	energy, virility, courage, ambition, leadership, great achievements; masculine, forceful, positive, lusty, power-hungry, daring, domineering, enterprising.
☉/♃ Sun/Jupiter	creativity, good fortune, wealth, fortunate birth, help through superiors, prominent or indulgent father, noble aims, social-climbing; lucky, generous, luxurious, magnanimous, indulgent.	tolerance, good humour, good health, advancement, honour, recognition; expansive, out-going, optimistic, materialistic, joyous, self-indulgent, well-liked.
☉/♄ Sun/Saturn	concentration, purposivity, ill-health, isolation, ambition, selfishness, strong paternal image; serious, egotistical, determined, monomaniacal, unfeeling, lonely, dedicated.	good father, slow advancement, responsibility, love of difficulties, loyalty, trust, dedication, working, sacrificing gladly; paternal, ambitious, sober, reserved, reliable, conservative, reliable.
☉/♅ Sun/Uranus	individualism to the point of anarchy, compulsive reforming, overpowering personality; insatiable, domineering, daemonic, restless, excitable, dynamic, explosive, alienated, eccentric.	leadership, originality, love of change, organizing abilities, positions of power, popularity; progressive, energetic, reforming, magnetic, respected.
☉/♆ Sun/Neptune	sensitivity, refinement, otherworldliness, psychic abilities, impressionability, music and art, ill-health; frail, delicate, inspired, visionary, unrealistic, mediumistic.	compassion, understanding, inspiration, inner vision, good taste, idealism, receptivity, enthusiasm, mysticism, soul-life, long journeys; sympathetic, imaginative, tender-hearted, tolerant.
☉/♇ Sun/Pluto	lust for power, craving for rulership, great advances and great reversals, an extraordinary and highly-fated individual; autocratic, ruthless, insanely ambitious, daemonic.	great achievements, leadership, belief in one's mission, organizing ability, pioneer spirit, creative power; forceful, magnetic, influential, indestructible.
☉/☊ Sun/Moon's Node	compulsive joining, clinging to associations, defining oneself through one's relationships.	happy relationships, working, educational and political associations, groups of men, cooperation, public relations; sociable, adaptable, popular.

Moon Aspects

	Moon/Conjunction Aspects	Moon/Positive Aspects
☾/ASC Moon/Ascendant	close personal ties, subjective attitude, women in the environment, obligingness, maternal attitude, taking care of others; easily moved, moody, kindly, changeable, receptive, mobile, animated.	many contacts with women, harmonious attitude, adaptability, influenced by women, easily moved; obliging, easy-going, relaxed, hospitable, sympathetic, feminine.

THE ROUND ART

Sun/Negative Aspects

mis-placed self-confidence, disadvantages through others, separations; pushy, ambitious, disliked, boisterous, braggardly, self-seeking.

egocentricity, misplaced self-confidence, lack of clarity, unrealistic goals, changing aims, professional difficulties; arrogant, misguided, conceited.

hypersentivity, ill-health, intelligence, financial difficulties, unfortunate marriage, schizophrenia; egotistical, ambitious, highly strung, irritable, gifted.

No Aspects Possible

No Aspects Possible

inability to relax, quarrels and contention, dissidence, hyper-activity, brutality, violence, overstrain, hastiness, many upsets, cardiac troubles; irrascible, headstrong.

extravagance, pretention, arrogance, conflicts with authorities, legal troubles, bad liver, over-indulgence, gluttony, bad taste; lazy, materialistic, ostentatious.

inferiority complex, difficult struggles, creative block, separation from father, cruel or weak father, ill-health, pessimism; weak, anxious, negative, lonely, maltreated.

excitement and upheaval, unending changes, forced readjustments, compulsion, self-destruction, occasional violence; excitable, rebellious, irritable, meddlesome

illness, unlucky speculation, seduction, scandal, bad taste, deception, over-indulgence, lack of self-control, weak father; over-emotional, easily led, romantic.

power mania brings destruction, ruthlessness, fanaticism, great losses, fall from power, physical suffering, danger to life, separation by providence.

lack of adaptability, estrangements, disharmonious attitude to others, short-lived relationships.

Sun/Conjunction Personalities

Moshe Dayan, Cecil DeMille, Dostoievsky, Mao Tse-tung, Paganini, U.S. Grant, Gounod, Charlton Heston

Cicero, Marcus Aurelius, Charlemagne, Balzac, Goethe, Thomas Mann, Khrushchev, DeGaulle, Himmler, Nicholas II

Beethoven, Queen Victoria, Alexandra, Swinburne, Marx, Brando, J.J. Rousseau, Lyndon Johnson, Ingrid Bergmann

Kant, Goethe, Marlowe, Henry Miller, Henry Ford, Mussolini, Edison, Dali, Valentino, H.C. Andersen, Bernhardt

Marie Antoinette, Wagner, Shelley, Liszt, Chopin, Keats, Robert Burns, Goya, James Joyce, F.D. Roosevelt, Chanel

Catherine the Great, Cervantes, Berlioz, Ivan the Terrible, Laing, Goebbels, John Glenn, P.T. Barnum, L.B. Johnson

William Blake, Kipling, Pushkin, Maria Callas, Khrushchev, Bob Dylan, Toulouse-Lautrec

Dante, Durer, Haydn, Mozart, Baudelaire, Walter Scott, Baruch Spinoza, George Wallace

Wellington, Pasteur, Shelley, Freud, Conan Doyle, Lewis Carroll, Dietrich, Walt Disney, Eugene O'Neill, H. Hughes

Savonarola, Handel, Keats, Pasteur, Leewenhoek, Madeleine Grey, William Randolph Hearst

Marcus Aurelius, Errol Flynn, Ibsen, Tito, W.R. Hearst, Susan Hayward, Princess Anne

Pope John XXIII, Stalin, John Lennon, Eleanor Roosevelt, Alexandra

Sun/Aspect Personalities

Martin Luther, Louis XIV, Carl Jung, Copernicus, Rudolf Steiner, Janis Joplin, Jackie Gleason

Machiavelli, Dickens, Hitler, Thomas Mann, Rachmaninoff, Elizabeth I, Jean Harlow, Charles Manson, Audrey Hepburn

Lenin, Disraeli, Gladstone, Prince Albert, Rembrandt, G.B. Shaw, Max Ernst, James Dean, Greta Garbo

No other aspects possible

No other aspects possible

Beethoven, Stravinsky, Franco, Jesse James, Al Capone, Muhammad Ali, Robert E. Lee, Amelia Earhart, Neil Armstrong, Jack London

Cellini, Julius Caesar, Wagner, Thomas Mann, Rodin, Oscar Wilde, Marx, Isadora Duncan, T.E. Lawrence, J.D. Rockefeller, Princess Anne

Oliver Cromwell, Stalin, Gandhi, Swedenborg, Thomas Hardy, Steiner, H. Hoover, C. Coolidge, Woodrow Wilson, F.D. Roosevelt

Richard I, Newton, Disraeli, Lenin, Raphael, John Dillinger, Thomas Mann, P.T. Barnum, Blavatsky, Bette Davis, Neil Armstrong

Louis XIV, Carl Jung, Mozart, Vermeer, Raphael, Tolstoi, Thomas Hardy, Rubens, Pushkin, Elvis Presley, Chopin

Erasmus, Caligula, Garibaldi, Nietzsche, Adler, Gurdjieff, Dulles, Clark Cable, Kahlil Gibran, Rudolf Nureyev

Gandhi, Schweitzer, M.L. King,Jr, Pope Paul VI, Helen Keller, R.F. Kennedy, Dulles, G.B. Shaw, Adlai Stevenson

Moon/Negative Aspects

disagreements with mother or women, disharmonious attitude, hypersensitivity; moody, changeable, easily annoyed, over-reactive, unreliable.

Moon/Conjunction Personalities

Queen Victoria, Trotsky, Rossini, Goya, Nehru, Charles Chaplin, Rose Kennedy, Shirley MacLaine, Pope Paul VI

Moon/Aspect Personalities

Liszt, Debussy, T.E. Lawrence, Carl Sandburg, Barbra Streisand, Andre Gide

Moon/Conjunction Aspects

☾ /MC
Moon/Midheaven rich soul life, intuitive understanding, changeable character, notoriety, contact with the public, women or mother exerts great influence on the destiny; impressionable, sentimental, loving,

☾ / ☿
Moon/Mercury fertile mind, talent for languages and business, intuitive understanding, perception, mental activity; quick witted, accomplished, facile, whimsical, talkative, eccentric, talented.

☾ / ♀
Moon/Venus tenderness, devotion, longing for love, affection, attraction for opposite sex, gain in wealth and possessions, artistic profession; demonstrative, romantic, aesthetic, kind, pleasure-loving, maternal.

☾ / ♂
Moon/Mars will power, fighting spirit, intense emotion, impulsiveness, vigour, inner tensions; easily angered, brave, straightforward, headstrong, impetuous, rebellious, independent.

☾ / ♃
Moon/Jupiter sociability, kindness, success, generosity, love of luxury, good fortune, practical idealism; responsive, indulgent, hedonistic, humanitarian, civilized, religious, hopeful, understanding.

☾ / ♄
Moon/Saturn intense concentration, dislike of mother, emotional repression, self-control, isolation, frigidity; hard-working, selfish, ascetic, critical, misanthropic, dour, melancholic, hard-hearted, ambitious, miserly.

☾ / ♅
Moon/Uranus eccentricity, the occult, tragic loves, intellectual specialization, peculiar interests, individualism, emotional tension; highly strung, electric, independent, incomprehensible.

☾ / ♆
Moon/Neptune sensitivity, heightened and refined feelings, peculiar disposition, drugs and alcohol, exaggerated romanticism; refined, misunderstood, solitary, precious, psychic, idealistic, frail, inspired.

☾ / ♇
Moon/Pluto extreme emotional reactions, fanatics, impulsiveness, fated relationships, devouring mother; compulsive, sadistic, violent, obsessed, dynamic, insatiable, impetuous, volcanic.

☾ / ☊
Moon/Moon's Node spiritual unions, devotion to another, family ties, exclusively female relationships, groups of women, blood relations, longing for another; devoted, loyal, emotional.

Moon/Positive Aspects

deep sentiment and feeling, great aspirations, desire to care for others, motherliness, domesticity, soul unions, spiritual relationship to women; flexible, mutable, emotional.

lucidity, good judgement, competence, mental balance, good humour; sane, optimistic, adaptable, fluid, reasonable, intelligent, productive, sympathetic, articulate.

good taste, ease, artistic ability, rich and happy emotional life; refined, cultured, gentle, attractive, sociable, popular, superficial, elegant, indolent, lyrical, feminine.

honesty, candour, sense of purpose, judging severely, whole-hearted pursuits; enterprising, candid, unpretentious, hard-working, sincere, energetic, enthusiastic, independent.

happiness, understanding others, generosity, tolerance, good humour, easy and fortunate contacts, social conscience, popularity, material advantages, foreign contacts, good mother; kind, obliging.

sense of duty, self-control, responsibilities, organization, business ability, respect for the mother, determined by family; conservative, reliable, serious, pragmatic, unimaginative, hard-working.

originality, ambition, expertise, sudden changes, sacrifices for a goal, strong convictions, colourful manner of expression, unusual accomplishments; intuitive, self-willed, progressive, scientific.

delicate perceptions, imagination, inspiration, romanticism, mysticism, platonic love, selflessness; cultured, refined, sympathetic, compassionate, quiet, gentle, subtle, humane, poetic, musical.

emotional transformations, great and deep expression of feeling, one-sidedness, great capacity for self-expression, dynamic unconscious; ardent, intense, dramatic, compelling.

many associations, happy unions, easy contact with women, love of the mother, emotional attitude toward all relationships; obliging, adaptable, communal.

Mercury Aspects

Mercury/Conjunction Aspects

☿ /ASC
Mercury/Ascendant fluent speech, intelligence, myriad social contacts; educable, inquiring, curious, eloquent, talkative, extraverted, witty, charming, facile.

☿ /MC
Mercury/Midheaven intellectual profession, higher education, advancement through social contact, passion for knowledge, powerful intellect; studious, well-read, analytical, rational, well-informed.

☿ / ♀
Mercury/Venus charm, artistic talent, facility, light relationships, female acquaintances, artistic friends; amusing, vain, agreeable, refined, sociable, graceful, merry, light-hearted and light-headed.

☿ / ♂
Mercury/Mars a sharp tongue, quick wit, incurring the wrath of others, repartee, thought power, penetrating intellect; hard-working, decisive, highly strung, rash, tactless, abrupt, frank, outspoken, quarrelsome.

☿ / ♃
Mercury/Jupiter fertile brain, positivism, literature and learning, wealth of ideas, conceit, business ability, popularity, publishing, travel; broadminded, intelligent, good-natured, philanthropic, well-read.

☿ / ♄
Mercury/Saturn concentration, inhibited expression, endurance, hard work, melancholia, discipline, pragmatism, deep thought; slow, dull, unimaginative, taciturn, scientific, profound, misunderstood.

Mercury/Positive Aspects

easy contacts, sociableness, facility, exchange of ideas, passion for discussion, many acquaintances, correspondence, business; analytical, articulate, diplomatic.

meditating and reflecting, planning ahead, professional advancement, well-defined aims, serious attitude, rapid progress.

love affairs, artistic ability, form sense, appreciation of beauty, graceful expression, hilarity; elegant, cheerful, superficial, refined, cultured, facile, silly, coquetish, sociable.

realization of ideas, determination, debate and argument, skill, dexterity, a good speaker; enterprising, quick, practical, decisive, competent, witty, arch, skeptical.

balanced mentality, sense of humour, business success, constructive mind, common sense, good speaker and writer, optimism, erudition; literary, scientific, positive, evolved, cultured, kindly, temperate

logic, concentration, science and philosophy, industriousness, slow but sure advancement; organized, methodical, pragmatic, serious, rational, studious, reliable, productive, quiet, thorough, earnest.

Moon/Negative Aspects

changing objectives, chequered career, difficulties with mother or women, many short-lived professions, vacillation; unreliable, indecisive, sentimental.

hypersensitivity, anxiety, indecision, ingeniousness, erratic intelligence, nervousness; imaginative, sarcastic, voluble, witty, clever, misunderstood, highly-strung.

frustrated love-longings, difficult births, over-indulgence, female complaints, moodiness, poverty, ungratified desires, bad taste; maltreated, shy.

rebelliousness, intolerance, fanatical independence, excitability, violent reactions, temper tantrums, fits, fear of restriction; quarrelsome, aggressive, rash.

religious and legal conflicts, rebellion, bad liver, faulty judgement, negligence, wastefulness, gluttony; sloppy, inefficient, neglectful, extravagant, speculative.

inferiority complex, melancholy, pessimism, lack of gratification, loneliness, estrangement from mother, anxiety, money troubles, ill-health, maltreatment;

extreme reactions, bizarre interests and attractions, the occult, self-willedness, exaggeration, overstrained nerves, desire for absolute independence; abrupt.

living in an unreal world, deception, fraud, spurious supernatural contacts, ill-health, scandal, longing for the impossible, peculiar tastes, addiction; seducible.

violent emotions, shocks, upheavals, insane demands, tantrums, fanatic attachments; jealous, devouring, tormented, insatiable, demanding, sadistic.

wanting relationships but becoming continually estranged, multiple relationships, lack of adaptability, inability to live with one's family; frustrated,

Moon/Conjunction Personalities

Galileo, Mary Stuart, Madame duBarry, Verlaine, Mary Astor, Luther Burbank, Pablo Casals, Cayce, Dali, Conan Doyle

Thoreau, Stravinsky, Tolstoi, Liberace, Lyndon Johnson, Howard Hughes, Dean Martin, Melina Mercouri

Louis XIV, Moliere, Rimbaud, Liberace, Renoir, Cary Grant, Madame Blavatsky, Hugh Hefner

Michaelangelo, Savonarola, Mussolini, Dumas, Khrushchev, Handel, Rembrandt, Henry Miller, Thomas Edison

Hitler, Leonardo, Copernicus, van Gogh, Nicholas II, Poe, Schubert, Bernhardt, Jules Verne, John L. Lewis

Jane Austen, Charlotte Bronte, Stalin, Keats, Truman Capote, Casanova, Rasputin, John Wilkes Booth, Zsa Zsa Gabor

Byron, George III, Marlowe, G.B. Shaw, Orson Welles, Mae West, Lindbergh

Robert L. Stevenson, Dickens, Dreyfuss, Berlioz, Edward Kennedy, Prince Philip, Lily Langtry

Cesare Borgia, Bette Davis, Zola, Gloria Swanson, Phyllis Diller

Picasso, Steinbeck, Paderewski, Dulles, Tito, Alexandra, Dietrich, C. Manson, Prince Charles, Ronald Reagan

Moon/Aspect Personalities

Proust, T.E. Lawrence, Rudolf Steiner, Alexander Hamilton, Douglas Fairbanks, Duke of Windsor, Shirley Temple

Machiavelli, William Blake, Dostoievsky, Hugo, Shaw, Sarah Bernhardt, Shelley, Wilde, Nelson Rockefeller, Fritz Kunkel

Jung, Einstein, Hugo, Renoir, Proust, Robert Browning, Toulouse-Lautrec, Mata Hari, Christine Jorgensen, Duchess of Windsor

King John, Hussein, Lindbergh, Admiral Byrd, Moshe Dayan, General Lee, J.F. Kennedy, Trotsky, Charlie Chaplin, Bob Hope

Mozart, Rubens, Shaw, Hardy, Gandhi, Valentino, Sir Richard Burton, Jack London, Louis Armstrong

Queen Victoria, Kant, Proust, Dulles, Brahms, John Dee, Savonarola, Schubert, Swift, Thomas Huxley

Durer, William Blake, Conan Doyle, Houdini, Rider Haggard, Madame Blavatsky, Wilde

Rubens, Freud, Kunkel, Laing, Gurdjieff, Verlaine, Charlotte Bronte, Poe, Gershwin, Marilyn Monroe, Brigitte Bardot, Gandhi

Havelock Ellis, Verlaine, John Baez, Puccini, John Lennon, Billy Graham, Hawthorne, M.L. King Jr, Gustav Mahler, Cellini

Mao Tse-tung, Picasso, Coco Chanel, Anastasia, Andy Warhol, Joan Baez, Liz Taylor, Mae West

Mercury/Negative Aspects

disharmonious attitude, poor judgement, gossip, criticism of others, quickly changing contacts; garrulous, superficial, unfriendly, offensive, flighty.

many professions, overestimation of self, changing goals, indecision, vacillation, aimlessness, lack of self-criticism, dishonest practices; unstable, unmotivated.

hedonism, vanity, conceit, short-lived relationships, extravagance; flighty, superficial, ostentatious, empty, luxury-loving, lazy, fatuous.

rashness, criticism, speech difficulties, irritability, disputes, thievery, plagiarism, lawsuits; nervous, edgy, fault-finding, obstinate, cynical, impudent, sarcastic.

negligence, frivolity, exaggeration, business failures, conceit, arrogance; wanton, mischievous, haphazard, unreliable, indiscreet, forgetful, imprudent, dishonest.

awkwardness, speech impediments, unhappy childhood, thrift, inhibitions, estrangements; suspecious; narrow-minded, conservative, obstinate, uncommunicative.

Mercury/Conjunction Personalities

Dante, Daniel Webster, T. Williams, Andy Warhol, Hemingway, W.R. Hearst

Nostradamus, Nietzsche, DeGaulle, Castro, Cicero, Wm. F. Buckley, Rubens, John Steinbeck, Henry Miller

Durer, Jung, Schumann, Rubens, Hardy, Chopin, Swinburne, Bach, Cellini, Erasmus, Milton, Nureyev, F. Scott Fitzgerald

Cicero, Voltaire, Mata Hari, Kipling, Zola, Salvadore Dali, Ralph Nader, Adlai Stevenson

William Blake, Rimsky-Korsakov, Toulouse-Lautrec, John Dee, Brahms, Brigitte Bardot, Shirley Temple

Einstein, Edgar Cayce, Jane Addams, Rider Haggard, Madame Blavatsky, Patrick Henry

Mercury/Aspect Personalities

Christopher Marlowe, Moliere, Victor Hugo, Picasso, Ravel, Bertrand Russell, Vermeer

Spinoza, Dostoievsky, Voltaire, Edison, Marie Curie, Cary Grant, Conan Doyle

Isaac Newton, Hawthorne, Gershwin, Paderewski, Peter Sellers, Walt Disney

Thomas More, Francis Bacon, Byron, FDR, James Joyce, Machiavelli, Cecil Rhodes, Sarah Bernhardt

Oscar Wilde, S.T. Coleridge, John Audubon, Ravel, Puccini, Mark Twain, Rachmaninoff, Edvard Grieg, Jerry Lewis

Leonardo, Isaac Newton, Darwin, Pasteur, Marconi, Ben Franklin, Thoreau, Pushkin, Lewis Carroll, J.W. Booth

Mercury/Conjunction Aspects

♀ / ♅
Mercury/Uranus the "mad genius", original but eccentric mentality, quick reactions, strange interests, specialization, brilliance; intellectual, self-willed, highly strung, erratic, unconventional, inspired, misunderstood.

♀ / ♆
Mercury/Neptune imagination, flights of fancy, idealism, sensitivity, delusions; wooly-minded, fey, inspired, unrealistic, gentle, credulous, deceptive, unclear, poetic, lyrical.

♀ / ♇
Mercury/Pluto influence through speaking or writing, sharp intellect, desire to be intellectually superior, nervous irritation, over-taxed mentality; influential, persuasive, implacable, dynamic, deranged.

♀ / ☊
Mercury/Moon's Node compulsively social, inability to be alone, needing to act with others, garrulousness, intellectual companions.

Mercury/Positive Aspects

inventive mind, mathematics and technology, intuition, innovation; astute, flexible, shrewd, articulate, independent, original, intelligent, quick-witted, resourceful.

sense of humour, active fantasy life, fertile mind, compassionate understanding, presentiment, spiritual longings, travel; whimsical, kind, imaginative, idealistic, subtle, open-minded, visionary.

quick grasp of every situation, biting wit, rapid and acute intellect, specialized speaking and writing, public recognition, diplomacy, intellectual triumph over others; restless, critical, acute, sly, cynical.

sociableness, social and business contacts, exchanging ideas with others, membership in societies, fellowship, a good companion, joint interests; group-orientated, communal.

Venus Aspects

Venus/Conjunction Aspects

♀ /ASC
Venus/Ascendant physical beauty, luxurious environment, self-adornment, easy circumstances, good taste, vanity; mannered, charming, youthful, flattering, attractive, well-bred, courteous, good-natured.

♀ /MC
Venus/Midheaven work in music or art, rich love life, sincere affection, an open and generous nature, aestheticism, professional contacts with women; loving, artistic, humanitarian, creative.

♀ / ♂
Venus/Mars passion, sensuality, excitability, sexual relationships, lack of tenderness and tact; Rabelaisian, impulsive, ardent, magnetic, coarse, libidinous, easily aroused.

♀ / ♃
Venus/Jupiter glamour, film-star mannerisms, sense of humour, popularity, love of luxury, grace of expression; hedonistic, extravagant, sociable, amorous, flamboyant, entertaining, artistic, lavish, fascinating.

♀ / ♄
Venus/Saturn emotions dominated by sense of duty, a cold heart, prostitution, emotional deprivation, inhibited pleasure principle, tragic love, jealousy; frigid, dutiful, repressed, lonely, prudish.

♀ / ♅
Venus/Uranus love at first sight, peculiar attractions, emotional tensions, rhythm, libido, excessive romanticism, eccentric tastes; misunderstood, avant-garde, highly strung, excitable.

♀ / ♆
Venus/Neptune delicate constitution, refined sentiments, animal lovers, disappointed love, dreamers, artists, mysticism; soft-hearted, sweet, overly sympathetic, musical, weak, unrealistic.

♀ / ♇
Venus/Pluto fanatic love, destructive relationships, compulsive attractions, heightened sexuality; rapacious, insatiable, sensual, demanding.

♀ / ☊
Venus/Moon's Node love affairs, cordial and agreeable disposition, artistic communities, humanitarianism; obliging, charming, diplomatic, flattering, fawning.

Venus/Positive Aspects

diplomacy, love affairs, sociableness, artistic environment, sense of beauty, kindness; gentle, relaxed, hospitable, warm-hearted, attractive, tactful, even-tempered.

harmonious nature, beauty and art, happy love life, felicitous contacts, true love, artistic profession; kind, gentle, affectionate, well-loved.

passionate love, artistic ability, liveliness, attractive to opposite sex, healthy sex drive, many loves; sensual, warm-hearted, expressive, prolific, creative.

grace, charm, tact, comfortable life, capacity for enjoyment, love of pleasure and amusement, happy loves; warm-hearted, gay, well-liked, tasteful, relaxed, expansive.

sense of duty, devotion, economy, fidelity, self-control, older partners, sacrifices for others; loyal, sober, reserved, respectable, unspontaneous, inhibited, straight-laced.

free love, exotic charm, many loves, original forms of artistic expression; alluring, fascinating, witty, flirtatious, unfaithful, easily roused.

refinement, ideal love, romanticism, receptivity for art and beauty, easy fortunes; dreamy, idealistic, sensitive, musical.

creative power, fanatic devotion to an artistic cause, special artistic gifts, sexuality; dramatic, unconventional, intense, talented, fascinating, magnetic.

engaging personality, a good companion, artistic friends, the ability to please, pleasant female associations, many love unions; popular, kindly, obliging, amusing, pleasant.

THE ROUND ART

Mercury/Negative Aspects

scattered energies, nervousness, overestimation of self, haste, eccentric actions, excitement, trouble-making; meddlesome, erratic, brutally frank, contradictory.

disturbed imagination, deception, fraud, faulty judgement, hyperaesthesia; devious, weak-minded, dishonest, fantastic, dissipated, vague, foolish.

nervous breakdown, libelous speech and writing, hasty thinking and speaking, over-estimation of self, overtaxing of strength, crude speech, tantrums;

the use of social contact for one's own benefit, chatter and gossip, disturbed relationships, superficial contacts; disloyal, unpopular, unsociable.

Mercury/Conjunction Personalities

William Lilly, Pasteur, Mata Hari, Renoir

Lenin, Rudolf Steiner, Walter Scott, Peter Sellers

Galileo, Lenin, Bismarck, Darwin, Hearst, Abraham Lincoln, Zola, Harry Truman, Baudelaire, Rossini, E.B. Browning

Nasser, Nelson Rockefeller, R. Hess, Edgar Cayce, Tennessee Williams, Shelley, Winters, Errol Flynn.

Mercury/Aspect Personalities

Voltaire, Shaw, Wilde, Nietzsche, Rimbaud, Ben Franklin, Tom Jefferson, Moshe Dayan, Trotsky, Wm. Buckley, Rodin

Cervantes, Shaw, Wilde, Debussy, Liszt, Joan of Arc, Richard Nixon, Byron, Samuel Hahnemann, Jack Benny

Keats, Jonathan Swift, Jack Benny, Winston Churchill, Franklin Roosevelt

Dali, Nureyev, Laurence Olivier, Orson Welles, Louis Armstrong, John Barrymore

Venus/Negative Aspects

a pleasure-seeking nature, tensions, attraction to unsavoury types, over-indulgence, wastefulness; extravagant, over-dressed, hypocritical, pretentious.

self-admiration, loss of friends and lovers, jealousy, conceit, superficiality, conflicts with women; vain, trivial, pleasure-loving, dissipated.

Don Juanism, tempestuous sex life, passion followed by coolness, difficult love relationships, infedelity, sexual diseases; impetuous, irritable, insatiable, tactless.

love conflicts, laziness, waste, excess emotion, many loves, infidelity, prodigality, self-indulgence, illness through rich living; sybaritic, cloying, indolent, vain.

unhappy love, emotional deprivation, poverty, exploitation, jealousy, unhealthy sex life, separations, a hard life, prostitution, self-torment; lonely, depressed.

inconstancy, numerous and short-lived love relationships, nervous troubles, rebellious love, estrangements; unconventional, indiscreet, loose.

weak character, erotic aberrations, false sense of love, impossible loves, hero worship, bad taste; seducible, deluded, fickle, cloying, overly romantic, escapist.

lust, tempestuous love life, sado-masochism, excessive sexuality; lascivious, lewd, self-destructive, coarse, vulgar.

difficulties with women, unhappy love affairs, separations, lack of adaptability, short-lived relationships; unreliable, flighty, flirtatious.

Venus/Conjunction Personalities

Debussy, Tennyson, Isadora Duncan, Alain Delon, Deborah Kerr, Sophia Loren, Rita Hayworth

Rubens, Goya, Rossini, Josephine, Henry VIII, Marilyn Monroe, Susan Hayward, J.P. Morgan

Baudelaire, Van Gogh, Verlaine, Balzac, Orson Welles, Paganini, Emily Bronte, Douglas Fairbanks, Chaplin, Hitler

Toscanini, Mahler, Max Ernst, Warhol, Ivan the Terrible, King John, Max Ernst, Krishnamurti, Robert Browning, Ed. Lear

Savonarola, Martin Luther, Pushkin, Tolstoi, Coleridge, Bogart, Bergmann, Dietrich

Zola, Verdi, Shelley, Dostoievsky, Warren Beatty, Steve McQueen, Liz Taylor

Coleridge, Valentino, Bach, Cezanne, Caruso, Dostoievsky, Errol Flynn, Sophia Loren, James Stewart

Yeats, Dickens, Hugo, Poe, B. Russell, Gina Lollobrigida, J.P. Morgan

Elvis Presley, James Stewart, John L. Lewis, Rachmaninoff

Venus/Aspect Personalities

Jane Austen, Durer, Leonardo, Nureyev, Clark Gable, Douglas Fairbanks

Wagner, Garbo, Freud, Marie Antoinette, Gloria Swanson, Paganini, Puccini, Pushkin, Richard Burton, Hugh Hefner

Schubert, Rossini, Yeats, Crowley, Rodin, Edward VII, Zsa Zsa Gabor, Tennessee Williams, Richard Burton, Stalin, Havelock Ellis

Liszt, Schubert, Ravel, Nell Gwynn, Marilyn Monroe, Edward VII, Liz Taylor

Freud, Hitler, Goering, Jackie Kennedy, Joan of Arc, Grace Kelly, Bette Davis, Emily Bronte

Goya, Max Ernst, William Blake, Dickens, Edgar Allan Poe, Madame duBarry

Rembrandt, Baudelaire, Goethe, Yeats, Poe, Brahms, Elizabeth Browning, Marie Antoinette

Josephine, Mozart, Rasputin, Elvis Presley, Eleanor Roosevelt, R.L. Stevenson

Chaplin, Zsa Zsa Gabor, Mahler, Stravinsky, Valentino, Harry Belafonte, Duchess of Windsor, F.D. Roosevelt, Capote, Fitzgerald

Mars Aspects

	Mars/Conjunction Aspects	Mars/Positive Aspects
♂ /ASC **Mars/Ascendant**	imposing one's will on others, physical strength and energy, an aggressive environment, advancement by means of force, fighting spirit; courageous, domineering, blunt, accident-prone, violent.	leadership, intense activity, self-assertion, work with others; dynamic, forceful, hard-working, practical, frank, honest, decisive, respected.
♂ /MC **Mars/Midheaven**	vigorous profession, concentration on an objective, ambition, drive, determination, independence, earned success; hard-working, purposeful, intent, earnest, pragmatic.	goal-consciousness, resolute action, attainment of objectives, professional advancement, organizing ability; determined, ambitious, independent, resourceful, business-like.
♂ / ♃ **Mars/Jupiter**	energy, drive, ambition, feats of prowess, leadership, rebellion; resourceful, daring, courageous, decisive, capable, positive, successful, jovial.	joie-de-vivre, spirit of enterprise, an active life, successful enterprises; honourable, independent, ardent, creative, proud, optimistic, irrepressible, bouyant, fortunate, expressive.
♂ / ♄ **Mars/Saturn**	destruction, negative energy, hardships, physical suffering, dangerous, situations, violence; accident-prone, sadistic, brutal, fanatical, hard-working, spartan.	endurance, persistence, pioneer spirit, power of resistance, survival instinct; enterprising, tough, indefatigable, ascetic, determined, disciplined, hard-working.
♂ / ♅ **Mars/Uranus**	great courage, struggles, haste, violence, temper, obstinacy, willfulness, intolerance, inability to relax, compulsive and erratic activity; nervous, danger-loving, dissatisfied, brutally frank, intense.	extraordinary energy emerging suddenly, attainment of goals, independence, courage, unusual achievements; hasty, decisive, hyper-active, unyielding, brave.
♂ / ♆ **Mars/Neptune**	longing for the impossible, treachery, lack of energy, secret enemies, dissatifaction, romanticism, drugs and alcohol, escapism; uncontrolled, insatiable, imaginative, fantastic, revelling	inspired actions, practical idealism, inspirations, many plans, help when needed; imaginative, artistic, idealistic, civilized, honourable.
♂ / ♇ **Mars/Pluto**	ruthlessness, cruelty, imposing one's will on others, power mania, sadism; obsessive, violent, indomitable, destructive, explosive, homicidal.	great self-confidence, working energy, extraordinary achievements, success through excessive efforts; powerful, courageous, macho, virile, obsessive, indefatigable, disciplined.
♂ / ☊ **Mars/Moon's Node**	sex unions, quarrels and disagreements, vigorous co-operation, groups of men, leadership, compulsive attractions, aggression.	comradeship, team spirit, energetic co-operation, shared success, organizing ability; frank, vigorous, whole-hearted, loyal, supportive.

Jupiter Aspects

	Jupiter/Conjunction Aspects	Jupiter/Positive Aspects
♃ /ASC **Jupiter/ Ascendant**	luxurious environment, magnaminity, charm, largesse, wealthy people; grandiose, regal, good humoured, imperturable, grandiloquent, extravagant, overweight.	good humour, positive attitude, profitable relationships, creation of a beautiful environment, recognition; generous, even-tempered, popular, agreeable, jovial, relaxed, tolerant, respected.
♃ /MC **Jupiter/ Midheaven**	good fortune, great objectives, nobility, easy life, wealth success; optimistic, content, calm, self-assured, expansive, lucky.	attainment of success, happiness, sense of purpose, calm, strength, advancement; generous, noble, humane, highly evolved, civilized, comfortable.
♃ / ♄ **Jupiter/Saturn**	perseverance, patience, slow advance, hard work, far-reaching objectives, manic-depression; dissatisfied, brooding, serious, plodding, possessive, suicidal.	patience, undertaking arduous tasks, happy seclusion, success after struggle, sense of duty, motivation, honesty; philosophical, determined, honourable, modest but confident, conscientious.
♃ / ♅ **Jupiter/Uranus**	desire for freedom and independence, unconventional views, religious and legal conflicts, restlessness, love of adventure; reformative, inventive, rebellious, disputatious, progressive.	individualism, originality, leadership, desire for knowledge, integrity, fortunate ideas, sudden realizations and changes, intuition; heroic, farsighted, enthusiastic, inventive, freedom-loving.
♃ / ♆ **Jupiter/Neptune**	idealism, mysticism, music and art, humanitarianism, selfless love; religious, visionary, dreamy, romantic, spectulative, overly generous, humane, tolerant, unrealistic.	altruism, intense imagination, gain without effort, visionary capacities, art and music, metaphysics; compassionate, expansive, speculative, generous, slack, Bohemian, lucky, kind-hearted,

THE ROUND ART

Mars/Negative Aspects

aggression, physical violence, conflicts; quarrelsome, contentious, competitive, agitated, disturbing, restless, violent, abrasive, coarse, uncivilized.

conflict with superiors, loss of position, misplaced aggression, premature action, disputes, failures; excitable, impulsive, misguided, hasty, strained.

rebelliousness, trouble with authority figures, hatred of rules and restrictions, exaggerated independence, haste, libertinism, disputes; intemperate, extremist, restless.

energy crises, disputes, separations, inability to finish anything, accidents, blowing hot and cold, harshness, brutality; ruthless, destructive, accident-prone.

struggle for survival, injuries, violence, temper tantrums, rage, fury, self-will, urge for freedom, fighting spirit, inability to rest or be satisfied;

seduction, dissipation, sexual fantasies, addiction, depravity, inability to take action, misuse of energy, moodiness, weakness; procrastinating, escapist.

attainment of objectives by force, cruelty, violent assaults, accidents, injuries; aggressive, inflammatory, obstinate, sadistic, ruthless, homicidal.

arguments, separations, dissident groups, anti-social conduct, breakdown of relationships, lack of tact; aggressive, trouble-making, subversive, disputative.

Mars/Conjunction Personalities

Simon Bolivar, DeGaulle, Moshe Dayan, Huey Long, Admiral Nelson, Paul Newman

Van Gogh, Eisenhower, George III, Marcus Aurelius, Ivan the Terrible

J.D. Rockefeller, J.P. Morgan, Casanova, Joe Kennedy, DeGaulle, Shelley, George Wallace, Krishnamurti, A. Earhart

Duke of Wellington, Howard Hughes, Marie Curie, Madame Blavatsky, Nostradamus

Haydn, Yehudi Menuhin, Mata Hari, John Wesley, Henry Miller, Nureyev, Olivier, Tennyson, John Wayne

Shelley, Blake, Paganini, Fitzgerald, Stalin, Napoleon, Robespierre, Manson, Pope Pius XII, Burt Lancaster

John L. Lewis, MacArthur, Marconi, Robert Mitchum, Mary Stuart, Will Rogers

Jane Addams, John Dillinger, Houdini, Rita Hayworth, Robert Redford

Mars/Aspect Personalities

Marx, Rasputin, George Washington, Mahler, Pasteur, Nureyev, Bette Davis

Gurdjieff, Orson Welles, Mark Twain, Chiang Kai-shek, Alain Delon, Erasmus, Amelia Earhart, T.E. Lawrence

Nietzsche, Helen Keller, Wagner, Blake, Dostoievsky, Mao Tse-tung, Jack London, Moliere, F.L. Wright, Melina Mercouri

Adler, Lenin, Leonardo, Zola, J.P. Morgan, Disraeli, Dickens, Cromwell, Edison, Gounod

Churchill, Princess Anne, Henry VIII, Napoleon, Voltaire, Rodin, Henry Ford, General Marshall

Yeats, Dickens, Dreyfuss, Helen Keller, Hawthorne, Mahler, Maximilian, James Pike, Pushkin

Einstein, Aliester Crowley, Rubens, Shelley, Muhammad Ali, Richard Nixon, Billy Graham, General Patton, Custer, Melina Mercouri

T.E. Lawrence, Trotsky, Lenin, DeGaulle, G.L. Rockwell, Toscanini, Mae West, Dayan, John Glenn, Richard Burton, L.B. Johnson

Jupiter/Negative Aspects

desire to be important, showing off, bragging, hypocrisy, misplaced generosity, conflicts with others; wasteful, extravagant, materialistic, conceited.

fluctuating circumstances, desire to be important, misplaced self-confidence, the ability to advance in one's profession, risks, changes in occupation; conceited.

discontent, instability, legal troubles, changing life-style, self-destructive; pessimistic, gloomy, depressive, unimaginative, prosaic, formal, distant, muddled.

opportunities missed, philosophical and religious arguments, non-conformity, rebelliousness, conflicts with superiors, rabble-rousing; anarchistic.

loss through speculation, unbalanced religious enthusiasm, gambling, scandal, instability, conflict between ideal and real, great expectations, seducible.

Jupiter/Conjunction Personalities

Brahms, Edward VII, DeGaulle, Disraeli, Errol Flynn, Mata Hari, Schweitzer, Theodore Roosevelt

Steiner, Charlemagne, George VI, R.F. Kennedy, Mahler, J.J. Rousseau, Rodin, Janis Joplin, Rita Hayworth

Shakespeare, Nostradamus, Galileo, Victor Hugo, Dumas, Newton, Marlowe, Joan Baez, Dostoievsky, M.B. Eddy

Himmler, Daniel Boone, Alexandra, Mary Stuart, Puccini, Bertrand Russell, Bob Dylan, Fidel Castro, Gypsy Rose Lee

Shelley, Disraeli, Pope John XXIII, Liberace, Olivier, F.D. Roosevelt, Rossini, Duke of Windsor

Jupiter/Aspect Personalities

Aleister Crowley, Coco Chanel, Thomas More, Schumann, Jonathan Swift, Frank L. Wright

Dulles, Raphael, Mendelssohn, John Lennon, Rembrandt, Tolstoi, Jackie Kennedy Onassis, Charles Lindbergh

Thomas Mann, Carl Jung, Rubens, Ibsen, Bertrand Russell, Christopher Wren

Thomas Beckett, Napoleon, Newton, Pasteur, J.F. Kennedy, F.D. Roosevelt, John Barrymore, Rommel, James Joyce

Goethe, Yeats, Crowley, Marilyn Monroe, Nelson, J.J. Rousseau, Swift, Zola, Tchaikowsky, Alexandra

Jupiter/Conjunction Aspects

♃ / ♇
Jupiter/Pluto
great achievements, desire to influence others, leadership, big ideas, plutocracy, extraordinary abilities, seizure of power; grandiose, self-confident, successful, imposing, dauntless.

♃ / ☊
Jupiter/Moon's Node
sociableness, associations with wealthy or influential people, governmental and legal organizations; good fellowship, trust, "gentlemen's agreements".

Jupiter/Positive Aspects

striving for physical or spiritual power, executive abilities, rebellions and uprisings, attainment of power, desire to lead the masses, organizing ability, large projects; enterprising, influential.

happy marriage, advantageous relationships, good connections, engagement or marriage, business advantages; adaptable, tactful, sociable, pleasant, harmonious.

Saturn Aspects

Saturn/Conjunction Aspects

♄ /ASC
Saturn/Ascendant
inhibited personality, seclusion, weak constitution, shyness, frustration, unsympathetic environment, difficult infancy; restrained, lonely, defensive, paranoid, anxious, nervous.

♄ /MC
Saturn/Midheaven
a hard life, slow and difficult advancement, stoicism, hard work, late acceptance, single-mindedness; highly restricted, inhibited, melancholic, hard-working, selfish.

♄ / ♅
Saturn/Uranus
great inner tensions, will power, violent behaviour, tenacity, accidents, involvement in difficult problems; self-willed, autocratic, tense, tough, hard, indestructible.

♄ / ♆
Saturn/Neptune
dual nature, conflict between materialism and idealism, peculiar character, mathematics and music, extraordinary abilities; self-obsessed, neurotic, humourless, ascetic.

♄ / ♇
Saturn/Pluto
homicidal tendencies, hatred of father, cruelty, physical suffering, bodily harm; hard-hearted, severe, brutal, frustrated, obsessive, violent, reactionary.

♄ / ☊
Saturn/Moon's Node
unhappy relationships, loyalty, associations with severe and unsympathetic people, depression due to others; inhibited, shy, anti-social, ungratified.

Saturn/Positive Aspects

old beyond one's years, preference for the company of older people, early experience; reserved, serious, composed, impenetrable, modest, retiring, paternal.

slow development, help from older persons, patient pursuit of objectives, clinging to hopes; self-absorbed, plodding, relentless, ambitious, conscientious.

perseverance, nervous energy, determination, late success, withstanding difficulties, dangerous situations, growing strength; stoical, scientific, capable, practical, unyielding.

foresight, sacrifice for others, self-restraint, caution, slow attainment of success, tedious work; methodical, painstaking, hard-working, patient, philosophical.

success in difficult undertakings, fanatic workers, hard struggles, great sacrifices, work in seclusion, research, record achievements; compulsive, indefatigable, painstaking, thorough, self-disciplined.

relationships with older people, father-figures, groups of elderly people and their sponsorship, fidelity, long-term associations, dutiful, loyal, self-effacing, devoted.

Uranus Aspects

Uranus/Conjunction Aspects

♅ /ASC
Uranus/Ascendant
exciting and quickly-changing environment, an erratic temperament, quick reactions, nervous haste; unconventional, excitable, restless, highly strung, scattered, disquieting, abrupt, outspoken.

♅ /MC
Uranus/Midheaven
sudden turns of fate, unusual profession, an exciting but unstable life, going one's own way, individualism, science and technology, unusual objectives; rebellious, tense, anarchistic, original.

♅ / ♆
Uranus/Neptune
extraordinary abilities and inclinations, strange occurrences, spiritual and occult sciences, eccentricity, self-will, genius, unusual people.

♅ / ♇
Uranus/Pluto
revolution, transformation, striving for the new, creation of a new life, great creative capacity, pioneers, reformers, exceptional people, super-human energy; heroic, daring, daemonic, foolhardy.

♅ / ☊
Uranus/Moon's Node
sudden attractions, intense but unstable relationships, difficulty in living with others, eccentric friends and lovers, upsetting others.

Uranus/Positive Aspects

love of change and variety, continual rearrangement of environment, original, high spirits, new contacts; inventive, unstable, quickly-responding, dynamic, fascinating.

fortunate turns of fate, zealous pursuit of objectives, originality, organization, peculiar methods, self-assertion; dynamic, decisive, energetic, lucky.

mysticism, strange pursuits, occult interests, visionary capacities, idealism, peculiar psychic states, long journeys; inspired, artistic, humanitarian, religious, mediumistic.

ceaseless activity, fighting for reforms, bringing about transformations, endurance; creative, untiring, progressive, rebellious, insistant, purposeful, self-aware.

many and changing contacts, shared experiences, quick associations, unusual, friendships, seeking new acquaintances; lively, spirited, witty, responsive.

THE ROUND ART

Jupiter/Negative Aspects

fanatical aims, taking risks, great gains and losses, financial disasters, falls from power, conflicts with authorities, arrest; wasteful, speculative, exploitative.

lack of good fellowship, unstable relationships, looking out for one's own gain first, social-climbing, anti-social conduct; hypocritical, exploitative.

Jupiter/Conjunction Personalities

Durer, Cervantes, Shaw, DeMille, Luther, Milton, Picasso, Vermeer, Gide, Khrushchev, Madame duBarry

F. Scott Fitzgerald, Himmler, Spencer Tracy, Audrey Hepburn, Dietrich, Judy Garland

Jupiter/Aspect Personalities

Michaelangelo, Goethe, Shelley, Balzac, Rembrandt, Rommel, Nixon, Andrew Carnegie

Jean Harlow, Cecil Rhodes, Maria Callas, Frank Lloyd Wright, Churchill, Caruso, Howard Hughes, Al Capone

Saturn/Negative Aspects

poverty, poor health, maltreatment, sad or inhibiting environment, lack of understanding, alienation; depressive, frail, pessimistic, fearful, lonely, awkward.

pessimism, doubt and fear, inferiority complex, inhibited self-expression, failure, professional difficulties, separations; self-doubting, negative.

tension, strain, eccentric father, repression by others, emotional conflicts, rebellion, upsetting others, separations, quarrels, use of force.

psychosomatic illnesses, insecurity, public troubles, secret enmities, thwarted ambitions, paranoia, peculiar neuroses, self-torment; inhibited, morose, suspicious.

severity, use of force, physical suffering, success denied, self-destruction, heavy losses, frustration, violence; fanatic, egoistic, hard-hearted, unfeeling, ruthless.

inability to relate to others, difficulties in co-operation, inhibited social function, separations and deaths, disadvantages through others; unco-operative.

Saturn/Conjunction Personalities

J.D. Rockefeller, Goethe, Cesare Borgia, Abraham Lincoln, Andrew Carnegie, U.S. Grant, Emerson, MacArthur, Marshall

Proust, Bernhardt, Elizabeth II, Picasso, Mao Tse-tung, Napoleon, Jack London, J. Edgar Hoover, Alfred Hitchcock

Goebbels, Muhammad Ali, Janis Joplin, Gloria Swanson, Hans Christian Andersen, Franklin Pierce

Darwin, Stravinsky, Edison, Lincoln, Pope John XXIII, Poe, G.L. Rockwell

Mussolini, Prince Albert, Orson Welles, Queen Victoria, General Sherman, Douglas Fairbanks

Yeats, Edgar Cayce, Dulles, Ralph Nader, Judy Garland

Saturn/Aspect Personalities

John Wesley, Joan of Arc, Pope Paul VI, Mahler, Andy Warhol, Dillinger, Calvin, Barry Goldwater

Lenin, Calvin, Castro, Luther, Robespierre, Peter the Great, Eugene O'Neill, Nicholas II, John Lennon

Churchill, Crowley, Chiang Kai-shek, Marx, Newton, Eichmann, Billy Graham, J.P. Jones, Lyndon Johnson, Rachmaninoff

Lenin, Rimbaud, Charlotte Bronte, Gide, Oscar Wilde, Mozart, Mark Twain, Pasteur, Jules Verne, Hugh Hefner

Kipling, Franco, Goering, Hemingway, R.F. Kennedy, T.E. Lawrence, Louis XIV, Rembrandt, John Wayne, Wren, Russell

Henry Ford, Rommel, Woodrow Wilson, Leonard Bernstein, James Joyce, Brando, Howard Hughes

Uranus/Negative Aspects

causing upsets to others, unexpected events, accidents, exciting and disturbing events, quick changes; inconstant, irritable, nervous, compulsive, rude.

many changes of profession, precipitancy, big upsets, sudden turns for the worse, checquered career; unreliable, temperamental, hasty, stubborn.

loss of consciousness, instability, impossible ideals, extremes of emotion, nervous sensitivity, confusion; psychic, muddle-headed, highly strung, easily upset.

fanaticism, violence, destruction mania, subversion, accidents, danger; rapacious, nervous, impatient, compulsive, scattered, ruthless.

disturbing influence on others, quarrels, separations, short-lived relationships; restless, flighty, irritable, excitable.

Uranus/Conjunction Personalities

R.D. Laing, Beethoven, Hitler, Stravinsky, Adler, Casanova, Edgar Cayce, Cromwell, Charles Manson, Voltaire, F.D. Roosevelt

Michaelangelo, F. Scott Fitzgerald, Christiaan Barnard, Moshe Dayan, Helen Keller, John L. Lewis, Garland

Baudelaire, Walt Whitman, Dostoievsky, Emily Bronte, Thomas More, M.B. Eddy, Clara Barton, U.S. Grant, Sherman

Cromwell, Van Gogh, Richard III, Van Dyck, J.J. Rousseau, Tchaikowsky

Himmler, Louis Armstrong, James Dean, Lenin, Frank Sinatra, Spencer Tracey

Uranus/Aspect Personalities

Mussolini, Havelock Ellis, Leonardo, Isadora Duncan, John Glenn, Thomas Huxley, Mozart, Christine Jorgensen

Beethoven, Cezanne, James Joyce, Voltaire, Toulouse-Lautrec, Robert Mitchum, Garibaldi

Francis Bacon, Rasputin, Katherine Hepburn, F.D. Roosevelt, Mary Astor

Dante, Lenin, Spinoza, Wagner, Napoleon, Liszt, Nostradamus, Walter Scott, Anastasia, Robert Burns

Thomas Mann, Jung, Hitler, Houdini, Dali, Chaplin, Cecil DeMille, Charlton Heston, Garbo, George Wallace

Neptune Aspects

	Neptune/Conjunction Aspects	**Neptune/Positive Aspects**
Ψ /ASC **Neptune/ Ascendant**	gullibility, deceived by others, sensitivity, insincerity, dishonesty, a misguided outlook; impressionable, weak, deluded, unreliable, unstable, vague, sentimental, flowery, gentle, kindly.	sympathy, compassion, refinement, unusual contacts; idealistic, easily led, romantic, sensitive, ingenuous, kind, understanding, unrealistic, artistic, responsive.
Ψ /MC **Neptune/ Midheaven**	scandal, notoriety, plans without action, exalted notions, self-deception, depressive psychoses, strange or artistic profession; mystical, idealistic, insecure, deluded, misunderstood.	longing for the impossible, unusual pursuits, selflessness, interest in the supernatural, films, music; soft-hearted, sentimental, utopian, otherwordly.
Ψ / ♇ **Neptune/Pluto**	mysticism, strange ideas, obsessional neuroses, peculiar objectives, the Supernatural, presentiments; otherworldly, mediumistic, fantastic.	occupation with unusual problems, intense soul life, spiritual experiences, dynamic unconscious, parapsychological investigations, great realizations, second sight; clairvoyant, mystical.
Ψ / ☊ **Neptune/Moon's Node**	strange or idealistic associations, expecting the impossible of others, undermined relationships, deceptive behaviour, inability to integrate into a group, disappointed by others, secret societies.	expecting too much of others, humanitarian and utopian organizations, spiritual unions, idealistic friends.

Pluto Aspects

	Pluto/Conjunction Aspects	**Pluto/Positive Aspects**
♇ /ASC **Pluto/Ascendant**	a fascinating personality, power and authority, domination of others, ruthlessness, egomania; unscrupulous, magnetic, autocratic, merciless, indomitable, destructive, violent, dramatic.	driving ambition, the exercise of power, unusual contacts, magical or psychic powers, control over the environment; influential, magnetic, compelling, peculiar, entertaining.
♇ /MC **Pluto/Midheaven**	fame, great professional success, exalted view of self, power-mania, dictatorship, expertise, specialization; individualistic, obsessive, single-minded, irresistible, indomitable, highly fated.	desire for importance, attainment of success, organizing ability, recognition, independence, acceptance of an important task; enterprising, visionary, authoritative, revolutionary.
♇ / ☊ **Pluto/Moon's Node**	fated relationships, tragic loves, wielding influence over a great many people, fanatical urge for recognition, public figures, powerful friends or lovers, contact with the masses.	multitudinous associations, desire to become a public figure, associations that are important to one's future, large business concerns, wielding influence over many.

Moon's Node Aspects

	Moon's Node/Conjunction Aspects	**Moon's Node/Positive Aspects**
☊ /ASC **Moon's Node/ Ascendant**	ability to relate to others, many loves, intense partnerships, a good companion, love of entertaining; sociable, extraverted, obliging, charming.	social conscience, concern for others, shared interests, dislike of living alone, happy associations; amenable, engaging, humane, communal.
☊ /MC **Moon's Node/ Midheaven**	individual associations, a destiny determined solely by relationships, idealistic attitude towards friendships, like-minded people.	advancement through one's associations, community spirit, fortunate contacts, working with others, joint aims, shared interests; humane, understanding, unselfish.

◁ THE ROUND ART ▷

Neptune/Negative Aspects

inability to succeed, influenced by others, betrayals, weak constitution, dishonesty; confused, disappointed, escapist, moody, insincere, fraudulent, hypocritical.

vague objectives, ill luck, lack of contact with reality, misguided notions, easily deceived, inferiority complex, mental disturbance; weak, unstable, hyper-sensitive.

fantastic notions, obsessed with an idea, delusion, drug and alcohol addiction, trickery, fraud, grave losses, confusion, soul suffering; obsessive, neurotic, peculiar.

deceiving or tricking others, exploitation, poor judgement of people, disappointed relationships, separation, alienation, anti-social behaviour, spying.

Neptune/Conjunction Personalities

James Pike, Rasputin, Ava Gardner, Gary Cooper, Abraham Lincoln, Renoir, Jonathan Swift, Robert Browning

Trotsky, Tchaikowsky, Shelley, Gable, Pope Paul VI, Machiavelli, Dean Martin, Bing Crosby, J.F. Kennedy, DeMille

Max Ernst, Charles Chaplin, Franco, Goering, Hess, Hitler, Nero, Khrushchev, Mao Tse-tung, Tito

Churchill, Bob Dylan, Rex Harrison, Bette Davis, Puccini, Charlton Heston, Herbert Hoover

Neptune/Aspect Personalities

Michaelangelo, Einstein, Houdini, Wilde, Mark Twain, Tolstoi, Verdi, Rex Harrison

Beethoven, Chopin, Grieg, Schubert, Verlaine, Schiller, Mozart, Poe, Louis XIV, James Joyce, Robert Louis Stevenson

Goethe, Beethoven, Rimsky-Korsakov, Raphael, Casanova, Machiavelli, Rembrandt, Thoreau

Truman Capote, Alfred Hitchcock, Gibran, Orson Welles, J. Edgar Hoover, Jane Addams, Steve McQueen, Warren Beatty

Pluto/Negative Aspects

repulsive behaviour, accidents, injuries, drastic changes in circumstances, violent disputes, fanatical urge to dominate; insatiable, brutal, crude, ruthless.

abuse of power, alienating others, ruin, disasters, many crises in life, sudden turns of fate; liscentious, foolhardy, danger-loving, anti-social, outspoken.

burdensome relationships, common tragic experiences, suffering through associations, destructive unions, revolutionary organizations, gangsters.

Pluto/Conjunction Personalities

Brando, Garbo, Judy Garland, Olivier, James Madison, Fred Astaire

Calvin, Walt Disney, Jean Harlow, Charlton Heston, Huey Long, J.P. Morgan

DeGaulle, Barry Goldwater, Marilyn Monroe, Christine Jorgensen

Pluto/Aspect Personalities

Toulouse-Lautrec, Orson Welles, Shelley, Houdini, Paganini, Napoleon, Stalin, G.L. Rockwell, Mata Hari, Ralph Nader

Hitler, Machiavelli, Moliere, Bill Graham, Martin Luther King Jr, Houdini, Dulles, Paul Newman, Joe Namath

Greta Garbo, Mata Hari, Joanne Woodward, Adlai Stevenson, Stravinsky, James Dean

Moon's Node/Negative Aspects

socially maladjusted, short-lived relationships, estrangements, inability to live with another, disturbed domestic and family life; antisocial, difficult.

exploiting others, social climbing, difficulty in relationships, inability to act with others; selfish, inconstant, aggravating, unpopular.

Node/Conjunction Personalities

Al Capone, Toulouse-Lautrec, Valentino, Tennessee Williams

Maria Callas, Calvin Coolidge, Hitler, Hess, Rose Kennedy, Katherine Hepburn, Errol Flynn

Node/Aspect Personalities

Elizabeth II, Mary Pickford, Mary Astor, Rex Harrison, Helen Keller, Shirley Temple, Warren Beatty, Fritz Kunkel

Bette Davis, Rex Harrison, Sophia Loren, Jackie Kennedy, Schweitzer, Lana Turner, Princess Anne

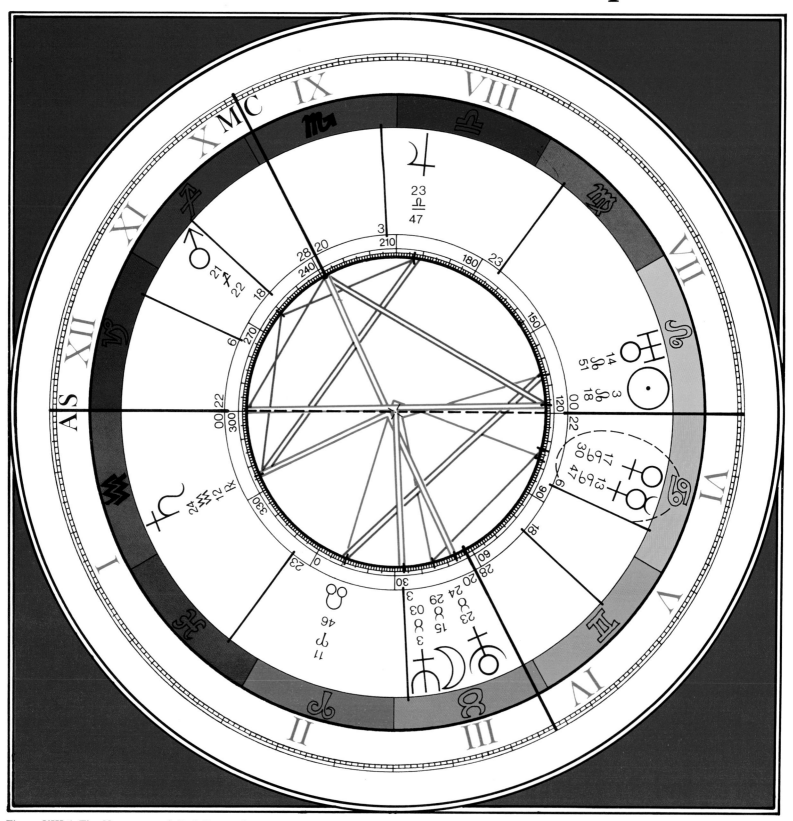

Figure VIII.1 The Horoscope of Carl Gustav Jung.

Traditional Methods of Interpretation

It is in the realm of interpretation that the use of Logarithmic Time Scale is truly revolutionary. The traditional approach takes each planet in a prearranged sequence, defines it by its sign and house qualities, and qualifies it by the aspects it makes to other planets. The sequence within which these planets are found is not considered. The various mechanisms of the individual are presented as though they all exist from birth and continue to operate through life as simultaneous qualities. Differentiation of values within the traditional method is created by the particular hierarchy of qualities that the astrologer personally accepts.

While this series of values usually starts with the Sun, Moon and Ascendant and follows with the other planets according to their distances away from the Sun, there is much variance about the exact sequence in which planets are interpreted. Current methods as described by Alan Leo, Margaret Hone, Ron Davison, Marc Edmund Jones, Jeff Mayo and Reinhold Ebertin all use a set hierarchy of planets as the initial — and sometime exclusive — method of ordering the interpretation. The houses of the horoscope, even though they are considered "divisions in time" or "spheres of life" by Jeff Mayo, or the "environment" by Alan Leo, are understood as mere conditioning factors which qualify the planets. There is no use of the natural sequence of houses.

Ebertin tries to eliminate the house system altogether. CSI "does not deal with any house interpretation".[1] He describes the traditional method very accurately in *"Man in the Universe"*:

> "Traditional astrology based its observation of the horoscope on the houses on the assumption that these corresponded to particular aspects of life, e.g., character was read from the 1st house, financial situation from the 2nd, marriage matters from the 7th, and vocation from the 10th house, etc. Each individual house was interpreted according to the stellar body occupying it, and in the case of there being no tenant, one merely took the 'ruler of the sign' on the 'cusp' and looked to see where this planet was located, etc. This kind of investigative method by no means fits into our modern times and is even less suited to scientific procedure. *This old division into houses with their correspondence to certain facets of life is so alluring that it makes it difficult for most students of this field of knowledge to renounce this method."* [2]

This renunciation is apparently difficult for Ebertin as well, since he is forced to postulate a "compilation of the potentials and areas according to Midheaven and Ascendant, which can serve as a foundation of disposition". He forms the individual factors into units:[3]

I. Vitality, health
II. Feeling, emotional disposition
III. Thinking, intellect, meditation
IV. Willpower and energy
V. Ego-consciousness, goal in life
VI. Contact, relationships with others
VII. Love, marriage, family
VIII. Trend of destiny

He then "orders the keywords" derived from an aspect analysis into this pattern of eight (why eight?) categories. The eminent scientist who can do without houses is forced to invent a totally unrelated hierarchy which includes many of the traditional "unscientific" categories.

Jeff Mayo divides the analysis into these section:[4]

I. General characteristics (Sun, Moon and their rulers)
II. Personality-Attitude (Ascendant, etc.)
III. Mentality (Mercury)
IV. Emotional Nature, Personal Contact
V. Business, Financial Interests, Career
VI. Travel
VII. Health

Within these classifications, Mayo considers three factors to be of prime importance — the Ascendant, Sun and Moon. In his opinion they should always be interpreted in that order. He walks even further out onto a limb by stating:

[1] Ebertin, *CSI,* p. 35.

[2] Ebertin, *Man in the Universe,* p. 67. My italics.

[3] Ebertin, *Man in the Universe,* p. 67.

[4] Mayo, *Astrology,* p. 167.

[5] Mayo, *Astrology,* p. 156. My italics.

"In fact, a very true assessment of an individual's character can be made from those three factors alone — judged from the signs they are associated with and houses and aspects involved, *or even just by signs.*" [5]

One wonders why the other planets and the house system he described earlier in his book are used, as they seem to have a relatively minor function.

Both of these approaches clearly demonstrate that a viable structure in analysis and interpretation is necessary. Both Ebertin and Mayo choose to invent eight or seven-stage processes which lose even the validity of the congruent house system. Both systems also require additional biographical information from the individual. Ebertin considers biography, handwriting and a photograph as "means of control". Mayo insists that he be given a few details concerning the general status of his client. "In this way the full value of the chart-pattern as a guide to character potentialities and future prospects is realized in the light of existing personal circumstances and problems." [6] One would think that the client might expect to have these circumstances discovered and identified by the astrologer.

[6] Mayo, *Astrology,* p. 167.

Although there is an element of the confessional in an astrological reading, this is not its central function. The astrologer seeks to unveil individual realities which are unconscious or unknown, and to verify those concepts which the individual already "knows".

In and Out of Time

> "The journey through the planetary houses boils down to becoming conscious of the good and the bad qualities in our character, and the apotheosis means no more than maximum consciousness; which amounts to maximal freedom of the will." [7]

The Logarithmic Time Scale correlated to the houses allows the interpretation to follow the growth, evolution and development of the individual. Life begins at the moment of conception on the cusp of the IXth house (Sagittarius). The horoscope is interpreted from this point on. The planetary positions in the time scale and their relevant events can be reconstructed in the proper sequence. Each stage of development is contingent upon those previously created and in turn conditions those which follow.

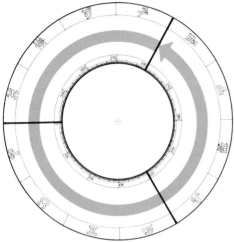

Figure VIII.2 Linear, Causal Reality.

There are two sets of values which work together in life. Movement around the periphery of the circle is equivalent to *linear, causal reality* where each event is ordered in succession according to the law of cause and effect. As Roland Fischer explains:

> "As a spider excretes his web, we excrete our dimensions of existence, spacetime, to catch as much world in it as we can. It is through this unidirectional web of time coupled to our metabolic rate that we learn about our lives, organic development, or the mathematical-physical world of Planck, Bohr and Heisenberg. Strangely, our concepts of the world evolve, as does our time, at an exponential rate, as in growth or aging." [8]

Following the periphery from conception, early events cause later events in a counterclockwise direction around the horoscope. (Figure VIII.2)

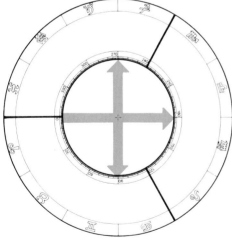

Figure VIII.3 Synchronistic, Acausal Reality.

The other set of values are aspect-patterns, which connect pairs of planets around the periphery through the centre. (Figure VIII.3) Aspects operate outside causal reality and are *acausal, synchronistic connections.* They link times as well as qualities, and their main function is to *transmit meaning from event to event.* Their connections are actually "outside time".

The combination of these two sets of values is described eloquently by Schopenhauer:

[7] Jung, *Mysterium Coniunctionis, CW 14,* p. 231.

[8] Fischer, *Voices of Time,* p. 376.

[9] Jung, *Synchronicity,* p. 427 from Schopenhauer, *via Parega und Paralipomena, I,* trans. Irvine, p. 49f.

> "All the events in a man's life stand in two fundamentally different kinds of connection: firstly, in the objective, causal connection of the natural process; secondly, in a subjective connection which exists only in relation to the individual who experiences it, and which is thus as subjective as his own dreams . . . . That both kinds of connection exist simultaneously, and the selfsame event, although a link in two totally different chains, nevertheless falls into place in both, so that the fate of one individual invariably fits the fate of the other, and each is the hero of his own drama while simultaneously figuring in a drama foreign to him — this is something that surpasses our powers of comprehension . . ." [9]

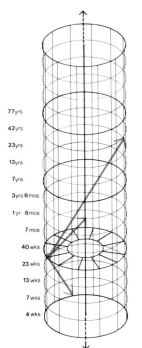

Figure VIII.4 Aspects on the Logarithmic Cylinder. A Grand Cross from the Ascendant.

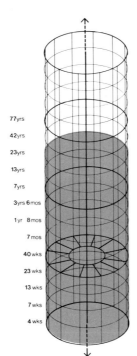

Figure VIII.5 Submersion of the Logarithmic Cylinder at 23 years old.

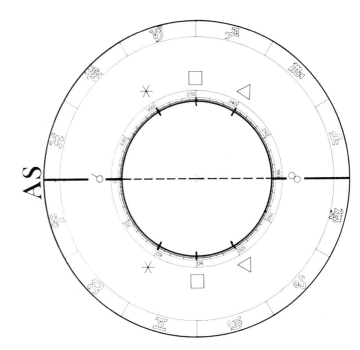

Figure VIII.6 Sensitive Points to the Ascendant.

Peripheral events are "objective" connections and aspects "subjective" connections, which only the individual experiences. Using the time scale it is possible to combine these two sets of values.

In the graded logarithmic cylinder of life, aspect connections move either *up* or *down* through the cylinder. Aspects back towards conception move down; aspects ahead move upwards to the transcendental octave. (Figure VIII.4) This temporal perspective is often very useful in interpretation. As the interpretation progresses, it is as though the cylinder were being filled with water (memories). As the water level rises with aging, all previous events, personifications and states of mind become successively submerged. (Figure VIII.5) Future events hover above the filled cylinder like rain-clouds waiting to discharge their moisture. Identifying previous experiences is a deep-sea salvage operation within the psyche. A clear memory indicates that the water filling the cylinder is crystal-clear, while hazy, ill-remembered events cloud the medium of communication. Only by bringing all memories to the surface can the individual clear his life of confusion.

In addition to the actual planetary positions there are *"sensitive points"*. Sensitive points are times when aspects register but no planets are present. (Figure VIII.6) The most critical are the squares and oppositions of each planet transferred to the time scale. These indicate parts of the psyche which are called the *Shadow*. The shadow is generally a negative figure in dreams which embodies qualities of which the individual is unconscious. To the extent that the personality is positive, the shadow is negative. Recognition and acceptance of contradictory qualities in one's psyche is equivalent to gradual consciousness of those qualities. The sensitive squares and oppositions are productive of continual tension and conflict: the motif of suffering. In the alchemists' coniunctio suffering produces such extreme heat that the opposing qualities melt and fuse together. (Figure VIII.7) Its intensity is a gauge of the degree to which we are intolerable to ourselves.[10] The whole individual experiences his conflict *consciously* and discovers that, paradoxically, both positive and negative qualities are necessary, but that the outcome of the confrontation is unknowable.

The psyche is affected not only by events, but also by internal processes not identifiable from an objective viewpoint. Psychic communications appear in *symbolic form* in the horoscope together with their coincident events. These may be most important to the individual and become the essence of the interpretation.

Figure VIII.7 The Alchemist's Furnace. (Geber, *De Alchimie,* 1532.)

[10] Jung, *Letters II, 1951-1961* p. 234.

A Pattern for Interpretation

To ensure correct interpretation, it is necessary to define the proper *pattern of approach*. All considerations proceed from the General to the Specific, starting from the initial visual impression of the horoscope. The following outline suggests an approach.

INTERPRETATION OUTLINE

I. General Considerations

A. Shape (Splay, Bowl, Bucket, Locomotive, Bundle, Sling and See-Saw)
B. Distribution by Octave (Octaves within which planets are located)
C. Major Aspect Patterns (Grand Trine, Grand Cross, T-square, Satellitium)
D. Constellations (Groupings which striate out from the whole horoscope)
E. Positive and Negative Planets (Fire and Air extravert and Earth and Water introvert)
F. Triplicities (Distribution of Elements)

Fire	(Aries, Leo, Sagittarius)
Air	(Gemini, Libra, Aquarius)
Earth	(Taurus, Virgo, Capricorn)
Water	(Cancer, Scorpio, Pisces)

G. Quadruplicities (Distribution of Modes)

Cardinal	(Aries, Cancer, Libra, Capricorn)
Fixed	(Taurus, Leo, Scorpio, Aquarius)
Mutable	(Gemini, Virgo, Sagittarius, Pisces)

H. House Modes (Distribution by House)

Angular	(I, IV, VII, Xth houses)
Succedent	(II, V, VIII, XIth houses)
Cadent	(III, VI, IX, XIIth houses)

I. Rulerships
J. Exaltations

II. Specific Considerations

A. Parental relationship before Conception (Sun and Moon aspects, signs, houses and relative order)
B. Conception Time (Signs, planets, aspects)
C. Individual Planets from Conception Time, including ASC and MC.

1. Gestation Octave
2. Childhood Octave
3. Maturity Octave
4. Transcendent Octave

Each planet interpreted according to:
a. Planetary nature and personifications
b. Registration age in the Time Scale.
c. House quality
d. Sign quality
e. Previous aspects and their ages ⎤⎡ personifications
f. Conjunctions ⎬⎨ correspondences
g. Forward aspects and their ages ⎦⎣ health significators

A. Shape

The first visual impression of the overall structure of the horoscope often gives an understanding which is verified by subsequent detailed investigation. The *shape* of the planetary configuration around the horoscope indicates the density, organization of the psyche and the "centre of gravity" of the individual. There are seven major shapes.

Note that the Ascendant, Midheaven and Moon's Nodes are not considered in the shapes.

By far the most common is the **Splay Shape,** where the ten planets are evenly distributed around the circle and throughout life. (Figure VIII.8) Every octave is occupied, and there is a *balance of viewpoint*. There may be aspect patterns which relate all planets to each other, or there may be very few connections. Valuation of the splay depends upon the degree of integration as determined by aspects and planets grouped around the ASC and MC positions. Examples of the well-integrated splay are the diplomat John Foster Dulles (Horoscope 14), the poet William Butler Yeats (Horoscope 48), the Nobel Prize Winner for Literature Thomas Mann (Horoscope 31) and the supreme artist Michaelangelo Buonarotti (Horoscope 33). They are all characterized by a vast scope of activities.

In the **Bowl Shape** all ten planets fall in one-half of the horoscope, usually enclosed by an opposition. (Figure VIII.9) The bowl relates everything to a *one-sided frame of reference* where all contact with the opposite half is by reflection. The critical planet in the bowl shape is the planet which "leads" the bowl through the signs, indicative of the half of the psyche activated. If all the planets are below the horizon as in Elizabeth Browning's (Horoscope 10), the individual is extremely subjective and unconscious, while all planets above the horizon, like Queen Victoria (Horoscope 46), produce an objective and conscious individual. The bowl often forces recognition of the vacant half of the horoscope. Karl Marx (Horoscope 32) has all planets in the left half, which indicates a dominant personal orientation compensated for with collective attitudes. Helen Keller (Horoscope 26) was born blind and deaf with all planets in the right half (the collective) and had to be cajoled out of herself, away from the personal. In most instances the bowl shape does not exactly coincide with the hemispheres as determined by the ASC-DES and MC-IC axes and therefore covers three quadrants. The central quadrant of the three indicates the *"centre of gravity"* of the individual, unless a majority of planets fall in either of the adjacent quadrants. The occupied bowl half indicates the part of the life which is formative, and the remainder is compensatory.

The **Bucket Shape** is a bowl with one planet (or a conjunction) outside acting as a "handle". (Figure VIII.10) *The handle must balance the influences of the remaining nine planets* as their only representative in the missing half, and is the channel through which they communicate. Planets within the bowl which aspect the handle indicate the nature of the channel. The handle compensates for the onesidedness of the bowl, and its effectiveness is dependent upon its strength by sign, house and aspect. The qualities of the handle often show where life energy directs itself. Again, the quadrants within which the bowl and the handle fall are important. In the case of Marcel Proust (Horoscope 37), where nine planets are below the horizon, the conscious handle (Saturn) must counterbalance all of the unconscious influences. Bucket individuals are highly focused, as the following examples show: composer Richard Wagner (Horoscope 47), physicist Albert Einstein (Horoscope 17), heretic Rasputin (Horoscope 39), dictator Adolf Hitler (Horoscope 24) and psychoanalyst Sigmund Freud (Horoscope 19). They are all men of extreme personal force.

In the **Locomotive Shape** one third of the horoscope is unoccupied, (Figure VIII.11) indicating that *one octave in life is not fully experienced*. The critical position is the planet which *leads* the other planets through the signs. A striking example is Anastasia of Russia (Horoscope 2) who had Saturn in Capricorn (political practicalities) as the leading planet register at the age of her early death (Mars square Saturn at 17 years old). Individuals with locomotive shapes often exaggerate the two strong octaves at the expense of the vacant one, producing an "Achilles Heel". The entire Octave of Gestation (creation of body) is missing in the horoscope of the footballer Joe Namath, who suffers from recurrent injuries. Other individuals with an octave missing concentrate upon the vacant octave, like Nicolai Lenin (Horoscope 29) overvaluating the physical; Leonardo da Vinci (Horoscope 30) transcending

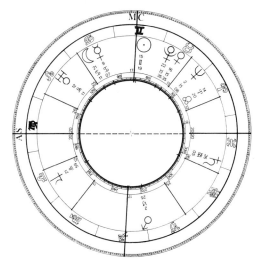
Figure VIII.8 The Splay Shape.

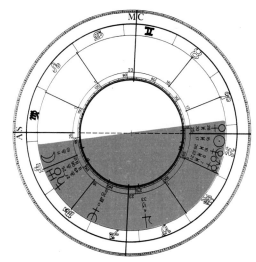
Figure VIII.9 The Bowl Shape.

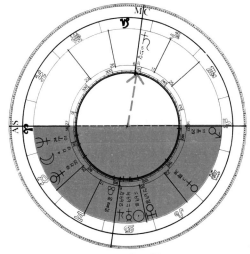
Figure VIII.10 The Bucket Shape.

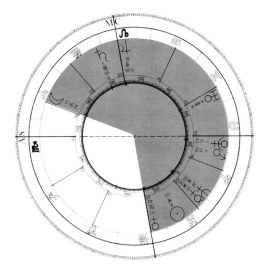

Figure VIII.11 The Locomotive Shape.

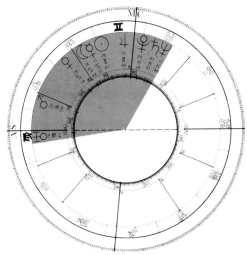

Figure VIII.12 The Bundle Shape.

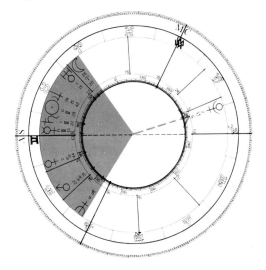

Figure VIII.13 The Sling Shape.

the physical through art; and Mary Baker Eddy (Horoscope 16), Founder of Christian Science, healing the body through the spirit. Rudyard Kipling (Horoscope 27) has an empty Octave of Childhood, yet his memorable stories for children seem to contradict this. Goethe (Horoscope 22) and Albrecht Durer (Horoscope 15) both lack planets in the Octave of Maturity, yet they are two of the most "mature" artists in history. *The locomotive shape allows the possibility of wholeness if the empty octave can be compensated for effectively.*

The **Bundle Shape** is the antithesis of the locomotive as all planets are within one trine (120°) and two-thirds of the horoscope is untenanted. (Figure VIII.12) It indicates individuals who are *highly concentrated* upon one set of values to the exclusion of all others. Only when the narrow range of qualities becomes universal can the individuals equilibrate. The compaction of bundle shapes is such that there can be only conjunctions, sextiles and squares, with the possibility of few trines. This produces a closely-knit complex with much tension and the necessity of confronting the absent two-thirds of the horoscope. The composer Igor Stravinsky (Horoscope 44) has all planets in the Octave of Gestation and his work reflects total involvement with the collective unconscious (The Rite of Spring) and transcendent states. By the time of his birth all the necessary influences had registered and all later events were reverberations of them. The highly-structured quality of his music and ballets certainly indicates this. Princess Anne of England (Horoscope 3) is confined to the same range as Stravinsky, and she functions as a symbol of the last remaining royalty on our planet — a matrix for the projections of a nation. The planets in Mussolini's horoscope (Horoscope 34) occupy the VIIth, VIIIth, IXth and Xth houses and corroborate his passion for domination of the conscious collective quadrant. His bundle is bounded by a Uranus/Neptune trine which indicates "the elimination of waking consciousness", producing the infantile fantasy which characterized his authoritarian regime. Bundle shapes produce individuals who have difficulty escaping from their obsessions, and are rare configurations.

The **Sling Shape** is to the bundle as the bucket is to the bowl shape. It is a bundle with one planet or a conjunction outside, (Figure VIII.13) which acts as the directing agent through which the bundled planets operate. With *concentration and an outlet,* this shape makes *very strong and highly focused individuals* who express themselves through one particular channel. The poets Dante (Horoscope 13), Baudelaire (Horoscope 8), Verlaine (Horoscope 45), Carl Sandburg, Robert Burns and John Greenleaf Whittier all have sling shapes. Baudelaire, Verlaine and Whittier focus upon the Moon, Sandburg on the outer planet Uranus, Burns on Neptune and Dante on Pluto. The character and direction of their poetry is related to the focusing planet. Two other sling shapes show how the same focus can manifest in very different ways. Both Clara Barton (Horoscope 7), founder of the Red Cross, and General William Tecumseh Sherman, American Civil War General, have sling shapes focused upon Mars (surgeons-nurses and fighters). The degree of integration of the separate planet into the bundle indicates the effectiveness of the horoscope, as there is an inherent danger of overloading the isolated planet.

The **See-Saw Shape** is composed of two dense constellations directly opposite one another. (Figure VIII.14) It produces individuals who have *highly tensioned extremes* in their character. The inherent oppositional nature of the shape can produce genius, but can also make for a very hazardous path through life. Strong see-saw shapes were possessed by the philosophers Nietzsche (Horoscope 35) and Spinoza (Horoscope 42) and the painters, Raphael (Horoscope 38) and Rubens (Horoscope 41). They all had extraordinary abilities, but in the case of Nietzsche, the opposites tore him apart and he was *non compos mentis* for the last ten years of his life. These shapes have multiple oppositions and create tensions without supplying trines or squares which can resolve them. They manifest at two opposing times in life which contradict each other, often leading to an abrupt about-face which is difficult to comprehend (for example Nixon and Nietzsche).

The shape is an indicator of the *"level of organization"* of the psyche. The splay is the least differentiated and could be compared to the amoeba which continually redefines its boundaries. The other shapes are more highly defined and rigid, producing lives metaphorical to their shapes. The more highly articulated the shape, the fewer examples are to be found. The mechanism of the horoscope allows choices within the disposition but does not allow alteration of the basic organization.

The shape has a further meaning through time, as the density of groupings implies the rate at which the planets unfold during life. The sequence of planets in the horoscope is activated through the Logarithmic Time Scale when transited each day by the Ascendant, each month by the Moon and each year by the Sun. If planets are grouped together in the birth horoscope, they will be concentrated during transits as well. If the horoscope is a bundle shape, the Moon will transit all planets in one-third of a month (ten days). In the case of Stravinsky (Horoscope 44), planets in the horoscope all register between the time just after conception (17° Taurus) and just after the birth moment (14° Virgo). Since the Sun passes 17° Taurus on the 8th of May each year and takes until the 7th of September to pass 14° Virgo, it is during this four month period of time that one would expect his creative activity to function at its strongest. This concept of shape clarifies the structure of each day, month and year for the individual, as well as the phases of his life.

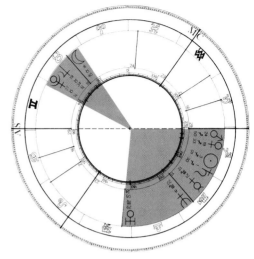

Figure VIII.14 The See-Saw Shape.

B. Distribution by Octave

The distribution of the planets by octave is closely related to the shape of the horoscope. The tenanted octaves define the developmental stages in life which are important (Figure VIII.15). As we found previously, the symbolism varies as we age, and interpretation becomes more and more specific.

In the **Octave of Gestation,** planets are most symbolic and are defined from the viewpoint of the mother. As this time is the realm of the Collective Unconscious, individuals who have a majority of their planets here have both attitudes and lives which are highly archetypal.

In the **Octave of Childhood,** events are interpreted relative to the mother and father within the structure of the family. All indications are connected to the development of the personality, but the fantasy factor of childhood must be recognized. Freud formulated his Oedipal Complex theory on confessions of his patients relating to childhood sexual experiences with their parents, and he did not discover until forty years later that a majority of these confessions were merely wish-fulfillment fantasies. Events clearly indicated in the horoscope which seem outlandish are often true during this time.

In the **Octave of Maturity,** events are usually within the memory of the individual, and hence verifiable, or else they occur in the future. Individuals with a majority of planets in this octave often feel throughout the first years of their lives that they have not yet 'begun to live', and this can be the case. They are the 'late-bloomers'.

In the **Octave of Transcendence,** influences are identical to those in the Gestation Octave, but they register only when the individual *realizes* their existence. This is often contingent upon how clear the individual is about the other experiences of his life as indicated by the integration level of his aspect-patterns.

A predominance of planets in any octave produces behaviour and attitudes which reflect the developmental stage of that octave. Many planets in the Childhood Octave tend to make childish adults, while many planets in the end of the Maturity Octave produce individuals who have an early maturity, etc. Distribution by octave is a prime consideration.

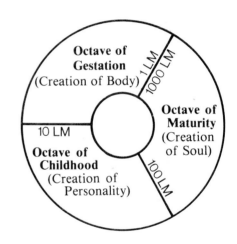

Figure VIII.15 The Three Octaves.

C. Major Aspect Patterns

The major aspect patterns — *Grand Trine, Grand Cross* and *T-Square* — are always critical, because they indicate archetypal combinations of planets. They often assimilate other planets and form very complex constellations which determine individual character.

The **Grand Trine** is composed of at least three planets or personal points each 120° apart. (Figure VIII.16) The three positions are usually in the same element and register in all octaves in the horoscope, producing an inner stability. The element of which the grand trine is composed indicates the nature of the unification. Beethoven (Horoscope 9) has an Earthy Grand Trine (sensation); Michaelangelo (Horoscope 33) has a Watery Grand Trine (feeling); Yeats (Hororscope 48) has an Airy Grand Trine (thinking); and Winston Churchill (Horoscope 11) has a Fiery Grand Trine (intuition). The qualities of the planets involved are indicative of the actual meaning of the Grand Trine. Beethoven's is extreme as the planets involved are the three slowest, Uranus, Neptune and Pluto, and both the Ascendant and the Midheaven are included as well.

Since orbs provide a leeway for the planets in the grand trine, participating planets may oc-

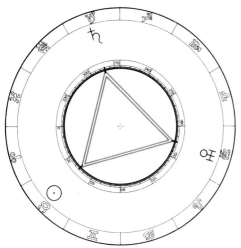

Figure VIII.16 Grand Trine.

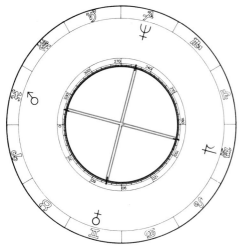

Figure VIII.17 Grand Cross.

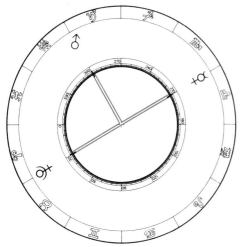

Figure VIII.18 T-Square.

cur at the very beginning or at the end of a sign, with one apex in a different element than the others. This is called a **Dissociate Grand Trine** and is only slightly less stable than the pure shape. Individuals with this formation include Jane Austen (Horoscope 6, earth and air) and Goethe (Horoscope 22, water and fire). The horoscope of the painter Max Ernst (Horoscope 18) is exceptional as it possesses both a pure Earthy Grand Trine and Dissociate Grand Trine in water and air.

The **Grand Cross** is the shape of maximum tension, but can produce the most exceptional beings if resolved. The Grand Cross is composed of four planets in mutual square and opposition. (Figure VIII.17). The Cardinal Grand Cross is the most aggressive, the Fixed Grand Cross the most difficult to resolve, while the Mutable Grand Cross is the easiest to work through. The American Secretary of State, John Foster Dulles (Horoscope 14), has a Mutable Grand Cross indicating an ability to handle enormously complex negotiations. When one of the positions in the grand cross occupies a mode different than the others, it is called a **Dissociate Grand Cross.**

The **T-Square** is a very dynamic shape and often appears in the horoscopes of strong individuals. (Figure VIII.18) The T-Square is an opposition with a third planet mutually square both ends. Richard Wagner (Horoscope 47) and Louis XIV have Fixed T-Squares, Jane Austen (Horoscope 6) and Max Ernst (Horoscope 18) have Mutable T-Squares, and Marcel Proust (Horoscope 37) has a Cardinal T-Square. The painter and diplomat Rubens (Horoscope 41) has both Cardinal and Fixed T-Squares, while the multi-faceted philosopher Baruch Spinoza (Horoscope 42) has both Fixed and Mutable T-Squares. Pairs of T-squares indicate individuals with complex realities and often the power to resolve them. The enigmatic but brilliant mystic Gurdjieff (Horoscope 23) has two Fixed T-Squares and one Dissociate T-Square, involving five planets and both personal points.

The psychologist Roberto Assagioli (Horoscope 5) has a Watery Grand Trine, a Mutable Grand Cross and a Fixed T-Square — which is appropriate since his psychology is called ''Psychosynthesis''! Although these three shapes include nine planets and both personal points, the remaining two planets, Mercury and Uranus, are unaspected. It is clear from a superficial investigation of this horoscope that Dr. Assagioli was forced to develop psychosynthesis to resolve his own dynamic psyche.

In the **Satellitium** (Figure VIII.19) more than four planets are mutually conjunct, producing a focus upon the sign or age it occupies. Baudelaire (Horoscope 8) has seven planets conjunct in the VIIIth house, verifying his overwhelming interest in passion and death. Galileo (Horoscope 20) has four planets in the sign Pisces, signifying work in seclusion.

D. Constellations

Constellations of planets indicate the flow of energy through life. Every horoscope has its unique system of aspects, and they can be diagrammed and analyzed. Certain combinations allow energy circulation, while others tend either to block, diffuse or to regress the flow of life force. Often series of planets striate out from the whole planetary pattern as self-contained complexes. Where pairs of planets are separate, whatever the aspect between them, the energy can only move back and forth. They have no alternative channel and can only participate in the whole by creating sympathetic resonances to the rest of the planets. The more complex the constellation, the more possible flow becomes, until in some horoscopes all ten planets and personal points are mutually connected. If every planet and personal point has at least two aspects, there is always a possibility of flexibility, but when a planet is isolated at the end of an aspect or has only square or opposition aspects, the flow tends toward a ''dead end''. In the horoscope of Adolf Hitler (Horoscope 24), Saturn in Leo is at the dead end of a square aspect, indicating the overwhelming personal inferiority which led to destructive impulses. Neptune and Pluto are conjunct (obsession and fanaticism) but only relate to the MC (Ego), where they must encounter the difficult dissociate T-square, producing an irresolute situation. In the horoscope of Gurdjieff (Horoscope 23), however, every planet is co-ordinated into the overall pattern, a supreme example of total integration.

In the following paragraphs we will analyze a few of the primary flow systems which occur in horoscopes.

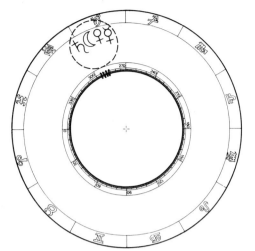

Figure VIII.19 Satellitium.

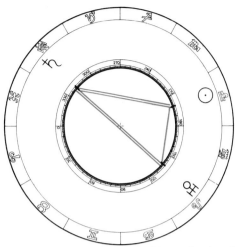

Figure VIII.20 The Opposition-Trine-Sextile Constellation.

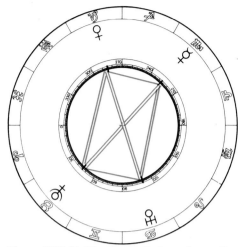

Figure VIII.21 The Constellation of two Oppositions, two Trines and two Sextiles.

The simplest constellation is a triangle composed of two planets in opposition with a third planet in trine to one and sextile to the other. (Figure VIII.20) Since energy flows along the line of least resistance, it will travel along the sextile-trine path and avoid the potential tension of the opposition. In Aleister Crowley's horoscope (Horoscope 12) Saturn and Uranus are opposed, and the Sun is sextile to Uranus and trine to Saturn. The opposition alone indicates tests of strength, while the introduction of the mediating Sun in Libra gives vitality leading to equilibration (Libra). The third planet softens the direct clash between the opposites. All three planets have two outlets for their energy. Dante (Horoscope 13) has this shape as the major constellation, and Nietzsche (Horoscope 35) has three stepping along in succession.

When this shape is doubled, it produces two oppositions with axes 60° apart, making two sextiles and two trines in the process (Figure VIII.21). It allows energy to circulate freely as both oppositions are resolute through the trines or sextiles. The energy can even move around the periphery of the shape and avoid the oppositions altogether. As the tension of oppositions is often beneficial to an individual's growth, this configuration can lead to lack of character or aversion to all difficulty. In any case it produces an alternation between extreme tension and great facility. The author Andre Gide (Horoscope 21) has this shape composed of a Venus-Uranus opposition (arousal of love) and a Mercury-Pluto opposition (acute observation and persuasive writing). His creativity results from the three graded energy outlets for each planet (sextile, trine and opposition). Usually all of the planets are in the same gender, except when they occur at the very beginning or end of signs. In Gide's case all planets are in water and earth signs: Taurus, Cancer, Scorpio and Capricorn.

When oppositions in either of the first two types of constellations become T-squares, the planet at the midpoint of the T-square becomes very critical and activates the whole shape. (Figure VIII.22) Galileo (Horoscope 20) has a Uranus-Neptune opposition which is trine and sextile to the ASC, with the Sun at the midpoint of the T-square. The triangle indicates confusion and one-sidedness afflicting the personality, but the introduction of the Sun gives the inventive aspect of Uranus a motivation and the result is revolutionary. It gives Galileo a true focus. The psychologist Carl Jung (Horoscope 25), the poet Verlaine (Horoscope 45) and the author Kipling (Horoscope 27) also have this shape.

When a constellation is composed mainly of sextiles and trines, participating squares provide an activation. (Figure VIII.23) Albert Einstein (Horoscope 17) has three planets in positive aspect to each other: Pluto is trine Mars (ambition and obsessive work) and the Sun is sextile to both, occupying their midpoint. The configuration indicates exceptional abilities but does not have the tension necessary for direction. The influences would naturally circulate and express themselves with increasing obsession but for the fact that Jupiter in Aquarius is square Pluto, producing organizational abilities and correct use of energy (relativity theory). The

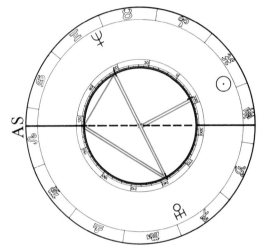

Figure VIII.22 The Opposition-Trine-Sextile-Square Constellation.

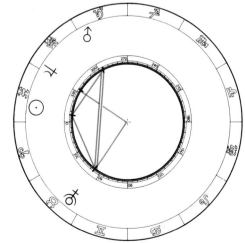

Figure VIII.23 The Activation of Squares.

meditative Jupiter agitates Pluto and transforms the whole constellation, producing extraordinary mental powers.

Beethoven (Horoscope 9) has all planets but Jupiter in one vast constellation, giving him access to a wide range of qualities. The unaspected Jupiter becomes a focus which counterbalances the force of the constellation, and indicates a philosophical attitude (Jupiter) towards practicalities (Capricorn) which resulted in his disastrous financial situation. His unaspected Venus in Capricorn conveys a distrust of artistic conventions, which also contributes to his instability. The flow in his horoscope always leads around the circle and back to the dead end at Mars in the IInd house (formal creative ability coupled with intractability), again raising the ugly financial question. Even though the Grand Trine in earth usually indicates power over physical matters, the irresolute unaspected planets whose flow terminates in Mars produce an individual who has great command but is able to transmit it only through aesthetic channels.

E. Positive and Negative Planets (Extraversion and Introversion)

Libido continually fluctuates and can have either a positive or negative charge. These charges correspond to the polarity of *extraversion* and *introversion* in psychology. Extraversion is an outward-turning of libido from subject to object, while introversion is an inward-turning of libido from object into subject. Everyone has both qualities, but the balance is critical. In astrology the dominant direction of libido rests upon the distribution of planets in their signs. Fire and air signs are positive and extravert, while earth and water signs are negative and introvert. (Figure VIII.24) As there are eleven positions to be evaluated in the horoscope (ten planets and the Ascendant), it is impossible for an individual to have an even balance. Everyone is inclined in one direction or the other. Horoscopes where all planets and the ASC are totally positive or negative are extremely rare.

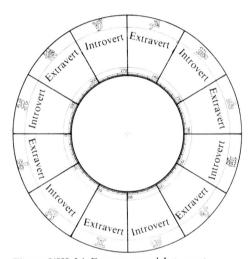

Figure VIII.24 Extravert and Introvert.

The following are positive extraverts:

Name and Occupation	Positive Fire & Air		Negative Earth & Water
Charles de Gaulle, General	10	—	1
Winston Churchill, Prime Minister	9	—	2
William Butler Yeats, Poet	9	—	2
Shirley Temple Black, Actress & Politician	8	—	3
Frederich Nietzsche, Philosopher	8	—	3

The following are negative introverts:

Name and Occupation	Positive Fire & Air		Negative Earth & Water
Rembrandt van Rijn, Painter	1	—	10
Pope John XXIII	1	—	10
Edgar Cayce, Clairvoyant Seer	2	—	9
Josef Stalin, Dictator	2	—	9
Marcel Proust, Author	3	—	8
Igor Stravinsky, Composer	3	—	8
Johann Wolfgang von Goethe, Poet	3	—	8

A majority of horoscopes have balanced distributions: 7-4, 6-5, 5-6 and 4-7. Individuals with balanced distribution tend to fluctuate between introversion and extraversion.

F. Triplicities (Distribution of Elements)

A finer level of distinction than positive and negative positions is indicated by the breakdown of elements, (Figure VIII.25) especially in balanced horoscopes. The distribution of some individuals who possess balanced positive-negative distributions follows:

Name and Occupation	Distribution Positive-Negative	Elemental Distribution			
		Fire	Air	Earth	Water
Carl Jung, Psychologist	6-5	3	3	3	2
Max Ernst, Painter	5-6	2	3	3	3
Mao Tse-tung, Chairman	6-5	2	4	3	2
Albert Einstein, Physicist	5-6	4	1	4	2
Leonardo da Vinci, Artist	5-6	2	3	3	3
Richard Wagner, Composer	5-6	2	3	4	2
Peter Paul Rubens, Painter	5-6	4	1	3	3

There are also individuals who have a balanced positive-negative distribution but extreme element distribution:

Ludwig von Beethoven, Composer	5-6	4	1	6	0

The elements very clearly correspond to Jung's four personality types: Fire to Intuition, Air to Thinking, Earth to Sensation and Water to Feeling. Thus Beethoven has dominant intuition and sensation and recessive thinking and feeling. The positive-negative evaluation should be combined with the dominant psychological type to indicate the overall disposition.

In some individuals one type is clearly dominant over the other three. When this occurs, there is often one element which has no planets at all. This seems to indicate an absence of the missing quality, but in practice there is unconscious compensation for the missing quality. The individual with no planets in water signs is often surrounded by others who continually display emotional attitudes.

The following table shows individuals with single element concentrations:

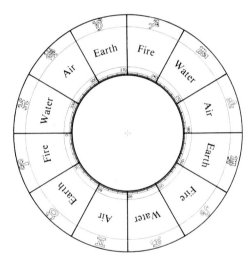

Figure VIII.25 Triplicities.

Name and Occupation	Positive-Negative Distribution	Triplicities			
		Fire	Air	Earth	Water
Fire-Intuition					
Emile Zola, Author	8-3	7	1	0	3
Fidel Castro, Revolutionary	7-4	6	1	2	2
Paul Verlaine, Poet	7-4	5	2	2	2
Charles Baudelaire, Poet	5-6	5	0	3	3
Air-Thinking					
F. Scott Fitzgerald, Author	7-4	0	7	2	2
Arthur Conan Doyle, Author	8-3	2	6	2	1
William Butler Yeats, Poet	9-2	3	6	2	0
Arthur Rimbaud, Poet	6-5	1	5	3	2
Earth-Sensation					
Louis Pasteur, Chemist	2-9	0	2	8	1
Kahlil Gibran, Author	3-8	2	1	8	0
Josef Stalin, Dictator	2-9	2	0	6	3
Ludwig von Beethoven, Composer	5-6	4	1	6	0
Pope John XXIII	1-10	1	0	7	3
Adolf Hitler, Dictator	6-5	2	4	5	0
Nicolai Lenin, Politician	4-7	3	1	4	3
Water-Feeling					
Longfellow, Poet	3-8	2	1	1	7
Giovanni Casanova, Lover	4-7	1	3	1	6
Rembrandt van Rijn, Painter	1-10	0	1	4	6
Schiller, Philosopher-Poet	3-8	3	0	2	6
Goethe, Philosopher-Poet	3-8	2	1	3	5
Michaelangelo, Artist	4-7	1	3	2	5
Rimsky-Korsakov, Composer	4-7	2	2	2	5

The triplicities determine the hierarchy of psychological types.

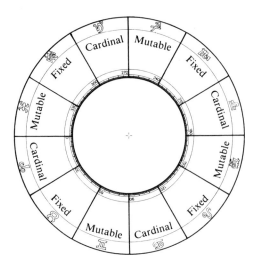

Figure VIII.26 Quadruplicities.

G. Quadruplicities (Distribution of Modes)

As the triplicities determine the quality of operation, the modes (Figure VIII.26) indicate individual strengths of groups of planets. Planets in **Cardinal Signs** (Aries, Cancer, Libra and Capricorn) are in the strongest positions in the zodiac and are *initiating influences*. Planets in **Fixed Signs** (Taurus, Leo, Scorpio and Aquarius) are stable and *sustaining influences*. Planets in **Mutable Signs** (Gemini, Virgo, Sagittarius and Pisces) are the weakest, *unstable influences*. The distribution of the quadruplicities show the relative *phasing of the individual mechanism*.

The following table shows individuals who have one dominant mode:

Name and Occupation	Cardinal (+)	Fixed (=)	Mutable (−)
Cardinal-Initiating			
Charles Baudelaire, Poet	8	0	3
Marcel Proust, Author	8	2	1
Francisco Goya, Painter	8	1	2
Paul von Hindenburg, Statesman	8	2	1
Fixed-Sustaining			
Herbert Hoover, President	1	9	1
Jack London, Author	1	8	2
Richard Wagner, Composer	1	7	3
Carl Jung, Psychologist	3	7	1
Mutable-Alternating			
Coco Chanel, Couturier	1	3	7
Francisco Franco, Dictator	2	2	7
Elizabeth Browning, Poetess	4	0	7
Nicholas Copernicus, Astronomer	1	3	7

Individuals with even distribution of the quadruplicities have balanced strengths.

Balanced Modalities			
Albert Einstein, Physicist	5	3	3
Dante Aligheri, Poet	4	3	4
Michaelangelo, Artist	4	3	4
R. D. Laing, Psychologist	4	3	4

H. House Modes (Distribution of Modes by House Position)

The position of the cardinal, fixed and mutable signs in the horoscope can vary, depending upon the mode of the ascendant. The distribution of the planets in the **Angular** (cardinal), **Succedent** (fixed) and **Cadent** (mutable) houses (Figure VIII.27) indicates the manner in which modes actually function through life. The following are individuals who have dominant house modes in one of the three categories:

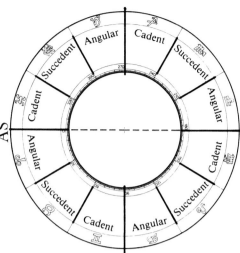

Name and Occupation	I, IV, VII, X Angular (+)	II, V, VIII, XI Succedent (=)	III, VI, IX, XII Cadent (−)
Angular-Strong			
Richard Wagner, Composer	7	1	2
Simon Bolivar, Statesman	7	1	2
Aleister Crowley, Magician	7	1	2
Francisco Goya, Painter	7	2	1
Succedent-Stable			
Charles Baudelaire, Poet	3	7	0
Ludwig von Beethoven, Composer	1	6	3
Galileo, Astronomer	1	6	3
Michaelangelo, Artist	3	6	1
Cadent-Weak			
Rubens, Painter and Diplomat	1	1	8
Baruch Spinoza, Philosopher	0	3	7
Victor Hugo, Author	2	1	7

Figure VIII.27 House Modes.

The ascendant position is not considered in this analysis because it is always angular, so the total number of positions are ten. When individuals have cardinal signs ascending, the house and sign positions by mode are usually identical, as in the horoscope of Goya. This is not true for either fixed or mutable signs rising. An additional strength factor for individuals with many angular planets is the implication that planets will tenant the strongest houses in the horoscope, the Ist and Xth.

Balanced house modes imply consistency of action. The following are examples of balanced distributions.

Balanced House Modes			
Albert Einstein, Physicist	4	3	3
Adolf Hitler, Dictator	3	4	3
Raphael, Painter	3	4	3
Thomas Mann, Author	3	3	4

I. Ruler and Detriment Planets

The planet which is most sympathetic to the qualities of each sign is the *Ruler* of that sign. The luminaries, the Sun and Moon, rule the two signs of the peak of summer, Leo and Cancer. The remaining five planets each rule two signs — one positive and one negative. The disposition of the rulerships is symmetrical around an axis through the cusp between Cancer and Leo as the accompanying illustration shows (Figure VIII.28).

Planetary Rulerships

Sun rules positive Leo	Moon rules negative Cancer
Mercury rules negative Virgo	Mercury rules positive Gemini
Venus rules positive Libra	Venus rules negative Taurus
Mars rules negative Scorpio	Mars rules positive Aries
Jupiter rules positive Sagittarius	Jupiter rules negative Pisces
Saturn rules negative Capricorn	Saturn rules positive Aquarius

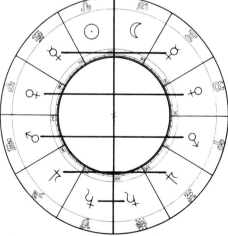

Figure VIII.28 Rulerships.

When a planet is in the sign it rules, it operates at its purest. In traditional astrology the planet ruling the ascendant (the *Lord of the Ascendant*) was considered very important, especially the house in which it resided. This supposedly gave the house quality through which the personality functioned, and if that house was angular or near the MC, the personality was then considered strong. Likewise, the planet which ruled each house cusp qualified the interpretation of that house. The attitude towards rulerships has declined recently and Ebertin dispenses with it altogether. Although the rulerships are very difficult to verify, they are included because they form an important part of the historical process of astrology and should at least be presented.

When a planet resides in the sign opposite to the sign it rules, it is in *Detriment.* This represents an unsympathetic location for the planetary qualities.

Planetary Detriments

Sun in detriment in Aquarius	Moon in detriment in Capricorn
Mercury in detriment in Pisces	Mercury in detriment in Sagittarius
Venus in detriment in Aries	Venus in detriment in Scorpio
Mars in detriment in Taurus	Mars in detriment in Libra
Jupiter in detriment in Gemini	Jupiter in detriment in Virgo
Saturn in detriment in Cancer	Saturn in detriment in Leo

As the outer planets were discovered, they were also given rulerships and detrimental signs.
Uranus rules Aquarius and is in detriment in Leo
Neptune rules Pisces and is in detriment in Virgo
Pluto rules Scorpio and is in detriment in Taurus

J. Exaltation and Fall Planets

Each planet has one sign where it operates at its strongest, called the sign of its *Exaltation* (Figure VIII.29). The opposite sign to the exaltation is the sign of the planet's *Fall,* where it is weakest. The planetary exaltations and falls follow:
Sun is exalted in Aries and in fall in Libra
Moon is exalted in Taurus and in fall in Scorpio
Mercury is exalted in Virgo and in fall in Pisces
Venus is exalted in Pisces and in fall in Virgo
Mars is exalted in Capricorn and in fall in Cancer
Jupiter is exalted in Cancer and in fall in Capricorn
Saturn is exalted in Libra and in fall in Aries
Uranus is exalted in Scorpio and in fall in Taurus
Neptune is exalted in Leo and in fall in Aquarius
Pluto is exalted in Aquarius and in fall in Leo
The Dragon's Head is exalted in Gemini and the Dragon's Tail is exalted in Sagittarius.

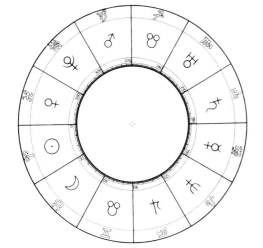

Figure VIII.29 Exaltations.

Blending Influences: The Ascendant of R. D. Laing

Once the General Considerations have been investigated, the individual planets and personal points must be analyzed. This is done by determining the age at which an influence operates, its sign and house position, the aspects it makes with other planets or personal points, and then blending the entire set of values. The following analysis of the Ascendant-Birth Moment of the psychiatrist R. D. Laing will illustrate this process.

R. D. Laing (1927-) has become interested in the maltreatment of children during and after birth. In his book *"The Facts of Life"* (Penguin Books, 1977), the liner notes state:

> "Some of the story of his own repressed and rather sad early life is told, but with amazing humour. He then moves from a discussion of our origin in sexual reproduction into the possibility that we remember, are haunted by and re-enact our conception, foetal life and birth, the loss of the cord and placenta. The result is a brilliant and moving attack on the 'heartless' science which is unaware of its own unconscious sadism — a book which is rich, disorderly, suggestive, inconclusive and humane."

An interpretation of the birth moment of Laing himself bears out all of these claims.

In Laing's horoscope, Horoscope 28 in the section of sample horoscopes, the Ascendant and its aspects (Figure VIII.30) will be considered and interpreted.

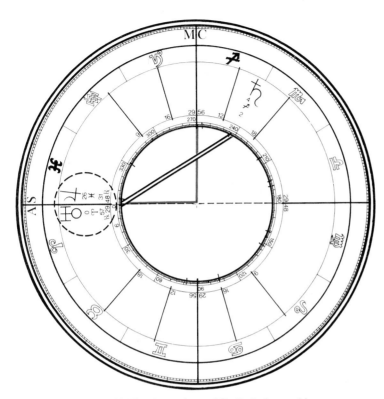

Figure VIII.30 The Ascendant of R. D. Laing and its aspects.

1. The Sign of the Ascendant

The ascendant is 29° Pisces 48′, which is only 12′ from the archetypal position of the ascendant (0° Aries 00′). Therefore, Laing's personality or mask is virtually archetypal. The position at the very end of Pisces in the Time Scale just precedes birth and indicates solitude, loneliness and the time of the first contractions.

2. Planets Aspecting the Ascendant

Jupiter at 26° Pisces 31′ is conjunct = *a philosophy of solitude, intoxication.*

Uranus at 00° Aries 57′ is conjunct = *peculiar assertion of the persona, an operation caused by blind zeal.*

MC at 29° Sagittarius is square = *intense striving for attainment of ego objectives (00° Capricorn 00′ is also the archetypal ego position!)*

Saturn at 4° Sagittarius 02′ is trine = *a seriously depressed philosophy, despair, psychological seriousness.*

Jupiter and Uranus bracket the ascendant, Jupiter occurring just before the birth and indicating expansion of self-sacrificial qualities or intoxication, while Uranus just after birth indicates a zealous incident or accident. The prelude to the birth was lonely and solitary, but the doctor's attitude was very aggressive (Uranus and Saturn). The square of the ascendant constellation to the MC indicates that the mother's involvement when she discovered that she was pregnant was highly tensioned by the actual experience of giving birth. Her personality as well as Laing's is more complicated than the ego motivating it. Saturn corresponds to a depressive factor registering just before Laing's conception which taints his birth, due to: "... my mother's father having died sometime earlier, shortly before I was conceived, I surmise." [11]

[11] Laing, *The Facts of Life,* p. 9.

3. Mutual Conjunctions

Jupiter/ASC (before birth)	= *an engaging manner, wealthy people (doctor?)* + *teamwork, recognition* − *environmental friction, differences, rebellion*
Uranus/ASC (just after birth)	= *unrest, scattered energy, nervous haste, excited people, sensitized skin nerves, trigeminal neuralgia* + *unstable, original, responsive personality* − *upsets, exciting experiences, an accident*
Jupiter/Uranus (entire process)	= *urge for independence, zealous one-sided views, convulsive fits, colics from irregular rhythm* + *sudden recognition, a successful speculation* − *arguments on outlook, exaggeration, magnification*

The conjunctions indicate the nature of the birth itself and also its phases — Jupiter, Ascendant, Uranus. The delivering doctor was concerned with his own recognition and proceded in a hasty manner, possibly cutting the umbilical cord prematurely (Jupiter/Uranus = an incident or accident). Laing's sensitive nerves were shocked and, although the doctor exaggerated the reasons for the rapid delivery, the speculation was successful for him.

> "'I used to be an obstetrician,' Dr. William Masters said, 'which is boring 90 per cent of the time. So every time I delivered a boy I used to engage in a little contest to see if I could cut the cord before he had an erection. I won about 50 per cent of the time.'"[12]

[12] Quoted by Laing, *The Facts of Life*, p. 97.

The doctor's act of expediting the delivery is a specific topic which concerns Laing. The rapid cutting of the cord can produce a temporary interruption of the rhythm of breathing, and Laing mentions his own mysterious obstructions of breath and allergenic reactions probably caused by his birth.[13] The astrological quality of the birth is definitely *traumatic*.

[13] Laing, *The Facts of Life*, p. 80, 82 and 83.

4. The Aspect Constellations —

The preceding information sets the scene for the total analysis of Laing's birth. Each of the pairs of aspects (Jup/ASC, Jup/Ura, Jup/MC, Jup/Sat, ASC/Ura, ASC/MC, ASC/Sat, Ura/MC, Ura/Sat) must be compared to the other planets in the constellation. We will see within this total range of interpretations the essence of Laing's psychology and, specifically, his justifiable attitude towards sadistic birth practices.

From *The Facts of Life* (Numbers in brackets indicate page numbers).

Jupiter Aspect Combinations

0980	Jup = Ura/ASC	=	*fortunate rearrangement of environment, co-operation*
0920	= Sat/ASC	=	*ignoring or by-passing difficulties, changed residence*
1112	= ASC/MC	=	*unhappiness in the family, unpopularity*
0992	= Ura/MC	=	*unhappy resolution of plans, inability to resolve tensions*
0849	Jup/ASC = ☌ Ura	=	*unfortunate rearrangement, unlucky guidance of others*
0853	= □ MC	=	*pleasant and harmonious personality*
0804	Jup/Ura = ☌ ASC	=	*inability to shape one's environment, peristalsis, convulsions, fits*
0800	= △ Sat	=	*tendency to have inhibitions, one-sided principles, obstinacy*
0865	Jup/MC = ☌ ASC	=	*depressive environment*
0861	= ☌ Ura	=	*lack of recognition, unsuccessful assertion of the ego*

Laing's mother assumed that having a child would improve her position and indicate her success as a woman, but she did not imagine the problems involved. She projected positively, but the response was not positive from her husband. She was ignored *(Jupiter in Pisces)*, possibly because of drinking problems in the family *(9-10)*. Laing's parents has ostendibly ceased sexual contact before his conception *(14)*, partially because they felt something 'immoral' about sex and children. There is no aspect between either the Sun (father) or Moon (mother) to the Ascendant, implying that neither parent was very close to Laing. This almost total lack of recognition existed even before the birth. This paralleled the inability of Laing's parents to recognize and resolve their own relationship's problems. This undercurrent of tension dominated Laing's gestation.

Ascendant Aspect Combinations

0914	Sat trine ASC	=	*an inhibited personality, lonely people, occupants and inmates of secluded establishments, drugs, alcoholism, chronic sense-organ disturbances*
0792	ASC = Jup/Sat	=	*inconstant or insecure attitude to others, a separation (from the mother?), relatives, professors, officials*
0997	= Ura/MC	=	*sudden adjustment to new circumstances or conditions, yoga*
0921	Sat/ASC = ♂ Ura	=	*self-willed, obstinate contact with others, enforced separation*
0925	= □ MC	=	*difficult growth of individual expression, suffering the actions of other people, inclination to feel depressed, oppressed, inhibited, frustrated or slighted*
1113	ASC/MC = △ Sat	=	*an inhibited type, moodiness*
1114	= ♂ Ura	=	*an excitable person, emotionalism, quick determination, upsets*
0981	Ura/ASC = △ Sat	=	*feeling hindered or oppressed by others, overcoming sudden difficulties jointly with others*
0985	= □ MC	=	*a restless character, constantly changing objectives*

During the birth, the doctor was nervous and hasty. The premature cutting of the umbilical cord produced a temporary heart-block *(Saturn/Uranus)* and an interruption of breathing and digestion, leading to colic after the birth. Pisces Ascendant is ruled by Neptune *(drugs, alcohol, anaesthetics)* implying that his mother was unconscious during the birth. This atmosphere still affects Laing: "At 17.15 almost every day for several years I feel like a drink. Why do I do it then? Has it anything to do with the time of my birth, 17.15?" *(76)* He continues to re-enact the placating effect of the drugs used during his birth. Immediately after birth Laing was removed from his mother and isolated in the children's ward with similarly-treated newborn individuals. This separation was repeated when he came home. "My father could not admit to anyone for several days that I was born." *(9)* The treatment during birth, the strangulation *(66-67)* and the separation make his personality severely oppressed and inhibited, and he equates doctors with suppression and the prevention of individual growth.

Uranus Aspect Combinations

0986	Ura square MC	=	*power of assertion, sudden rearrangement of the environment, original personalities, breathing activity (yoga)*
1114	Ura = ASC/MC	=	*an excitable person, emotionalism*
0877	Sat/Ura = □ MC	=	*making the highest demands upon one's own strength, rebellion, provocation, the act of separating oneself from others*

As Uranus indicates eccentricity, rhythm and change, after his birth Laing developed an obstinate personality together with the other children in his ward — a rebellion against their common savage treatment. An unspoken communication existed among them. The first two at-home nurses who cared for him were alcoholics and he did not rejoin his mother until months after his birth. By this time he was totally cut off from his family.

The following is a poem from *The Facts of Life:*
> *the world is crushing me*
> *the world is falling in on me*
> *I am crib'd, cabined, confined,*
> *I have no room*
> *no room to manoeuvre*
> *no room to turn*
> *I am suffocated*
> *I am stifled*
> *I am smothered*
> *there is pressure from all sides,*
> > *from all directions*[14]

and:

> *my own birth*   *world collapse*
> *my own destruction*
> *crushed*
> *chucked out*[15]

and:

"In my opinion, the shattering of the natural bonds at birth is a premonition of insanity in later life." [16]

From this analysis of the birth moment of R. D. Laing, it is clear that his interest in birth-trauma therapy is directly related to his own experiences. He initially concentrated upon the problems of the family (see *Sanity, Madness and the Family*) but has obviously moved back through his own life to the crucial registration of his personality at birth. The correct identification of these critical times in the life of an individual can be demonstrated by the use of the astrological Time Scale, as his case shows.

[14] Laing, *The Facts of Life,* p. 66.

[15] Laing, *The Facts of Life,* p. 66.

[16] Laing, *Psychology* Magazine, Sept. 1977.

A Complete Horoscope Analysis of Carl Gustav Jung

The complete interpretation of a birth horoscope involves the analysis of each planetary position as we have analyzed the ascendant of R. D. Laing. Through the horoscope from conception until the Transcendent Octave each planet and personal point is correlated to the proper age, its sign and house positions are identified, and all of its aspect combinations investigated.

In the horoscope of **Carl Gustav Jung** (Horoscope 25) there are two distinct levels of interpretation. The first level is the determination of external events in his life — residence changes, ages at which accidents or other traumatic situations occurred, the timing and overt implications of school life, occupational changes and many others. But this is only the surface of Jung's life. The second level of interpretation concerns the inner world of the psyche. Obviously, Jung is an individual who lived a vital psychic life, and for this reason his horoscope is particularly interesting. In the analysis there is a distinct leaning towards the profound inner events which so strongly affected his outer life. The following quotation from the Introduction of his autobiographical *"Memories, Dreams and Reflections"*, written by his collaborator, Aniela Jaffe, shows a similar situation as the interpretation of Jung's horoscope.

> "The genesis of the book to some extent determined its contents. The chapters are rapidly moving beams of light that only fleetingly illuminate the outward events of Jung's life and work. In recompense, they transmit the atmosphere of his intellectual world and the experience of a man to whom the psyche was a profound reality. I often asked Jung for specific data on outward happenings, but I asked in vain. Only the spiritual essence of his life's experience remained in his memory, and this alone seemed to him worth the effort of telling." [17]

[17] Jung and Jaffe, *Memories, Dreams and Reflections,* p. 9.

Most of the indications in his horoscope parallel outer events of his early life, but also form the basis of his psychology and humanity for the remainder of his life. The actual events as located by the Time Scale cover the period from his conception until the age of 31, with one planet, Jupiter, registering after the time of his death at the advanced age of 86. This is identical to his autobiography, where there are chapters on his early life up until the completion of his medical studies in 1900. He then wrote the chapter *"On Life after Death"*. This approach corresponds exactly to the structure of his horoscope, with Jupiter indicating the direction of his life and his final observations. Only later did he fill in the central portion of the book with brief episodes.

Concentration upon his youth brought back connections of those earliest events with his later psychological ideas.

> "Fate will have it — and this has always been the case with me — that all the 'outer' aspects of my life should be accidental. Only what is interior has proved to have substance and a determining value. As a result, all memory of outer events has faded, and perhaps these 'outer' experiences were never so very essential anyhow, or were so only in that they coincided with phases of my inner development." [18]

[18] Jung and Jaffe, *Memories, Dreams and Reflections,* p. 11.

The interpretation of Jung's horoscope is organized in two parallel columns. The left-hand column is a notation of the planetary positions, the ages at which they register and their aspect constellations. These are correlated to the numbered interpretations in Ebertin's *The Combination of Stellar Influences,* [19] and are taken quite literally to prevent 'bending the truth'. The right-hand column is a series of dreams, visions and observations and are taken from Jung's autobiography. Every effort has been made to render this interpretation as 'objective' as possible, although it would have been possible to elaborate endlessly upon the information given.

[19] Ebertin, *The Combination of Stellar Influences,* pages 70-225.

I. General Considerations

A. Shape — *Jung's horoscope is a Splay Shape, indicating an even distribution of events throughout his life, and a balanced overall viewpoint.*

B. Distribution by Octave — *There are five planets each in the octaves of Childhood and Maturity, and one planet (Mars) and the MC in the octave of Gestation and Transcendence. It is interesting to note that six planets make aspects to either Mars or the MC within the Gestation Octave, or to the ASC at the end of that octave: Saturn, Moon's Node, Neptune, Pluto, Sun and Jupiter. This fact balances the emphasis upon the two later octaves.*

C. Major Aspect Patterns — *Jung has two Fixed T-Squares. ASC square Neptune square Sun indicates extreme sensitivity, difficult advancement in life, association with men in the public eye, and mysticism. MC square Saturn square Pluto indicates concentration upon shaping individuality, a destined struggle leading to emergence as a great authority in a specific field, and the life of a magician. These Fixed T-Squares are highly dynamic and show a complex reality successfully battling static life conditions.*

D. Constellations — *Every planet and personal point in Jung's horoscope is linked together, indicating a profound possibility of integration. The most problematic planet is Neptune, which is at the dead-end of one of the T-Squares. Jung must overcome the unconscious pull to destructive mediumship and exaggerated sensitivity which this produces.*

E. Positive and Negative Planets — *Jung has a balanced distribution between six extravert (Fire and Air) and five introvert (Earth and Water) signs. He is therefore balanced with a tendency towards extraversion. Although Jung considered himself an introvert, he acknowledged that this was a very fine distinction.*

F. Triplicities — *Jung has three planets each in Fire (intuition), Air (thinking) and Earth (sensation) and two planets in Water (feeling). This balanced distribution reflects Jung's interest in the potential parity of the four psychological types. His opinion of his own dominant function varied through his life, although he favoured the Intuition Function. This may have been caused by the fact that the Sun and Uranus in Leo register in the time scale from 25 years until his death.*

G. Quadruplicities — *Jung has three planets in Cardinal Signs, six planets and the ASC in Fixed Signs and one planet, Mars, in a Mutable Sign. His life is characterized by a sustained belief in certain principles, which originated in early childhood, and continued to dominate his whole life.*

H. House Modes — *Jung has three planets in Angular houses, two planets in Succedent houses and five planets in Cadent houses. Jung always found it very difficult to obtain recognition and felt he was fighting an uphill battle. The emphasis upon Cadent Houses produces a tendency to explore and expand rather than to concentrate.*

I. Rulerships — *The Sun is in its sign Leo, and Saturn is in its sign Aquarius. Both of these masculine planets are in their strongest positions, indicating a conflict between the extraverted self-interest of Sun/Leo and the serious and restrained humanitarianism of Saturn/Aquarius. Pluto is in detriment in Taurus (necessary concentration upon physical security, or conservative attitudes towards change), and Uranus is in detriment in Leo (extreme individualism, a spirit of enterprise and a love of personal freedom).*

J. Exaltations — *The Moon is exalted in Taurus, indicating constancy, deep feelings and a very strong maternal imago — all of which were reflected in his psychology.*

II. Specific Considerations

(Note: The letter ''r'' after the CSI reference numbers denote repeated aspects.)

Biographical Parallels (Reference numbers in parentheses from *Memories, Dreams and Reflections).*

Before Conception

Sun Leo VII (Father)	=	*Ambitious, desires importance in public, highly mannered, child will supplement his Ego, the Father is extremely paternal.*
Moon Tau III (Mother)	=	*Emotionally constant, reserved, despondent, moody.*

There is no mutual aspect, therefore there is a weak relationship between them. They are socially respectable and communicate minimally.

Jung's Father was a small-town Protestant pastor who desired a large family, but due to the delicacy of his wife was unable to have one. Externally he was very self-confident, but inwardly he was riddled by doubts about himself and religious matters *(MDR, 60)*. Jung's Mother was sensitive, moody, nervous about childbirth, and had many fears which were eventually justified. She was hospitalized after Jung's birth, and remained semi-invalid for the rest of her life. She preferred to be silent about her husband's wishes and to relent.

Conception

Conception

Conception point Scorpio	=		*Father is aggressive, violent, passionate, normally conservative sexually, disharmonious union.*
	= □ Sun	=	*Mother's disharmonious attitude towards sex union, tension with Father, sense relation to passive perception.*
	= ⚹ Nep	=	*Mother dominated by others (Father), a peculiar contact, Mother physically weak, physical harm to Mother.*

Due to Mother's reticence about virtually all contact with her husband, the Father was obviously the initiator of the conception. That the conception was violent is borne out clearly by a dream Jung had at four years old when the opposite Neptune registered. Her reaction is mentioned in the dream. *(See Neptune at four years old)*

MC Scorpio

28 weeks before Birth (12 weeks after Conception)

MC Scor		=	*Mother separated from Ego-consciousness, overtaxed, hard work for Mother, Mother contemplates separation from Father, Mother has suppressed ambition for a child.*

His Mother had very little sense of her own strength, and usually shied away from all but the most conventional attitudes. Jung later described her as a kindly, fat old woman who hid her true nature beneath conventionalities *(66).*

1106	MC/ASC sextile	=	*Relationship between Lower Self (Personality) and Higher Self (Ego), interest in individual synthesis, personality directed by the Ego.*
1107	= △ Sun	=	*Relationship between Body and Soul, attitude towards others, strong male principle (Father), Father happy.*
1113	= □ Sat	=	*Depression (Mother), inhibition, inferiority*
1116	= ⚹ Plu	=	*Fascinating personality.*

Jung's mother had a dual personality, which Jung himself inherited from her. She preferred to keep the internal struggle to herself rather than mentioning it to her husband *(66)*. Jung was more sympathetic to his Mother because of this, but simultaneously he felt compassionate towards his Father. He appeared strong, but in reality was quite weak *(40)*. This was probably the root of Jung's idea that the persona was a compensatory mechanism hiding the true self within.

0926	MC/Sat square	=	*Hindered growth, insanity, loss of Ego, disintegration of the Ego, mental disorder, restrictive idealism.*
0937	= ⚹ ASC	=	*Anxiety with others, lonely person.*
0935	= ⚹ Plu	=	*A destined struggle, difficult success.*
0927	= △ Sun	=	*Insufficient defenses, depression, restriction.*

His Mother knew that her path through the pregnancy would be quite difficult but that she had to endure it. This attitude fore-shadowed Jung's own difficulty in differentiating between his reserved and introverted No.2 personality and his conventional No.1 personality.

1070	MC/Plu opposition	=	*Shaping individuality, organization, recuperation, vocation seen as a mission.*
1081	= ⚹ ASC	=	*Recognition, fame, important position personally.*
1077	= □ Sat	=	*Self-sacrifice, toil, object gained through sacrifice.*

Both parents felt overwhelmed by what was expected of them, and Jung resolved the dilemma later by organizing his family structure as a barrier to the outside world. (''It was most essential for me to have a normal life in the real world as a counterpoise to that strange inner world.'' *214)*

0314	MC/Sun trine	=	*Individuality as the goal of life, awareness of one's mission, a positive attitude, individual advancement, the Father's rôle.*
0325	= ⚹ ASC	=	*Personal relations, individual attitude towards others.*
0320	= □ Sat	=	*Reserve, inhibitions, difficult decisions.*
0323	= △ Plu	=	*Leadership by force, extraordinary and unusual plans.*

Jung's Mother displayed a positive exterior even when she was most depressed. This was primarily to protect the insecurity of her husband *(40)*. Her withdrawl seemed to have been conscious, just as Jung's was in his later life. The square to the MC, at 41 years old in 1916, is in the midst of his ''confrontation with the unconscious''.

Mars Sagittarius XIth

22 weeks before Birth (18 weeks after Conception)

Mar Sag XI		=	*Religious desires, strife, need to convince others, reform, disagreements with men, violation.*

Jung's Mother took refuge in a religious attitude as she began being overwhelmed by the pressures of her pregnancy.

0698	Mar/Sat sextile	=	*Harmful or destructive energy, destroyed vitality, resistance, the more energy available, the more difficulties.*
0703	= ⚹ Jup	=	*Complete concentration upon a particular objective, improvement during an illness, easy death.*
0686	Mar/Jup sextile	=	*Successful creative activity, joy and activity, occupational success.*
0691	= ⚹ Sat	=	*Difficulty with decisions, terminated relationship.*

As Mars rules the blood, she may possibly have had internal complications during pregnancy. The trine to this time, at 21° Leo in 1913, produced a series of dreams where entire populations of people were deluged by "rivers of blood" *(199)*. This was followed by a dream *(200)* where frightful cold descended upon mankind leaving only a leaf-bearing tree without fruit. The leaves were transformed by the frost into sweet grapes full of healing juices. Jung believed that this tree represented his "tree of life", and it seems to imply that he almost did not survive pregnancy due to the complications.

ASC Aquarius — Birth (1875)

| ASC Aquarius | | = | *Reformed environment, adaptable, dominant soul life, irregular heart.* |

Jung's Mother's attitudes were improved at the time of the birth, but she was further alienated by her husband's attitudes towards the newborn Carl.

1106r	ASC/MC sextile	=	*Individual synthesis, Ego-directed persona, relationship between Higher and Lower Self.*
1107	= ☍ Sun	=	*Difficulties with the male principle, opposition to the Father.*
1115	= □ Nep	=	*Ill at ease in the family, feigning, experiencing disappointments, drugged birth.*

Father's initial opinion was that the child was weak and small. This lack of approval by the masculine principle plagued Jung for the rest of his life. The baby Carl had to compensate through exerting fascination upon his parents. The Neptune contact implies that his Mother was anaesthetized during the birth, and Carl possibly received medication as well.

1022	ASC/Nep square	=	*Impressionable personality, mediumship, sensitive, peculiar contacts with others in the environment, eczema.*
1033	= ⚹ MC	=	*Lacks resistance, influenced by others.*
1023	= ☍ Sun	=	*Physical weakness, physical harm, humiliation from Father.*

This produced an isolation from the surrounding world. As this contact also indicates skin problems (eczema), this principle becomes a physical reality as well as a psychological one. His contact with his Mother was highly sensitized and operated upon a psychic level, while with his Father the relationship centred upon physical strength.

1058	ASC/Plu trine	=	*Fascinating persona, strong will, ambition, utilizing magical and psychic powers, continual readjustment to the environment.*
1069	= ⚹ MC	=	*Attainment of power and authority, success through the personality.*
1067	= □ Nep	=	*Deceit in the environment, awkward situations.*
1059	= ☍ Sun	=	*Ruthless conduct by the Father, esteem through strength.*

The newborn Carl's ability to accept the censure of his Father and the distance from his Mother led to the detached viewpoint associated with Aquarius ascending. The psychic involvement with his parents, in spite of the more problematic overt relationship with them, formed a pattern which his later approach to psychoanalysis bears out. He felt that the doctor must attempt to communicate with his patient within a common reality, rather than imposing upon him any rigid doctrine. He developed and implemented this concept at the opposite time to the Ascendant, 23 years old.

0302	ASC/Sun opposition	=	*Personal attitude towards others, disharmony due to the Father, over-accentuated self-confidence.*
0313	= ⚹ MC	=	*Desire for soul-unions, attainment of esteem, seeks mental and intellectual contact with men.*
0310	= □ Nep	=	*Hyper-sensitive to others, anger, degradation from others.*
0311	= △ Plu	=	*Fighting for independence.*

Since Jung's health at birth was poor, he was forced to struggle to maintain his position in the world. This is echoed in his life-long quest to prove the validity of his ideas.

Saturn Aquarius Ist — 6 months old (1876)

| Saturn Aquarius I | | = | *Self restraint, elders protect, serious people, eczema, social aspirations, older people.* |

Jung's family moved to the vicarage of Laufen above the Falls of the Rhine. Jung was cared for by an elderly aunt and a maid *(22)*.

0926r	Sat/MC square	=	*Slow development, feeling sick.*
0931	= ⚹ Mars	=	*Docility, defenselessness, suffering oppression, accepting one's destiny, enforced separation.*
0935r	= □ Plu	=	*Destined fateful struggle.*
0932	= △ Jup	=	*Plainness, simplicity, changed residence.*

The eczema, which was undoubtedly latent from his birth, began to become more problemmatic, cutting him off from most contact with others. Jung remembered an incident of this time, when he was not permitted to go with school children to a picnic in the Alps because he was "too small, and nothing could be done about it" *(22)*.

0698	Sat/Mars sextile	=	*Inhibited vitality, resistance.*
0709	= □ MC	=	*Suffering with dignity, difficulties.*
0706	= □ Plu	=	*A death, injury, accidents, affecting the masses.*
0703r	= △ Jup	=	*Concentration upon particular objectives, dissolution of the body.*

Another incident he mentions is that local fishermen found a corpse near the Falls — apparently a frequent phenomenon. Jung was "extraordinarily interested" in all of these things. This closeness to death is related to many incidents.

| 0890 | Sat/Plu square | = | *Cruelty, magicians and adepts, martyrdom, eczema, deeply searching scientists, silent activity.* |
| 0901 | = □ MC | = | *Self sacrifice, ascetic habits, the magician, flight, suicidal tendencies.* |

He talks about having an "unconscious suicidal urge or a fatal resistance to life" related to his later (within the next two years) near-fall off of the bridge over the Falls. He also was obsessed with water: ". . . without water, I thought, nobody

0895	= *Mars	=	Brutality, violence, maltreatment, suicide.
0896	= △Jup	=	Difficult illness, religious fanaticism.

could live at all." (22). He lived an isolated life here: "The muted roar of the Rhine Falls was always audible, and all around lay a danger zone."

0782	Sat/Jup trine	=	Patience, chronic skin ailments, seclusion, a happy separation.
0793	= □MC	=	Desire for solitude, the philosopher.
0787	= *Mars	=	Separation, lack of endurance, discontent.
0790	= □Plu	=	Violence.

Jung had no playmates, and observed his Father burying and praying for many people who had perished in the Falls. This coupled with his "vague fears at night" and the things he saw walking the halls of the gloomy vicarage led for the first time to fantasies and superstitions about religion and death.

Dragon's Head Aries IInd 2 years 3 months old (1877)

Dragon's Head Aries II		=	One sided associations, facing danger, self expression in associations, permanent unions.

Jung's parents were having much trouble with each other, and Jung associates this with his eczema (Also Sat/Jup). His mother went away to the hospital for several months, and Jung was tended by an elderly aunt.

0542	DH/Mer square	=	Exchanged ideas, unsociable, disturbances.
0549	= △Ura	=	Stimulated by others, quick exchanges of ideas.
0545	= □Ven	=	Associations with others of similar ideas or artistic taste.
0650	DH/Ven square	=	Little interest in obliging others, artistic interests.
0653	= □Mer	=	Difficulties in contact with others, but desire to make the contacts.
0657	= △Ura	=	Unease in making contacts, short relationships.

This troubled him, but simultaneously created the nucleus of his attitude towards men and women. "From then on, I always felt mistrustful when the word 'love' was spoken. The feeling I associated with 'woman' was for a long time that of innate unreliability. 'Father', on the other hand, meant reliability and powerlessness. That is the handicap I started off with" (23).

0962	DH/Ura trine	=	Shared experiences, variety, disturbing dreams, inner vision, dominant dreamlife.
0965	= □Mer	=	Quick comprehension, sudden understanding.
0966	= □Ven	=	Intensified feelings with others, sudden attachments, experiences in artistic comprehension.

Jung experienced a sudden contact with a young woman who came to care for him. She was dark and strange, and he associated her with extreme mystery. "The feeling of strangeness which she conveyed, and yet of having known her always, was a characteristic of that figure which later came to symbolize for me the whole essence of womanhood" (23). She foreshadowed his concept of the anima.

Neptune Taurus IIIrd 4 years old (1879)

Neptune Taurus III		=	Hallucinations, hospital, mediumship, fantasies, moody, mystic sensitivity, faculty to understand others.
1022r	Nep/ASC square	=	Mediumship, sensitivity, sensitive persona, eczema, impressionable, peculiar contact with others.
1023r	= □Sun	=	Humiliation by the Father.
0266	Nep/Sun square	=	Sensitive, weakness, illness, susceptibility, drugs, mediumship, being exploited.
0276	= □ASC	=	Negative environment, hospital, sick people.

Jung went into hospital for his eczema, and probably received drug treatment, producing peculiar feelings and heightening his already delicate sensibilities. He also had a dream which affected his psyche for the rest of his life (27). He dreamed that he entered an underground arched chamber, and followed a red carpet to an enthroned phallus-like object made of flesh. The top of the phallus had one upward-pointing eye, and Jung was paralyzed with fear, although the phallus had a halo of light. His Mother called out, "Yes, just look at him. That is the man-eater!" As this is opposite his conception moment, it was a dream of *his own conception*. He also associated this with his fears of religion.

Moon Taurus IIIrd 5 years old (1880)

Moon Taurus III		=	Clinging to Mother, reserved women, stubbornness, manifold emotional expressions, moody, short journeys with women, changes in emotional life.
0326	Moon/Mer sextile	=	Thinking influenced by feelings, protection from a woman (Mother), stimulation by women.
0328	= *Ven	=	Love, beauty and art, young women.
0332	= □Ura	=	Sudden thoughts, independent thinking, a young woman.
0338	Moon/Ven sextile	=	Love and devotion, art talent, grace, happy family life.
0340	= *Mer	=	Longing for love, artists, problems.
0344	= □Ura	=	Acting by feelings, emotional fits, epilepsy.

Jung was surrounded by women and influenced by them during his childhood, as shown by the following memory image: "A young, very pretty and charming girl with blue eyes and fair hair is leading me, on a blue autumn day, under golden maple and chestnut trees along the Rhine. The sun is shining through the foliage, and yellow leaves lie on the ground" (23). This woman later became his mother-in-law. His earliest memories of art date to this time. "Often I would steal into the dark, sequestered room and sit for hours in front of the pictures, gazing at all this beauty. It was the only beautiful thing I knew" (31).

0386	Moon/Ura square	=	Emotional tension, sudden unions manifest, self will, overstrained emotions, clairvoyance, craving independence, inherited schizophrenia, anxiety, female reformers.
0388	= *Mer	=	Intuition, suggestion, sudden cognition and perceptions.
0389	= *Ven	=	Artistic ambitions, self-willed love.

Jung felt his mother's tension. He saw her as having two sides. During the day she was warm and loving, but at night she became "a priestess in a bear's cave" (68). Jung inherited his dual personalities from his Mother, and this led to his interest in dementia praecox (schizophrenia).

Pluto Taurus IIIrd — 6 years old (1881)

Pluto Taurus III		=	*Gaining possessions, assertion of individuality, adventurous behaviour, a transformation.*
1070r	Plu/MC opposition	=	*Shaped individuality, vocation, expertise, daring, resistance, antisocial, a destined change.*
1081r	= △ ASC	=	*Fame.*
1077r	= □ Sat	=	*Self sacrifice, toilsome existence.*
1058r	Plu/ASC trine	=	*Fascinating persona, magical-psychic powers, a physical transformation, unusual contacts.*
1069r	= ♂ MC	=	*Fascinating personality, sense of authority.*
1065r	= □ Sat	=	*Forced suppression, coercion, emotional suffering.*
0890r	Plu/Sat square	=	*Cruelty, toughness, violence, martyrdom, self-destructive energy.*
0901r	= ♂ MC	=	*Onesidedness, severity, flight.*
0900r	= △ ASC	=	*Separation, a difficult situation.*

Jung became interested in antiquities when his aunt took him to a museum, and he became totally engrossed in the medieval sculptures *(31)*.

His reactions to other children were often crude and violent. He proudly beat up a 'high-class' child, and was admonished by his Mother: "Now look at these nice children, so well brought up and polite, but you behave like a little lout" *(66)*. He also fell upon the altar in church, gashed his head, and was taken to hospital with fits and rages. He played alone and his sensitivity was channeled into imaginary battles and sieges *(33)*. At this time his Father began tutoring him in Latin. He was also fascinated by a book on exotic eastern religions. He considered his Mother's attitude to the 'heathens' as faulty. He felt an affinity with them, which he protected as an "original revelation" and kept secret from her. He began school which further accentuated the split from his Mother *(32-33)*.

VIth house cusp in Gemini = 11, Jung went to the Basel Gymnasium school.

Mercury Cancer VIth — 17 years old (1892)

Mercury Cancer VI		=	*Gaining perceptions, interrelating thinking and feeling, memory, immersion in thought, thirst for knowledge, special skills, critical and criticised.*
0458	Mer/Ven conjunction	=	*Love and beauty, grace, light-hearted, artistic ability.*
0467	= □ DH	=	*Unsociable, unstimulated by others.*
0460	= ✳ Moon	=	*Shaping plane surfaces, susceptible to beauty.*
0542	Mer/DH square	=	*Common plans are difficult, unsociable, disliked by others.*
0545	= ♂ Ven	=	*Urge to separate oneself from others, lonely art.*
0544	= ✳ Moon	=	*Secretive nature (troubles), emotions withheld, exchanges with women.*
0326r	Mer/Moon sextile	=	*Thinking governed by feeling, women stimulate, external horizons attract.*
0328r	= ♂ Ven	=	*Art and beauty.*
0335	= □ DH	=	*No exchanges with others, few contacts (especially with women).*

"Between my sixteenth and nineteenth years the fog of my dilemma slowly lifted, and my depressive states of mind improved. No.1 personality emerged more and more distinctly. I began systematically pursuing questions I had consciously framed. I read a brief introduction to the history of philosophy and in this way gained a bird's-eye view of everything that had been thought in this field" *(87)*.

"I had some facility in drawing, although I did not realise that it depended upon the way I was feeling. I could draw only what stirred my imagination" *(45)*.

Jung's two personalities constantly warred with each other, and the boredom of school *(43)* combined with that to make him shy and introverted. His inner dialogue was very important to him and was source of security.

"Naturally, I could not talk with anyone about these things. I knew of no one to whom I might have communicated them except, possibly, my mother." *(65)* She thought along the same lines as Jung, but it was an impossible contact, so he kept the ideas to himself. As a symbol of this want, he began to desire to go to the mountains. His Father took him, but due to lack of money, *only Jung could ascend.* His Father said: "You can ride up to the peak alone. I'll stay here, it's too expensive for the two of us. Be careful not to fall down anywhere." *(96)* He went ahead alone!

Venus Cancer VIth — 18 years old (1893)

Venus Cancer VI		=	*Deep emotions, artistic nature, moral sense is puritanical, heart suppressed by practicalities.*
0458r	Ven/Mer conjunct	=	
0467r	= □ DH	=	*Same as above for Mer/Ven conjunction.*
0460r	= ✳ Moon	=	
0650r	Ven/DH square	=	*Lack adaptability, little interest in being obliging.*
0653r	= ♂ Mer	=	*No desire for contact with others.*
0652	= ✳ Moon	=	*No understanding of others.*
0338r	Ven/Moon sextile	=	*Love and devotion to women, artistic talent, Mother-love.*

"I regretted Faust's behaviour, for to my mind he should not have been so one-sided and so easily tricked. He should have been clever and also more moral" *(78)*.

He visited his Father near the hermitage of the saint Brother Klaus, and was surprised to learn that his Father was communicating with a Catholic priest.

In the process, he walked into the mountains and met a peasant girl. He felt embarrassed and realized that she did not

| 0340r | | = ♂ Mer | = | *Longing for Mother, artistic talent.* |
| 0347 | | = □ DH | = | *Longing for tenderness, association with the Mother.* |

know what he knew about philosophy. "She still dwells in the distant land of innocence, but I have plunged into reality, into the splendour and cruelty of creation" *(99)*. This related to his Mother: "As Goethe says of the Mothers, 'Even to speak of them dismays the bold.'" *(101)* But also: "My mother was a very good mother to me." *(65)*

Sun Leo VIIth   25 years old (1900)

Sun Leo VII		=	*Confidence, formative energy, creativity, assurance, personal rise, harmony, public spirit, mannered, strong desire for importance, vanity.*

In 1900 Jung began as a privat-docent (doctor) at Burghölzli Mental Hospital in Zurich. "Life took on an undivided reality — all intention, consciousness, duty and responsibility." *(133)*

0314r	Sun/MC trine	=	*Many goals, individuality, devotion to personality, self knowledge, attained position, strong constitution, professional advancement, successes.*
0325r	= ♂ ASC	=	*Personal relations with others, associations important.*
0322	= □ Nep	=	*Lack of clarity, experiencing disappointments.*

He realized that insane ideas and hallucinations contained a germ of meaning, and tried to understand his patients. This created a stir in his colleagues. He also found that this had implications about himself as well. "At bottom we discover nothing new and unknown in the mentally ill; rather, we encounter the substratum of our our natures." *(149)*

0302r	Sun/ASC opposition	=	*Accentuated self-confidence, men in the environment, difficult relationships, separations.*
0313r	= △ MC	=	*Seeking mental-intellectual contacts, esteem, respect, an individual attitude towards others.*
0310r	= □ Nep	=	*Hypersensitive, easily upset, degradation, illnesses.*

And, as he had already known: "Delusions have human meaning." *(131)* His Basle friends did not understand why he left them, and his colleagues avoided discussion with him. They all diagnosed patients according to rigid doctrines, and were unable to accept the patients as individuals.

0290	Sun/DH loose trine	=	*Intellectual associations with men, public affairs, colleagues, shared experiences with others.*
0301	= △ MC	=	*Fighting others, battles, emotional relationships.*
0300	= ♂ ASC	=	*Seeking contact with others.*
0298	= □ Nep	=	*Easily annoyed by others, quickly disappointed.*

Jung believed that the cure should grow naturally out of the patient. *(see the Tree dream in Mars)* "I treat every patient as individually as possible, because the solution of the problem is always an individual one." *(152)* "The crucial point is that I confront the patient as one human being to another. Analysis is a dialogue demanding two partners." *(153)*

0266r	Sun/Nep square	=	*Rejection of drug therapy, peculiar ideas, mediumship, contact with sick, mystic experiences, scandals.*
0277	= △ MC	=	*Sensitive, periodic depression, mental stress.*
0276r	= ♂ ASC	=	*Difficult advancement, hospital, sick persons.*
0275	= △ DH	=	*Association with sick persons.*

At this point, Jung began to understand duality, because it existed within him. He had patients who had been routinely drugged for lack of any other solution to their problems, and he felt that this degraded them. His attitudes were highly original, and they threatened the other doctors. "Clinical diagnoses are important since they give the doctor a certain orientation; but they do not help the patient!" *(145)*

Uranus Leo VII   31 years old (1906-7)

Uranus Leo VII		=	*Enterprising, boldness, determined freedom, a difficult gamble, inspiration, empathy, public reforms, irregular attitudes, peculiar partnerships of short duration.*

In 1907, Jung met Freud in Vienna, but he had been familiar with Freud's technique since 1900. Although Jung realized that Freud had shortcomings, he saw in Freud an ally and a cause.

| 0962r | Ura/DH trine | = | *Shared experiences, lively and active associations, new experiences with others, searching for new approaches, inner vision and memory, the dreamlife, political reforms, commencement of an association.* |
| 0964 | = □ Moon | = | *Excitable with others, quick enthusiasm for others.* |

". . . the discovery that my association experiments were in agreement with Freud's theories was far from pleasant to me." *(170-171)* Their common ground was the importance of the dream. But: "I was never able to agree with Freud that the dream is a 'façade' behind which its meaning lies hidden." *(185)* "To me dreams are a part of nature, which harbours no intention to deceive, but expresses something as best it can." *(185)*

| 0386r | Ura/Moon square | = | *Emotional tension, unconditional pursuit of convictions, striving for a goal, striving for absolute independence, schizophrenia, sacrifice for special aims, sudden successes, help from friends, overstrain.* |
| 0395 | = △ DH | = | *Excitable contact with others, association with ambitious women.* |

Freud styled Jung as his heir apparent and acted paternally toward him. He also tried to get Jung to promise never to abandon the sexual theory of psychology, which Jung was unable to accept in the first place. The paper Jung wrote at this time which ended their association was *"The Psychology of Dementia Praecox"* — an analysis of a woman schizophrenic. He also sought the empathy of his wife in preference to Freud's paternalism.

Jupiter Libra VIIIth   after the end of life

Jupiter Libra VIII		=	*Philosophical interests, metaphysical, just, striving for public recognition, social contacts, popularity, dependence upon others, expansion in death (peaceful), heart trouble.*

For the remainder of Jung's life after 1907, his quest became more and more internalized — although he always wished to be publicly recognized. The C.G. Jung Institute was formed by his pupils and patients, and spread his ideas over most of

0686r	Jup/Mars sextile	=	*Fortunate decision, success in creative activity, will power directed towards goals, harmonious life, joy of life, urge to activity, honour, creative power, propaganda, results in professional activity, (the completed birth!).*
0691r	= △ Sat	=	*Difficulties in religious matters, tending to let opportunities slip.*
0782r	Jup/Sat trine	=	*Success through perseverance, patience, industry philosophical thinking, tenacious, pursuit of plans, professors and teachers, realizations in seclusion, further development in isolation.*
0787r	= ✳ Mars	=	*Endurance and tenacity, the act of separation.*

Europe and America, but he never received recognition comparable to Freud's. After 1912, when he split with Freud, he also vacated his Presidency of the International Psychological Association to carry on his work alone. Instead of being collectivized, Jung preferred to become a self-reliant, whole individual, enriching the world through this very independence. He gradually became involved in alchemy — the conjunction of opposites — and this led to the idea of the *"individuation process"* which is a rebirth of the psyche. Due to many Christian influences in alchemy, he also had extensive dialogues with theologians. (see particularly Father Victor White in Letters II.) "As a child I felt myself to be alone, and I am still, because I know things and must hint at things which others apparently know nothing of, and for the most part do not want to know." *(388)* The man of superior insight "has seen and experienced worth and worthlessness, and at the end of his life desires to return into his own being, into the eternal unknowable meaning. The archetype of the old man who has seen enough is eternally true." *(392,* written at the age of 84 years old.) His death was peaceful.

CONIVNCTIO SIVE

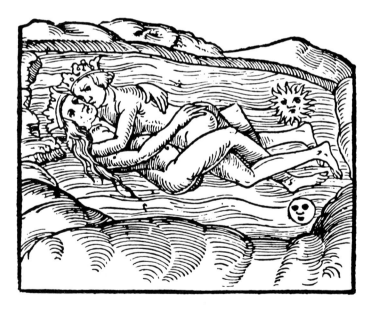

O Luna durch meyn vmbgeben/vnd suffe mynne/
Wirstu schön/starck/vnd gewaltig als ich byn.

O Sol/du bist vber alle liecht zu erkennen/
So bedarffstu doch mein als der han der hennen.

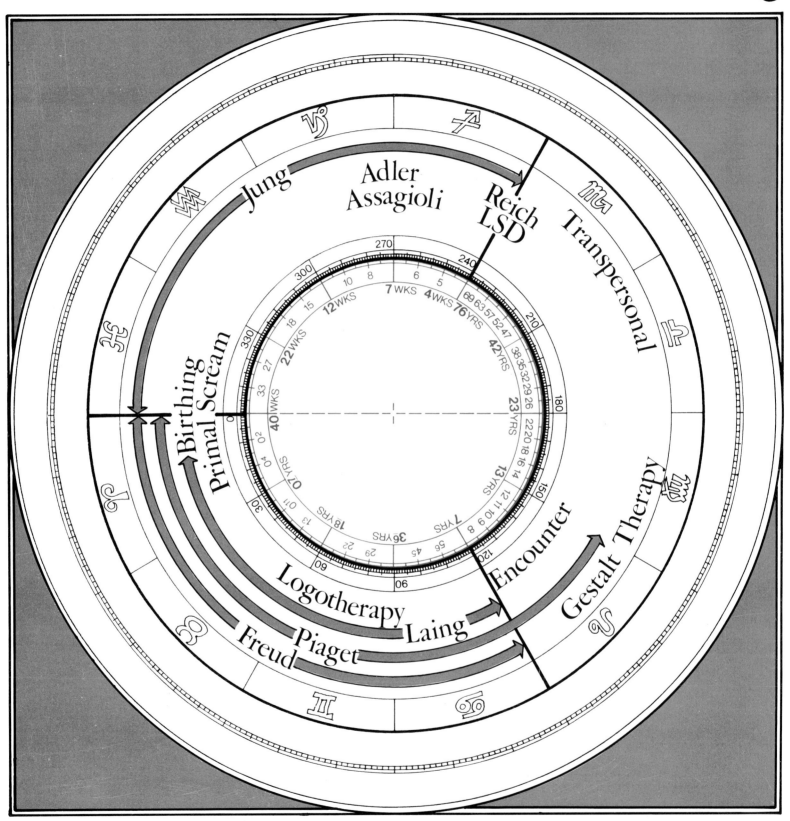

Figure IX.1 The Wheel of Psychology.

The Astrological Reading

Although everyone interested in Astrology does not necessarily want to practice the art, understanding the mechanism involved has always been shrouded in mystery, partially because astrologers have not understood it clearly themselves. With the development and acceptance of psychology in this century, it has become possible to clarify the process of the reading. The psyche is mysterious and often ambiguous, and techniques which attempt to describe it must respect this fact.

Astrology is frequently represented as metaphysical doctrine requiring belief, but in reality it is as 'logical' as psychology or medicine. It is an active, dynamic and perpetually evolving natural science and art for every successive generation that utilizes its mechanism. The structure is consistent, but its mode of communication and the problems to which it addresses itself must be qualified by the language and psychological reality of the times. The pronouncements of Ptolemy in the Second Century A.D. are not relevant to us now, but considering the level of understanding in his time, his appoach *was* valid. People wanted to know whether they would be victorious in battle or how many of their children would survive, rather than the nature of their psychological structure. His interpretations were perfectly adequate for prognostication; and, though they would not do for Twentieth-Century Man, they are not necessarily invalidated. Cultures, civilizations, languages and religions all continually change, yet remain major forces throughout history. Astrology changes in the same way.

The practice of Astrology is in low repute in this century mainly because of its practitioners' misconceptions. Aleister Crowley made this situation painfully clear in *"The Complete Astrological Writings"* in 1917 by describing his contact with "the most famous astrologer in the United States" at the time, Evangeline Evans. She made from astrology:

> ". . . fifty thousand dollars a year (but) did not know that the solar system was essentially a disk. In thirty years of daily use of the ephemeris, she had never observed that Neptune takes fifteen years or so to pass through a sign of the Zodiac, and told her clients that Neptune being in such and such a sign at their birth, they must possess various curious powers. When I pointed out that this applied to everyone born in three lustres (one lustre equals five years), she was at first bewildered, then incredulous; and, proof being produced, angry and insulting." [1]

[1] Crowley, *The Complete Astrological Writings*, p. 8.

This scathing observation is unfortunately all too true, but the problem should be remedied. Crowley's *Preface* to the book is extremely ironic. He observes:

> "Astrologers sometimes make mistakes. From this fact, which even they are scarcely sufficiently brazen to dispute, it follows with mathematical certainty that astrology is not a science but a sham, a quackery and a fraud. Contrast its shameful uncertainty with medicine, where no doctor ever lost a patient; with law where no lawyer ever lost a case; or even with arms, where no soldier ever lost a battle!" [2]

[2] Crowley, *The Complete Astrological Writings*, p. 13.

Astrology requires its practitioners to be aware, intelligent, sensitive, rational and honest. If the qualities of the astrologer are deficient, his readings reflect this and he gives his clients an incorrect picture of astrology itself. This is true of all individuals who provide personal services to others, but the importance of the astrologer's understanding is magnified because he deals with *the being of another individual* — the supreme responsibility. He is subject to the same rules and restrictions as the psychologist, psychiatrist, priest or doctor. Astrology is not a game of chance or a parlour amusement, but a serious pursuit of the intelligent.

The astrological reading is a two-way process which involves the understanding of both the astrologer and his client. The contact can potentially alter the level of awareness of the client and has an equal effect upon the astrologer. Every individual expands his reality when he tries to comprehend another point of view. Everyone sees the universe from a different vantage point, and the more viewpoints one can assimilate, the more complete one is. Every event, every person and every reality is a component of the whole. To achieve wholeness it is essential to bring to consciousness as many contradictory fragments as possible.

Many believe that the sole purpose of astrology is predicting the future. While this is an integral part of the process, it is not its only object. The reading presents events, connections between events, states of mind and other components of the psyche as integral facets of a

whole. It evaluates existing and future information and orders it according to its relationship to the present. Most individuals do not remember accurately anything before the age of seven, although the most critical influences are often registered before this time. A description of the first two octaves — from conception until seven — is similar to the process of analysis in psychology.

Psychoanalysis and the Reading

Striking parallels exist between psychoanalysis and the astrological reading. Both analyze the structure and dynamics of the psyche, and the relationship between the analyst and analysand in psychoanalysis is distinctly similar to that between the astrologer and his client. In both methods there is a confrontation between an individual's subjective attitudes and those of an objective observer. The analyst and the astrologer expose not only personal traits but the impersonal and objective facts which produce them.

While the psychic content is the same in both processes, the *context* within which it is discovered is different. Astrology derives all information from the horoscope and this is disseminated by the astrologer in one session. In psychology, on the other hand, the relevant information is drawn from the patient by association, hypnosis, dreams or memories, and the entire analysis often takes years to complete. Astrology is a highly compacted form of reverse psychoanalysis.

In psychoanalysis, associations, dreams, fantasies and memories are subjected to careful scrutiny by the analyst, and then transferred into symbolic form in the Jungian method or reduced to psychological and physiological processes in that of Freud. In both cases the analyst must allow for the possibility of faulty memory or overt lies. Most traumatic events are initially hidden — consciously or unconsciously — and this constitutes a major problem to psychology. In the astrological reading the process *begins with symbols and proceeds to associations*. This is advantageous because the individual has no opportunity to mislead the astrologer.

Astrology is unique in simultaneously combining a causal, linear sequence and an acausal, synchronistic structure. In psychoanalysis associations rarely follow any logical order, and often it is impossible to reconstruct the actual temporal positions of critical complexes. Analysis works from the present moment backwards in time, while the astrological reading starts at conception and works towards the present. Complexes are seen in context, and this reliving of events is a beneficial curative operation.

The factor of time is also an advantage in astrology. Psychoanalysis takes years of twice- or thrice-weekly sessions as well as being very laborious and expensive, and even then rarely shows therapeutic results. Astrology introduces the individual to the ideas and methodology of self-analysis, which can be ultimately more beneficial. The usual length of a complete horoscope reading is three to four hours, during which time it is possible to identify all major events and complexes of a lifetime. A correct reading uncovers the same complexes which will occupy an analyst for years. Through the aspect-patterns, complexes which originated in early life are not only identified by their quality and age, but also by the times of their reccurence.

In the astrological reading, the initial reference point is a time before conception. The individual must momentarily try to erase his existence from his mind and try to place himself outside his lifetime. This process is identical to religious-meditative procedures and oracular techniques; it is not far removed from the deep breath taken by the athlete before acting under stress, or from the expectancy of the movie-goer just before the magic screen lights up the darkened theatre. Once this state is achieved, the reading proceeds through life from conception in the same sequence in which it was lived. When archetypal motifs come into play they are relived and confronted.

The astrologer presents a range of metaphors which has a two-fold purpose — to describe the initial event, and to determine its implications when it is keyed off at a later time. Many psychological complexes remain unresolved, and any form of analysis must respect this fact. Complexes are all alive, not static, and *this is the way they should be*. They are activated each day by the movement of the Ascendant, each month by the Moon, each year by the Sun, and at longer intervals by the other planets, and it is unrealistic to believe that they will ever disappear. In the astrological view, complexes are always there waiting to be reactivated.

Techniques of Psychotherapy and the Time Scale

"Every psychotherapist not only has his own method — he himself is that method." [3]

[3] Jung, *The Practice of Psychotherapy, CW 16*, p. 88.

Various psychotherapies in use today relate to archetypal ages in the Time Scale. The orientation of a therapy is determined by the stage of life to which it corresponds, and often parallels a need felt by its originator. Freud was notoriously neurotic and sexually inhibited; Adler spent his life trying to resolve his own will to power; Jung spent the nine years from 1911 until 1920 totally possessed by the unconscious: *their therapies are symbolic of their own psychological dilemmas*. The relationship of modern therapies to each other and to astrology is shown in the accompanying Circular Diagram of the Therapies and Therapists (Figure IX.1).

Psychologists with more universal scope occupy greater range around the circle, and compensatory therapies occupy opposite positions across the circle. Overlaps indicate common ground, and the areas which aspect each other indicate therapies which either harmonize or tension each other.

The therapy of **Wilhelm Reich** (1897-1957), an early student of Freud, was based upon the *"Function of the Orgasm"*. His therapy corresponds to conception moment (the cusp of the IXth house) as well as to the death moment. That conception *is* the orgasm formed the basis of Reich's ideas:

"Orgastic longing, which plays such a gigantic rôle in the life of animals, appears now as an expression of this 'striving beyond oneself' as 'longing' to reach *beyond* the narrow sack of one's own organism. 'We wonder' — to use an apt phrase — for the beyond of ourselves. Perhaps here lies the solution of the riddle why the idea of death so often represents the orgasm. In dying, too, the biological energy reaches beyond the boundaries of the material sack which holds it prisoner." [4]

[4] Wilhelm Reich, *Selected Writings*, p. 217.

At the MC (the cusp of the Xth house), the registration of the Ego and seat of the Will, are the power-oriented therapies of **Alfred Adler** (1870-1937) and **Roberto Assagioli** (1888-). Adler's method encourages the application of individual power — through proper conditioning — towards normalization and social adaptation. The MC as the 'centre of the field of consciousness' explains Adler's undervaluation of the unconscious. Roberto Assagioli is associated with both Freud and Jung and attempts to create an individual *"psychosynthesis"* of love and will, as expressed in his book *"The Act of Will"*. The diagram on page 14 of his book shows his positioning of the 'transpersonal self' in the place of the MC (Figure IX.2).

The province of **Carl Jung** is the broadest of all modern therapies, including simultaneously the first octave of Gestation and the fourth octave of Transcendence — the realm of the Collective Unconscious. His interest in "sychronicity" is indicative of an attempt to co-ordinate these two levels of the psyche. In astrological interpretation the fourth octave is totally symbolic and this would explain Jung's symbolic approach to psychology.

The Ascendant is concerned with Personality and Birth therapies. Prime examples are the *"Birthing"* process of **Elizabeth Fehr** (1920-1974), which is a re-enactment of the pressure upon the crown of the head during the compression of birth; and the *"Primal Scream Therapy"* of **Arthur Janov**, which is based upon a repetition of the original scream of release after birth. Also relevant is the therapy of **Abraham Maslow** as defined in his "Motivation and Personality".

The area devoted to **Sigmund Freud** is the Octave of Childhood from the Ascendant birth moment until 7 years old. Freud reduced the life of the psyche to social and biological factors affecting infantile sexuality and the child-parent relationship. All psychic disturbances, according to Freud, originate with the sexual disturbances of childhood. Freud prized consciousness — a compensation for the unconsciousness of his own psychic reality. His reductive analysis and the projected "Father-image" he evoked in his patients verify this correlation of childhood with his psychoanalysis. He adjoins Jung at the birth moment, implying that their contact was persona-oriented.

Piaget (1896-) covers the time from birth until the end of Leo at 15, and his grading of childhood developmental periods coincides with the Time Scale houses as we have seen.

There are other more specific therapies within the Octave of Childhood. The

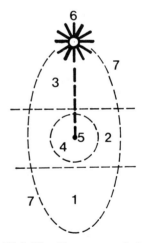

Figure IX.2 The Transpersonal Self. (After Assagioli, *The Act of Will,* p. 14.)
1. The Lower Unconscious
2. The Middle Unconscious
3. The Higher Unconscious, or Superconscious
4. The Field of Consciousness
5. The Conscious Self, or "I"
6. The Transpersonal Self
7. The Collective Unconscious

"logotherapy" of **Frankl** is related to the Gemini time of communication, as is the concept of *"general semantics"*.

The early work of **R. D. Laing** concentrated upon the Cancer, IVth house time. In *"Sanity, Madness and the Family"* and *"The Politics of the Family"* he postulated the idea that in cases of "madness" the family and its values were often at fault rather than the individual. Laing organized "Philadelphia Houses" where he and his patients could retreat into the world of childhood which spawned their dilemmas, but out of range of parental figures. He has recently become concerned with the process of birth and its implications. *"The Facts of Life"* (1976) explores the insensitivity of doctors during birth, and the ensuing psychological difficulties caused by this treatment. He also had contact with Elizabeth Fehr's "Birthing".[5] For a more complete analysis of Laing's connection to the birth moment, see the analysis of his Ascendant in Part VIII.

Gestalt therapies occupy the time from 7 until 23 years old (Vth house Leo and VIth house Virgo) and are involved with the relationship between the Self and others during puberty. As this area of the horoscope is opposite the province of Jung, Gestalt therapy is non-symbolic. These therapies are physically active and anti-intellectual, being more "good old common sense" and hard work than true psychoanalysis. They are equivalent to a transference of the game-playing outpouring of Self during the Leo time to adults who never were able to progress beyond that point.

Encounter Groups and **Transpersonal Psychology** relate to the Libra time from 23 years until 43 years old; the VIIth house. These therapies try to compensate for the fact that external relationships are mainly projections and lay prime emphasis upon the group at the expense of the individual. They assume that if a group becomes familiar physically, it will follow that a security will be generated which is beyond the reach of any individual participant. The integral mechanism is the establishment of sensory connections which approximate primitive survival states (for example, hunting, roving, running from or after, the campfire, darkness, etc.). Encounter is the antithesis of Freudian therapy since incestuous tendencies are encouraged instead of blocked.

The last therapy on the scale of the life is **LSD Therapy** used with terminal cancer patients and the elderly anticipating death. This completes the circle and re-iterates the central ideas of Reichian release from "armouring", and lessens the fear of death which characterizes Western Man. LSD therapy allows the individual access to the entire lifespan back to conception. The distortion of time produced by hallucenogenic drugs provides a liberating perspective which allows death to be understood as a totally natural phenomenon. Like initiation, this release from the boundary of the mortal coil is the ultimate therapy.

The Transcendent Octave is the higher level of the Gestation Octave, and therapies which operate there function on both levels. Thus, Reich, Adler, Assagioli and Jung all participate in the highest and lowest levels of the psyche, while Elizabeth Fehr, Janov, Freud and Laing abut them. The diagrams typical of Reich indicate this linkage (Figure IX.3). The diagram of wholeness used by Assagioli is biassed towards the MC part of the oval. Jung's mandalas show balance and equilibration indicative of his interest in the quaternary nature of the psyche.

Each therapy in the diagram serves individuals with problematic planets or constellations grouped in the corresponding area. Splay-shaped horoscopes tend to sample many therapies, while more highly differentiated shapes like the bowl or bundle show extremists advocating the specific therapy with which they converge. The entire spectrum of therapies is necessary to modern man, but the relativity of each must eventually be recognized. Astrology provides just such an overview of them.

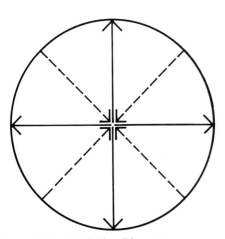

Figure IX.3 A Reichian Diagram.

[5] Laing, *The Facts of Life,* p. 67-69.

"Obviously astrology has much to offer psychology, but what the latter can offer its elder sister is less evident. So far as I can judge, it would seem to me advantageous for astrology to take the existence of psychology into account, above all the psychology of the personality and of the unconscious. I am almost sure that something could be learnt from its symbolic method of interpretation; for that has to do with the interpretation of the archetypes (the gods) and their mutual relations, the common concern of bother arts." [6]

[6] Jung, *Letters II,* May, 1954.

THE ROUND ART

The Importance of the Magic Circle

The structure of astrology is integral to the circle, and the process of the reading uses the circle in a way which could be considered magical. Like the mandala, the circle is a magical reflection of the universe (Figure IX.4). The periphery of the circle represents the time-bound life and the centre is a timeless point — a unity out of which all comes and into which all is poured. The circle is a sacred zone within which there is total balance and harmony. Although external influences may be chaotic, it affords a protected zone where the interchange between the astrologer and the individual takes place. Entrance into the circle begins the reading, the dialectic takes place within it, and the termination of the reading is an exit from the circle. The circle protects the psyches of both participants from outside infiltration and from each other. It encourages pure interchange. The eastern mystic uses his mandala to transform himself into the ideal Atman (Universal Self), and the Christian performs his rituals within the sacred precinct of the Church. (Figure IX.5) The horoscope is a sacred zone within which both participants can channel their experience of consciousness toward unity.

The ritual form of the reading has definite purposes. The astrologer uses the same format for every reading because it focuses his conscious and unconscious being upon a universal process. This gives meaning beyond the purely personal confrontation and unites past and present in an elevated realm. Just as the process of individuation in psychology is a dialectical confrontation of the Ego with the "emptiness" of the centre, so in the reading the individual and the astrologer are confronted with their common centre.

The ritual for entering the circle is an encapsulated version of Parts III, IV, V and VII of this book. The horoscope is presented to the individual by the astrologer and its orientation in space and time is explained. The horizon is shown to be coincident to the Ascendant-Descendant axis of the horoscope at the time and place of the individual's birth. The cardinal points are identified, and the horoscope sheet is tilted from horizontal the equivalent number of degrees to the latitude of the place of birth (Figure IX.6). The tilting approximates the inclination of the plane of the solar system. The MC coincides with the Sun's position at noon and the IC with the midnight position. The locations of the luminaries and planets can then be understood as if the reading were actually occurring at the time and place of the birth. This orients the individual to the physical reality of the horoscope.

The astrologer next describes how the horoscope diagram interfaces with time. Due to the simultaneity of time systems, the horoscope represents a circular matrix for the movements of the planets and for the Logarithmic Time Scale relative to the individual's life. The individual must imagine the planets all revolving around the circle. This temporal viewpoint initiates the individual to the dynamic aspect of the horoscope.

The matrix of logarithmic time is then compared and co-ordinated with the individual's horosocope. The conception point is identified as the cusp of the IXth house, the birth moment as the Ascendant, the end of childhood as the cusp of the Vth house and the death point as the cusp of the IXth house. The dual nature of the Transcendent Octave must be stressed. If the individual's horoscope has planets in this octave, he will be more likely to understand their significance, while if there are no planets there, he may not relate to them at all. Once this complete circuit has been described, *the circle is closed and the astrologer and the individual are within its protected sacred zone until the termination of the reading.* As no specific information is mentioned about the individual, he is forced to try to understand the system from an objective standpoint.

The introduction is like the Preliminary Evocation during a magical ritual, where the environment is purified by recognizing the four cardinal directions. The closure of the circle announces the nature of the Great Work.

The second stage of the reading is a brief capitulation of the twelve archetypal house positions and their qualities. Again, no personal observations are made — the individual must try to understand the *context* of life in its purest sense. Each house is explained with as little embellishment as possible, from conception until the end of the transcendent level, as shown below.

Figure IX.4 The Circle as a Magical Reflection of the Universe.

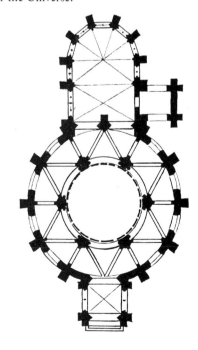

Figure IX.5 The Church as a Mandala.

Figure IX.6 Holding the Horoscope.

House Correspondences

Order	House	Archetypal Sign	Key Words
1.	IXth	Sagittarius	Self-realization of the Mother
2.	Xth	Capricorn	Recognition of the conception
3.	XIth	Aquarius	Planning and idealism of the Mother
4.	XIIth	Pisces	Isolation and self-sacrifice before birth
5.	Ist	Aries	Self-assertion and birth-personality
6.	IInd	Taurus	Undifferentiated matter and the physical world
7.	IIIrd	Gemini	Communication and speech
8.	IVth	Cancer	Emotional reaction to home and family
9.	Vth	Leo	Self exteriorization and gameplaying
10.	VIth	Virgo	Differentiated matter and health
11.	VIIth	Libra	Sublimation and partnership
12.	VIIIth	Scorpio	End of life and metaphysical reality
13.	IXth	Sagittarius	Self-realization
14.	Xth	Capricorn	Willful transcendence
15.	XIth	Aquarius	Humanitarianism
16.	XIIth	Pisces	Self-sacrificial transcendence

This second circumambulation creates within the individual an identification with the entire range of values on the archetypal periphery of the circle — the second stage of the reading is complete. Although no individual has more than ten houses occupied, he unconsciously associates with certain of the archetypal qualities and energies within himself and, without being aware of it, adopts particular attitudes towards the entire circle. Even if he has difficulty comprehending all of the information presented to him — and this is expected — his unconscious mechanism will begin to function.

The signs and houses around the periphery of the circle are analogous to the psychic "whole", and the individual experiences *potential wholeness* as described in the Brhadaranyaka Upanishad:

> "As all the spokes are connected both with the hub and with the rim, so all
> creatures, all Gods, all worlds, all organs are bound together in that soul." [7]

This is the *"mystic lotus"* of the Buddhists, and the second circumambulation is paralleled by a similar process in mandala meditation:

> "The first creation is in space and time, the second starts from this limitation
> but, by transcending the process of becoming, accomplishes (through con-
> templation) that qualitative 'leap' by means of which the spirit of the
> meditator finds itself transported into a different and more exalted sphere." [8]

When two circumambulations are completed, the individual is tuned into the circle as frame of reference, and the astrologer has eliminated from his own mind any external or subjective biases — there exists a parity between them. This is critical because the reading of the horoscope involves an *exchange of rôles*. The astrologer assumes the identity indicated by the horoscope, and the individual becomes an objective observer of his own life. This mechanism is paralleled by the use of the rosary, where circumambulations are accompanied by repetitive prayers (in the east, mantras). Through the circumambulations and the magical nature of the circle both participants are psychically protected from external influences and no energy enters or leaves the circle during the remainder of the reading. A channel of communication to the unconscious is created and the level of response is heightened to the point where the other exchange mechanisms of the reading can begin to function. The interchange during the reading is identical to the psychological 'transference'. This relativity of the astrologer, the individual and circle will be further investigated in the next section.

The third stage of the reading is an introduction to the "cast of characters" — the planetary archetypes (Figure IX.7). The astrologer presents the planets and their many metaphors in their purest form without ascribing any direct personal significance to them.

[7] Tucci, *Theory and Practice of the Mandala*, p. 26.

[8] Tucci, *Theory and Practice of the Mandala*, p. 28.

Again, the individual will relate intimately with some, but not all. The process of the reading is like a highly condensed language course where the alphabet, the vocabulary, the syntax and the proper usage precede actual contact with the language in text or conversation. In describing the planets it is stressed that their function is archetypal, because as symbols they have many layers of meaning. Each planet in turn, starting with the major pair of the Sun and Moon, is identified by its correspondences. The individual unconsciously or consciously compares the archetypes to his personal indentifications.

Figure IX.7 Planetary Archetypes.

Planetary Correspondences

Planet	Gender	Principle	Personifications
Sun	Masculine	Spirit, energy, vitality	Father, men, paternal figures
Moon	Feminine	Soul, feelings, emotion	Mother, women, maternal figures
Mercury	Neutral	Mind, intellect, communication, mediation	Thinkers, mediators, communicative individuals
Venus	Feminine	Harmony, attraction, form	Feminine sexuality, maidens, artists
Mars	Masculine	Desire, conflict, willpower	Masculine sexuality, fighters
Jupiter	Feminine	Expansion, wisdom, generosity	Optimists, altruists, the manic
Saturn	Masculine	Contraction, seriousness	Pessimists, depressives, the serious
Uranus	Neutral	Eccentricity, invention, independence, inspiration	Eccentrics, inventors, the independent
Neptune	Feminine	Psychic reality, fantasy, imagination, mediumship	Psychics, mediums, sensitives, fantasizers, dreamers
Pluto	Masculine	Regeneration, revolution, magical powers	Revolutionaries, transformers
Moon's Node	—	Association, adaptability	Socialities, family, groupies

For the individual with no foreknowledge of astrology and its symbolism, the breadth of imagery and metaphor involved is often overwhelming. This is beneficial, as the virtue of astrology is its capacity to communicate directly to the unconscious. The necessary haze of words is similar to "association tests" in psychology — individual's response to verbal stimuli often betrays his true rather than his conditioned attitudes.[9] The confusion of the conscious mind is counterbalanced by the advantage of eliminating the preconceptions with which most individuals enter an astrological reading. It also helps dissolve psychological "armouring" — the blocking mechanism which preserves the rigidity of character from influences which threaten its stasis. If left to its own devices, the conscious mind tries to depotentiate any material which evokes unconscious responses.

[9] See Jung's *Studies in Word Association, CW 1* (1904).

After describing the planetary metaphors, the aspects are explained. The differentiation in dynamics of trines and sextiles in green, and squares and oppositions in red, is pointed out, as well as the unity of the conjunction. The transmission from age to age is stressed. When the aspects have been covered, the introductory stage of the reading is complete and the individual is prepared for the actual analysis of his horoscope.

The importance of the introduction, which takes half an hour, is inestimable. It constitutes a compacted lesson in the dynamics and mechanisms of astrology, which is usually necessary even if the individual has had some previous knowledge of the subject. After many readings, the introduction eventually becomes a mantra. The principles involved are linked to the conscious and unconscious being of the astrologer, a connection which is essential to the proper practice of the art and science of astrology. As we will see in the section on transference, this has a protective function against the hazard of absorbing extraneous psychic energies.

During the introduction, the psychic reaction of the individual can often be productive of a "realization" by the astrologer which guides him during the reading. As the circumambula-

tions are explained, the astrologer constructs the horoscope in his mind's eye and resolves the basic flow of the life. Preparation for the reading before the individual arrives serves to make the astrologer consciously familiar with the material, while the explanation of the introduction makes him unconsciously familiar.

After the preliminary operations enclose both participants within the circle, the reading proper can begin. The format of the reading follows the sequence and procedure of the complete analysis explained in Part VIII, on pages 188-213. Upon completion of the analysis the third circumambulation is complete, and the ritual terminates. Each of the three stages is successively more complex and personal as the reading ranges from general archetypal images to the specific. This gradual descent from the realm of the archetypes into the "real" world is helpful as it allows each participant to deacclimate from his subjective realities into the unique psychic space within which astrology operates. It also provides an intermediate frame of reference which minimizes personality differences between the astrologer and the individual.

Once the circle has been rent at the end of the reading, there is a rush back to subjectivity, often accompanied by feelings of elation.

The Transference and Energy-Exchange Mechanisms [10]

The *Transference* is the relationship between the analyst and the analysand in psychoanalysis, and the astrological reading produces a similar phenomenon. Transference phenomena denote a turn for the better in some cases, a totally negative response in others and in a few are virtually unimportant.[11] This is also true in astrological readings. As the reading is highly compacted in comparison to psychoanalysis, so the transference phenomena are compressed and exaggerated.

Transference in the reading is based upon many factors, most of which can be determined beforehand by virtue of a preliminary analysis of the horoscope. The first variable is the attitude of the individual towards astrology as he comes to the reading. Types of individuals who come to an astrologer are usually:

1. Individuals who have or profess complete, but purely subjective, belief in astrology and its mechanisms.
2. Individuals who have or profess complete belief in astrology and its mechanisms because it has been previously demonstrated to them or to a close aquaintance. In some cases these people are interested in opinions of different astrologers and, depending upon the previous experiences of such people, it can be easier or more difficult to do the reading.
3. Individuals who are sceptics but feel that astrology is worth giving a try and could potentially be taken seriously.
4. Individuals who are total sceptics or have a 'scientific' orientation and require proof that it works without really expecting or believing that proof.
5. Individuals who have no predetermined opinion either way.
6. Individuals who profess to know astrology, but cannot do it themselves.
7. Individuals who are in the midst of life-crises and will try anything which might give satisfaction or relief.
8. Ego-maniacal individuals who will enter any situation as long as the central topic is themselves.
9. Individuals who are extremely superstitious and will believe anything.
10. Individuals who are solely attracted to the personality of the astrologer.

The type of client qualifies the transference. They are all — even the sceptics — drawn into the contact with some expectation. As a rule, the individual's attitude is initially compensatory. Since his unconscious content is in some way locked up inside and trying to break through to consciousness, it projects itself onto the astrologer. Thus, *the sceptic is actually sceptical of his own unconscious processes*. Negative forms of transference such as dislike, resistance or hate endow astrology and the astrologer with great importance from the beginning. Some individuals try to put every possible obstacle in the way of a positive relationship, thus manifesting their own internal obstacles. But, whether the projections are positive or negative,

[10] Many of the points to be discussed are presented from the psychoanalytic viewpoint as documented in Jung's article, ''The Psychology of the Transference'' in *The Practice of Psychotherapy, CW 16*, p. 164-323.

[11] Jung, *The Practice of Psychotherapy, CW 16*, p. 164.

the unconscious of the individual falls into a relationship anyway. The only approach for the astrologer is not to alter the content of the reading nor to act defensively whatever the initial attitudes of his client. The more sceptical, objective and scientific the individual appears, the greater the chance that his unconscious is raging behind the surface of his personality and crying to get out. The information in the horoscope will not lie, but the individual often will. The sooner this is realized, the better.

Many individuals have qualified their own pasts to such an extent that the "real" events are totally obscured. The individual's opinion of his past becomes slightly altered for the sake of a "better story", but many individuals begin to believe their fabrications and then to elaborate upon them. The true function of the astrologer is to provide a view of the individual which is untainted by the subjective need to tell a good story. Paradoxically, the real circumstances of most people are infinitely more interesting than fictions. They seem to be the only ones who cannot see this. Another paradox is that most individuals are horrified at being exposed, but come to an astrologer seeking precisely that. Often the most extreme reactions come from sceptics who do not believe in astrology at all. The reading is a profound unmasking, but it is not personal and should not threaten the individual. It is protected like the confessional or a doctor's examination.

The astrologer must simultaneously be an analyst, confessor, parent, critic and sympathizer; above all, he must understand that *the reading is a reversible process.* The reading may change the individual's attitudes, but there will always be an equivalent transformation in the astrologer's psyche. Within the circle (the Self) the symbol and the goal of the process is the confrontation of opposites. Both parties project their opposite or "shadow" sides onto each other. As the shadow is the sum of qualities repressed for the sake of the Ego, it appears as a dark figure, often very sinister and menacing. The individual often projects his shadow upon the astrologer as a representative of the darkness of his own psyche, while the astrologer in exchange projects his own shadow onto the individual as a symbol of his ignorance. There is always drama.

The only attitude the aware astrologer can take is that every reading is a potential key to his own shadow, and by extension, to his unconscious. The assumption could be made that *the astrologer is called to his profession because of the need to comprehend his own complex reality.* No matter how mundane or tedious the client may seem at first, he temporarily becomes the astrologer's shadow, and as such is very interesting indeed. The aim of the reading is not to change either party, but to expose the path by which each individual may re-establish the internal dialogue to which he has lost access.

The reading is an exchange of rôles, personalities and Egos for a brief period of time within the confines of the circle. The astrologer, in recreating the life of his client, identifies with that individual's reality so totally that they temporarily *become each other.* To the extent that the astrologer and his client can assume each other's identities, the reading is successful. If the astrologer succeeds in becoming the individual from the beginning, since they are both protected in the circle, the only identity the individual can adopt is that of the astrologer. In the successful reading, *the individual sees his own life and identity from the point of view of the astrologer.* To the extent the astrologer can adopt the thoughts, feelings, sensations and intuitions of the individual, the individual will see his own behaviour from an outside, objective viewpoint. The laws of conservation of energy and momentum hold true within this closed system, so unless there is a total lack of identity the reading will produce the correct response.

During the exchange of identities, the specific information related becomes secondary to the wonder of being able to look at oneself through the eyes of another. It is equally astonishing to the astrologer on every occasion. (The author has experienced this exchange on over four hundred occasions, and it is invariably amazing each time. Even in readings tape-recorded for distant clients, the clients have reported this phenomenon after playing the tape back.)

The reality of the transference in psychology is linked to the reciprocal problem of the *Counter-transference* — the termination of the transference at the end of the analysis or reading. During the reading, unconscious contents are projected onto the personality of the analyst-astrologer in the form of unreal intimacy; fatherly, motherly, sisterly, brotherly feelings; resistances or even neuroses (called by Freud "transference neuroses"). Freud countered this problem by his famous technique of sitting behind his patient. He believed that transference was to be avoided at all costs, and that the proper position of the doctor was as an omnipotent paternal figure. This attitude is safe for the analyst, but places a negative value upon the patient from the beginning. Freud found not only that the transference happened anyway, but that it was impossible to terminate. Freudian analysis can last virtually a lifetime unless the analyst can convince the analysand that their relationship should be terminated.

The transference should be regarded as a natural adjunct of the reading and be neither encouraged nor rejected. There are parallel phenomena deriving from the reading which also have value to the individual, as the following opinion of Jung suggests:

> "I personally am always glad when there is only a mild transference or when it is practically unnoticeable. Far less claim is then made upon one as a person, and one can be satisfied with other therapeutically effective factors. Among these the patient's own insight plays an important part, also his goodwill, the doctor's authority, suggestion, good advice, understanding, sympathy, encouragement, etc. Naturally the more serious cases do not come into this category." [12]

12 Jung, *The Practice of Psychotherapy, CW 16,* p. 173.

These "more serious cases" constitute potential danger to the astrologer. Transference with psychotic or schizophrenic individuals can be extremely difficult, but the astrologer of true calling must be aware of these states and be able to understand their potential existence in himself. The only solution to these dilemmas is to bring them to consciousness with total honesty. The protective nature of the magic circle is critical in these cases. The individual temporarily adopts the astrologer's viewpoint. This should allow the individual a first-hand experience of the dissociated side of his reality. It should also permit stabilizing mechanisms within the psyche to be directed towards corrective measures. If the individual is irrevocably split, he hears what is being said about his dissociated personality but does not remember it afterwards. Although this sounds illogical, it works in practice. Disturbed individuals are more easily drawn into the circle in the first place and hence are more effectively protected from problematic reactions.

The essence of the reading is to make constellated (unconscious) contents available to consciousness. Whereas in psychoanalysis, unconscious contents are usually projected onto the analyst and reburied at a later stage, in the astrological reading contents are reburied simultaneously with the end of the reading. If the individual assumed the astrologer's point of view during the reading, he will have reacted with the same objectivity as the astrologer himself.

The competent astrologer learns to allow projections either to reflect from his own psyche like a mirror, or to be able to transmit them so fluidly through his centre, like a superconductor, that they seem to have been conscious all along. The only way to convince an individual to put all his energy and consciousness into the reading is for the astrologer to set an example. The astrologer's ability and willingness to involve himself with the complicated internal dialogue involved shows the individual that it is possible.

Psychoanalysts always experience an initial "training analysis" where they are analysed themselves, and this is also true of astrologers. The astrologer learns the technique of interpretation from his own horoscope, and his first readings reflect his honesty with himself. It is always more difficult to be honest with oneself than with others, especially in astrology, which is essentially self-analytical. As the astrologer's ability to discover central dilemmas and bring them to consciousness increases with experience, he finds that a mechanism develops which safeguards him from submersion in the underworld of the unconscious. Directness and total honesty are his only infallible protection. Difficulty resolving particular horoscopes indicates to the astrologer that he is not as honest with himself as he should be. Eventually the astrologer understands that his own reality is intimately related to the reality of all of his clients, all other individuals and the Universal Psyche. This is the object of astrology.

Figure IX.8 Solomon's Ring Mandala.

Part X

Horoscopes

This section includes the horoscopes of forty-eight individuals. The particular horoscopes were chosen for a variety of reasons. Some of them have very clear examples of the Major Aspects Patterns, some have unusual distributions, some are uniquely positioned by octave, some have interesting constellations or overall patterns, and many represent clear verifications of the workings of the Logarithmic Time Scale. The horoscopes are intended for reference, interest and study.

The horoscopes stretch back in time to the birth of Dante in 1265. This has been done instead of choosing horoscopes of contemporary individuals, because the distributions of the slow-moving planets (Uranus, Neptune and Pluto) change significantly only over hundreds of years. An attempt has also been made to choose individuals from a wide range of professions, cultures, physical descriptions and historical positions to allow as much latitude as possible.

For each individual horoscope the following information is given:
— A photograph or etching of the individual for correlation to the Physical Descriptions in the Tables of Correspondences.
— The Date and Place of birth.
— The Shape of the horoscope.
— The Ruling Planet of the horoscope.
— Major Aspect Patterns are listed, together with the planets and personal points which compose them.

Horoscope 1.
Alfred Adler, Psychologist
7 February 1870
Vienna, Austria

Loose Bowl Shape: Uranus leads
Ruling Planet: Moon Taurus XI

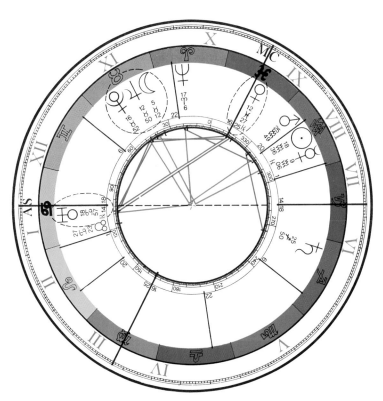

Adler
1

Element Distribution

Fire	2	5 pos
Air	3	
Earth	3	6 neg
Water	3	

Mode Distribution

Cardinal	3
Fixed	6
Mutable	2

House Distribution

Angular	2
Succedent	5
Cadent	3

Mary Evans Picture Library

Horoscope 2.
Anastasia of Russia
18 June 1901
Leningrad, Russia

Locomotive Shape: Saturn leads
Ruling Planet: Sun Gemini XI

Mutable T-Square: ♀ □ ♂ □ ♅

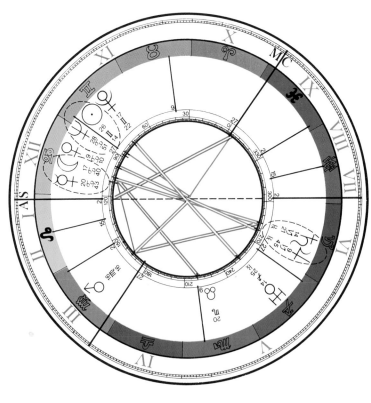

Anastasia
2

Element Distribution

Fire	2	5 pos
Air	3	
Earth	3	6 neg
Water	3	

Mode Distribution

Cardinal	5
Fixed	1
Mutable	5

House Distribution

Angular	0
Succedent	3
Cadent	7

Princess Anne
3

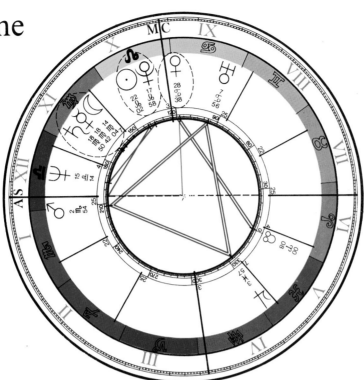

Element Distribution

Fire	2	
Air	2	4 pos
Earth	3	
Water	4	7 neg

Mode Distribution

Cardinal	4
Fixed	3
Mutable	4

House Distribution

Angular	4
Succedent	3
Cadent	3

Camera Press

Horoscope 3.
Princess Anne of England
15 August 1950
London, England

Sling Shape: Jupiter handle
Ruling Planet: Venus Cancer IX

Watery Grand Trine: ♂ △ ♃ △ ♅

Armstrong
4

Element Distribution

Fire	3	
Air	2	5 pos
Earth	4	
Water	2	6 neg

Mode Distribution

Cardinal	4
Fixed	1
Mutable	6

House Distribution

Angular	5
Succedent	4
Cadent	1

Camera Press

Horoscope 4.
Neil Armstrong, Astronaut
5 August 1930
Wapahoneta, Ohio, USA

Bucket Shape: Moon-Saturn handle
Ruling Planet: Mercury Virgo IV

Dissociate Grand Trine: ☽ △ ♀ ♆ △ ⚷

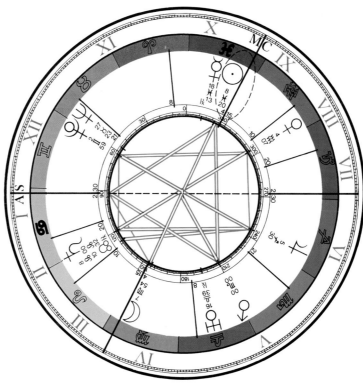

Assagioli
5

Horoscope 5.
Roberto Assagioli, Psychologist
27 February 1888
Venice, Italy

Splay Shape
Ruling Planet: Sun Pisces X

Watery Grand Trine: *ASC* △ ☉ *MC* △ ♂
Mutable Grand Cross: ♀ ♓ □ ☉ *MC* □ ♃ □ ☾
Fixed T-Square: ♄ □ ♂ □ ♀

Element Distribution

Fire	2	5 pos
Air	3	
Earth	2	6 neg
Water	4	

Mode Distribution

Cardinal	2
Fixed	4
Mutable	5

House Distribution

Angular	3
Succedent	4
Cadent	3

Austen
6

Mary Evans Picture Library

Horoscope 6.
Jane Austen, Author
16 December 1775
Steventon, England

Sling Shape: Jupiter-Uranus handle
Ruling Planet: Jupiter Gemini X

Airy Grand Trine: ♅ △ ♆ △ ♀
Mutable T-Square: ♃ *MC* □ *ASC* □ ♀

Element Distribution

Fire	2	7 pos
Air	5	
Earth	3	4 neg
Water	1	

Mode Distribution

Cardinal	3
Dixed	2
Mutable	6

House Distribtuion

Angular	4
Succedent	4
Cadent	2

Barton
7

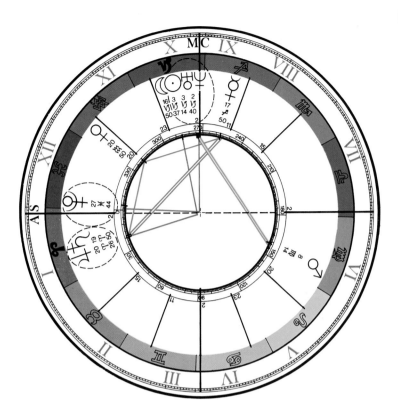

Element Distribution

Fire	4	5 pos
Air	1	
Earth	5	6 neg
Water	1	

Mode Distribution

Cardinal	7
Fixed	1
Mutable	3

House Distribution

Angular	6
Succedent	0
Cadent	4

Horoscope 7.
Clara Barton, Red Cross Founder
25 December 1821
Oxford, Massachusetts, USA

Sling Shape: Mars handle
Ruling Planet: Sun Capricorn X

Baudelaire
8

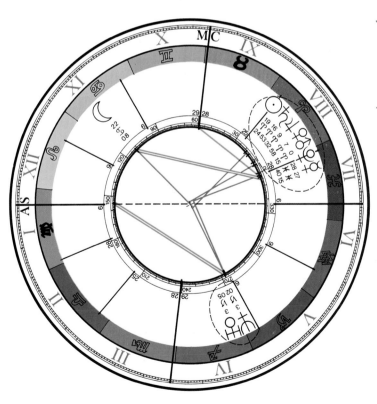

Element Distribution

Fire	5	5 pos
Air	0	
Earth	3	6 neg
Water	3	

Mode Distribution

Cardinal	8
Fixed	0
Mutable	3

House Distribution

Angular	3
Succedent	7
Cadent	0

Horoscope 8.
Charles Baudelaire, Poet
9 April 1821
Paris, France

Sling Shape: Moon handle
Ruling Planet: Moon Cancer XI

Mary Evans Picture Library

Horoscope 9.
Ludwig van Beethoven, Composer
16 December 1770
Bonn, Germany

Splay Shape
Ruling Planet: Venus Capricorn X

Earthy Grand Trine: *ASC* ♅ △ ♀ *MC* △ ♆

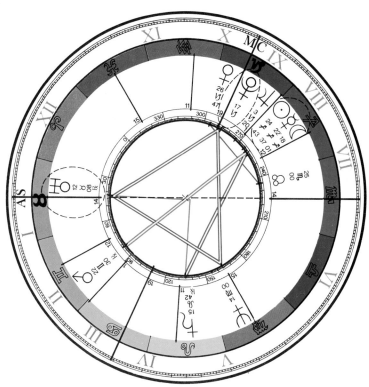

Beethoven
9

Element Distribution
Fire	4	5 pos
Air	1	
Earth	6	6 neg
Water	0	

Mode Distribution
Cardinal	3
Fixed	3
Mutable	5

House Distribution
Angular	1
Succedent	6
Cadent	3

Mary Evans Picture Library

Horoscope 10.
Elizabeth Barrett Browning, Poetess
3 March 1806
Durham, England

Bowl Shape: Venus leads
Ruling Planet: Mercury Pisces VI

Mutable T-Square: ♀ □ *MC* □ *ASC*

Browning
10

Element Distribution
Fire	1	4 pos
Air	3	
Earth	2	7 neg
Water	5	

Mode Distribution
Cardinal	4
Fixed	0
Mutable	6

House Distribution
Angular	3
Succedent	2
Cadent	5

Churchill
11

Element Distribution
Fire   5   9 pos
Air   4
Earth   1   2 neg
Water   1

Mode Distribution
Cardinal 4
Fixed   5
Mutable   2

House Distribution
Angular   2
Succedent 6
Cadent   2

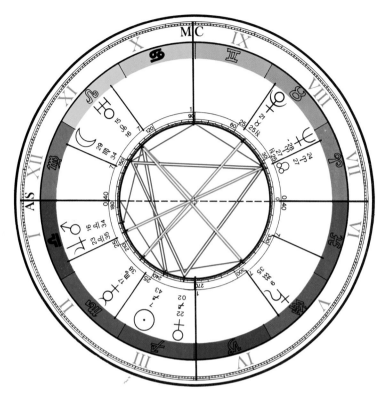

Horoscope 11.
Winston Churchill, Prime Minister
30 November 1874
Blenheim Palace, England

Splay Shape
Ruling Planet: Venus Sagittarius III

Fiery Grand Trine: ♆ ☊ △ ☾ △ ♀

Crowley
12

Element Distribution
Fire   2   5 pos
Air   3
Earth   3   6 neg
Water   3

Mode Distribution
Cardinal 3
Fixed   7
Mutable   1

House Distribution
Angular   7
Succedent 1
Cadent   2

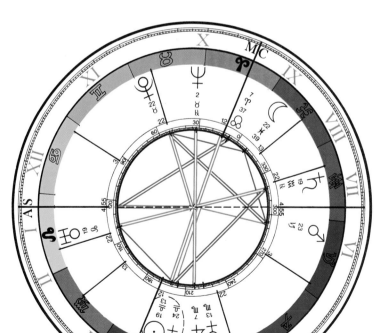

Horoscope 12.
Aleister Crowley, Magician
12 October 1875
Leamington, England

Splay Shape
Ruling Planet: Sun Libra IV

Fixed T-Square: ♀ □ ASC □ ♃

Horoscope 13.
Dante Aligheri, Poet
14 May 1265
Florence, Italy

Sling Shape: Pluto handle
Ruling Planet: Mercury Gemini XII

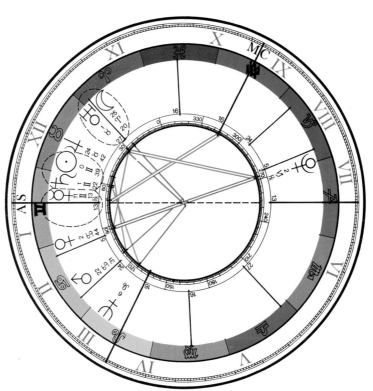

Mary Evans Picture Library

Dante
13

Element Distribution

Fire	2	6 pos
Air	4	
Earth	3	5 neg
Water	2	

Mode Distribution

Cardinal	4
Fixed	3
Mutable	4

House Distribution

Angular	2
Succedent	2
Cadent	6

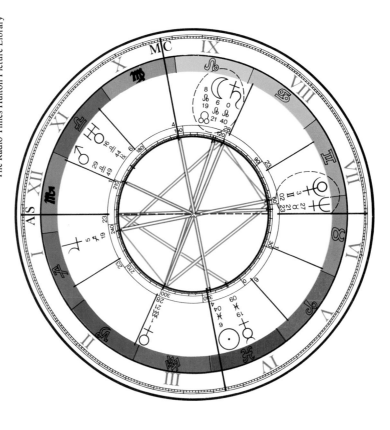

The Radio Times Hulton Picture Library

Horoscope 14.
John Foster Dulles, Diplomat
25 February 1888
Washington, D.C., USA

Splay Shape
Ruling Planet: Mars Libra XI

Mutable Grand Cross: ♃ □ *MC* □ ♀ □ ☉
Dissociate T-Square: ♄ □ ♂ □ ♀

Dulles
14

Element Distribution

Fire	3	7 pos
Air	4	
Earth	1	4 neg
Water	3	

Mode Distribution

Cardinal	2
Fixed	4
Mutable	5

House Distribution

Angular	5
Succedent	2
Cadent	3

Durer
15

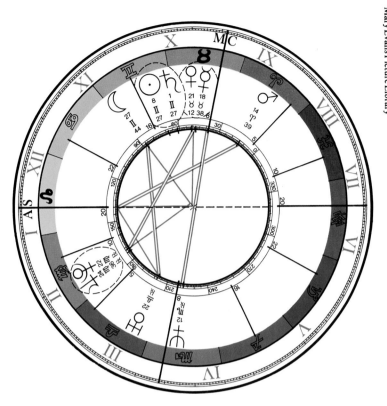

Element Distribution

Fire	2	6 pos
Air	4	
Earth	4	5 neg
Water	1	

Mode Distribution

Cardinal	2
Fixed	4
Mutable	5

House Distribution

Angular	5
Succedent	3
Cadent	2

Eddy
16

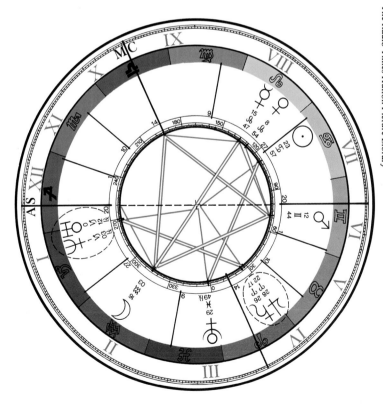

Element Distribution

Fire	5	7 pos
Air	2	
Earth	2	4 neg
Water	2	

Mode Distribution

Cardinal	5
Fixed	3
Mutable	3

House Distribution

Angular	5
Succedent	3
Cadent	2

Horoscope 15.
Albrecht Durer, Artist
21 May 1471
Nuremburg, Germany

Bucket Shape: Mars handle
Ruling Planet: Sun Gemini X

Horoscope 16.
Mary Baker Eddy, Christian Scientist
16 July 1821
Bow, New Hampshire, USA

Locomotive Shape: Mercury leads
Ruling Planet: Jupiter Aries IV

Airy Grand Trine: ☾ △ ♂ △ MC

Mary Evans Picture Library

Horoscope 17.
Albert Einstein, Physicist
14 March 1879
Ulm, Germany

Bucket Shape: Uranus handle
Ruling Planet: Sun Pisces X

Einstein
17

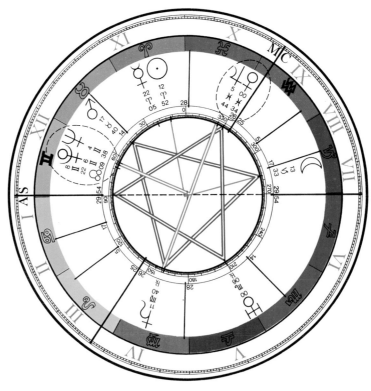

Element Distribution

Fire	4	5 pos
Air	1	
Earth	4	6 neg
Water	2	

Mode Distribution

Cardinal	5
Fixed	3
Mutable	3

House Distribution

Angular	4
Succedent	3
Cadent	3

Camera Press

Horoscope 18.
Max Ernst, Painter
2 April 1891
Bruhl, Germany

Splay Shape
Ruling Planet: Venus Jupiter Pisces X

Earthy Grand Trine: ☽ △ ♂ △ ♄
Dissociate Grand Trine: ASC △ ♅ △ MC ♀ ♃
Mutable T-Square: ♄ ☐ ☊ ♀ ☐ ♃

Ernst
18

Element Distribution

Fire	2	5 pos
Air	3	
Earth	3	6 neg
Water	3	

Mode Distribution

Cardinal	3
Fixed	2
Mutable	6

House Distribution

Angular	4
Succedent	3
Cadent	3

Freud/Galileo

THE ROUND ART

Freud
19

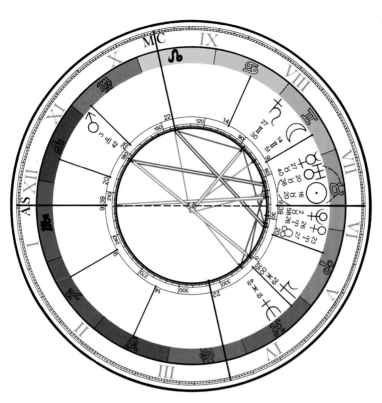

Element Distribution

Fire	1	4 pos
Air	3	
Earth	4	7 neg
Water	3	

Mode Distribution

Cardinal	2
Fixed	5
Mutable	4

House Distribution

Angular	4
Succedent	4
Cadent	2

Galileo
20

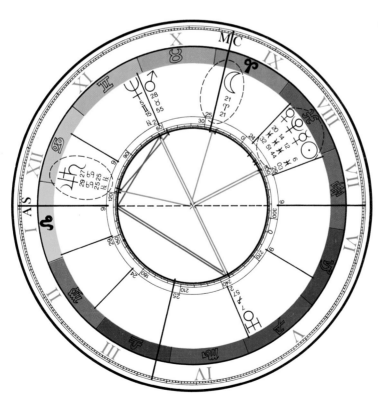

Element Distribution

Fire	3	4 pos
Air	1	
Earth	1	7 neg
Water	6	

Mode Distribution

Cardinal	3
Fixed	2
Mutable	6

House Distribution

Angular	1
Succedent	6
Cadent	3

Mary Evans Picture Library

Horoscope 19.
Sigmund Freud, Psychoanalysis Founder
6 May 1856
Freiburg, Czechoslovakia

Sling Shape: Mars handle
Ruling Planet: Pluto Taurus VI

Dissociate T-Square: ♃ □ ♄ □ ♂

Mary Evans Picture Library

Horoscope 20.
Galileo Galilei, Astronomer
15 February 1564
Pisa, Italy

Bucket Shape: Uranus handle
Ruling Planet: Sun Pisces VIII

Mutable T-Square: ♅ □ ☉ □ ♀

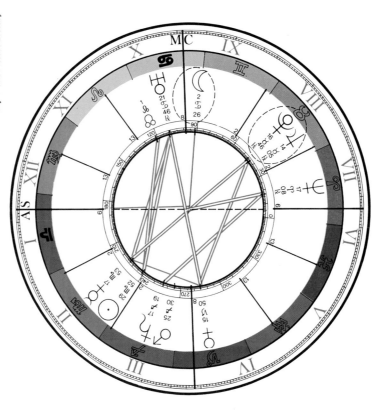

Gide
21

Horoscope 21.
Andre Gide, Novelist
22 November 1869
Paris, France

See-Saw Shape
Ruling Planet: Moon Cancer IX

Cardinal T-Square: ♀ □ ♆ □ ♅

Element Distribution

Fire	3	4 pos
Air	1	
Earth	3	7 neg
Water	4	

Mode Distribution

Cardinal	5
Fixed	4
Mutable	2

House Distribution

Angular	3
Succedent	4
Cadent	3

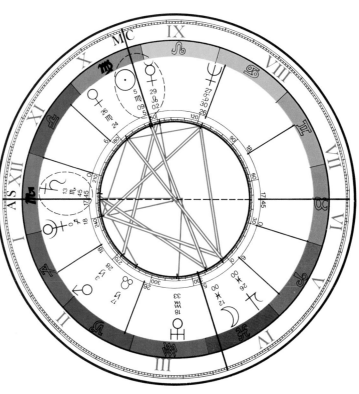

Goethe
22

Horoscope 22.
Johann Wolfgang von Goethe, Poet
28 August 1749
Frankfurt am Main, Germany

Locomotive Shape: Jupiter leads
Ruling Planet: Sun Virgo X

Dissociate Grand Trine: ♃ △ ♆ △ ♀

Element Distribution

Fire	2	3 pos
Air	1	
Earth	3	8 neg
Water	5	

Mode Distribution

Cardinal	2
Fixed	4
Mutable	5

House Distribution

Angular	3
Succedent	1
Cadent	4

Gurdjieff
23

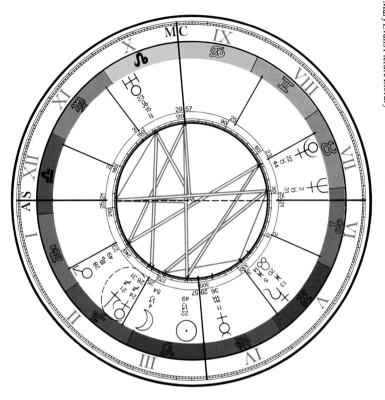

Element Distribution

Fire	3	5 pos
Air	2	
Earth	4	6 neg
Water	2	

Mode Distribution

Cardinal	3
Fixed	5
Mutable	3

House Distribution

Angular	4
Succedent	4
Cadent	2

Horoscope 23.
George Ivanovich Gurdjieff, Mystic
13 January 1887
Caucasus

Bucket Shape: Uranus handle
Ruling Shape: Venus Sagittarius II

Fixed T-Square: ♂ □ ♅ □ ♀
Cardinal T-Square: ☉ □ ASC □ MC
Dissociate T-Square: ♆ □ MC □ ASC

Hitler
24

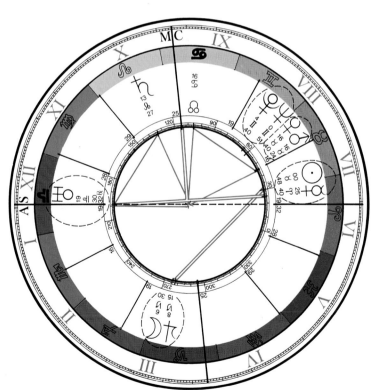

Element Distribution

Fire	2	6 pos
Air	4	
Earth	5	5 neg
Water	0	

Mode Distribution

Cardinal	5
Fixed	4
Mutable	2

House Distribution

Angular	3
Succedent	4
Cadent	3

Horoscope 24.
Adolf Hitler, Dictator
20 April 1889
Brauau, Austria

Bucket Shape: Moon-Jupiter handle
Ruling Planet: Uranus Libra XII

Cardinal T-Square: ASC ♅ □ MC □ ♀

Mary Evans Picture Library

Horoscope 25.
Carl Gustav Jung, Psychoanalyst
26 July 1875
Kesswil, Switzerland

Splay Shape:
Ruling Planet: Saturn Aquarius I

Fixed T-Square: $ASC \square \Psi \square \odot$
Fixed T-Square: $\female \square \saturn \square MC$

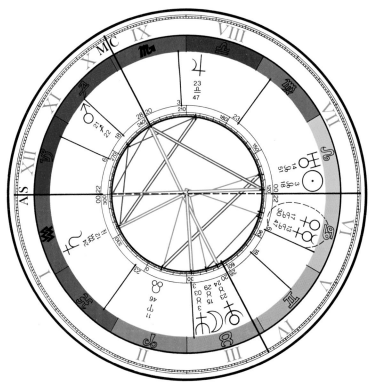

Jung
25

Element Distribution

Fire	3	6 pos
Air	3	
Earth	3	5 neg
Water	2	

Mode Distribution

Cardinal	3
Fixed	7
Mutable	1

House Distribution

Angular	3
Succedent	2
Cadent	5

Mary Evans Picture Library

Horoscope 26.
Helen Keller, Blind-Deaf Author
27 June 1880
Tuscumbia, Alabama

Bowl Shape: Moon leads
Ruling Planet: Mars Leo IX

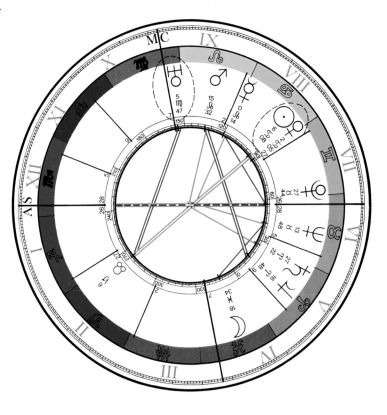

Keller
26

Element Distribution

Fire	4	4 pos
Air	0	
Earth	3	7 neg
Water	4	

Mode Distribution

Cardinal	4
Fixed	5
Mutable	2

House Distribution

Angular	2
Succedent	5
Cadent	3

Kipling
27

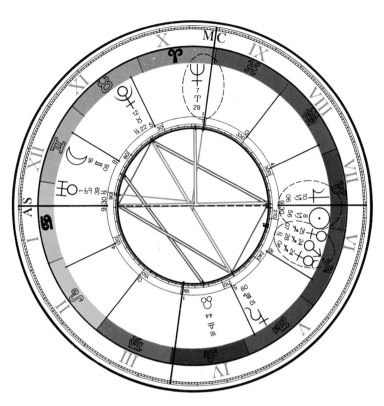

Element Distribution

Fire	4	5 pos
Air	1	
Earth	3	6 neg
Water	3	

Mode Distribution

Cardinal	5
Fixed	2
Mutable	4

House Distribution

Angular	2
Succedent	2
Cadent	6

Mary Evans Picture Library

Horoscope 27.
Rudyard Kipling, Author
30 December 1865
Bombay, India

Locomotive Shape: Uranus leads
Ruling Planet: Neptune Aries X

Cardinal T-Square: ♃ ☉ □ ♆ □ *ASC*

Laing
28

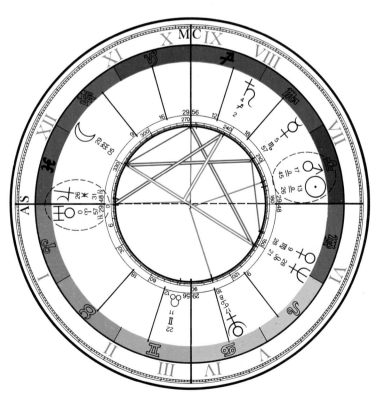

Element Distribution

Fire	3	6 pos
Air	3	
Earth	1	5 neg
Water	4	

Mode Distribution

Cardinal	4
Fixed	3
Mutable	4

House Distribution

Angular	4
Succedent	2
Cadent	4

Camera Press

Horoscope 28.
R.D. Laing, Psychiatrist
7 October 1927
Glasgow, Scotland

Splay Shape
Ruling Planet: Jupiter Pisces XII

Dissociate T-Square: ☽ □ ♄ □ ♆

Mary Evans Picture Library

Horoscope 29.
Nikolai Lenin, Revolutionary
22 April 1870
Simbirsk, Russia

Bucket Shape: Uranus handle
Ruling Planet: Pluto Taurus VI

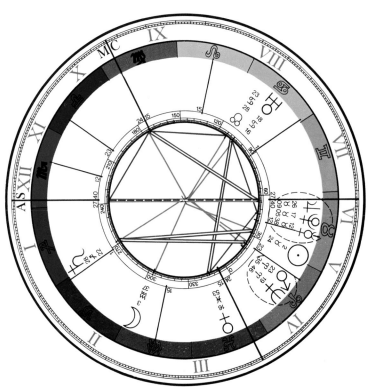

Lenin
29

Element Distribution

Fire	3	4 pos
Air	1	
Earth	4	7 neg
Water	3	

Mode Distribution

Cardinal	3
Fixed	6
Mutable	2

House Distribution

Angular	2
Succedent	4
Cadent	4

Mary Evans Picture Library

Horoscope 30.
Leonardo da Vinci, Artist
15 April 1452
Vinci, Italy

Locomotive Shape: Saturn leads
Ruling Planet: Saturn Libra VIII

Fixed T-Square: ♂ □MC □ ♀

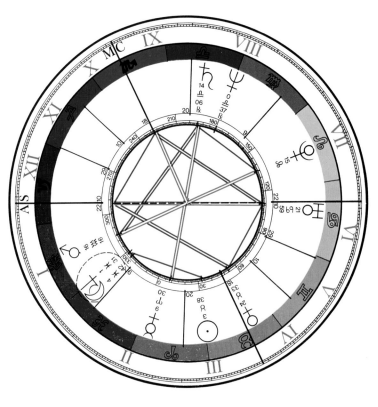

Leonardo
30

Element Distribution

Fire	2	5 pos
Air	3	
Earth	3	6 neg
Water	3	

Mode Distribution

Cardinal	5
Fixed	4
Mutable	2

House Distribution

Angular	5
Succedent	3
Cadent	2

Mann
31

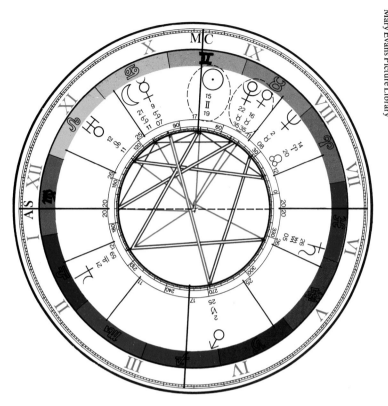

Element Distribution

Fire	1	4 pos
Air	3	
Earth	5	7 neg
Water	2	

Mode Distribution

Cardinal	4
Fixed	5
Mutable	2

House Distribution

Angular	3
Succedent	3
Cadent	4

Horoscope 31.
Thomas Mann, Author
6 June 1875
Lubeck, Germany

Splay Shape
Ruling Planet: Sun Gemini IX

Marx
32

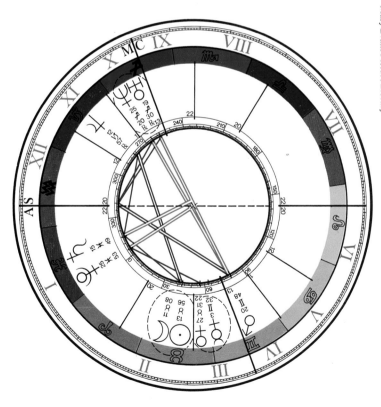

Element Distribution

Fire	2	5 pos
Air	3	
Earth	4	6 neg
Water	2	

Mode Distribution

Cardinal	1
Fixed	4
Mutable	6

House Distribution

Angular	5
Succedent	3
Cadent	2

Horoscope 32.
Karl Marx, Revolutionary
5 May 1818
Trier, Germany

Bowl Shape: Uranus leads
Ruling Planet: Uranus Sagittarius X

Mutable T-Square: ♂ □ ♀ □ ♆
Mutable T-Square: ♂ □ ♄ □ ♅

Michaelangelo
33

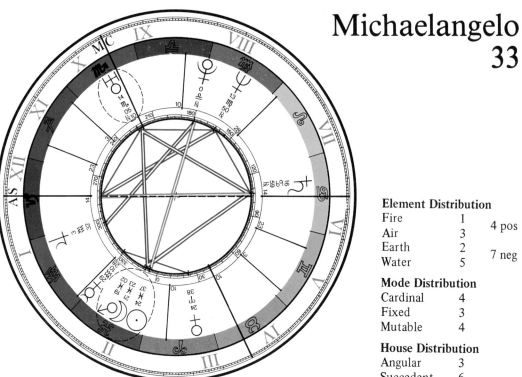

Horoscope 33.
Michaelangelo Buonarotti, Artist
6 March 1475
Caprese, Italy

Splay Shape
Ruling Planet: Uranus Scorpio X

Watery Grand Trine: ☾ ♂ △ ♄ ♅ *MC*

Element Distribution

Fire	1	4 pos
Air	3	
Earth	2	7 neg
Water	5	

Mode Distribution

Cardinal	4
Fixed	3
Mutable	4

House Distribution

Angular	3
Succedent	6
Cadent	1

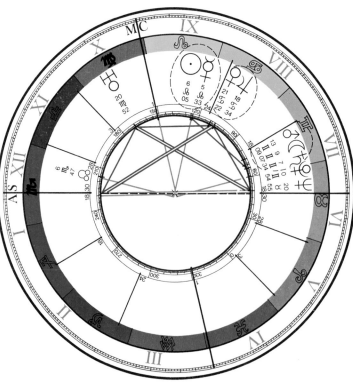

Mussolini
34

Horoscope 34.
Benito Mussolini, Dictator
29 July 1883
Dovia, Italy

Bundle Shape: Uranus leads
Ruling Planet: Mars Pluto Gemini VII

Element Distribution

Fire	2	6 pos
Air	4	
Earth	2	5 neg
Water	3	

Mode Distribution

Cardinal	2
Fixed	4
Mutable	5

House Distribution

Angular	6
Succedent	2
Cadent	2

Nietzsche
35

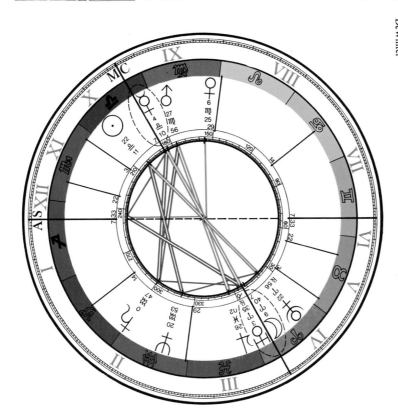

Element Distribution

Fire	4	8 pos
Air	4	
Earth	2	3 neg
Water	1	

Mode Distribution

Cardinal	5
Fixed	2
Mutable	4

House Distribution

Angular	3
Succedent	2
Cadent	5

Horoscope 35.
Friederich Nietzsche, Philosopher
15 October 1844
Lutzen, Germany

See-Saw Shape
Ruling Planet: Jupiter Pisces III

Nostradamus
36

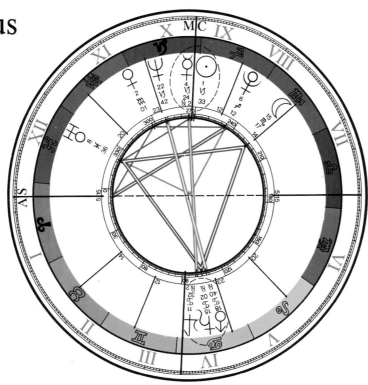

Element Distribution

Fire	2	5 pos
Air	3	
Earth	1	6 neg
Water	5	

Mode Distribution

Cardinal	7
Fixed	2
Mutable	2

House Distribution

Angular	5
Succedent	3
Cadent	2

Horoscope 36.
Michel de Nostradamus, Astrologer
14th December 1503
St. Remy, France

Sling Shape: Mars-Jupiter-Saturn handle
Ruling Planet: Sun Capricorn IX

Watery Grand Trine: ☾ △ ♅ △ ♃ ♄

Mary Evans Picture Library

Horoscope 37.
Marcel Proust, Author
10 July 1871
Paris, France

Bucket Shape: Saturn handle
Ruling Planet: Saturn Capricorn IX

Earthy Grand Trine: ☾ △ ♀ ♄ MC
Cardinal T-Square: ♃ □ ♂ □ ♄ MC
Cardinal T-Square: ♂ □ ♃ □ ASC

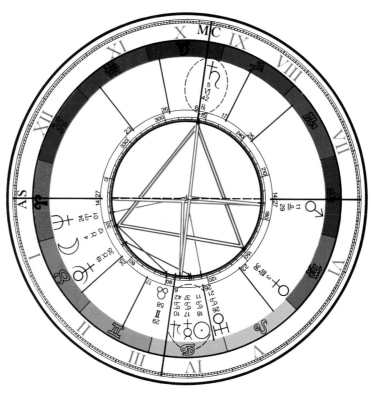

Proust
37

Element Distribution

Fire	2	3 pos
Air	1	
Earth	4	8 neg
Water	4	

Mode Distribution

Cardinal	8
Fixed	2
Mutable	1

House Distribution

Angular	6
Succedent	1
Cadent	3

The Radio Times Hulton Picture Library

Horoscope 38.
Raphael, Artist
6 April 1483
Urbino, Italy

See-Saw Shape
Ruling Planet: Mercury Taurus IX

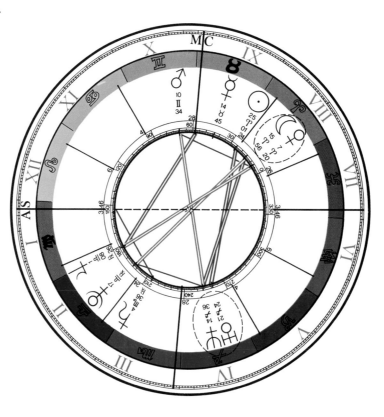

Raphael
38

Element Distribution

Fire	5	8 pos
Air	3	
Earth	2	3 neg
Water	1	

Mode Distribution

Cardinal	5
Fixed	2
Mutable	4

House Distribution

Angular	3
Succedent	4
Cadent	3

Rasputin
39

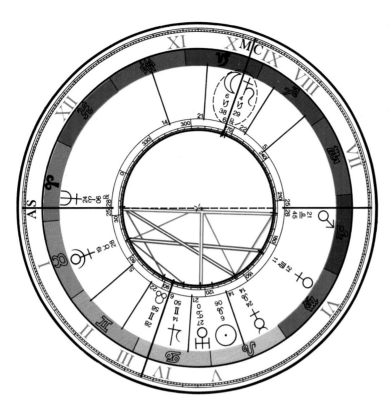

Element Distribution

Fire	4	5 pos
Air	1	
Earth	4	6 neg
Water	2	

Mode Distribution

Cardinal	7
Fixed	3
Mutable	1

House Distribution

Angular	3
Succedent	2
Cadent	5

Horoscope 39.
Grigori Rasputin, Demagogue
29 July 1871
Pokrovskoe, Russia

Bucket Shape: Moon-Saturn handle
Ruling Planet: Saturn Capricorn IX

Cardinal T-Square: ♂ □ ♅ □ ♆ ASC

Rimsky-Korsakov
40

Element Distribution

Fire	2	4 pos
Air	2	
Earth	2	7 neg
Water	5	

Mode Distribution

Cardinal	3
Fixed	4
Mutable	4

House Distribution

Angular	4
Succedent	5
Cadent	1

Horoscope 40.
Nicolas Rimsky-Korsakov, Composer
18 March 1844
Tischwin, Russia

Bundle Shape: Mars leads
Ruling Planet: Moon Pisces X

Mary Evans Picture Library

Horoscope 41.
Peter Paul Rubens, Artist
29 June 1577
Siegen, Germany

See-Saw Shape
Ruling Planet: Mars Leo IX

Fixed T-Square: ♂ □ ASC □ ♅
Cardinal T-Square: ☾ ♄ □ ♀ □ ♆

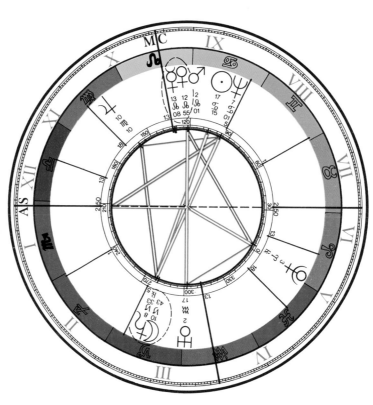

Rubens
41

Element Distribution

Fire	4	5 pos
Air	1	
Earth	3	6 neg
Water	3	

Mode Distribution

Cardinal	5
Fixed	5
Mutable	1

House Distribution

Angular	1
Succedent	1
Cadent	8

Mary Evans Picture Library

Horoscope 42.
Baruch Spinoza, Philosopher
24 November 1632
Amsterdam, Holland

See-Saw Shape
Ruling Planet: Mercury Scorpio VI

Mutable T-Square: ♂ □ ♅ □ ASC
Fixed T-Square: ♃ □ ♀ □ MC

Spinoza
42

Element Distribution

Fire	4	5 pos
Air	1	
Earth	4	6 neg
Water	2	

Mode Distribution

Cardinal	0
Fixed	5
Mutable	6

House Distribution

Angular	0
Succedent	3
Cadent	7

Steiner
43

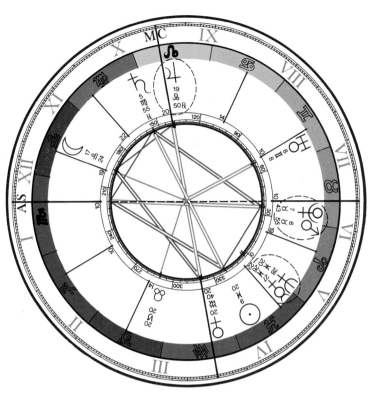

Element Distribution

Fire	1	4 pos
Air	3	
Earth	3	7 neg
Water	4	

Mode Distribution

Cardinal	1
Fixed	5
Mutable	5

House Distribution

Angular	4
Succedent	3
Cadent	3

Horoscope 43.
Rudolf Steiner, Occultist
27 February 1861
Darmstadt, Germany

Splay Shape
Ruling Planet: Mars-Pluto Taurus VI

Mutable T-Square: ☉ □ ♅ □ ♄

Stravinsky
44

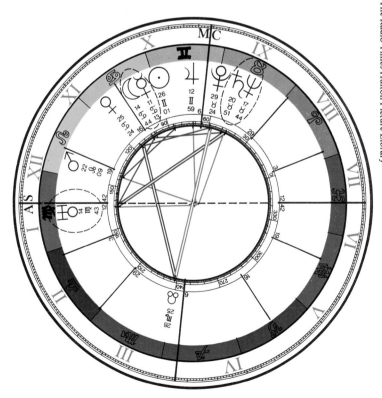

Element Distribution

Fire	1	3 pos
Air	2	
Earth	5	8 neg
Water	3	

Mode Distribution

Cardinal	3
Fixed	4
Mutable	4

House Distribution

Angular	5
Succedent	1
Cadent	4

Horoscope 44.
Igor Stravinsky, Composer
17 June 1882
Oranienburg, Russia

Bundle Shape: Uranus leads
Ruling Planet: Mercury Cancer X

Horoscope 45.
Paul Verlaine, Poet
30 March 1844
Paris, France

Bowl Shape: Moon leads
Ruling Planet: Moon Leo X

Fixed T-Square: ☾ *MC* □ ♆ □ ♀ ♂

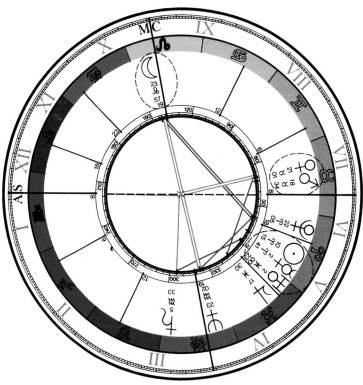

Verlaine
45

Element Distribution

Fire	5	7 pos
Air	2	
Earth	2	4 neg
Water	2	

Mode Distribution

Cardinal	4
Fixed	6
Mutable	1

House Distribution

Angular	5
Succedent	3
Cadent	2

Horoscope 46.
Queen Victoria of England
24 May 1819
London, England

Bowl Shape: Moon leads
Ruling Planet: Sun-Moon Gemini XII

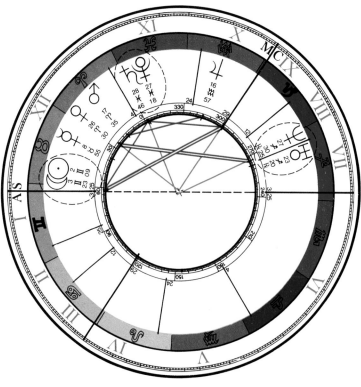

Victoria
46

Element Distribution

Fire	4	8 pos
Air	4	
Earth	1	3 neg
Water	2	

Mode Distribution

Cardinal	2
Fixed	2
Mutable	7

House Distribution

Angular	2
Succedent	3
Cadent	5

Wagner
47

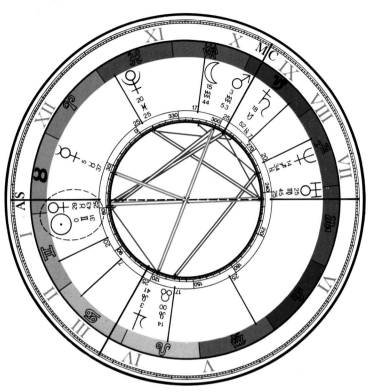

Element Distribution

Fire	2	5 pos
Air	3	
Earth	4	6 neg
Water	2	

Mode Distribution

Cardinal	1
Fixed	7
Mutable	3

House Distribution

Angular	7
Succedent	1
Cadent	2

Yeats
48

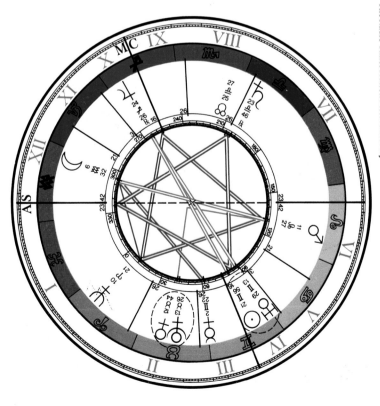

Element Distribution

Fire	3	9 pos
Air	6	
Earth	2	2 neg
Water	0	

Mode Distribution

Cardinal	2
Fixed	5
Mutable	4

House Distribution

Angular	4
Succedent	2
Cadent	4

Horoscope 47.
Richard Wagner, Composer
22 May 1813
Leipzig, Germany

Bucket Shape: Jupiter handle
Ruling Planet: Venus Taurus I

Fixed T-Square: ♃ □ ♀ □ ♂

Horoscope 48.
William Butler Yeats, Poet
13 June 1865
Dublin, Ireland

Splay Shape
Ruling Planet: Saturn Libra VII

Fiery Grand Trine: ♂ △ ♆ △MC
Airy Grand Trine: ♄ ☌ △ ☉ ♅ △ASC

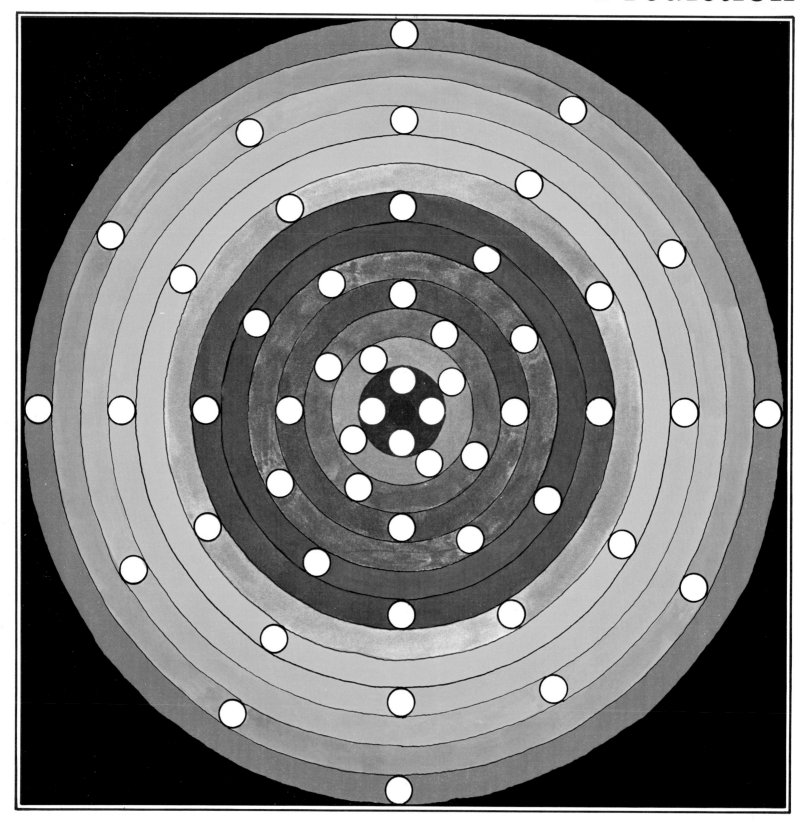

Part XI

Figure XI.1 The Horoscope Mandala.

THE ROUND ART

Available Techniques and the Time Factor

The birth horoscope is used with the Logarithmic Time Scale to indicate major trends in an individual's life. This is an improvement over traditional methods of interpretation where there is no similar chronology. The method we outline is a head-start on the prediction of future events and a reference diagram against which other predictive techniques are compared. Predictive techniques fall into two distinct categories, differentiated by their relationship to time and whether they are actual or symbolic.

Transits are continuous *natural movements* of the planetary bodies in relation to the horoscope — the daily positions in the ephemeris. Transits of the horoscope are identified by the prefix T. (T.Sat = transit of Saturn) The influence of transits is determined by the length of time taken to move through one degree of the zodiac. Their influences range from the rapid movement of the Moon, which takes two to three hours to move one degree, to the slowest planet Pluto, which takes several months. Transits represent *"short-term"* influences.

Directions are *symbolic movements* of planetary bodies determined by one of four similar methods.

1. *Solar Arc Directions* (SA) move planetary bodies according to the formula:
   1 degree = 1 year of life
   For example, in the 45th year of life, each planetary body has advanced 45° from its radix position. This is called the *"One-degree Method"* and is primarily used to estimate solar arcs.

2. *"Naibod Arcs"* use the Sun's average daily arc as equivalent to one year. Since the daily movement of the Sun varies from a minimum of 57′05′′ to a maximum of 1°01′10′′, the Naibod Arcs use a mean of 59′08′′ per year. This method does not account for the time of year when an individual is born.

3. The *"One Day per Year"* method of determining solar arcs uses the formula:
   1 day's actual motion of the Sun after birth = 1 year of life
   To calculate the solar arc for any year, the position of the Sun on the day of birth in the ephemeris is translated into the number of degrees from 0° Aries and used as a base. The solar arc for the desired year of life is found by counting an equivalent number of days ahead in the ephemeris, translating the position of the Sun on that day into degrees from 0° Aries, and then subtracting the former from the latter. The number of degrees away from 0° Aries is indicated on the innermost ring of the horoscope form. (Figure XI.2)

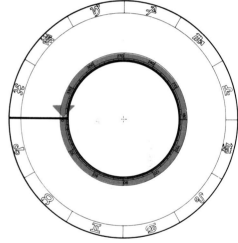

Figure XI.2 Degrees from 0° Aries. The degrees are indicated in red.

For example, on 18 August 1943, the position of the Sun is 24° Leo 40′01′′. Since 0° Leo is 120° from 0° Aries, the position of the Sun is 24°40′01′′ + 120° = 144°40′01′′. The solar arc for 32 years old would be the position of the Sun on 19 September 1943; 25° Virgo 40′20′′ + 150° = 175°40′20′′ minus 144°40′01′′ = SA 30°00′19′′. Every planetary body and personal point advances by adding 31°00′19′′ to the birth horoscope position.

This method for determining solar arcs is the most accurate.

4. *Progressions* are considered "Secondary Directions" and are calculated by counting the number of days after the birthday equivalent to the year in question, and then taking the actual positions of the planetary bodies directly from the ephemeris. The position of the Sun is identical to solar arc method 3, but the positions of the other planetary bodies are different.

   The primary problem with progressions is that while the Sun, Moon, Mercury, Venus and Mars move enough to form many aspects, the outer planets beyond Mars only advance a few degrees each in a lifetime. Pluto only advances 1° in 80 years. The use of progressions is the oldest technique, but its use has declined in favour of solar arcs.

The "One-degree Method" and "Naibod Arcs" are too generalized for accurate use, and Progressions only function reasonably for the inner planets, so we can confine our study to the "One Day per Year" solar arc directions. Solar arc directions are *"long-term"* influences in the horoscope.

For the greatest accuracy in prediction, transits are used together with solar arcs. Solar arcs determine the *years* when critical influences are felt, while transits indicate the specific *days or weeks* when the actual events occur. The essence of correct prediction is the blending of solar arcs and transits with the birth horoscope.

The specificity of prediction is intimately related to the mechanism of prediction in science as presented in Part II, *"Astrology and Physics"*. The duality of waves and particles in the physical world is parallel to that of solar arc directions and transits in astrology. Solar arc directions have a wave-like nature because their movements are regular throughout life, and shift gradually into and out of critical maxima and minima. It is relatively easy to determine the energy of solar arcs, but difficult to find exactly when they occur. Transits have a particle nature — they can be specifically located in time, their movements are often irregular when planets are in retrograde motion or direct, but their precise impact is difficult to ascertain. Fritjof Capra states:

> "... we can never know both the time at which an event occurs and the energy involved in it with great accuracy. Events occurring inside a short time span *(transits)* involve a large uncertainty in energy; events involving a precise amount of energy *(solar arcs)* can be localized only within a long period of time." [1]

The problem of "uncertainty" in physics is paralleled in astrological prediction. In both cases an intelligent co-ordination between the short- and long-term events allows accurate prediction. A factor which increases the efficacy of prediction is the density of events in time and an understanding of the "trigger mechanisms" which actualize potential events.

In astrology, transits are triggering mechanisms for solar arc directions, especially transits of the Sun, Moon and Mercury. When constellations of solar arc planets or slow-moving transits form exact aspects, conjunction, square or opposition transits by any of these three triggers key off the full effects of the constellation. For example, if Saturn is transitting in opposition to a planet in the birth horoscope, the period of time within which the aspect is exact is approximately one month. The event indicated by Saturn is keyed off when the Sun, Moon or Mercury transit Saturn's position in the zodiac. There is a potential event during the entire month, but the *actual event* only happens when it is triggered off by a faster-moving planet. The greater the number of planets participating in a constellation, the more certain the occurrence of an event.

The disparate natures of planets in a constellation are also considered. There is greater surety when involved planets have similar natures than when they have contradictory natures. When Mars and Pluto — both of which indicate violence and extreme tension — are involved in a constellation, the event is highly likely to have an element of violence even if they are triggered by the totally passive Moon or Mercury. The triggering planets — the Sun, Moon and Mercury — have little individual nature. They take on the qualities of the planets they key off.

Transits of the slow-moving planets, Uranus, Neptune and Pluto, take so long to occur that they are partially activated by six or seven lunar transits. In these situations the possibility of precise prediction lessens, unless other fast-moving planets enter the constellation. As the transitting period increases there is a decrease in predictability.

The unification of solar arc directions and transits is similar to "complementarity" in physics. Three systems enter this complementary calculation — the birth horoscope indicates the general framework within which the event occurs; solar arc directions define the amount of energy involved; and transits are triggering mechanisms. When these three systems are correctly weighed against each other, very accurate prediction results. As in physics, correct prediction is more a function of experience and intuition than specific formulae.

In the branch of physics called "quantum mechanics", prediction is a central concern. Quantum physicists analyse waves in such a way that the specific moment of energy or an event is quite exact. A wave of constant wavelength and amplitude is regular throughout its length, and due to this regularity it is difficult to locate a particle since there is an identical probability anywhere along its length. (Figure XI.3). Often, however, physicists can determine boundaries for the wave. In the description of an electron in an atom, the possibilities of finding the electron can be increased by confining its location to a certain region. Outside that region the probability is zero. This distortion of a wave pattern is a "wave packet". When an electron is confined, its velocity increases, and the corresponding amplitude increases towards the centre of the wave packet (Figure XI.4).The particle is most likely to be found in the centre

[1] Capra, *The Tao of Physics,* p. 164, with my parentheses.

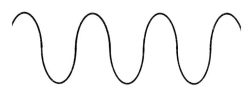

Figure XI.3 A Wavelength of constant amplitude.

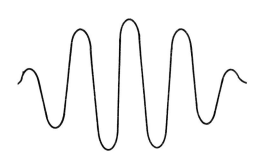

Figure XI.4 A Wave Packet.

of the wave packet, and the length of the wave packet represents the uncertainty of the location of the particle. Since uncertainty operates in time as well as in space, it is analogous to astrological processes.

In astrological prediction, the solar arc directions are regular waves, and as such their energy (amplitude) can be determined. The transitting planets make wave packets when they form aspects, determined by the length of time it takes them to move one degree. An event occurs when the wave packet of the transit coincides with the peak of solar arc, distorting the solar arc wave to greater amplitude (Figure XI.5). This agitates the birth horoscope planet involved to a greater velocity, and an event is produced to release the energy. Finding the time of these critical events is the essence of prediction.

The value of the logarithmic time scale in prediction is profound. Solar arcs and transits move around the periphery of the birth horoscope and key off latent constellations at particular ages. Every event is a combination of the influences of many different ages related to a predictable moment. These events combine and are relived through a series of *"present moments"* which interrelate with each other through time.

This mechanism is also at the heart of psychoanalysis. Contents evoked by the analyst during a particular session correspond to previous experiences in the analysand's life which are triggered on that day. They seem to be random fragments, but this is the result of the juxtaposition of moments. An unconscious individual is subject to a flood of images from his past and possibly his future, and he is unable to differentiate those images from the present moment. When the individual cannot return to a clear present moment, the resultant confusion is then defined as "madness". Everyone is more or less disoriented in time, but prediction can help clarify the individual's relationship to his past, present and future.

The important point is astrological prediction is that life is circular rather than linear. When life conceived is as a straight line trailing off into infinity, the reality of the past which forms the substrata for all our experiences is lost. This is a rejection of the Theory of Relativity and its curvature of space and time. When circular reality is accepted, events may not alter, but they can be understood in their proper context. It will be made abundantly clear that astrological prediction can be very accurate and extremely relevant. In all types of prediction the transitting or solar arc planets are related by aspect to planetary positions in the birth horoscope.

Transits [2]

The positions of transiting planets for a specific time can be read directly from the ephemeris on the day required. They are then entered in the outermost ring around the periphery of the birth horoscope and prefixed by the letter T.

Richard Nixon resigned the Presidency of the United States on 9 August, 1974, after the debilitating effects of the Watergate cover-up had made his position untenable. The positions of the planets on that day (Figure XI.6) were as follows:
(The positions need only be given to the nearest degree.)
12.00 Noon, 9 August, 1974.

T.Sun	:16° Leo
T.Moon	:28° Aries
T.Mercury	: 7° Leo
T.Venus	:23° Cancer
T.Mars	: 8° Virgo
T.Jupiter	:16° Pisces Retrograde
T.Saturn	:13° Cancer
T.Uranus	:24° Libra
T.Neptune	: 6° Sagittarius Retrograde
T.Pluto	: 5° Libra
T.No. Node	:16° Sagittarius

The transit analysis for this date includes a check not only of the planets in exact aspect to the birth horoscope, but also of planets that have just moved out of aspect and those which are moving into aspect. It is necessary to follow the movements of all planets in the ephemeris during the entire month within which the specific date falls.

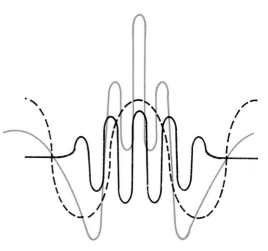

Figure XI.5 The Superimposition of waves.

[2] The best reference book is *"Transits"* by Ebertin, translated by Linda Kratzsch.

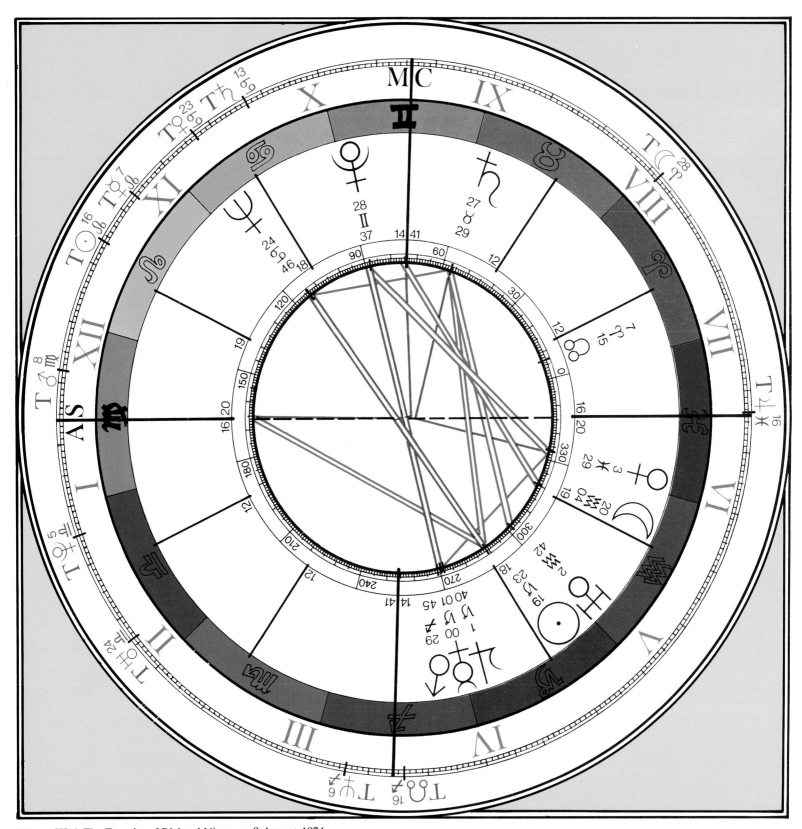

Figure XI.6 The Transits of Richard Nixon on 9 August 1974.

⊳⧉◁ THE ROUND ART ▷⧉◁

It can be seen in the transits of Richard Nixon that T.Jupiter and T.Neptune are *"Retrograde"* (moving backwards through the zodiac). When a planet is in retrograde motion it travels backwards for a period of time and then appears to stop altogether (Figure XI.7). In this static state the planet is *"stationary"*. If a transitting planet is stationary while in exact aspect with a birth horoscope planet, the power of any resultant event is increased. The slow-moving planets from Jupiter outwards from the Sun are stationary for a month or more before they continue their forward motion.

If a planet passes an exact aspect while retrograding, after it has gone direct again it passes the exact aspect a second time. Neptune and Pluto often go retrograde, and in some instances pass over an aspect many times during a period of months before moving out of range. An example of this movement is T.Neptune in Nixon's transits. The R.North Node in his birth horoscope is positioned at 7° Aries 15′, and at the time of his resignation the North Node is trined by T.Neptune at 6° Sagittarius 52′. This aspect indicates:

> *unreality, vagueness, lying, lack of discrimination, strange or idealistic associations, expecting the impossible from others, undermined relationships, deceptive behaviour and disappointment.*

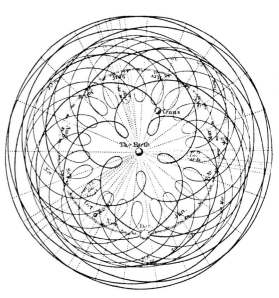

Figure XI.7 A diagram of Retrograde Motion as seen from the Earth.

These qualities were certainly in operation on 9 August 1974, but a check of the motion of T.Neptune before and after the resignation discloses that this influence operated over a very long period of time. T.Neptune first aspects the R.North Node from 2 January 1973 until 10 February 1973, the period of time it takes to pass through the one degree of critical orb for the transit (from 6° Sagittarius 15′ to 7° Sagittarius 15′). On 12 March 1973 T.Neptune goes retrograde, and from 4 April 1973 until 21 May 1973 it passes back through the critical degree. On 18 August 1973 T.Neptune goes direct, and by 5 November 1973 it has gone into the critical degree yet again until 2 December 1973. On 14 March 1974 it goes retrograde again. On 9 July 1974 it passes back into the critical degree of the R.North Node trine, where it remains throughout the time we are analyzing. T.Neptune finally goes direct on 22 August 1974, and passes out of orb for the last time on 27 September 1974. Over a period of 20 months, Richard Nixon was haunted by this T. Neptune trine R.North Node four times!

The following table indicates the average time of planetary motions through one critical degree in transit:

T.Sun	**1 day.**
T.Moon	**2 to 3 hours.**
T.Mercury	**1 to 3 days.**
T.Venus	**1 to 3 days.**
T.Mars	**2 to 3 days.**
T.Jupiter	**2 to 10 days; 30 days stationary.**
T.Saturn	**8 to 12 days; 8 weeks stationary.**
T.Uranus	**2 to 10 weeks; 10 weeks stationary.**
T.Neptune	**4 to 8 weeks; 3 weeks stationary; multiple passes can last up to 2 years.**
T.Pluto	**3 to 6 months.**
T.North Node	**2 to 3 weeks (always moves backwards).**

Since the Moon moves approximately 11 to 14 degrees each day, it often passes many aspect positions during a particular day. The entire range must be considered, although lunar conjunctions are the most important. As may be seen in the analysis to follow, the T.Moon makes aspects with R.Pluto, R.Neptune, R.Mars and R.Uranus on the 9th of August. These four aspects describe Nixon's emotional response to the longer-term influences which produced his resignation in the first place.

(Planets in the birth horoscope are prefixed by R, indicating "radix".

Transit/Sign/ House	Aspect	Radix/Sign/ House	Interpretation
Sun Transits			
T.Sun/Leo/XI	opp	R.Moon/Aqu/VI (14th August)	*Hypersensitivity, ill health, financial difficulties, an unfortunate relationship, schizophrenia, egotism, ambition; highly strung, irritable, self-doubting.*

Moon Transits

T.Moon/Ari/VIII	sex	R.Plu/Gem/X	*Emotional transformation, one-sidedness, deep feelings, dynamic unconscious impulses; intensity, compulsion, drama.*
	squ	R.Nep/Can/XI (early on the 9th August)	*Living in unreality, deception, fraud, ill health, scandal, longing for the impossible, peculiar tastes, instability, delusion.*
	tri	R.Mars/Sag/IV (late on the 9th August)	*Honesty, candour, severe judgement; candid, sincere, enthusiastic, independent.*
	squ	R.Ura/Aqu/V (late on the 9th August)	*Extreme reactions, bizarre interests, self-willedness, exaggeration, strain; nervous, abrupt, eccentric, restless, melodramatic.*

Mercury Transits

T.Mer/Leo/XI	tri	R.Node/Ari/VII	*Family group orientation, fellowship, exchanging ideas with others, business contacts.*

Venus Transits

T.Ven/Can/XI	con	R.Nep/Can/XI	*Delicate constitution, disappointment, dreaming; unrealistic, weak, overly sympathetic, hero worship, delusion, escapism.*

Mars Transits

T.Mars/Vir/XII	no aspects		*Suspended desire to organize and arrange, adaptation to isolation; nervousness, procrastination, revelling in depravity.*

Jupiter Transits

T.Jup/Pis/VII Retrograde	opp	R.Asc/Virgo	*Desire to be important, hypocrisy, bragging, conflicts with others, waste, extravagance, conceit, materialism.*
	squ	R.MC/Gemini (21st August)	*Fluctuating circumstances, desire for importance, misplaced self-confidence, risks, changed occupation, conceit.*

Saturn Transits

T.Sat/Can/X	sex	R.Asc/Virgo (28th August)	*Repressed emotions, difficult family life, paranoia, guilt, jealousy, inhibited personality, seclusion, weak constitution, shyness, frustration, unsympathetic environment; lonely, defensive, paranoid, anxious.*

Uranus Transits

T.Ura/Lib/II	squ	R.Nep/Can/XI	*Instability, impossible ideals, extreme emotion, nervous sensitivity, confusion; highly-strung, muddled, fanatical, intolerant.*

Neptune Transits

T.Nep/Sag/III Retrograde	tri	R.Node/Ari/VII	*Unrealistic, untruthful, vague; lack of discrimination, strange or idealistic associations, expecting the impossible from others, undermined relationships, deceptive behaviour, idealistic friends and family, great disappointment.*

Pluto Transits

T.Plu/Lib/I	opp	R.Node/Ari/VII (19th September)	*Burdensome relations, common tragic experiences, suffering through an association, destructive unions, gangsters, subversive activities, termination of associations.*

North Node Transits

T.Node/Sag/IV	squ	R.Asc/Virgo	*Socially maladjusted, estrangements, inability to live with others, disturbed domestic life, antisocial attitudes; unreliable, untrustworthy.*
	opp	R.MC/II (8th September)	*Exploiting others, difficult relations, inability to act with others, extreme selfishness, aggravation.*

These transit interpretations are taken directly from the Tables of Aspects in Part VII of this book, and are sufficiently clear that no explanation is necessary. The incredible publicity this day received in the press and its description by Bernstein and Woodward, Erlichmann and Haldeman in their books on the Nixon days all serve to verify this transit prognostication. The exceptional factor is that every planet except Mars makes one or more aspects to the birth horoscope, and they all agree in character. Truly, a dismal day for a dismal individual.

To evaluate the effects of transits correctly it is necessary to understand the following mechanisms:

— Conjunctions of transiting planets to radix planets are evaluated by the nature of the planets involved and the constellation of the radix planet. If the constellation is positive, aspects to the birth horoscope, even by malefics like Mars, Saturn or Pluto, do not necessarily produce negative effects.

— Sextiles and trines usually indicate static states or attitudes.

— Squares and oppositions usually indicate events.

— The Sun, Moon and Mercury are *triggers* and adopt the qualities of the constellations that they trigger off.

— In birth horoscopes with a preponderance of sextiles and trines, transiting planets forming square and opposition aspects are beneficial, while conjunctions, sextiles and trines have a neutral effect. In birth horoscopes with a preponderance of conjunctions and oppositions, sextiles, squares and trines are beneficial, while conjunctions and oppositions are neutral. Transit square aspects have a dynamic effect whatever the basic disposition of the birth horoscope.[3]

— Each transiting planet should be evaluated according to its sign, its equivalent age in the Logarithmic Time Scale, its octave of development and its house qualities, as well as the aspects it makes to radix planets. This is especially important with planets which do not make aspects to the radix horoscope.

— When transiting planets are near the personal points — the ASC and MC — it is important to recognize the constellations formed, as well as the pair of bodies directly forming the aspect. This is especially true when the radix horoscope is an approximation based upon an assumed birth time. When this is the case, the exact time when an event manifests can enable the astrologer to correct the position of the ASC or the MC. This will be further discussed in Appendix B, Rectification.

— The positions of New and Full Moons are critical. Since there are one of each in every monthly lunar cycle, when the position of the Sun and Moon align or oppose they tend to agitate profoundly birth horoscope constellations which aspect them.

The primary use of transits is in determining the *time* of events, rather than as a gauge of the power or importance of an event. They are a continuous system of prognostication to be checked on a day-to-day basis.

[3] Ebertin, *Transits,* p. 28-29.

Solar Arc Directions[4]

Solar arc directions locate the years of critical influences which operate throughout an entire lifetime. While the Time Scale locates the thirteen most important ages for archetypal events, the solar arcs usually provide one or more events within each year. Solar arcs are intermediaries between the Time Scale and transits.

Logarithmic Time Scale	=	Archetypal life events
Solar arc directions	=	Critical years in the life
Transits	=	Specific events within each year, or triggers of events

The solar arcs, prefixed by the letter "S", are entered in the first ring outside the birth horoscope (Figure XI.8). As transits are entered in the outermost ring outside the birth horoscope, all three systems can be easily compared. Taken altogether, the birth horoscope in the centre is the base around which the yearly solar arcs and the daily transits revolve. As one proceeds outwards from the centre, influences indicated become more temporary and less critical.

In practice, solar arcs are entered each year (equivalent to the year in the life in question), but for the following analysis, the complete lifetime solar arc distribution of **Adolf Hitler** is used. In the interpretation of solar arcs, sextile and trine aspects are not used as their effects

[4] The best references are *"Directions"* and *"Applied Cosmobiology"* by Ebertin.

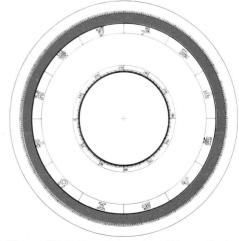

Figure XI.8 The Solar Arc Ring of the Horoscope.

THE ROUND ART

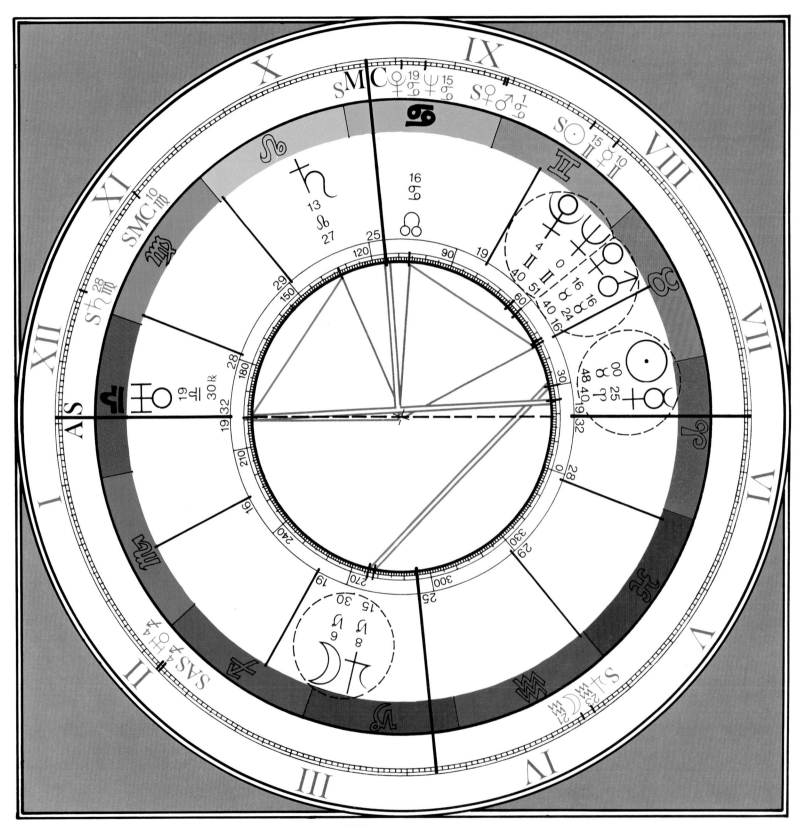

Figure XI.9 The Solar Arc Directions of Adolf Hitler for the year 1936.

THE ROUND ART

are often unnoticeable. The concentration is upon *conjunctions,* which are the most important solar arc aspects, *squares* and *oppositions.* This gives solar arcs an emphasis upon events rather than states of being.

The calculation for solar arc directions has already been described, and the computation technique is fully explained in Appendix C. In the life analysis of Hitler (Figure XI.9), the years of his life within which solar arcs register are shown in chronological order.

Figure XI.9 The Solar Arc Directions of Adolf Hitler for the year 1936. The Solar Arc aspects occurring during this year are: S.ASC opposition R.Pluto, S.Uranus opposition R.Pluto, S.Pluto square R.Uranus and S.Pluto square R.ASC.

Year	Solar Arc/ Sign/House	Aspect	Radix/Sign/ House	Interpretation	Life Events
1891	S.Moon/Cap/III	conj	R.Jup/Cap/III	= *Mother, kindness, generosity, practical idealism; indulgent, civilized, socially conscious.*	Adolf Hitler's mother was the niece of her husband, and was also 23 years younger.
1892	S.Sat/Leo/X	squ	R.Mars/Tau/VIII	= *Energy crises, disputes, separations, inability to finish anything, harshness, brutality; ruthless, destructive, maltreated, vengeful, hard-hearted.*	She had had three miscarriages before Adolf's birth, and was very happy and indulgent with her child in his early years. Adolf's father was violent and whipped Adolf repeatedly during this time. Adolf observed his drunken father raping his mother, and was extremely jealous and angry. His parents were very unhappy because of the difference in their ages, and domestic life was depressed. His father continually moved his family and was very unreliable.
		squ	R.Ven/Tau/VIII	= *Unhappy love, emotional deprivation, poverty, exploitation, jealousy, separations, a hard life, self-torment; lonely.*	
	S.Node/Can/IX	squ	R.Ura/Lib/XII	= *Disturbing influence upon others, quarrels, separations, short-lived relationships; restless, flighty, irritable.*	
		squ	R.ASC/Lib	= *Socially maladjusted, estrangements, inability to live with others, disturbed domestic and family life; antisocial, difficult, unreliable, untrustworthy.*	
1893	S.Nep/Gem/VIII	conj	R.Plu/Gem/VIII	= *Mysticism, strange ideas, obsessional neuroses, peculiar objectives, the Supernatural, presentiments; mediumistic.*	Adolf continually fantasized about his mother's rape — it haunted him for the rest of his life.
1894	S.MC/Leo/X	squ	R.Sun/Tau/VII	= *Father, egocentricity, misplaced self-confidence, lack of clarity, unrealistic goals, changing aims, professional difficulties; arrogant, misguided, pretentious, conceited.*	His father transferred to Linz due to failure in business. He bought and sold farms, but had severe monetary problems. His outward demeanor was superficially strong and successful, but totally misleading.
1895	S.ASC/Lib/I	opp	R.Mer/Ari/VII	= *Disharmonious attitudes, poor judgement, gossip, criticism, quickly changing contacts; garrulous, unfriendly, flighty.*	A brother was born. This shifted mother's attentions away from Adolf, but he still vied for them. He entered public school in Linz and was often chastised for bringing knives and hatchets into school. Simultaneously, he was a good student. His father continued trading farms although he became more and more unsuccessful.
		squ	R.MC/Can	= *Compromising personality tensions maternal dominance.*	
	S.Ura/Lib/I	opp	R.Mer/Ari/VII	= *Scattered energies, nervousness, haste, eccentricity, excitement, trouble-making; meddlesome, erratic, brutal, quarrelsome, tactless, highly strung, contradictory.*	
		squ	R.MC/Can	= *Changes of profession, precipitancy, upsets, sudden turns for the worse, checquered career; unreliable, temperamental.*	
1897	S.Jup/Cap/III	opp	R.Node/Can/IX	= *Lack of fellowship, unstable relationships, one's gain first, social-climbing, anti-social conduct; hypocritical.*	Each time his father failed, Adolf was forced to change schools.
1898	S.Node/Can/IX	conj	R.MC/Can	= *Exploiting others, difficult relationships, inability to act with others; selfish, inconstant, aggravating, unpopular.*	He entered a cloister school of Benedictines and worshipped the Abbot, but his behaviour contradicted his expressed desire to become a religious man. After one year he again went to public school, and continually bullied others.
		squ	R.Mer/Ari/VII	= *Using social contact for benefit, gossip, disturbed relations, superficial contacts; disloyal, unpopular, unsociable.*	
1899	S.Moon/Cap/III	opp	R.Node/Can/IX	= *Wanting relationships but becoming estranged, lack of adaptability, inability to live with one's family; frustrated, changeable, flighty, easily injured.*	He became disillusioned with his family after his brother died. His attention in school deteriorated until he was not promoted to secondary school.
1901	S.ASC/Sco/I	opp	R.Sun/Tau/VII	= *Disadvantages through others (father), separations; pushy, ambitious, disliked, boisterous, braggardly, self-seeking.*	He argued with his father about an ambition to be a painter. His views of himself were inflated. He was also accused of sexual perver-

	S.Jup/Cap/III	squ	R.ASC/Lib	=	*Desire for importance, showing off, bragging, hypocrisy, conflicts with others; wasteful, conceited.*	sities by the school authorities. Due to a sexual deformity (undescended testicle), puberty was difficult for him, and he compensated by making perpetual trouble for his schoolmasters. His behaviour ranged from shyness to extreme violence and anger.
		squ	R.Ura/Lib/XII	=	*Opportunities missed, philosophical arguments, non-conformity, rebelliousness, conflicts with superiors, rabble-rousing; anarchistic, trouble-making, provocative, argumentative.*	
	S.Ura/Sco/I	opp	R.Sun/Tau/VII	=	*Individualism to the point of anarchy, overpowering personality, upheaval, forced readjustments, occasional violence; excitable, rebellious, irrational, magnetic.*	
1903	S.Sun/Tau/VII	squ	R.Sat/Leo/X	=	*Inferiority complex, difficult struggles, cruel father, separation from father, ill-health, pessimism, misunderstood.*	His father became more violent, but then suddenly suffered a painful death. Adolf was then raised by his mother and her sisters in a totally feminine environment. His mother became the light of his life again. Upon taking his first communion he spat the host back onto the altar. Although he was well treated at home, he became successively more lazy and unreasonable at school. He maintained that this was the result of his father's irresponsible and cruel behaviour.
	S.Moon/Cap/III	squ	R.ASC/Lib	=	*Close contact with mother, maternal care, obliging, adaptability, easily moved, femininity, sympathy.*	
		squ	R.Ura/Lib/XII	=	*Tragic loves, peculiar interests, emotional tension, interest in the occult, strain, independence desired; abrupt.*	
	S.Node/Leo/X	squ	R.Sun/Tau/VII	=	*Estrangement from father, clinging to associations (mother), short-lived associations, disharmonious with others.*	
1904	S.Mars/Gem/VIII	conj	R.Nep/Gem/VIII	=	*Longing for the impossible, treachery, lack of energy, dissatisfaction, romanticism, escapism; uncontrolled, imaginative, revelling, fantastic.*	He revelled in the fantasy that he was a great man, and first dreamed of power. He was very slight in build, and it was suspected at this time that he had inherited the lung trouble which killed his father. He fantasized about this for the rest of his life.
	S.Ven/Gem/VIII	conj	R.Nep/Gem/VIII	=	*Delicate constitution, erotic abherations, false sense of love, hero worship, idealism, artists, dreamers, mystics; unrealistic, weak.*	
1905	S.Sun/Tau/VIII	conj	R.Mars/Tau/VII	=	*Desire to be in the lime-light, competition, danger, quarrels, contention, dissidence, brutality, violence, upsets.*	Since he could not reconcile his fantasies with school he dropped out, became lazier and more violent, but still desired to become a great artist.
		conj	R.Ven/Tau/VIII	=	*Artistic ability, romanticism, lack of recognition.*	
1906	S.Jup/Cap/IV	opp	R.MC/Can	=	*Fluctuating circumstances, desire for importance, mis-placed self-confidence, risks; materialistic.*	Adolf left home for art school in Vienna, where he was continually refused promotion. He applied for a place in architectural school, but was rejected because he had not completed secondary school.
		squ	R.Mer/Ari/VII	=	*Negligence, frivolity, exaggeration, failures, arrogance, unreliability; undisciplined, dishonest, imprudent.*	
1907	S.MC/Leo/X	conj	R.Sat/Leo/X	=	*A hard life, slow and difficult advancement.*	He was penniless and lonely. He felt that there was a conspiracy against his greatness, and this depressed him even further. He had difficulty making relationships, especially with women. His unproven lung ailment was the cause of much anxiety.
	S.Mer/Tau/VIII	squ	R.Sat/Leo/X	=	*Awkwardness, unhappiness, inhibitions, thrift; suspicious, defensive, shy, graceless, melancholic.*	
	S.Sat/Vir/XI	squ	R.Nep/Gem/VIII	=	*Psychosomatic illness, insecurity, public troubles, secret enmities, paranoia, peculiar neuroses, self-torment; morose.*	
1908	S.Moon/Cap/IV	opp	R.MC/Can	=	*Changing objectives, checquered career, difficulties with women, short-lived professions, vacillation; indecisive.*	His mother died of cancer and Adolf's family life terminated. He remained in abject poverty, and lived with his friend, Hanisch, in a hostel frequented by homosexual vagrants. Although he finally accused his friend of theft, this was the only person he associated with. Again he vacillated between insatiable lust for power, and total dejection and loneliness.
		squ	R.Mer/Ari/VII	=	*Hypersensitivity, anxiety, erratic intelligence, nerves; highly strung, misunderstood, frustrated ideas.*	
	S.Ven/Gem/VIII	conj	R.Plu/Gem/VIII	=	*Insatiable loves, destructive relationships, compulsive attractions, heightened sexuality without satisfaction.*	
	S.Mars/Gem/VIII	conj	R.Plu/Gem/VIII	=	*Ruthlessness, cruelty, imposing one's will upon others, power mania, sadism; obsessive, violent, homicidal, destructive.*	
1910	S.MC/Leo/X	squ	R.Ven/Tau/VIII	=	*Self-admiration, loss of friends and lovers, jealousy, conceit.*	After his abortive accusations to police about his former friend, he left Vienna with a Jew clothes salesman, Neumann. His behaviour with others was perfunctory and repellant, although he wished that others would
		squ	R.Mars/Tau/VIII	=	*Conflict with superiors, loss of position, misplaced aggression, premature actions, failures; strained, restless.*	

	S.Mer/Tau/VIII	conj	R.Mars/Tau/VIII	= *Sharp tongue, quick wit, incurring the wrath of others, repartee, penetrating intellect; decisive, rash, tactless.*	recognize his greatness.
1911	S.Jup/Aqu/IV	squ	R.Sun/Tau/VII	= *Pretention, arrogance, conflicts with authorities, bad taste; undisciplined.*	He was arrested for theft, but it was never proven. He worked painting furniture and curios, but was unreliable and usually had to give up his commissions due to an inability to complete them.
	S.Mer/Tau/VIII	conj	R.Ven/Tau/VIII	= *Artistic aspirations, vanity, superficiality, hedonism, short-lived relationships, flighty, ostentatious.*	
1913	S.Moon/Aqu/IV	squ	R.Sun/Tau/VII	= *Hypersensitivity, ill-health, intelligence, financial difficulties, unfortunate with women, schizophrenia; self-doubting, nervous, immoderate, gifted.*	He moved to Munich, where he became weaker and less able to work than before. He avoided women while idolizing them from a distance.
1914	S.ASC/Sco/I	squ	R.Sat/Leo/X	= *Poverty, poor health, maltreatment, sad, inhibiting environment, alienation, depression, frailty; lonely, repressed.*	He wandered the streets as a beggar, becoming dirtier and more alienated. He enlisted in the military, but was rejected due to poor health.
	S.Ura/Sco/I	squ	R.Sat/Leo/X	= *Tension, strain, repressed by others, emotional conflicts, rebellion, upsetting others, separations, limited freedom.*	
1917	S.ASC/Sco/II	opp	R.Mars/Tau/VIII	= *Aggression, physical violence, conflicts, contention, coarse, pleasure-seeking, tensions,*	Eventually he was accepted and served in World War I as an orderly. He was insanely patriotic and aggressive, winning the Iron Cross Ist and 2nd grades during the war. His whole being was channeled towards hatred of the enemy. He was gassed and temporarily blinded, necessitating hospitalization. He continued to believe that he was superior to his commanding officers.
		opp	R.Ven/Tau/VIII	= *attraction to unsavoury types.*	
	S.Node/Leo/X	conj	R.Sat/Leo/X	= *Unhappy relationships, loyalty, severity, inhibition; ungratified.*	
	S.Ura/Sco/II	opp	R.Mars/Tau/VIII	= *Struggle for survival, injuries, violence, temper, rage, fury, fighting spirit, dissatisfaction, argumentative.*	
		opp	R.Ven/Tau/VIII	= *Inconstancy, nervous troubles, rebellion, estrangements.*	
1920	S.Sun/Gem/VIII	conj	R.Nep/Gem/VIII	= *Sensitivity, otherworldness, psychic abilities, inspiration, visionary attitudes; mediumistic, unrealistic.*	He became interested in astrology through the Thule Occult Society, and joined the German Workers Party as head of propaganda. When there was a right-wing coup, he was imprisoned for one month, although he was also elevated to President of the tiny Party afterwards.
	S.Node/Leo/X	squ	R.Mars/Tau/VIII	= *Arguments, separations, dissident groups, anti-social conduct, breakdown of relationships, lack of tact; trouble-making.*	
		squ	R.Ven/Tau/VIII	= *Difficulties with women, separations, lack of adaptability.*	
1923	S.Plu/Can/IX	opp	R.Moon/Cap/III	= *Violent emotions, shocks, upheavals, insane demands, tantrums, fanatic attachments; devouring, tormented, insatiable, sadistic.*	His Münich Beer-Hall Putsch attempted an overthrow of the government, but failed and landed him in jail.
1924	S.Sun/Gem/VIII	conj	R.Plu/Gem/VIII	= *Lust for power, craving for rulership, great advances and equivalent reversals, a highly fated individual; ruthless, insanely ambitious, daemonic.*	While imprisoned he wrote "Mein Kampf" (My Struggle) and became a hero of his Party. He began again to desire complete overthrow of the government by brutality, being able to verbally inflame his colleagues into violent frenzy.
	S.Plu/Can/IX	opp	R.Jup/Cap/III	= *Fanatical aims, taking risks, great gains and losses, financial disaster, fall from power, conflict with authorities, arrest; seditious.*	
1925	S.MC/Vir/XI	squ	R.Nep/Gem/VIII	= *Ill luck, lack of contact with reality, misguided emotions, easily deceived, inferiority complex, mental disturbance.*	When he was freed he lived in poverty with his sister. The government banned him from making public speeches. He gained absolute power in his Party by discrediting others for their lack of voilence, and frequently became insanely excited while writing the second part of his book. He continually made promises to the government that he advocated peaceful politics, but his actions belied this.
	S.Jup/Aqu/IV	opp	R.Sat/Leo/X	= *Discontent, instability, legal troubles, changing life-style; pessimistic, gloomy, depressive, prosaic.*	
	S.Mer/Gem/VIII	conj	R.Nep/Gem/VIII	= *Imaginative intellect; lyrical, poetic, idealistic, sensitive, deluded, inspired, credulous, deceptive.*	
1926	S.Nep/Can/IX	opp	R.Moon/Cap/III	= *Living in unreality, deception, fraud, spurious supernatural contacts, scandal, longing for the impossible.*	He accused both his party associates and the government of being homosexual conspirators.
1927	S.Moon/Aqu/IV	opp	R.Sat/Leo/X	= *Inferiority complex, melancholy, pessimism, lack of gratification, estrangement, anxiety, money trouble; fearful.*	He spoke at the Nuremburg Rally of 1927, and while gaining support for his party, he had financial troubles due to the inflation of the mark.

Year						
1928	S.Jup/Aqu/IV	squ	R.Mars/Tau/VIII	=	*Rebelliousness, trouble with authorities, hatred of rules and restrictions, exaggerated independence; manic.*	The authorities again restricted him from public speeches. He finally met an aristocratic circle of friends and used the women for gaining financial assistance for his party. His platform became primarily anti-Jewish.
		squ	R.Ven/Tau/VIII	=	*Waste, excess emotion, many loves, infidelity, indulgence; sybaritic, indolent, luxury-loving.*	
	S.Nep/Can/IX	opp	R.Jup/Cap/III	=	*Loss through speculation, unbalanced religious enthusiasm, gambling, scandal, conflict between the real and the ideal.*	
1929	S.MC/Vir/XI	squ	R.Plu/Gem/VIII	=	*Abuse of power, alienating others, ruin, disasters, many crises, sudden turns of fate; danger-loving, outspoken, abusive.*	The Nazi Party was formed with Hitler as leader, but roundly lost the election against Hindenburg. He had only a small contingent of supporters, but wrote many articles in newspapers owned by his friends. His ideas became very clear and lucid.
	S.Mer/Gem/VIII	conj	R.Plu/Gem/VIII	=	*Great influence through speaking and writing, sharp intellect, desire to be intellectually superior, irritation; influential, persuasive, implacable, dynamic, deranged.*	
1930	S.Moon/Aqu/IV	squ	R.Mars/Tau/VIII	=	*Fanatical independence, intolerance, rebelliousness, violent reactions, temper-tantrums, fits, aggression, rashness,*	As he was unable and unwilling to co-operate with anyone else, he lost another election but gained greater support from disenchanted officers and hooligans in Munich. He lived with his young niece.
		squ	R.Ven/Tau/VIII	=	*Frustrated loves, females troublesome, ungratified desires; overly romantic.*	
1931	S.Plu/Can/IX	conj	R.Node/Can/IX	=	*Fated relationships, tragic loves, wielding influence over a great many people, fanatical urge for recognition, a public figure, powerful friends and lovers, the masses.*	When his niece committed suicide, he began living with Eva Braun. Support gathered, and the Nazis benefited from the financial troubles of the government.
1932	S.ASC/Sag/II	opp	R.Nep/Gem/VIII	=	*Inability to succeed, influenced by others, betrayals, weak constitution, dishonesty; hypocondriac, escapist.*	The elected government weakened but, although the Nazis and their allies held a majority, Hitler did not yet want total power. Secret intrigues against Hindenburg were mounted. Compromises were necessary.
	S.Ura/Sag/II	opp	R.Nep/Gem/VIII	=	*Instability, impossible ideals, extreme emotion, nervous sensitivity, confusion; psychic, highly strung, easily upset.*	
1935	S.Node/Vir/XI	squ	R.Nep/Gem/VIII	=	*Deceiving or tricking others, exploitation, disappointed relationships, separation, alienation, anti-social behaviour, subversive groups, spying, secret organizations.*	Hitler became Chancellor in 1934, and deceived Britain and Europe to allow Germany to rearm. The Third Reich was formed and other nations were in dissaray at Hitler's tactics.
1936	S.ASC/Sag/II	opp	R.Plu/Gem/VIII	=	*Repulsive behaviour, accidents, injuries, drastic changes in circumstances, violent disputes, fanatical urge to dominate.*	Hitler's SA troops began a campaign of terror, assassinating all those who opposed them within Germany. He also made an alliance with the Italian Fascist Mussolini for the domination of Europe. Everyone in Hitler's way was unceremoniously annihilated.
	S.Ura/Sag/II	opp	R.Plu/Gem/VIII	=	*Fanaticism, violence, destruction mania, subversion, danger, accidents; rapacious, nervous, impatient, compulsive.*	
	S.Plu/Can/IX	squ	R.Ura/Lib/XII	=	*(Same as the above, but exaggerated)*	
	S.Plu/Can/IX	squ	R.ASC/Lib	=	*Repulsive behaviour, exercise of power, unusual contacts, magical or psychic powers, control over the masses; compelling, influential, insatiable, brutal, crude, ruthless.*	
1937	S.Nep/Can/IX	conj	R.Node/Can/IX	=	*Idealistic associations, expecting the impossible from others, undermined relations, deceptive behaviour.*	Although his earlier policies were to include the voice of the masses, his power became a majority of one, and he ruthlessly eliminated all dissenters.
1938	S.Sun/Gem conj to the IXth cusp			=	*Successful travel, aspirations. (the death-conception point)*	In 1937 he annexed Austria to "free the Austrian people". Czechoslovakia and Poland followed. The British and French entered the war, which had disastrous effects upon the Reich. Hitler had previously managed to separate the European countries from each other.
1939	S.Node/Vir/XI	squ	R.Plu/Gem/VIII	=	*Burdensome relationships, common tragic experiences, suffering through associations, destructive unions, revolutionary organizations, gangsters, subversive activities, the violent termination of an association.*	
1940	S.Nep/Can/IX	squ	R.Ura/Lib/XII	=	*Instability, impossible ideals, extreme emotion, nervous sensitivity, confusion, catastrophes, heavy losses; fanatical.*	Denmark and Norway were invaded. Hitler branched out with conquests over Europe. The Italians and Mussolini were weak and Hitler was forced to cover-up for them in the Mediterranean.
		squ	R.ASC/Lib	=	*Influenced by others, inability to succeed, betrayals, dishonesty, disappointment, escapism; moody, fraudulent.*	

1941	S.Mars/Can/IX	opp	R.Moon/Cap/III	= *Rebelliousness, intolerance, fanatical independence, violent reactions, temper-tantrums, fear of restriction, rashness, aggression, crudeness.*	Europe was a blood-bath, and the concentration camps were decimating Jews and enemies of the Reich. The USA and Russia entered the war, making two fronts. Hitler's anger and paranoia were rampant. He isolated himself and fantasized more and more.
	S.Ven/Can/IX	opp	R.Moon/Cap/III	= *Frustration through women, over-indulgence, moodiness, ungratified desires, maltreatment, carelessness.*	
1942	S.Plu/Can/X	conj	R.MC/Can	= *Abuse of power, alienating others, ruin, disgrace, disasters, many crises, sudden turns of fate; danger-loving, anti-social, outspoken, abusive, purposefully difficult.*	The two-front split led to defeats at Stalingrad and El Alamein. Hitler grew paranoid about the SS and his own generals.
1943	S.Jup/Pis/V	squ	R.Nep/Gem/VIII	= *Loss through speculation, unbalanced religious views, gambling, scandal, instability, waste, real-ideal conflict.*	The extermination of the Jews accelerated. Hitler began being dependent upon drugs to cure suspected Addison's Syndrome, and he became a doubtful leader to his nation, although his quest was still fanatically pursued.
	S.Plu/Can/X	squ	R.Mer/Ari/VII	= *Nervous breakdown, libelous speech, hasty thinking and speaking, over-estimation of self, overtaxing strength, tantrums, back-biting, fanatically critical.*	
1944	S.Sat/Lib/XII	squ	R.Moon/Cap/III	= *Inferiority complex, melancholy, pessimism, separation (possibly death), lack of gratification, money troubles, maladjustment, doubt; self-protective, fearful.*	Hitler was almost assassinated by a group of his generals. Germany had monetary problems, and the manufacture of war materials suffered from allied bombings.
1945	S.Mars/Can/IX	opp	R.Jup/Cap/III	= *Rebelliousness, trouble with authorities, hatred of rules and restrictions, exaggerated independence, haste, disputes.*	His fear of his own staff heightened until he rarely left his bunker in Berlin. The Allies invaded Germany and destroyed the very ground around him. He still believed that Germany would win the war and sent millions to their deaths in hopeless defence of the Fatherland. When he finally realized the fight was hopeless, he and his paramour Eva Braun took cyanide.
	S.Venus/Can/IX	opp	R.Jup/Cap/III	= *Conflicts, laziness, waste, excessive emotion, many loves, infidelity, self indulgence; vain, luxury-loving.*	
	S.Sat/Lib/XII	squ	R.Jup/Cap/III	= *Discontent, instability, legal troubles, changing life-style, self-destruction, pessimism; gloomy, depressive, formal.*	
	S.Moon/Pis/V	squ	R.Nep/Gem/VIII	= *Living in unreality, deception, spurious supernatural contacts, ill-health, drugs, addiction; unstable, deluded, weak.*	

The complete analysis of solar arc directions for Adolf Hitler very accurately covers the developments during his lifetime. The patterns of behaviour which manifested in his youth continued to determine his behaviour throughout his life until his suicide in the Berlin Bunker in 1945. Hitler's solar arcs are appropriate becuase there is a definite predominance of Mars, Saturn, Uranus and Pluto aspects as well as many aspects to the VIII house, all of which indicate excessive violence. When planets are conjunct in the birth horoscope — in Hitler's case, Neptune-Pluto, Ascendant-Uranus, Venus-Mars and Moon-Jupiter — they travel together through the signs, producing additional emphasis upon their qualities. Hitler's horoscope is one of the few which clearly indicates the time of death in the Time Scale, with Pluto registering at the age of 56. While Hitler's solar arcs are extreme, they do reflect the reality of the greatest monster of the Twentieth Century.

The Solar Return

The *Solar Return* is a technique for predicting events which occur during any year in life — from birthday to birthday. The character of a year is implicit in the positions of the planets at the precise moment when the Sun makes its yearly return to the exact degree, minute and second it occupied at the moment of birth (For computation details, see Appendix D). When this moment is determined, the horoscope is erected and compared to the positions in the radix horoscope. The resultant aspects define a series of events throughout the year — one for each planet and personal point.

The ascendant in the solar return is equivalent to the birthday beginning the year in question. Since there are 360° around the horoscope and 365 days in a year, each degree from the ascendant through the signs in a counter-clockwise direction is approximately equal to one day

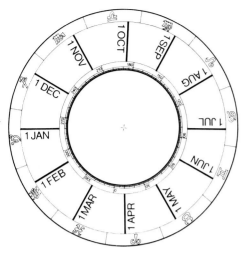

Figure XI.10 Solar Return Day Determination. The relationship between the degrees of the horoscope and the days during a year are noted in red.

[5] The Sun moves more or less than one degree each day, so the solar return formula of one degree equals one day is an approximation. The use of Leap Years also effects the correlation between the zodical position of the Sun and the calendar date.

in the year (Figure XI.10). Each thirty degree increment around the horoscope is approximately equal to one month. Every planet and personal point (ASC and MC) can be located to within two days throughout the year. When a planet is located, the aspects it makes to radix planets and personal points are interpreted.

The structure of the solar return follows the symbolic division of the zodiac. From the birthday-ascendant until the descendant exactly one-half year later, all planets in the lower half of the horoscope indicate events which are *subjective, unconscious* and *indirect,* while the second half of the year shows the planets which are *objective, conscious* and *direct.* The aspects within the solar return connect events throughout the year to each other. Conjunctions indicate events which happen in rapid succession; sextiles and trines indicate events which link up harmoniously; and squares and oppositions indicate events which tension each other. A planetary position can relate to previous events in the year and in turn condition later events.

Planetary positions in the solar return denote events, frames of mind, individuals, or the behaviour of those in one's environment, according to the aspects they make to the birth horoscope. While the events are very accurately located in time, their real impact is difficult to determine as they are actually transits.

The solar return planetary positions do not create events themselves, but rather *condition* latent mechanisms in the birth horoscope. The solar return is an opportunity for the individual to comprehend his life mechanisms through specific events each year. A planet in the solar return is a medium through which combinations of birth planets actualize themselves. When a solar return planet aspects three or more birth horoscope planets, the archetypal qualities involved are blended through the event. Each year of life consists of permutations of our inherent structure carried through mundane events. The purpose of the solar return is to determine, test and prove the reality of archetypal modes of behaviour which are determinate factors in our lives.

The ascendant in the solar return indicates the Personality the individual assumes throughout the entire year. Since the calendar is slightly irregular in relation to the movement of the Sun through the zodiac,[5] the registration time of the Sun's return can be on the actual calendar date of the birthday, or on the day before or after the calendar birthday. Throughout life the individual has an opportunity to experience all twelve ascendants, although not necessarily in succession. This is the reason why some years an individual feels either disoriented or highly focused — he is temporarily donning a *new* (Solar return) personality and comparing it to his *essential* (radix) personality. The same principle holds true for the MC-Ego. Every year the position of the MC in the solar return varies, and therefore the direction and desires of the individual undergo short-term variations. A great value of the solar return is that the individual can prepare for this yearly change of focus and learn through time how to find his essence behind the illusion of temporal experiences.

The following example solar return is for the revolutionary **Lenin (Vladimir Ilyich Ulyanov)** during the year 1917-1918 (Figure XI.11). Although Lenin's birthday is 22 April 1870, the Sun returns to its position at the time of his birth, 2° Taurus 24′ (See Horoscope 29), on 23 April 1917 at 5.46 a.m. GMT. A horoscope is constructed as though he were born in Petrograd (later Leningrad), where he lived at the time. The ascendant of 14° Gemini 19′ is equivalent to 23 April 1917. The solar return governs the time from 23 April 1917 until 22 April 1918.

An interesting peculiarity of Lenin's solar return is that during the year 1918, Russia changed its calendar system from the antique and incorrect Julian Calendar to the Gregorian Calendar, which most of Europe had used since 1752. On 14 February 1918, 13 days were added to the Julian Calendar, bringing it into synchronization with the Gregorian Calendar. On the solar return horoscope both dates will be given. Lenin's birthday was 23 April 1917 (Gregorian), and 10 April 1917 (Julian).

In addition to the registration times of the planets and personal points in the solar return, the house cusps are also important. The locations of the house cusps show when changes in the pattern of the year occur.

A factor to keep in mind when interpreting solar returns is that events are often in the process of formation from days to weeks before they happen, and have future repercussions as well. Each planetary position produces an event or frame of mind which has a duration of a few days, but the influence's residue remains until the next planet occurs. This is shown in the

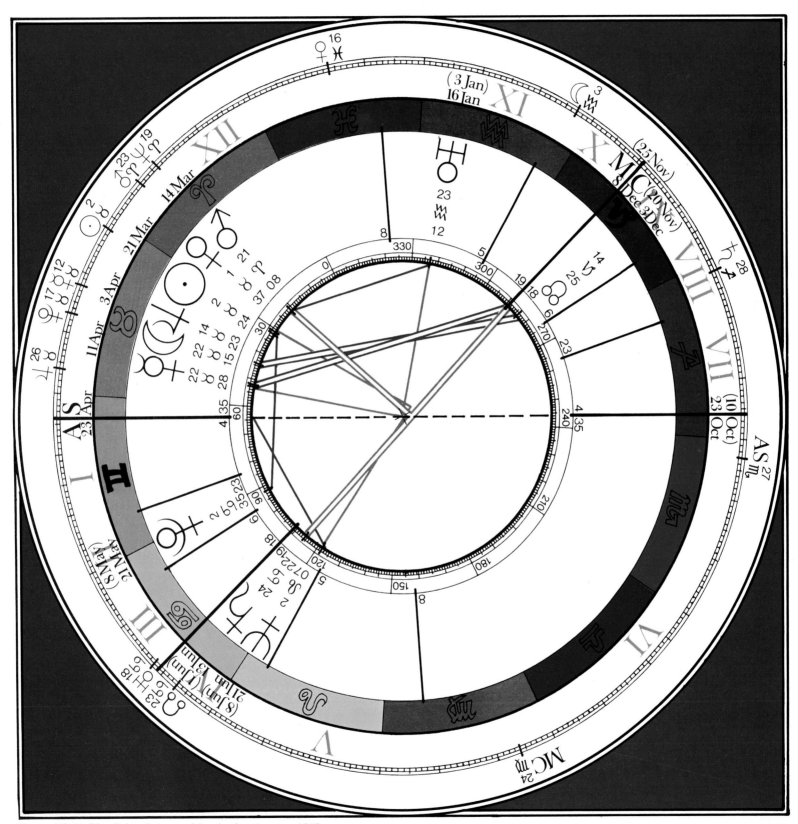

Figure XI.11 The Solar Return of Lenin for the year 1917.

vacant portion of Lenin's solar return. from the registration of Neptune in Leo on 29 May 1917, until the Descendant on 10 October 1917, during which time Lenin was forced to go into hiding from the police before the October Revolution. The function of the solar return is not to identify *all* events during a year, but rather to indicate those situations which are critical to the individual himself.

(The Julian dates are shown in italics under the Gregorian dates.)

Date	Solar Return	to	Radix Horoscope	Interpretation	Life Events (All dates given in Gregorian Calendar)
23 Apr *10 Apr*	ASC/Gem	opp	R.ASC/Sco	= *Dualism, compromise instead of violence, a mask, writing and speaking, opposing personalities.*	Lenin returned to Petrograd from exile in Switzerland on 16 April to find a conflict between his Bolsheviks and the three other parties composing the Provisional Government.
		tri	R.Moon/Aqu/II	= *Making many acquaintances, harmonious attitudes, environmental splits, emotionally idealistic.*	
21 May *8 May*	Plu/Can/II	opp	R.Sat/Sag/I	= *Severity, use of force, success denied, heavy losses, violence, change in philosophy, opposition.*	His "April Theses" were presented, but were voted down because they opposed the continuance of the German War. Lenin was forced to adopt and demand a policy of "All power to the Soviets". Continuous demonstrations by the peasants amplified this.
		sex	R.Sun/Tau/V	= *Great achievements, leadership, belief in a mission, organizing ability, forceful, magnetic, influential.*	
13 Jun *1 Jun*	Sat/Can/IV	conj	R.Node/Can/VIII	= *Inhibited associations, unhappy relationships (women), depression due to others, separations.*	He lost control of the government to Kerensky in an election and was branded a traitor. The government tried to continue WWI, but the peasants refused to fight. Lenin had to wait until the right time for takeover presented itself. He was separated from his wife over policies. Russia lacked food and industrial production, so the pressure upon all politicians was great. At the Ist All-Russian Congress of the Soviets, Lenin's Bolsheviks got only ¹/₈th of the votes, and his guidance was even rejected by those in his own party.
		sex	R.MC/Vir	= *Slow development, help from elders, clinging to hopes, conscientious, patient, pursuit of objectives.*	
		tri	R.ASC/Sco	= *Reservation, composed, impenetrable, retiring, paternal, maturity, restrictive separations.*	
		squ	R.Nep/Ari/IV	= *Insecurity, thwarted ambitions, paranoia, self torment, public troubles, secret enmities.*	
		squ	R.Mars/Ari/V	= *Energy crises, disputes, separations, harshness, brutality, vengeance, non-submission.*	
		sex	R.Jup/Tau/VI	= *Patience, arduous tasks, happy in seclusion, duty, motivation expands, determination; conscientious.*	
21 Jun *10 Jun*	Nep/Leo/IV	opp	R.Moon/Aqu/II	= *Living in unreality, deception, ill-health, scandals, longing for the impossible, delusion, dependence.*	Lenin's health was poor and he was totally governed by circumstances beyond his control. His hard-line attitudes were rejected by the Provos, and he was forced to escape to Finland.
		squ	R.Sun/Tau/V	= *Illness, unlucky speculation, scandal, deception, lack of self-control, weak leadership, exploitation.*	
23 Oct *10 Oct*	DES/Sag			= *Objective half-year is far-sighted, philosophical, and realized.*	Lenin returned to Petrograd just before the October Revolution on the 24th. He became Chairman.
3 Dec *20 Nov*	Node/Cap/IX	sex	R.Ven/Pis/III	= *Engaging personality, ability to please, popular, obliging, pleasant experiences, harmonious association.*	Russia was financially depleted and attacked by the Germans on the Western Front. Lenin's desire for peace and reconstruction was denied by the Constituent Assembly and the Red Guard was formed to revolutionize the people. There was internal dissention among the leaders and Lenin proposed a decree allowing for the future disbanding of all assemblies.
		tri	R.Mer/Tau/VI	= *Sociable, business associations, exchanging ideas with others, societies, fellowship, joint interests.*	
		tri	R.Plu/Tau/VI	= *A changed relationship to the world (revolutionary!), fateful relationships.*	
		opp	R.Ura/Can/VIII	= *Disturbing influence upon others, quarrels, irritation, separations, restlessness, short-lived relationships.*	
8 Dec *25 Nov*	MC/Cap	squ	R.Mars/Ari/V	= *Conflict with superiors, misplaced aggression, premature actions, loss of position, disputes, failure.*	Negotiations for the end of the war with Germany and Austro-Hungary began with Lenin being unco-operative. This play for time led to the threat of German advances into Russia. Lenin had a crisis of conscience, as he did not want to yield, but feared the collapse of the Soviets. The negotiations were abandoned and the coalition with the Social Revolutionaries
		squ	R.Nep/Ari/IV	= *Vague objectives, ill luck, lack of contact with reality, deception, mental disturbance, confusion, haplessness.*	
		opp	R.Node/Can/VIII	= *Difficulties in joint activities, contemplation of the withdrawl from an association.*	

		tri	R.MC/Vir	= *Practicalities of assertion rest upon details.*	was short-lived. Lenin sought support from revolutionary socialists in other European countries, but did not succeed.
		opp	R.Ura/Can/VIII	= *Many changes, precipitancy, upsets, hastiness, heroism, sudden turns for the worse, chequered successes.*	Lenin decreed that proportional representation within the government would be ended and nationalized major industries. Lenin virtually never saw his wife during this time, and lived with another woman while writing policy speeches.
		tri	R.Plu/Tau/VI	= *Desire for power, attained success, organizing, independence desired, an important revolutionary task.*	
		sex	R.Ven/Pis/III	= *Individual love and affection, well-loved, felicitous contacts, artistic communications.*	
16 Jan *3 Jan*	Ura/Aqu/XI	sex	R.Mars/Ari/V	= *Sudden emergence of extraordinary energy, courage, attaining goals, unusual events, decisions.*	On 2 January there was an assassination attempt on Lenin. The German demands for truce were brutal and the negotiations were ended again. His policy of peaceful termination of the war forced him to disband the Soviet Constituent Assembly and he threatened to resign from chancellorship.
		squ	R.Jup/Tau/VI	= *Missed opportunity, philosophical arguments, rebelliousness, conflicts with others, anarchy.*	
		squ	R.ASC/Sco	= *Causing upsets, unexpected events, disturbing events, quick changes, non-conformity.*	

CALENDAR CHANGES FROM JULIAN TO GREGORIAN ON THE 14th FEBRUARY, 1918.

14 Mar	Mars/Ari/XII	conj	R.Nep/Ari/IV	= *Longing for the impossible, treachery, dissatisfaction, being harmed, secret enmities.*	The Brest-Litovsk Treaty was signed, giving away 32% of all Russian land. The economic and social aftermath was disastrous. The White Guards returned from war and fought the Bolsheviks for power. Criticism was banned, and the peasants were militantly organized. Lenin left Petrograd for Moscow and the Kremlin. German troops still occupied Kiev and threatened Russian security.
		conj	R.Mars/Ari/V	= *Ruthlessness, aggressive energies, violence, disputes.*	
		squ	R.Ura/Can/VIII	= *Struggle for survival, violence, temper, rage, urge for freedom, fighting spirit, aggression.*	
		squ	R.Node/Can/VIII	= *Arguments, separations, dissidents, disputes, breakdown of relationships, trouble-making.*	
19 Mar	Ven/Tau/XII	conj	R.Sun/Tau/V	= *Love affairs, romanticism, praise, recognition, help from the opposite sex, demonstrative.*	The difficult organization of the country after the end of the war was "idealism confronting reality". Lenin organized subversive groups to restore property to the peasants throughout Russia.
		squ	R.Moon/Aqu/II	= *Disagreements, a difficult birth, indulgence, moodiness, poverty, ungratified desires.*	
21 Mar	Sun Returns to XIIth House			= *Reserve, secret stability, absorption, moodiness, seclusion; self-sacrificial.*	Lenin had difficulties. The populace believed that he had given away too much to Germany, so many towns revolted against the Germans and repelled them. He disagreed with Trotsky about the evacuation of Czech troops still on the Western Front.
		squ	R.Moon/Aqu/II	= *Hypersensitivity, intelligent action, ambition, financial difficulties, practical matters tension ideals.*	
3 Apr	Jup/Tau/XII	sex	R.Ura/Can/VIII	= *Originality, leadership in seclusion, integrity, fortunate ideas, sudden relationships, heroism.*	Lenin feared wholesale intervention as the Japanese entered Vladavostok with the British, but he remained silent and concentrated upon the many domestic problems which produced continuous rioting.
		sex	R.Ven/Pis/III	= *Charm, tact, comfortable life, love of amusement, warm-heartedness, well-liked, expansive.*	
11 Apr	Mer/Tau/XII	sex	R.Node/Can/VIII	= *Social and business contacts, exchanging ideas with others, membership in societies, joint interests.*	His tasks were mainly supervision of the organization of the government and compromises with his colleagues — especially Trotsky. They annihilated and disbanded the Black Guards and anarchists. Although the entire country was totally chaotic, his policies and leadership were respected by the people as truly unyielding. His political motives changed from earlier idealism to the recognition that both he and the people had to be re-educated.
		tri	R.MC/Vir	= *Meditating and reflecting, planning, professional advancement, well-defined aims, rapid progress.*	
	Moon/Tau/XII	conj	R.Jup/Tau/VI	= *Sociability, success, generosity, good fortune, practical idealism, humanitarian, civilized, hopeful.*	
		sex	R.Node/Can/VIII	= *Many associations, happy unions, contact with women, emotional relationships, communal activities.*	
		tri	R.MC/Vir	= *Deep sentiment, great aspirations, caring for others, domesticity, soul unions, spiritual relations with women.*	

When a planet in the solar return makes many aspects to planets in the radix horoscope, there are often contradictory influences at work. In these situations an entire range of qualities blend into the event. Thus the real complexity of life is illustrated, rather than a simple-minded and one-sided false picture. Every individual encounters both his positive and negative sides simultaneously throughout the events of his life, and all must be recognized for the attainment of unity.

Fate and Free Will

The question of free will is critical in astrology — especially in connection with prediction. Is life predetermined to the degree that the individual is chained to a specific series of events that cannot be changed?

The answer to this question in astrology is similar to the answer the physicist would give to the question of whether his "laws of the universe" are absolute and binding. *All natural laws are statistical laws,* and statistics takes into account the factor of uncertainty. The statistical laws of the physicist are valid in *most* situations, but by definition are not valid in *all* situations. Statistics imply that there must be deviations, otherwise the laws would be absolute and totally predictable. The same situation is true in astrology.

The importance of astrological or physical laws is that they are "workable models" which mathematically approximate reality and hold true in a majority of cases accurately enough to allow reasonable prediction. A light-bulb illuminates a room because electricity is assumed to follow the path of least resistance from its source to the bulb, but the true nature of electricity is unknown. Electricity has been discovered, harnessed and utilized through a process of "trial and error" which has betrayed certain of its qualities — barely enough to allow physicists to predict its behaviour. Astrologically, libido inevitably follows a path of least resistance (aspect connections) until it illuminates a certain part of the psycho-physical organism of an individual. The aspect patterns of the horoscope are analogous to the wiring scheme of a house. There are always local failures, alternations in the overall energy of the system and unpredictable events. The activations are, however, mainly predictable and the margin of error is minimal.

Jung believed that maximum free will was equivalent to maximum consciousness. The individual is never free to change most components of his being, but he has the option to be aware or unaware of these essential characteristics. The less conscious an individual is of his determining characteristics, the more mechanically he lives his life. Most individuals are so unaware of their true Self that they have no control at all over their lives. They fight against restrictions which are inherent in them, and never realize that they are Self-created. The conscious man understands that there are limiting factors integral to his being and that he must live with them in mind. He must make the best of the qualities he does possess and not waste time and life warring with inevitabilities. The individual who is not born beautiful is foolish to devote his/her life trying to counteract that fact. Everyone has limitations which are necessary to define the scope of his reality. The sooner an individual accepts the strictures he is born with, the more freedom he possesses. Limitations, like difficult events in life, function as mechanisms to awaken an individual from the undifferentiation of the unconscious, primitive being which resides within him.

Medical Diagnosis

The birth horoscope and techniques of prediction are useful in determining the state of an individual's health. Health is a gauge of the ease with which an individual relates to his body and to the external world. A lack of integration is "dis-ease". Physical disease is a resistance to oneself which manifests itself in the physical organism, while a healthy state is a dynamic equilibrium where all internal and external forces are circulated and utilized effectively. The flow of libido is metaphorical to the proper dynamic functioning of the psyche and the body. The components of the horoscope indicate bodily and psychic mechanisms:

Sun	= *Vitality, the heart and circulation, the whole organism.*
Moon	= *Soul, bodily fluids and lymphatic systems, menstruation.*
Dragon's Head	= *Astral body, hereditary factors.*
Ascendant	= *Physical appearance, birth, the environment, personality.*
The Planets	= *Cell and functional systems, the endocrine glands, the chakras.*
Aspect-patterns	= *System interrelationships.*
The Signs	= *The physiology.*
The Houses	= *The time factor of potential and release.*

(The specific correspondences are listed in Part VI.)

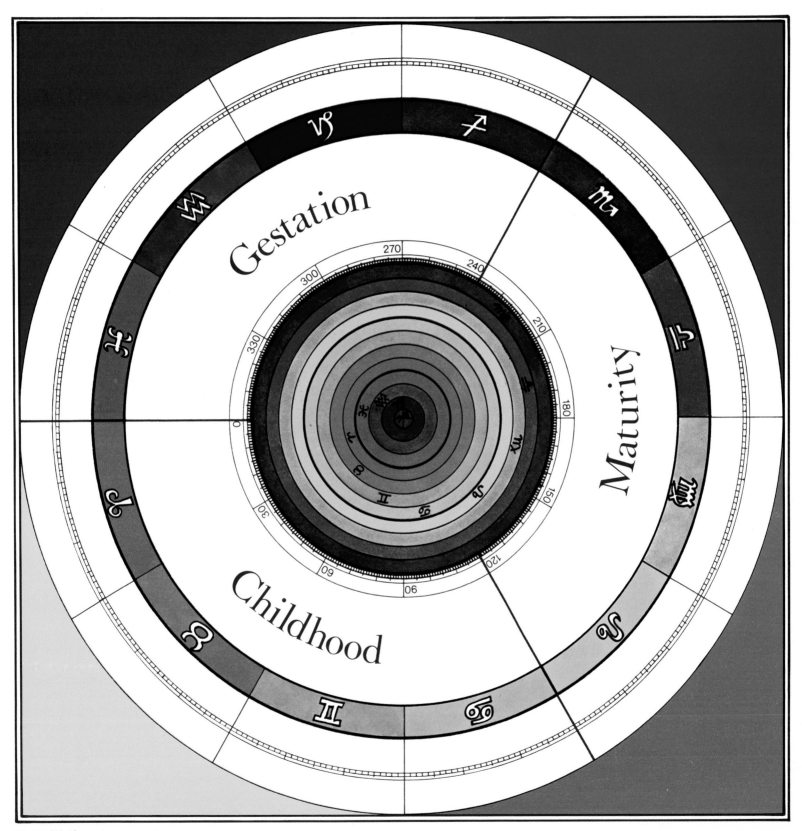

Figure XI.12

The structure of the horoscope indicates the *potential* for disease. The position of each planet in the Time Scale locates the time of its maximum affliction, and the sensitive points indicate other times in the life when the same or similar ailments are likely to manifest (especially square and opposition points).

The signs tenanted by malefic planets (Mars, Saturn, Uranus, Pluto and sometimes Neptune) or by planets afflicted by aspect, show the body parts affected. These positions in every horoscope determine the weakest bodily parts. Mars (inflammations, accidents, operations) in the sign Taurus would indicate a propensity for mumps, swollen glands in the neck, inflammations of the throat. In addition, the opposite sign can be reciprocally affected. Afflictions in Taurus (throat, tonsils) have a reciprocal effect upon the Scorpio parts (sex organs). To use commonly-known examples, the voice changes at puberty, and in other days castrati were valued for their voices. The body part opposites are shown graphically in medieval illustrations where the human body is wrapped around the inside of the zodiacal circle.

Disease or affliction is caused either by an exaggeration of the qualities of a planet (Jupiter exalted in Cancer produces overindulgence and weight gain), or a weak position (Sun in Aquarius, opposite its rulership Leo can produce heart trouble). Disease is imbalance.

The octave within which an affliction is indicated also gives information about the nature of the disease. The cylindrical Time Scale of the Four Octaves illustrates this hierarchy of disease and is analogous to the concept of the "Four Bodies" of Plato.

Octave of Transcendence = Spirit
Octave of Maturity = Mind
Octave of Childhood = Emotion
Octave of Gestation = Body

Every individual is conceived with a certain hereditary predisposition towards particular afflictions via the genetic code. All physical, emotional, mental and spiritual predispositions are activations of the genetic reservoir which links every individual back to the beginning of life on Earth. Disease occurs when latent propensity is echoed in external conditions which support manifestation. The octave in the horoscope which contains an afflicted planet tells much about the origin of diseases, and also how they may be cured.

Afflictions in the Gestation Octave indicate hereditary diseases, diseases or afflictions derived from the health of the mother, chronic diseases and faults in the *physical body* itself. If these diseases do not manifest by the time of birth, they do so when their square and opposition aspects occur during the life. These afflictions we come into the world possessing.

Afflictions in the Childhood Octave have their primary effect upon the *emotional body*. Brutality or accidents during delivery, improper care during the first years of life, childhood diseases or accidents during childhood all produce emotional injuries later in life. Childhood diseases are often more critical and remembered for the restriction they force, reactions of the parents or side-effects upon the personality, than for their actual effects upon the physical organism. The child who never experiences childhood illnesses (chickenpox, measles, mumps, tonsils, etc.) is less well prepared to accept minor and major afflictions later in life because he does not possess the emotional equipment to understand that they happen and pass.

Afflictions during the Octave of Maturity have their major effect upon the *mental body*. Psychosomatic illnesses, nervous disturbances, tension, sensory organ degeneration and others are all related to the psychological state of the individual. Retaining the resiliancy of childhood implies a frame of mind which remains fluid and active. Many individuals begin to crystallize and harden as their psychological perspective narrows during maturity. The ability of the individual to manifest his mental potential reflects itself in the state of his health. Afflicted sight implies a restrictive view of oneself (Saturn in Aries); throat cancer would result from oververbalization (Sun afflicted in Taurus = Freud). Due to the extension of time in the maturity octave, illnesses during this time tend to have long duration and subsequently require long periods for recuperation.

Afflictions during the Octave of Transcendence are conditioned by the planets in the Octave of Gestation. The ability to achieve the transcendent state is equivalent to making supreme use of *the constitution as a whole*. Acceptance and manifestation of the entire range of abilities and weaknesses distinguishes the true artist and unified individual. Specific

personal qualities and afflictions must be surmounted in favour of whole. The individual and collective viewpoints must be united in the mystery of the opposites. The transcendent function is the regulatory mechanism which allows the meaning of life to express itself. The life is the art, and inability to co-ordinate the parts with the whole results in the most extreme illness of all — the alienation of the Self. As the perspective of life is reviewed before entering the Transcendent Octave, all traumas and afflictions are represented and confronted, and all weaknesses become known. The quality of one's death is a compensatory reaction to the process of life, and if the irrationals of an individual's existence are confronted, death is the total release it is intended to be. The elderly gradually assume the reality of helplessness in the womb, borne by the Great Mother. Thus the highest and the lowest octaves finally unite in death.

Afflictions also communicate themselves from octave to octave within life. The transcendent level, being the finest in energy, perceives imbalances first, and if these are not properly equilibrated, the imbalance communicates itself to the mental body as a disturbance of thought. If the mental apparatus perceives the imbalance, responds to the warning and reorganizes itself, it can be a catalyst for expression of the imbalance — its cure. If the imbalance is suppressed, ignored or blocked by the mental body, the dilemma is communicated down to the emotional body as feelings of disorientation. The feelings then condition the mentality, until the mind cannot re-create order. Attempts to rationalize the problem only lead to the abyss of conflicting feelings. The feelings attach themselves to all contents perceived, and they exaggerate the initial imbalance. When the three highest bodies become inoperative in this way, the imbalance becomes physical and produces physical symptoms to express itself. The physical symptom is the last step in the process and an indication that the imbalance has affected the entire organism and psyche. The symptom is the last line of control and shows abuse of the higher levels. Successful diagnosis and treatment mean a successive regeneration of all bodies from the lowest to the highest.

In the astrological framework, the depth of an affliction is related to the number of aspects in an afflicted constellation and to the octave that it affects. One pair of planets — each afflicting the other — indicates an ambiguity and a necessity to relate the two levels involved. The dualism implies that the affliction is primarily mental and that the *idea* of disease is in operation. Three planets afflicting each other show an emotional involvement in the imbalance. The affliction is 'felt', although there may not be physical symptoms, and these feelings can offset stability and permeate all three octaves. When four planets afflict each other, the imbalance can be considered chronic. The word chronic is an imbalance which continues through time *(chron- = time)*. Once the temporal equilibrium is disturbed in this way, the other bodies become similarly disoriented.

Cure can only be effected by understanding the relationship between all four bodies. The physical symptom must imply its emotional basis, the feeling must lead the mind to the faulty ideas, and the spiritual integration must be discovered and synthesized into a healthy whole again. The circular process of disease and cure is identical to the circular reality of life.

Appendices

Appendix A
Construction of the Birth Horoscope

The calculation and construction of the birth horoscope is a ritualistic and meditative act. Once the procedure is understood and practiced many times, it becomes second-nature to the astrologer. The process of calculation and construction allows the astrologer to follow the evolution of the horoscope from the base information; in the meantime he programmes himself with all relevant information before an interpretation is attempted. Structural familiarity is of great assistance during the interpretation and the reading.

The calculations are not so complex that they require profound mathematical skills, but are rather an elementary exercise in logic. The object is to translate a birth-time and birth-place into the symbolic representation of the horoscope.

The calculation and construction of the horoscope involves three operations:

I. The *Sidereal Time of Birth* is calculated from the date, time and place. From this the longitude of the Ascendant, MC and the intermediate house cusps are obtained. The house cusps are then entered on the horoscope form.

II. The *Planetary Positions* are based upon the calculation of the GMT (Greenwich Mean Time) of birth. The planetary positions are then entered on the horoscope form.

III. The *Mutual Aspects* are determined and indicated upon the horoscope form.

To construct the birth horoscope, the following information is necessary:

Name: The full name of the individual for whom the horoscope is constructed. This may be the name given at birth, the married name, or any name preferred by the individual.

Birth Date: The Day, Month and Year of birth.

Birth Time: The Birth Time must be as accurate as possible. For a reasonably accurate horoscope it is necessary to know the time of birth to within ten minutes. Even birth times in hospital records or on birth certificates are often only accurate to the nearest quarter of an hour. The birth time should be given in hours and minutes, AM or PM. Any question of the accuracy of the given time should be noted.

Often the time of birth is not known to within one half hour; this can produce an inaccuracy of up to ten degrees for the Ascendant and other house cusps. In these cases it is advisable to follow the procedure called *Rectification* — the correction of the Ascendant. Rectification is described in Appendix B.

Birth Place: The name of the City and Country of birth. When the birth has occurred in the countryside, the nearest city should be given.

The *Latitude* (north or south of the equator) and the *Longitude* (east or west of Greenwich) are necessary. They can be found in an Atlas or Gazetteer. The degree and, if possible, the minute of latitude and longitude are necessary.

The following reference books are necessary:

Ephemeris: The Ephemeris shows the Sidereal Time and the positions of the luminaries, planets and north node at either noon or midnight each day.
Noon (12 hr.) Ephemerides: *Raphael's Ephemeris* for individual years from 1820 to the present. (Swiss) *Ephemeriden 1890-1950. Simplified Scientific Ephemeris,* ten year volumes from 1857-1979. *Die Deutsche Ephemeride,* 1850-1930.
Midnight (0 hr.) Ephemerides: *Die Deutsche Ephemeride,* 1931-1980. *The American Ephemeris,* 1930-1980. *The Complete Planetary Ephemeris,* 1950-2000.

Tables of Houses: The Tables of Houses show the positions of the ASC, MC and the intermediate house cusps for approximately each four minute interval of sidereal time. Use a Table of Houses within one degree of the desired latitude of the birth place.

Raphael's Tables of Houses for Northern Latitudes from the Equator to 50° North 0', also for Leningrad 59° North 56'.

Raphael's Tables of Houses for Great Britain.

Simplified Scientific Tables of Houses, Latitudes 0 to 66 Degrees.

Tools of Astrology: Houses. Tables of houses for Alcabitius, Campanus, Placidus, Porphyry, Regiomontanus and Zariel methods of house computation.

Time Changes: These show the Standard Time Zones and changes due to Summer Time, War Time or local variation. This facilitates the translation of the Local Time of birth to GMT.

Time Changes in the World, by Doris Chase Doane.

Time Changes in the USA, by Doris Chase Doane.

Time Changes in Canada and Mexico, by Doris Chase Doane.

Atlas or Gazetteer: A gazetteer is a list of cities with their latitude and longitude. An atlas may be used by interpolating the location of a city.

The *Simplified Scientific Tables of Houses* has a gazetteer included.

The (Swiss) *Ephemeriden 1890-1950* has a gazetteer.

Although many astrological textbooks attempt to include these reference works in simplified fashion, there is no substitute for the original sources.

I. Calculation of Sidereal Time

The following is a worksheet for use in calculating sidereal time.

Worksheet for the Calculation of Sidereal Time

1. **Name:** _____

2. **Birth Date:**

Day	Month	Year

3. **Birth Time:** (AM/PM)

Hours	Minutes	Seconds

4. **Birth Place:** Latitude (N/S)

Degrees	N/S	Minutes

Longitude (E/W)

Degrees	E/W	Minutes

	Hours	Minutes	Seconds
5. **Local Birth Time:**	____	____	____
6. **Zone Standard:** (E − , W +)	____	____	____
7. **Summer Time:** (− 1 hour)	____	____	____
o r			
8. **Double Summer Time:** (− 2 hours)	____	____	____
9. **Greenwich Mean Time of Birth:** (5 + / − 6 − 7 or 8)	____	____	____

10. **GMT Date:**

Day	Month	Year

	Hours	Minutes	Seconds
11. **Sidereal Time (ST) Noon GMT:** (or Midnight)	____	____	____
12. **Interval To/From Noon** (AM − , PM +)	____	____	____
13. **Acceleration on the Interval** (10′′ per hour) (AM − , PM +)	____	____	____
14. **Sidereal Time at Greenwich** (11 + / − 12 + / − 13)	____	____	____
15. **Longitude Equivalent** (E + , W −)	____	____	____
16. **Sidereal Time at Birth** If greater than 24 hours, subtract 24 hours. (14 + / − 15)	____	____	____

THE ROUND ART

Let us erect the horoscope of a woman born in London, England, on 18 August 1952, at 7:22 PM.

1. **Name:**   Miss A.

2. **Birth Date:**   18 August 1952

3. **Birth Time:**   7 hours 22 minutes PM

4. **Birth Place:**   London, England
                                                                          51° North 32′ x
                                                                          00° West 06′

	Hours	Minutes	Seconds	
5. **Local Birth Time:**	07	22	00	PM
6. **Zone Standard:** (E −, W +)	00	00	00	

London, England is on Greenwich Mean Time, so there is no correction for Zone Standard. If the Zone Standard is West of GMT, it must be added to Local Birth Time. If the Zone Standard is East of GMT, it must be subtracted from the Local Birth Time.

7. **Summer Time:**	− 01	00	00	

Time Changes in the World or Whitaker's Almanack show that Summer Time was in effect from 20 April 1952 until 26 October 1952. One hour must be subtracted from the Local Birth Time.
or

8. **Double Summer Time:**	00	00	00	

Double Summer Time was only in effect from 1941 until 1947 and from 1967 until 1972 in England. When Double Summer Time is operative an additional hour must be subtracted from the Local Birth Time.

9. **Greenwich Mean Time of Birth:**	06	22	00	PM

10. **GMT Date:**   18 August 1952

The GMT Date in this case is the same. If, however, the Local Birth Time is just after the midnight beginning of day (0:00 hr.), and the Zone Standard requires hours to be subtracted, the GMT Date may be the previous day. If the Local Birth Time is just before midnight (24:00 hrs) and the Zone Standard requires hours to be added, the GMT Date may be the following day. In our two other examples, both of these possibilities are explored.

11. **Sidereal Time at Noon GMT:**	09	47	10	

from the accompanying ephemeris excerpt
The Sidereal Time is found by reading across from 18 August under the heading ST. (Figure A.1) In the German or Swiss ephemerides, Sidereal Time is called Sternzeit or SZ. As our excerpt is a noon ephemeris, our Sidereal Time is for noon. With midnight ephemerides it is usual to take the Sidereal Time for the midnight closest to the GMT of Birth. In our case the Sidereal Time for midnight on the 19th of August would be used.

12. **Interval To/From Noon:** (AM −, PM +)	+ 06	22	00	

Since our GMT is PM, it must be added to the ST at noon. 06:22.00 is six hours, 22 minutes and 00 seconds after noon. If a midnight ephemeris is used, the GMT would be subtracted from the ST at the following midnight (12:00.00 − 06:22.00 = − 05:38.00, to be subtracted from the midnight ST). If the Local Birth Time is either before the preceding midnight or after the following midnight, it is necessary to subtract or add as much as 24 hours to the ST at noon. Many astrologers choose to take the earlier Sidereal Time noon so that this operation is additive.

13. **Acceleration on the Interval:**	+ 00	01	04	

(10′ per Hour) (AM −, PM +)
Because the Mean Solar Day is equal to 24 hours 03 minutes and 56.6 seconds of Sidereal

Time, the Solar Time used thus far must be corrected. Although the actual acceleration correction is 9.84 seconds per hour of Solar Time, the approximation of 10 seconds per hour is satisfactory. The maximum acceleration in 12 hours of Sidereal Time is 2 minutes, and the maximum acceleration in 24 hours of Sidereal Time is 4 minutes. The Acceleration on the Interval is added when the Interval is added, and subtracted when the Interval is subtracted.

14. *Sidereal Time at Greenwich:* 16 10 14
In this case both the Interval (Step 12) and the Acceleration on the Interval (Step 13) are added to the GMT Sidereal Time at noon. When the Interval is before noon, steps 12 and 13 are subtracted. This gives us the Sidereal Time at Greenwich Meridian. The next operation transposes the GMT ST to the actual location of the individual.

15. **Longitude Equivalent:** (E +, W −) −00 00 24
To correlate the Sidereal Time at Greenwich to the place of birth, the longitude of the place of birth (Step 4) must be translated into time. The formulae for this calculation are:

Longitude		Time			
1°	=	4 minutes	15°	=	1 hour
1′	=	4 seconds	360°	=	24 hours

In some ephmerides (the Swiss Ephemeriden), the longitudes of most major cities are translated into time. If the birth place is East of Greenwich, the Longitude Equivalent is added to ST(G), while if the birth place is West of Greenwich, the Longitude Equivalent is subtracted from ST(G). The operation of this step is always the opposite of Step 6 above.

16. **Sidereal Time at Birth:** 16 hrs. 09 mins. 50 secs.
From the Sidereal Time at Birth, the positions of the house cusps are determined. If the result is greater than 24 hours, 24 hours must be subtracted.

Figure A.1 A Sample Ephemeris for August 1952.

	Sidereal Time H. M. S.	☉ Long. ° ′ ″	☊ Long. ° ″	☾ Long. ° ′ ″	☿ Long. ° ′	♀ Long. ° ′	♂ Long. ° ′	♃ Long. ° ′	♄ Long. ° ′	♅ Long. ° ′	♆ Long. ° ′	♇ Long. ° ′
1 F	8 40 9	9 ♌ 9 20	22 ♒ 11	9 ♐ 27 0	26 ♌ 52	19 ♌ 33	15 ♏ 42	18 ♉ 34	10 ♎ 21	15 ♋ 46	19 ♎ 13	20 ♌ 48
2 S	8 44 5	10 6 44	22 8	23 40 21	26 ℞ 36	20 46	16 11	18 41	10 26	15 49	19 14	20 50
3 S	8 48 2	11 4 9	22 5	8 ♑ 18 23	26 14	22 0	16 41	18 48	10 30	15 53	19 15	20 51
4 M	8 51 58	12 1 34	22 1	23 16 3	25 48	23 14	17 10	18 54	10 35	15 56	19 16	20 53
5 T	8 55 55	12 59 1	21 58	8 ♒ 25 46	25 17	24 28	17 40	19 1	10 40	15 59	19 17	20 55
6 W	8 59 52	13 56 28	21 55	23 38 20	24 41	25 42	18 11	19 7	10 45	16 3	19 18	20 57
7 T	9 3 48	14 53 57	21 52	8 ♓ 44 12	24 2	26 56	18 42	19 13	10 50	16 6	19 19	20 59
8 F	9 7 45	15 51 27	21 49	23 34 53	23 19	28 10	19 12	19 19	10 55	16 9	19 20	21 0
9 S	9 11 41	16 48 58	21 45	8 ♈ 4 5	22 33	29 24	19 44	19 25	11 1	16 13	19 22	21 3
10 S	9 15 38	17 46 30	21 42	22 8 5	21 46	0 ♍ 38	20 15	19 31	11 6	16 16	19 23	21 4
11 M	9 19 34	18 44 4	21 39	5 ♉ 45 45	20 57	1 52	20 47	19 37	11 11	16 19	19 24	21 6
12 T	9 23 31	19 41 39	21 36	18 58 7	20 8	3 6	21 19	19 42	11 17	16 22	19 26	21 8
13 W	9 27 27	20 39 16	21 33	1 ♊ 47 40	19 19	4 20	21 51	19 47	11 22	16 25	19 27	21 10
14 T	9 31 24	21 36 54	21 30	14 17 46	18 32	5 34	22 24	19 52	11 28	16 28	19 28	21 12
15 F	9 35 21	22 34 34	21 26	26 32 13	17 47	6 47	22 57	19 57	11 33	16 32	19 30	21 14
16 S	9 39 17	23 32 15	21 23	8 ♋ 34 48	17 6	8 1	23 30	20 2	11 39	16 35	19 31	21 16
17 S	9 43 14	24 29 58	21 20	20 29 5	16 29	9 15	24 3	20 6	11 45	16 38	19 32	21 18
18 M	**9 47 10**	**25 27 42**	**21 17**	**2 ♌ 18 18**	**15 57**	**10 29**	**24 37**	**20 11**	**11 50**	**16 41**	**19 34**	**21 19**
19 T	9 51 7	26 25 28	21 14	14 5 20	15 31	11 43	25 11	20 15	11 56	16 44	19 35	21 21
20 W	9 55 3	27 23 15	21 11	25 52 46	15 11	12 57	25 45	20 19	12 2	16 47	19 37	21 23
21 T	9 59 0	28 21 3	21 7	7 ♍ 42 53	14 59	14 11	26 19	20 23	12 8	16 50	19 38	21 25
22 F	10 2 56	29 18 53	21 4	19 37 55	14 54	15 25	26 54	20 26	12 14	16 53	19 40	21 27
23 S	10 6 53	0 ♍ 16 44	21 1	1 ♎ 40 4	14 56	16 39	27 28	20 30	12 20	16 56	19 42	21 29
24 S	10 10 50	1 14 37	20 58	13 51 41	15 6	17 53	28 4	20 33	12 26	16 58	19 43	21 31
25 M	10 14 46	2 12 31	20 55	26 15 15	15 24	19 7	28 39	20 36	12 32	17 1	19 45	21 33
26 T	10 18 43	3 10 26	20 51	8 ♏ 53 29	15 50	20 21	29 14	20 39	12 38	17 4	19 46	21 34
27 W	10 22 39	4 8 23	20 48	21 49 6	16 24	21 35	29 50	20 42	12 45	17 7	19 48	21 36
28 T	10 26 36	5 6 20	20 45	5 ♐ 4 44	17 6	22 49	0 ♐ 26	20 44	12 51	17 10	19 50	21 38
29 F	10 30 32	6 4 19	20 42	18 42 25	17 55	24 3	1 2	20 47	12 57	17 12	19 52	21 40
30 S	10 34 29	7 2 20	20 39	2 ♑ 43 11	18 52	25 16	1 38	20 49	13 4	17 15	19 53	21 42
31 S	10 38 25	8 0 22	20 36	17 6 31	19 56	26 31	2 15	20 51	13 10	17 17	19 55	21 44

THE ROUND ART

The following table shows the calculation procedure we have followed for determining the Sidereal Time of Birth for Miss A, and the calculations for two other individuals born on the same day. Mr. B was born at 9:56 PM in New York City, USA, and Mr. C was born at 3:25 AM in Tokyo, Japan. New York City is in the Eastern Standard Time Zone, 5 hours West of Greenwich. Tokyo is in Japan Time Zone (Japanische Zeit), 9 hours East of Greenwich. It is interesting to notice that when the Local Birth Time of Mr. B is correlated to GMT, it falls at 01:54.00 AM on the following day, the 19th of August 1952. In the case of Mr. C, his standard time zone is so far East of Greenwich that his GMT is 06:25.00 PM on the previous day, the 17th of August 1952.

		Miss A			Mr B			Mr C		
1. **Name:**		18 August 1952			18 August 1952			18 August 1952		
2. **Birth Date:**										
3. **Birth Time:**	(AM/PM)	07:22.00 PM			09:56.00 PM			03:25.00 AM		
4. **Birth Place:**		London, England			New York City, USA			Tokyo Japan		
	(Lat)	51° N. 31′ x			40° N. 43′ x			35° N. 40′ x		
	(Long)	00° W. 06′			73° W. 57′			139° E. 45′		
		H	M	S	H	M	S	H	M	S
5. **Local Birth Time:**		07	22	00	09	54	00	03	25	00
6. **Zone Standard:**	(E −, W +)	00	00	00	+05	00	00	−09	00	00
7. **Summer Time or**	(−1 hour)	−01	00	00	−01	00	00	00	00	00
8. **Double Summer Time**	(−2 hour)	00	00	00	00	00	00	00	00	00
9. **GMT of Birth**		06	22	00	01	54	00	06	25	00
10. **GMT Date**		18 August 1952			19 August 1952			17 August 1952		
11. **Sidereal Time Noon GMT**		09	47	10	09	47	10	09	47	00
12. **Interval To/From Noon** (AM −, PM +)		+06	22	00	+13	54	00	−17	35	00
13. **Acceleration on the Interval**		+	1	04	+	2	19	−	2	56
14. **Sidereal Time Greenwich**		16	10	14	23	43	29	16	09	14
15. **Longitude Equivalent** (E +, W −)		−00	00	24	−04	55	54	+09	19	00
16. **Sidereal Time**		16	09	50	18	47	35	25	28	14
								−24	00	00
								1	28	14

Determining the Ascendant, Midheaven and House Cusps

The Ascendant, Midheaven and house cusps are found in the Tables of Houses for the latitude nearest to the birth place. Most Tables of Houses have a table converting Sidereal Time to the house cusps for each 1° increment of latitude. The Tables of Houses for each latitude give the Sidereal Time in approximate 4′ intervals throughout the entire sidereal day of 24 hours. Adjacent each 4′ increment of Sidereal Time are the longitudes of the Xth (10th or MC) house cusp, the XIth house cusp, the XIIth house cusp, the Ascendant, the IInd house cusp and the IIIrd house cusp. Only these six cusps are necessary as the opposite house cusps are the same degree and minute, but in the opposite signs. The cusp longitudes in the ephemeris are usually given according to the Placidean House System. If the Xth cusp (the MC) is 17° Virgo 20′, then the opposite IVth cusp is 17° Pisces 20′, etc.

In the majority of horoscopes the time of birth as given is only accurate to within five minutes. This five minute 'margin of error' converts to about one degree of longitude. Therefore, in most cases the positions of the house cusps may be taken directly from the Tables of Houses adjacent to the nearest sidereal time of the calculated Sidereal Time of Birth.

When the birth time is given to the exact hour and minute, the following calculation gives the house cusps of the Ascendant and MC to within a few minutes' accuracy. While this accuracy is not necessary in most cases, it is occasionally necessary for determining the exact days of Transits, for computing exact Solar Arc Directions and for the calculation of the Solar Return yearly analysis.

To calculate the house cusps for Miss A, the Table of Houses for London, latitude 51° North 31′ is used. Miss A's Sidereal Time of Birth has been determined as 16 hrs 09 mins 50 secs. We use the two lines of sidereal times and house cusps between which her computed Sidereal Time falls.

	Sidereal Time			10(Xth) ♐ °	11(XIth) ♐ °	12(XIIth) ♑ °	Ascendant ♒ ° ′	2(IInd) ♈ °	3(IIIrd) ♉ °
	H	M	S						
Earlier	16	08	00	4	22	10	3 16	3	11
Later	16	12	13	5	23	11	4 53	5	12

Since the MC passes through 1° of longitude between the Earlier ST of 16:08.00 and the Later ST of 16:12.13, we want to find the proportion of that 1° which has passed at the Sidereal Time of 16:09.50. To do this we find the total interval between the Earlier and Later Sidereal Times, and the interval between the Earlier ST and our computed Sidereal Time of Birth. This proportion is then multiplied by the total interval the MC has moved.

Computed ST	16	09	50
− Earlier ST	16	08	00
Interval A	00	01	50

Later ST	16	12	13
− Earlier ST	16	08	00
Interval B	00	04	13

These intervals are converted into seconds to make our proportion:

$$\frac{\text{Interval A}}{\text{Interval B}} = \frac{01'\ 50''}{04'\ 13''} \text{ converted to seconds} = \frac{110''}{253''}$$

The proportion $\frac{110}{253}$ is multiplied times 1° (60′) and equals 24′. This result is then added to the Earlier MC of 4° Sagittarius, to give a final MC of 4° Sagittarius 24′.

The same proportion is used to find the Ascendant. Between the Earlier ST and the Later ST, the Ascendant has moved:

Later ASC	4°	53′
− Earlier ASC	3	16
Interval	1°	37′

This ASC Interval is converted into minutes: 1° 37′ = 97′.

$\frac{110}{253}$ times 97′ = 43′ added to the Earlier ASC 3° Aquarius 16′ gives a final Ascendant of 3° Aquarius 59′.

Since the computed Sidereal Time is closer to the Earlier ST as given in the Tables of Houses, the intermediate house cusps are taken from that row. The list of house cusps are as following:

Given From Tables of Houses and the Computation		The Opposite House Cusps	
Xth (MC)	4° Sagittarius 24′	IVth (IC)	4° Gemini 24′
XIth	22° Sagittarius	Vth	22° Gemini
XIIth	10° Capricorn	VIth	10° Cancer
Ist (ASC)	3° Aquarius 59′	VIIth (DES)	3° Leo 59′
IInd	3° Aries	VIIIth	3° Libra
IIIrd	12° Taurus	IXth	12° Scorpio

These house cusps may then be entered on a horoscope form. (Figure A.2) The Ascendant and Descendant should be shown as darker lines extending past the edge of the circle of the signs, and should have a dashed line (the horizon) connecting them. The MC and IC should also be drawn as darker lines extending beyond the circle of the signs. This allows the four 'cardinal points' to be identified at a glance.

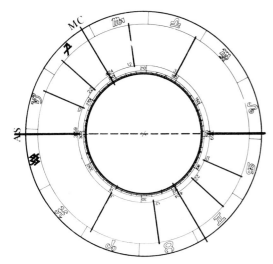

Figure A.2 House Cusps Entered on the Horoscope Blank

In our example, two house cusps occupy the signs Sagittarius and Gemini, while the signs Virgo and Pisces have no cusps within them. The signs Virgo and Pisces are "Intercepted". Intercepted signs indicate extended periods of development according to their location in the Logarithmic Time Scale.

House Cusps in the Southern Hemisphere

The tilt of the Earth's axis necessitates a further calculation for determining house cusps in the Southern Hemisphere. The signs of Long Ascension in the Northern Hemisphere are signs of Short Ascension in the Southern Hemisphere, and vice versa. Since the Tables of Houses give only information for the Northern Hemisphere, the following conversion is necessary:

If Miss A were born at the same time but at 51° South 31' latitude, the calculations for determining the Sidereal Time are the same except that *12 hours are added* to the computed Sidereal Time at Birth, and the resultant house cusps found in the Tables of Houses for Northern Latitudes must be changed to their *opposite signs*.

Sidereal Time of Birth	16	09	50
Add	+ 12	00	00
Converted ST	28	09	50
Subtract 24 hours	− 24	00	00
Final ST	04	09	50

The house cusps found in the row nearest to the ST of 04:09.50 are then converted to their opposite signs:

	Xth	XIth	XIIth	ASC	IInd	IIIrd
Tables of Houses	4 ♊	11 ♋	14 ♌	10 ♍ 17	2 ♎	29 ♎
Converted	4 ♐	11 ♑	14 ♒	10 ♓ 17	2 ♈	29 ♈

Although this conversion is necessary for the house cusps, the planetary positions are not reversed in the Southern Hemisphere.

II. Calculation of Planetary Positions

The planetary positions are based upon the Greenwich Mean Time of Birth (Step 9 above). The longitudes of the planetary bodies are given in the ephemeris at noon on each successive day (or at midnight, according to the ephemeris used). If the Sidereal Time of birth is exactly noon the planetary positions can be taken directly from the ephemeris. If the GMT is after noon a proportional movement must be *added* to the noon position, and if the GMT is before noon a proportional movement must be *subtracted* from the noon positions.

Since the GMT of Miss A is 06 hrs 22 minutes after noon on the 18th of August 1952, we add the proportional movements to the planet's positions at noon on 18 August 1952. We calculate the proportion of time between noon on 18 August and noon on 19 August, and multiply it by the motion of each planet during the same time. The time between the two noons is 24 hours, and the amount of time elapsed until the time of birth is 6 hours 22 minutes. To make the proportion, both times are converted into minutes.

$$\frac{06 \text{ hrs } 22 \text{ min}}{24 \text{ hrs } 00 \text{ min}} = \frac{382'}{1440'} = .27$$

The interval of motion for each planet is determined by subtracting the longitude on 18 August at noon from the longitude on 19 August at noon, converting the interval into minutes, multiplying by .27, and then adding the result to the positions on 18 August. The most effective way to do this is in tabular form. When a planet in the ephemeris is Retrograde (moving backwards) the process is reversed. The planetary longitude on 19 August is subtracted from the longitude on 18 August, the result is multiplied by the factor .27, and then subtracted from the longitude on 18 August.

Table for Calculating Planetary Positions

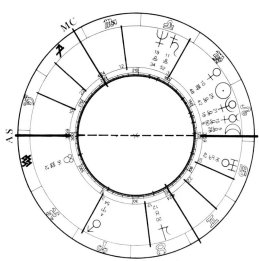

Figure A.3 Planets Entered on the Horoscope

Planet	Longitude at Noon 19 August	Longitude at Noon 18 August	Difference Daily Motion	x .27 Proportional Factor	Added to 18 August
Sun	26° ♌ 25′	25° ♌ 27′	58′	+ 15′	25° ♌ 42′
Moon	14° ♌ 05′	2° ♌ 18′	11° 47′ = 707′	+190′ = 3° 10′	5° ♌ 28′
Mercury R	15° ♌ 31′	15° ♌ 57′	26′	− 7′	15° ♌ 50′ R
Venus	11° ♍ 43′	10° ♍ 29′	74′	+ 19′	10° ♍ 48′
Mars	5° ♏ 41′	4° ♏ 37′	64′	+ 17′	4° ♏ 54′
Jupiter	20° ♉ 15′	20° ♉ 11′	4′	+ 1′	20° ♉ 12′
Saturn	11° ♎ 56′	11° ♎ 50′	6′	+ 2′	11° ♎ 52′
Uranus	16° ♋ 44′	16° ♋ 41′	3′	+ 1′	16° ♋ 42′
Neptune	19° ♎ 35′	19° ♎ 34′	1′	+ 0′	19° ♎ 34′
Pluto	21° ♌ 19′	21° ♌ 18′	1′	+ 0′	21° ♌ 18′
Moon's Node	21° ♒ 14′	21° ♒ 17′	3′	− 1′	21° ♒ 16′

When the planetary positions have been calculated they are entered on the horoscope form. (Figure A.3) On the innermost circle of 360° a mark is made for each planet. The appropriate planetary glyph and the degree and minute of each planet is entered.

An easier and faster method for determining planetary positions is to use tables which are made for the purpose. The American Federation of Astrologers publish the *'Tables of Diurnal Planetary Motion'*, Ebertin publishes *'Auxiliary Tables for Calculating the Stellar Positions'*, and the Swiss Epheriden contains the *'Bewegung Der Gestirne' (Planetary Motions)*. The use of these tables is explained in each source.

Determining Aspects With the Logarithmic Time Scale Disk

When the planetary positions have been entered on the horoscope, the aspect lines connecting them must be determined and drawn. For ease in differentiation, the Trines and Sextiles are drawn in green, and the Squares and Oppositions are drawn in red. (See the sample horoscopes in Part X.) They are first drawn lightly in pencil as they are discovered.

Each planet is taken in turn from the position of the Ascendant through the twelve houses. To start, take the transparent Logarithmic Time Scale disk included in this book and insert a map tack or pin through the centre of the disk, then through the centre of the horoscope. (Figure A.5) This allows the disk to revolve around the centre point. Each planet in turn is aligned with the Birth-Ascendant position on the disk, and the radiating lines point out the seven aspect positions around the horoscope. If any planet is within proper orb of any of these aspect positions, the aspect is drawn lightly in pencil. Sextiles, Trines and Oppositions are indicated as straight lines joining the planetary bodies, Conjunctions are indicated by a dashed line surrounding the planets, and Squares are right-angled lines which intersect the centre of the horoscope.

After all of the aspects have been found and indicated in pencil, they are redrawn in red and green. The information required on the horoscope form is then entered, and the horoscope is ready for interpretation. (Figure A.5 on page 291.)

Appendix B
Rectification — Correction of the Birth Time

One of the central and virtually insurmountable problems of traditional astrology is the determination of the correct time of birth. Ebertin compared birth time information he received from clients to hospital or registrar records. He found that in 80% of the cases the birth time produced an ascendant correct within 30° (one whole sign). The number of birth times which fall within an acceptable accuracy of 5° is minimal.

When asked his birth time, an individual often replies, "I was born in the middle of the night. It must have been 12 midnight." Or, "My mother said I was born just as Father returned from playing polo. Since he always returns at 4:30 in the afternoon, that must be my birth time.'' Most individuals only know their time of birth to the nearest hour or half-hour. Often an individual places his birth time, ''Between eight o'clock and nine o'clock''. Even when birth times are recorded in hospitals, they are often rounded off to the nearest half-hour, or only determined after the child has been spanked, had his cord cut, been talcumed and removed to a nursery.

In traditional astrology, the exactitude of the Ascendant is of minimal importance, since there is no inherent time system in the horoscope circle itself. With the Logarithmic Time Scale the position of the Ascendant is of critical importance. Since the ascendant moves one degree every 4 minutes, a half-hour margin of error in a birth time results in an 8 degree variance. In the early part of life, until the age of seven, this error only amounts to a period of six months, but by the age of 23 it amounts to 5 years. The process of correcting the birth time is called 'Rectification'. The use of the time scale allows a unique method of doing this quickly and accurately. With practice, it can and should be used for every horoscope the astrologer constructs.

The rectification procedure becomes clear when applied to an actual case. Mr. Smith was born on 4 July 1939 in London, England, and his birth time was only known to be between 3:00 PM and 4:00 PM. The following is a step-by-step procedure for the rectification of Mr. Smith's horoscope.

1. Within the range of given times of birth, calculate the mean Sidereal Time of birth. If the total range is one hour, make the ST calculation for the half-hour. When the ST is found, take the nearest ascendant from the Tables of Houses. To find the range of possible ascendants, subtract 30 minutes from the mean ST to find the earliest possible ascendant, and add 30 minutes to the mean ST to find the latest possible ascendant. From the mean ascendant, construct a horoscope.

    Mr. Smith's margin of possible birth times is the one hour between 3:00 PM and 4:00 PM, so the calculation is made for 3:30 PM. This gives a ST of 9:16.26, and an ascendant of 5° Scorpio. To find the ascendant for 3:00 PM, 30 minutes are subtracted from 9:16.26, giving a ST of 8:46.26, and an ascendant of 29° Libra. To find the ascendant for 4:00 PM, 30 minutes are added to 9:16.26, giving a ST of 9:46.26, and an ascendant of 10° Scorpio. The range of possible ascendants is therefore between 29° Libra and 10° Scorpio.

2. The physical appearance is used to narrow the range of possible ascendants. In Part VI of this book, *Sign Correspondences,* are general Physical Descriptions of the signs, and a specific description for each 5° Face. The physical description of the individual is compared to the descriptions of the Faces determined by Step 1. When the range of possible ascendants falls on the borderline between two signs, the selection of the correct ascendant is usually easier. This is because the positive signs (Fire and Air) tend to be tall and fair, while the negative signs (Earth and Water) tend to be short, stocky and dark.

    If planets conjunct or aspect the ascendant, they influence the physical description:

    Sun — Makes the body taller and stronger, the complexion is often redder, the hair curlier, the eyes larger.

    Moon — Makes the body fuller, the face rounder and fairer, shorter arms and legs, a greater delicacy of figure.

    Mercury — Makes the body taller and thinner, the forehead higher, the hair more profuse, and the constitution more nervous.

    Venus — Makes the face rounder, the hair of mixed colouring and lighter than the eyebrows, the physique shorter but well shaped, and the eyes darker.

    Mars — Makes the body shorter but stronger, the hair redder, the complexion ruddier, the nose more pronounced, and the whole demeanor more dynamic, with a possibility of head scars.

    Jupiter — Makes the body more upright, taller; fuller and fleshier, the forehead higher, the hair and eyes light, larger arms, legs and feet, but well-proportioned.

    Saturn — Makes the body bonier, straighter, darker hair and eyes, thicker nose and mouth, thinner beard, yellowish complexion.

    Uranus — Makes the body taller, straighter, stiffer, stronger above the waist than below,

fuller in the face, lighter hair, scars.

Neptune — Makes the body rounder, more amorphous, more delicate, fairer hair and eyes, finer features, peculiarities.

Pluto — Makes the body harder and harsher, more changeable demeanor, violent appearance.

Mr. Smith is 5 feet 8 inches tall, corpulent, with light brown hair and eyes, short in the legs and arms, and not physically attractive. The possible range of ascendants include the Sixth Face of Libra (25° to 30°), the First Face of Scorpio (0° to 5°) and the Second Face of Scorpio (5° to 10°). Since the Sixth Face of Libra is tall, slender, very fair and beautiful, this can be eliminated. Mr. Smith's description could be either of the first two faces of Scorpio, and he fits the general Scorpio description very well. Since he is corpulent and not particularly attractive, we can safely assume his ascendant to be in the Second Face of Scorpio, between 5° and 10°.

3. The clear plastic Logarithmic Time Scale disk is placed over the horoscope so that the Birth Time on the disk coincides with the approximate ascendant as determined in Step 1. This shows the ages at which planets in the horoscope register, as well as the planets which aspect the ascendant.

The disk is placed over the horoscope of Mr. Smith with the Birth Time on 5° Scorpio — the first degree in the Second Face of Scorpio. In this location the ascendant is squared by Mercury in Leo and Mars in Aquarius, and loosely in trine to the Sun in Cancer.

4. The most effective planets for locating events are the malefics, which indicate dramatic impairments of health. These are *Mars* (surgery, broken bones and accidents), *Saturn* (rheumatism, broken bones, ruptures, bronchial trouble and constriction), *Uranus* (operations, rhythmic disturbances, nervous breakdowns, breathing trouble and migraines), *Neptune* (anaesthetics, drugs, prominent dreams, paralysis, weakness and drowning) and *Pluto* (residence changes, violence, serious disorders, serious accidents). When any of these planets occur in the life they can be expected to produce events which the individual will remember. Their influences are even more pronounced when they aspect each other in the horoscope, in which case their effects combine. When malefics fall in the same constellation, the combined influence operates at the planetary position of each participating planet or personal point in the constellation. The aspect combinations and their specific influences are most easily found in Ebertin's *"The Combination of Stellar Influences"*, although the tables in Part VI of this book give a good idea of what influences to look for.

5. The locations of Mars, Saturn, Uranus, Neptune and Pluto in each individual horoscope determine traumatic ages. In an optimal situation, one of these malefics falls between the age of 7 and the present age of the individual. Most individuals have only a vague idea exactly when illnesses, accidents or other critical influences occurred before 7 years old. In addition, ages after 7 are defined degree by degree, making it easier to locate planets exactly.

With the Time Scale disk set to 5° Scorpio, it is seen that Mars registers at the age of 3 years 4 months, Saturn registers at 20 years 9 months and Uranus registers at 31 years 6 months. Mars is in the sign Aquarius (blood poisoning), in square to Saturn (bronchial infection), and is opposed to Pluto (disability). Since Mars is in the IIIrd house, which governs the development of speech, it is reasonable to assume that this affliction concerns breathing. Saturn is in Aries (restriction of the brain) and is square to Mars (bronchial infection as before) and to Pluto (inflammatory injuries, near death). Because Saturn is in the same constellation as Mars, it is reasonable to assume that these two events at 3 and 20 are related. Uranus is in a different constellation, and therefore represents another ailment. Uranus in Taurus indicates a disturbance of rhythm centring in the throat or neck (spasmodic contractions or throat disorder) or nervous breakdown. As Neptune (drugs) is in trine to Uranus, it is reasonable to assume that the constriction was caused by drugs or septic conditions (Neptune in Virgo). These ailments constitute the critical health dispositions of Mr Smith.

6. Once these critical events have been located and metaphorically described, the individual is asked to try to remember if and when events of a similar kind happened. Often the crises are described exactly, but in many cases the metaphor allows the individual to remember what variation actually occurred, and the age at which it happened.

Mr. Smith remembered that he had had pneumonia between 3 and 5 years old (Mars). He also had a repercussion of lung trouble and near-suffocation at the age of 20, associated with a serious fever (Saturn and Mars). At the age of 30 he was travelling in a foreign country (Uranus trine Neptune) and required treatment for a minor ailment. The drug he was given produced an allergic reaction, resulting in coma and near death. During the same year Mr. Smith had a nervous breakdown, again requiring hospitalization (Uranus trine Neptune in Virgo).

7. When the indicated cirses have been located, the time scale is rotated until the equivalent ages align with the planets indicating the crises. The position of the ascendant changes to the 'new' ascendant. When two or three planetary crises are all aligned with their equivalent ages, the position of the ascendant is correct. The corrected ascendant is then checked with the Face description. (Figure B.1.).

The crises described by Mr. Smith are very close to the ages found with the ascendant at 5° Scorpio, but in the case of Saturn and Uranus, the planetary locations are slightly late. The disk is rotated until Saturn aligns with 20 years old, and Uranus is aligned with 30 years old. They both align perfectly! This adjustment places Mars at 3 years 2 months old. With this corrected alignment, the ascendant moves to between 7° and 8° Scorpio. This ascendant is within the Face determined by Step 2 — an additional verification.

8. Step 7 should be repeated with as many malefics as are available to provide a cross-check to the corrected ascendant.

9. If the events coincide with their appropriate ages, and the physical description tallies, the ascendant is correct!

10. To find the corrected birth time, the calculations for the Sidereal Time of birth are worked backwards. The ascendant is correlated with its correct ST from the Tables of Houses and, the Longitude Equivalent is either added or subtracted to the ST (the opposite operation to that performed in Step 1). By adding or subtracting from the GMT Sidereal Time at noon (again the opposite operation from Step 1), the result is obtained. The Interval allows the calculation of the GMT, and hence the exact time of birth. Since the corrected ascendant is correct to within one degree, the birth time is correct to within four minutes!

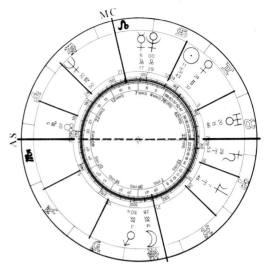

Figure B.1 Correct Alignment.

Birth Time	03	46	35	PM	A.	*Birth Time*
Summer Time (− 1)	− 1	00	00		G.	*Add 1 hour Summer Time*
Zone Standard (E −, W +)	00	00	00		F.	*No Zone Standard*
GMT of Birth	02	46	35	PM	E.	*The Interval gives the Birth GMT*
ST(GMT) at Noon	06	46	24		D.	*Subtract ST(GMT) at Noon*
Interval (PM +, AM −)	+2	26	35			*from Greenwich ST(Step C)*
Acceleration	+		25			*to find the Interval*
ST at Greenwich	09	33	58		C.	*ST at Greenwich*
Longitude Equivalent	−		23		B.	*Add London Longitude Equivalent*
Sidereal Time	09	33	35		A.	*ST from Tables of Houses*

Mr. Smith was born at 3:46 PM on 4 July 1939.

Every time a horoscope is calculated and constructed the astrologer should check the physical description with the Face of the Ascendant. If the physical description is wildly off base, the preceding rectification process should be used. With practice it can be done in a matter of minutes.

Appendix C
The Determination of Solar Arc Directions

The reference book necessary for determining Solar Arc Directions is the Ephemeris for the year of the individual's birth. Two other references may be used when solar arcs are done regularly. Ebertin's *"Tables of Events"* contain tables of the daily arc of the Sun throughout the year, and allows direct access to solar arcs during any year of life. Ebertin's *"Directions — Co-Determinants of Fate"* is a complete study of directions and their interpretation.

There are two types of operations for calculating solar arc directions. One involves finding the solar arcs in a certain year in an individual's life, the other finding which year a certain planetary solar arc configuration is to take place.

The first operation is used in solar arc analyses like the life analysis of Adolf Hitler in Part XI. To demonstrate this method, we will calculate a table for the first 12 years of Hitler's life. All solar arc directions are based upon the position of the Sun at noon on the day of Hitler's birth, 20 April 1889. For each following year of his life, every planet in his horoscope moves the same distance as the Sun does during each day following his birthday. The amount of the solar arc is found by subtracting the position of the Sun on each following day from the Sun's longitude at his birth.

Year	Age	Key Day	Sun Longitude	Calculation		Solar Arc
1889	Birth	20 April 1889	00° Taurus 35'			
1890	1	21 April 1889	01 Taurus 33	01:33 — 00:35	=	**00°:58'**
1891	2	22 April 1889	02 Taurus 31	02:31 — 00:35	=	**01°:56'**
1892	3	23 April 1889	03 Taurus 30	03:30 — 00:35	=	**02°:55'**
1893	4	24 April 1889	04 Taurus 28	04:28 — 00:35	=	**03°:53'**
1894	5	25 April 1889	05 Taurus 26	05:26 — 00:35	=	**04°:51'**
1895	6	26 April 1889	06 Taurus 25	06:25 — 00:35	=	**05°:50'**
1896	7	27 April 1889	07 Taurus 23	07:23 — 00:35	=	**06°:48'**
1897	8	28 April 1889	08 Taurus 21	08:21 — 00:35	=	**07°:46'**
1898	9	29 April 1889	09 Taurus 19	09:19 — 00:35	=	**08°:44'**
1899	10	30 April 1889	10 Taurus 18	10:18 — 00:35	=	**09°:43'**
1900	11	1 May 1889	11 Taurus 16	11:16 — 00:35	=	**10°:41'**
1901	12	2 May 1889	12 Taurus 15	12:15 — 00:35	=	**11°:40'**

Once the solar arc has been determined for the year in question, the longitude of the solar arc is added to the radix longitude of every planet and personal point in the horoscope. This may also be tabulated.

Solar Arc Directions for 12 Years Old in 1901 for Adolf Hitler

Radix Planet or	Radix	Added		Solar Arc Positions
Ascendant	19° Libra 32'	+ 11°40'	=	**01° Scorpio 12'**
MC	25 Cancer 00	+ 11 40	=	**06 Leo 55**
Sun	00 Taurus 48	+ 11 40	=	**12 Taurus 28**
Moon	06 Capricorn 30	+ 11 40	=	**06 Capricorn 55**
Mercury	25 Aries 40	+ 11 40	=	**06 Taurus 55**
Venus	16 Taurus 40	+ 11 40	=	**06 Gemini 55**
Mars	16 Taurus 24	+ 11 40	=	**06 Gemini 55**
Jupiter	08 Capricorn 15	+ 11 40	=	**06 Capricorn 55**
Saturn	13 Leo 27	+ 11 40	=	**06 Leo 55**
Uranus	19 Libra 32R	+ 11 40	=	**06 Scorpio 55**
Neptune	00 Gemini 51	+ 11 40	=	**06 Gemini 55**
Pluto	04 Gemini 40	+ 11 40	=	**06 Gemini 55**
Moon's Node	16 Cancer 00	+ 11 40	=	**06 Cancer 55**

These solar arcs are entered in the circle around the radix horoscope and are all prefaced with the letter S to indicate Solar Arc. (Figure C.1) The aspects between the solar arc planetary bodies and the radix planetary bodies can be found with the Logarithmic Time Scale disk as explained in Appendix A.

If total accuracy is desired, the above computations may be done not only with the degree and minute of longitude of each planet, but with the seconds as well. This also allows the determination of the exact month a solar arc becomes due. Since the Sun moves approximately one degree per year, it moves about 05' per month during each year. This accuracy is rarely necessary because the function of solar arc directions is primarily to determine the years within which major events occur.

The second type of operation locates the exact year when a solar arc event occurs. To find the year when Hitler's S. Sun became conjunct to R. Pluto, the following calculation is made. (Figure C.2)

1. The longitude of R. Sun is subtracted from the longitude of R. Pluto.

R. Pluto	04° Gemini 40'	=	64°40' from 0° Aries
− R. Sun	00° Taurus 48'	=	30°48' from 0° Aries
Solar Arc		=	33°52'

2. An estimate of 1° per year is made to find the approximate year of the aspect. This would yield the approximate age of 34 years. As the actual yearly solar arc of Hitler is 00°58', the Sun would take more than 34 years to travel the 33°52'.

3. The longitude of the Sun during the 34th, 35th and 36th years of Hitler's life are found on the 34th, 35th and 36th days after 20 April 1889. The 34th day is 24 May 1889, the 35th day is 25 May 1889, and the 36th day is 26 May 1889. The longitude of the Sun at Hitler's birth is subtracted from the Sun's longitude on each of these days.

Age	Key Day	Sun Longitude	Minus the Sun's Birth Longitude		Solar Arc
34	24 May 1889	03° Gemini 27'	− 00° Taurus 48'	=	32°53'
35	25 May 1889	04° Gemini 25'	− 00° Taurus 48'	=	33°51'
36	26 May 1889	05° Gemini 22'	− 00° Taurus 48'	=	34°48'

The S. Sun was conjunct Pluto when Hitler was 35, in 1924.

With practice is it possible to do the above calculations in seconds.

Appendix D
Solar Return Construction

The Solar Return yearly analysis is a horoscope for a specified year of life, erected at the moment when the transiting Sun returns to its exact position at Birth. First the astrologer must determine when this occurs. Once the moment of the Sun's return is known, the second stage involves the erection of a horoscope for that moment. It is necessary to have a Birth Horoscope of the individual, and to know his location on his birthday in the year in question. Although the positions of the planets in the signs remain the same, the Ascendant, MC and intermediate house cusps are determined by his location.

Because the calendar year does not exactly coincide with the astronomical year, it often happens that the day on which the Sun returns to its Radix position is different than the original birthday. The margin of possible Solar Return birthdays is 2 days on either side of the calendar birthday.

In the following description of the procedure for calculating and constructing a Solar Return, the mechanics of each step are accompanied by a sample construction — the Solar Return of Mr. M. Mr. M was born on 18 August 1943 at 3:05 PM in Auburn, New York, USA (this horoscope appears on page 7 of this book). The Solar Return is to be constructed for the year from his birthday in 1952 until his birthday in 1953. Mr. M was in New York City, USA on his birthday in 1952. The ephemeris used is for August, 1952, reproduced in Appendix A, on page 278.

Finding the GMT of the Sun's Return

Since the ephemeris uses GMT for Sidereal Time and the planetary positions, we must calculate the GMT when the Sun returns to its radix longitude. We then work *forward* to find

the Sidereal Time of the solar return and *backward* to find the Local Time of the solar return.

1. The longitude of the Sun in the radix horoscope is necessary. Often the longitude of the Sun is calculated in degrees, minutes and seconds, but for the purposes of the solar return it is only necessary to know the Sun's longitude to the exact degree and the nearest minute. The margin of error in a Solar Return is one day, so calculations involving seconds are unnecessary.

   The Sun's longitude at the birth moment of Mr. M is 24° Leo 57'.

2. The ephemeris lists the longitude of the Sun at noon on each successive day in the year. The radix longitude of the Sun must be located between the noon longitudes of the Sun on two successive days. This determines the 24 hour period during which the Sun's return occurs.

   Mr. M's radix Sun is 24° Leo 57'. In the year 1952, the radix position falls between longitude 24° Leo 29'58'' on 17 August at noon, and longitude 25° Leo 27'42'' on 18 August at noon. Therefore the Sun returns to its birth position at some moment between noon on 17 August and noon on 18 August, both noons being GMT.

3. To find the moment when the Sun returns to its radix position, it is necessary to make a proportion between the motion of the Sun from noon to the longitude of its return, and the total daily motion of the Sun from noon to noon. When this proportion is multiplied by the total time from noon to noon (24 hours), the result will be the length of time after the Earlier noon that the Return occurs.

   First, the position of the Sun at the Earlier of the two noon dates is subtracted from the Radix longitude of the Sun.

Sun's Radix longitude	in degrees and minutes
— Sun's Earlier noon longitude	in degrees and minutes
Interval after noon	in degrees and minutes

   The longitude of the Sun at noon on 17 August is subtracted from the Radix longitude of Mr. M's Sun:

Sun's Radix longitude	*24° Leo 57'*
— Sun's Earlier noon longitude	*24° Leo 30'*
Interval after noon	*00° 27'*

4. The total daily motion of the Sun between the two successive noons is found by subtracting the Earlier noon longitude from the Later noon longitude.

   The longitude of the Sun at noon on 17 August is subtracted from the longitude of the Sun at noon on 18 August.

Sun's Later noon longitude	*25° Leo 28'*
— Sun's Earlier noon longitude	*24° Leo 30'*
Sun's total daily motion	*58'*

5. The proportion $\dfrac{\text{Interval after noon}}{\text{Total daily motion}}$ must be multiplied by the total time interval between the two successive noons (24 hours). To simplify the calculations, all times must be converted into minutes.

$$24 \text{ hours} = 1440 \text{ minutes}$$

   For Mr. M: $\dfrac{27'}{58'} \times 1440' = 670' = 11 \text{ hours } 10 \text{ minutes}$

   this represents the length of time after noon on 17 August when the Sun returns to its radix longitude. Therefore, the time of the return is 11:17 PM GMT on 17 August 1952.

The Ascendant, MC and Intermediate House Cusps

6. To find the Ascendant, MC and the intermediate house cusps, it is necessary to follow the procedure described in Appendix A, from Step 11 to Step 16 on the Worksheet, for

calculating Sidereal Time.

11. Sidereal Time Noon GMT		*09 43 14*
The Sidereal Time is taken for noon on 17 August 1952 from the ephemeris.		
12. Interval To/From Noon (AM−, PM+)		*+11 10 00*
The Interval is found from Step 5 above.		
13. Acceleration on the Interval	*+*	*1 52*
The acceleration is 10'' per hour of the interval of 11 hours 10 minutes.		
14. Sidereal Time Greenwich		*20 55 06*
The Interval and the Acceleration are added to the ST(GMT) at noon.		
15. Longitude Equivalent (E+, W−)		*− 4 44 54*
The longitude of New York of 73° West 57' is translated into hours, minutes and seconds.		
16. Sidereal Time		*15 59 02*

7. The Ascendant, MC and intermediate house cusps are found in the Tables of Houses for the latitude of the individual on his birthday. Since the margin of error is one degree for the personal points (ASC and MC), it is only necessary to take the nearest Sidereal Time in the Tables of Houses and read off the house cusps directly.

In the Table of Houses for New York, latitude 40° North 43', the nearest Sidereal Time to 15:59.02 is 15:59.36. This gives house cusps of:

Xth(MC)	*02° Sagittarius*
XIth	*23° Sagittarius*
XIIth	*15° Capricorn*
Ist(ASC)	*11° Aquarius 56'*
IInd	*00° Aries*
IIIrd	*06° Taurus*

And the cusps for the opposite half of the horoscope:

IVth(IC)	*02° Gemini*
Vth	*23° Gemini*
VIth	*15° Cancer*
VIIth(DES)	*11° Leo 56'*
VIIIth	*00° Libra*
IXth	*06° Scorpio*

The ASC, MC and the other house cusps are constructed on a blank horoscope form.

The Planetary Positions

8. The planetary positions are calculated from the GMT of the Solar Return according to the standard procedure explained in Appendix A. The planetary longitudes must only be accurate to the nearest degree so an approximation may be used to estimate the minutes for each planet.

The daily motion of the planets are found by subtracting their longitude on 17 August from their longitude on 18 August, and the difference is multiplied by the factor of:

$$\frac{11 \ hr \ 10 \ min}{24 \ hr \ 00 \ min} = \frac{670 \ minutes}{1440 \ minutes} = .47$$

This gives the following planetary positions:

Sun	*24° Leo*	*57'*	*(same as radix longitude)*
Moon	*25° Cancer*	*54'*	
Mercury	*16° Leo*	*13'*	*Retrograde*
Venus	*09° Virgo*	*53'*	
Mars	*24° Scorpio*	*20'*	
Jupiter	*20° Taurus*	*08'*	
Saturn	*11° Libra*	*47'*	
Uranus	*16° Cancer*	*39'*	

Neptune	*19° Libra*	*33'*
Pluto	*21° Leo*	*18'*
Moon's Node	*21° Aquarius*	*18'*

The planets are then entered on the horoscope from in their appropriate houses. (Figure D.2)

9. The aspects between planets and personal points in the Solar Return are found and drawn as explained in Appendix A. (Figure D.1)

10. The dates of planetary events throughout the year from birthday to birthday are entered in the first ring around the periphery of the horoscope circle, outside the circle of the zodiacal signs. (Figure D.1) This process of determining dates starts with the degree of the SR ascendant — designated the Solar Return birthday. After the ascendant, in the direction of the signs (counter-clockwise), each 30° increment represents one month of the year. (See Figure XI.10, on page 266.) Each planet in the Solar Return, as well as the Descendant and the MC are located throughout the year.

    Mr. M's Solar Return ascendant of 11° Aquarius is equivalent to 17 August 1952. Therefore, as an approximation throughout the year, 11° Pisces is 17 September, 11° Aries is 17 October, 11° Taurus is 17 November, 11° Gemini is 17 December, 11° Cancer is 17 January 1953, etc. By counting forwards and backwards from these approximate dates, each planet may be located throughout the year.

11. The planets, the moon's node and the personal points of the radix horoscope are then entered in the outermost ring of the horoscope blank. This allows the astrologer to see at a glance the relative positions of all planets in both the Solar Return and the Radix.

12. Each planetary position in the Solar Return, beginning with the ascendant is defined by the date at which it registers, the sign and house within which it falls, and by the aspects it makes to the planets in the radix around the outermost ring of the horoscope.

13. To find the True Local Time of the Solar Return, an additional calculation is necessary. As we know the GMP of the solar return, we must work backwards through the first four steps in the usual calculation of a horoscope. To do this we reverse the addition and subtraction operations for each step.

From Appendix A	Step	Normal Operation	Reverse	Hours	Minutes	Seconds
				°	'	''
9	GMT	—	—	11	10	00 PM
	The Greenwich Mean Time calculated for the solar return.					
8	Double Summer Time	—	—	—	—	—
	There is no Double Summer Time in New York.					
7	Summer Time	− 1 hour	+ 1 hour	12	10	00
	There is Daylight Savings Time in New York City.					
6	Zone Standard (W +)	+ 5 hours	− 5 hours	07	10	00

New York City is in Eastern Standard Time Zone, 5 hours west of Greenwich. Since normally this 5 hours would be added to the Local Birth Time, in this case it is subtracted from the result of Steps 9, 8 and 7 above.

5	Local Birth Time	—	—	07	10	00 PM

The Local Time in New York City when the Solar Return was constructed was 7:10 PM Eastern Standard Time on 17 August 1952.

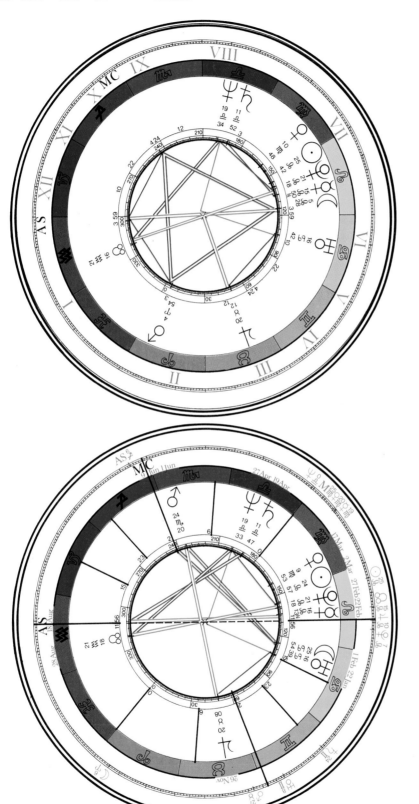

Figure A.4 The Completed Horoscope.

Figure D.1 The Completed Solar Return

Logarithmic Time Scale Tables

The Logarithmic Time Scale Tables are the basis of the timing system in The Round Art. Due to the size of the transparent Logarithmic Time Scale Disk overlay, it is not possible to include the equivalent ages for every degree of the horoscope. These tables remedy this shortcoming.

In Table A, the positive signs are adjacent to each other and the negative signs are also adjacent to each other. By reading across any line, the sextile and trine sensitive points may be determined. In Table B, the cardinal, fixed and mutable signs are aligned. By reading across any line, the square and opposition sensitive points may be determined.

Every critical age throughout the lifetime is correlated with two astrological positions. The first column shows the Archetypal Zodiacal Position if the Ascendant is 0° Aries. The second column shows the position in degrees from the Ascendant when the Ascendant is other than 0° Aries. The calculation technique for finding these positions is explained on pages 134 and 135 in Part V, The Houses of the Horoscope.

In the Octave of Gestation (Sagittarius through Piscus), times are graded in weeks and days after conception for every 5° interval. In the Octave of Childhood (Aries through Cancer), times are graded in years and months after birth for every 5° interval. In the Octave of Maturity (Leo through Scorpio), times are graded in years and months after birth for every 1° interval. For ages past the archetypal maximum of 76 years old, an addendum is included for an additional 15°. This allows determination of events until the age of 101 years old.

Table A
Sextile and Trine
Sensitive Points

Position	Degree	Week	Day	Position	Degree	Week	Day	Position	Degree	Year	Month	Position	Degree	Year	Month	Position	Degree	Year	Month	Position	Degree	Year	Month
00°	240°	4	0	00°	300°	12	3	00°	00°	00	00	00°	60°	1	8	00°	120°	6	10	00°	180°	23	5
01	241			01	301			01	01			01	61			01	121	7	1	01	181	23	11
02	242			02	302			02	02			02	62			02	122	7	2	02	182	24	4
03	243			03	303			03	03			03	63			03	123	7	4	03	183	24	10
04	244			04	304			04	04			04	64			04	124	7	6	04	184	25	4
05	245	4	2	05	305	13	5	05	05	0	1	05	65	1	11	05	125	7	8	05	185	25	10
06	246			06	306			06	06			06	66			06	126	7	10	06	186	26	4
07	247			07	307			07	07			07	67			07	127	8	0	07	187	26	11
08	248			08	308			08	08			08	68			08	128	8	2	08	188	27	5
09	249			09	309			09	09			09	69			09	129	8	4	09	189	28	0
10	250	4	5	10	310	15	1	10	10	0	2	10	70	2	2	10	130	8	6	10	190	28	6
11	251			11	311			11	11			11	71			11	131	8	8	11	191	29	1
12	252			12	312			12	12			12	72			12	132	8	10	12	192	29	8
13	253			13	313			13	13			13	73			13	133	9	0	13	193	30	3
14	254			14	314			14	14			14	74			14	134	9	3	14	194	30	11
15 ♐	255	5	2	15 ♒	315	16	4	15 ♈	15	0	3	15 ♊	75	2	5	15 ♌	135	9	5	15 ♎	195	31	6
16	256			16	316			16	16			16	76			16	136	9	7	16	196	32	2
17	257			17	317			17	17			17	77			17	137	9	10	17	197	32	9
18	258			18	318			18	18			18	78			18	138	10	0	18	198	33	5
19	259			19	319			19	19			19	79			19	139	10	3	19	199	34	1
20	260	5	6	20	320	18	2	20	20	0	4	20	80	2	9	20	140	10	5	20	200	34	9
21	261			21	321			21	21			21	81			21	141	10	8	21	201	35	5
22	262			22	322			22	22			22	82			22	142	10	10	22	202	36	2
23	263			23	323	2		23	23			23	83			23	143	11	1	23	203	36	10
24	264			24	324			24	24			24	84			24	144	11	4	24	204	37	7
25	265	6	3	25	325	20	1	25	25	0	6	25	85	3	2	25	145	11	7	25	205	38	4
26	266			26	326			26	26			26	86			26	146	11	10	26	206	39	1
27	267			27	327			27	27			27	87			27	147	12	1	27	207	39	11
28	268			28	328			28	28			28	88			28	148	12	4	28	208	40	8
29	269			29	329			29	29			29	89			29	149	12	7	29	209	41	6
00	270	7	0	00	330	22	1	00	30	0	7	00	90	3	6	00	150	12	10	00	210	42	3
01	271			01	331			01	31			01	91			01	151	13	1	01	211	43	2
02	272			02	332			02	32			02	92			02	152	13	4	02	212	44	0
03	273			03	333			03	33			03	93			03	153	13	8	03	213	44	10
04	274			04	334			04	34			04	94			04	154	13	11	04	214	45	9
05	275	7	5	05	335	24	3	05	35	0	9	05	95	4	0	05	155	14	2	05	215	46	8
06	276			06	336			06	36			06	96			06	156	14	6	06	216	47	7
07	277			07	337			07	37			07	97			07	157	14	9	07	217	48	6
08	278			08	338			08	38			08	98			08	158	15	1	08	218	49	5
09	279			09	339			09	39			09	99			09	159	15	4	09	219	50	5
10	280	8	3	10	340	26	6	10	40	0	11	10	100	4	5	10	160	15	8	10	220	51	5
11	281			11	341			11	41			11	101			11	161	16	0	11	221	52	5
12	282			12	342			12	42			12	102			12	162	16	4	12	222	53	6
13	283			13	343			13	43			13	103			13	163	16	8	13	223	54	6
14	284			14	344			14	44			14	104			14	164	17	0	14	224	55	7
15 ♑	285	9	2	15 ♓	345	29	4	15 ♉	45	1	0	15 ♋	105	5	0	15 ♍	165	17	4	15 ♏	225	56	8
16	286			16	346			16	46			16	106			16	166	17	8	16	226	57	10
17	287			17	347			17	47			17	107			17	167	18	1	17	227	58	11
18	288			18	348			18	48			18	108			18	168	18	5	18	228	60	1
19	289			19	349			19	49			19	109			19	169	18	10	19	229	61	3
20	290	10	2	20	350	32	4	20	50	1	3	20	110	5	6	20	170	19	2	20	230	62	6
21	291			21	351			21	51			21	111			21	171	19	7	21	231	63	9
22	292			22	352			22	52			22	112			22	172	20	0	22	232	65	0
23	293			23	353			23	53			23	113			23	173	20	4	23	233	66	3
24	294			24	354			24	54			24	114			24	174	20	9	24	234	67	7
25	295	11	2	25	355	35	6	25	55	1	5	25	115	6	2	25	175	21	2	25	235	68	11
26	296			26	356			26	56			26	116			26	176	21	7	26	236	70	3
27	297			27	357			27	57			27	117			27	177	22	1	27	237	71	7
28	298			28	358			28	58			28	118			28	178	22	6	28	238	73	0
29	299			29	359			29	59			29	119			29	179	22	11	29	239	74	5
00	300	12	3	00	360	40	4	00	60	1	8	00	120	6	10	00	180	23	5	00	240	75	11

Table B
Square and Opposition Sensitive Points

Columns 1 (♈ Aries / ♉ Taurus / ♊ Gemini)

Archetypal Zodiacal Position	Degree	Year	Month
00°	00°	00	00
01	01		
02	02		
03	03		
04	04		
05	05	0	1
06	06		
07	07		
08	08		
09	09		
10	10	0	2
11	11		
12	12		
13	13		
14	14		
15 (♈)	15	0	3
16	16		
17	17		
18	18		
19	19		
20	20	0	4
21	21		
22	22		
23	23		
24	24		
25	25	0	6
26	26		
27	27		
28	28		
29	29		
00	30	0	7
01	31		
02	32		
03	33		
04	34		
05	35	0	9
06	36		
07	37		
08	38		
09	39		
10	40	0	11
11	41		
12	42		
13	43		
14	44		
15 (♉)	45	1	0
16	46		
17	47		
18	48		
19	49		
20	50	1	3
21	51		
22	52		
23	53		
24	54		
25	55	1	5
26	56		
27	57		
28	58		
29	59		
00	60	1	8
01	61		
02	62		
03	63		
04	64		
05	65	1	11
06	66		
07	67		
08	68		
09	69		
10	70	2	2
11	71		
12	72		
13	73		
14	74		
15 (♊)	75	2	5
16	76		
17	77		
18	78		
19	79		
20	80	2	9
21	81		
22	82		
23	83		
24	84		
25	85	3	2
26	86		
27	87		
28	88		
29	89		
00	90	3	6

Columns 2 (♋ Cancer / ♌ Leo / ♍ Virgo)

Archetypal Zodiacal Position	Degree	Year	Month
00°	90°	3	6
01	91		
02	92		
03	93		
04	94		
05	95	4	0
06	96		
07	97		
08	98		
09	99		
10	100	4	5
11	101		
12	102		
13	103		
14	104		
15 (♋)	105	5	0
16	106		
17	107		
18	108		
19	109		
20	110	5	6
21	111		
22	112		
23	113		
24	114		
25	115	6	2
26	116		
27	117		
28	118		
29	119		
00	120	6	10
01	121	7	1
02	122	7	2
03	123	7	4
04	124	7	6
05	125	7	8
06	126	7	10
07	127	8	0
08	128	8	2
09	129	8	4
10	130	8	6
11	131	8	8
12	132	8	10
13	133	9	0
14	134	9	3
15 (♌)	135	9	5
16	136	9	7
17	137	9	10
18	138	10	0
19	139	10	3
20	140	10	5
21	141	10	8
22	142	10	10
23	143	11	1
24	144	11	4
25	145	11	7
26	146	11	10
27	147	12	1
28	148	12	4
29	149	12	7
00	150	12	10
01	151	13	1
02	152	13	4
03	153	13	8
04	154	13	11
05	155	14	2
06	156	14	6
07	157	14	9
08	158	15	1
09	159	15	4
10	160	15	8
11	161	16	0
12	162	16	4
13	163	16	8
14	164	17	0
15 (♍)	165	17	4
16	166	17	8
17	167	18	1
18	168	18	5
19	169	18	10
20	170	19	2
21	171	19	7
22	172	20	0
23	173	20	4
24	174	20	9
25	175	21	2
26	176	21	7
27	177	22	1
28	178	22	6
29	179	22	11
00	180	23	5

Columns 3 (♎ Libra / ♏ Scorpio / ♐ Sagittarius)

Archetypal Zodiacal Position	Degree	Year	Month
00°	180°	23	5
01	181	23	11
02	182	24	4
03	183	24	10
04	184	25	4
05	185	25	10
06	186	26	4
07	187	26	11
08	188	27	5
09	189	28	0
10	190	28	6
11	191	29	1
12	192	29	8
13	193	30	3
14	194	30	11
15 (♎)	195	31	6
16	196	32	2
17	197	32	9
18	198	33	5
19	199	34	1
20	200	34	9
21	201	35	5
22	202	36	2
23	203	36	10
24	204	37	7
25	205	38	4
26	206	39	1
27	207	39	11
28	208	40	8
29	209	41	6
00	210	42	3
01	211	43	2
02	212	44	0
03	213	44	10
04	214	45	9
05	215	46	8
06	216	47	7
07	217	48	6
08	218	49	5
09	219	50	5
10	220	51	5
11	221	52	5
12	222	53	5
13	223	54	6
14	224	55	7
15 (♏)	225	56	8
16	226	57	10
17	227	58	11
18	228	60	1
19	229	61	3
20	230	62	6
21	231	63	9
22	232	65	0
23	233	66	3
24	234	67	7
25	235	68	11
26	236	70	3
27	237	71	7
28	238	73	0
29	239	74	5
00	240	75	11
01	241	4	0
02	242		
03	243		
04	244		
05	245	4	2
06	246		
07	247		
08	248		
09	249		
10	250	4	5
11	251		
12	252		
13	253		
14	254		
15 (♐)	255	5	2
16	256		
17	257		
18	258		
19	259		
20	260	5	6
21	261		
22	262		
23	263		
24	264		
25	265	6	3
26	266		
27	267		
28	268		
29	269		
00	270	7	0

Columns 4 (♑ Capricorn / ♒ Aquarius / ♓ Pisces)

Archetypal Zodiacal Position	Degree	Week	Day
00°	270°	7	0
01	271		
02	272		
03	273		
04	274		
05	275	7	5
06	276		
07	277		
08	278		
09	279		
10	280	8	3
11	281		
12	282		
13	283		
14	284		
15 (♑)	285	9	2
16	286		
17	287		
18	288		
19	289		
20	290	10	2
21	291		
22	292		
23	293		
24	294		
25	295	11	2
26	296		
27	297		
28	298		
29	299		
00	300	12	3
01	301		
02	302		
03	303		
04	304		
05	305	13	5
06	306		
07	307		
08	308		
09	309		
10	310	15	1
11	311		
12	312		
13	313		
14	314		
15 (♒)	315	16	4
16	316		
17	317		
18	318		
19	319		
20	320	18	2
21	321		
22	322		
23	323	2	
24	324		
25	325	20	1
26	326		
27	327		
28	328		
29	329		
00	330	22	1
01	331		
02	332		
03	333		
04	334		
05	335	24	3
06	336		
07	337		
08	338		
09	339		
10	340	26	6
11	341		
12	342		
13	343		
14	344		
15 (♓)	345	29	4
16	346		
17	347		
18	348		
19	349		
20	350	32	4
21	351		
22	352		
23	353		
24	354		
25	355	35	6
26	356		
27	357		
28	358		
29	359		
00	360	40	4

Addendum for Old Age

Archetypal Zodiacal Position	Degree	Year	Month
00°	240°	75	11
01	241	77	5
02	242	78	11
03	243	80	6
04	244	82	0
05	245	83	6
06	246	85	4
07 (♐)	247	86	11
08	248	88	8
09	249	90	5
10	250	92	2
11	251	94	0
12	252	95	10
13	253	97	8
14	254	99	7
15	255	101	7

Bibliography

Astrological

Bills, Rex E. **The Rulership Book.** 1971, Macoy Publishing & Masonic Supply Company, Richmond, Virginia.

Carus, Paul, **Chinese Astrology.** 1974 (1907). Open Court, La Salle, Illinois.

Copper, Michael and Weaver, Andrew. **An Astrological Index to the World's Famous People.** 1975, Doubleday, New York.

Cornell, Dr. H. L. **Encyclopedia of Medical Astrology.** Revised Edition. 1972, Llewellyn Publications and Samuel Weiser, New York.

Crowley, Aleister. **The Complete Astrological Writings.** Edited by John Symonds and John Grant. 1974, Gerald Duckworth, London.

Davison, R. C. **Astrology.** 1963, Arco Publishing Company, New York.

De Luce, Robert. **Complete Method of Prediction.** 1935, The De Luce Publishing Company, New York.

Ebertin, Reinhold. **The Annual Diagram.** 1973, Ebertin-Verlag, Aalen.

    Applied Cosmobiology. Translated by Heidi Langman and Jim ten Hove. 1972, Ebertin-Verlag, Aalen.

    The Combination of Stellar Influences. Translated by Dr. Alfred G. Roosedale and Linda Kratzsch. 1940, Ebertin-Verlag, Aalen.

    Directions. Translated by Linda Kratzsch. 1976 (1931), Ebertin-Verlag, Aalen.

    Man in the Universe. Translated by Linda Kratzsch. 1973, Ebertin-Verlag, Aalen.

    Rapid and Reliable Analysis. Translated by Patrick Harding. 1970, Ebertin-Verlag, Aalen.

    Transits. Translated by Linda Kratzsch. 1971 (1928), Ebertin-Verlag, Aalen.

Eisler, Robert. **The Royal Art of Astrology.** 1946, Herbert Joseph, London.

Gauquelin, Michel. **Science and Astrology.** Translated by James Hughes. 1969 (1966), Peter Davies, London.

George Llewellyn. **A to Z Horoscope Maker and Delineator.** 1968 (1910), Llewellyn Publications, St. Paul, Minnesota.

Heindel, Max and Augusta Foss. **The Message of the Stars.** 1927, The Rosicrucian Fellowship, Oceanside, California.

Hone, Margaret. **The Modern Textbook of Astrology.** 1951, L. N. Fowler, London.

Landscheidt, Dr. Theodor. **Cosmic Cybernetics.** Translated by Linda Kratzsch. 1973, Ebertin-Verlag, Aalen.

Lilly, William. **An Introduction to Astrology.** Originally published in 1647. 1972, Newcastle Publishing Company, Hollywood, California.

Lorenz, Dona Marie. **Tools of Astrology: Houses.** 1973, Eomega Grove Press, Topanga, California.

Mayo, Jeff. **Astrology.** 1964, Hodder and Stoughton, London.

Penfield, Marc. **An Astrological Who's Who.** 1972, Arcane Publications, York Harbour, Maine.

Ptolemy. **Tetrabiblos.** Translated and Edited by F. E. Robbins. 1971 (1940), Harvard University Press, Cambridge, Massachusetts.

Randolph, Ludwig. **Meaning of the Planets in the Houses.** The theory of houses according to Witte. 1973, Witte-Verlag, Hamburg.

Rele, Dr. V. G. **Directional Astrology of the Hindus.** 1965, D. B. Taraporevala Sons, Bombay.

Rosenblum, Art. **Natural Birth Control.** 1971, Aquarian Research Foundation, Philadelphia.

Rudhyar, Dane. **Astrology and the Modern Psyche.** 1976, CRCS Publications, Davis, California.

Simmonite, W. J. **Complete Arcana of Astral Philosophy.** 1916, Foulsham & Company, London.

Shethlage, Francesca. **Navities of Famous Musicians.** 1976, Edizione F. Capone, Torino, Italy.

West, John Anthony and Toonder, Gerhard. **The Case for Astrology.** 1970, MacDonald and Company, London.

General

Beard, Ruth M. **An Outline of Piaget's Developmental Psychology.** 1969, Routledge & Kegan Paul, London.

Calder, Nigel. **The Key to the Universe.** 1977, British Broadcasting Corporation, London.

Capra, Fritjof. **The Tao of Physics.** 1975, Wildwood House, London.

Collin, Rodney. **The Theory of Celestial Influence.** 1954, Robinson and Watkins, London.

    The Theory of Eternal Life. 1950, Robinson and Watkins, London.

Cowen, Painton. **Rose Windows.** 1978, Thames and Hudson, London.

Crowley, Aleister. **The Qabalah of Aleister Crowley (Liber 777).** 1973, Samuel Weiser, New York.

Du Noüy, Lecomte. **Biological Time,** 1936, Methuen, London.

Eliade, Mircea. **Myth and Reality.** 1964, Allen and Unwin, London.

    Myths, Dreams and Realities. Translated by Philip Mairet. 1968, Collins, London.

    The Myth of the Eternal Return. Translated by Willard Trask. 1954, Bollingen Foundation, New York.

    Shamanism: Archaic Techniques of Ecstacy. Translated by Willard Trask. 1964, Bollingen Foundation, Princetown, New Jersey.

Eranos Yearbook. **Man and Time.** Edited by Joseph Campbell. 1957, Bollingen Foundation, New York.

Franz, Marie Louise von. **Number and Time.** 1974 (1970), Northwestern University Press. Translated by Andrea Dykes. 1974, Rider & Company, London.

Fraser, J. T. **The Voices of Time.** Edited by J. T. Fraser. 1968, Allen Lane and the Penguin Press, London.

Freud, Sigmund. **Letters of Sigmund Freud 1873-1939.** Edited by Ernest L. Freud. Translated by Tania and James Stern. 1961, Hogarth Press, London.

Jung, Carl Gustav. **C. G. Jung Letters, Volume One 1906-1950.** Translated by R. F. C. Hull. 1973, Routledge & Kegan Paul, London.

    C. G. Jung Letters, Volume Two 1950-1961. Translated by R. F. C. Hull. 1977, Routledge & Kegan Paul, London.

    Psychological Types, CW 6. Translated by R. F. C. Hull. 1921, Routledge & Kegan Paul, London.

    The Structure and Dynamics of the Psyche, CW 8. Translated by R. F. C. Hull. 1960, Routledge & Kegan Paul, London.

    The Archetypes and the Collective Unconscious, CW 9, Part I, Translated by R. F. C. Hull, 1959, Routledge & Kegan Paul, London.

    Aion, CW 9, Part II. Translated by R. F. C. Hull, 1951, Routledge & Kegan Paul, London.

    Psychology and Alchemy, CW 12. Translated by R. F. C. Hull. 1966 (1953), Routledge & Kegan Paul, London.

    Alchemical Studies, CW 13. Translated by R. F. C. Hull, 1966, Routledge & Kegan Paul, London.

    Mysterium Coniunctionis, CW 14. Translated by R. F. C. Hull. 1963 (1955-56), Routledge & Kegan Paul, London.

    The Practice of Psychotherapy, CW 16. Translated by R. F. C. Hull. 1966 (1954), Routledge & Kegan Paul, London.

Jung, Carl Gustav and Pauli, Wolfgang. **The Interpretation and Nature of the Psyche.** 1955, Routledge & Kegan Paul, London.

Laing, R. D. **The Facts of Life.** 1976, Allen Lane, London.

Mann, Thomas. **Joseph and His Brothers.** Translated by H. T. Lowe-Porter. 1950, Secker and Warburg, London.

Neumann, Erich. **The Great Mother.** 1955, Routledge & Kegan Paul, London.

Plato, **Timaeus and Critias.** Translated by Desmond Lee. 1965, Penguin, London.

Reich, Wilhelm. **Wilhelm Reich: Selected Writings, An Introduction to Orgonomy.** 1961, The Noonday Press, London.

Rugh, Roberts and Shettles, Landrum B. **From Conception to Birth.** 1971, Allen and Unwin, London.

Russell, Bertrand. **A History of Western Philosophy.** 1945, Simon and Schuster, New York.

Schwaller de Lubicz, R. A. **The Temple in Man.** 1949. Translated by Robert and Deborah Lawlor in 1977, Autumn Press, Cambridge, Massachusetts.

Watson, James D. **The Double Helix.** 1968, Weidenfeld and Nicholson, London.

Yates, Frances A. **The Art of Memory.** 1966, Routledge & Kegan Paul, London.

Glossary

Afflicted — A planet with a predominance of square and opposition aspects; or a planet with aspects to Mars, Saturn, Uranus or Pluto.

Air Signs — Gemini, Libra and Aquarius. These indicate mentality and communication.

Angles (Angular Houses) — The houses which occupy the east, west, north and south points in the horoscope. Also, the Ist, IVth, VIIthe and Xth houses. The angles are the most powerful positions in the horoscope.

Applying Aspect — A planetary aspect which is approaching exactitude. The 'potential' of an event.

Arc — The spherical angle formed by the intersection of two great circles measured in degrees.

Armillary Sphere — A renaissance astronomical device showing the skeleton of the circles which define the celestial sphere.

Ascendant (ASC or AS) — The degree and sign on the eastern horizon; the Ist house; the indictor of the moment of birth; and the intersection between the ecliptic and the horizon. It indicates the personality. It is also called the *'Rising Sign'*.

Aspect — The angular relationship in degrees between a pair of planetary bodies as seen from the Earth.

Astrology — From the Greek *'astros'*, a star and *'logos'*, knowledge. The knowledge of the stars.

Autumnal Equinox (Fall Equinox) — The point where the Sun passes the equator moving from north to south, designated 0° Libra.

Benefics — Planets which possess positive influences. Venus and Jupiter.

Biological Time — The relationship of time perception to a living being.

Birth Horoscope — The horoscope constructed for the moment of birth. Also called the *Radix,* the *Natal Horoscope* or the *Genethliological Chart.*

Bowl Shape — An horoscope with all planets in half of the signs, enclosed within an opposition. A one-sided individual.

Bucket Shape — An horoscope with all planets in half of the signs, but with a single planet or conjunction of planets outside that half.

Bundle Shape — An horoscope with all planets within a 120° (trine) segment. A highly concentrated individual.

Cadent Houses — The four houses which precede the angles. The IIIrd, VIth, IXth and XIIth houses. They are the weakest positions in the horoscope.

Cardinal Points — The north, south, east and west points of the heavens.

Cardinal Signs — Aries, Cancer, Libra and Capricorn. The equinoctial and solstitial signs, considered the most dynamic signs in the zodiac.

Celestial Poles — The points on the celestial sphere equivalent to the north and south poles on Earth. The celestial sphere rotates around the celestial poles.

Celestial Sphere — An imaginary sphere with its centre coincident to the centre of the Earth. The movements of planetary bodies are registered upon the surface of the celestial sphere.

Circumpolar Stars — The stars which surround the north or south celestial poles. The most important circumpolar stars are in the constellation Ursa Major near the north celestial pole, and the Southern Cross near the south celestial pole.

Collective Unconscious — A term coined by Jung defining a dimension of the unconscious psyche which contains the totality of human experience.

Combust — A planet within three degrees from the sun's longitude. The sun's strength overwhelms the influence of combust planet.

Conjunction — Two or more planets with the same longitude. The closer together the planets, the stronger the influence.

Constellation — A series of planets or personal points inter-related by aspects.

Cosmobiology — A scientific discipline exploring the correlations between the cosmos and man through the medium of cosmic rhythms. It has become well-known through the vision and practice of Reinhold Ebertin.

Counter-transference — The termination of the psychoanalysis and its effects. In astrology, the process of ending the reading of the horoscope.

Culminating — A planet coinciding with the meridian on the celestial sphere.

Cusp — The 3° of longitude which precedes the first degree of a sign or house.

Daylight Savings Time — Used in the USA to preserve daylight. Clocks are turned one hour ahead in the spring and one hour back in the fall.

Decanate — Ten degree increments of each sign of the zodiac. First decanate is 0° to 10°, second decanate is 10° to 20°, and third decanate is 20° to 30°. Decanates were used by the Egyptians and Greeks to locate fixed stars.

Declination — The distance of a planetary body north or south of the equator.

Decile — An aspect of 36° between a pair of planets. Half of a quintile.

Degree — The 360th part of a circle, or the 30th part of a zodiacal sign.

Descendant — The point where the ecliptic intersects the western horizon, opposite to the ascendant. Also, the VIIth house.

Detriment — A planet which resides in the sign opposite to that which it rules. This position weakens the influence of the planet.

Dignified — A planet in an angular house; in the sign which it rules; or in exaltation.

Direction (Arc of Direction) — The movement of planetary bodies through the horoscope usually according to the formula one day equals one year. The aspects directions make to the birth horoscope determine events. *(See Primary Directions and Secondary Directions.)*

Direct Motion (D) — The natural counter-clockwise movement of the planets through the signs of the zodiac. Its opposite is *Retrograde motion,* when a planet appears to move backwards through the signs. After a period of Retrograde motion the planet appears to stop — it is *stationary* — and then direct motion resumes.

Diurnal Circles — Small circles parallel to the equator. Planets declined above or below the equator move along diurnal circles.

Diurnal Arcs — The part of the ecliptic above the horizon. Also, the upper half of the horoscope above the ascendant-descendant axis. The diurnal arc is equivalent to consciousness and objectivity.

Dispositor — The planet which rules the sign containing another planet or planets. If Jupiter is in Aries, which is ruled by Mars, then Mars is the dispositor or governor of Jupiter. The dispositor is strongest when it is in its own sign.

Double Summer Time (DST) — From 1941 until 1945 in the United Kingdom, War Time was used as well as Summer Time. Double Summer Time means that clocks were turned two hours ahead of GMT.

Dragon's Head *(Caput Draconis)* — The position where the Moon crosses the ecliptic from south to north. Also called the *Moon's North Node* or *Rahu.*

Dragon's Tail *(Carda Draconis)* — The position where the Moon crosses the ecliptic from north to south. Also called the *Moon's South Node* or *Ketu.*

Earth Signs — Taurus, Virgo and Capricorn. They indicate the physical world.

Ecliptic — A great circle which indicates the plane of the solar system and the path which the Sun apparently follows around the Earth. The plane of the ecliptic is inclined at an angle of 23½° to the plane of the equator. The signs of the zodiac are equal 30° divisions of the ecliptic.

Elevation — The height in degrees above the horizon of a planetary body.

Ephemeris — An almanac containing the sidereal time and planetary positions at noon or midnight every day. The standard reference work for determining planetary positions and constructing the horoscope.

Ephemeris Time (ET) — In 1956 the introduction of ET altered the definition of the second from 1/86400th of the day to 1/31556925.9747 of the tropical year of 365.242199 . . . days. The first computed time standard.

Equal House System *(Modus Equalis)* — The oldest and simplest method of house division. Each house is found by adding equal 30° increments of longitude to the position of the ascendant. Ptolemy used this system.

Equator — The great circle perpendicular to the polar axis of the Earth, and equidistant from the north and south poles. The celestial equator is the equivalent great circle around the celestial sphere, equidistant from the north and south celestial poles.

Equinox — The two points at which the Sun crosses the equator, and day is equal to night. *(See Autumnal Equinox and Vernal Equinox.)*

Exaltation — The sign in which a planet is strongest and its qualities are most exaggerated.

Face — The sixth part of a sign, equal to 5°. A face is half of a decanate.

Fall — A planet in the sign opposite to its exaltation. The weakest position for a planet.

Feminine Signs — The earth and water signs, which are considered to be introverted and passive. Taurus, Cancer, Virgo, Scorpio, Capricorn and Pisces.

Fire Signs — Aries, Leo and Sagittarius. They indicate energy.

Figure — A nineteenth century designation for the horoscope.

Fixed Signs — The four signs which occupy the centres of the zodiacal quadrants. Taurus, Leo, Scorpio and Aquarius. Also called the Four Sacred Beasts.

Fixed Stars — Stars which have no apparent movement.

Galactic Centre — The centre of the Milky Way Galaxy, located by radio-astronomers at 26° Sagittarius 30'. It moves one degree every 70 years.

Genethliological Astrology — An obsolete term for the judgement of the birth horoscope.

Geocentric — Earth-centred. All astrological and astronomical data are computed from the centre of the Earth.

Gestation Octave — The time period from conception until birth in the Logarithmic Time Scale. During this time the body is created and all influences are received through the medium of the mother.

Grand Cross — Four planets or personal points at 90° intervals around the horoscope. Two oppositions in square to each other. Grand Crosses usually occur among four planets or personal points in the same mode (for example; *Cardinal Grand Cross, Fixed Grand Cross* and *Mutable Grand Cross)*. This is the constellation of maximum tension.

Grand Trine — Three planets or personal points mutually in trine with each other. Grand Trines usually occur among three planets or personal points in the same element (for example; *Fiery Grand Trine, Earthy Grand Trine, Airy Grand Trine* and *Watery Grand Trine)*. This constellation indicates maximum harmony and stability.

Great Circle — Any plane which intersects the centre of a sphere forms a great circle.

Greenwich Mean Time (GMT) — The standard time for which all ephemerides are calculated, and to which all longitudes on Earth are compared. GMT is based on the Greenwich Meridian, designated 0° Longitude. Every standard time zone is defined by its position in relation to GMT.

Greenwich Meridian — The meridian which passes through Greenwich, England. The standard meridian of Greenwich Mean Time (GMT).

Heliacal Rising — A planet rising with the Sun, but just visible to the east of him. The Egyptian calendar was based upon the heliacal rising of the star Sirius, which signalled the flooding of the Nile.

Heliocentric — Sun-centred. Planetary positions in relation to the Sun as the observation point.

Horary Astrology — The art of foreseeing events by erecting a horoscope for the moment a question is propounded. This branch of astrology was the basis for most predictions in the Middle Ages and the Renaissance.

Horizon — A great circle formed by a plane perpendicular to the direction of gravity and passing through the centre of the celestial sphere. Not to be confused with the visual horizon, a plane tangent to the surface of the Earth at the observer's location.

Hour Circles — Great circles which pass vertically through the celestial poles.

House Circles — Great circles which intersect the north and south points of the horizon.

Houses — Twelve divisions of the ecliptic related to the position of the ascendant. The houses are numbered with Roman Numerals from I to XII counter-clockwise from the ascendant. The houses may be either equal or unequal according to the method used to compute them.

Immum Coeli (IC or Lower Midheaven) — The point of intersection between the ecliptic and the northern arc of the meridian, which is equivalent to the position of the Sun at midnight. The centre of the field of the unconscious or the Non-ego.

Individual — The term denoting the person for whom the horoscope is erected. It is equivalent to the older term native.

Individuation — The process of achieving wholeness, according to Jung.

Interception — A zodiacal sign which is totally enclosed within one house in the horoscope. When a sign is intercepted, its opposite is also.

Latitude — The distance in degrees north or south of the plane of the ecliptic on the celestial sphere. Latitude on Earth is the distance north or south of the equator.

Libido — All of the diverse expressions of psychic energy and its field.

Locomotive Shape — Planets in all but one 120° segment of the horoscope. There is usually a lack of awareness of the missing octave and a necessity to compensate for its absence.

Logarithmic Time Scale — A method for correlating biological time to the circle of the horoscope and determining the exact ages in life of all house cusps and planetary positions. Also the transparent disk used for this purpose.

Long Ascension — Signs which take more than two hours to pass the ascendant. The signs Cancer, Leo, Virgo, Libra, Scorpio and Sagittarius. These signs of long ascension in the northern hemisphere are signs of short ascension in the southern hemisphere. *(See Short Ascension.)*

Longitude — The distance of any body on the celestial sphere from the first point of the zodiac, 0° Aries, along the ecliptic in the direction of the signs (counter-clockwise). On the Earth, longitude is measured in degrees east or west of Greenwich Meridian.

Lord of the Ascendant — The planet which rules the sign of the ascendant in the horoscope. Also called the *Ruling Planet.* Its strength is determined by its house and sign position. If the ascendant is Aries, the lord of the ascendant is Mars. The lord of the ascendant is strongest when it is near the MC or the ASC.

Luminaries — The Sun and the Moon.

Lunation Cycle — The period of time from New Moon until the following New Moon, approximately 29½ days. The four subdivisions of the lunation cycle are the phases of the moon. It is also called the *Synodic Month.*

Malefics — Planets which produce negative effects. Mars, Saturn, Uranus and Pluto.

Masculine Signs — The fire and air signs, which are considered to be active and extravert. Aries, Gemini, Leo, Libra, Sagittarius and Aquarius.

Maturity Octave — The time period in the Logarithmic Time Scale from seven years old until death, during which the Creation of Soul occurs.

Mean Solar Time — The average length of the solar day throughout the year. It coincides over the length of the solar year, but rarely with the actual length of a rotational day.

Medium Coeli (MC or Midheaven) — The point of intersection between the ecliptic and the southern arc of the meridian, which is equivalent to the position of the Sun at noon. The centre of the field of consciousness and the position of the *Ego.*

Meridian — A great circle passing through the zenith, nadir, north and south celestial poles as determined by the terrestrial longitude of the observer.

Midheaven — The Medium Coeli.

Midpoint — The point in the horoscope exactly halfway between two planetary positions which is a sensitive point manifesting their combined influences. Since the midpoint is determined by an axis bisecting the angle of the two planets, there are two midpoints for every pair of planets at opposite points in the horoscope. *A Direct Midpoint* is a planet positioned at the midpoint of a pair of planets. An *Indirect Midpoint* is two pairs of planets which share the same axis, or a third planet aspecting the midpoint of a pair of planets.

Mode — The quadruplicity of a sign. Cardinal, Fixed or Mutable modes.

Mundane Astrology — The art of foreseeing natural catastrophes or other physical phenomena from the stars.

Mutable Signs — Gemini, Virgo, Sagittarius and Pisces. These signs occupy the last third of each quadrant and are the weakest signs in the zodiac.

Nadir — The lowest point on the celestial sphere as determined by a plumb line. The nadir is opposite the zenith.

Natal Horoscope — The *Birth Horoscope* or *Radix.*

Native — The person for whom the horoscope is erected.

Nativity — The *Birth Horoscope* or *Radix.*

Neurosis — A pathological, one-sided development of the personality.

Nocturnal Arc — The part of the ecliptic below the horizon. Also, the lower half of the horoscope below the ascendant-descendant axis. The nocturnal arc is equivalent to the unconscious and subjectivity.

Nodes — The nodes of the Moon are the points where the Moon passes the ecliptic. The nodes move backwards through the zodiac, making a complete revolution every 18 years. (See *Dragon's Head* and *Dragon's Tail.)*

Occidental — The West. The western half of the horoscope which includes the descendant and is bounded by the MC and the IC. The occidental half indicates the collective reality.

Opposition — Two planets 180° apart from each other. An aspect of maximum tension.

Orb — The sphere of influence of a planet or aspect. The orb varies in traditional textbooks of astrology from 1° on either side of the exact aspect to 15° on either side. The size of the planetary orb depends upon the size and strength of the planet and the type of aspect involved.

Oriental — The East. The eastern half of the horoscope which includes the ascendant and is bounded by the IC and the MC. The oriental half indicates the individual reality.

Parallel — Two planets with the same declination, whether north or south of the equator. Similar to a conjunction aspect.

Pars Fortunae (Part of Fortune) — A so-called *'Arabic Part'* which signifies good luck, especially for finances. The Part of Fortune is found by calculating where the Moon would be if the Sun were exactly on the ascendant. The sign and house of the Part of Fortune indicates its qualities. (ASC long. + Moon long. – Sun long. = Part of Fortune)

Partile — A conjunction in which two planets are no more than 5 minutes apart. This is the most perfect and powerful aspect.

Persona — The personality in the Greek sense *(persona = mask)*. The persona is determined by the ascendant and its aspects.

Personal Points — The ascendant (ASC) and the midheaven (MC) as equivalents of the personality and ego of an individual. They move about one degree every four minutes.

Planetary Body — Any of the ten planets, including the Sun and Moon.

Planetary Picture — A diagram illustrating a constellation of planets related by aspect. The method of indicating constellations popularized by Ebertin's Cosmobiology.

Platonic Month — The period of time necessary for the equinoctial point to process one complete sign through the zodiac. The 'Age of Aquarius' is a Platonic Month. (Approximately 2,140 years)

Platonic Year — The period of time necessary for the equinoctial point to move through the entire zodiac. (Approximately 25,500 years)

Polar Axis — The Earth's axis — a line between north and south poles.

Polar Elevation — The latitude of geographical location.

Pole Star — The star Polaris, towards which the north polar axis points.

Precession of the Equinoxes — The backwards movement of the polar axis through the signs of the zodiac, caused by the wobble of the polar axis. This phenomenon is responsible for the *Platonic Year*.

Primary Direction — The movement of planets according to the formula: One day after birth = One year of life. The position of the Sun on the days after birth indicates the movement applied to all planets. These 'Solar Arcs' are compared to the birth horoscope to predict events.

Progression — Also called a *Secondary Direction*. Directing the planets in the birth horoscope to their positions in the ephemeris on the days after birth according to the formula: One day = One year. The fortieth day after birth indicates the positions of the progressed planets in the fortieth year of life.

Quadrant Method — A method of house division wherein the four quadrants are divided into three equal parts to calculate the intermediate house cusps. It is used in the house systems of Porphyry, Campanus and Regiomontanus.

Quadruplicities — Groups of signs with similar modes. Cardinal, Fixed and Mutable modes.

Quartile — A square aspect of 90° between a pair of planets. Considered a tensioning aspect and likely to produce events.

Quaternity — Groups of four symbols which constitute a pattern of potential wholeness.

Quincunx — An aspect of 150°, or five complete signs. It is considered a favourable aspect, although largely obsolete. Also called *Inconjunct*.

Quintile — An aspect of 72°, or one-fifth of the circle. Considered a beneficial aspect, although largely obselete.

Radix — The birth horoscope, especially when other planetary positions are compared to it.

Reception (Mutual Reception) — Two planets posited in the signs of each other's ruler. For example, when the Sun is in Sagittarius and Jupiter is in Leo, the Sun and Jupiter are in mutual reception.

Rectification — Correcting the ascendant birth time of an horoscope. Rectification is often necessary as birth times are notoriously inaccurate.

Reading — The explanation of the horoscope by an astrologer to an individual.

Retrograde Motion — The apparent backward movement of a planet through the zodiac due to the geocentric viewpoint of Earth. This usually indicates a debility to the planet involved.

Right Ascension (RA) — The distance from 0° Aries on the plane of the equator.

Ruler (Ruling Planet) — Usually the planet which rules the sign on the ascendant. The planet which is the natural resident in a sign. Also, the planet in an horoscope which is closest to the MC.

Satellitium — A group of planets which are mutually conjunct. Often a sequence of planets are conjunct to their adjacent planets, but the total range is beyond a commonly accepted conjunction aspect. For example, when Jupiter is at 4° Leo, the Sun at 7° Leo, Venus at 11° Leo and Mars at 14° Leo. Even though Jupiter and Mars are not really conjunct, they are integral parts of the entire satellitium.

Secondary Direction — (See *Progression*)

See-Saw Shape — All planets disposed in two groups or satellitia opposed to each other. It produces extreme tension.

Self — The pattern of wholeness implicit in an individual (Jung).

Semi-arc — One quadrant of the horoscope houses in an unequal house system.

Semi-sextile — An aspect of 30°, or one sign of the zodiac. Obsolete.

Semi-square — An aspect of 45°, and the midpoint of the square aspect. It is considered an very important aspect by Ebertin as a harmonic of the square.

Sensitive Point — A position in the horoscope which has no planet in residence, but which is either a midpoint or an exact aspect away from a radix planet. When sensitive points are passed in the Time Scale they reactivate previous events.

Separation — A planet moving beyond the orb of exactitude of an aspect. The influence of the aspect is residual.

Sesquiquadrate — An aspect of 135°, related to the semi-square. Ebertin considers this important as an harmonic of the square. An aspect of tension.

Sextile — An aspect of 60°, and the midpoint of a trine aspect. An important aspect which indicates a spiritual linkage.

Shape — The overall disposition of planets in the birth horoscope. (See *Bowl, Bucket, Bundle, Locomotive, See-Saw, Sling* or *Splay* Shapes.)

Short Ascension — Signs which take less than two hours to pass the ascendant. The signs Capricorn, Aquarius, Pisces, Aries, Taurus and Gemini. These signs of short ascension in the northern hemisphere are signs of long ascension in the southern hemisphere. (See *Long Ascension.*)

Sidereal Time (ST) — Star Time. The true right ascension on the meridian at noon.

Sidereal Zodiac — A zodiac based upon the actual constellation in which the equinoctial point falls. According to sidereal astrology, an individual born in 1970 in the sign of Aries is actually an Aquarius.

Sling Shape — All planets in the horoscope in a bundle (120°) except for one planet or a conjunction. The single planet must compensate for all the others. A very tense and difficult shape.

Small Circle — The circle derived by passing a plane through a sphere which does not pass through the centre.

Solar Arc Direction — A way of directing the planets so that each planet moves the same amount as the Sun. Each day after birth equals one year of life.

Solar Apex — The position towards which the Sun is moving, thought to be the star Hercules.

Solstices — The two points where the Sun reaches its greatest declination above and below the plane of the equator. The Winter Solstice is near 21 December, and the Summer Solstice is near 21 June.

Splay Shape — Planets distributed evenly around the entire horoscope. The most common and least specialized shape.

Spring Equinox — (See *Vernal Equinox.*)

Square — A major aspect of 90°, which indicates a tension relationship usually resulting in an event. Also called a *Quartile*.

Standard Time — An international time standard based upon GMT.

Standard Time Zone — The standard time of a given longitude, usually indicated in an even number of hours east or west of Greenwich.

Stationary — The apparent cessation of planetary motion after Retrograde Motion.

Stellar Body — The planets and the luminaries. A term used by Ebertin.

Succedent Houses — The houses which occupy the positions just before the angles. They are considered the weakest houses. The IIIrd, VIth, IXth and the XIIth houses.

Summer Time (ST) — Used in many countries to preserve daylight. Clocks are turned ahead one hour in the spring and back one hour in the autumn. (See *Daylight Savings Time.*)

Syzygy — The New and Full Moons, and the conjunctions and oppositions of any planets.

Tables of Houses — Tables showing the positions of the house cusps, usually according to the Placidean House System. An essential reference book.

Transcendent Octave — The higher level of the Gestation Octave. The octave of the realized self and the individual who has created a Soul.

Transference — A psychoanalytical term denoting the relationship between the analyst and the analysand. In astrology it denotes the relationship between the astrologer and his client.

Transit — The daily movement of planets indicated in the ephemeris, especially when they pass over or aspect radix planets. Transits are usually short-term influences, except by the outer planets.

Trine — An aspect of 120°, one-third of the horoscope. An important aspect indicating harmony and easy communication.

Triplicity — Groups of signs with similar elements. Fire, Earth, Air and Water triplicities. They are correspondent positions in each octave.

Tropical Zodiac — The zodiac which defines the vernal equinox as 0° Aries. The zodiacal equinoxes reflect astronomical and seasonal qualities rather than actual constellations.

T-Square — A constellation with an opposition and another planet in square to both ends of the opposition. It indicates great stress but maximum potential.

Universal Time (UTO) — A calculated time standard which includes the effects of wobble and precession. *Universal Time One (UTI)* excludes wobble effects.

Vernal Equinox (Spring Equinox) — The point where the Sun passes the equator moving from south to north, designated 0° Aries. The first point of the astronomical and astrological year.

Vertical Circles — Great circles perpendicular to the plane of the horizon which intersect the zenith and the nadir. The *Prime Vertical* also intersects the east and west points on the horizon.

War Time (WT) — War Time was instituted in the United Kingdom during the Second World War, between 1941 and 1945. Clocks were turned ahead one hour from GMT during this entire time.

Water Signs — Cancer, Scorpio and Pisces. They indicate emotions and feelings.

Wobble — The axis of the Earth wanders in relation to the Pole Star over long periods of time. This wobble accounts for a difference in year lengths and for the precession of the equinoxes.

Zenith — The position on the celestial sphere directly above an observer as determined by a plumb line.

Zodiac — *From the Greek zoidiakos kyklos,* meaning *'wheel of animals'.* The zodiac is a band of constellations which follow the path of the ecliptic. It is used to locate planetary motions and is the basis of the calendar.

Zone Standard Time (ZST) — The standard time of a given longitudinal area, usually indicated in even hours east or west of Greenwich. Some countries use the longitude of their capitals instead. (Iran, for example.)

Index